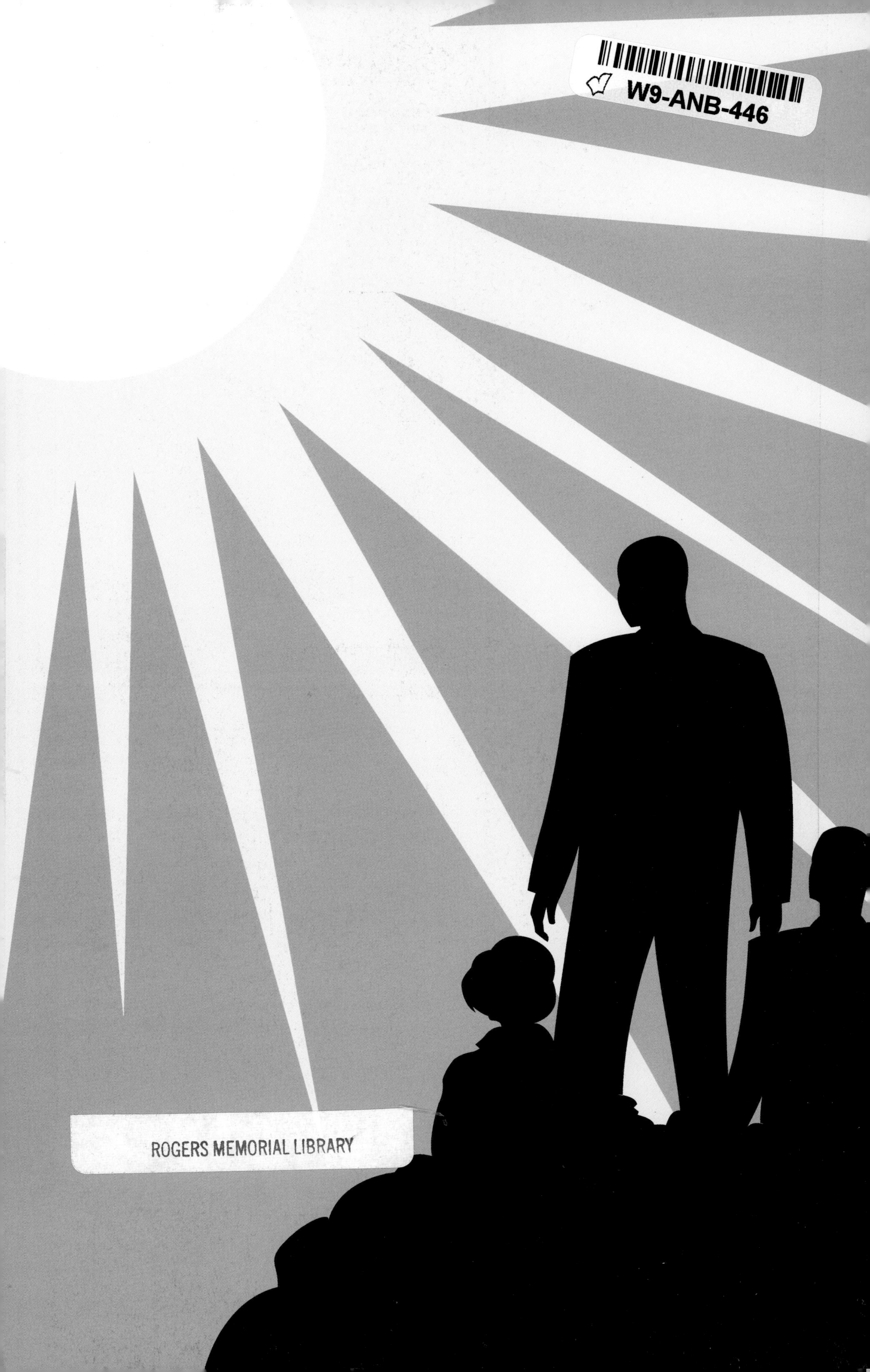

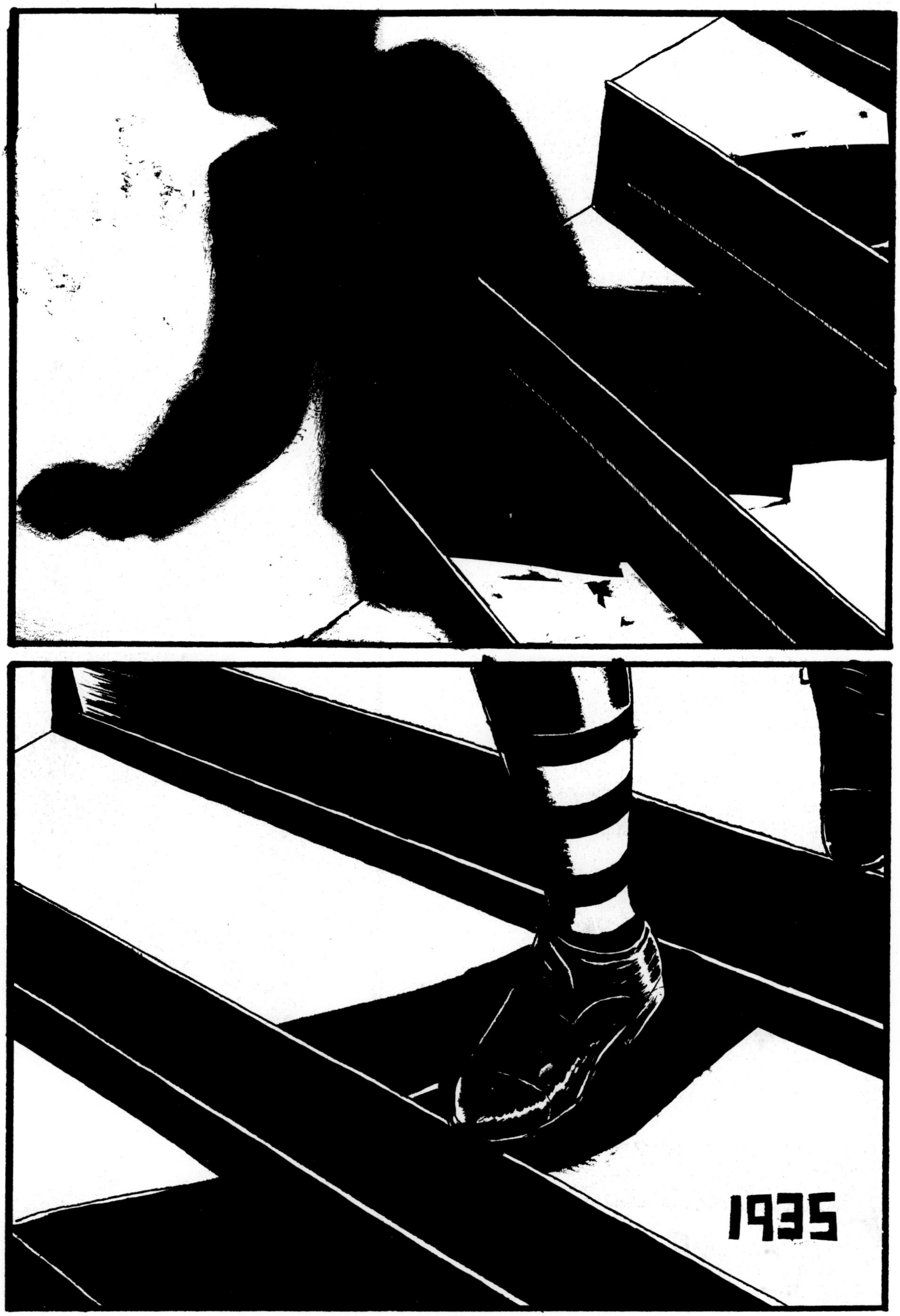
1935

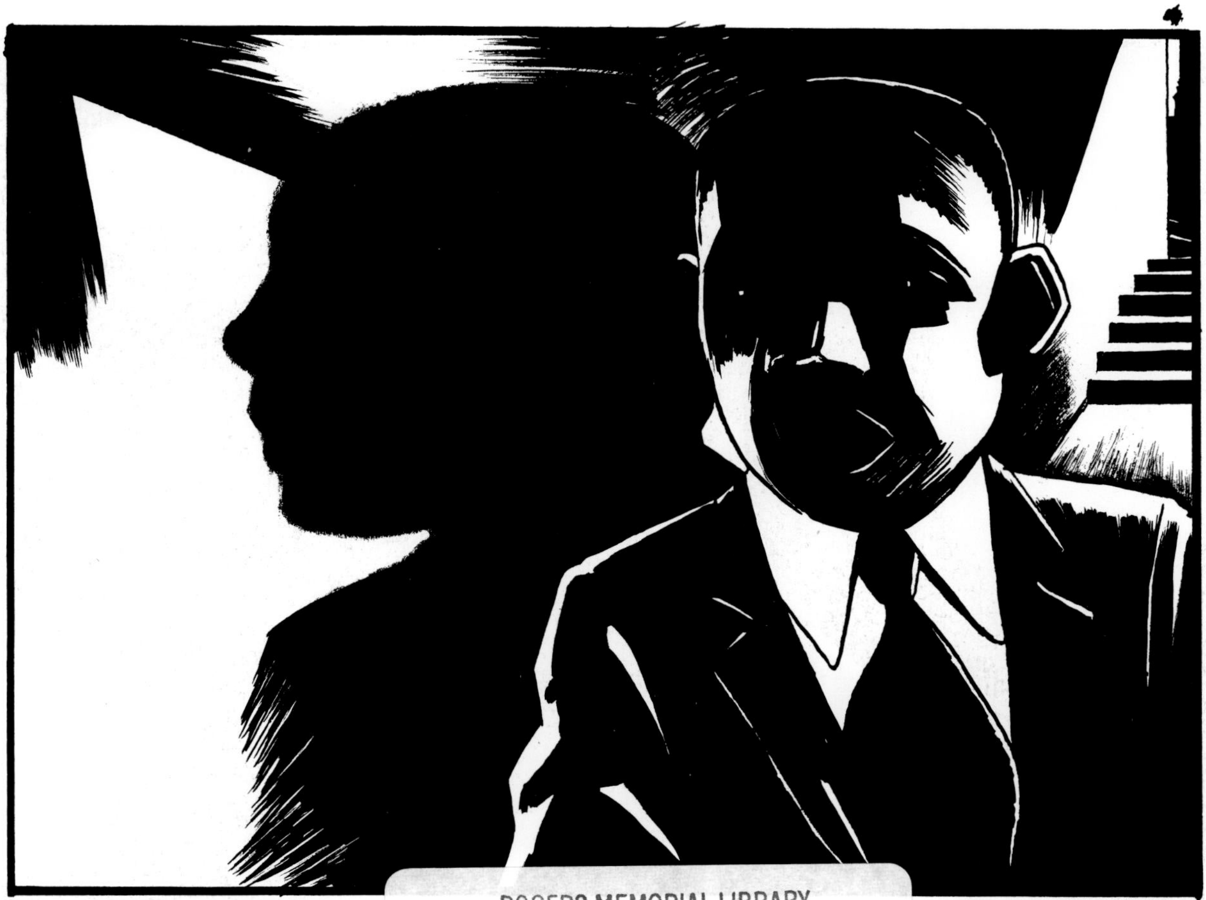

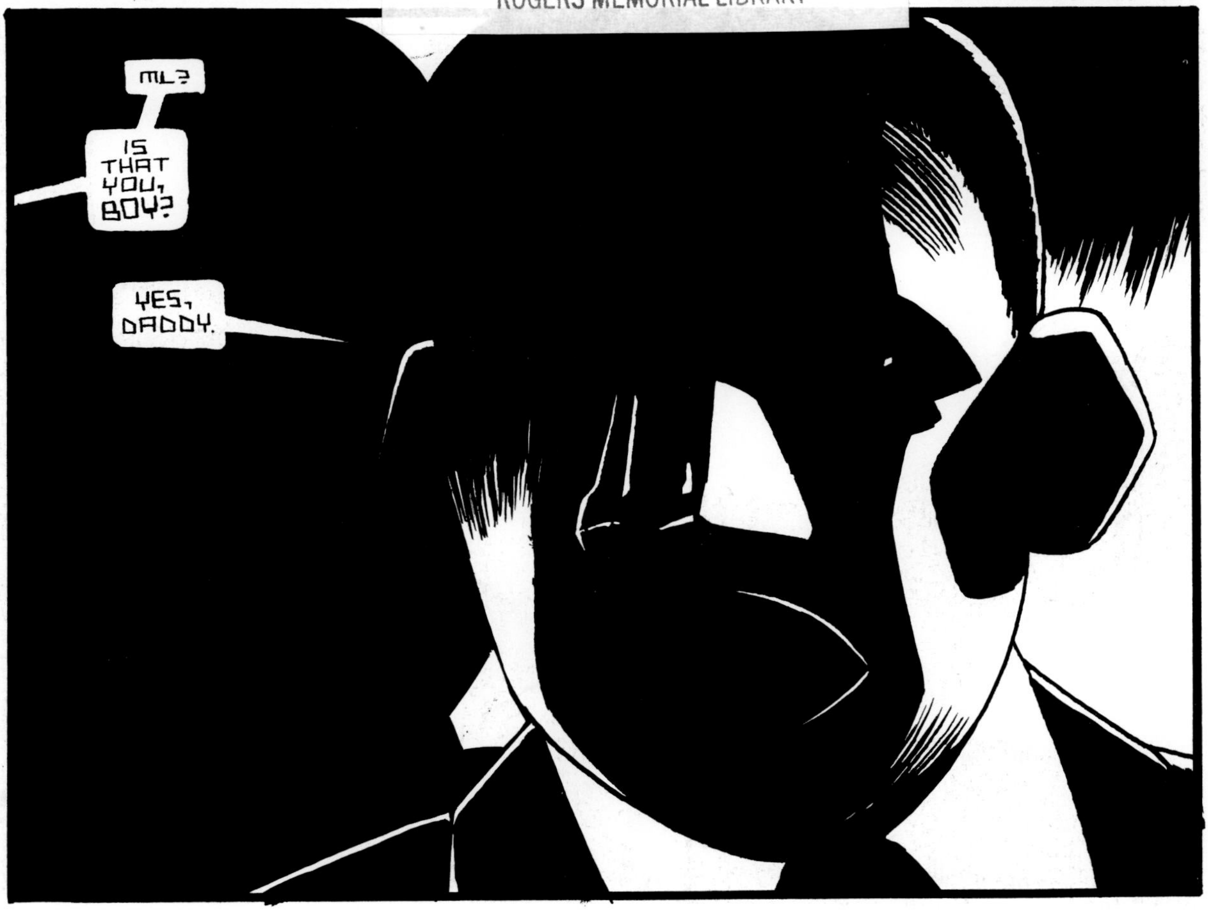
ML?
IS THAT YOU, BOY?
YES, DADDY.

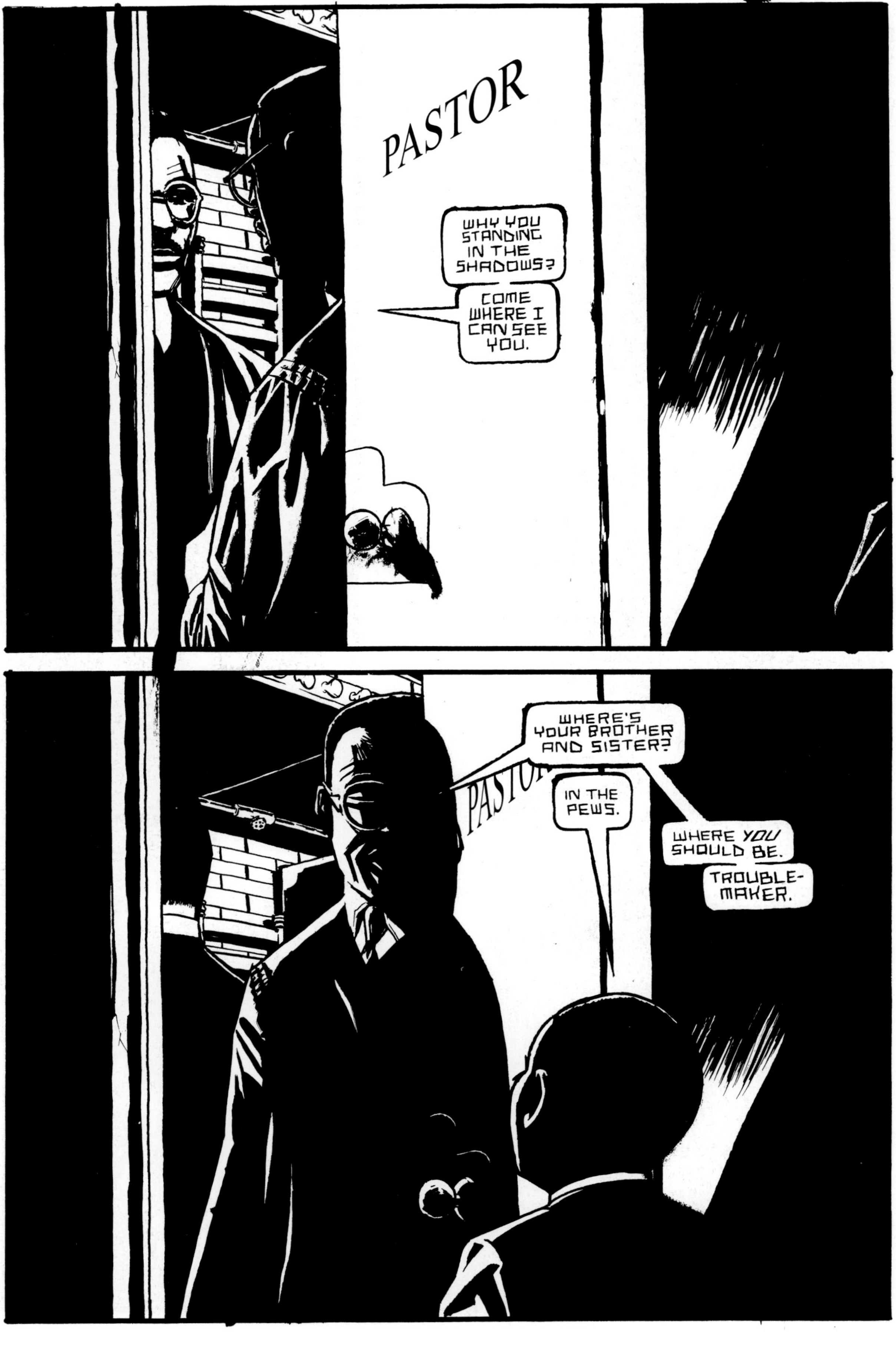
PASTOR
WHY YOU STANDING IN THE SHADOWS?
COME WHERE I CAN SEE YOU.
WHERE'S YOUR BROTHER AND SISTER?
IN THE PEWS.
WHERE *YOU* SHOULD BE.
TROUBLE-MAKER.

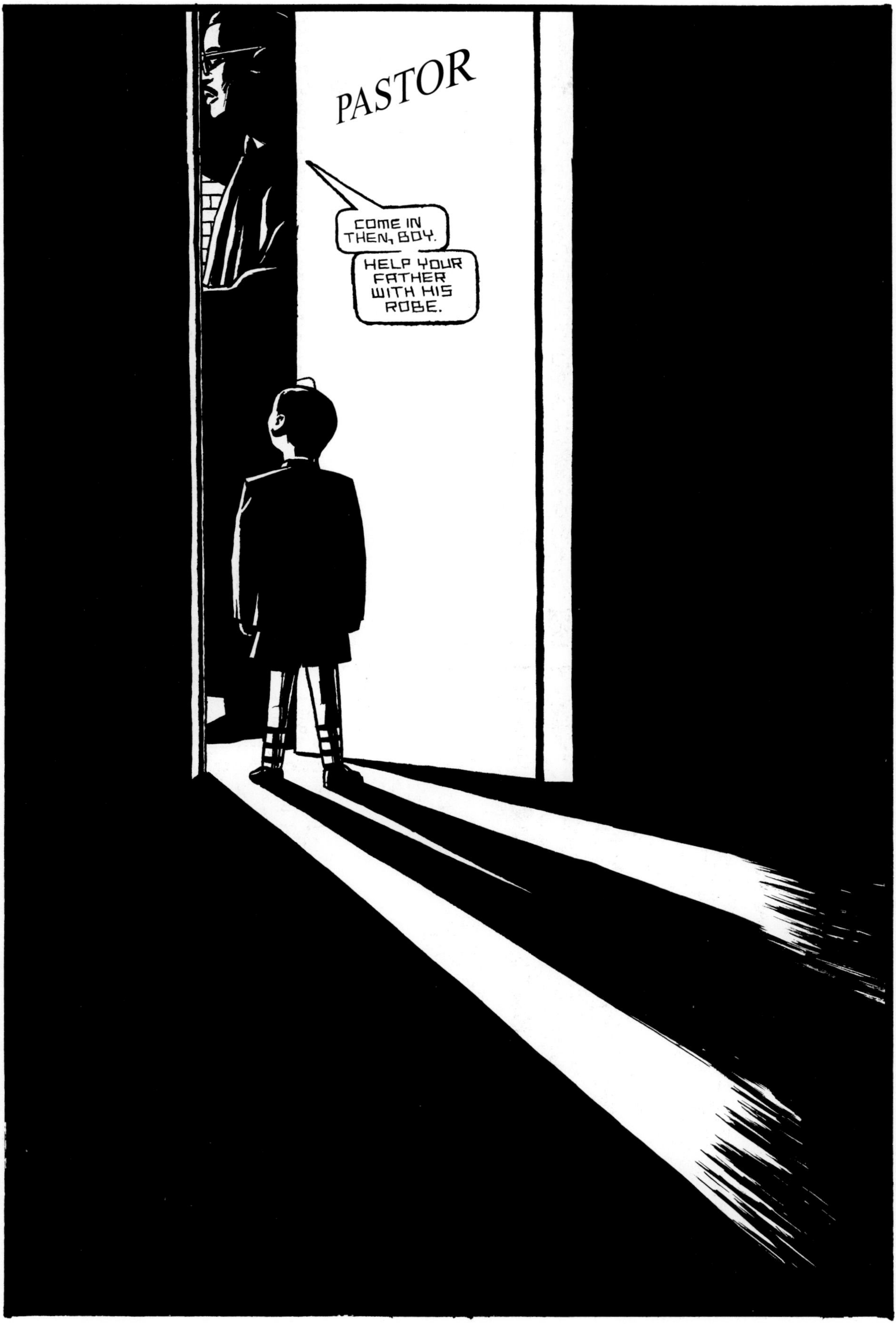
PASTOR
COME IN THEN, BOY.
HELP YOUR FATHER WITH HIS ROBE.

A COMIC BOOK BIOGRAPHY

KING

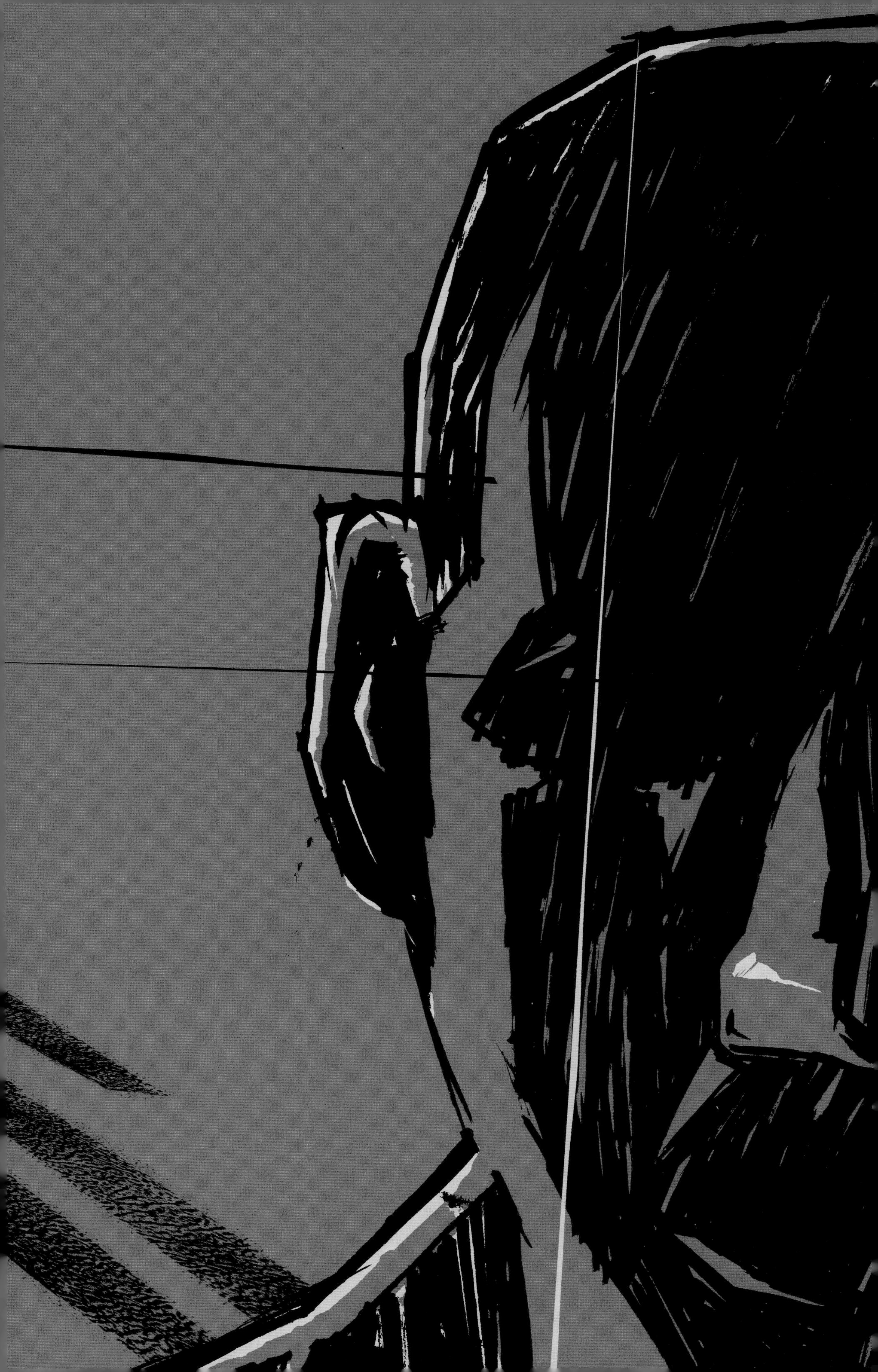

Fantagraphics Books
7563 Lake City Way
Seattle, WA 98115 USA.

Edited by Gary Groth
Promotion by Eric Reynolds
Published by Gary Groth & Kim Thompson

First Fantagraphics Books edition: February, 2005

ISBN 1-56097-622-5

Printed in Korea

A King in Comics

Introduction by Stanley Crouch

In this comic book (or "graphic novel") Ho Che Anderson offers an epic telling of the story of Martin Luther King, Jr. We are given a mix of fact and fiction, an interpretation for the purposes of entertainment, and a jumbling together of imagined conversations and relationships that puts it as much in the realm of fiction as biography. It is neither an insult nor an evasion of the size of the man or his struggle; it is a recognition of the fact that King now resides in many aspects of our culture. This book is proof of how far the image, the story, the legend, the myth, the varied meanings, and the endurance of the tale travel in our society. In our technological time we measure how important the meaning of a person is—particularly one who arrives outside the electronic auction block of advertising—by how many places in our communication network acknowledge the existence of the person, living or dead. In that sense, a once obscure man who rose to fame on the shoulders of a turbulent time became a conqueror while alive and an ever greater conqueror after his death.

This is so true that Martin Luther King, Jr. is now celebrated as a national hero with a holiday usually given over to sound bites. Though born the descendant of a group of people brought here purely for the purposes of forced labor, his birth is now marked by a brief vacation from work, a closing of city, state, and federal offices. It is a day set aside for the end of governmental business. Every American child, looking forward to that play day, knows Martin Luther King's name and may wonder who he is other than someone who said four words in Washington, D.C. a long time ago: "I have a dream." So he is now part of the national heritage. He has left his blood family to represent a high point of individual achievement in the family of man. The breadth of his significance has inspired newspaper articles, essays, biographies; there are conspiracy theories, documentaries, and television shows that use invented dialogue for what are known as "docudramas." Martin Luther King's image can be seen on posters, in paintings, sculpture, and in the voodoo dolls of vulgar representation that are part of the doom of all great men in a commercial culture of souvenirs. That he can be both elevated and trivialized, the subject of serious contemplation, scholarship, and conferences on the one hand, and the puppet of perfectly insane projections on the other, seals the fate of his tale. Martin Luther King's story has been taken across the wilderness of our needs and placed in the cultural and historical pyramids reserved for those whose journeys have taught us something in high relief about the hope and the troubles of the species.

Mr. Anderson understands this and wants this book to be taken as "an independent work on its own, but also an introduction to the story of the man. Some people might think this is not enough. If that's the way they see it, this should be an inspiration to go

to other sources if they want to get a more complex and nuanced picture of the man. My problem was to make a compelling visual narrative out of a cartoon book. Cartoons were never intended for nuance and all that. They are supposed to be simple and direct. But this is part of my protest against that. That's what separates our time from the old time cartoonists. Modern cartoonists can protest simplistic ideas by bringing their own sense of what makes something complex. That's what I did. This man was many things. He was a tragic hero, he was a martyr, he was from a privileged class and might have felt some guilt. He was chosen by history to *make* history instead of watching history happen—*and* he had flaws like we all do. What I learned from six months of reading books about the man and studying documentaries about him and the civil rights movement grounded me in his story. There are books that came out after I did this that I wish were available when I was preparing myself to create my version of the story. But you never get it *all*. You take what is there and you do the best that you can, which is where all the artistry comes in. No matter how much you know, you still have to *create*. You have to imagine how things looked and how they felt. That's what I wanted to do. I wanted to create *my* version of this story. The life of Martin Luther King was the script. I had to be the director. These aren't cartoon versions of photographs. These are my camera angles, my close-ups, my decisions of when it's going to be black and white or in color or whatever. That's what I want to be judged by because that's where *I* come in."

I think it is good to take Mr. Anderson at his word and to judge his work within its ambitions and its inevitable limits. I find the mix of drama and melodrama, of fact and fantasy, of the tale of a man whose life ended in tragedy more than a bit interesting. This is especially true for me when we think that the telling of any tale that does not start at the beginning and go straight to the end is a form of fiction, since fiction is about imposed form while life seems to be about successions of events that are largely electro-magnetic and chemical. Purpose, the facts or fantasies of good and evil, are all human creations, unless we explain things in terms of faith (there ain't nothing wrong with that). Though we would be mad if we were to compare the cartoonist to the Renaissance painter of religious subjects—doing some kind of insubstantial twisting in which far too broad generalizations are made for the purposes of comparison—there are still things we can think about. We should be able to recognize that that both the Renaissance painter of religious subjects and the cartoonist labor within the same arena of decisions, however different their dimensions. Both are improvisors whose creations arrive in the form of design. The heritage and the traditions out of which each comes are, surely, vast in their distinctions. The Renaissance artist draws upon a line of tradition that leads back to Greece and the attempt to bring the human being into three dimensions from stone. Above all else, the painter of a biblical subject has to decide on the perspective, the time of day or the quality of night. The faces, the facial expressions, the colors of the clothes and the surroundings come from him. Familiarity does not impose strict limits on the images. The cartoonist arrives with abstraction, simplifications or satirizing images, when not the rendering of fantastical creatures and places. The cartoonist is also heir to a much larger world of visual images, plastic and not.

That is where Mr. Anderson makes his statement. All of the photographs and moving images and all of the cartoons in the entire world are part of his heritage. He also knows that the moving picture itself is an illusion of single shots moving too fast for the eye to notice. So he calls upon everything and creates very impressive conditions of movement and contemplation. His ambition to make a good piece of entertainment is achieved. There is a level of complexity and a superb capturing of the range of Afro-American features, which include the frequent varieties of lighter skins and the patches of facial freck-les that do appear very often in fine art paintings of black people by black people. Figure that one out for yourself. But notice that Mr. Anderson achieves this in black and white alone, which is a high mark of skill. Perhaps what is most interesting is how the images themselves move from the world of Brenda Starr all the way over to the abstractions of the last third of the book when the characters appear to be totemic, standing or striding in a world now completely mythical, the land of dreams and tragic finality. Taken for what it is, I think the reader will move through this book more than a few times, stop-ping frequently along the way to study a surprising or emotionally provocative image. Neither a writer nor an illustrator could ask for more than that.

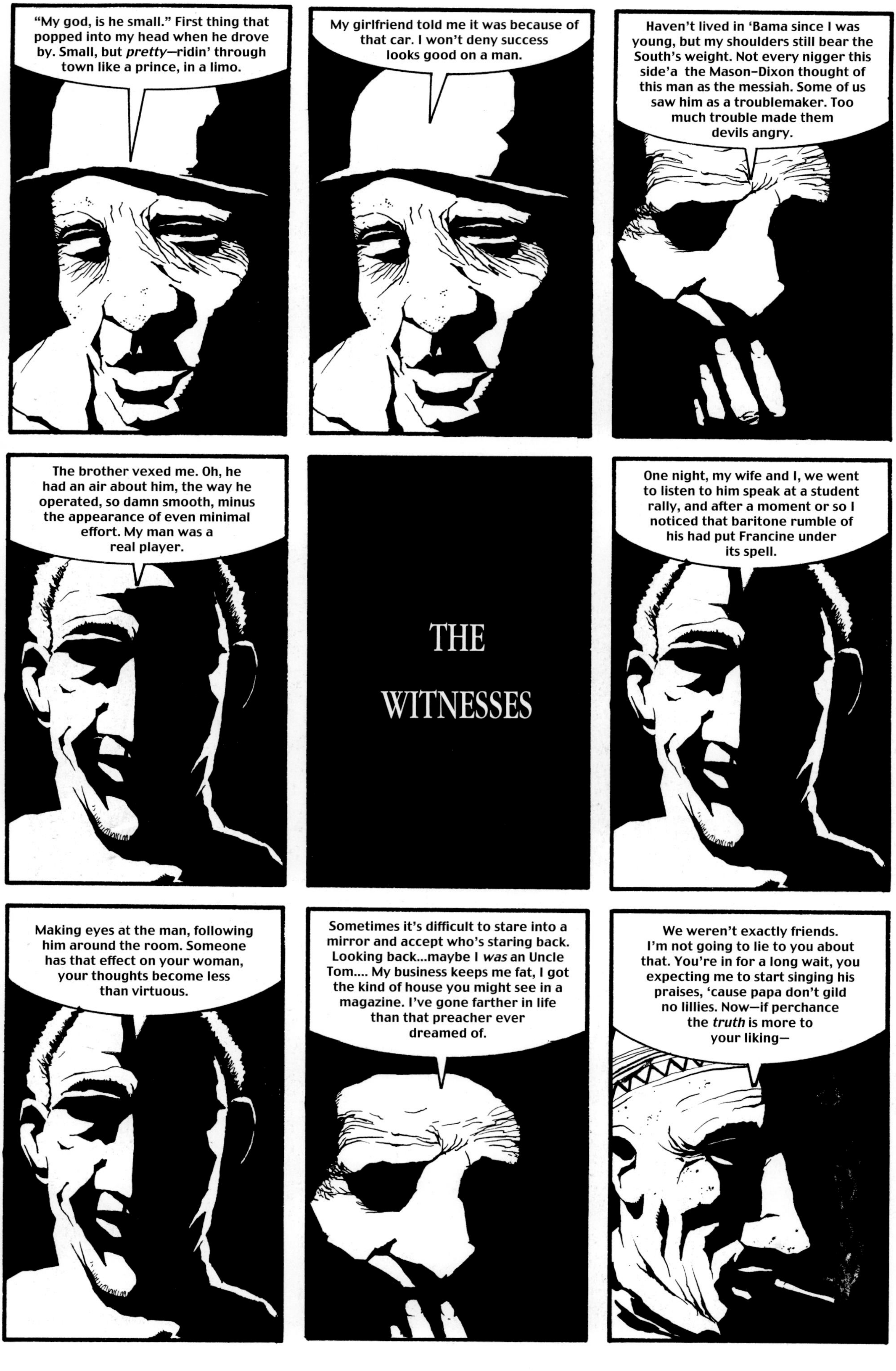
"My god, is he small." First thing that popped into my head when he drove by. Small, but *pretty*—ridin' through town like a prince, in a limo.
My girlfriend told me it was because of that car. I won't deny success looks good on a man.
Haven't lived in 'Bama since I was young, but my shoulders still bear the South's weight. Not every nigger this side'a the Mason-Dixon thought of this man as the messiah. Some of us saw him as a troublemaker. Too much trouble made them devils angry.
The brother vexed me. Oh, he had an air about him, the way he operated, so damn smooth, minus the appearance of even minimal effort. My man was a real player.
THE WITNESSES
One night, my wife and I, we went to listen to him speak at a student rally, and after a moment or so I noticed that baritone rumble of his had put Francine under its spell.
Making eyes at the man, following him around the room. Someone has that effect on your woman, your thoughts become less than virtuous.
Sometimes it's difficult to stare into a mirror and accept who's staring back. Looking back...maybe I *was* an Uncle Tom.... My business keeps me fat, I got the kind of house you might see in a magazine. I've gone farther in life than that preacher ever dreamed of.
We weren't exactly friends. I'm not going to lie to you about that. You're in for a long wait, you expecting me to start singing his praises, 'cause papa don't gild no lillies. Now—if perchance the *truth* is more to your liking—

The church was what made him. The church was who he was. It gave his whole world order, gave it balance. It made him special—he was the *reverend's* boy. The *reverend's* boy wasn't *allowed* to feel anger.

White folks? What can I say? They never wanted any part of us so I decided early I didn't want no part of them. It's like they ain't happy 'less they fuckin' with the Black man. And this man wanted to *integrate?* With *them?*

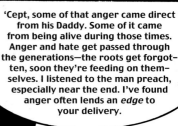

'Cept, some of that anger came direct from his Daddy. Some of it came from being alive during those times. Anger and hate get passed through the generations—the roots get forgotten, soon they're feeding on themselves. I listened to the man preach, especially near the end. I've found anger often lends an *edge* to your delivery.

Though I'd love to forget, I vividly remember making such a *buffoon* of myself at the sit-ins. I had such a crush on Dr. King. My girlfriends thought he was too dark, but I just *threw* myself at him, my god.

I saw the struggle he had to endure, giving out constantly, rarely stopping to take anything in. That kind of existence, you take comforts where you can find them. I'm a woman—I'm not condoning some of his actions on the road, but I can't bring myself to judge. Maybe he didn't always *do* the right thing—but he always *tried.*

He was just a man. Full stop. No better'n the rest of us, no worse'n the rest of us. Don't talk to me about myths and legends, I don't have no interest in that stuff—

There was a point he had no time for the pulpit, he wrestled with the church's role in his life. The South's all about the church, and I'll tell you, he could rock the church house like few ever have.

For a man so devoted to peace to live such a violent life.... And his wife—oh, that woman, so beautiful, so much like my daughter in her way.

People like this aren't built very often. The *life* this man led— I met him once, at a party. We had an argument about the power of love. Actually, I've got a *couple* of stories—if you're interested.

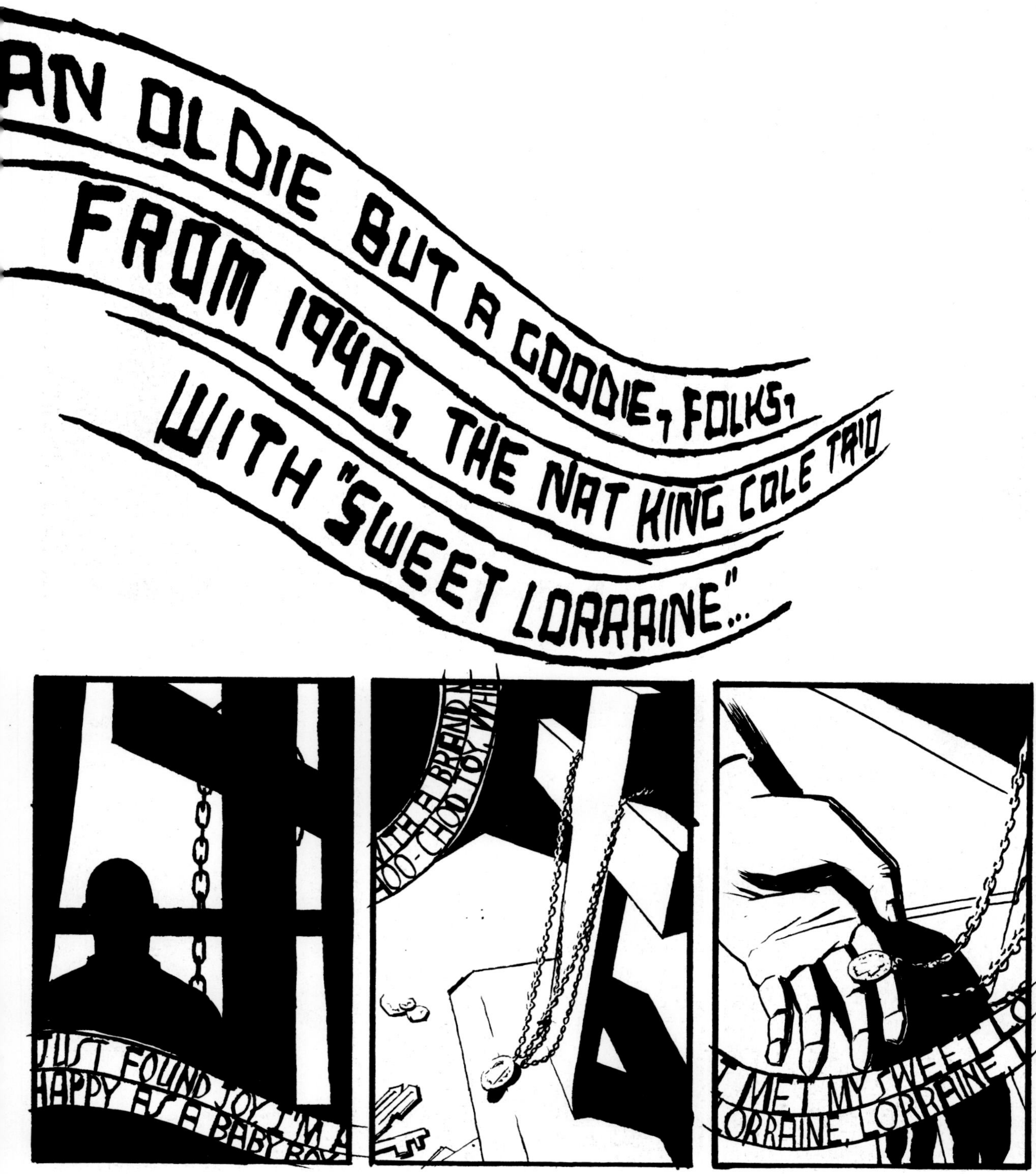

AN OLDIE BUT A GOODIE, FOLKS,
FROM 1940, THE NAT KING COLE TRIO
WITH "SWEET LORRAINE"...
JUST FOUND JOY I'M A
HAPPY AS A BABY BOY
WITH A BRAND N
OO-CHOO TOY, WH
MET MY SWEET LO
LORRAINE, LORRAINE

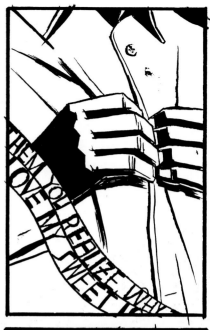
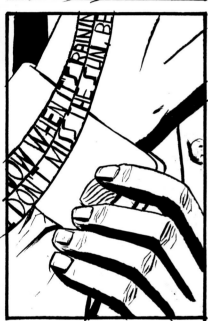

BOSTON

UNIVERSITY.

1952

Coretta Scott? Guess who. Mary said it'd be OK if I called.

Is it OK?

So these are the tones you inspire.... I've been trying to reach you all week.

Nothing too sinister. Dinner... perhaps a drink to wind things down, we can risk an evening of excess, just this once.

15

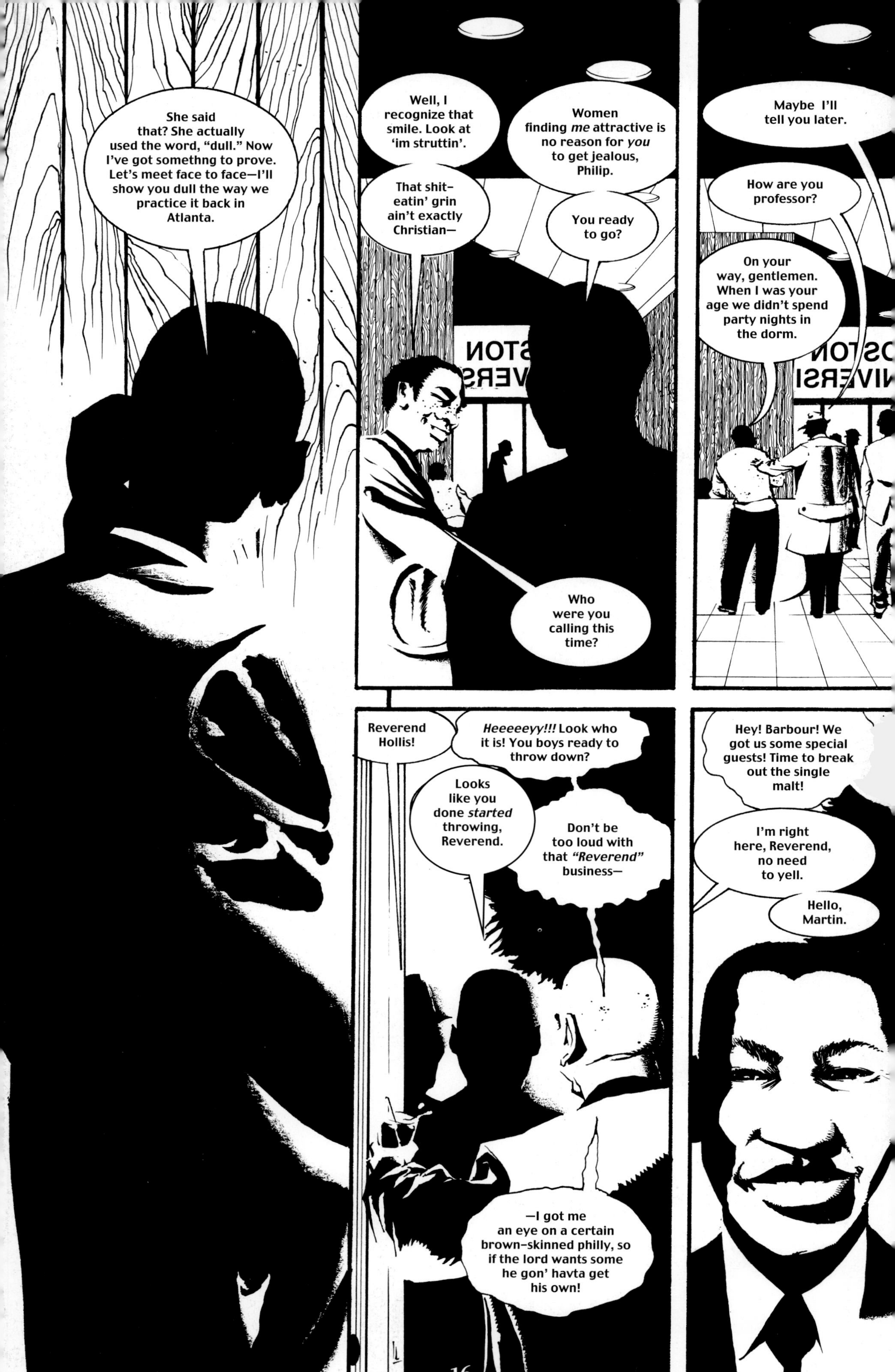
She said that? She actually used the word, "dull." Now I've got somethng to prove. Let's meet face to face—I'll show you dull the way we practice it back in Atlanta.
Well, I recognize that smile. Look at 'im struttin'.
That shit-eatin' grin ain't exactly Christian—
Women finding *me* attractive is no reason for *you* to get jealous, Philip.
You ready to go?
Who were you calling this time?
Maybe I'll tell you later.
How are you professor?
On your way, gentlemen. When I was your age we didn't spend party nights in the dorm.
Reverend Hollis!
Heeeeeyy!!! Look who it is! You boys ready to throw down?
Looks like you done *started* throwing, Reverend.
Don't be too loud with that *"Reverend"* business—
—I got me an eye on a certain brown-skinned philly, so if the lord wants some he gon' havta get his own!
Hey! Barbour! We got us some special guests! Time to break out the single malt!
I'm right here, Reverend, no need to yell.
Hello, Martin.

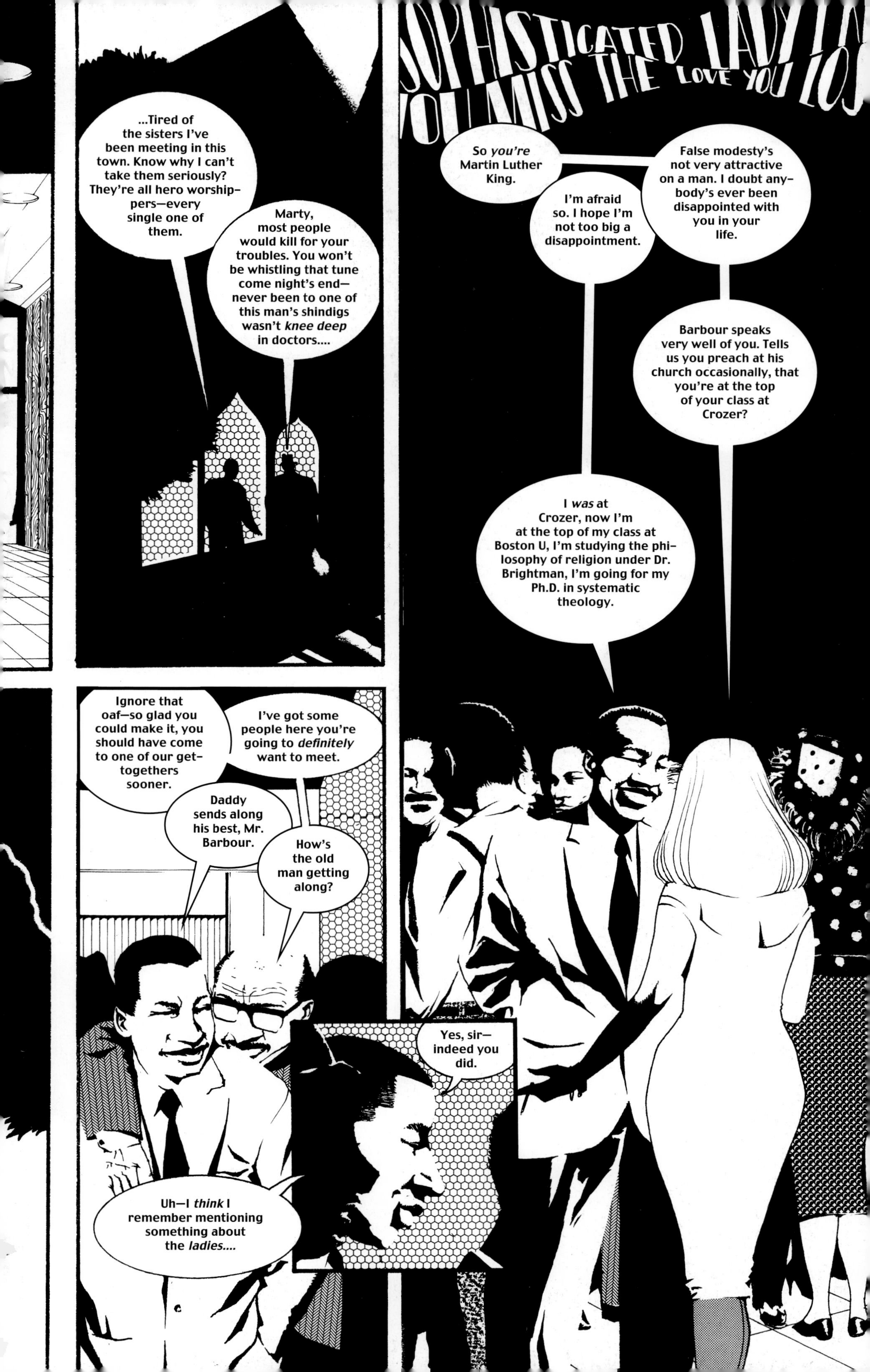
...Tired of the sisters I've been meeting in this town. Know why I can't take them seriously? They're all hero worship-pers—every single one of them.
Marty, most people would kill for your troubles. You won't be whistling that tune come night's end—never been to one of this man's shindigs wasn't *knee deep* in doctors....
Ignore that oaf—so glad you could make it, you should have come to one of our get-togethers sooner.
I've got some people here you're going to *definitely* want to meet.
Daddy sends along his best, Mr. Barbour.
How's the old man getting along?
Uh—I *think* I remember mentioning something about the *ladies*....
Yes, sir—indeed you did.
SOPHISTICATED LADY
YOU MISS THE LOVE YOU
So *you're* Martin Luther King.
I'm afraid so. I hope I'm not too big a disappointment.
False modesty's not very attractive on a man. I doubt any-body's ever been disappointed with you in your life.
Barbour speaks very well of you. Tells us you preach at his church occasionally, that you're at the top of your class at Crozer?
I *was* at Crozer, now I'm at the top of my class at Boston U, I'm studying the phi-losophy of religion under Dr. Brightman, I'm going for my Ph.D. in systematic theology.

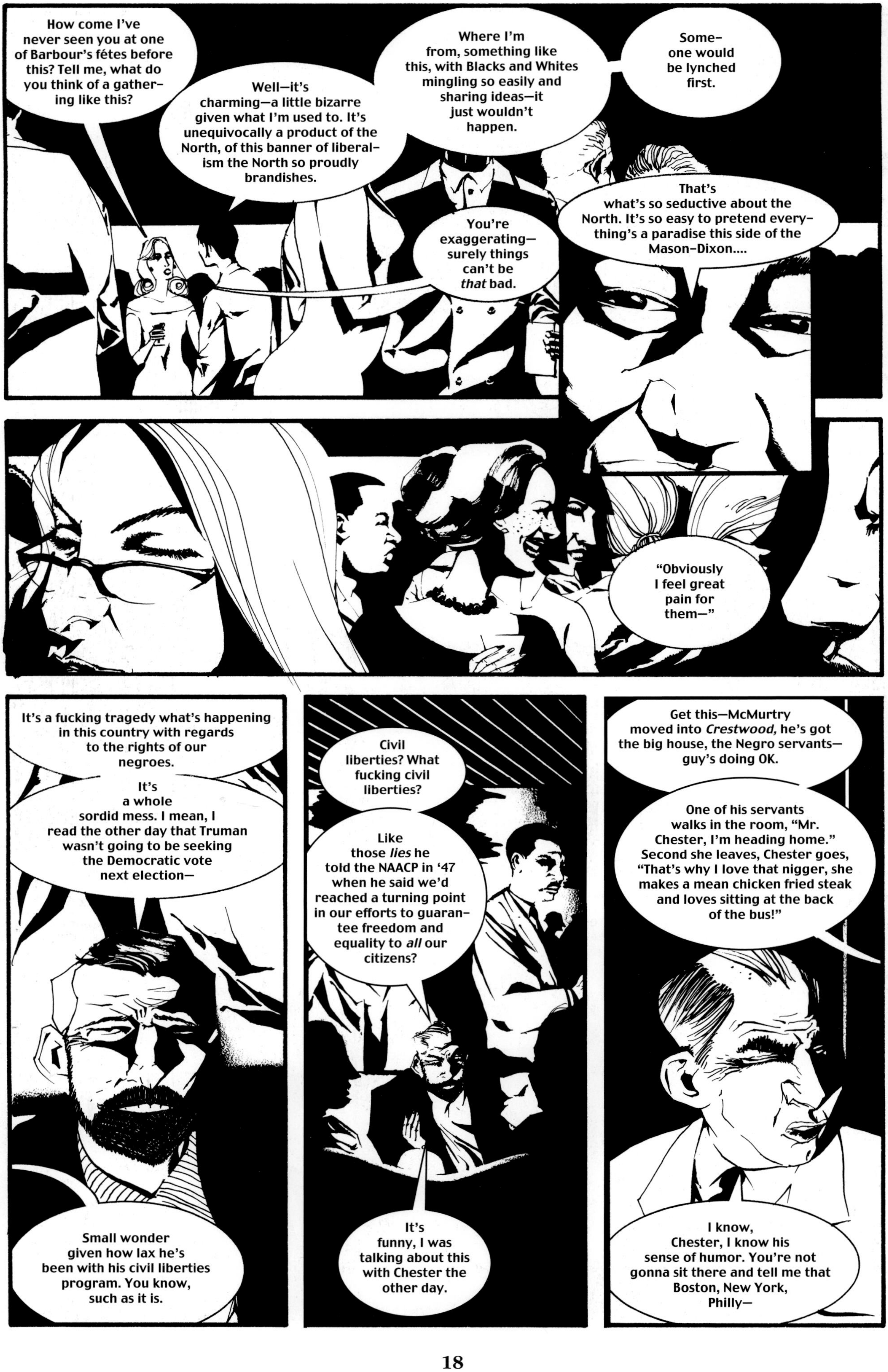
How come I've never seen you at one of Barbour's fêtes before this? Tell me, what do you think of a gathering like this?
Well—it's charming—a little bizarre given what I'm used to. It's unequivocally a product of the North, of this banner of liberalism the North so proudly brandishes.
Where I'm from, something like this, with Blacks and Whites mingling so easily and sharing ideas—it just wouldn't happen.
Someone would be lynched first.
You're exaggerating—surely things can't be *that* bad.
That's what's so seductive about the North. It's so easy to pretend everything's a paradise this side of the Mason-Dixon....
"Obviously I feel great pain for them—"
It's a fucking tragedy what's happening in this country with regards to the rights of our negroes.
It's a whole sordid mess. I mean, I read the other day that Truman wasn't going to be seeking the Democratic vote next election—
Small wonder given how lax he's been with his civil liberties program. You know, such as it is.
Civil liberties? What fucking civil liberties?
Like those *lies* he told the NAACP in '47 when he said we'd reached a turning point in our efforts to guarantee freedom and equality to *all* our citizens?
It's funny, I was talking about this with Chester the other day.
Get this—McMurtry moved into *Crestwood,* he's got the big house, the Negro servants—guy's doing OK.
One of his servants walks in the room, "Mr. Chester, I'm heading home." Second she leaves, Chester goes, "That's why I love that nigger, she makes a mean chicken fried steak and loves sitting at the back of the bus!"
I know, Chester, I know his sense of humor. You're not gonna sit there and tell me that Boston, New York, Philly—

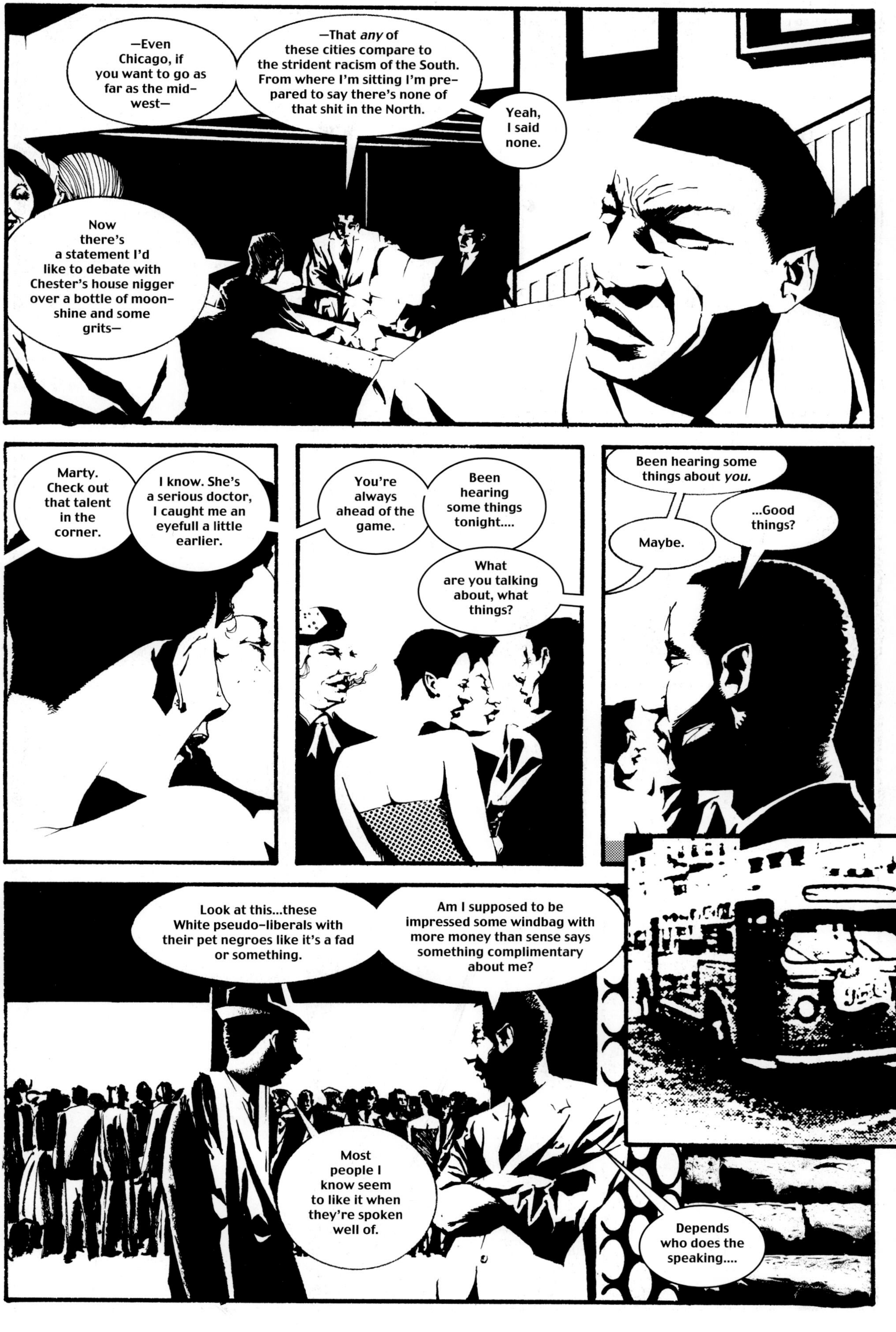
—Even Chicago, if you want to go as far as the mid-west—
—That *any* of these cities compare to the strident racism of the South. From where I'm sitting I'm pre-pared to say there's none of that shit in the North.
Yeah, I said none.
Now there's a statement I'd like to debate with Chester's house nigger over a bottle of moon-shine and some grits—
Marty. Check out that talent in the corner.
I know. She's a serious doctor, I caught me an eyefull a little earlier.
You're always ahead of the game.
Been hearing some things tonight....
What are you talking about, what things?
Been hearing some things about *you.*
Maybe.
...Good things?
Look at this...these White pseudo-liberals with their pet negroes like it's a fad or something.
Am I supposed to be impressed some windbag with more money than sense says something complimentary about me?
Most people I know seem to like it when they're spoken well of.
Depends who does the speaking....

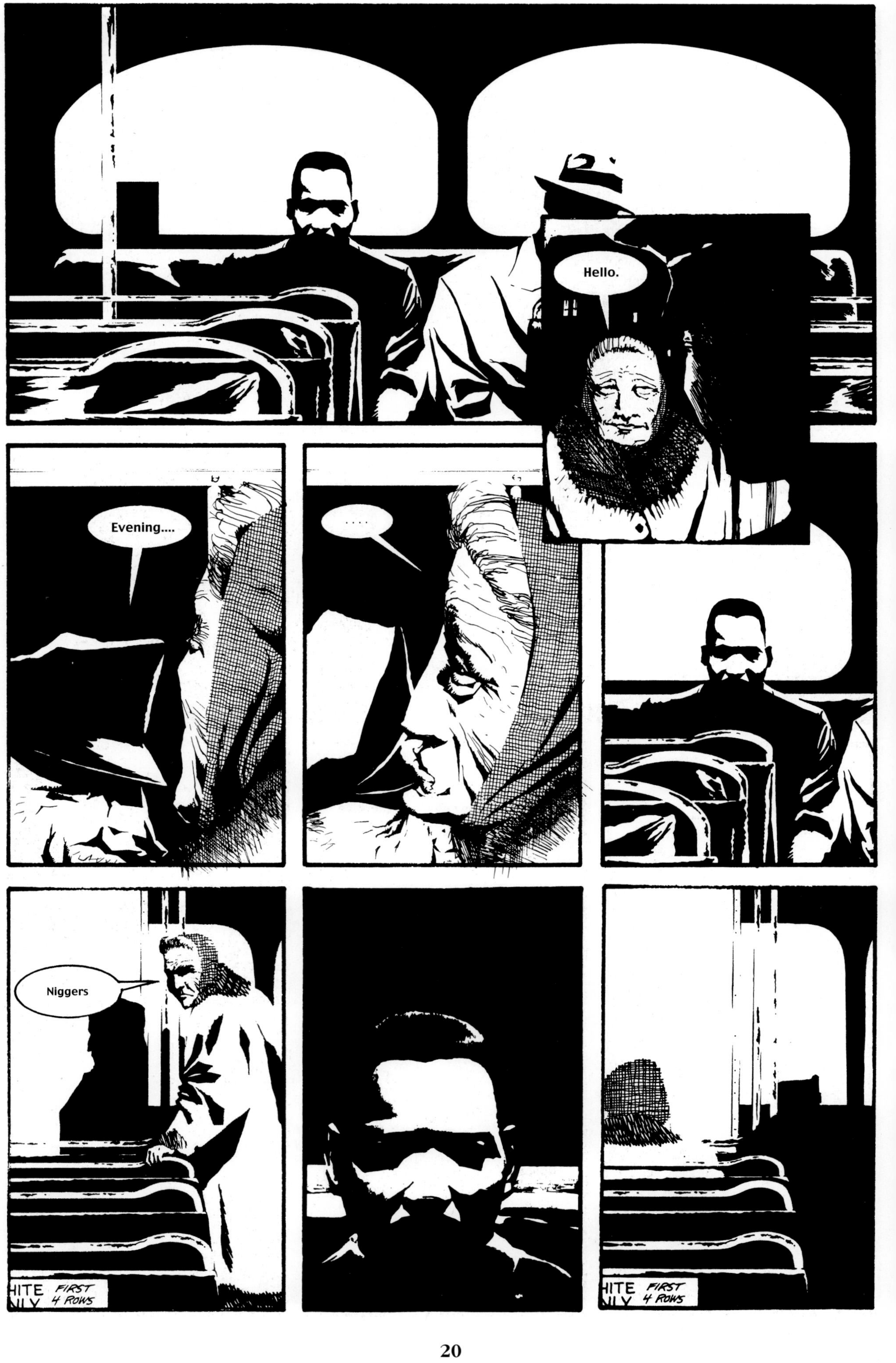
Hello.
Evening....
....
Niggers
HITE FIRST
NLY 4 ROWS
HITE FIRST
NLY 4 ROWS

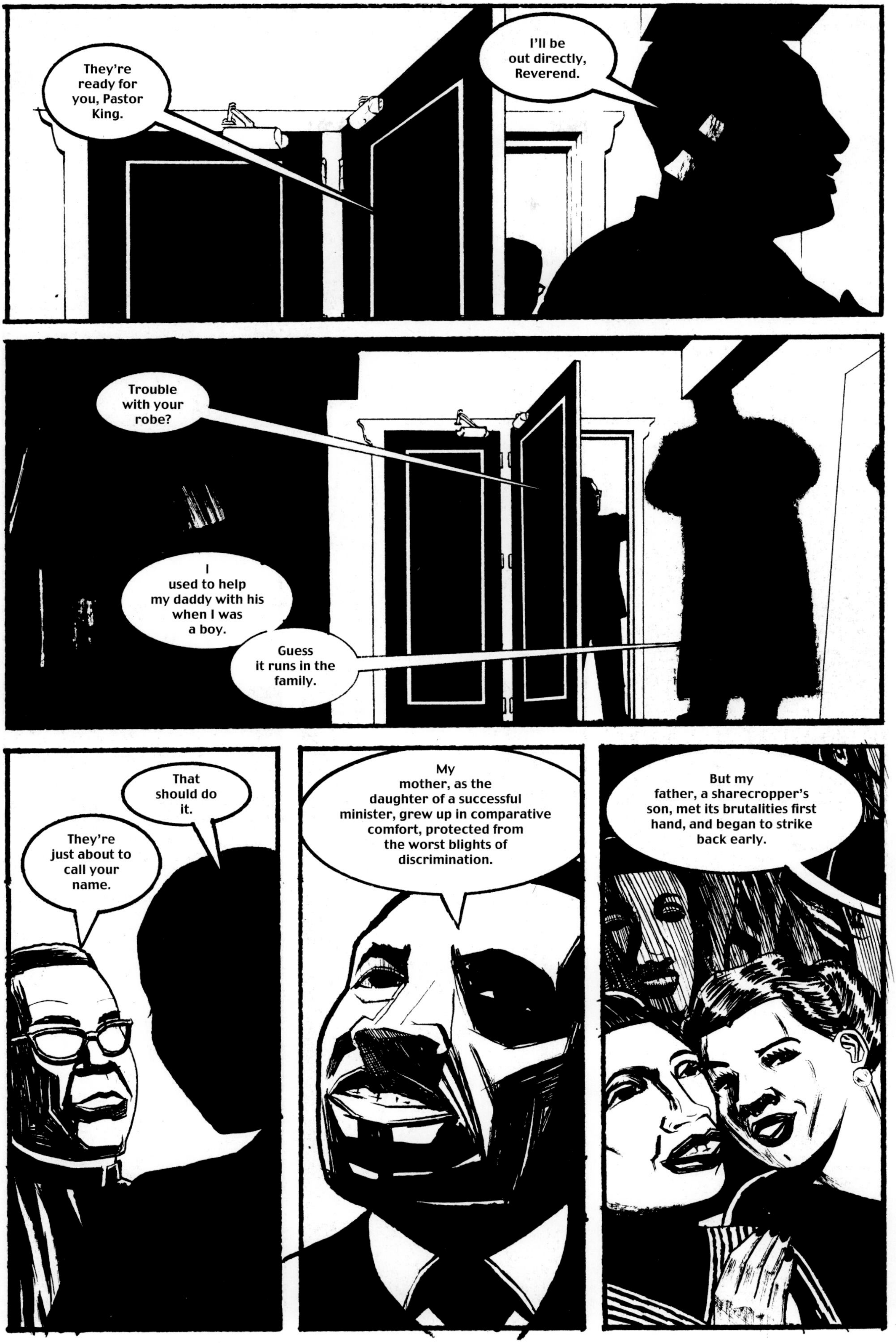
They're ready for you, Pastor King.
I'll be out directly, Reverend.
Trouble with your robe?
I used to help my daddy with his when I was a boy.
Guess it runs in the family.
They're just about to call your name.
That should do it.
My mother, as the daughter of a successful minister, grew up in comparative comfort, protected from the worst blights of discrimination.
But my father, a sharecropper's son, met its brutalities first hand, and began to strike back early.

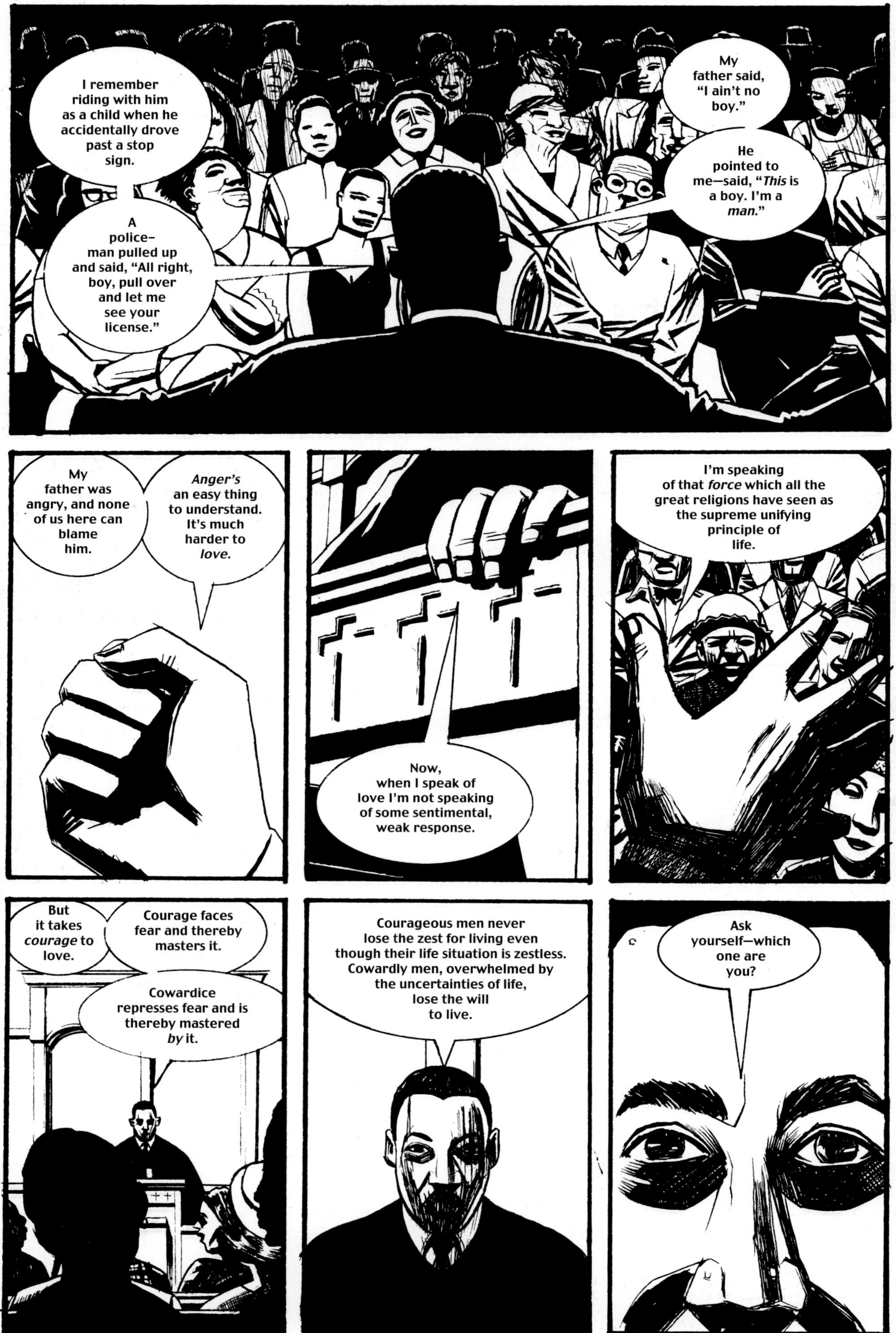
I remember riding with him as a child when he accidentally drove past a stop sign.
A police–man pulled up and said, "All right, boy, pull over and let me see your license."
My father said, "I ain't no boy."
He pointed to me—said, "*This* is a boy. I'm a *man*."
My father was angry, and none of us here can blame him.
Anger's an easy thing to understand. It's much harder to *love.*
Now, when I speak of love I'm not speaking of some sentimental, weak response.
I'm speaking of that *force* which all the great religions have seen as the supreme unifying principle of life.
But it takes *courage* to love.
Courage faces fear and thereby masters it.
Cowardice represses fear and is thereby mastered *by* it.
Courageous men never lose the zest for living even though their life situation is zestless. Cowardly men, overwhelmed by the uncertainties of life, lose the will to live.
Ask yourself—which one are you?

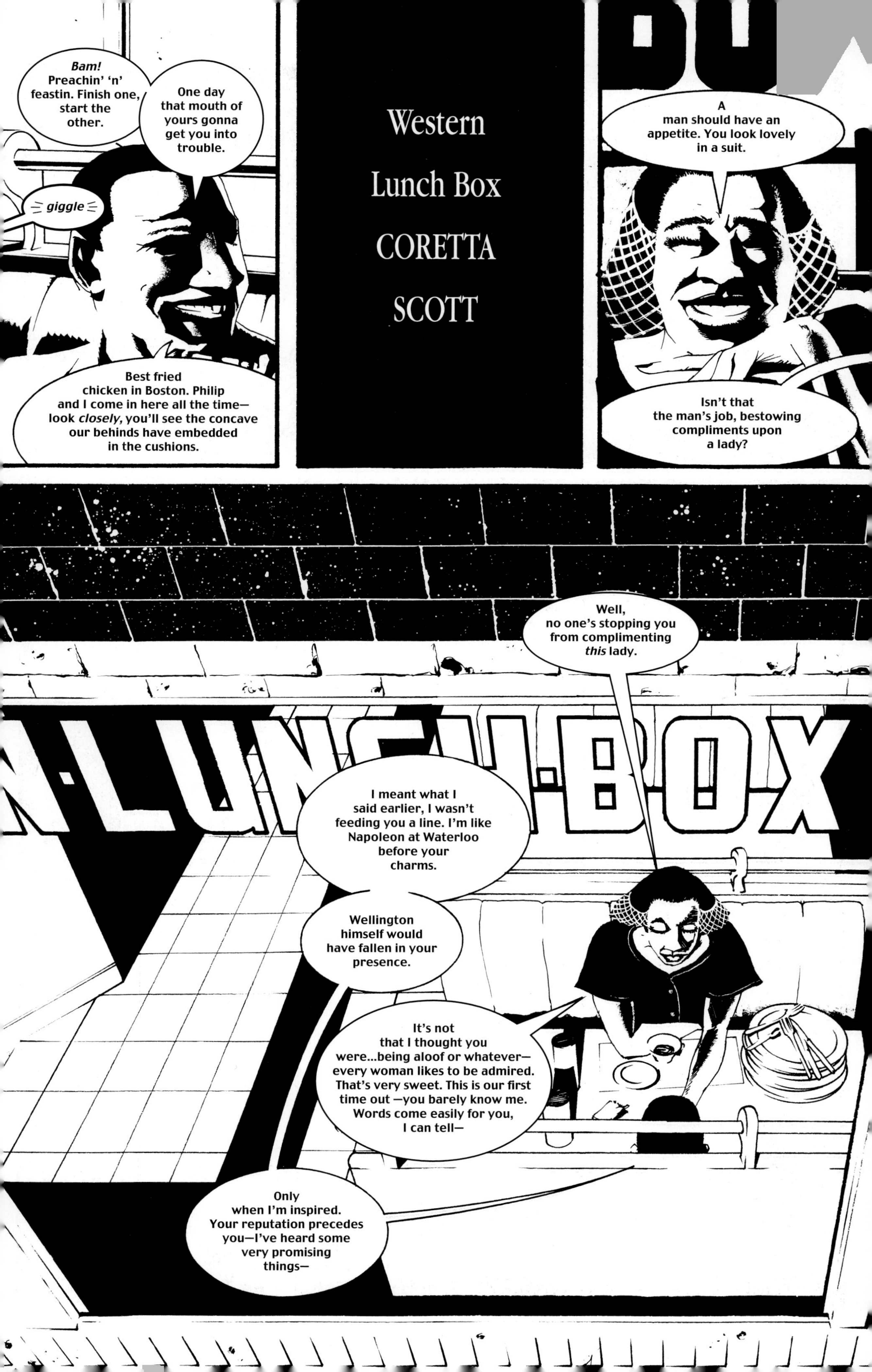

Bam! Preachin' 'n' feastin. Finish one, start the other.
One day that mouth of yours gonna get you into trouble.
giggle
Best fried chicken in Boston. Philip and I come in here all the time—look closely, you'll see the concave our behinds have embedded in the cushions.
Western Lunch Box CORETTA SCOTT
A man should have an appetite. You look lovely in a suit.
Isn't that the man's job, bestowing compliments upon a lady?
Well, no one's stopping you from complimenting this lady.
I meant what I said earlier, I wasn't feeding you a line. I'm like Napoleon at Waterloo before your charms.
Wellington himself would have fallen in your presence.
It's not that I thought you were...being aloof or whatever—every woman likes to be admired. That's very sweet. This is our first time out —you barely know me. Words come easily for you, I can tell—
Only when I'm inspired. Your reputation precedes you—I've heard some very promising things—

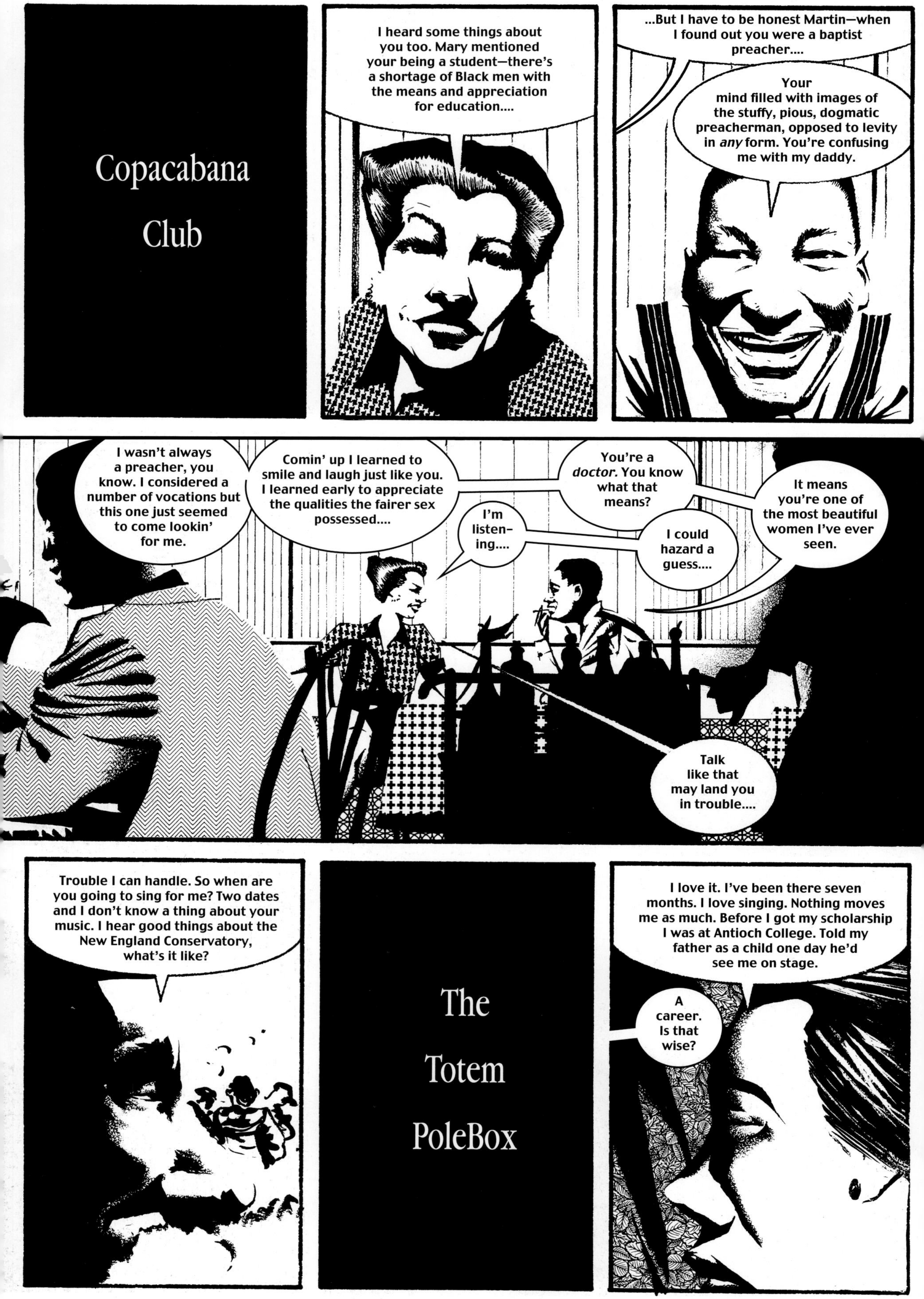
Copacabana Club
I heard some things about you too. Mary mentioned your being a student—there's a shortage of Black men with the means and appreciation for education....
...But I have to be honest Martin—when I found out you were a baptist preacher....
Your mind filled with images of the stuffy, pious, dogmatic preacherman, opposed to levity in *any* form. You're confusing me with my daddy.
I wasn't always a preacher, you know. I considered a number of vocations but this one just seemed to come lookin' for me.
Comin' up I learned to smile and laugh just like you. I learned early to appreciate the qualities the fairer sex possessed....
I'm listen-ing....
You're a *doctor.* You know what that means?
I could hazard a guess....
It means you're one of the most beautiful women I've ever seen.
Talk like that may land you in trouble....
Trouble I can handle. So when are you going to sing for me? Two dates and I don't know a thing about your music. I hear good things about the New England Conservatory, what's it like?
The Totem PoleBox
I love it. I've been there seven months. I love singing. Nothing moves me as much. Before I got my scholarship I was at Antioch College. Told my father as a child one day he'd see me on stage.
A career. Is that wise?

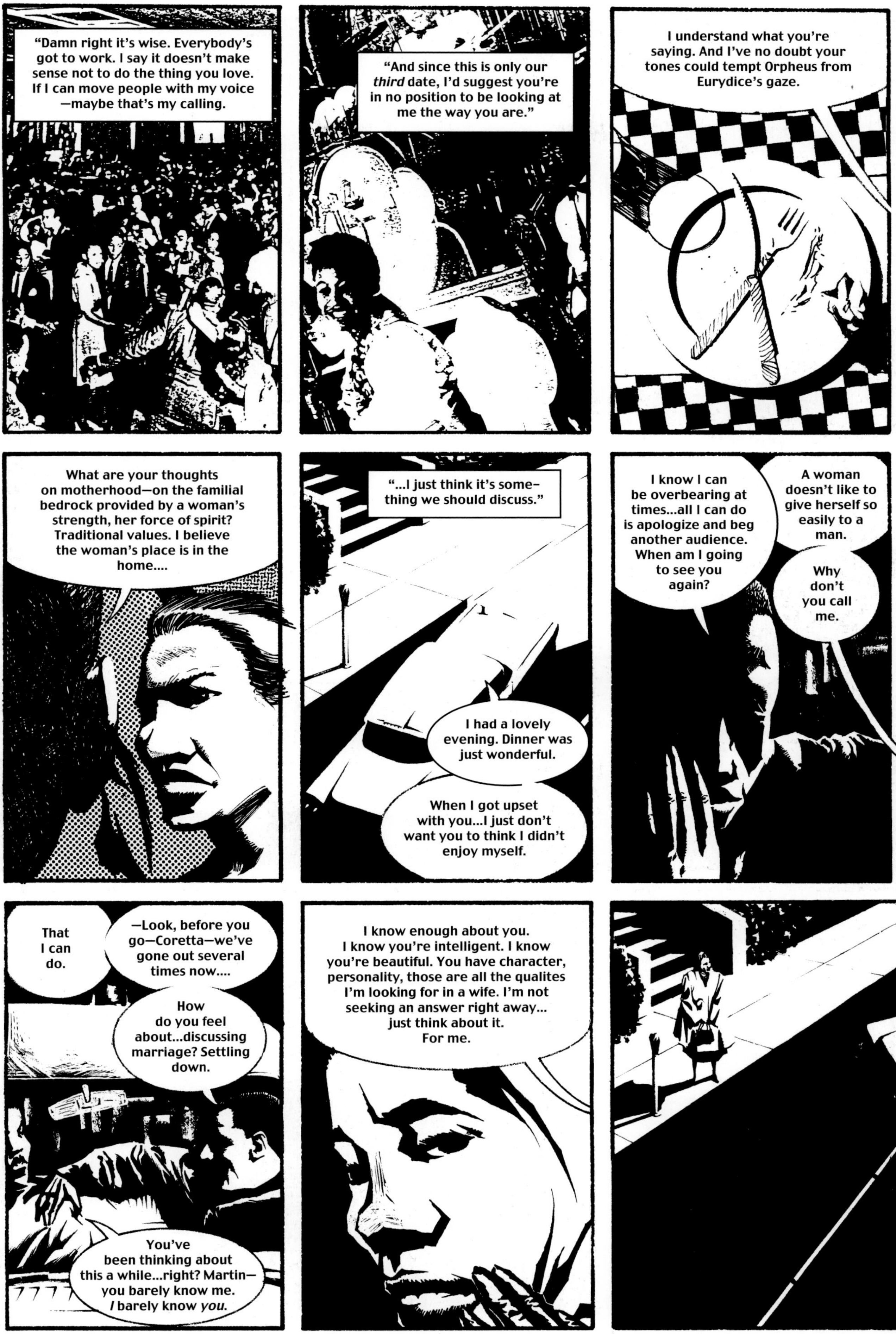
"Damn right it's wise. Everybody's got to work. I say it doesn't make sense not to do the thing you love. If I can move people with my voice —maybe that's my calling.
"And since this is only our *third* date, I'd suggest you're in no position to be looking at me the way you are."
I understand what you're saying. And I've no doubt your tones could tempt Orpheus from Eurydice's gaze.
What are your thoughts on motherhood—on the familial bedrock provided by a woman's strength, her force of spirit? Traditional values. I believe the woman's place is in the home....
"...I just think it's something we should discuss."
I had a lovely evening. Dinner was just wonderful.
When I got upset with you...I just don't want you to think I didn't enjoy myself.
I know I can be overbearing at times...all I can do is apologize and beg another audience. When am I going to see you again?
A woman doesn't like to give herself so easily to a man.
Why don't you call me.
That I can do.
—Look, before you go—Coretta—we've gone out several times now....
How do you feel about...discussing marriage? Settling down.
You've been thinking about this a while...right? Martin—you barely know me. *I* barely know *you*.
I know enough about you. I know you're intelligent. I know you're beautiful. You have character, personality, those are all the qualites I'm looking for in a wife. I'm not seeking an answer right away... just think about it. For me.

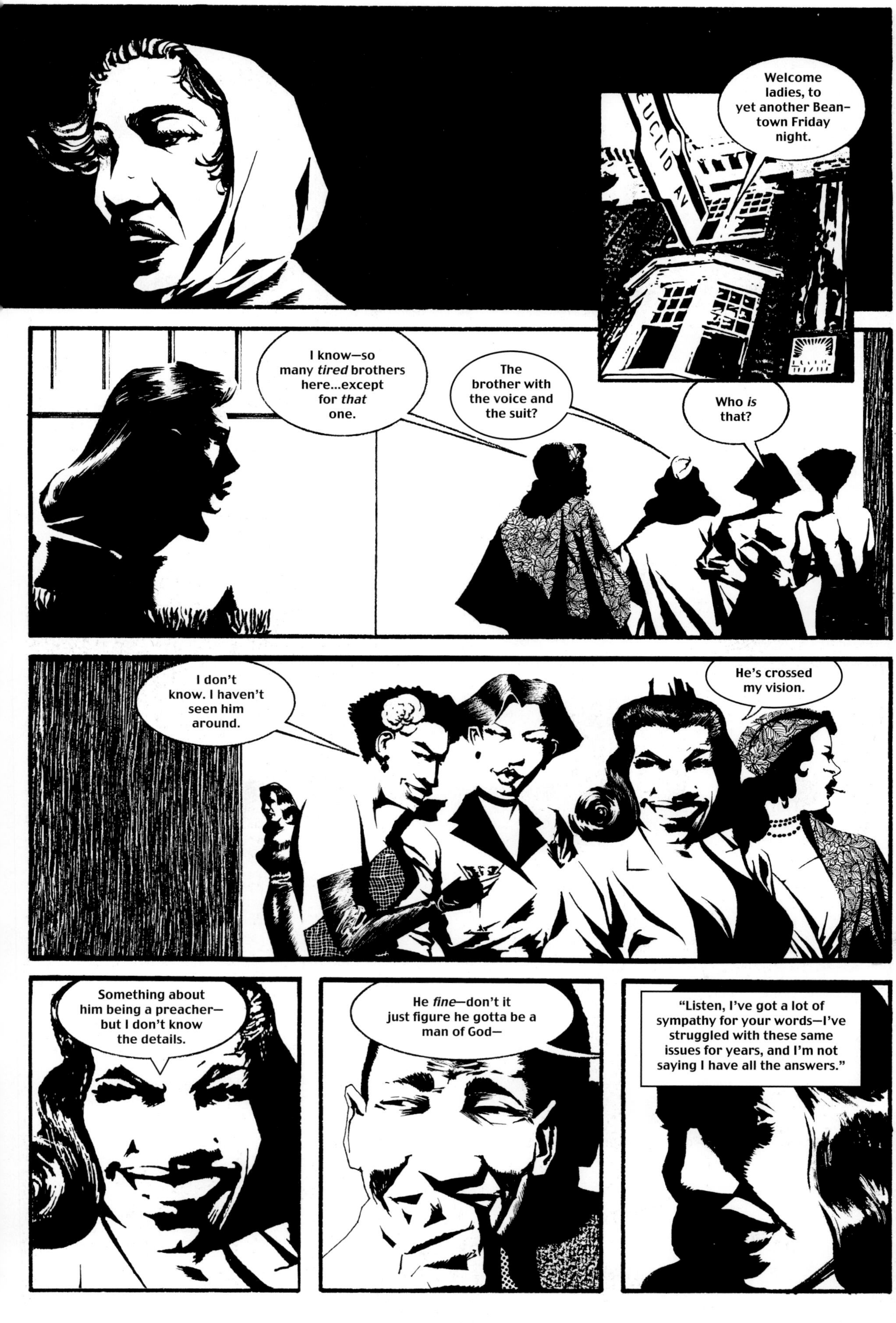
Welcome ladies, to yet another Bean-town Friday night.
I know—so many *tired* brothers here...except for *that* one.
The brother with the voice and the suit?
Who *is* that?
I don't know. I haven't seen him around.
He's crossed my vision.
Something about him being a preacher—but I don't know the details.
He *fine*—don't it just figure he gotta be a man of God—
"Listen, I've got a lot of sympathy for your words—I've struggled with these same issues for years, and I'm not saying I have all the answers."

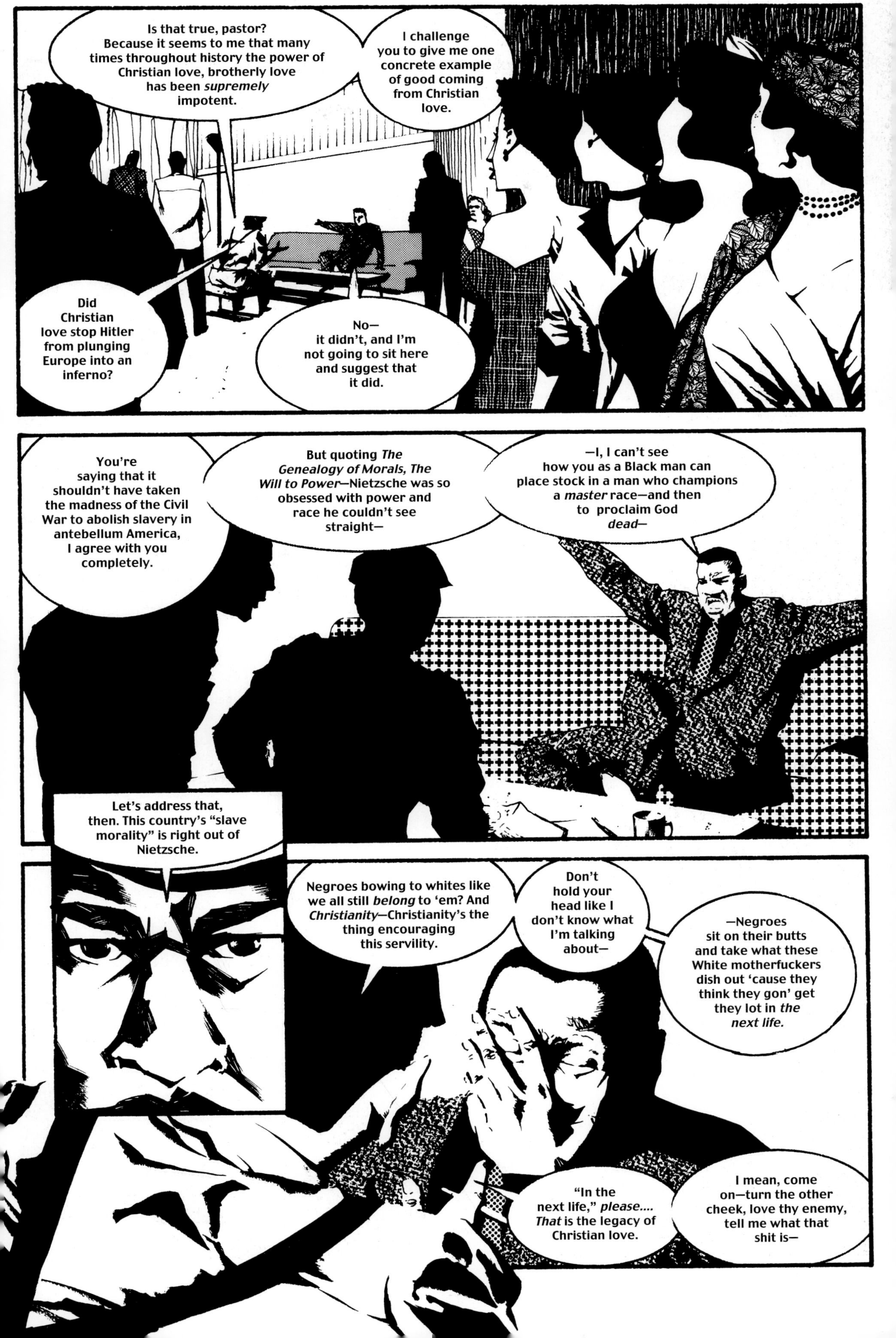
Is that true, pastor? Because it seems to me that many times throughout history the power of Christian love, brotherly love has been *supremely* impotent.
I challenge you to give me one concrete example of good coming from Christian love.
Did Christian love stop Hitler from plunging Europe into an inferno?
No— it didn't, and I'm not going to sit here and suggest that it did.
You're saying that it shouldn't have taken the madness of the Civil War to abolish slavery in antebellum America, I agree with you completely.
But quoting *The Genealogy of Morals, The Will to Power*—Nietzsche was so obsessed with power and race he couldn't see straight—
—I, I can't see how you as a Black man can place stock in a man who champions a *master* race—and then to proclaim God *dead*—
Let's address that, then. This country's "slave morality" is right out of Nietzsche.
Negroes bowing to whites like we all still *belong* to 'em? And *Christianity*—Christianity's the thing encouraging this servility.
Don't hold your head like I don't know what I'm talking about—
—Negroes sit on their butts and take what these White motherfuckers dish out 'cause they think they gon' get they lot in *the next life.*
"In the next life," *please....* *That* is the legacy of Christian love.
I mean, come on—turn the other cheek, love thy enemy, tell me what that shit is—

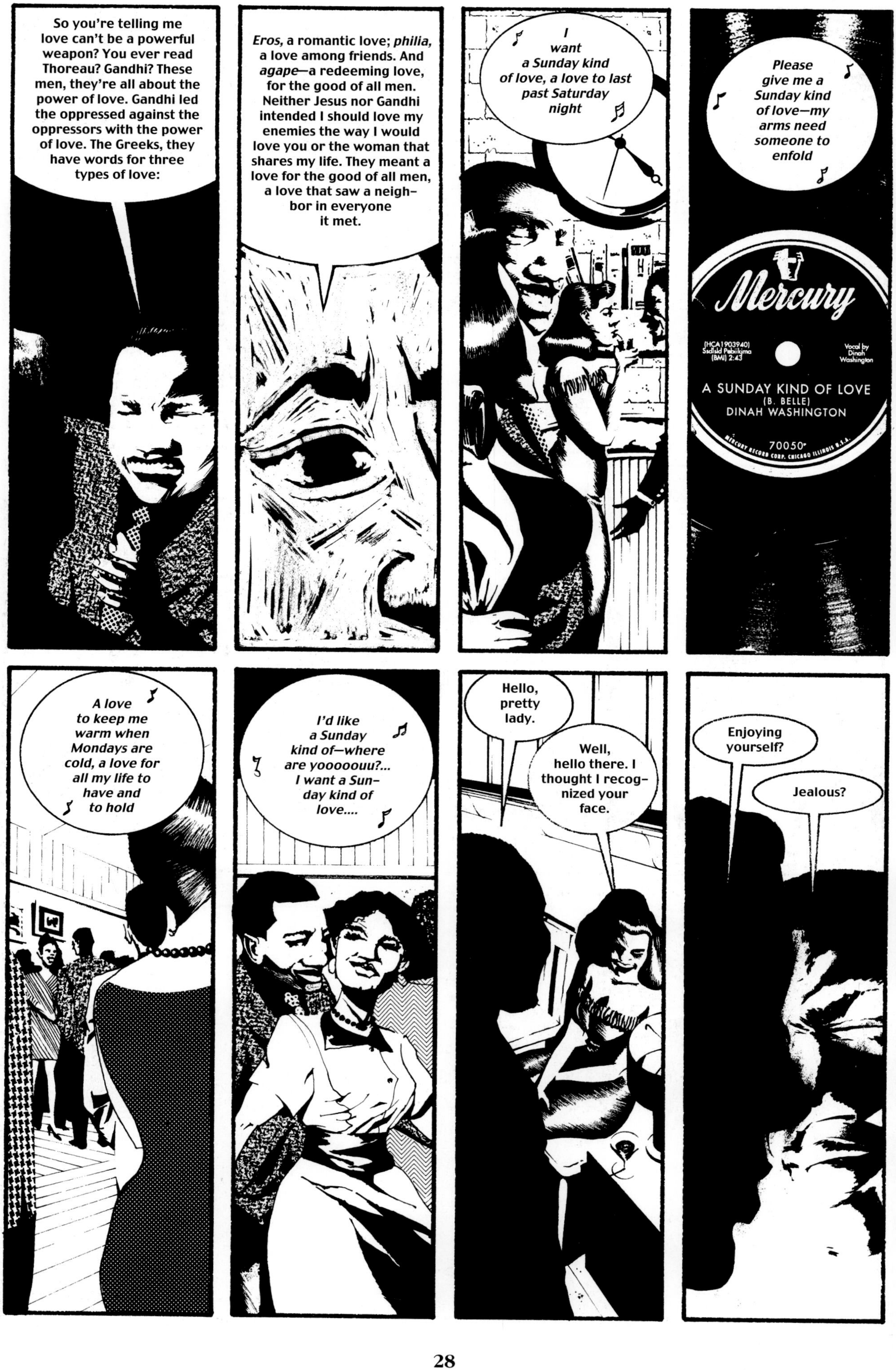

So you're telling me love can't be a powerful weapon? You ever read Thoreau? Gandhi? These men, they're all about the power of love. Gandhi led the oppressed against the oppressors with the power of love. The Greeks, they have words for three types of love:
Eros, a romantic love; *philia*, a love among friends. And *agape*—a redeeming love, for the good of all men. Neither Jesus nor Gandhi intended I should love my enemies the way I would love you or the woman that shares my life. They meant a love for the good of all men, a love that saw a neighbor in everyone it met.
I want a Sunday kind of love, a love to last past Saturday night
Please give me a Sunday kind of love—my arms need someone to enfold
Mercury
Vocal by Dinah Washington
A SUNDAY KIND OF LOVE
(B. BELLE)
DINAH WASHINGTON
70050
A love to keep me warm when Mondays are cold, a love for all my life to have and to hold
I'd like a Sunday kind of—where are yoooooUU?... I want a Sunday kind of love....
Hello, pretty lady.
Well, hello there. I thought I recognized your face.
Enjoying yourself?
Jealous?

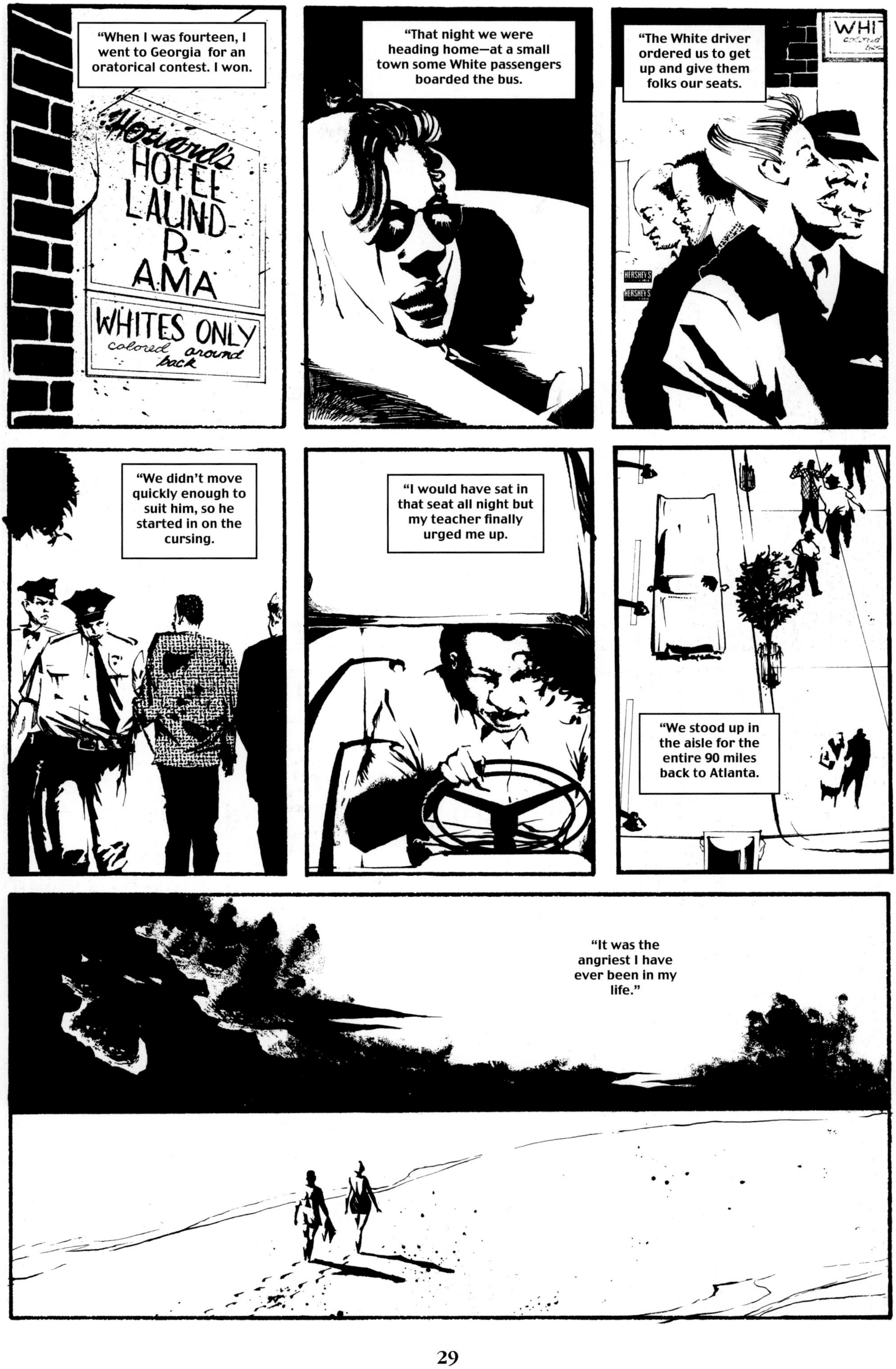
"When I was fourteen, I went to Georgia for an oratorical contest. I won.
Howard's HOTEL LAUND-R-AMA
WHITES ONLY colored around back
"That night we were heading home—at a small town some White passengers boarded the bus.
"The White driver ordered us to get up and give them folks our seats.
HERSHEY'S
HERSHEY'S
"We didn't move quickly enough to suit him, so he started in on the cursing.
"I would have sat in that seat all night but my teacher finally urged me up.
"We stood up in the aisle for the entire 90 miles back to Atlanta.
"It was the angriest I have ever been in my life."

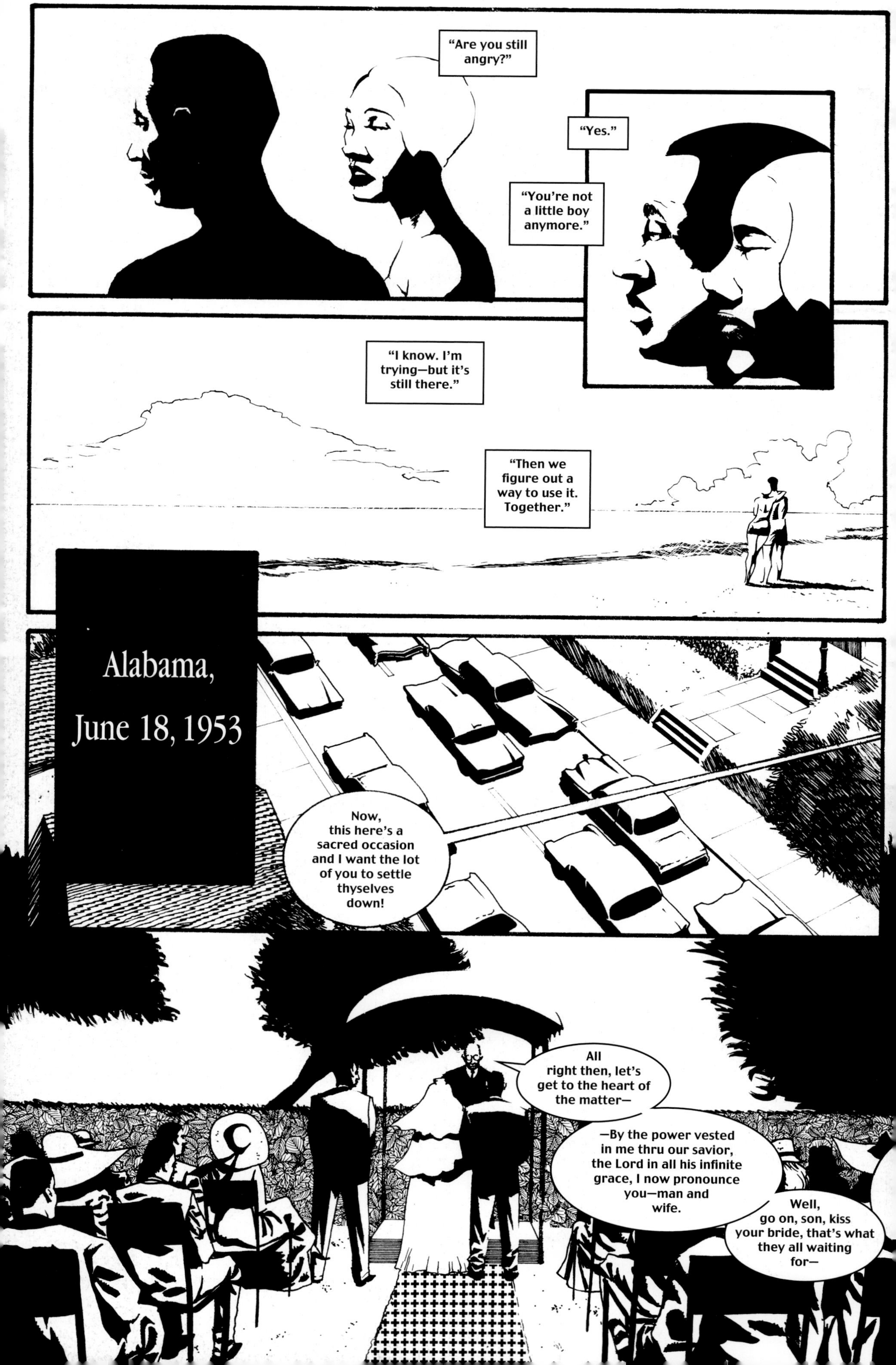

"Are you still angry?"
"Yes."
"You're not a little boy anymore."
"I know. I'm trying—but it's still there."
"Then we figure out a way to use it. Together."
Alabama, June 18, 1953
Now, this here's a sacred occasion and I want the lot of you to settle thyselves down!
All right then, let's get to the heart of the matter—
—By the power vested in me thru our savior, the Lord in all his infinite grace, I now pronounce you—man and wife.
Well, go on, son, kiss your bride, that's what they all waiting for—

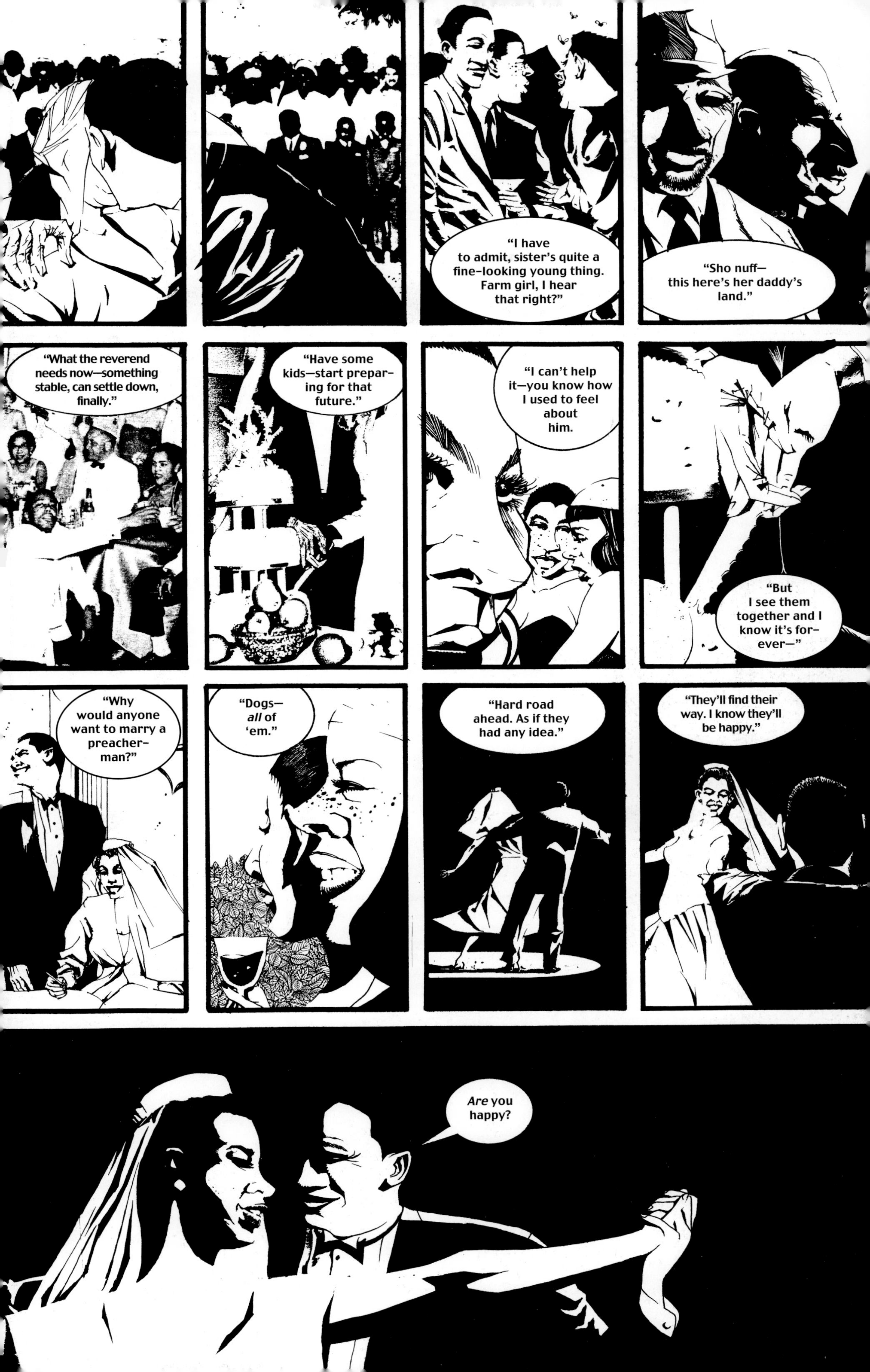
"I have to admit, sister's quite a fine-looking young thing. Farm girl, I hear that right?"
"Sho nuff—this here's her daddy's land."
"What the reverend needs now—something stable, can settle down, finally."
"Have some kids—start preparing for that future."
"I can't help it—you know how I used to feel about him.
"But I see them together and I know it's forever—"
"Why would anyone want to marry a preacher-man?"
"Dogs—*all* of 'em."
"Hard road ahead. As if they had any idea."
"They'll find their way. I know they'll be happy."
Are you happy?

In '54...I think it was April, Martin accepted an offer to preach at the Dexter Avenue Baptist Church in Montgomery, Alabama, to make it his own. That's when I heard the news, I was still living in Boston at the time.

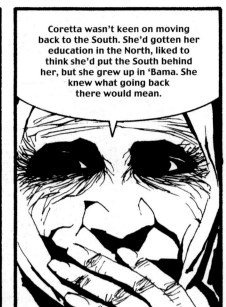

Coretta wasn't keen on moving back to the South. She'd gotten her education in the North, liked to think she'd put the South behind her, but she grew up in 'Bama. She knew what going back there would mean.

The schools were segregated. In the White schools the students were taught by competent professionals in a clean, comfortable setting. The Black schools? You gotta pass the outhouse on the way to class, and good luck finding some can teach you to write more than your own name.

I don't even think she was worried so much for herself, more for the children they planned on. The South does things to Black folks it don't do to other people.

Every Sunday, you'd find my behind in one of those Dexter pews. I can tell you brotherman was some kind of stiff in his preaching—you use words like *"Satyagraha"* in your oratories and most folks eyes are like t'glaze over.

Some folks said his preaching was maybe a little too refined. The reverend had some schooling, that wasn't anything he could help. Maybe he didn't speak to every- one with his preaching near the beginning—

And I tell you that any religion that professes to be concerned with the souls of men and is not concerned with the shanties that damn him—

Tell it, doctor!

—And the social conditions that cripple them is a dry-as-dust religion. Religion deals with both Heaven and Earth, time and eternity, not only to integrate man with God, but man with man.

—But he sure made up for that in record time. He moved you. His words found a home inside you.

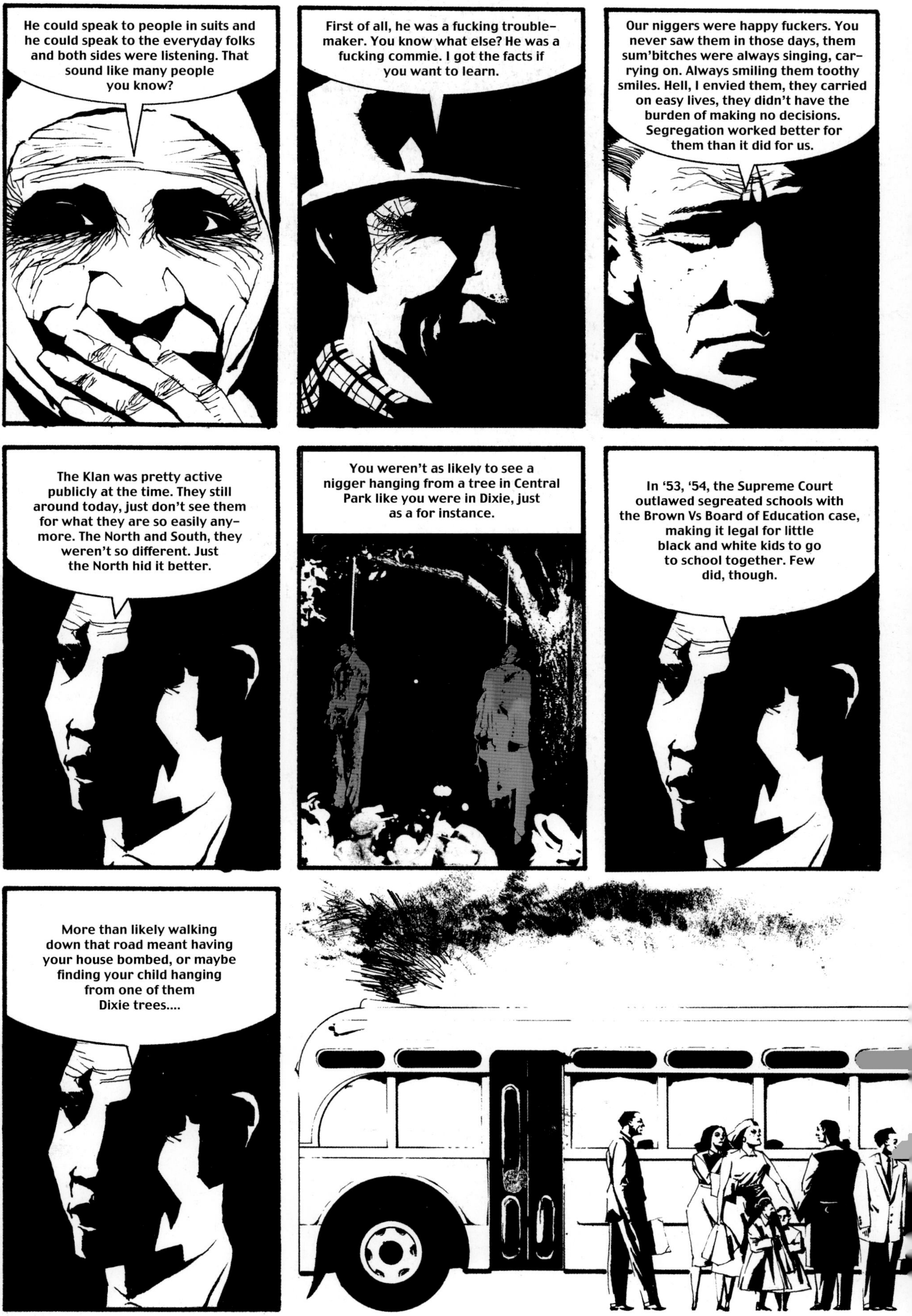
He could speak to people in suits and he could speak to the everyday folks and both sides were listening. That sound like many people you know?
First of all, he was a fucking trouble-maker. You know what else? He was a fucking commie. I got the facts if you want to learn.
Our niggers were happy fuckers. You never saw them in those days, them sum'bitches were always singing, car-rying on. Always smiling them toothy smiles. Hell, I envied them, they carried on easy lives, they didn't have the burden of making no decisions. Segregation worked better for them than it did for us.
The Klan was pretty active publicly at the time. They still around today, just don't see them for what they are so easily any-more. The North and South, they weren't so different. Just the North hid it better.
You weren't as likely to see a nigger hanging from a tree in Central Park like you were in Dixie, just as a for instance.
In '53, '54, the Supreme Court outlawed segregated schools with the Brown Vs Board of Education case, making it legal for little black and white kids to go to school together. Few did, though.
More than likely walking down that road meant having your house bombed, or maybe finding your child hanging from one of them Dixie trees....

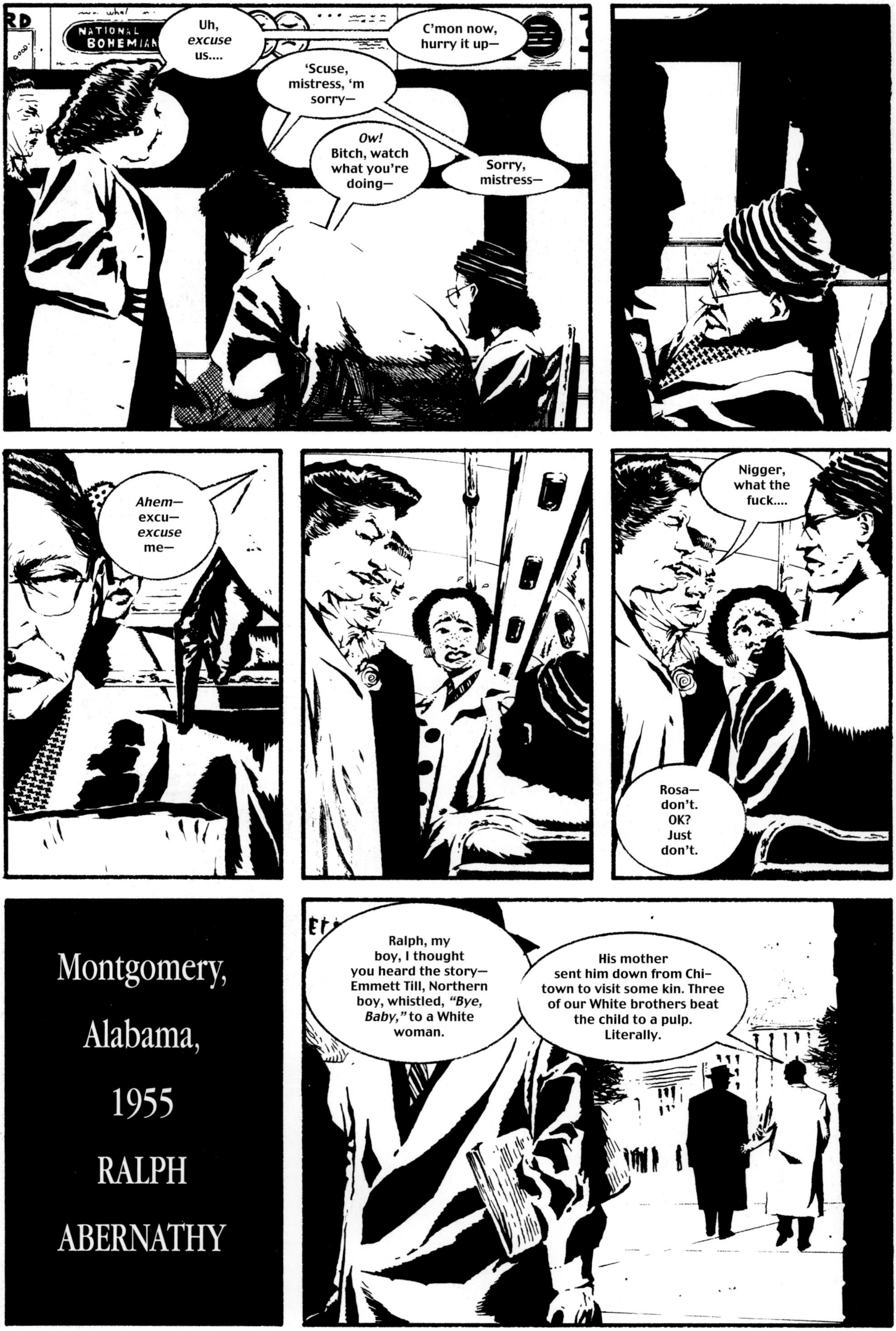
NATIONAL BOHEMIAN
Uh, *excuse* us....
C'mon now, hurry it up—
'Scuse, mistress, 'm sorry—
Ow! Bitch, watch what you're doing—
Sorry, mistress—
Ahem— excu— *excuse* me—
Nigger, what the fuck....
Rosa— don't. OK? Just don't.
Montgomery, Alabama, 1955
RALPH ABERNATHY
Ralph, my boy, I thought you heard the story— Emmett Till, Northern boy, whistled, *"Bye, Baby,"* to a White woman.
His mother sent him down from Chi-town to visit some kin. Three of our White brothers beat the child to a pulp. Literally.

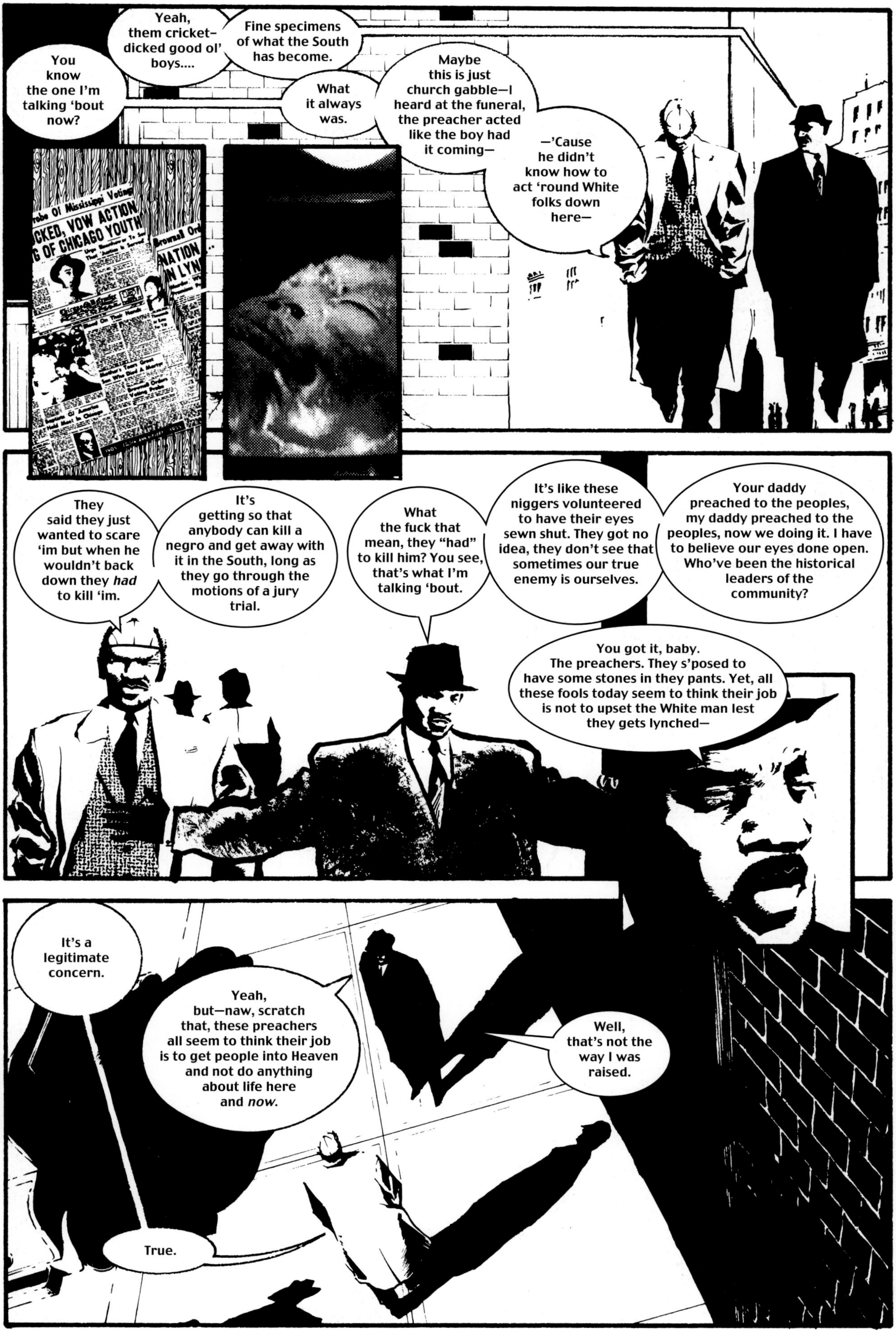
You know the one I'm talking 'bout now?
Yeah, them cricket-dicked good ol' boys....
Fine specimens of what the South has become.
What it always was.
Maybe this is just church gabble—I heard at the funeral, the preacher acted like the boy had it coming—
—'Cause he didn't know how to act 'round White folks down here—
They said they just wanted to scare 'im but when he wouldn't back down they *had* to kill 'im.
It's getting so that anybody can kill a negro and get away with it in the South, long as they go through the motions of a jury trial.
What the fuck that mean, they "had" to kill him? You see, that's what I'm talking 'bout.
It's like these niggers volunteered to have their eyes sewn shut. They got no idea, they don't see that sometimes our true enemy is ourselves.
Your daddy preached to the peoples, my daddy preached to the peoples, now we doing it. I have to believe our eyes done open. Who've been the historical leaders of the community?
You got it, baby. The preachers. They s'posed to have some stones in they pants. Yet, all these fools today seem to think their job is not to upset the White man lest they gets lynched—
It's a legitimate concern.
Yeah, but—naw, scratch that, these preachers all seem to think their job is to get people into Heaven and not do anything about life here and *now*.
Well, that's not the way I was raised.
True.

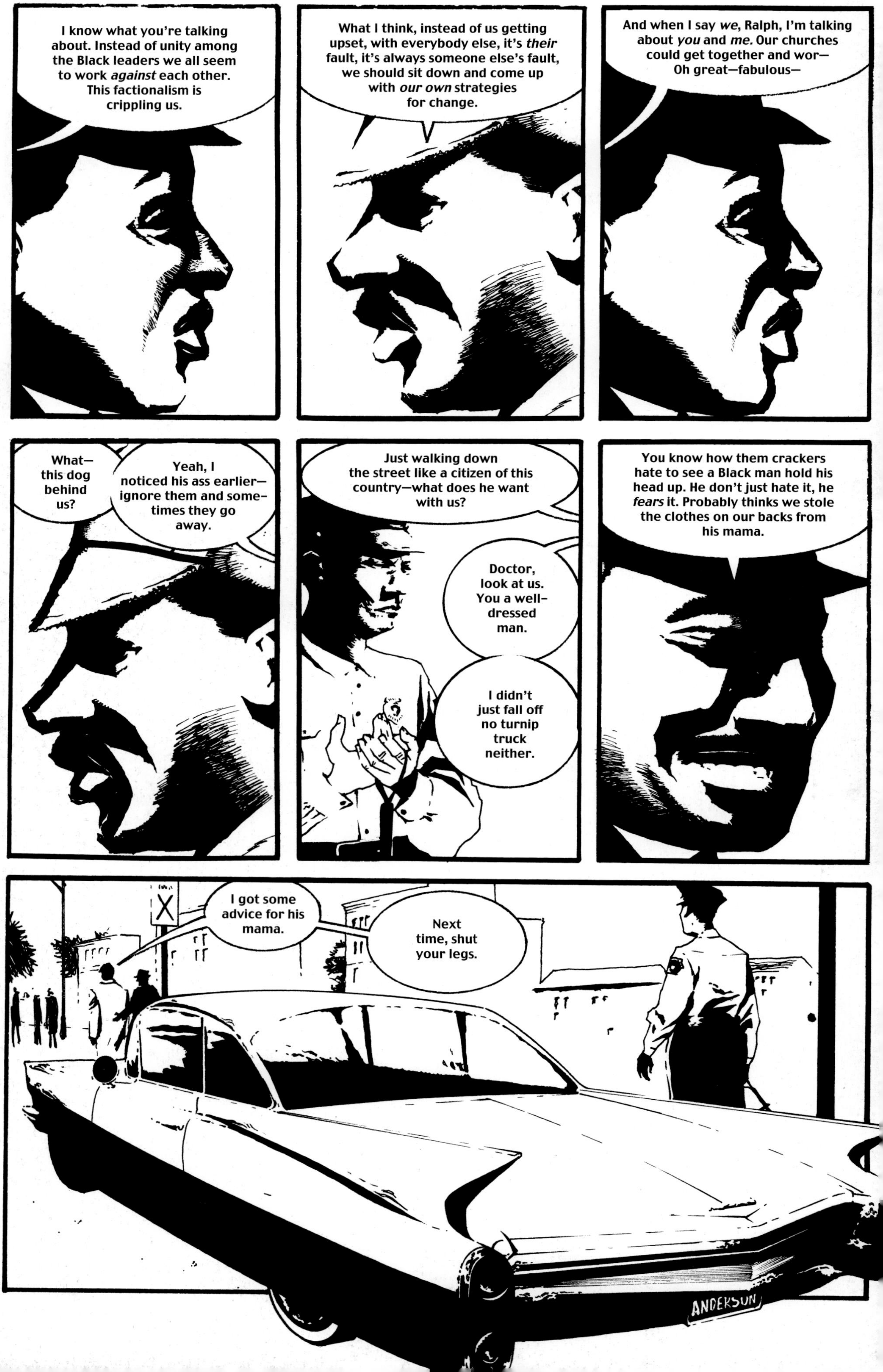
I know what you're talking about. Instead of unity among the Black leaders we all seem to work *against* each other. This factionalism is crippling us.
What I think, instead of us getting upset, with everybody else, it's *their* fault, it's always someone else's fault, we should sit down and come up with *our own* strategies for change.
And when I say *we*, Ralph, I'm talking about *you* and *me*. Our churches could get together and wor— Oh great—fabulous—
What— this dog behind us?
Yeah, I noticed his ass earlier— ignore them and sometimes they go away.
Just walking down the street like a citizen of this country—what does he want with us?
Doctor, look at us. You a well-dressed man.
I didn't just fall off no turnip truck neither.
You know how them crackers hate to see a Black man hold his head up. He don't just hate it, he *fears* it. Probably thinks we stole the clothes on our backs from his mama.
I got some advice for his mama.
Next time, shut your legs.
ANDERSON

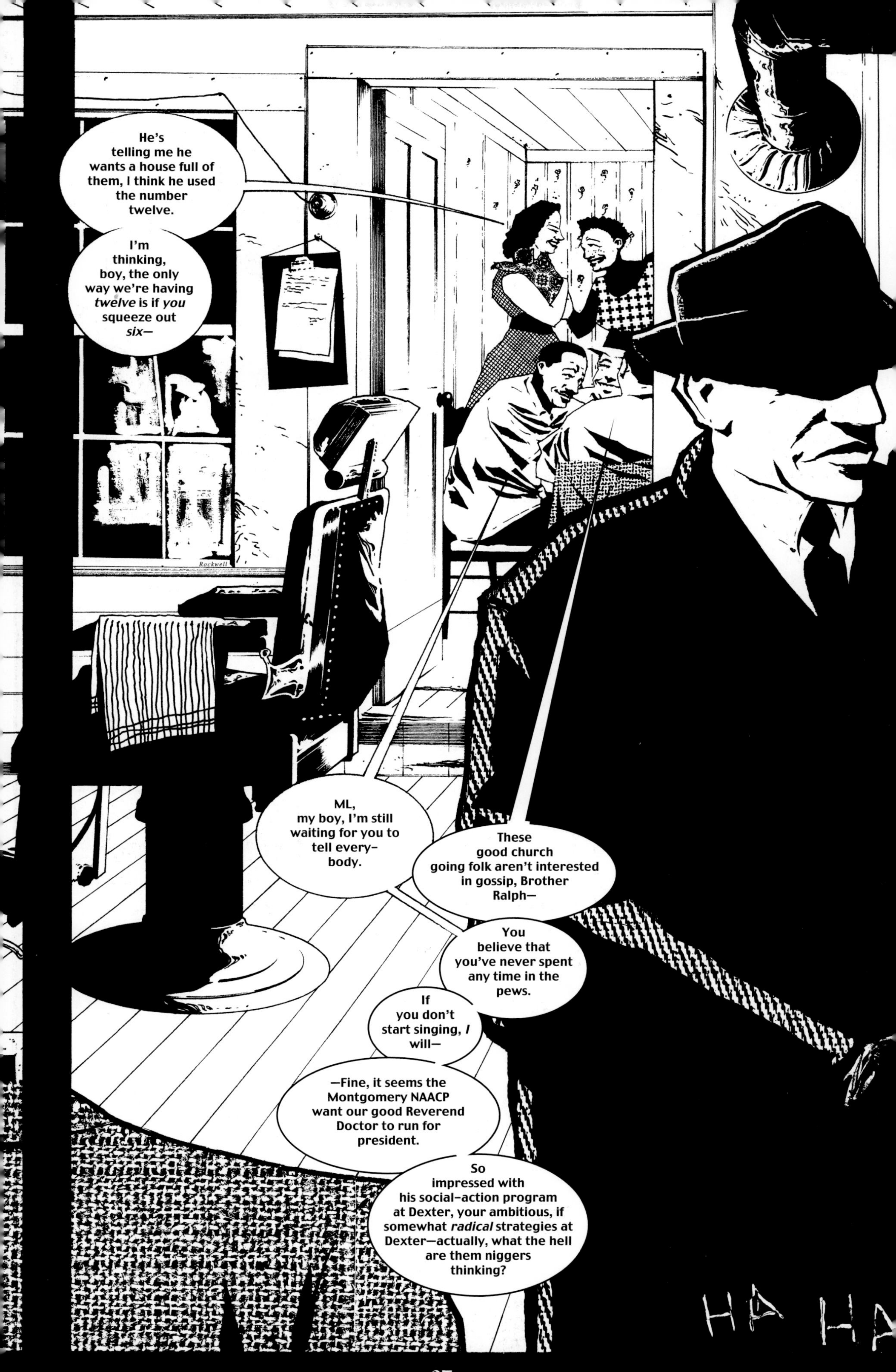
He's telling me he wants a house full of them, I think he used the number twelve.
I'm thinking, boy, the only way we're having *twelve* is if *you* squeeze out *six*—
Rockwell
ML, my boy, I'm still waiting for you to tell every-body.
These good church going folk aren't interested in gossip, Brother Ralph—
You believe that you've never spent any time in the pews.
If you don't start singing, *I* will—
—Fine, it seems the Montgomery NAACP want our good Reverend Doctor to run for president.
So impressed with his social-action program at Dexter, your ambitious, if somewhat *radical* strategies at Dexter—actually, what the hell are them niggers thinking?
HA HA

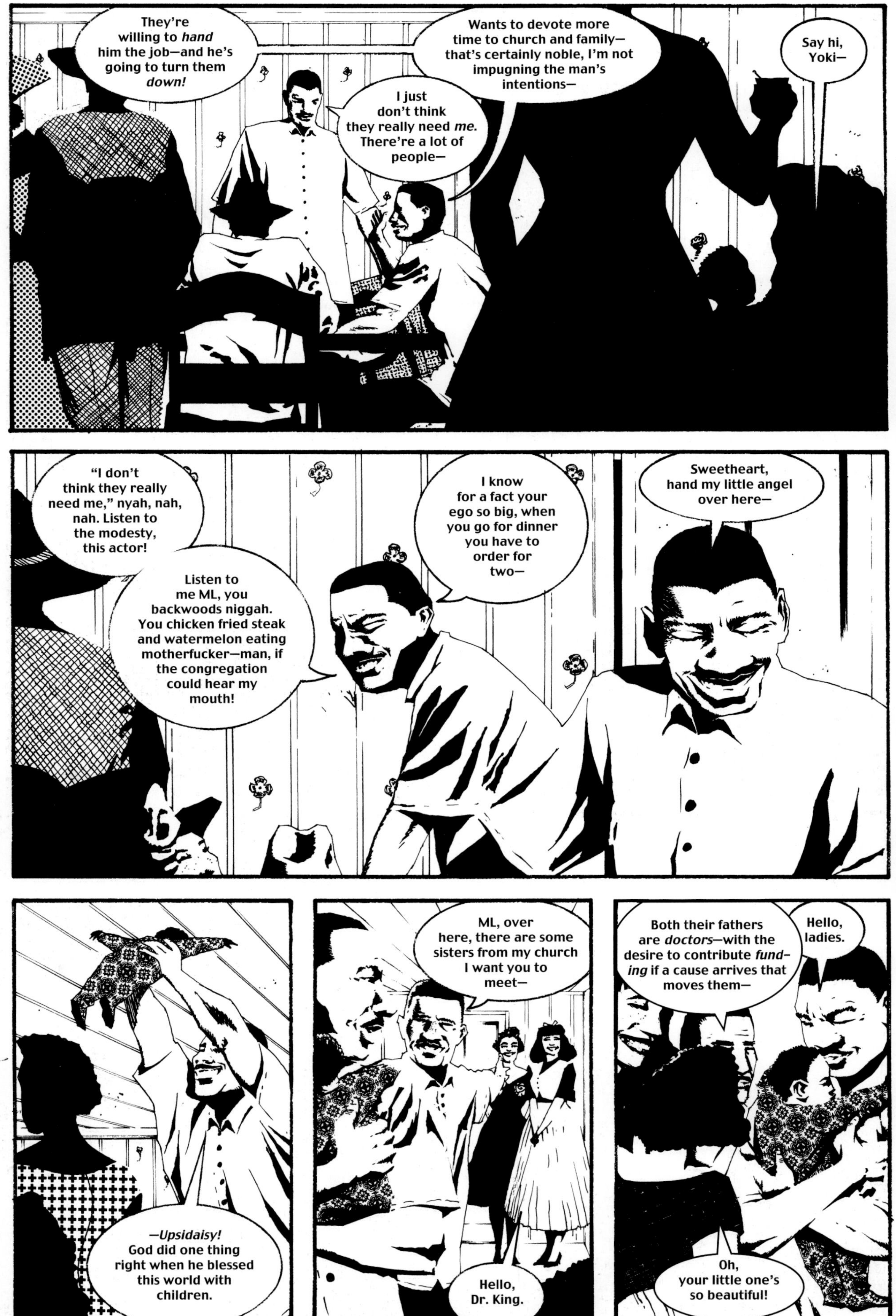
They're willing to *hand* him the job—and he's going to turn them *down!*
Wants to devote more time to church and family—that's certainly noble, I'm not impugning the man's intentions—
I just don't think they really need *me.* There're a lot of people—
Say hi, Yoki—
"I don't think they really need me," nyah, nah, nah. Listen to the modesty, this actor!
Listen to me ML, you backwoods niggah. You chicken fried steak and watermelon eating motherfucker—man, if the congregation could hear my mouth!
I know for a fact your ego so big, when you go for dinner you have to order for two—
Sweetheart, hand my little angel over here—
—*Upsidaisy!* God did one thing right when he blessed this world with children.
ML, over here, there are some sisters from my church I want you to meet—
Hello, Dr. King.
Both their fathers are *doctors*—with the desire to contribute *fund-ing* if a cause arrives that moves them—
Hello, ladies.
Oh, your little one's so beautiful!

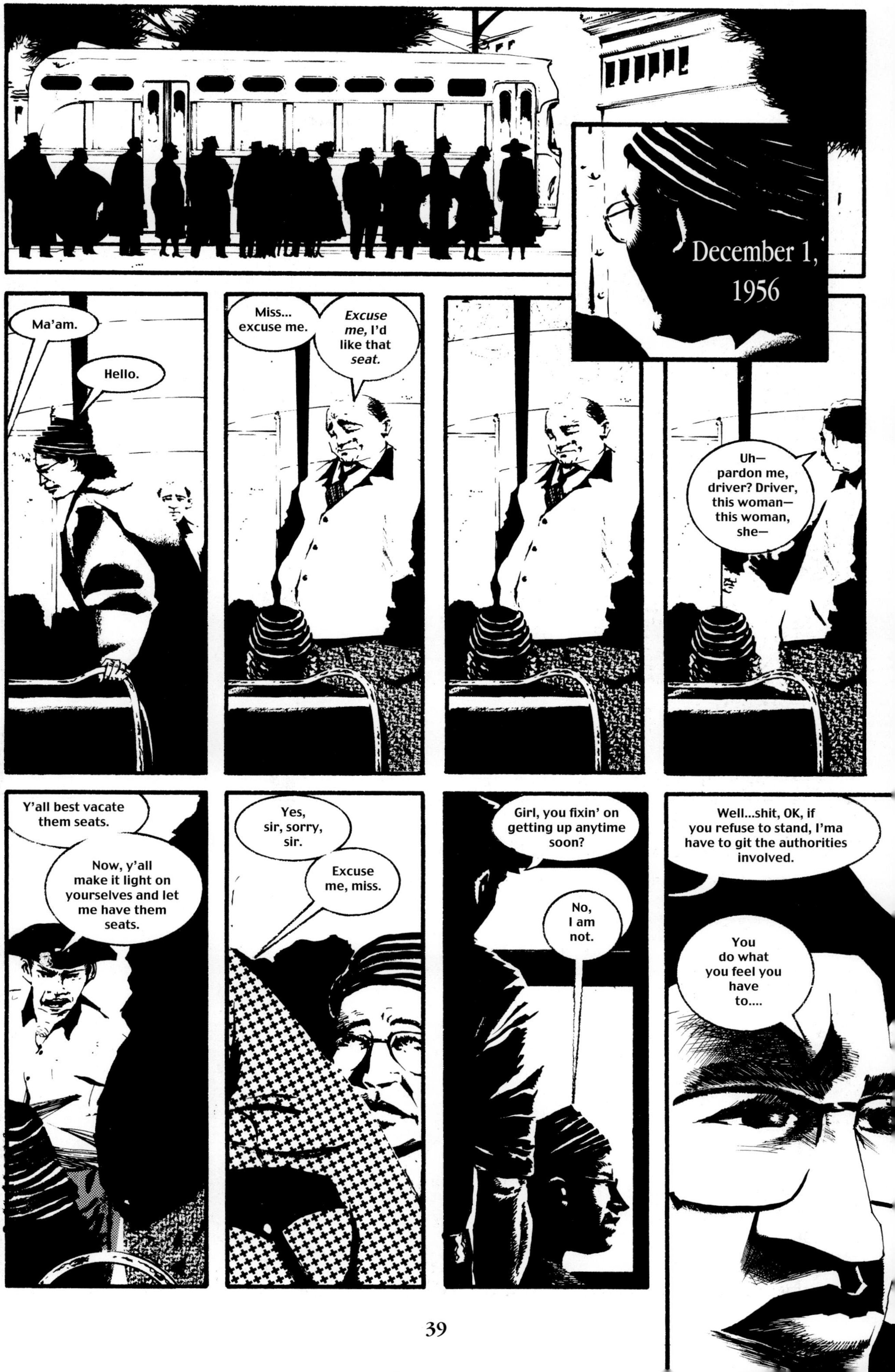
December 1, 1956
Ma'am.
Hello.
Miss... excuse me.
Excuse me, I'd like that *seat.*
Uh— pardon me, driver? Driver, this woman— this woman, she—
Y'all best vacate them seats.
Now, y'all make it light on yourselves and let me have them seats.
Yes, sir, sorry, sir.
Excuse me, miss.
Girl, you fixin' on getting up anytime soon?
No, I am not.
Well...shit, OK, if you refuse to stand, I'ma have to git the authorities involved.
You do what you feel you have to....

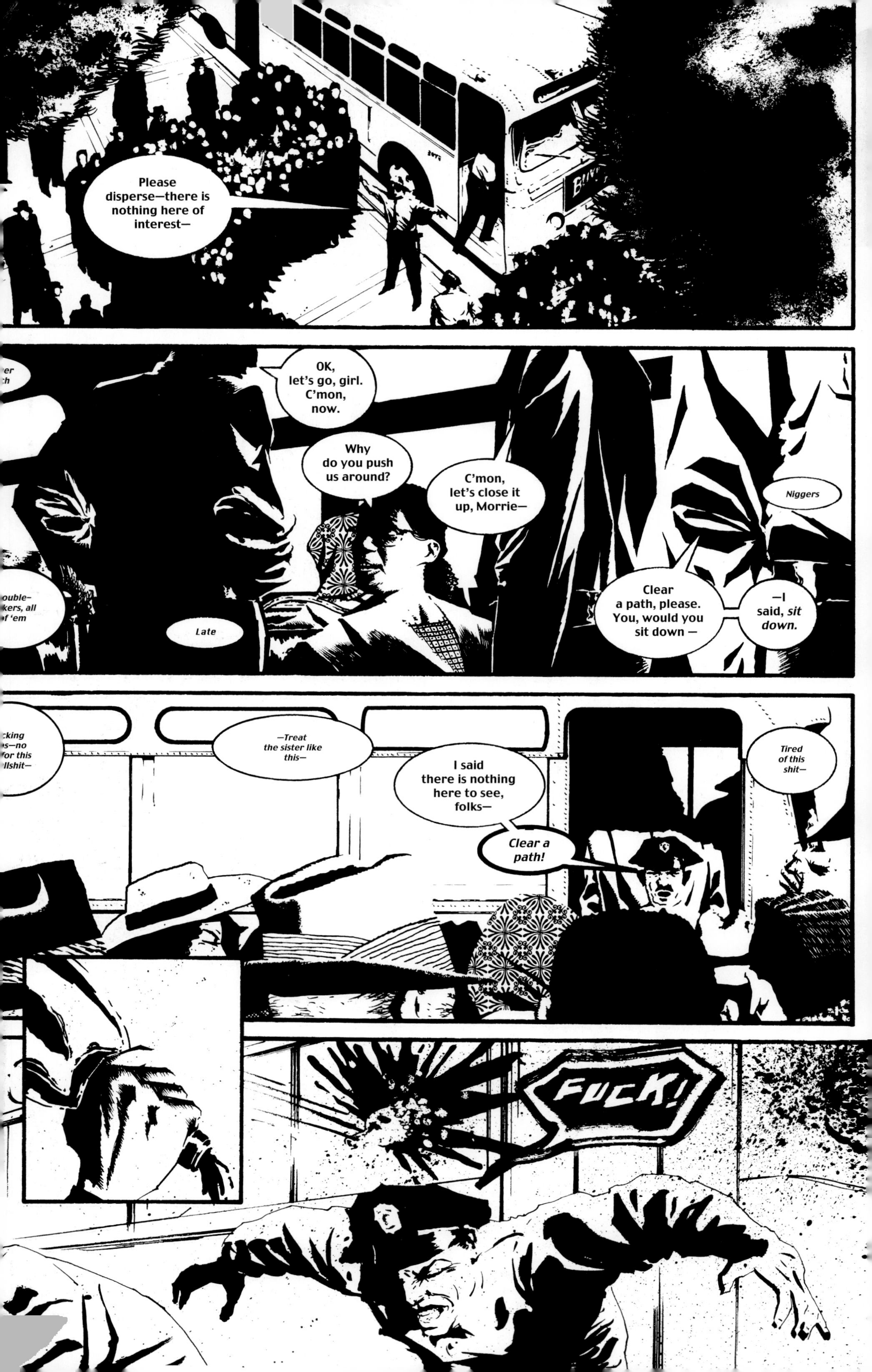
Please disperse—there is nothing here of interest—
OK, let's go, girl. C'mon, now.
Why do you push us around?
Late
C'mon, let's close it up, Morrie—
Niggers
Clear a path, please. You, would you sit down —
—I said, *sit down.*
—Treat the sister like this—
I said there is nothing here to see, folks—
Clear a path!
Tired of this shit—
FUCK!

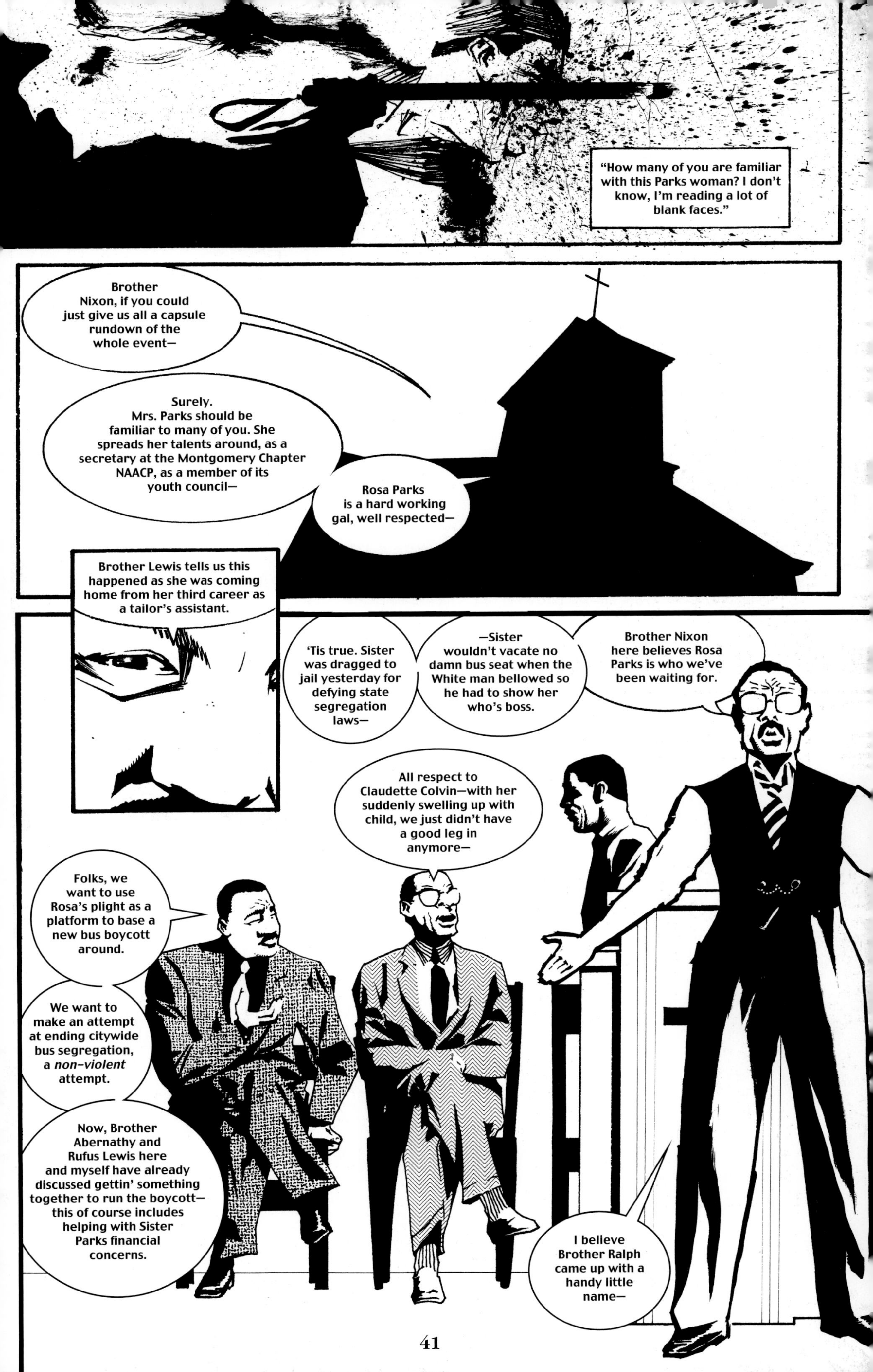
"How many of you are familiar with this Parks woman? I don't know, I'm reading a lot of blank faces."
Brother Nixon, if you could just give us all a capsule rundown of the whole event—
Surely. Mrs. Parks should be familiar to many of you. She spreads her talents around, as a secretary at the Montgomery Chapter NAACP, as a member of its youth council—
Rosa Parks is a hard working gal, well respected—
Brother Lewis tells us this happened as she was coming home from her third career as a tailor's assistant.
'Tis true. Sister was dragged to jail yesterday for defying state segregation laws—
—Sister wouldn't vacate no damn bus seat when the White man bellowed so he had to show her who's boss.
Brother Nixon here believes Rosa Parks is who we've been waiting for.
All respect to Claudette Colvin—with her suddenly swelling up with child, we just didn't have a good leg in anymore—
Folks, we want to use Rosa's plight as a platform to base a new bus boycott around.
We want to make an attempt at ending citywide bus segregation, a *non-violent* attempt.
Now, Brother Abernathy and Rufus Lewis here and myself have already discussed gettin' something together to run the boycott—this of course includes helping with Sister Parks financial concerns.
I believe Brother Ralph came up with a handy little name—

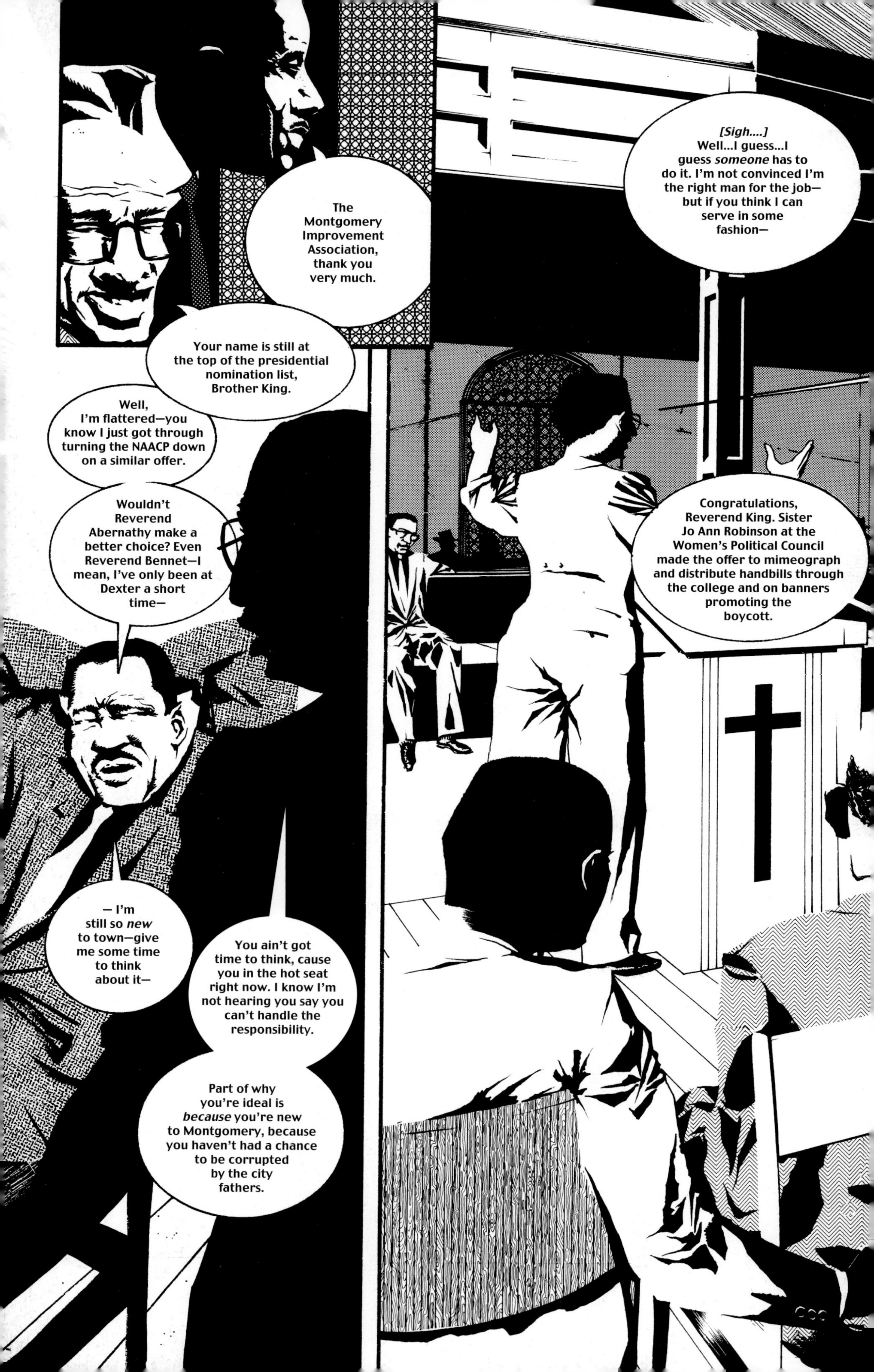
The Montgomery Improvement Association, thank you very much.
Your name is still at the top of the presidential nomination list, Brother King.
Well, I'm flattered—you know I just got through turning the NAACP down on a similar offer.
Wouldn't Reverend Abernathy make a better choice? Even Reverend Bennet—I mean, I've only been at Dexter a short time—
— I'm still so *new* to town—give me some time to think about it—
You ain't got time to think, cause you in the hot seat right now. I know I'm not hearing you say you can't handle the responsibility.
Part of why you're ideal is *because* you're new to Montgomery, because you haven't had a chance to be corrupted by the city fathers.
[Sigh....] Well...I guess...I guess *someone* has to do it. I'm not convinced I'm the right man for the job—but if you think I can serve in some fashion—
Congratulations, Reverend King. Sister Jo Ann Robinson at the Women's Political Council made the offer to mimeograph and distribute handbills through the college and on banners promoting the boycott.

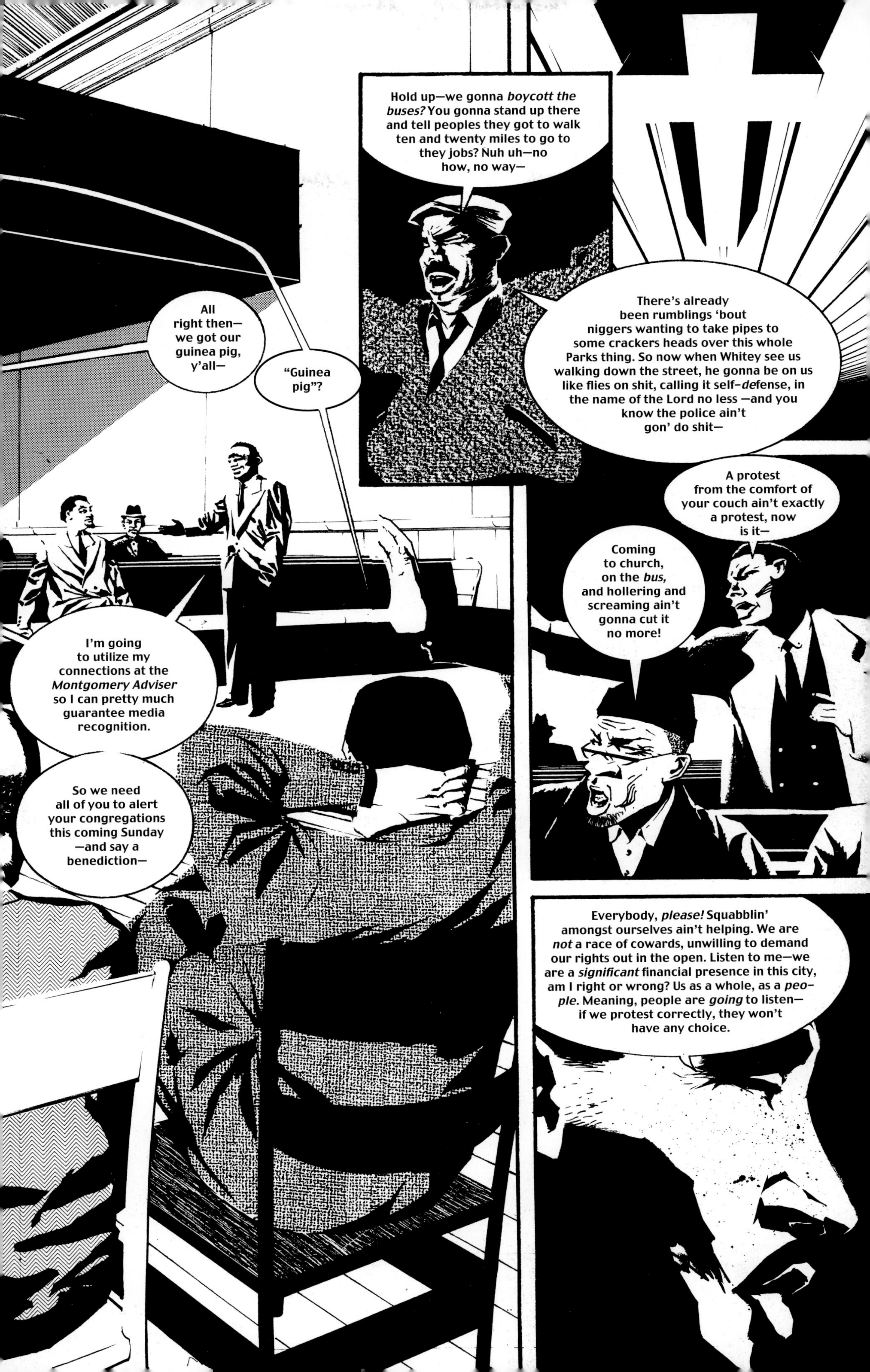
All right then—we got our guinea pig, y'all—
"Guinea pig"?
Hold up—we gonna *boycott the buses?* You gonna stand up there and tell peoples they got to walk ten and twenty miles to go to they jobs? Nuh uh—no how, no way—
There's already been rumblings 'bout niggers wanting to take pipes to some crackers heads over this whole Parks thing. So now when Whitey see us walking down the street, he gonna be on us like flies on shit, calling it self-*de*fense, in the name of the Lord no less —and you know the police ain't gon' do shit—
I'm going to utilize my connections at the *Montgomery Adviser* so I can pretty much guarantee media recognition.
So we need all of you to alert your congregations this coming Sunday —and say a benediction—
A protest from the comfort of your couch ain't exactly a protest, now is it—
Coming to church, on the *bus,* and hollering and screaming ain't gonna cut it no more!
Everybody, *please!* Squabblin' amongst ourselves ain't helping. We are *not* a race of cowards, unwilling to demand our rights out in the open. Listen to me—we are a *significant* financial presence in this city, am I right or wrong? Us as a whole, as a *peo-ple.* Meaning, people are *going* to listen—if we protest correctly, they won't have any choice.

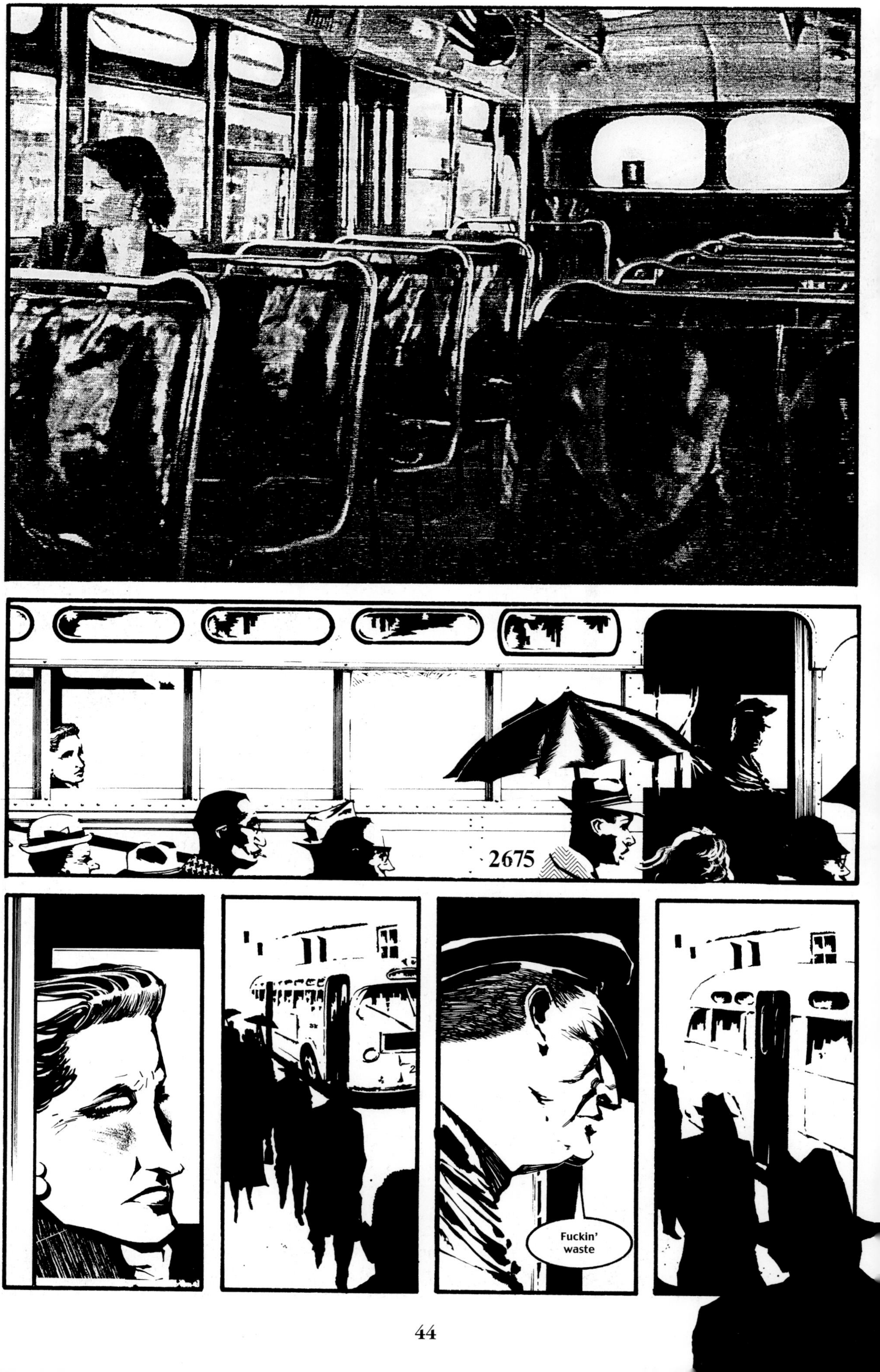
2675
Fuckin' waste

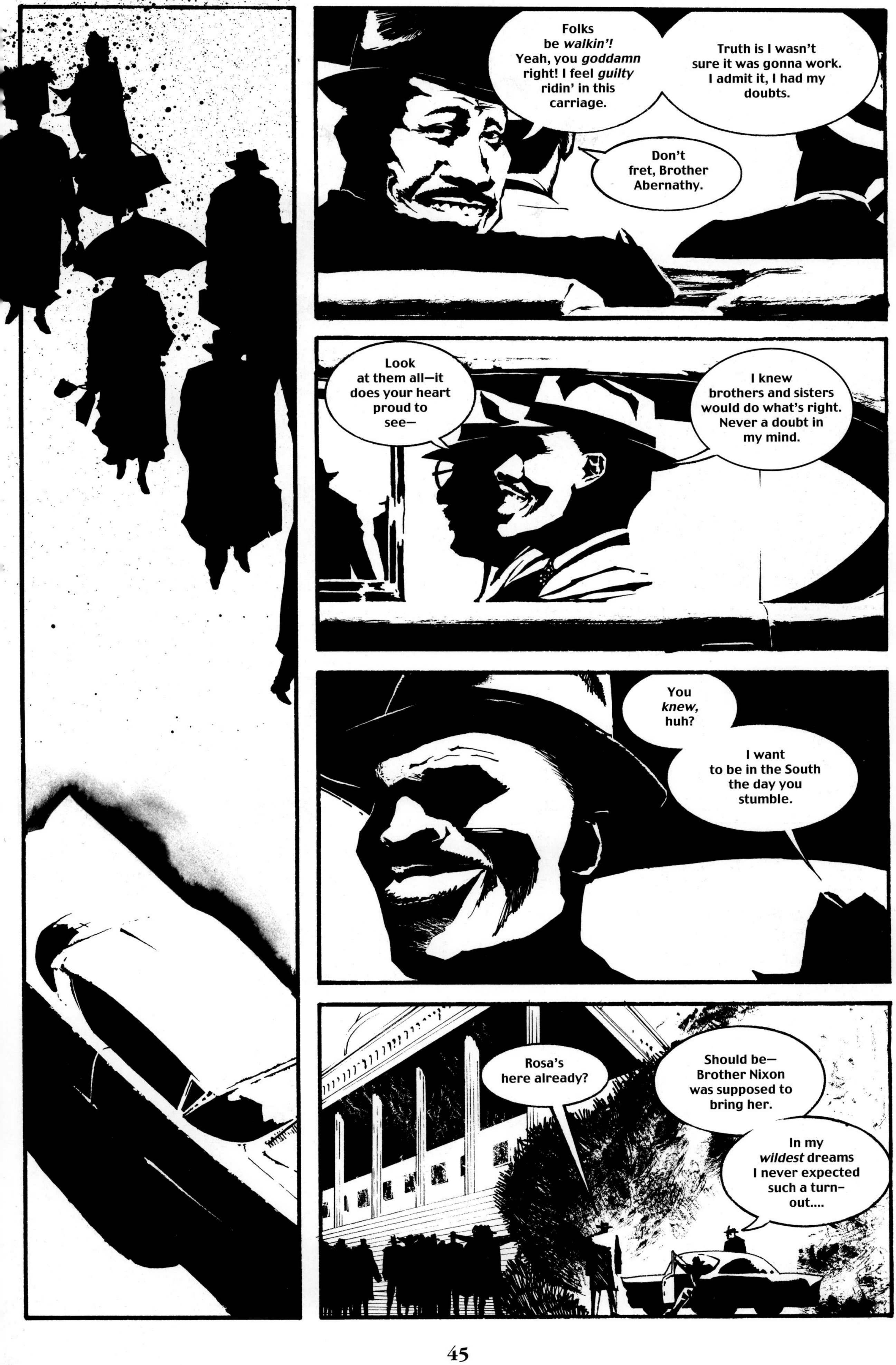
Folks be *walkin'!* Yeah, you *goddamn* right! I feel *guilty* ridin' in this carriage.
Truth is I wasn't sure it was gonna work. I admit it, I had my doubts.
Don't fret, Brother Abernathy.
Look at them all—it does your heart proud to see—
I knew brothers and sisters would do what's right. Never a doubt in my mind.
You *knew,* huh?
I want to be in the South the day you stumble.
Rosa's here already?
Should be— Brother Nixon was supposed to bring her.
In my *wildest* dreams I never expected such a turn-out....

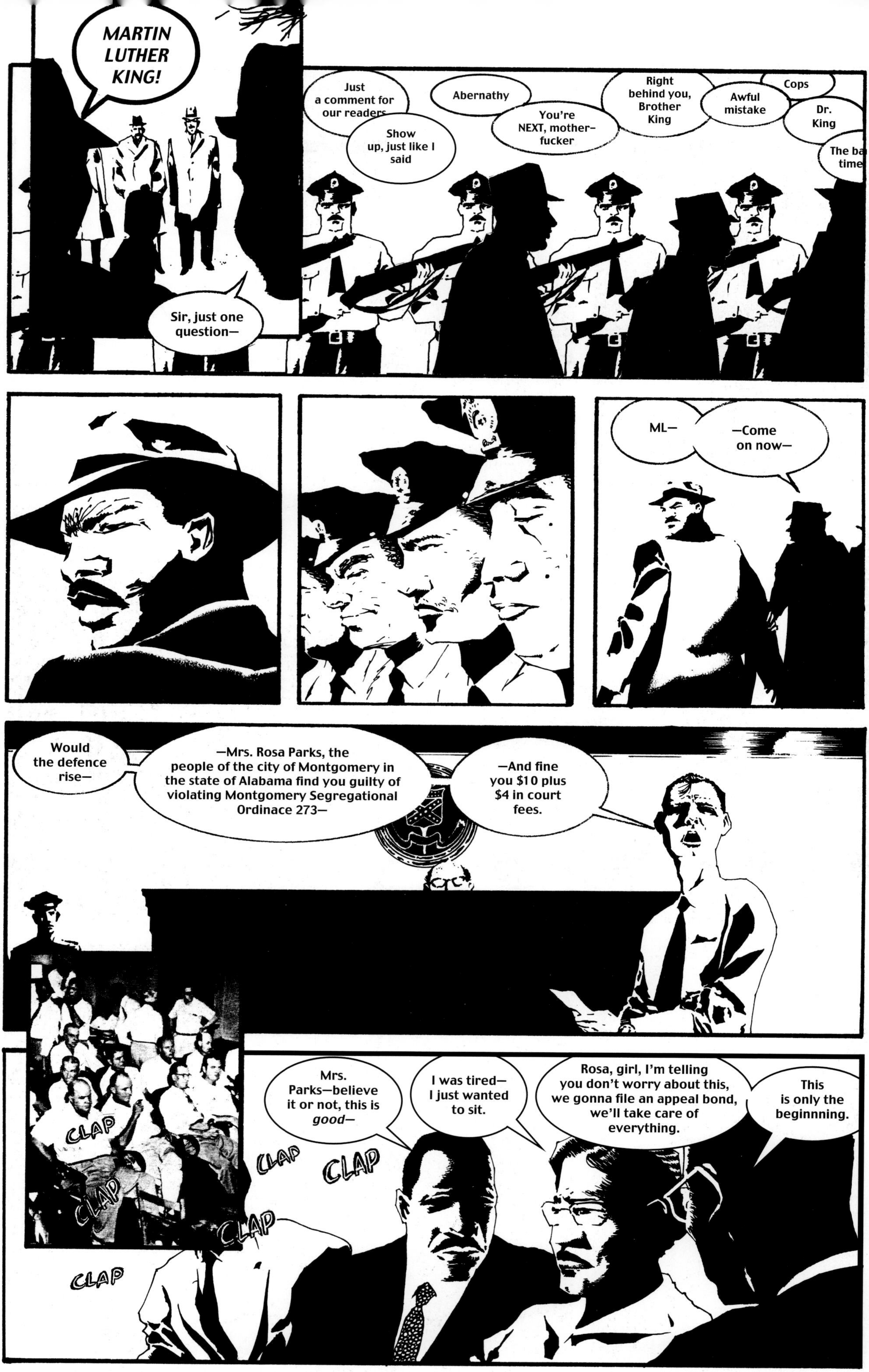
MARTIN LUTHER KING!
Sir, just one question—
Just a comment for our readers
Show up, just like I said
Abernathy
You're NEXT, mother-fucker
Right behind you, Brother King
Awful mistake
Cops
Dr. King
ML—
—Come on now—
Would the defence rise—
—Mrs. Rosa Parks, the people of the city of Montgomery in the state of Alabama find you guilty of violating Montgomery Segregational Ordinace 273—
—And fine you $10 plus $4 in court fees.
CLAP
CLAP
CLAP
CLAP
CLAP
CLAP
Mrs. Parks—believe it or not, this is *good*—
I was tired—I just wanted to sit.
Rosa, girl, I'm telling you don't worry about this, we gonna file an appeal bond, we'll take care of everything.
This is only the beginnning.

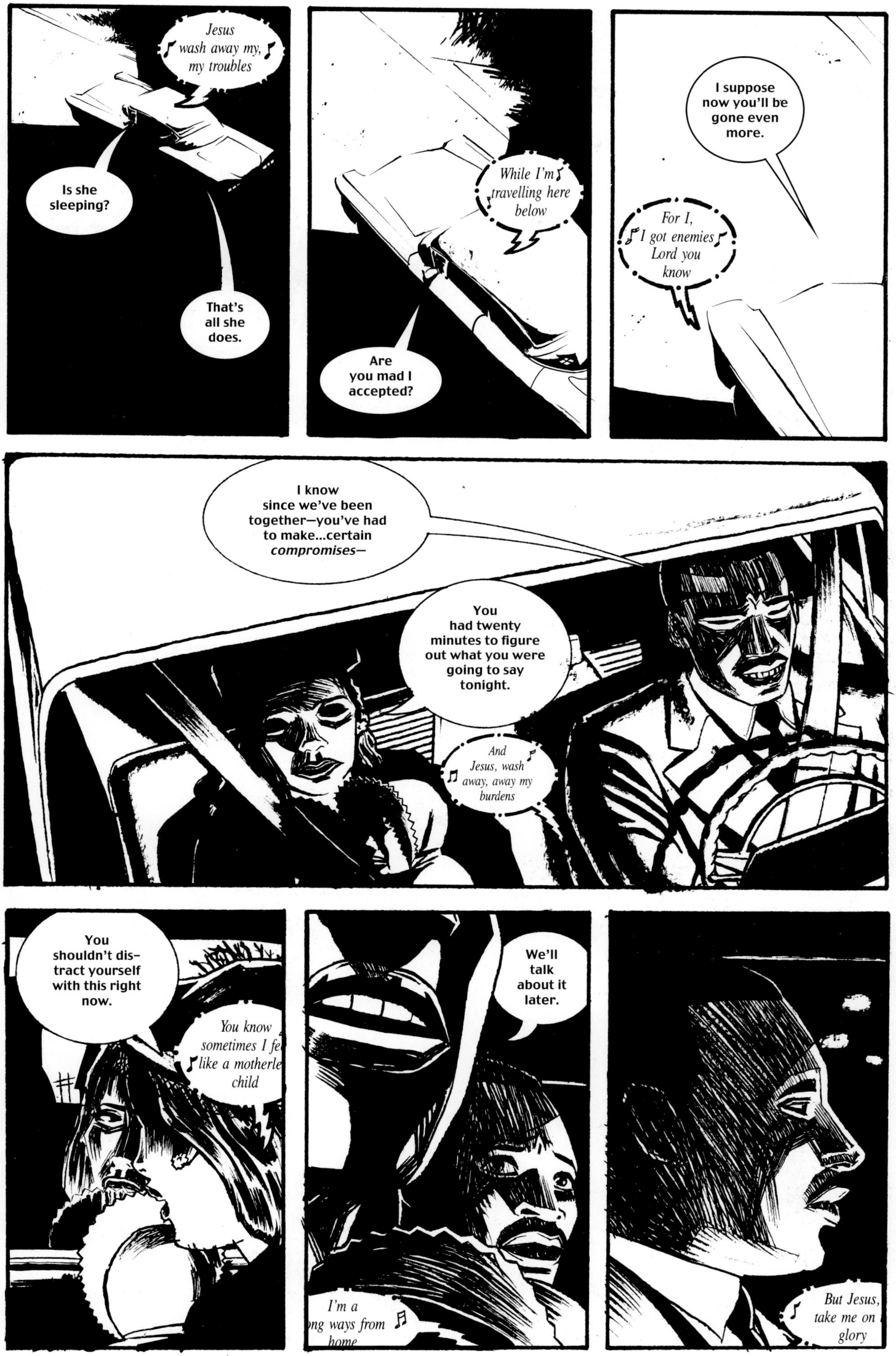

Jesus wash away my, my troubles
Is she sleeping?
That's all she does.
While I'm travelling here below
Are you mad I accepted?
I suppose now you'll be gone even more.
For I, I got enemies Lord you know
I know since we've been together—you've had to make...certain *compromises*—
You had twenty minutes to figure out what you were going to say tonight.
And Jesus, wash away, away my burdens
You shouldn't distract yourself with this right now.
You know sometimes I fe like a motherle child
We'll talk about it later.
I'm a ng ways from home
But Jesus, take me on glory

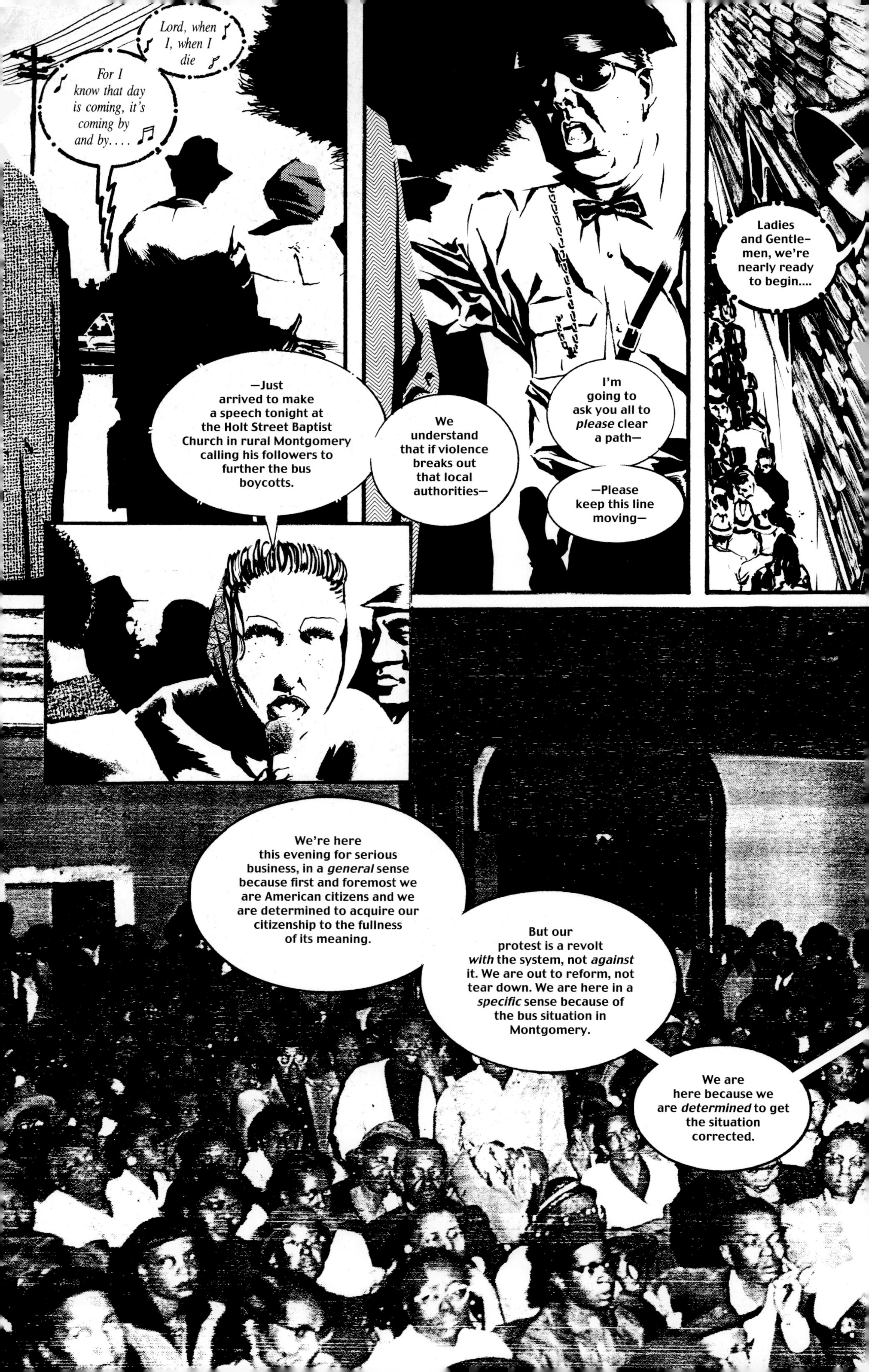
Lord, when I, when I die
For I know that day is coming, it's coming by and by....
Ladies and Gentle– men, we're nearly ready to begin....
—Just arrived to make a speech tonight at the Holt Street Baptist Church in rural Montgomery calling his followers to further the bus boycotts.
We understand that if violence breaks out that local authorities—
I'm going to ask you all to *please* clear a path—
—Please keep this line moving—
We're here this evening for serious business, in a *general* sense because first and foremost we are American citizens and we are determined to acquire our citizenship to the fullness of its meaning.
But our protest is a revolt *with* the system, not *against* it. We are out to reform, not tear down. We are here in a *specific* sense because of the bus situation in Montgomery.
We are here because we are *determined* to get the situation corrected.

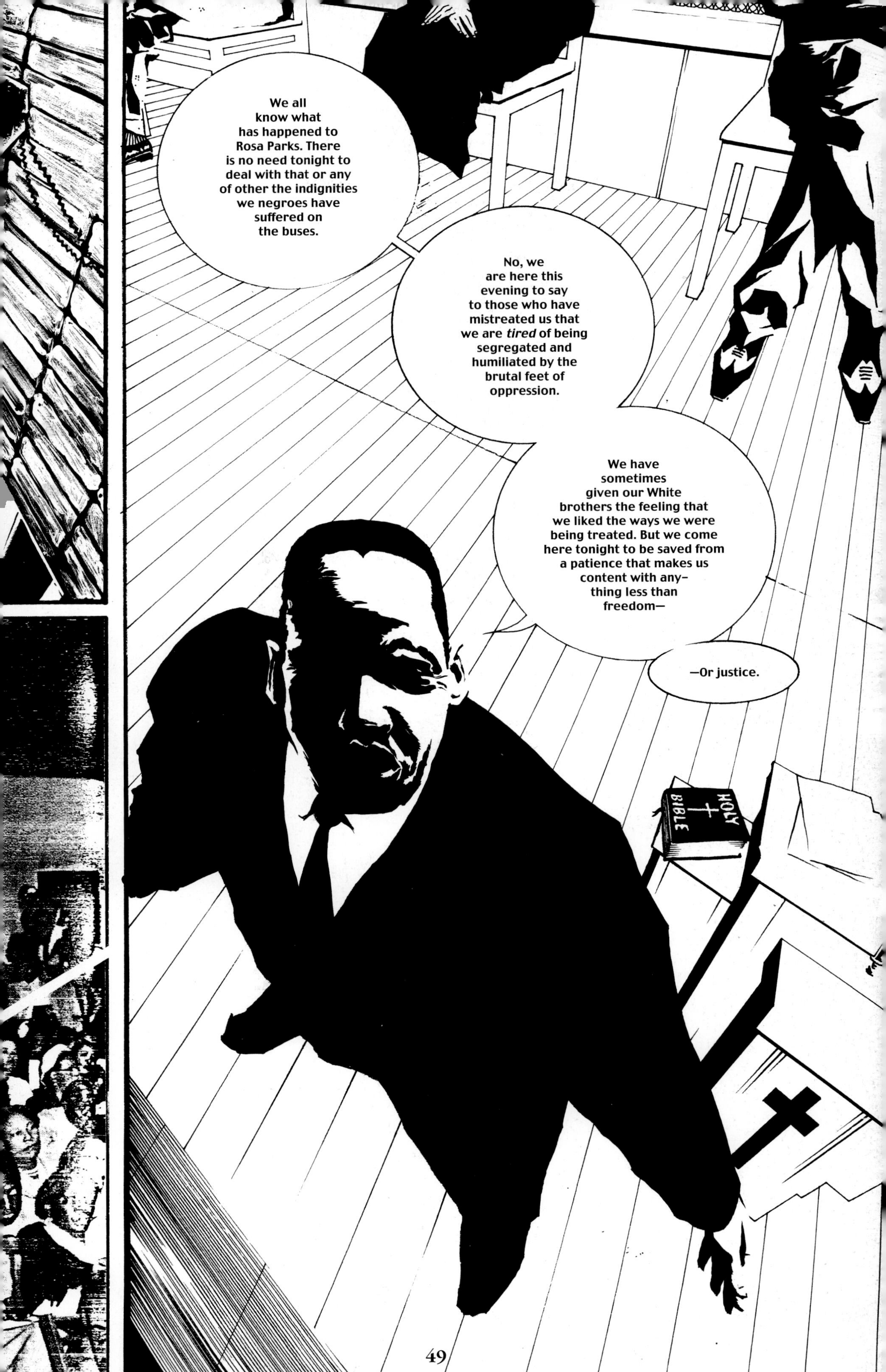
We all know what has happened to Rosa Parks. There is no need tonight to deal with that or any of other the indignities we negroes have suffered on the buses.
No, we are here this evening to say to those who have mistreated us that we are *tired* of being segregated and humiliated by the brutal feet of oppression.
We have sometimes given our White brothers the feeling that we liked the ways we were being treated. But we come here tonight to be saved from a patience that makes us content with any-thing less than freedom—
—Or justice.
HOLY BIBLE

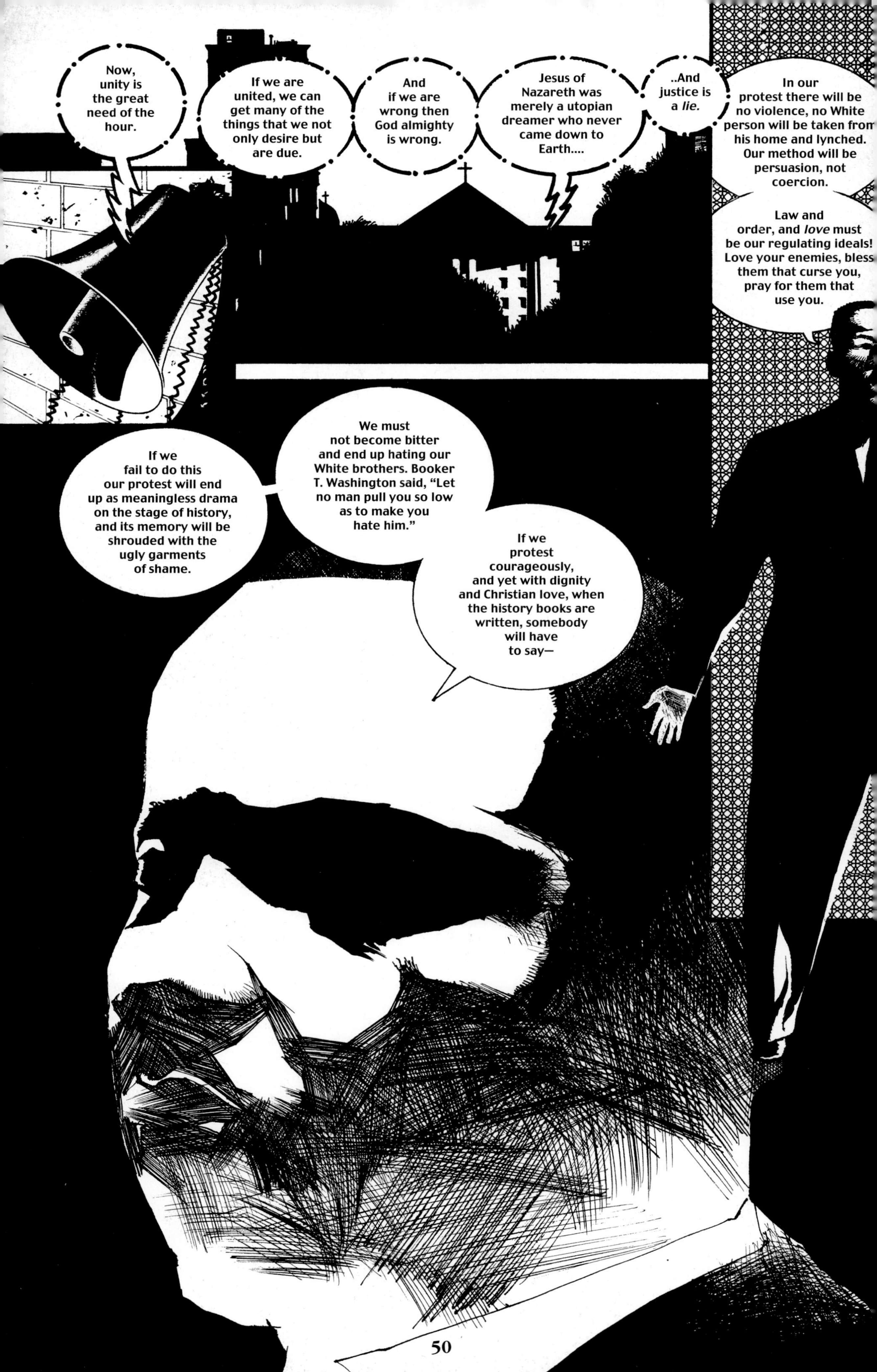
Now, unity is the great need of the hour.
If we are united, we can get many of the things that we not only desire but are due.
And if we are wrong then God almighty is wrong.
Jesus of Nazareth was merely a utopian dreamer who never came down to Earth....
..And justice is a *lie.*
In our protest there will be no violence, no White person will be taken from his home and lynched. Our method will be persuasion, not coercion.
Law and order, and *love* must be our regulating ideals! Love your enemies, bless them that curse you, pray for them that use you.
If we fail to do this our protest will end up as meaningless drama on the stage of history, and its memory will be shrouded with the ugly garments of shame.
We must not become bitter and end up hating our White brothers. Booker T. Washington said, "Let no man pull you so low as to make you hate him."
If we protest courageously, and yet with dignity and Christian love, when the history books are written, somebody will have to say—

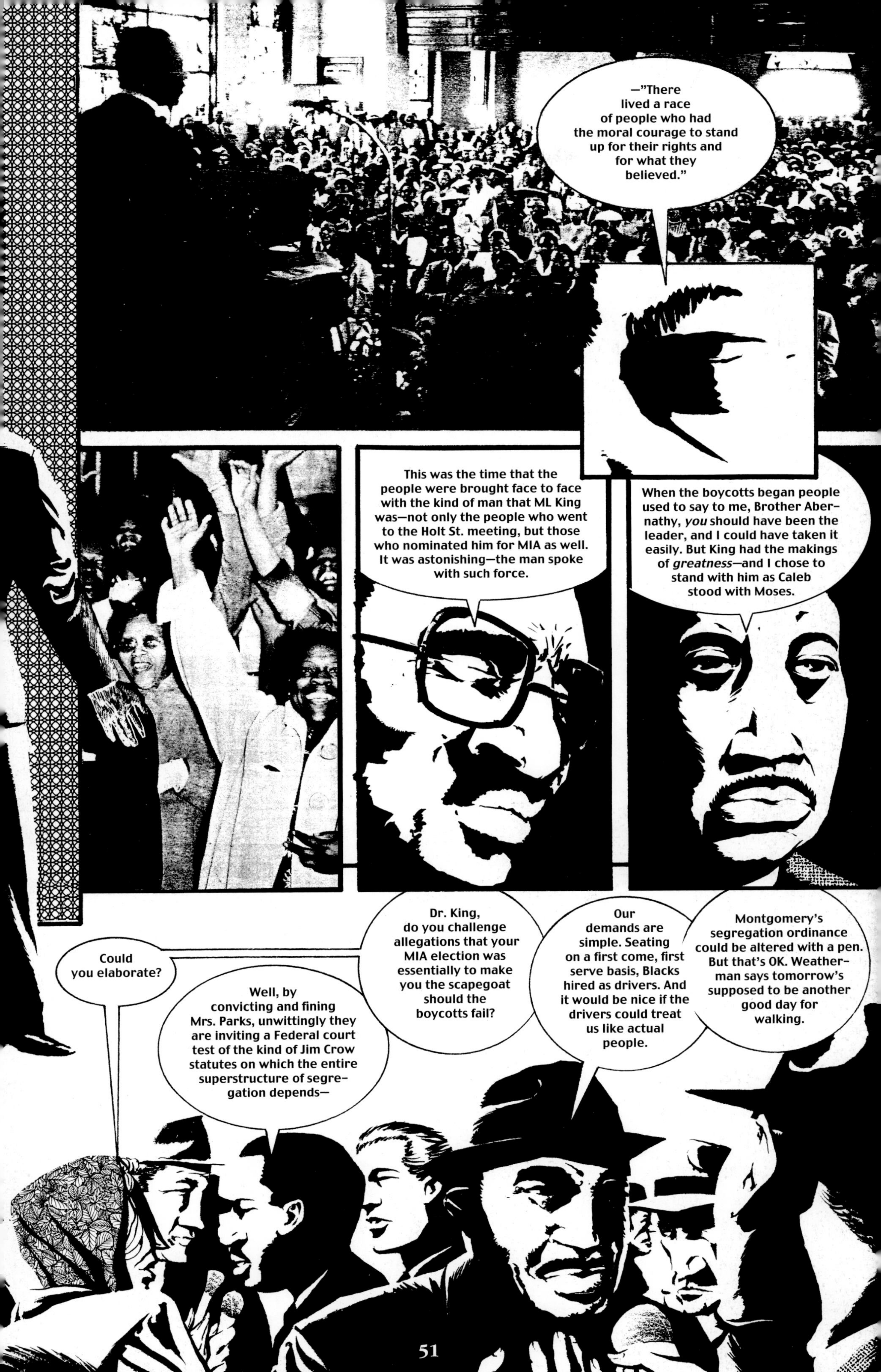
—"There lived a race of people who had the moral courage to stand up for their rights and for what they believed."
This was the time that the people were brought face to face with the kind of man that ML King was—not only the people who went to the Holt St. meeting, but those who nominated him for MIA as well. It was astonishing—the man spoke with such force.
When the boycotts began people used to say to me, Brother Abernathy, *you* should have been the leader, and I could have taken it easily. But King had the makings of *greatness*—and I chose to stand with him as Caleb stood with Moses.
Could you elaborate?
Well, by convicting and fining Mrs. Parks, unwittingly they are inviting a Federal court test of the kind of Jim Crow statutes on which the entire superstructure of segregation depends—
Dr. King, do you challenge allegations that your MIA election was essentially to make you the scapegoat should the boycotts fail?
Our demands are simple. Seating on a first come, first serve basis, Blacks hired as drivers. And it would be nice if the drivers could treat us like actual people.
Montgomery's segregation ordinance could be altered with a pen. But that's OK. Weatherman says tomorrow's supposed to be another good day for walking.

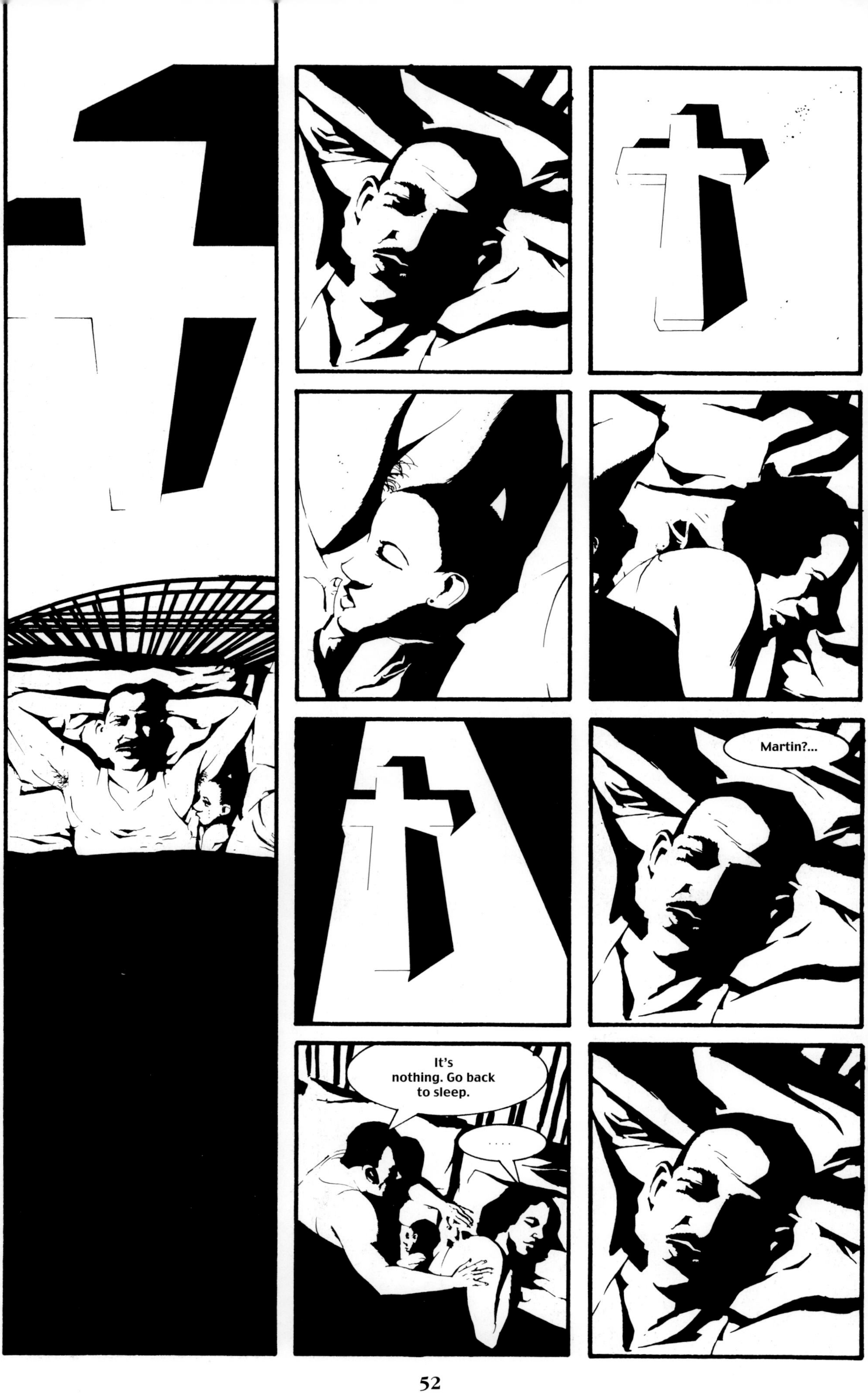
Martin?...
It's nothing. Go back to sleep.
. . . .

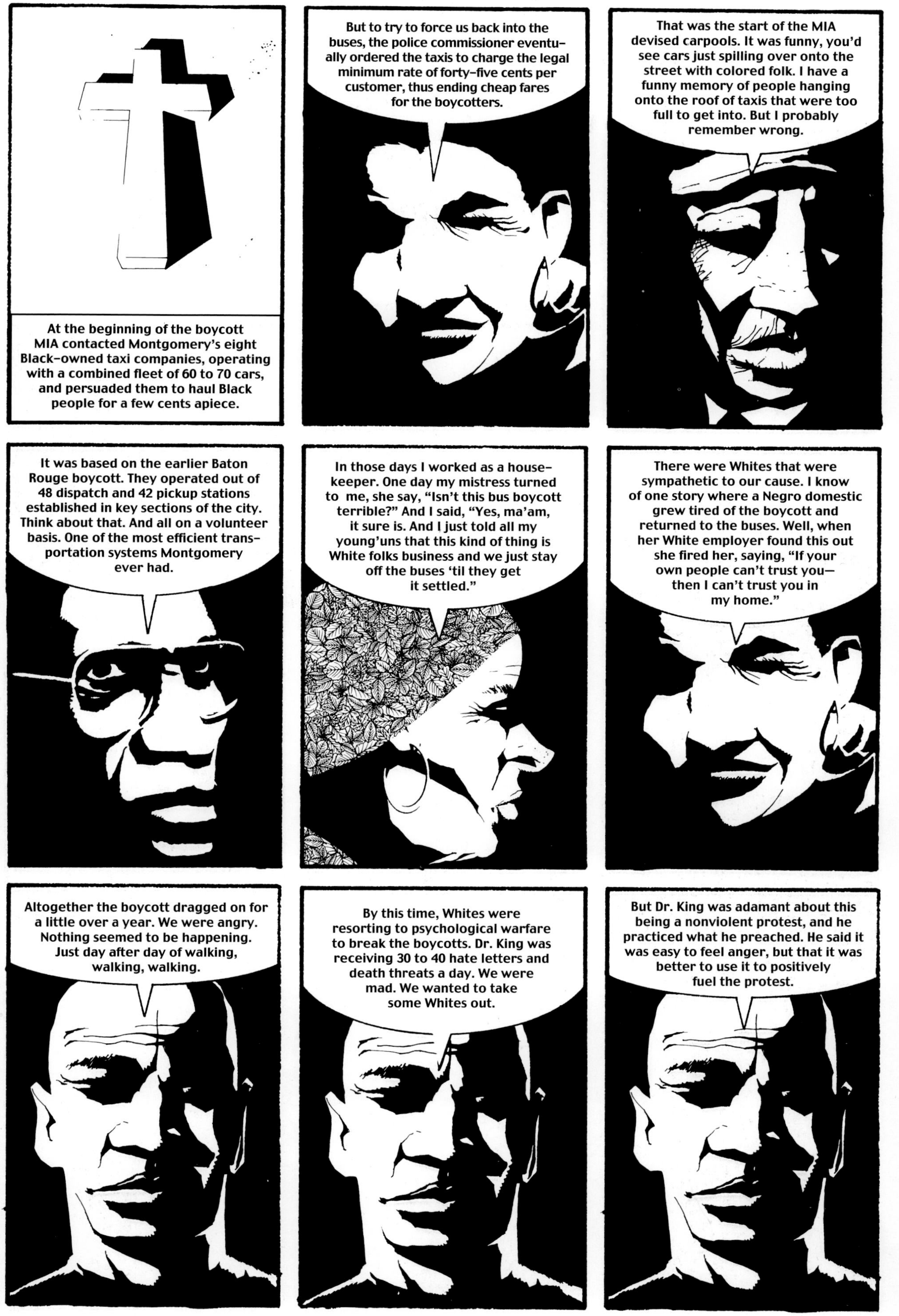
At the beginning of the boycott MIA contacted Montgomery's eight Black-owned taxi companies, operating with a combined fleet of 60 to 70 cars, and persuaded them to haul Black people for a few cents apiece.
But to try to force us back into the buses, the police commissioner eventually ordered the taxis to charge the legal minimum rate of forty-five cents per customer, thus ending cheap fares for the boycotters.
That was the start of the MIA devised carpools. It was funny, you'd see cars just spilling over onto the street with colored folk. I have a funny memory of people hanging onto the roof of taxis that were too full to get into. But I probably remember wrong.
It was based on the earlier Baton Rouge boycott. They operated out of 48 dispatch and 42 pickup stations established in key sections of the city. Think about that. And all on a volunteer basis. One of the most efficient transportation systems Montgomery ever had.
In those days I worked as a housekeeper. One day my mistress turned to me, she say, "Isn't this bus boycott terrible?" And I said, "Yes, ma'am, it sure is. And I just told all my young'uns that this kind of thing is White folks business and we just stay off the buses 'til they get it settled."
There were Whites that were sympathetic to our cause. I know of one story where a Negro domestic grew tired of the boycott and returned to the buses. Well, when her White employer found this out she fired her, saying, "If your own people can't trust you— then I can't trust you in my home."
Altogether the boycott dragged on for a little over a year. We were angry. Nothing seemed to be happening. Just day after day of walking, walking, walking.
By this time, Whites were resorting to psychological warfare to break the boycotts. Dr. King was receiving 30 to 40 hate letters and death threats a day. We were mad. We wanted to take some Whites out.
But Dr. King was adamant about this being a nonviolent protest, and he practiced what he preached. He said it was easy to feel anger, but that it was better to use it to positively fuel the protest.

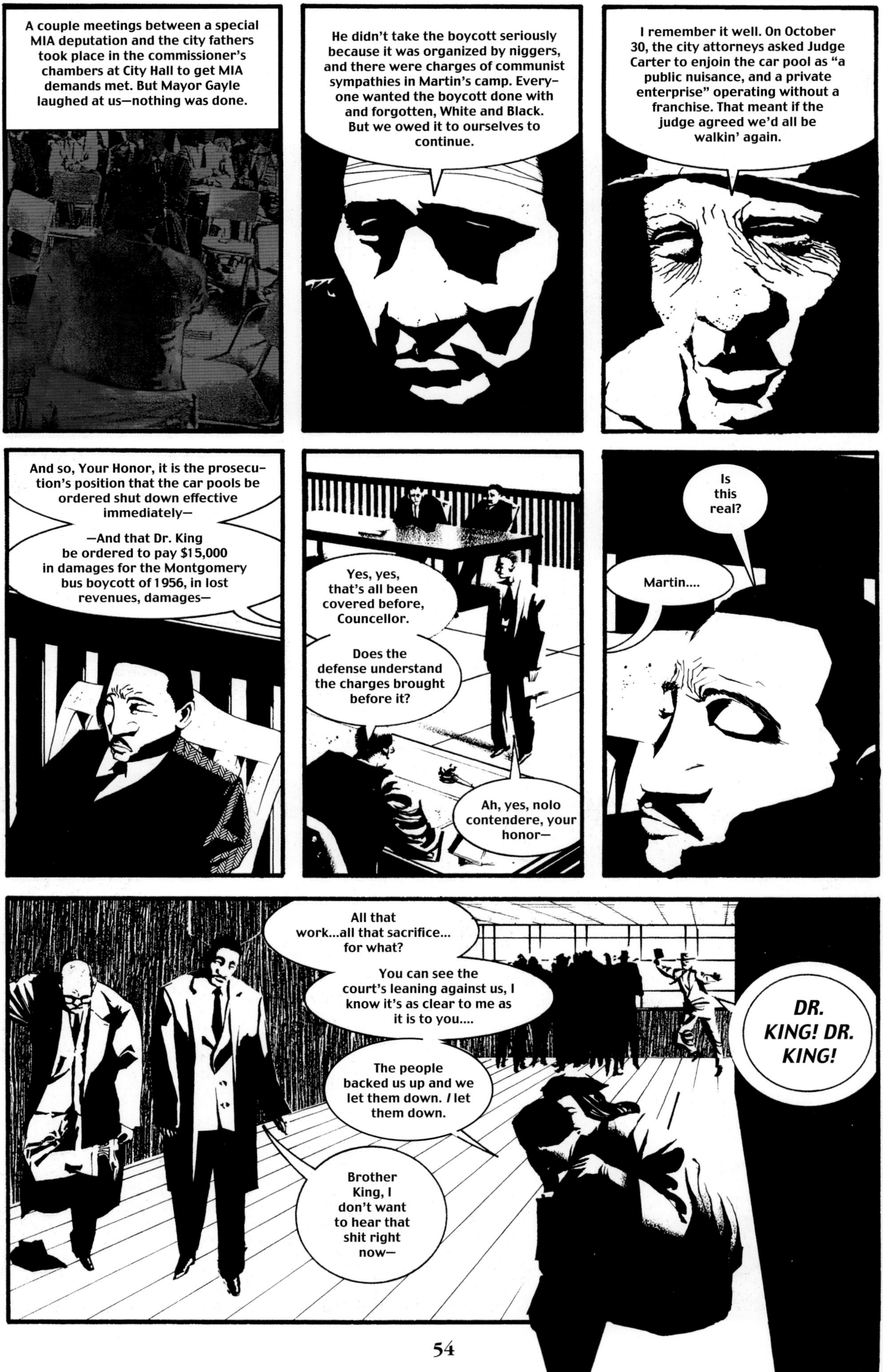
A couple meetings between a special MIA deputation and the city fathers took place in the commissioner's chambers at City Hall to get MIA demands met. But Mayor Gayle laughed at us—nothing was done.
He didn't take the boycott seriously because it was organized by niggers, and there were charges of communist sympathies in Martin's camp. Everyone wanted the boycott done with and forgotten, White and Black. But we owed it to ourselves to continue.
I remember it well. On October 30, the city attorneys asked Judge Carter to enjoin the car pool as "a public nuisance, and a private enterprise" operating without a franchise. That meant if the judge agreed we'd all be walkin' again.
And so, Your Honor, it is the prosecution's position that the car pools be ordered shut down effective immediately—
—And that Dr. King be ordered to pay $15,000 in damages for the Montgomery bus boycott of 1956, in lost revenues, damages—
Yes, yes, that's all been covered before, Councellor.
Does the defense understand the charges brought before it?
Ah, yes, nolo contendere, your honor—
Is this real?
Martin....
All that work...all that sacrifice... for what?
You can see the court's leaning against us, I know it's as clear to me as it is to you....
The people backed us up and we let them down. *I* let them down.
Brother King, I don't want to hear that shit right now—
DR. KING! DR. KING!

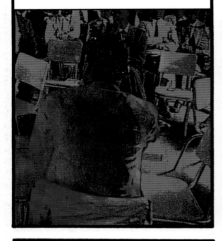

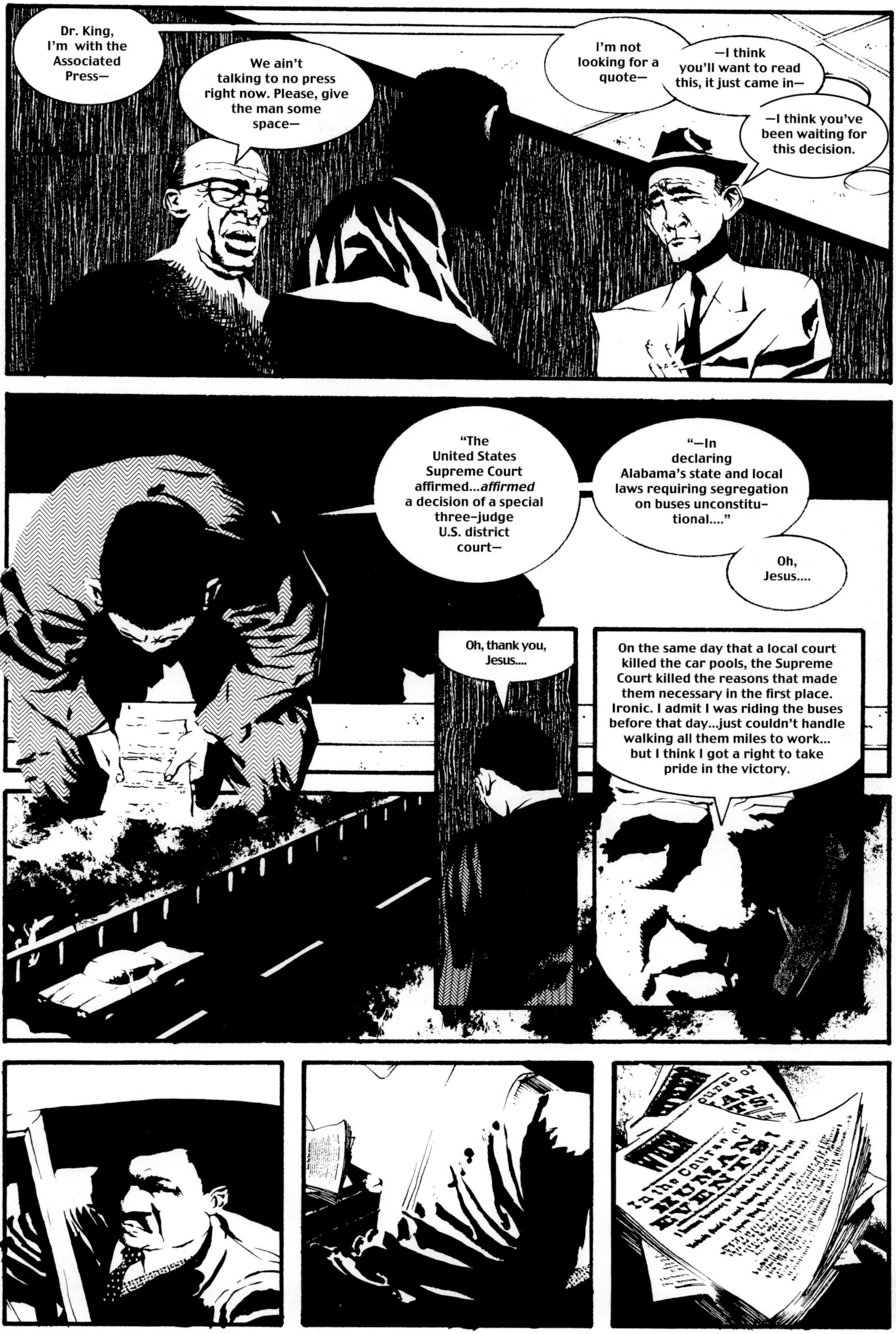
Dr. King, I'm with the Associated Press—
We ain't talking to no press right now. Please, give the man some space—
I'm not looking for a quote—
—I think you'll want to read this, it just came in—
—I think you've been waiting for this decision.
"The United States Supreme Court affirmed...*affirmed* a decision of a special three-judge U.S. district court—
"—In declaring Alabama's state and local laws requiring segregation on buses unconstitu- tional...."
Oh, Jesus....
Oh, thank you, Jesus....
On the same day that a local court killed the car pools, the Supreme Court killed the reasons that made them necessary in the first place. Ironic. I admit I was riding the buses before that day...just couldn't handle walking all them miles to work... but I think I got a right to take pride in the victory.

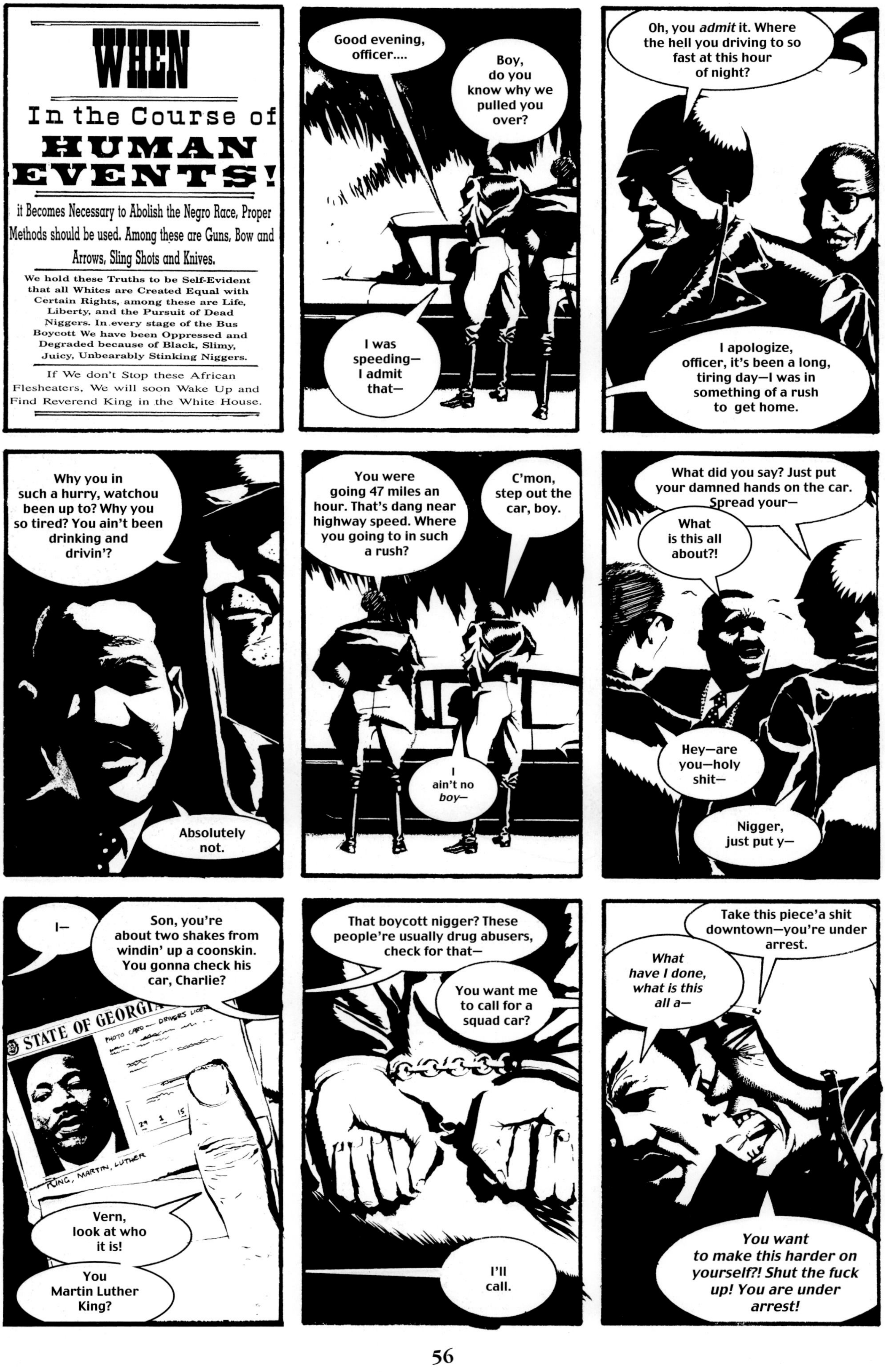
WHEN
In the Course of
HUMAN EVENTS!
it Becomes Necessary to Abolish the Negro Race, Proper Methods should be used. Among these are Guns, Bow and Arrows, Sling Shots and Knives.
We hold these Truths to be Self-Evident that all Whites are Created Equal with Certain Rights, among these are Life, Liberty, and the Pursuit of Dead Niggers. In every stage of the Bus Boycott We have been Oppressed and Degraded because of Black, Slimy, Juicy, Unbearably Stinking Niggers.
If We don't Stop these African Flesheaters, We will soon Wake Up and Find Reverend King in the White House.
Good evening, officer....
Boy, do you know why we pulled you over?
I was speeding—I admit that—
Oh, you *admit* it. Where the hell you driving to so fast at this hour of night?
I apologize, officer, it's been a long, tiring day—I was in something of a rush to get home.
Why you in such a hurry, watchou been up to? Why you so tired? You ain't been drinking and drivin'?
Absolutely not.
You were going 47 miles an hour. That's dang near highway speed. Where you going to in such a rush?
C'mon, step out the car, boy.
I ain't no *boy*—
What did you say? Just put your damned hands on the car. Spread your—
What is this all about?!
Hey—are you—holy shit—
Nigger, just put y—
I—
Son, you're about two shakes from windin' up a coonskin. You gonna check his car, Charlie?
STATE OF GEORGIA
KING, MARTIN, LUTHER
Vern, look at who it is!
You Martin Luther King?
That boycott nigger? These people're usually drug abusers, check for that—
You want me to call for a squad car?
I'll call.
Take this piece'a shit downtown—you're under arrest.
What have I done, what is this all a—
You want to make this harder on yourself?! Shut the fuck up! You are under arrest!

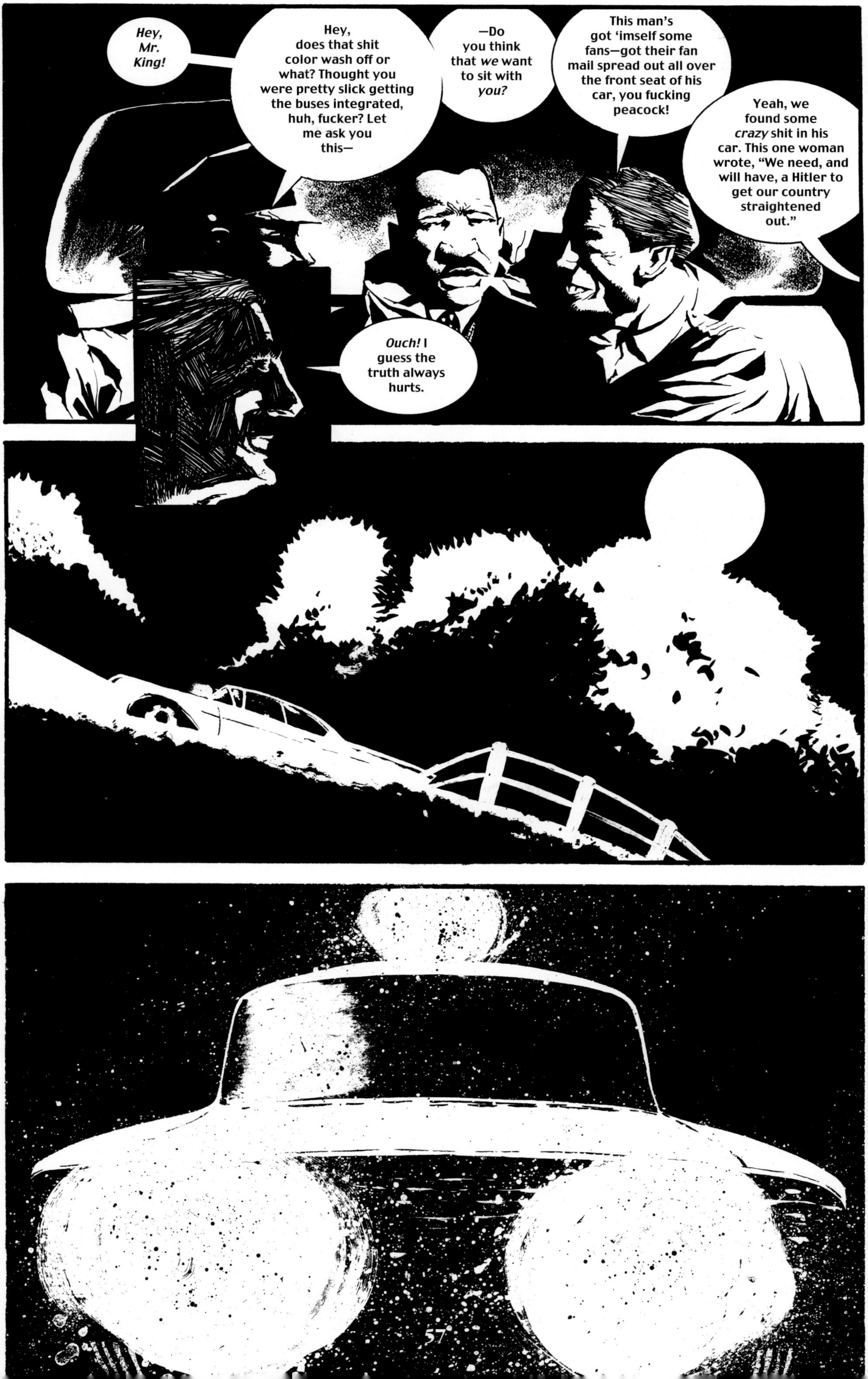
Hey, Mr. King!
Hey, does that shit color wash off or what? Thought you were pretty slick getting the buses integrated, huh, fucker? Let me ask you this—
—Do you think that *we* want to sit with *you?*
This man's got 'imself some fans—got their fan mail spread out all over the front seat of his car, you fucking peacock!
Yeah, we found some *crazy* shit in his car. This one woman wrote, "We need, and will have, a Hitler to get our country straightened out."
Ouch! I guess the truth always hurts.

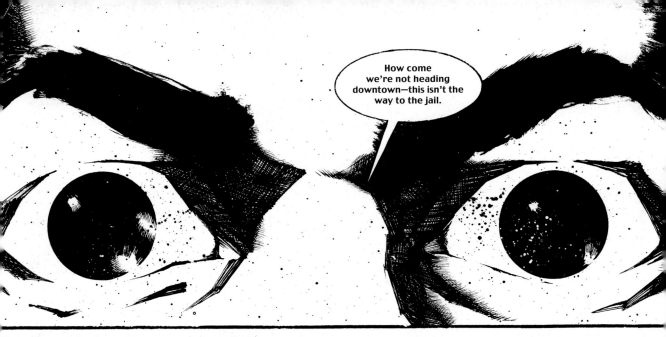

How come we're not heading downtown—this isn't the way to the jail.

Shut up.

Please, where are you taking me, I just want to kn—

I told you to shut that fucking pie-hole—

I just wanna know where you're taking me, I just—

Christ, will you *shut him up* back there!

Quiet down now, nigger—

Oh my Lord, where are you taking me

MONTGOMERY JAIL

This is where we're taking you, fucker.

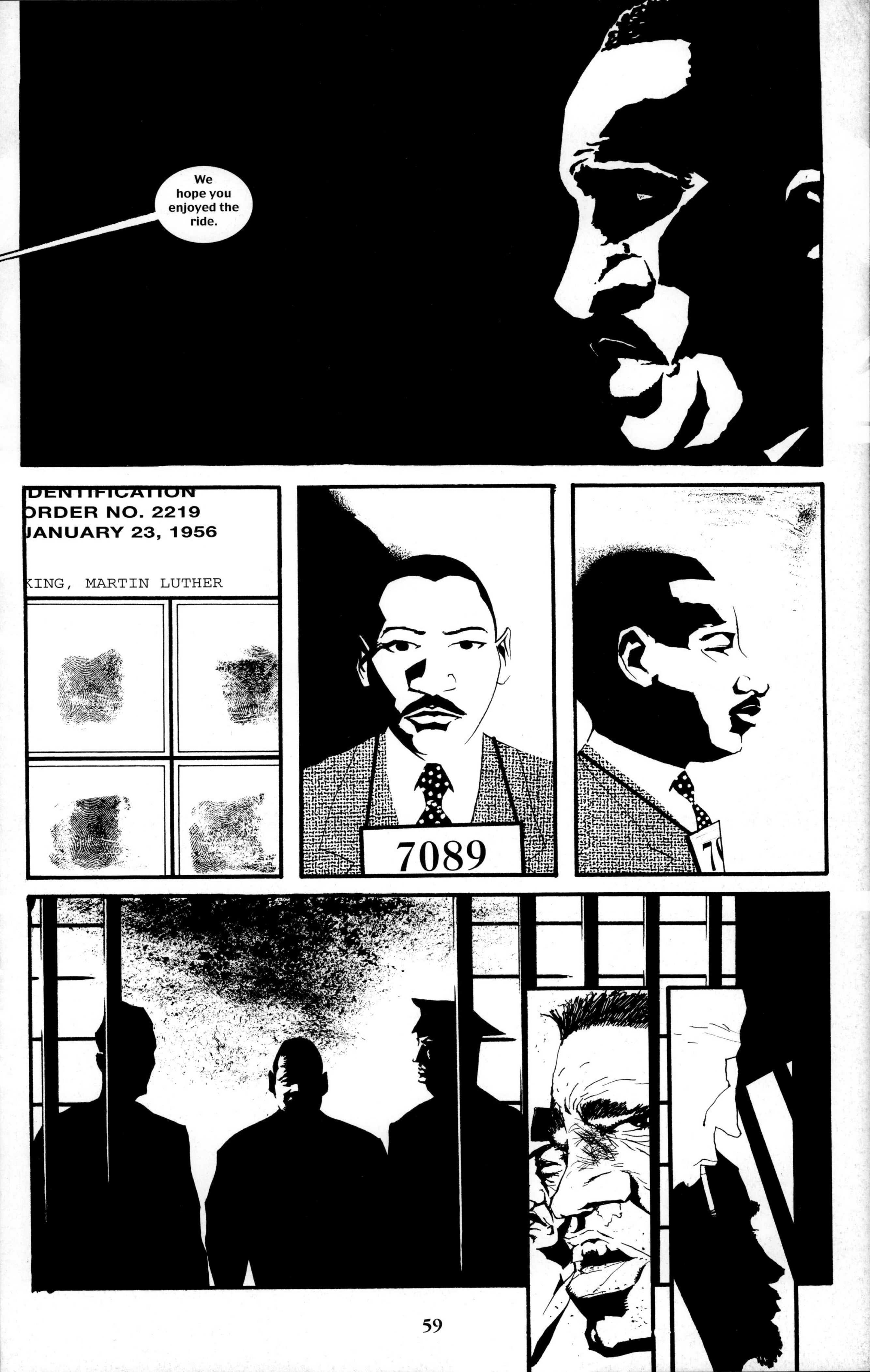
We hope you enjoyed the ride.
IDENTIFICATION
ORDER NO. 2219
JANUARY 23, 1956
KING, MARTIN LUTHER
7089

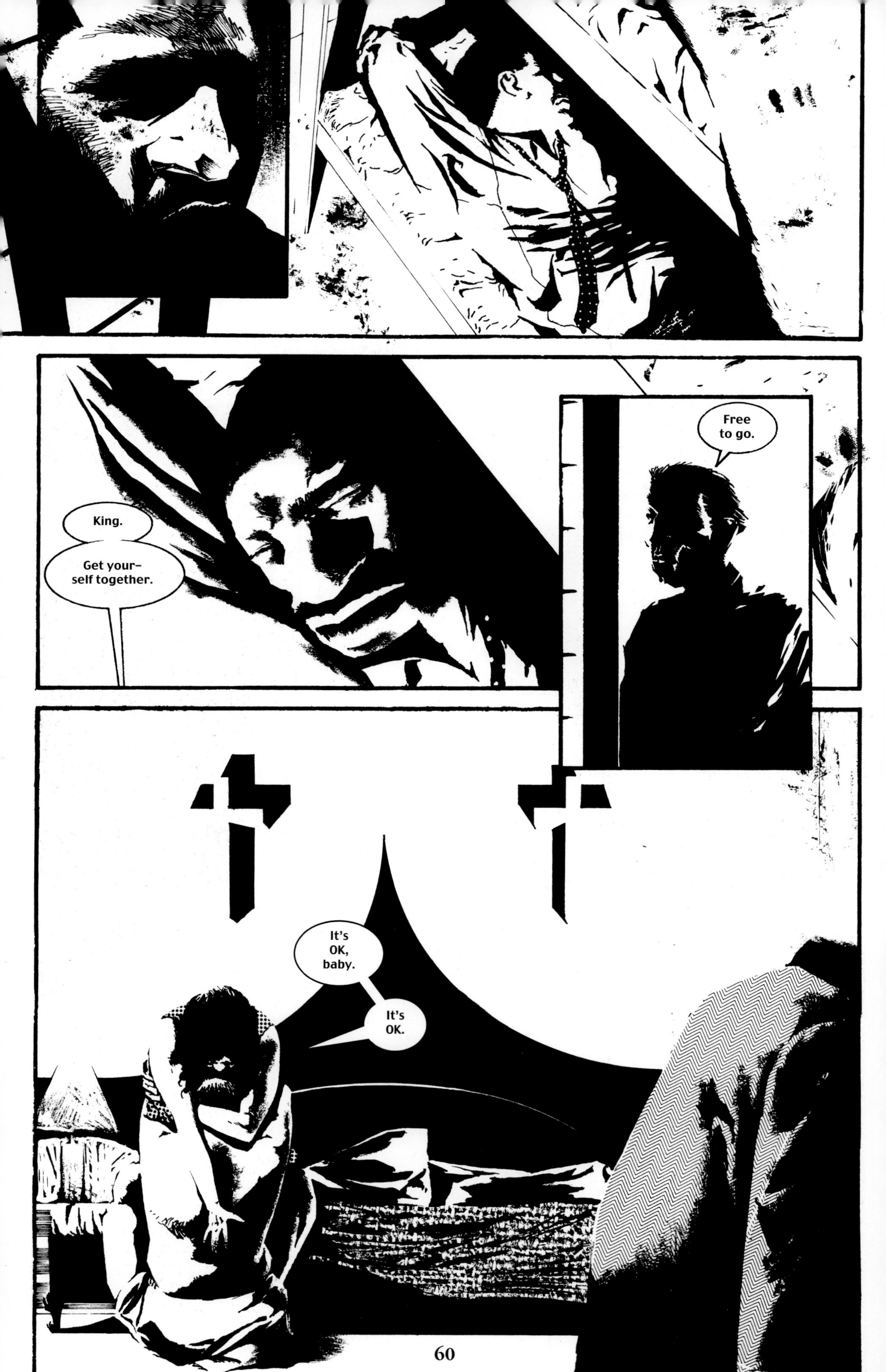
King.
Get your-self together.
Free to go.
It's OK, baby.
It's OK.

In December the Supreme Court mandate finally took effect in Montgomery, which meant we could all stampede on to the buses like a pack o' wild buffalo and not have to move to the back of the bus.

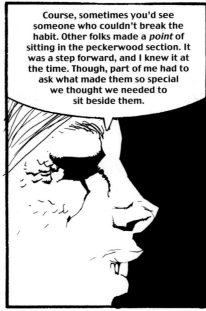

Course, sometimes you'd see someone who couldn't break the habit. Other folks made a *point* of sitting in the peckerwood section. It was a step forward, and I knew it at the time. Though, part of me had to ask what made them so special we thought we needed to sit beside them.

Martin and Abernathy and Nixon and the rest stepped on the bus that morning. They all got on with a White preacher if memory serves, Glenn Smiley.

The first integrated bus in Montgomery.

It was a new order. For the most part...people just found a way to accept what had happened and moved on....

Jesus Christ

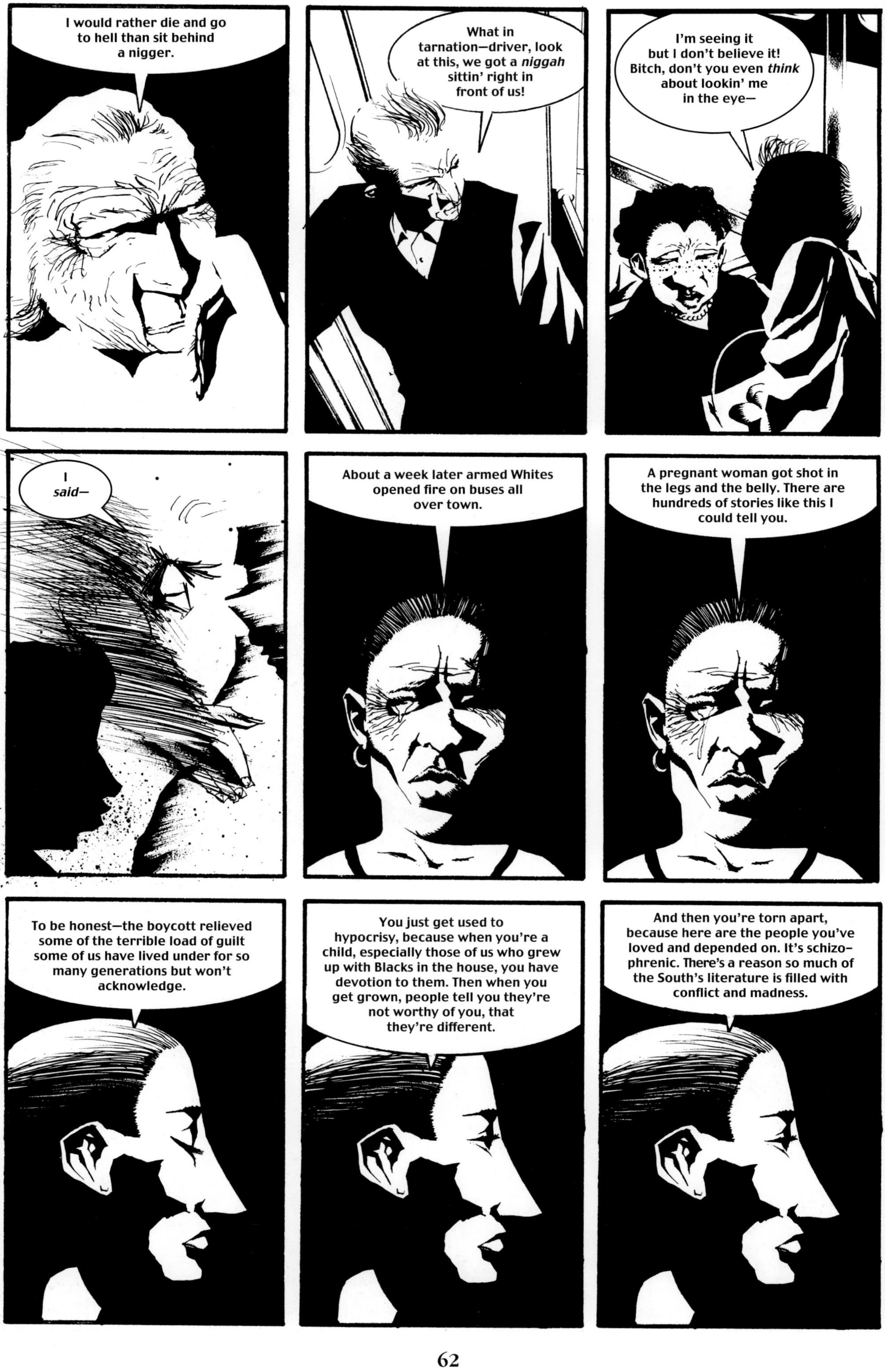
I would rather die and go to hell than sit behind a nigger.
What in tarnation—driver, look at this, we got a *niggah* sittin' right in front of us!
I'm seeing it but I don't believe it! Bitch, don't you even *think* about lookin' me in the eye—
I *said*—
About a week later armed Whites opened fire on buses all over town.
A pregnant woman got shot in the legs and the belly. There are hundreds of stories like this I could tell you.
To be honest—the boycott relieved some of the terrible load of guilt some of us have lived under for so many generations but won't acknowledge.
You just get used to hypocrisy, because when you're a child, especially those of us who grew up with Blacks in the house, you have devotion to them. Then when you get grown, people tell you they're not worthy of you, that they're different.
And then you're torn apart, because here are the people you've loved and depended on. It's schizo-phrenic. There's a reason so much of the South's literature is filled with conflict and madness.

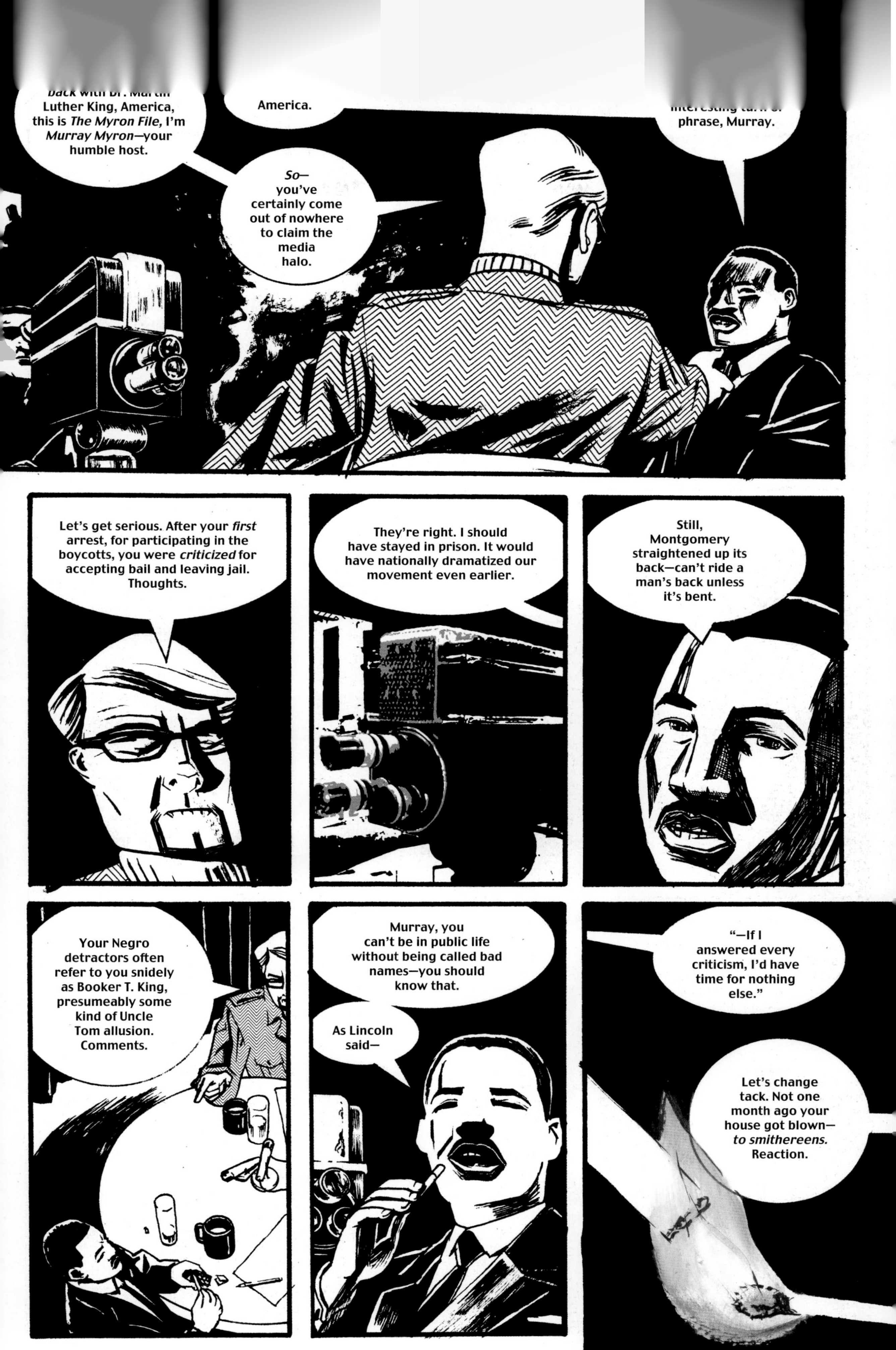
Luther King, America, this is *The Myron File,* I'm *Murray Myron*—your humble host.
America.
So— you've certainly come out of nowhere to claim the media halo.
phrase, Murray.
Let's get serious. After your *first* arrest, for participating in the boycotts, you were *criticized* for accepting bail and leaving jail. Thoughts.
They're right. I should have stayed in prison. It would have nationally dramatized our movement even earlier.
Still, Montgomery straightened up its back—can't ride a man's back unless it's bent.
Your Negro detractors often refer to you snidely as Booker T. King, presumeably some kind of Uncle Tom allusion. Comments.
Murray, you can't be in public life without being called bad names—you should know that.
As Lincoln said—
"—If I answered every criticism, I'd have time for nothing else."
Let's change tack. Not one month ago your house got blown—*to smithereens.* Reaction.

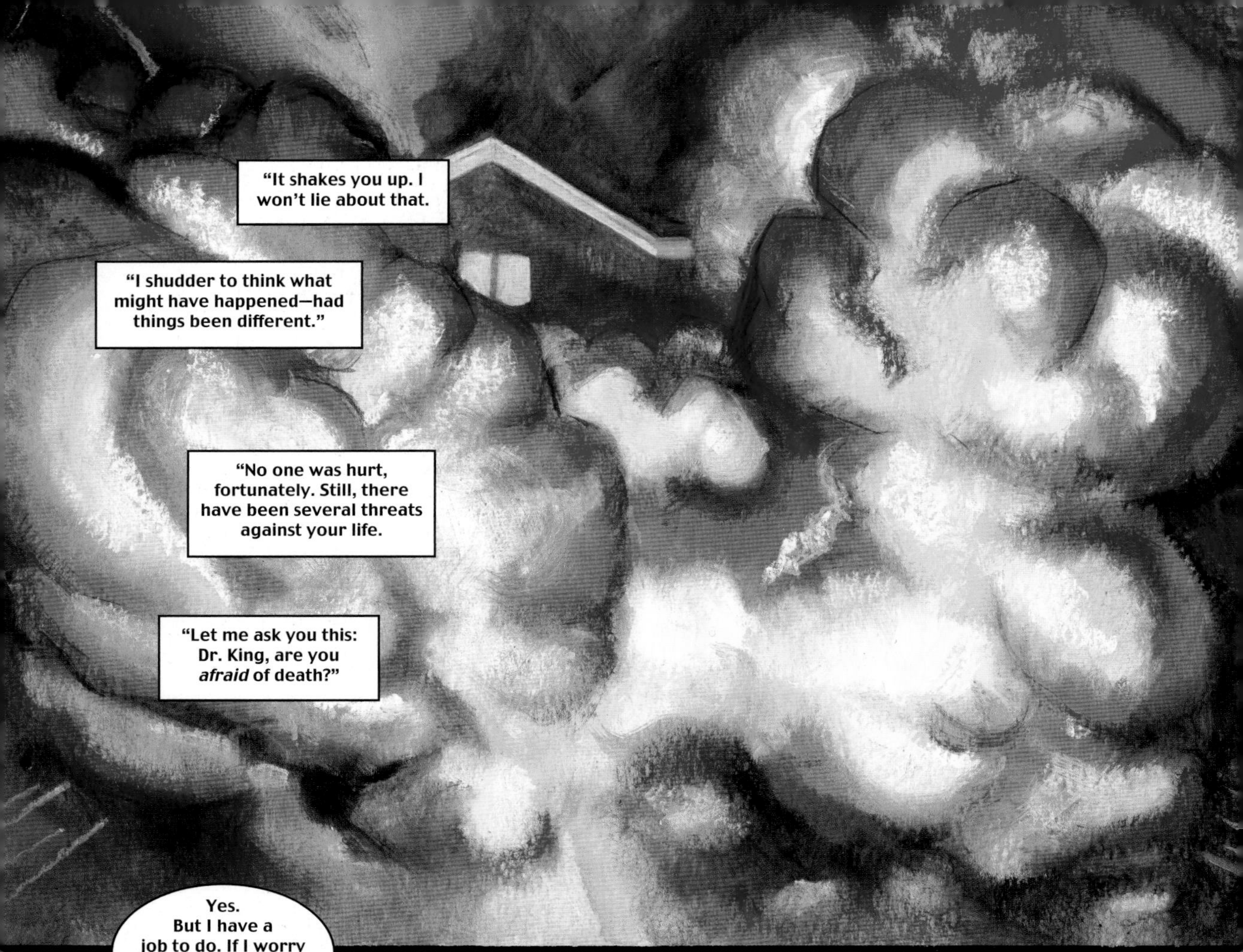
"It shakes you up. I won't lie about that.
"I shudder to think what might have happened—had things been different."
"No one was hurt, fortunately. Still, there have been several threats against your life.
"Let me ask you this: Dr. King, are you *afraid* of death?"

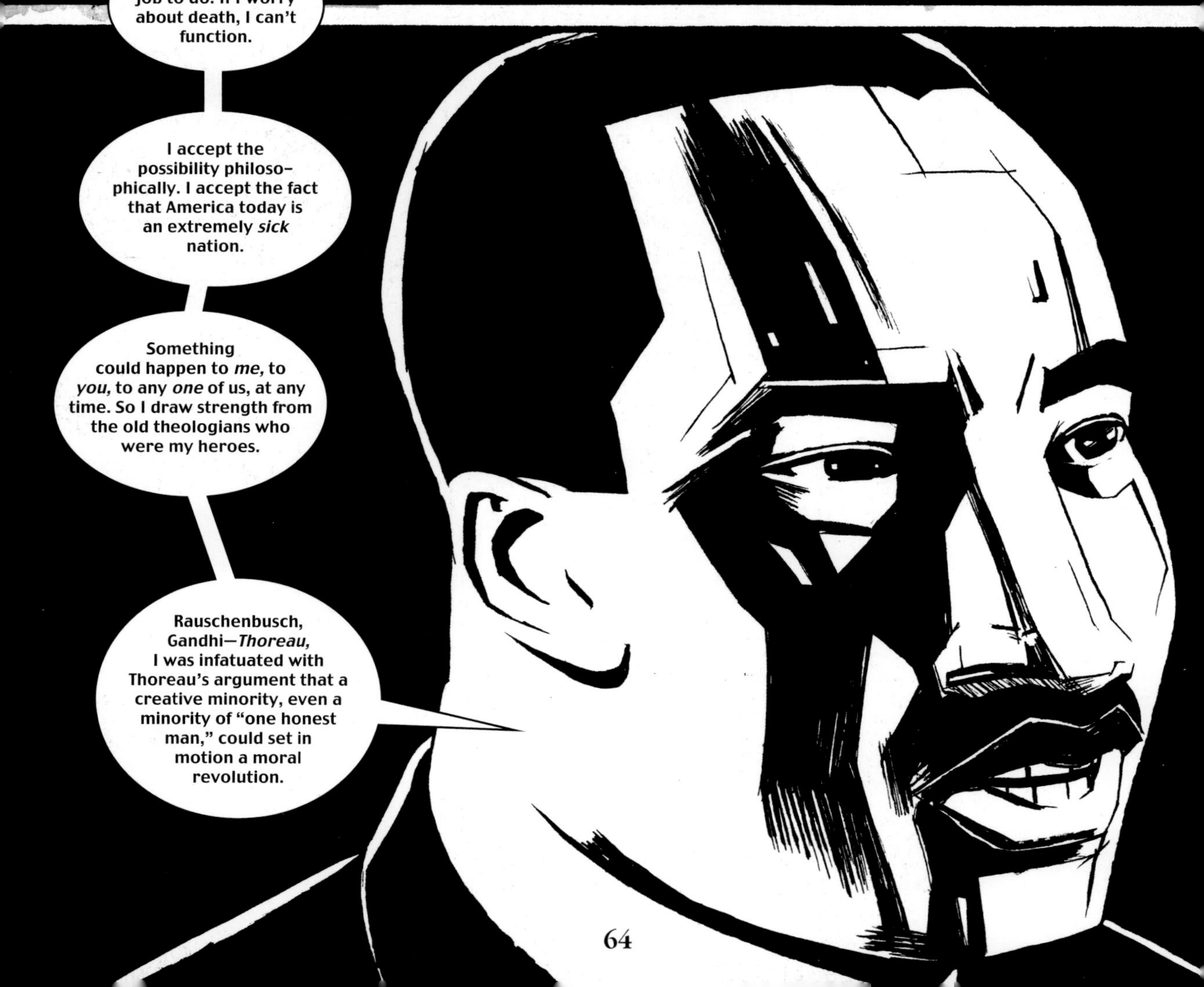
Yes. But I have a job to do. If I worry about death, I can't function.
I accept the possibility philoso-phically. I accept the fact that America today is an extremely *sick* nation.
Something could happen to *me,* to *you,* to any *one* of us, at any time. So I draw strength from the old theologians who were my heroes.
Rauschenbusch, Gandhi—*Thoreau,* I was infatuated with Thoreau's argument that a creative minority, even a minority of "one honest man," could set in motion a moral revolution.

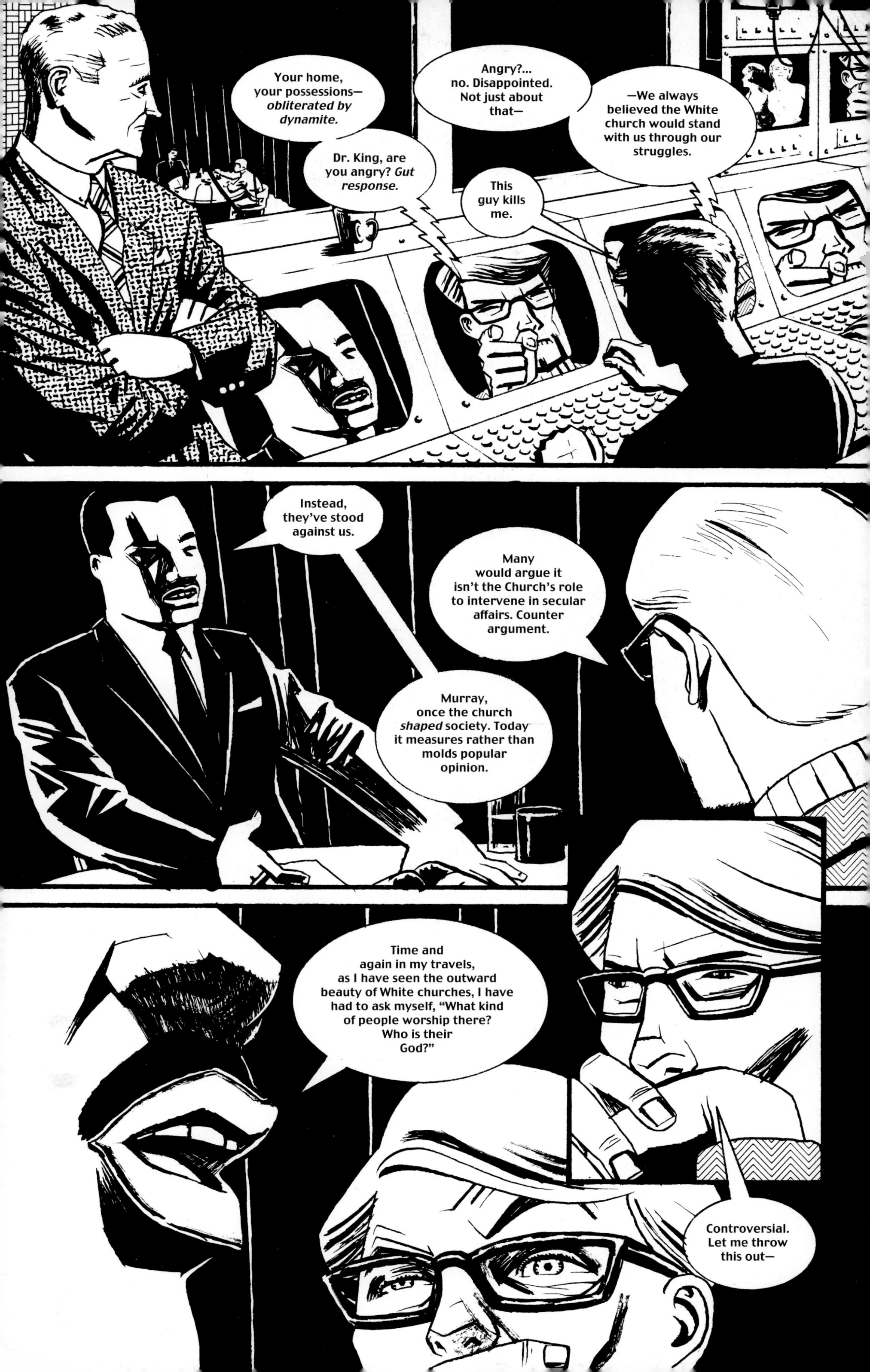
Your home, your possessions—*obliterated by dynamite.*
Dr. King, are you angry? *Gut response.*
Angry?... no. Disappointed. Not just about that—
This guy kills me.
—We always believed the White church would stand with us through our struggles.
Instead, they've stood against us.
Many would argue it isn't the Church's role to intervene in secular affairs. Counter argument.
Murray, once the church *shaped* society. Today it measures rather than molds popular opinion.
Time and again in my travels, as I have seen the outward beauty of White churches, I have had to ask myself, "What kind of people worship there? Who is their God?"
Controversial. Let me throw this out—

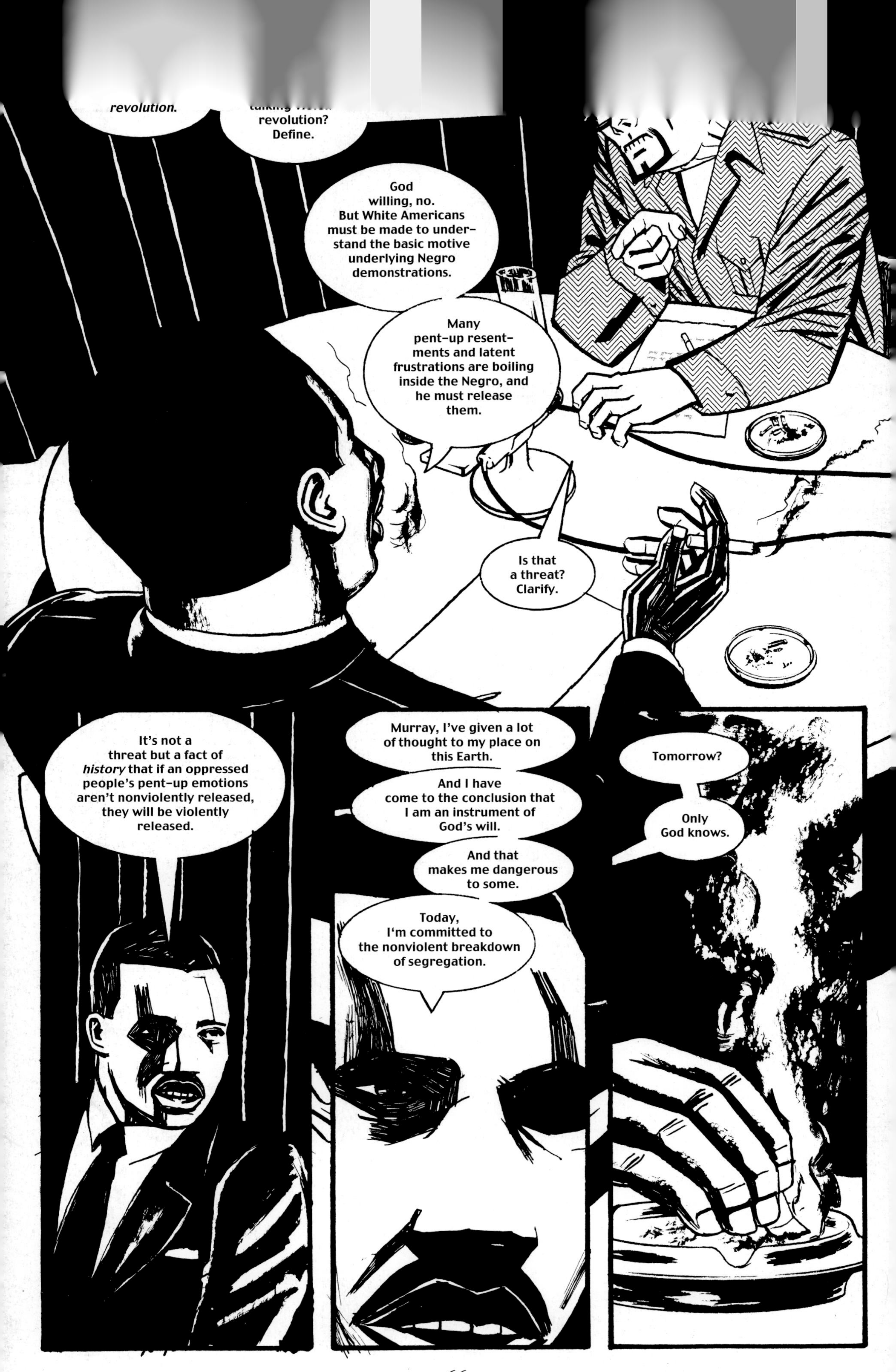
revolution.
revolution? Define.
God willing, no. But White Americans must be made to understand the basic motive underlying Negro demonstrations.
Many pent-up resentments and latent frustrations are boiling inside the Negro, and he must release them.
Is that a threat? Clarify.
It's not a threat but a fact of *history* that if an oppressed people's pent-up emotions aren't nonviolently released, they will be violently released.
Murray, I've given a lot of thought to my place on this Earth.
And I have come to the conclusion that I am an instrument of God's will.
And that makes me dangerous to some.
Today, I'm committed to the nonviolent breakdown of segregation.
Tomorrow?
Only God knows.

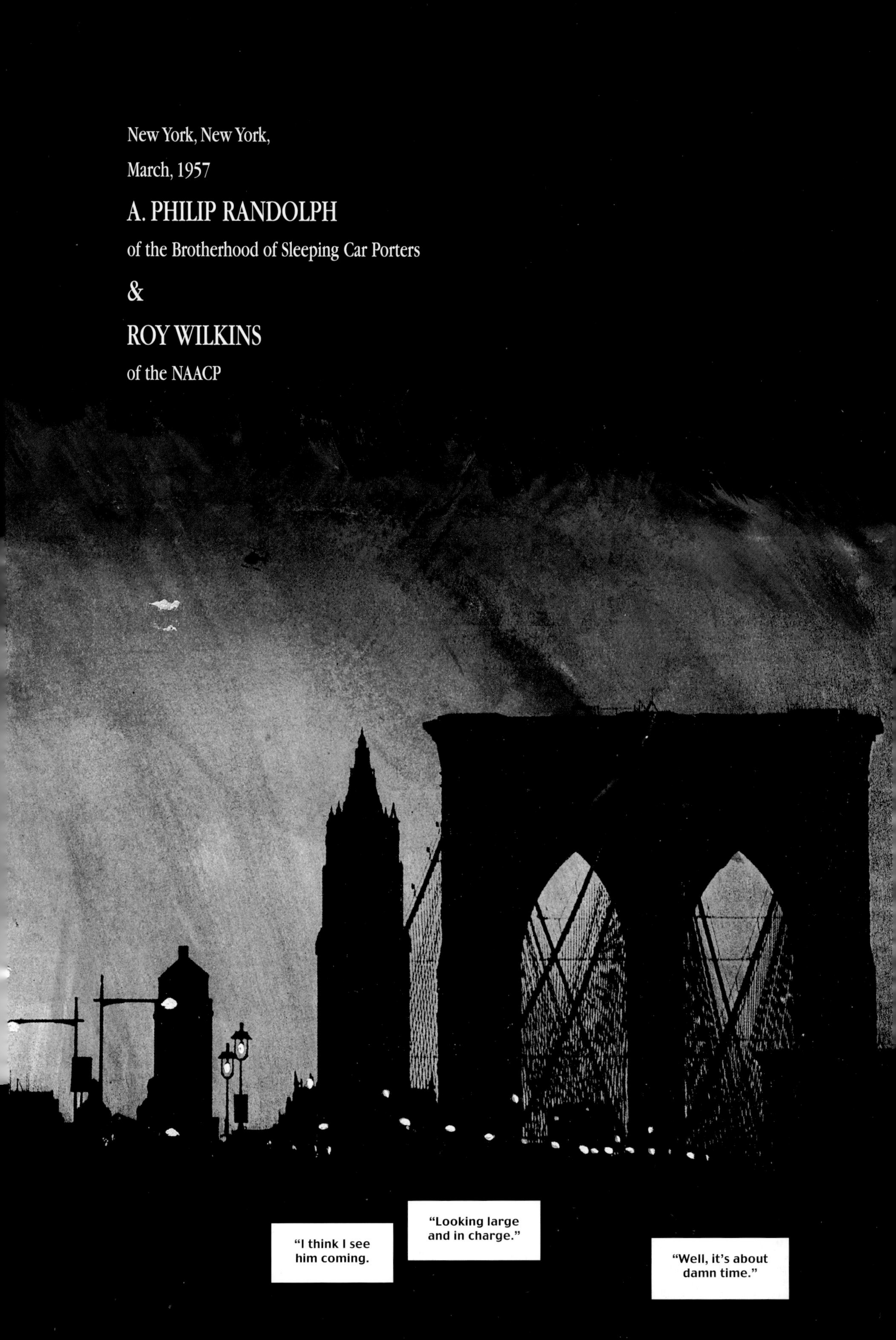
New York, New York,
March, 1957
A. PHILIP RANDOLPH
of the Brotherhood of Sleeping Car Porters
&
ROY WILKINS
of the NAACP
"I think I see him coming.
"Looking large and in charge."
"Well, it's about damn time."

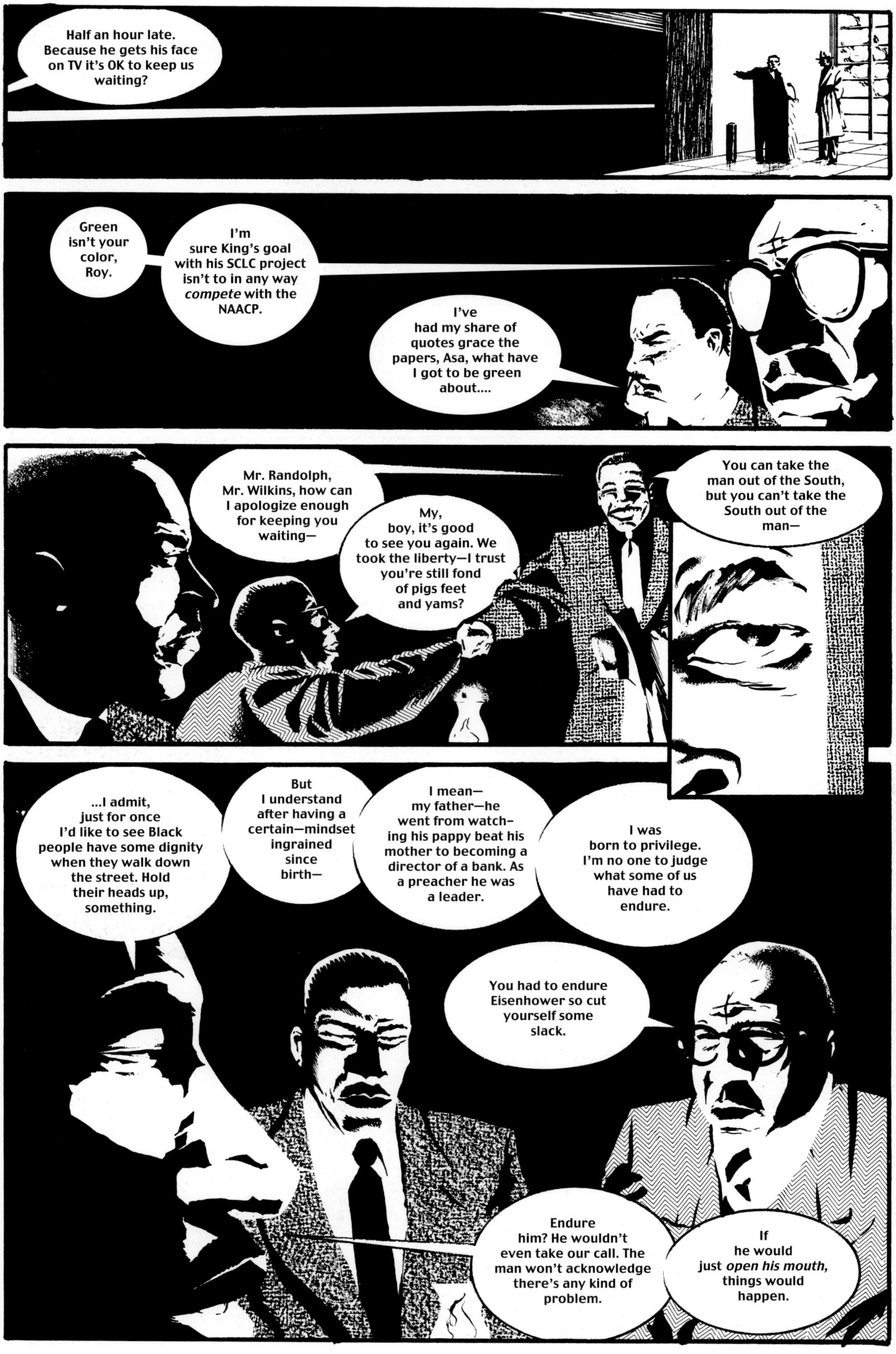
Half an hour late. Because he gets his face on TV it's OK to keep us waiting?
Green isn't your color, Roy.
I'm sure King's goal with his SCLC project isn't to in any way *compete* with the NAACP.
I've had my share of quotes grace the papers, Asa, what have I got to be green about....
Mr. Randolph, Mr. Wilkins, how can I apologize enough for keeping you waiting—
My, boy, it's good to see you again. We took the liberty—I trust you're still fond of pigs feet and yams?
You can take the man out of the South, but you can't take the South out of the man—
...I admit, just for once I'd like to see Black people have some dignity when they walk down the street. Hold their heads up, something.
But I understand after having a certain—mindset ingrained since birth—
I mean— my father—he went from watching his pappy beat his mother to becoming a director of a bank. As a preacher he was a leader.
I was born to privilege. I'm no one to judge what some of us have had to endure.
You had to endure Eisenhower so cut yourself some slack.
Endure him? He wouldn't even take our call. The man won't acknowledge there's any kind of problem.
If he would just *open his mouth,* things would happen.

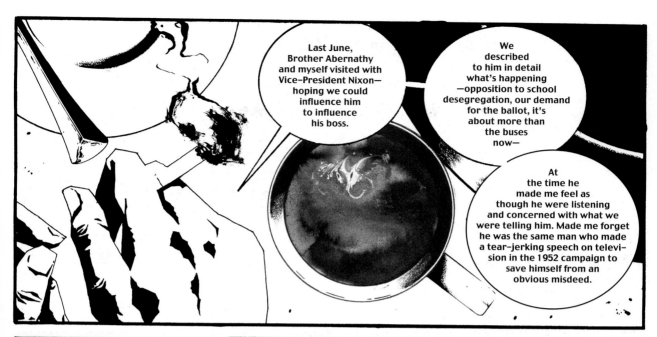

Last June, Brother Abernathy and myself visited with Vice-President Nixon—hoping we could influence him to influence his boss.

We described to him in detail what's happening—opposition to school desegregation, our demand for the ballot, it's about more than the buses now—

At the time he made me feel as though he were listening and concerned with what we were telling him. Made me forget he was the same man who made a tear-jerking speech on television in the 1952 campaign to save himself from an obvious misdeed.

I heard that that Texas senator, Johnson, didn't he herd a civil rights bill through the Senate?

Yes, sir, but in doing so he bartered away any injunctive power the Attorney General might have to enforce school desegragation.

What the hell was Johnson thinking?

Lyndon Johnson managed to push the first civil rights legislation since the Reconstruction—I think he deserves—

I don't know, Roy—I have to say I agree with Martin. The bill all but ignores the school problem or voting rights.

That's where the Southern Christian Leadership Conference comes in.

Bayard Rustin and myself called 115 Negro leaders, mostly church folk, to Montgomery to plan a counter-offensive.

Mr. Wilkins, we're trying to avoid any overlap. Unlike the NAACP's membership model, we've planned SCLC to consist of local affiliates—for our purposes it's a more effective strategy.

Fundamentally, what we want is to operate through the churches and function as a service agency to coordinate local civil rights activity by means of bi-annual conventions with delegates of the various affiliates.

69

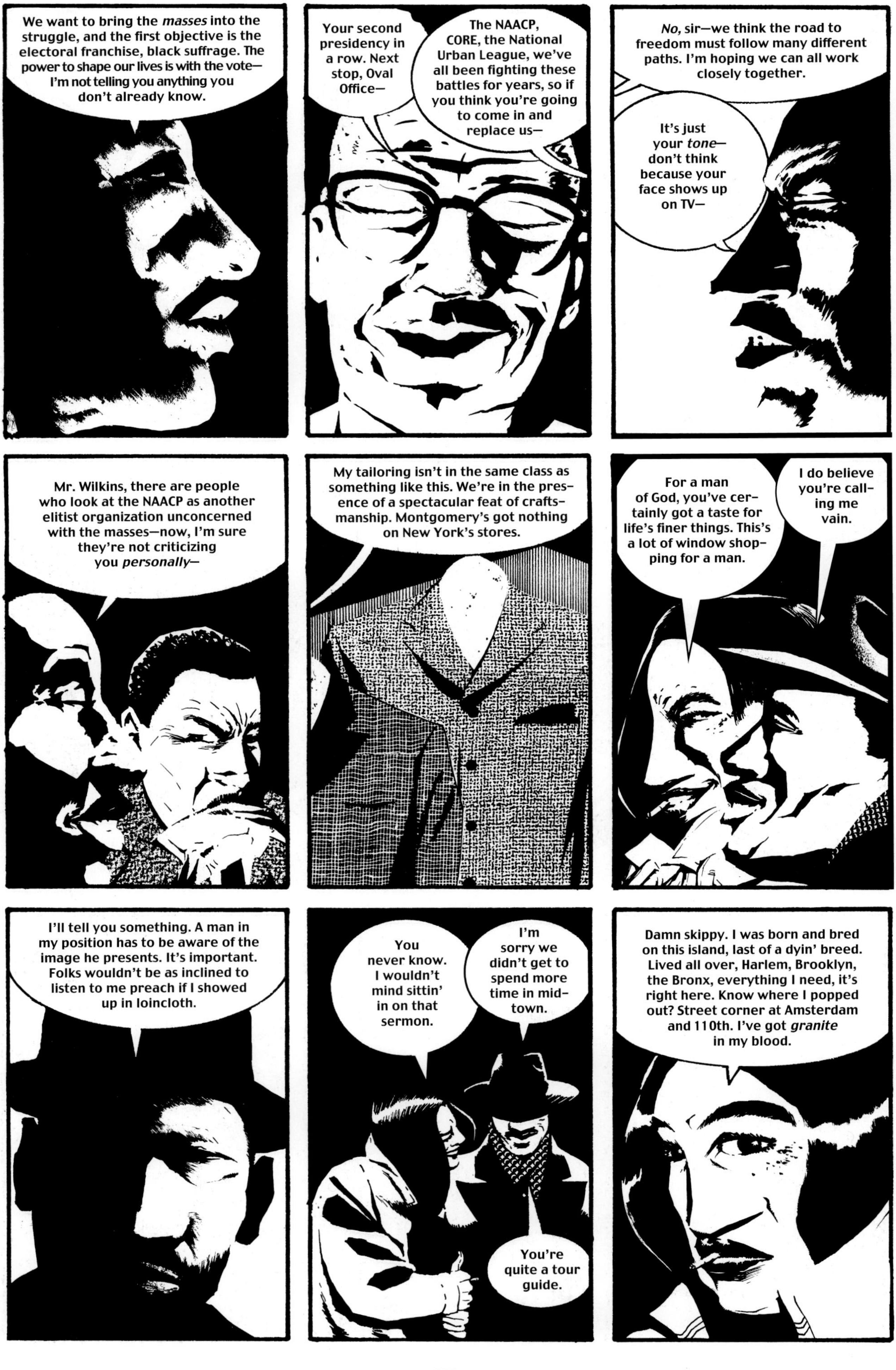
We want to bring the *masses* into the struggle, and the first objective is the electoral franchise, black suffrage. The power to shape our lives is with the vote—I'm not telling you anything you don't already know.
Your second presidency in a row. Next stop, Oval Office—
The NAACP, CORE, the National Urban League, we've all been fighting these battles for years, so if you think you're going to come in and replace us—
No, sir—we think the road to freedom must follow many different paths. I'm hoping we can all work closely together.
It's just your *tone*—don't think because your face shows up on TV—
Mr. Wilkins, there are people who look at the NAACP as another elitist organization unconcerned with the masses—now, I'm sure they're not criticizing you *personally*—
My tailoring isn't in the same class as something like this. We're in the presence of a spectacular feat of craftsmanship. Montgomery's got nothing on New York's stores.
For a man of God, you've certainly got a taste for life's finer things. This's a lot of window shopping for a man.
I do believe you're calling me vain.
I'll tell you something. A man in my position has to be aware of the image he presents. It's important. Folks wouldn't be as inclined to listen to me preach if I showed up in loincloth.
You never know. I wouldn't mind sittin' in on that sermon.
I'm sorry we didn't get to spend more time in midtown.
You're quite a tour guide.
Damn skippy. I was born and bred on this island, last of a dyin' breed. Lived all over, Harlem, Brooklyn, the Bronx, everything I need, it's right here. Know where I popped out? Street corner at Amsterdam and 110th. I've got *granite* in my blood.

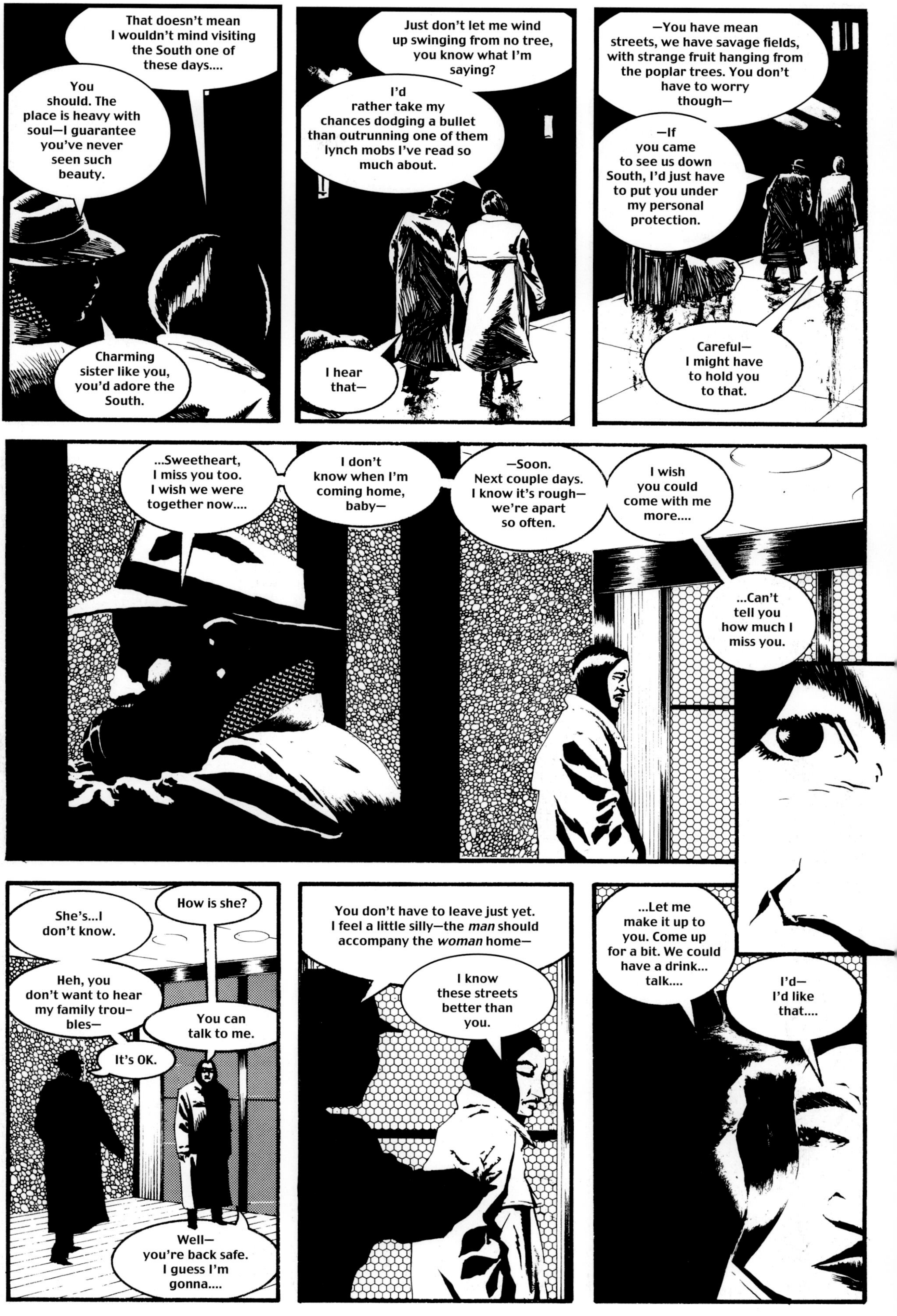
That doesn't mean I wouldn't mind visiting the South one of these days....
You should. The place is heavy with soul—I guarantee you've never seen such beauty.
Charming sister like you, you'd adore the South.
Just don't let me wind up swinging from no tree, you know what I'm saying?
I'd rather take my chances dodging a bullet than outrunning one of them lynch mobs I've read so much about.
I hear that—
—You have mean streets, we have savage fields, with strange fruit hanging from the poplar trees. You don't have to worry though—
—If you came to see us down South, I'd just have to put you under my personal protection.
Careful—I might have to hold you to that.
...Sweetheart, I miss you too. I wish we were together now....
I don't know when I'm coming home, baby—
—Soon. Next couple days. I know it's rough—we're apart so often.
I wish you could come with me more....
...Can't tell you how much I miss you.
She's...I don't know.
How is she?
Heh, you don't want to hear my family troubles—
You can talk to me.
It's OK.
Well—you're back safe. I guess I'm gonna....
You don't have to leave just yet. I feel a little silly—the *man* should accompany the *woman* home—
I know these streets better than you.
...Let me make it up to you. Come up for a bit. We could have a drink... talk....
I'd—I'd like that....

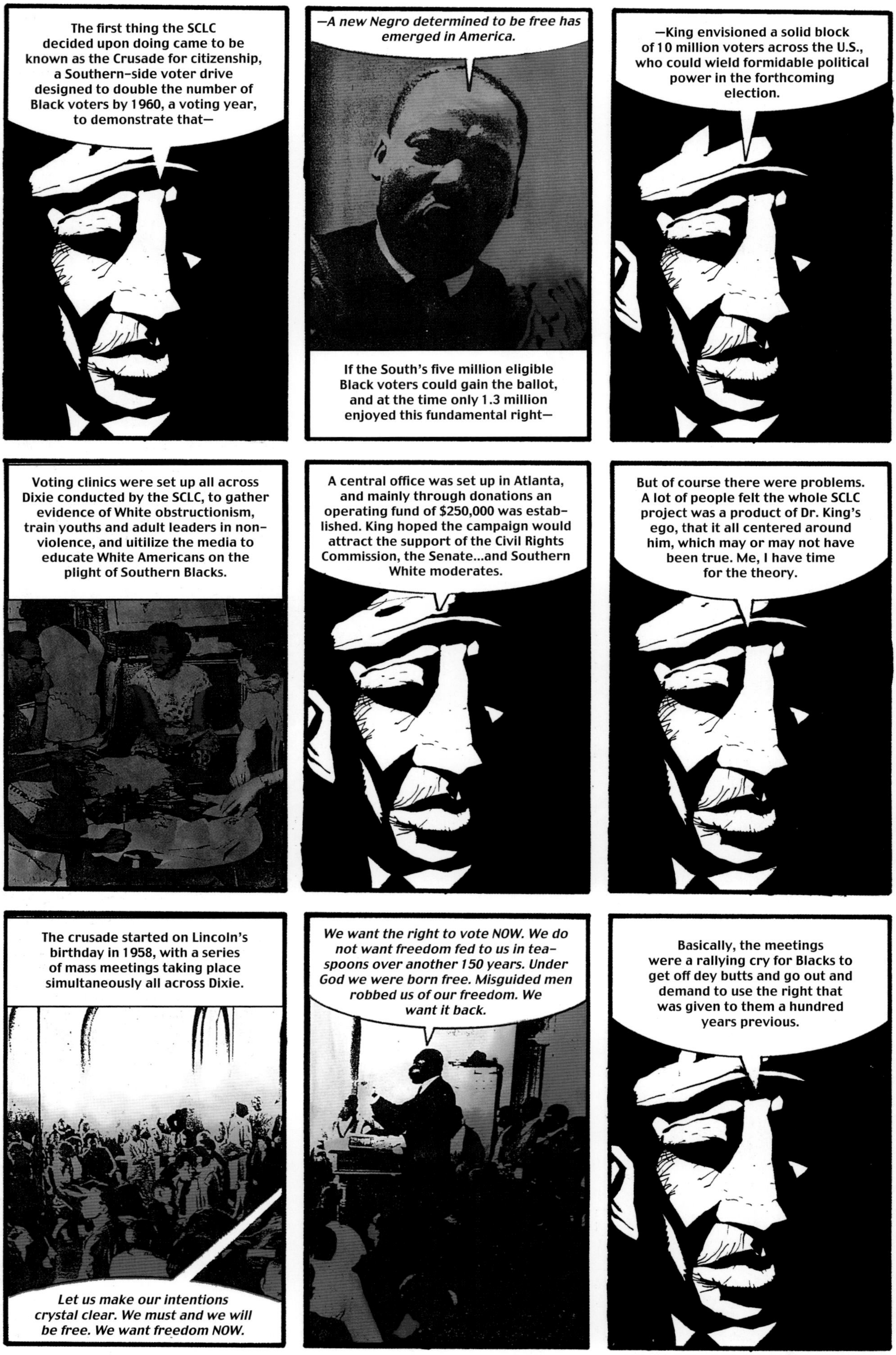

The first thing the SCLC decided upon doing came to be known as the Crusade for citizenship, a Southern-side voter drive designed to double the number of Black voters by 1960, a voting year, to demonstrate that—
—A new Negro determined to be free has emerged in America.
If the South's five million eligible Black voters could gain the ballot, and at the time only 1.3 million enjoyed this fundamental right—
—King envisioned a solid block of 10 million voters across the U.S., who could wield formidable political power in the forthcoming election.
Voting clinics were set up all across Dixie conducted by the SCLC, to gather evidence of White obstructionism, train youths and adult leaders in non-violence, and uitilize the media to educate White Americans on the plight of Southern Blacks.
A central office was set up in Atlanta, and mainly through donations an operating fund of $250,000 was estab-lished. King hoped the campaign would attract the support of the Civil Rights Commission, the Senate...and Southern White moderates.
But of course there were problems. A lot of people felt the whole SCLC project was a product of Dr. King's ego, that it all centered around him, which may or may not have been true. Me, I have time for the theory.
The crusade started on Lincoln's birthday in 1958, with a series of mass meetings taking place simultaneously all across Dixie.
Let us make our intentions crystal clear. We must and we will be free. We want freedom NOW.
We want the right to vote NOW. We do not want freedom fed to us in tea-spoons over another 150 years. Under God we were born free. Misguided men robbed us of our freedom. We want it back.
Basically, the meetings were a rallying cry for Blacks to get off dey butts and go out and demand to use the right that was given to them a hundred years previous.

The right to play a hand in shaping their own lives. The right to vote.

Whoa! Where in the Sam Hill do you think you're headin' off to, nigger-man?

I asked you a question, you walkin' 'round'a shit.

I'm going to vote.

Is that a fact, Sambo?

Heh, you hear that, Billy Bob?

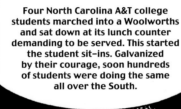

Eventually SCLC resolved to file voter registration complaints with the CRC.

SCLC strongly supported its recommendation that federal registrars be deployed in Southern areas where Blacks were systematically kept off the voting rolls and out of politics.

February 2, 1960

Four North Carolina A&T college students marched into a Woolworths and sat down at its lunch counter demanding to be served. This started the student sit-ins. Galvanized by their courage, soon hundreds of students were doing the same all over the South.

This was another form of protest to force desegregation. King was delighted that finally students were getting up and doing something to make their lives better, becoming involved in the struggle.

WE WANT TO SIT DOWN LIKE ANYONE ELSE

On the 13th the largest sit-in was staged when 500 students crowded into White lunch counters in Nashville. King urged the students to follow the "Montgomery way," to not shove back when Whites shoved them and screamed at them.

In the eyes of the Lord, who looks worse, the oppressed or the oppressor?

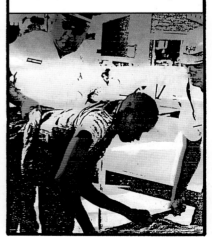

In March students held a demonstration at the county courthouse in Alabama. In retaliation, police invaded the campus of Alabama State College with shotguns, rifles, and tear gas, and threatened to arrest the entire student body.

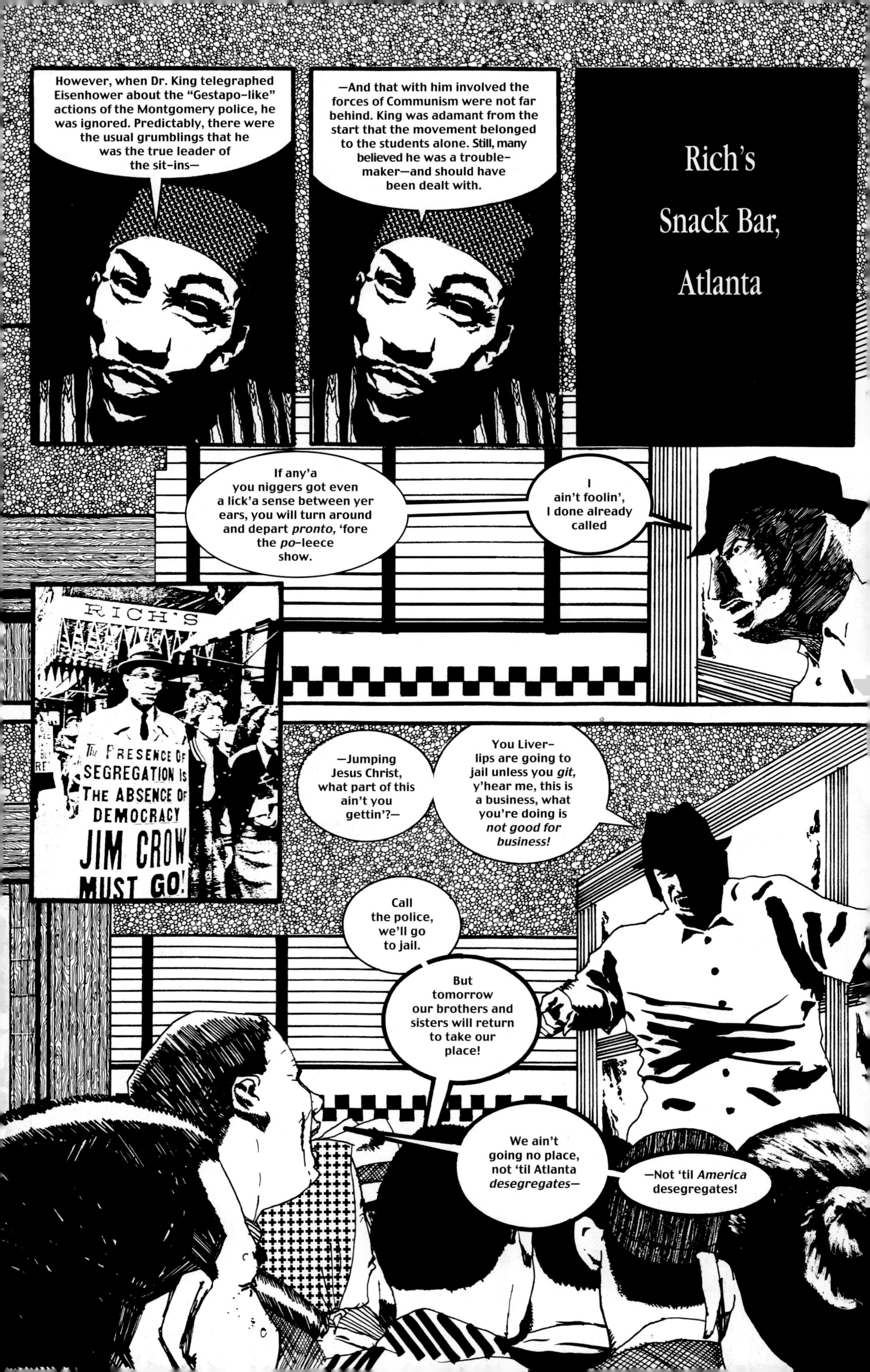
However, when Dr. King telegraphed Eisenhower about the "Gestapo-like" actions of the Montgomery police, he was ignored. Predictably, there were the usual grumblings that he was the true leader of the sit-ins—
—And that with him involved the forces of Communism were not far behind. King was adamant from the start that the movement belonged to the students alone. Still, many believed he was a trouble-maker—and should have been dealt with.
Rich's Snack Bar, Atlanta
If any'a you niggers got even a lick'a sense between yer ears, you will turn around and depart *pronto,* 'fore the *po*-leece show.
I ain't foolin', I done already called
RICH'S
The PRESENCE OF SEGREGATION IS THE ABSENCE OF DEMOCRACY JIM CROW MUST GO!
—Jumping Jesus Christ, what part of this ain't you gettin'?—
You Liver-lips are going to jail unless you *git,* y'hear me, this is a business, what you're doing is *not good for business!*
Call the police, we'll go to jail.
But tomorrow our brothers and sisters will return to take our place!
We ain't going no place, not 'til Atlanta *desegregates*—
—Not 'til *America* desegregates!

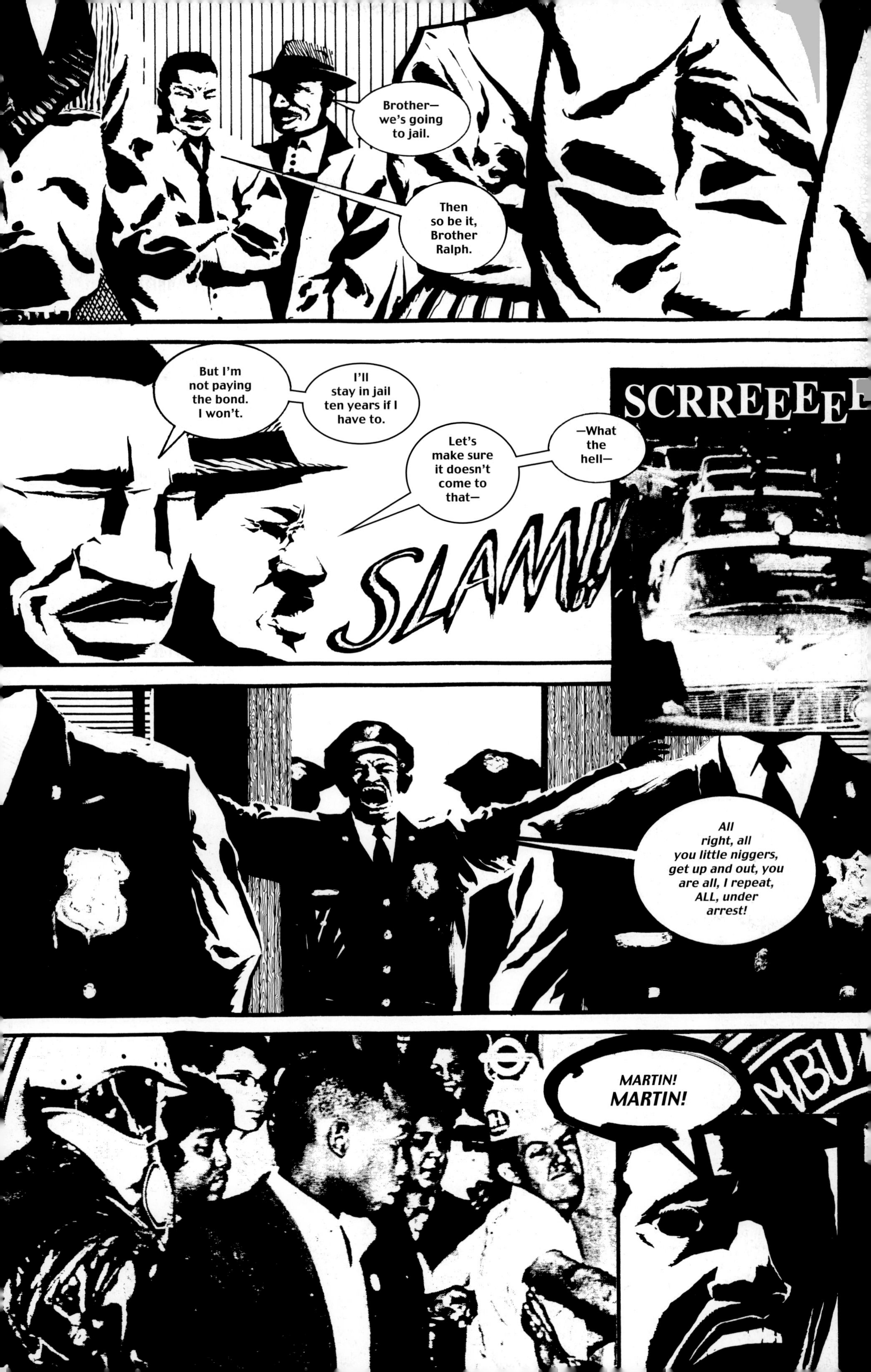
Brother— we's going to jail.
Then so be it, Brother Ralph.
But I'm not paying the bond. I won't.
I'll stay in jail ten years if I have to.
Let's make sure it doesn't come to that—
—What the hell—
SCRREEEE
SLAM!!
All right, all you little niggers, get up and out, you are all, I repeat, ALL, under arrest!
MARTIN! MARTIN!

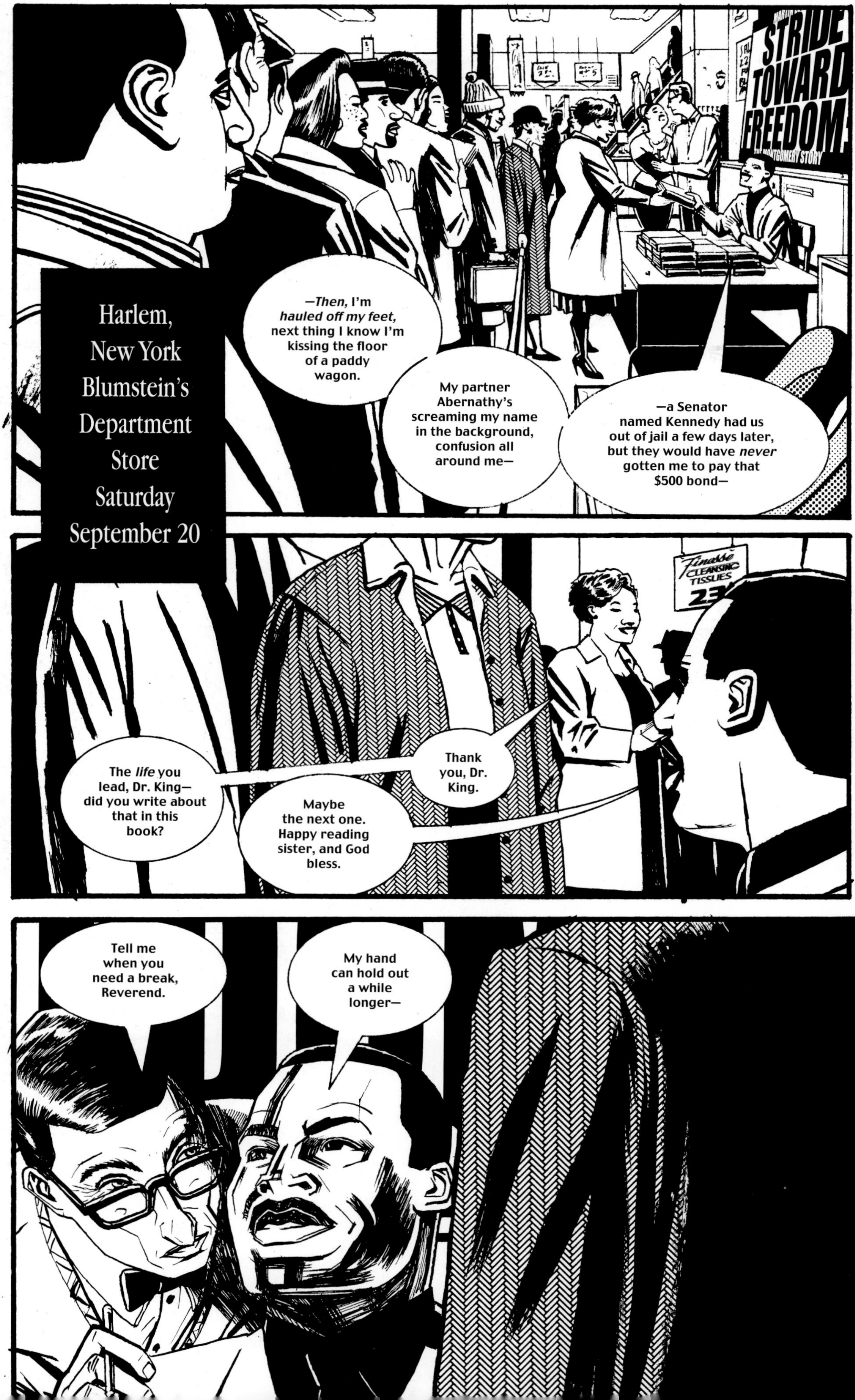
Harlem, New York Blumstein's Department Store Saturday September 20
—*Then,* I'm *hauled off my feet,* next thing I know I'm kissing the floor of a paddy wagon.
My partner Abernathy's screaming my name in the background, confusion all around me—
—a Senator named Kennedy had us out of jail a few days later, but they would have *never* gotten me to pay that $500 bond—
STRIDE TOWARD FREEDOM
THE MONTGOMERY STORY
The *life* you lead, Dr. King—did you write about that in this book?
Thank you, Dr. King.
Maybe the next one. Happy reading sister, and God bless.
Finesse CLEANSING TISSUES
Tell me when you need a break, Reverend.
My hand can hold out a while longer—

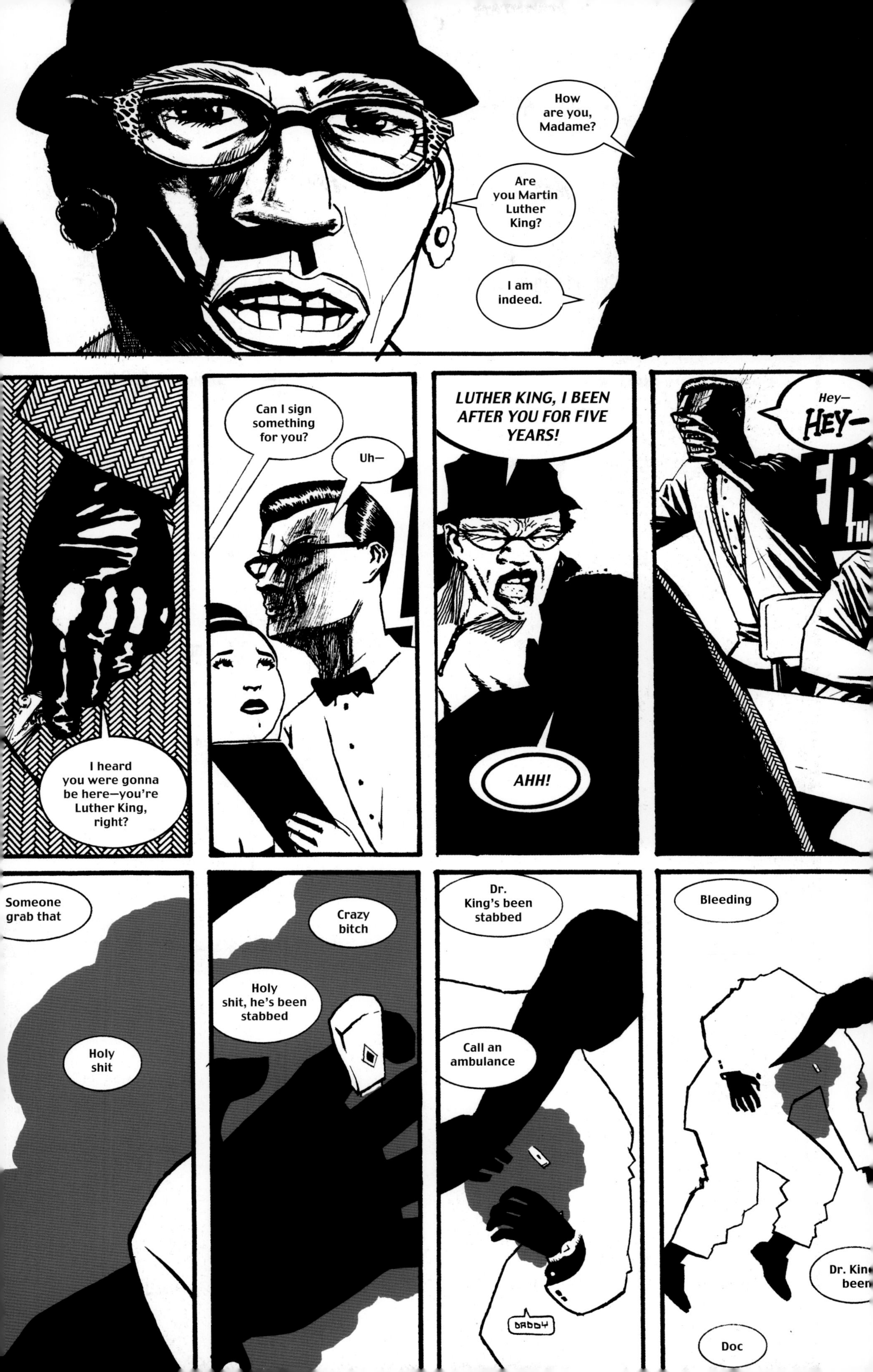
How are you, Madame?
Are you Martin Luther King?
I am indeed.
I heard you were gonna be here—you're Luther King, right?
Can I sign something for you?
Uh—
LUTHER KING, I BEEN AFTER YOU FOR FIVE YEARS!
AHH!
Hey—
HEY—
Someone grab that
Holy shit
Crazy bitch
Holy shit, he's been stabbed
Dr. King's been stabbed
Call an ambulance
DADDY
Bleeding
Doc

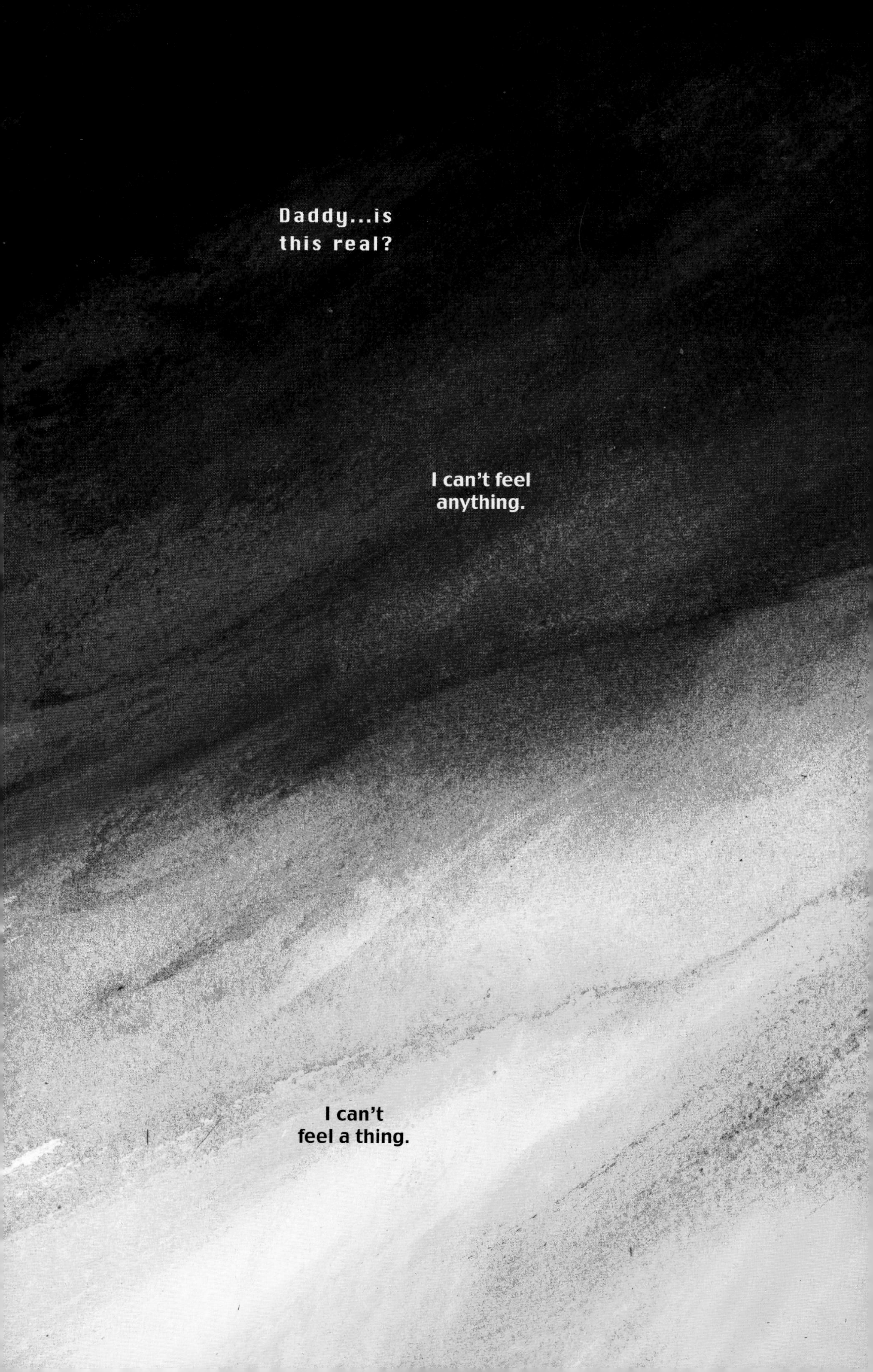
Daddy...is this real?
I can't feel anything.
I can't feel a thing.

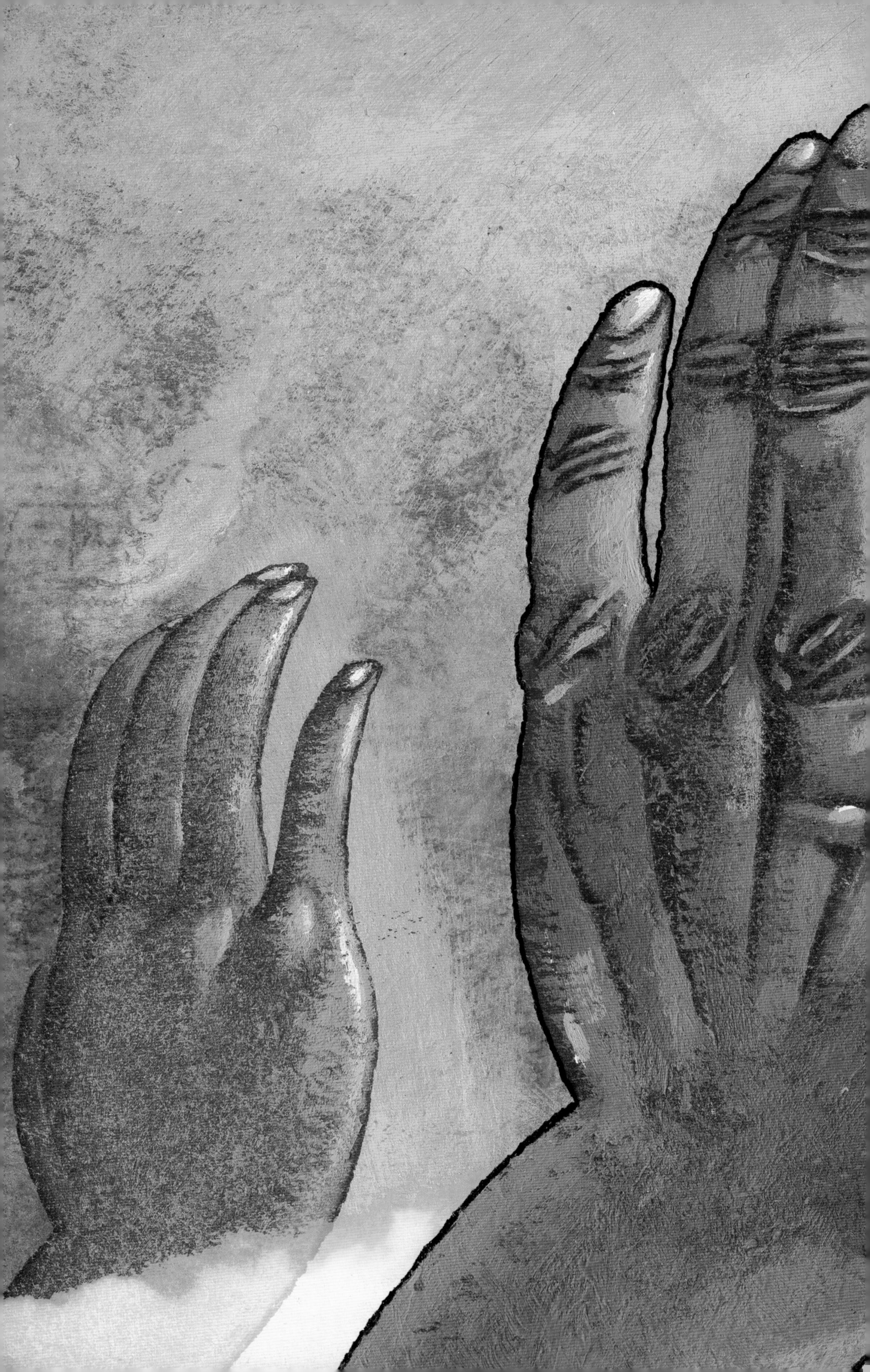

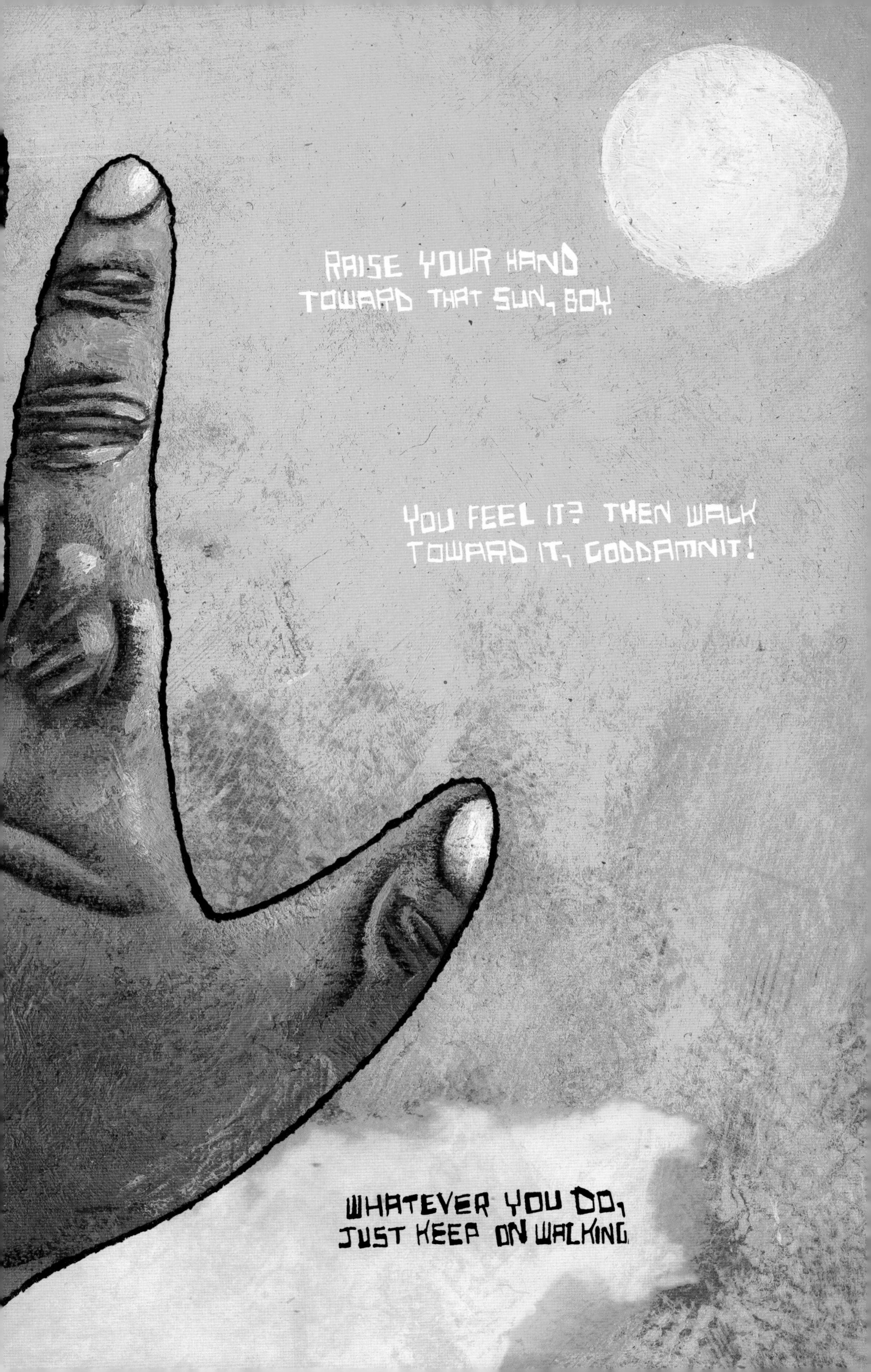
RAISE YOUR HAND TOWARD THAT SUN, BOY.
YOU FEEL IT? THEN WALK TOWARD IT, GODDAMNIT!
WHATEVER YOU DO, JUST KEEP ON WALKING.

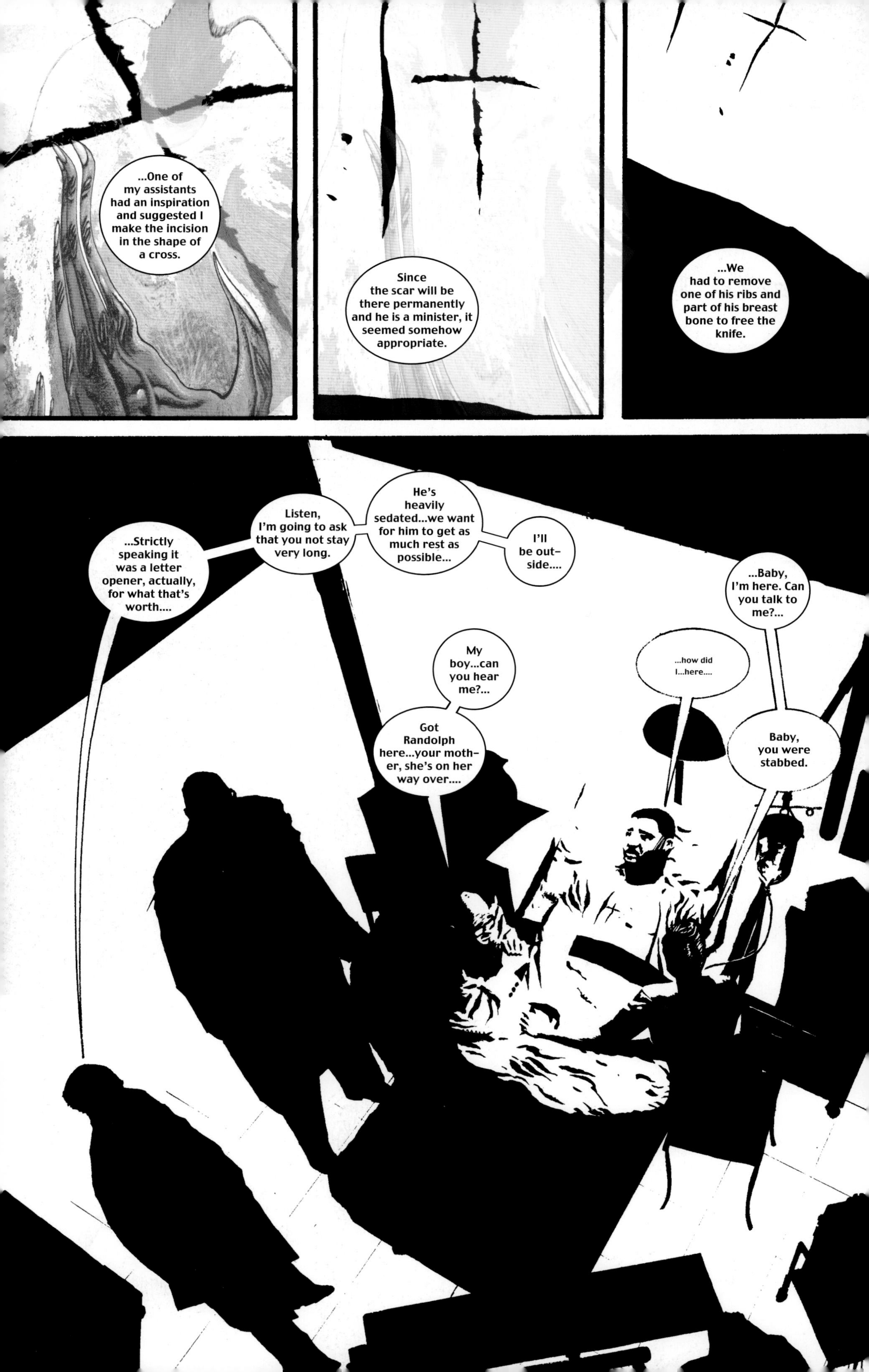
...One of my assistants had an inspiration and suggested I make the incision in the shape of a cross.
Since the scar will be there permanently and he is a minister, it seemed somehow appropriate.
...We had to remove one of his ribs and part of his breast bone to free the knife.
...Strictly speaking it was a letter opener, actually, for what that's worth....
Listen, I'm going to ask that you not stay very long.
He's heavily sedated...we want for him to get as much rest as possible...
I'll be out-side....
My boy...can you hear me?...
Got Randolph here...your moth-er, she's on her way over....
...how did I...here....
...Baby, I'm here. Can you talk to me?...
Baby, you were stabbed.

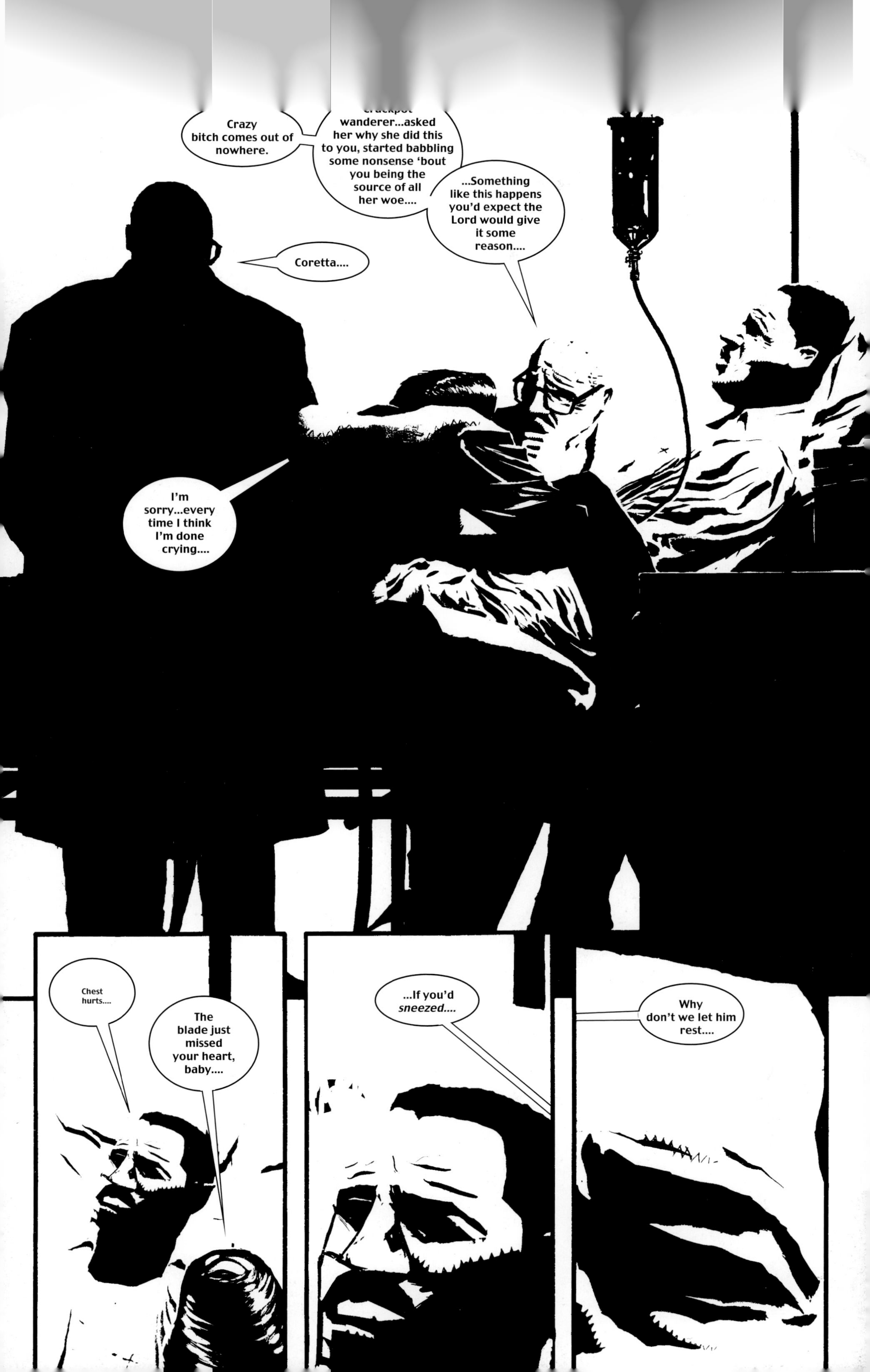
Crazy bitch comes out of nowhere.
wanderer...asked her why she did this to you, started babbling some nonsense 'bout you being the source of all her woe....
...Something like this happens you'd expect the Lord would give it some reason....
Coretta....
I'm sorry...every time I think I'm done crying....
Chest hurts....
The blade just missed your heart, baby....
...If you'd *sneezed....*
Why don't we let him rest....

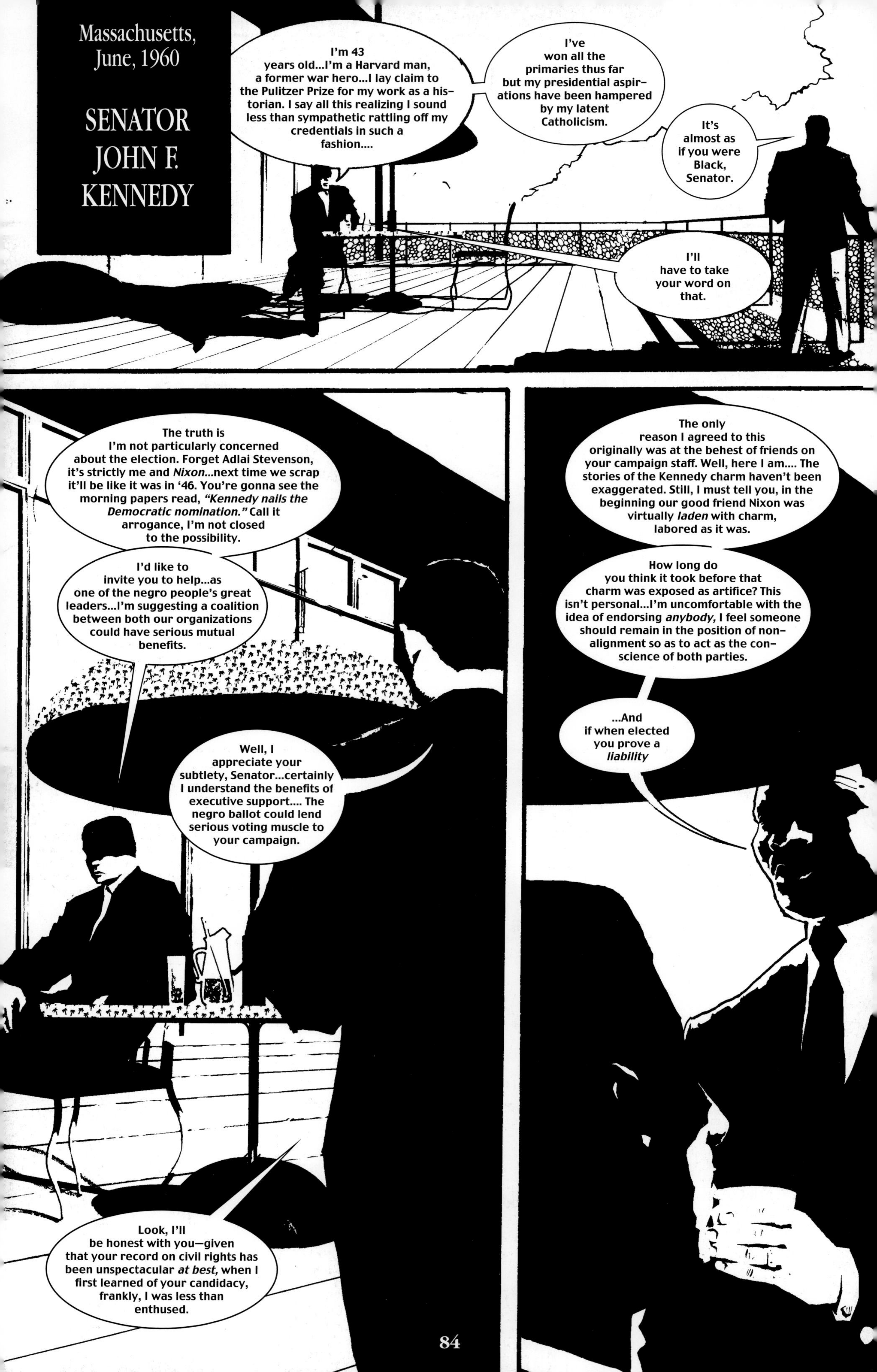
Massachusetts, June, 1960
SENATOR JOHN F. KENNEDY
I'm 43 years old...I'm a Harvard man, a former war hero...I lay claim to the Pulitzer Prize for my work as a historian. I say all this realizing I sound less than sympathetic rattling off my credentials in such a fashion....
I've won all the primaries thus far but my presidential aspirations have been hampered by my latent Catholicism.
It's almost as if you were Black, Senator.
I'll have to take your word on that.
The truth is I'm not particularly concerned about the election. Forget Adlai Stevenson, it's strictly me and *Nixon*...next time we scrap it'll be like it was in '46. You're gonna see the morning papers read, *"Kennedy nails the Democratic nomination."* Call it arrogance, I'm not closed to the possibility.
I'd like to invite you to help...as one of the negro people's great leaders...I'm suggesting a coalition between both our organizations could have serious mutual benefits.
Well, I appreciate your subtlety, Senator...certainly I understand the benefits of executive support.... The negro ballot could lend serious voting muscle to your campaign.
Look, I'll be honest with you—given that your record on civil rights has been unspectacular *at best,* when I first learned of your candidacy, frankly, I was less than enthused.
The only reason I agreed to this originally was at the behest of friends on your campaign staff. Well, here I am.... The stories of the Kennedy charm haven't been exaggerated. Still, I must tell you, in the beginning our good friend Nixon was virtually *laden* with charm, labored as it was.
How long do you think it took before that charm was exposed as artifice? This isn't personal...I'm uncomfortable with the idea of endorsing *anybody,* I feel someone should remain in the position of non-alignment so as to act as the conscience of both parties.
...And if when elected you prove a *liability*

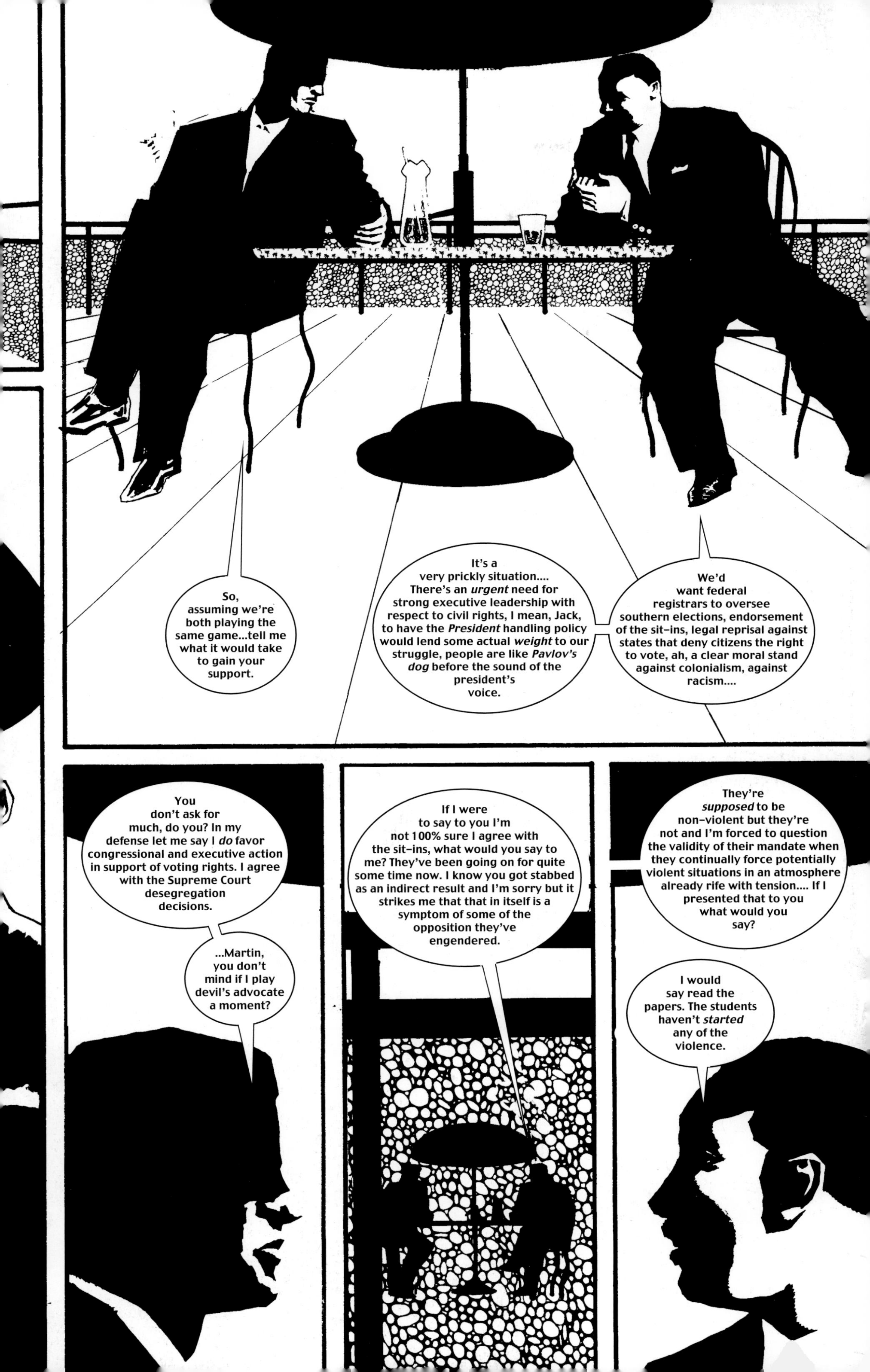
So, assuming we're both playing the same game...tell me what it would take to gain your support.
It's a very prickly situation.... There's an *urgent* need for strong executive leadership with respect to civil rights, I mean, Jack, to have the *President* handling policy would lend some actual *weight* to our struggle, people are like *Pavlov's dog* before the sound of the president's voice.
We'd want federal registrars to oversee southern elections, endorsement of the sit-ins, legal reprisal against states that deny citizens the right to vote, ah, a clear moral stand against colonialism, against racism....
You don't ask for much, do you? In my defense let me say I *do* favor congressional and executive action in support of voting rights. I agree with the Supreme Court desegregation decisions.
...Martin, you don't mind if I play devil's advocate a moment?
If I were to say to you I'm not 100% sure I agree with the sit-ins, what would you say to me? They've been going on for quite some time now. I know you got stabbed as an indirect result and I'm sorry but it strikes me that that in itself is a symptom of some of the opposition they've engendered.
They're *supposed* to be non-violent but they're not and I'm forced to question the validity of their mandate when they continually force potentially violent situations in an atmosphere already rife with tension.... If I presented that to you what would you say?
I would say read the papers. The students haven't *started* any of the violence.

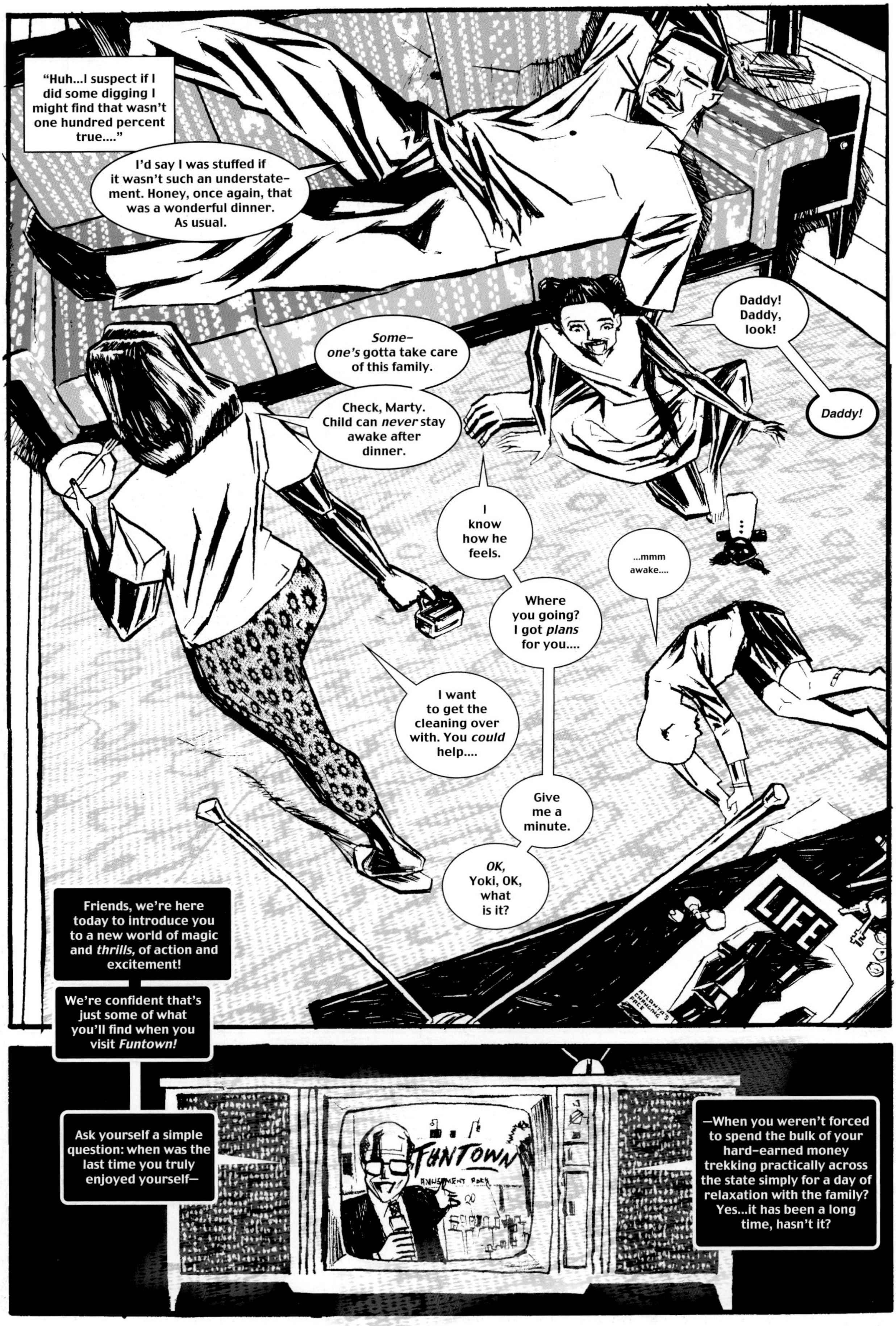
"Huh...I suspect if I did some digging I might find that wasn't one hundred percent true...."
I'd say I was stuffed if it wasn't such an understatement. Honey, once again, that was a wonderful dinner. As usual.
Some-one's gotta take care of this family.
Check, Marty. Child can *never* stay awake after dinner.
Daddy! Daddy, look!
Daddy!
I know how he feels.
...mmm awake....
Where you going? I got *plans* for you....
I want to get the cleaning over with. You *could* help....
Give me a minute.
OK, Yoki, OK, what is it?
LIFE
Friends, we're here today to introduce you to a new world of magic and *thrills,* of action and excitement!
We're confident that's just some of what you'll find when you visit *Funtown!*
Ask yourself a simple question: when was the last time you truly enjoyed yourself—
FUNTOWN
—When you weren't forced to spend the bulk of your hard-earned money trekking practically across the state simply for a day of relaxation with the family? Yes...it has been a long time, hasn't it?

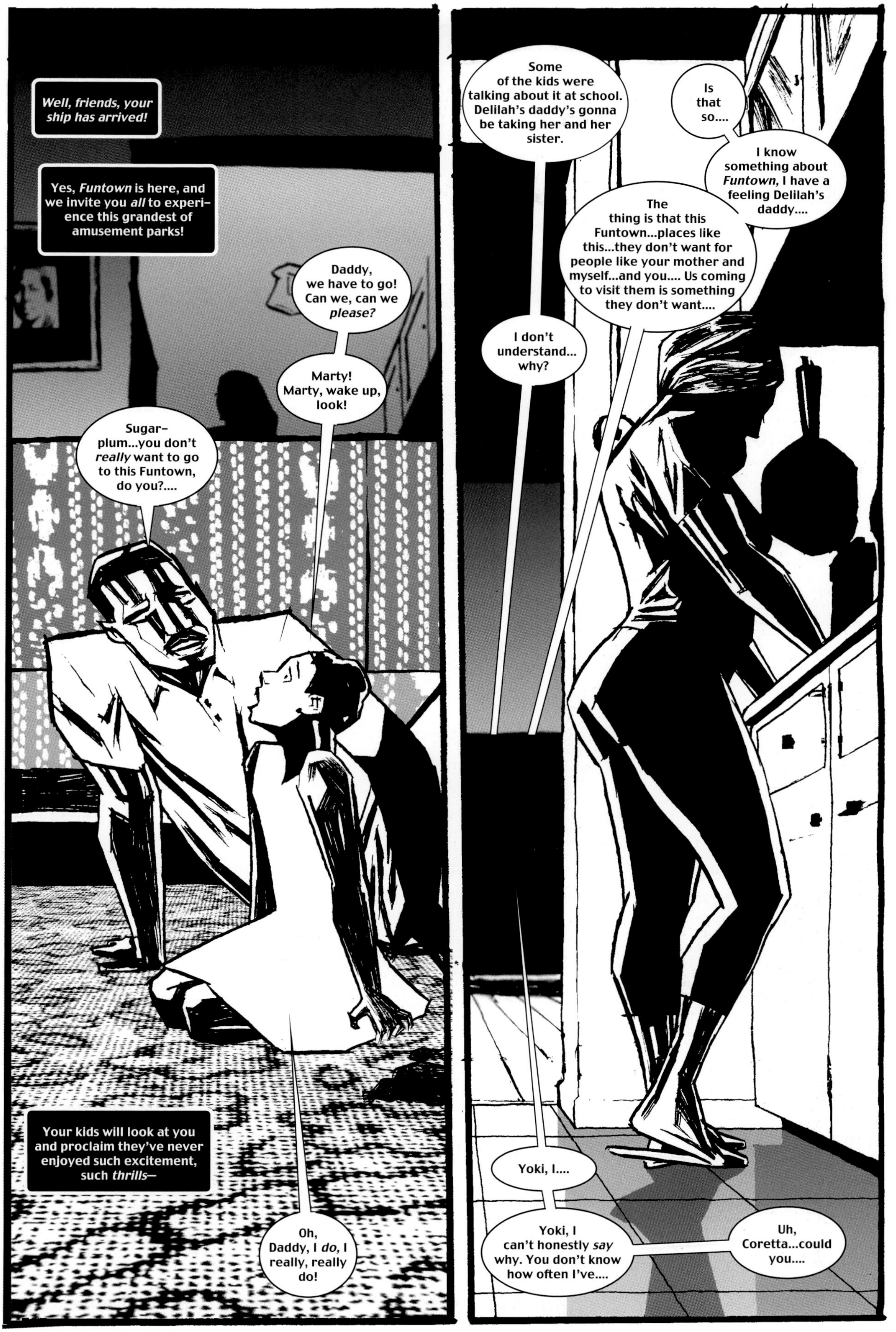
Well, friends, your ship has arrived!
Yes, *Funtown* is here, and we invite you *all* to experience this grandest of amusement parks!
Daddy, we have to go! Can we, can we *please?*
Marty! Marty, wake up, look!
Sugar-plum...you don't *really* want to go to this Funtown, do you?....
Your kids will look at you and proclaim they've never enjoyed such excitement, such *thrills*—
Oh, Daddy, I *do,* I really, really do!
Some of the kids were talking about it at school. Delilah's daddy's gonna be taking her and her sister.
Is that so....
I know something about *Funtown,* I have a feeling Delilah's daddy....
The thing is that this Funtown...places like this...they don't want for people like your mother and myself...and you.... Us coming to visit them is something they don't want....
I don't understand... why?
Yoki, I....
Yoki, I can't honestly *say* why. You don't know how often I've....
Uh, Coretta...could you....

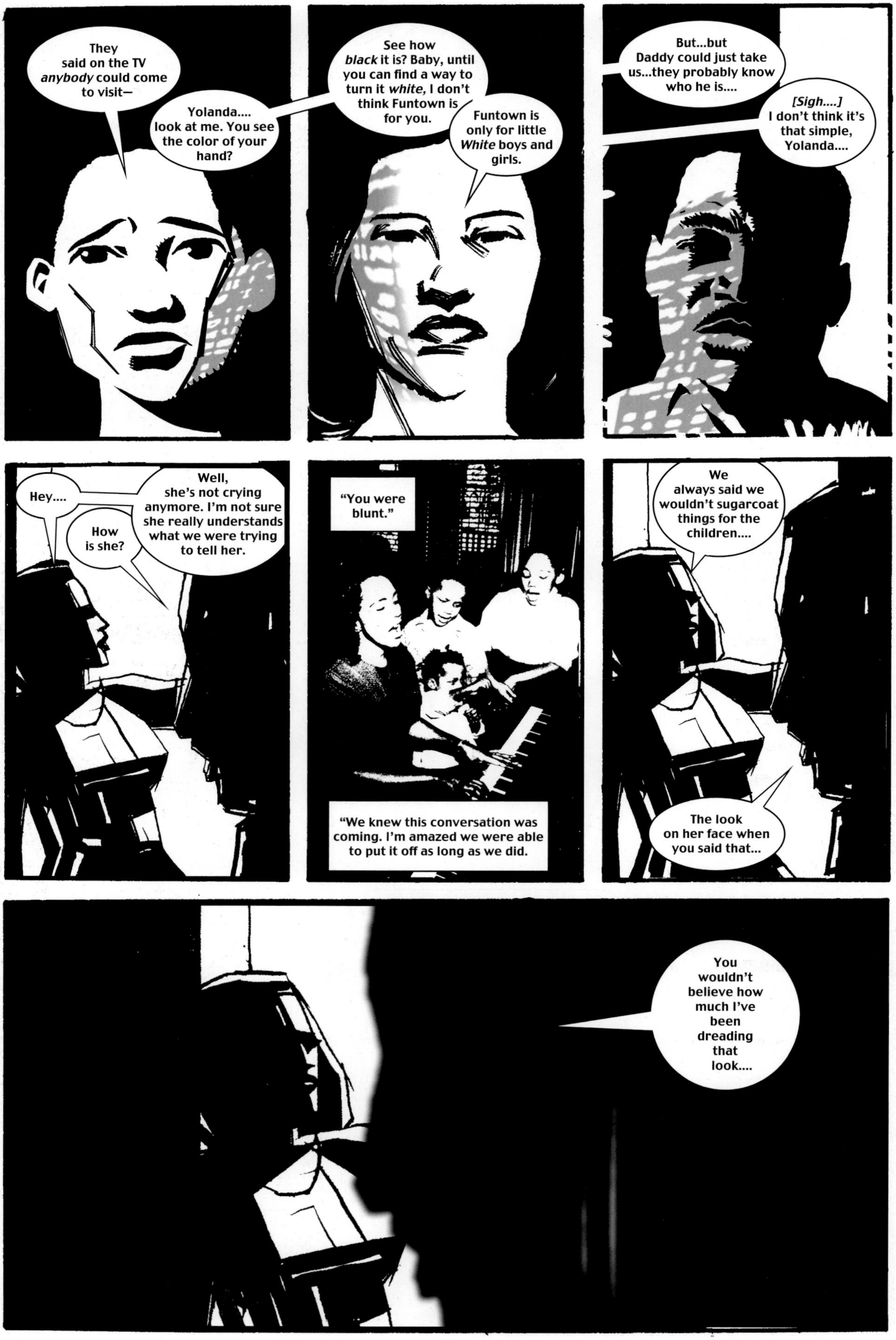
They said on the TV *anybody* could come to visit—
Yolanda.... look at me. You see the color of your hand?
See how *black* it is? Baby, until you can find a way to turn it *white,* I don't think Funtown is for you.
Funtown is only for little *White* boys and girls.
But...but Daddy could just take us...they probably know who he is....
[Sigh....] I don't think it's that simple, Yolanda....
Hey....
How is she?
Well, she's not crying anymore. I'm not sure she really understands what we were trying to tell her.
"You were blunt."
"We knew this conversation was coming. I'm amazed we were able to put it off as long as we did.
We always said we wouldn't sugarcoat things for the children....
The look on her face when you said that...
You wouldn't believe how much I've been dreading that look....

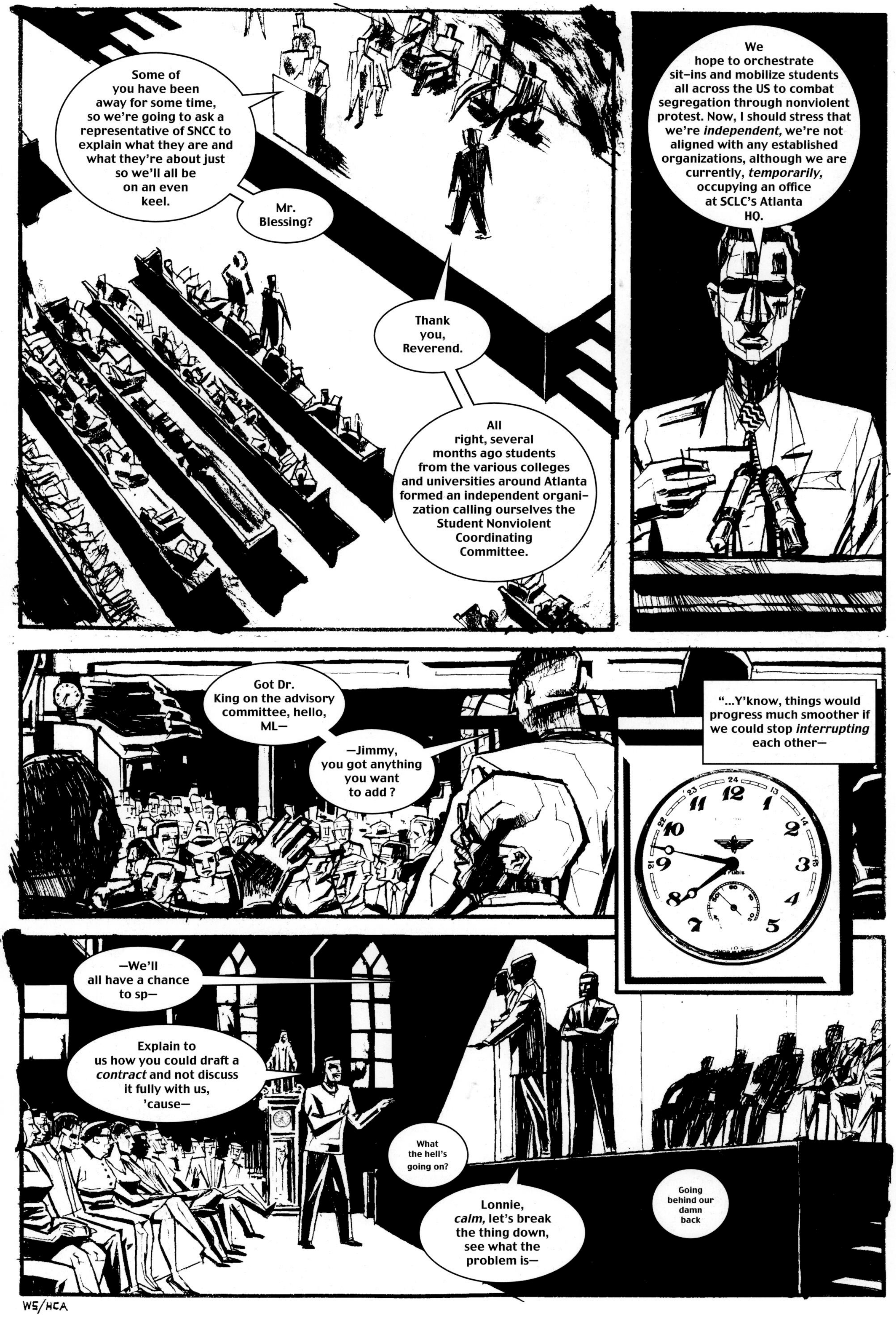

Some of you have been away for some time, so we're going to ask a representative of SNCC to explain what they are and what they're about just so we'll all be on an even keel.
Mr. Blessing?
Thank you, Reverend.
All right, several months ago students from the various colleges and universities around Atlanta formed an independent organization calling ourselves the Student Nonviolent Coordinating Committee.
We hope to orchestrate sit-ins and mobilize students all across the US to combat segregation through nonviolent protest. Now, I should stress that we're *independent,* we're not aligned with any established organizations, although we are currently, *temporarily,* occupying an office at SCLC's Atlanta HQ.
Got Dr. King on the advisory committee, hello, ML—
—Jimmy, you got anything you want to add ?
"...Y'know, things would progress much smoother if we could stop *interrupting* each other—
—We'll all have a chance to sp—
Explain to us how you could draft a *contract* and not discuss it fully with us, 'cause—
What the hell's going on?
Lonnie, *calm,* let's break the thing down, see what the problem is—
Going behind our damn back
WS/HCA

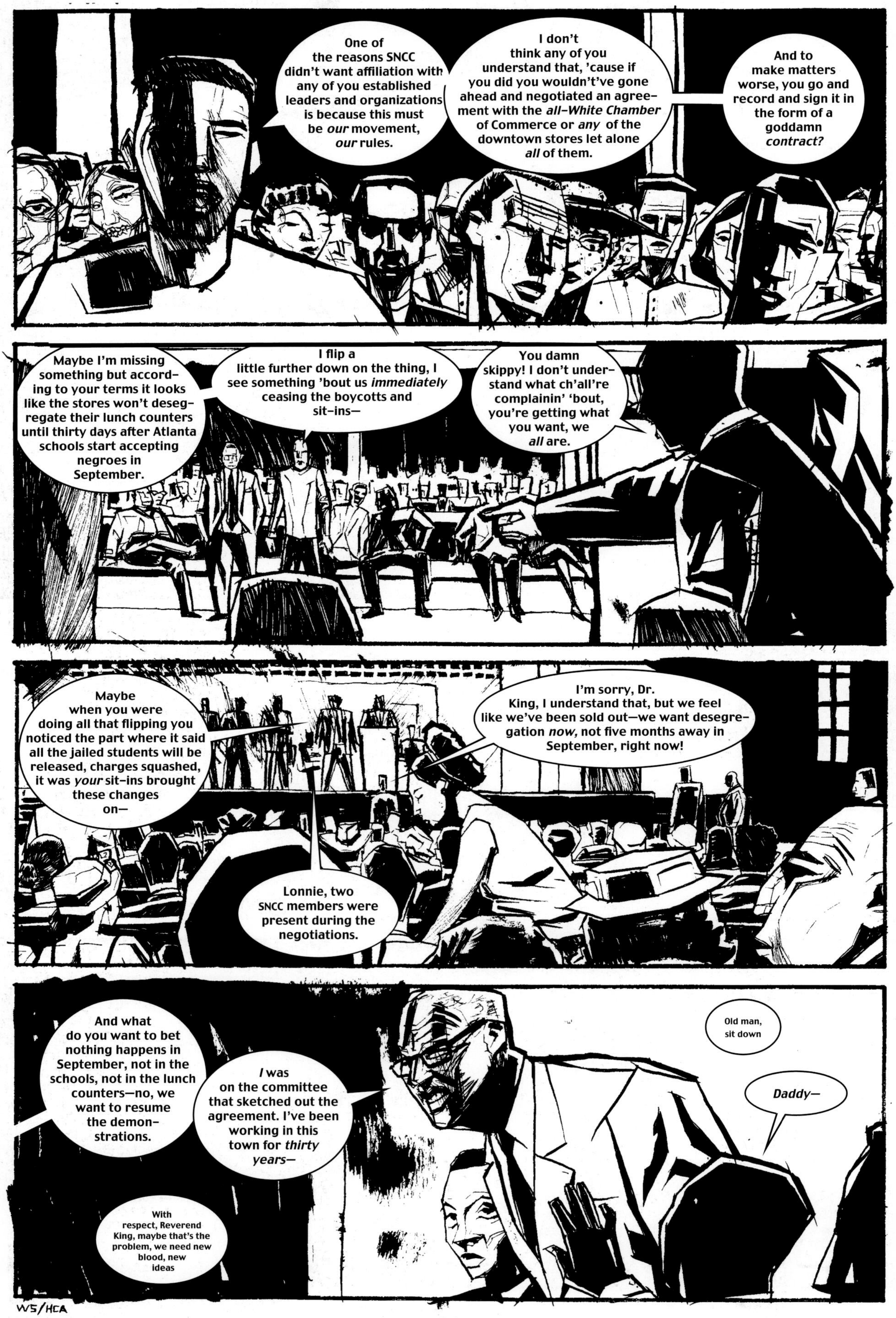
One of the reasons SNCC didn't want affiliation with any of you established leaders and organizations is because this must be *our* movement, *our* rules.
I don't think any of you understand that, 'cause if you did you wouldn't've gone ahead and negotiated an agreement with the *all-White Chamber* of Commerce or *any* of the downtown stores let alone *all* of them.
And to make matters worse, you go and record and sign it in the form of a goddamn *contract?*
Maybe I'm missing something but according to your terms it looks like the stores won't desegregate their lunch counters until thirty days after Atlanta schools start accepting negroes in September.
I flip a little further down on the thing, I see something 'bout us *immediately* ceasing the boycotts and sit-ins—
You damn skippy! I don't understand what ch'all're complainin' 'bout, you're getting what you want, we *all* are.
Maybe when you were doing all that flipping you noticed the part where it said all the jailed students will be released, charges squashed, it was *your* sit-ins brought these changes on—
I'm sorry, Dr. King, I understand that, but we feel like we've been sold out—we want desegregation *now,* not five months away in September, right now!
Lonnie, two SNCC members were present during the negotiations.
And what do you want to bet nothing happens in September, not in the schools, not in the lunch counters—no, we want to resume the demonstrations.
I was on the committee that sketched out the agreement. I've been working in this town for *thirty years*—
With respect, Reverend King, maybe that's the problem, we need new blood, new ideas
Old man, sit down
Daddy—
WS/HCA

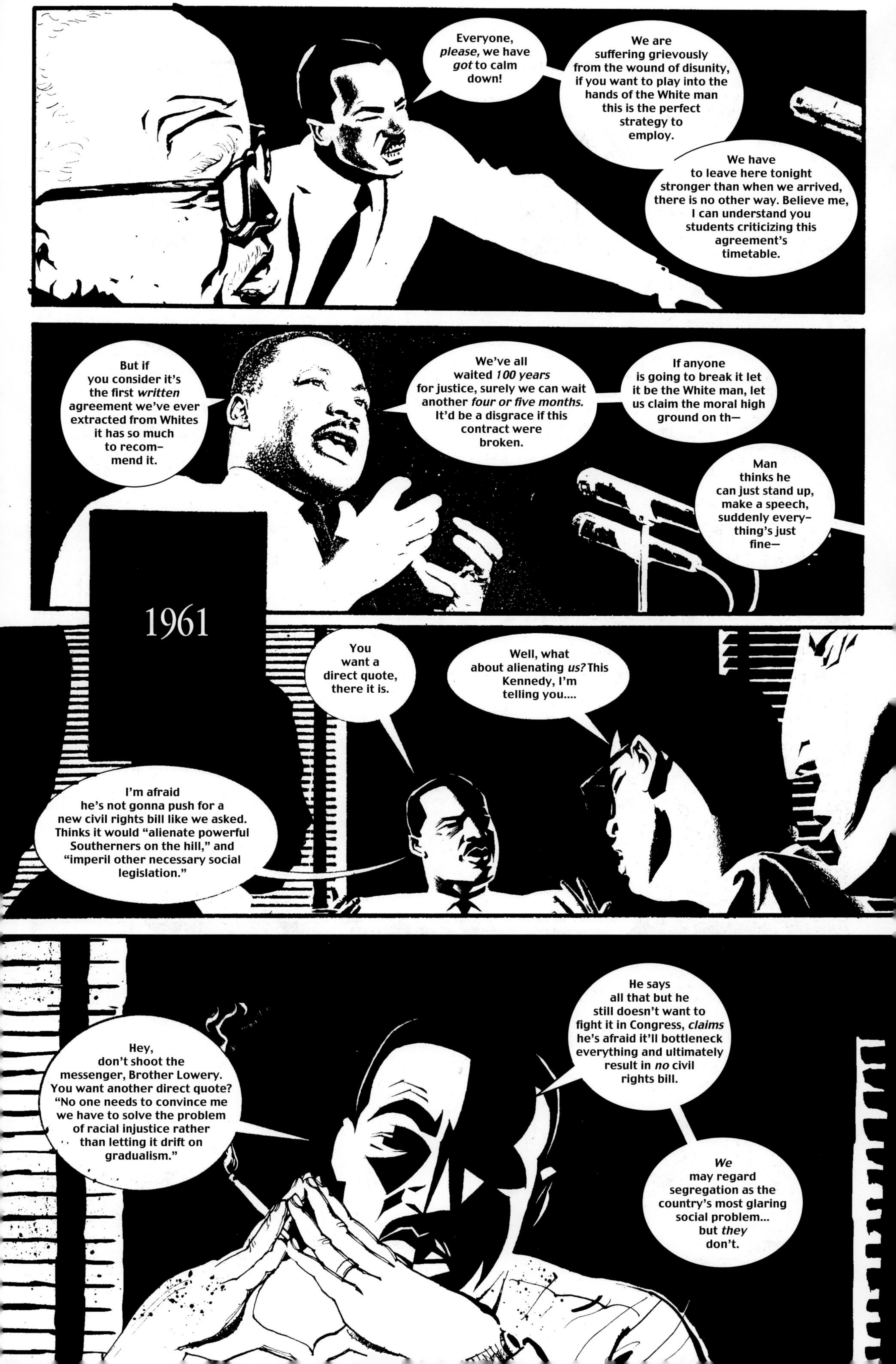
Everyone, *please,* we have *got* to calm down!
We are suffering grievously from the wound of disunity, if you want to play into the hands of the White man this is the perfect strategy to employ.
We have to leave here tonight stronger than when we arrived, there is no other way. Believe me, I can understand you students criticizing this agreement's timetable.
But if you consider it's the first *written* agreement we've ever extracted from Whites it has so much to recom-mend it.
We've all waited *100 years* for justice, surely we can wait another *four or five months.* It'd be a disgrace if this contract were broken.
If anyone is going to break it let it be the White man, let us claim the moral high ground on th—
Man thinks he can just stand up, make a speech, suddenly every-thing's just fine—
1961
You want a direct quote, there it is.
Well, what about alienating *us?* This Kennedy, I'm telling you....
I'm afraid he's not gonna push for a new civil rights bill like we asked. Thinks it would "alienate powerful Southerners on the hill," and "imperil other necessary social legislation."
Hey, don't shoot the messenger, Brother Lowery. You want another direct quote? "No one needs to convince me we have to solve the problem of racial injustice rather than letting it drift on gradualism."
He says all that but he still doesn't want to fight it in Congress, *claims* he's afraid it'll bottleneck everything and ultimately result in *no* civil rights bill.
We may regard segregation as the country's most glaring social problem... but *they* don't.

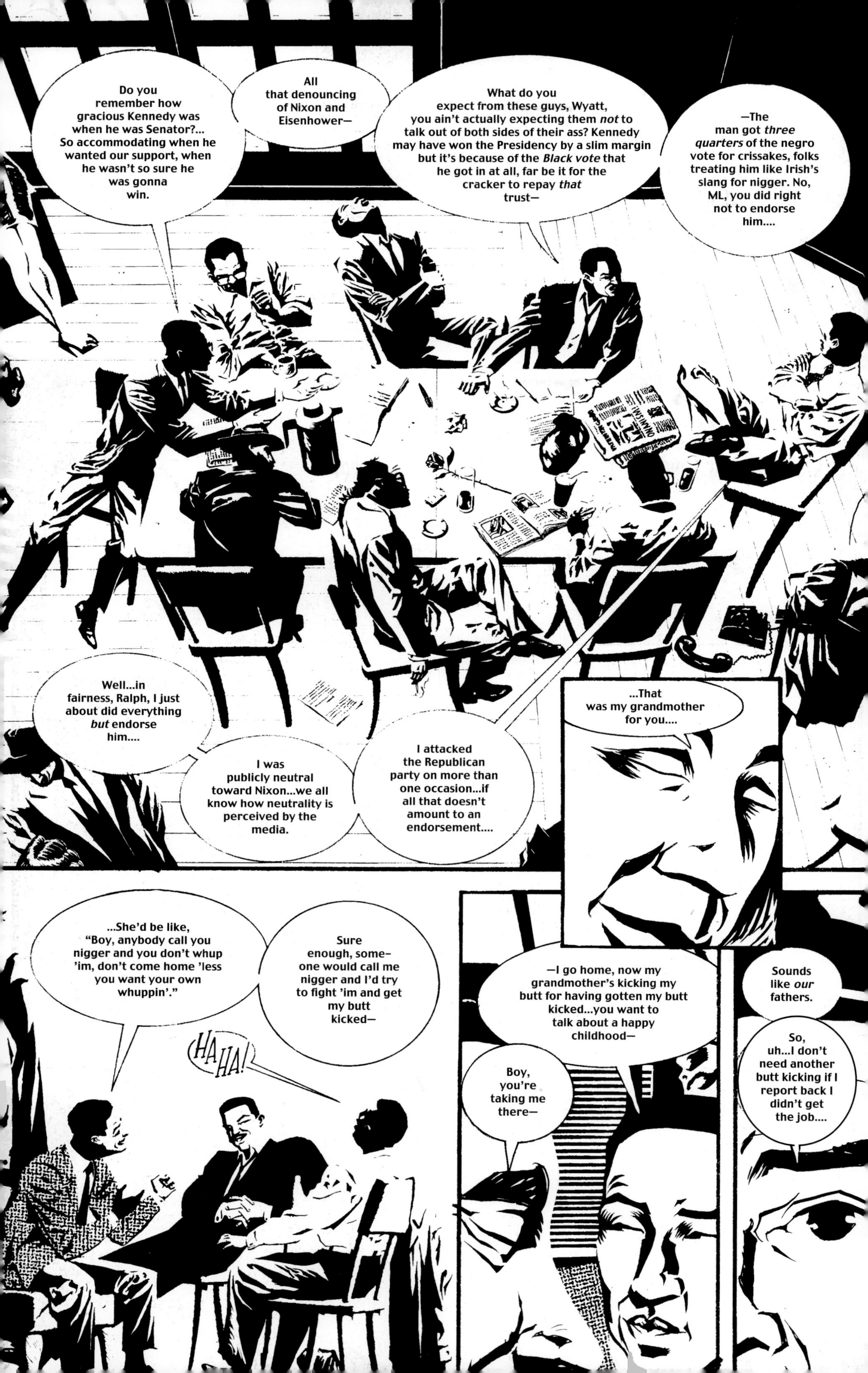
Do you remember how gracious Kennedy was when he was Senator?... So accommodating when he wanted our support, when he wasn't so sure he was gonna win.
All that denouncing of Nixon and Eisenhower—
What do you expect from these guys, Wyatt, you ain't actually expecting them *not* to talk out of both sides of their ass? Kennedy may have won the Presidency by a slim margin but it's because of the *Black vote* that he got in at all, far be it for the cracker to repay *that* trust—
—The man got *three quarters* of the negro vote for crissakes, folks treating him like Irish's slang for nigger. No, ML, you did right not to endorse him....
Well...in fairness, Ralph, I just about did everything *but* endorse him....
I was publicly neutral toward Nixon...we all know how neutrality is perceived by the media.
I attacked the Republican party on more than one occasion...if all that doesn't amount to an endorsement....
...That was my grandmother for you....
...She'd be like, "Boy, anybody call you nigger and you don't whup 'im, don't come home 'less you want your own whuppin'."
Sure enough, some-one would call me nigger and I'd try to fight 'im and get my butt kicked—
HA HA!
—I go home, now my grandmother's kicking my butt for having gotten my butt kicked...you want to talk about a happy childhood—
Boy, you're taking me there—
Sounds like *our* fathers.
So, uh...I don't need another butt kicking if I report back I didn't get the job....

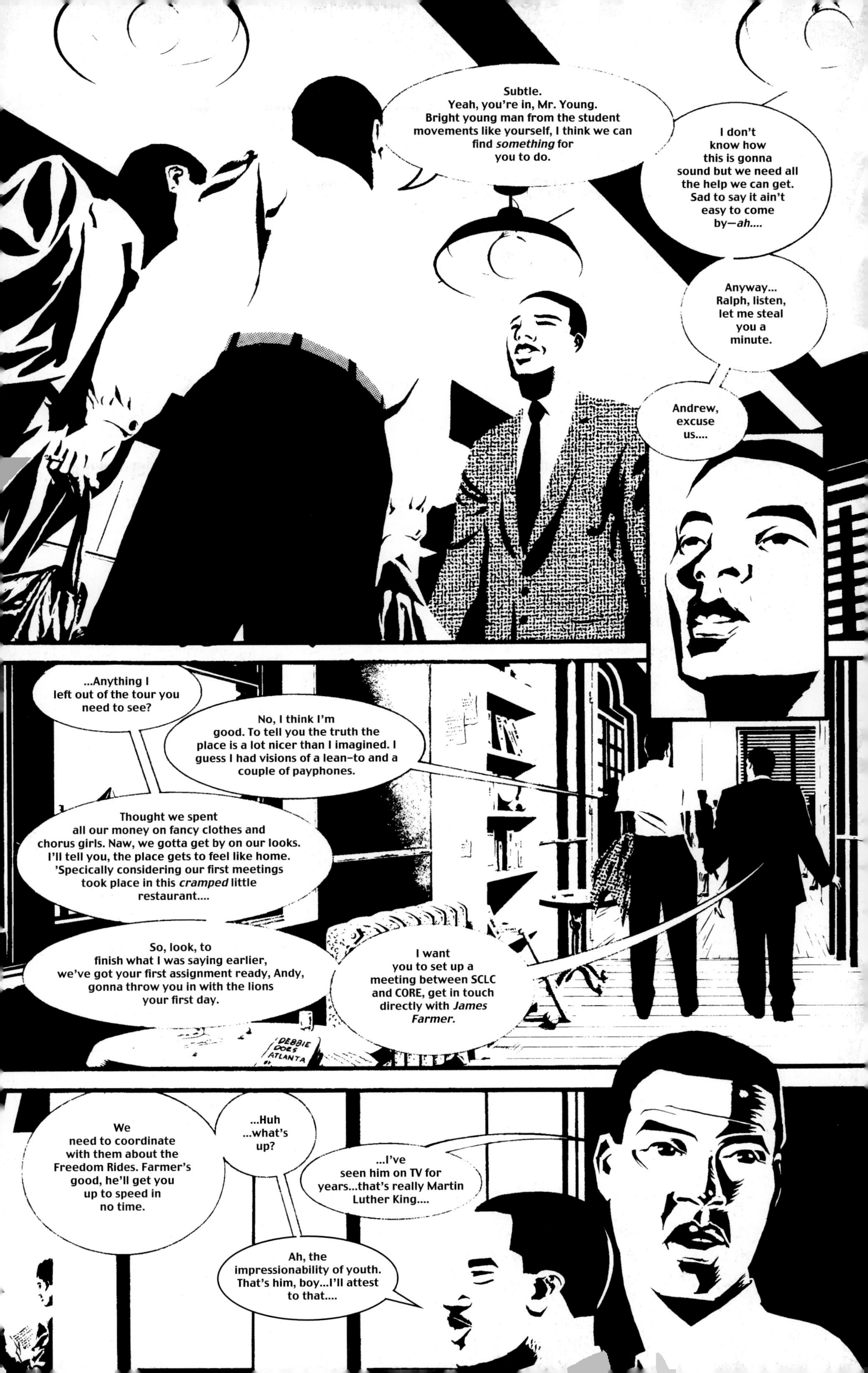
Subtle. Yeah, you're in, Mr. Young. Bright young man from the student movements like yourself, I think we can find *something* for you to do.
I don't know how this is gonna sound but we need all the help we can get. Sad to say it ain't easy to come by—*ah*....
Anyway... Ralph, listen, let me steal you a minute.
Andrew, excuse us....
...Anything I left out of the tour you need to see?
No, I think I'm good. To tell you the truth the place is a lot nicer than I imagined. I guess I had visions of a lean-to and a couple of payphones.
Thought we spent all our money on fancy clothes and chorus girls. Naw, we gotta get by on our looks. I'll tell you, the place gets to feel like home. 'Specically considering our first meetings took place in this *cramped* little restaurant....
So, look, to finish what I was saying earlier, we've got your first assignment ready, Andy, gonna throw you in with the lions your first day.
I want you to set up a meeting between SCLC and CORE, get in touch directly with *James Farmer.*
DEBBIE DOES ATLANTA
We need to coordinate with them about the Freedom Rides. Farmer's good, he'll get you up to speed in no time.
...Huh ...what's up?
...I've seen him on TV for years...that's really Martin Luther King....
Ah, the impressionability of youth. That's him, boy...I'll attest to that....

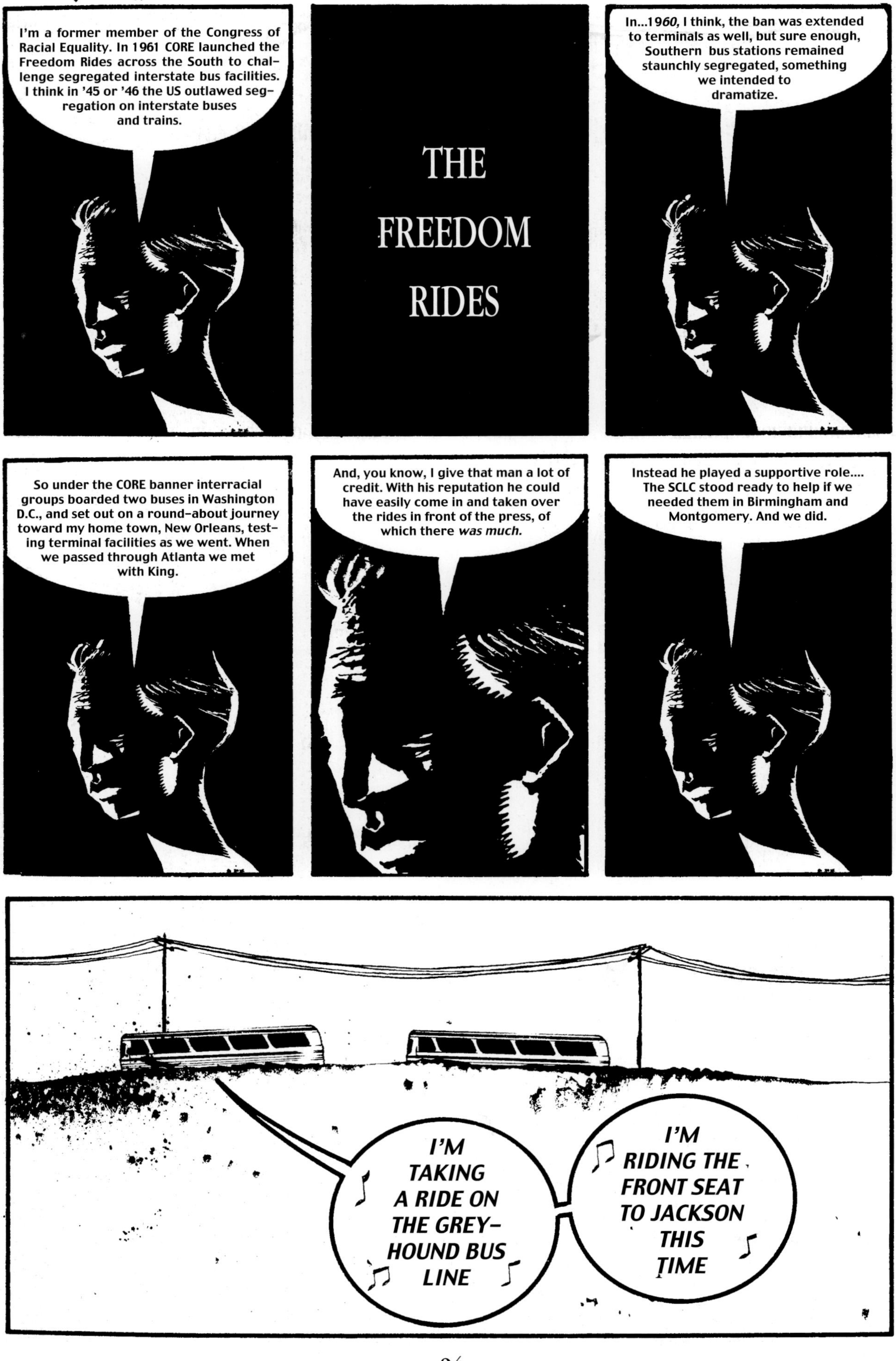
I'm a former member of the Congress of Racial Equality. In 1961 CORE launched the Freedom Rides across the South to challenge segregated interstate bus facilities. I think in '45 or '46 the US outlawed segregation on interstate buses and trains.
THE FREEDOM RIDES
In...1960, I think, the ban was extended to terminals as well, but sure enough, Southern bus stations remained staunchly segregated, something we intended to dramatize.
So under the CORE banner interracial groups boarded two buses in Washington D.C., and set out on a round-about journey toward my home town, New Orleans, testing terminal facilities as we went. When we passed through Atlanta we met with King.
And, you know, I give that man a lot of credit. With his reputation he could have easily come in and taken over the rides in front of the press, of which there *was much.*
Instead he played a supportive role.... The SCLC stood ready to help if we needed them in Birmingham and Montgomery. And we did.
I'M TAKING A RIDE ON THE GREY-HOUND BUS LINE
I'M RIDING THE FRONT SEAT TO JACKSON THIS TIME

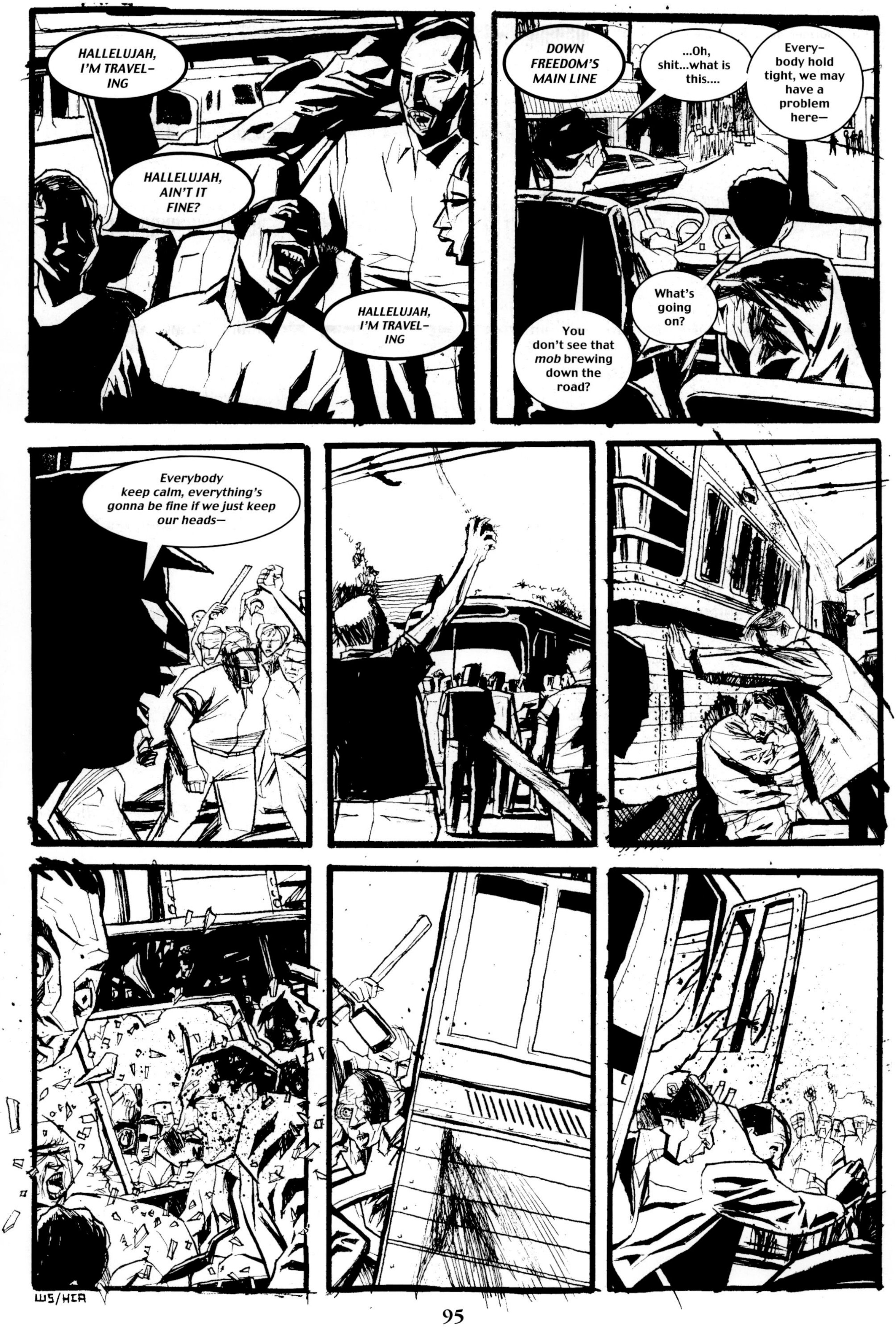
HALLELUJAH, I'M TRAVEL-ING
HALLELUJAH, AIN'T IT FINE?
HALLELUJAH, I'M TRAVEL-ING
DOWN FREEDOM'S MAIN LINE
...Oh, shit...what is this....
Every-body hold tight, we may have a problem here—
What's going on?
You don't see that *mob* brewing down the road?
Everybody keep calm, everything's gonna be fine if we just keep our heads—
WS/HIA

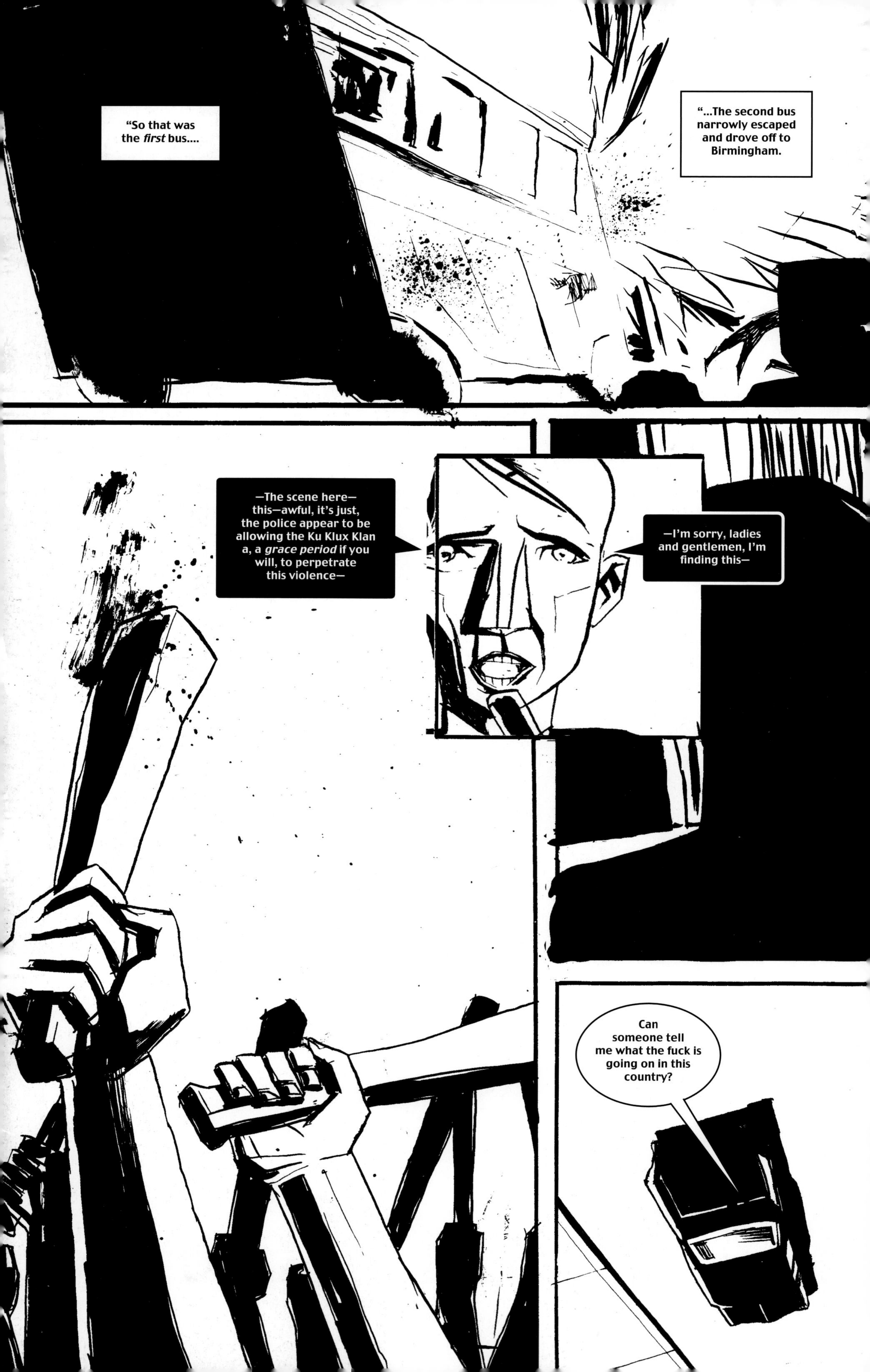
"So that was the *first* bus....
"...The second bus narrowly escaped and drove off to Birmingham.
—The scene here— this—awful, it's just, the police appear to be allowing the Ku Klux Klan a, a *grace period* if you will, to perpetrate this violence—
—I'm sorry, ladies and gentlemen, I'm finding this—
Can someone tell me what the fuck is going on in this country?

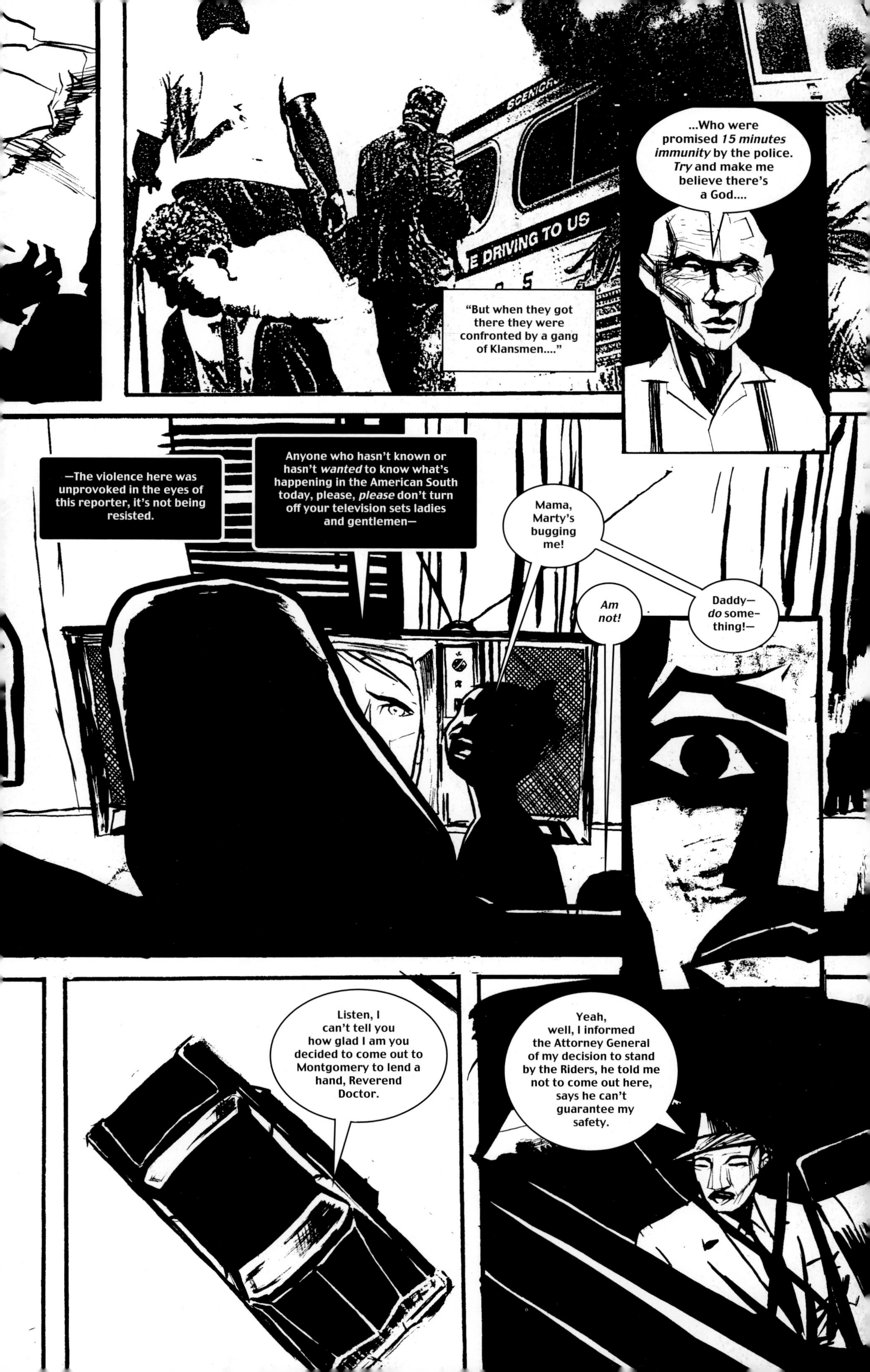

...Who were promised *15 minutes immunity* by the police. *Try* and make me believe there's a God....
"But when they got there they were confronted by a gang of Klansmen...."
E DRIVING TO US
—The violence here was unprovoked in the eyes of this reporter, it's not being resisted.
Anyone who hasn't known or hasn't *wanted* to know what's happening in the American South today, please, *please* don't turn off your television sets ladies and gentlemen—
Mama, Marty's bugging me!
Am not!
Daddy— *do* some-thing!—
Listen, I can't tell you how glad I am you decided to come out to Montgomery to lend a hand, Reverend Doctor.
Yeah, well, I informed the Attorney General of my decision to stand by the Riders, he told me not to come out here, says he can't guarantee my safety.

I'm there telling him this is about more than the safety of one man, but I think that fact may have been lost on him....

Well, that's a *Kennedy* for you.

Speaking of which, did you hear what our friend the Governor had to say about the violence up in Birmingham against the Riders?

...In fairness he did say he was going to try sending out Federal Marshals since it's obvious Governor Patterson won't lift a hand to help...still....

No WAY I'ma send in the National Guard to protect no Freedom Rider. There's nobody in the whole country got the spine to stand up to the goddamned nigger 'cept me and the city of Birmingham.

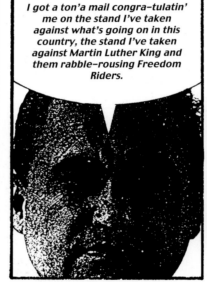

I got a ton'a mail congra-tulatin' me on the stand I've taken against what's going on in this country, the stand I've taken against Martin Luther King and them rabble-rousing Freedom Riders.

Another thing: you can tell the Attorney General di-rect from me, if the schools desegregate, by God, blood's gonna flow in the streets of America.

Martin!

So you finally decided to show up, you old dog, how you been, brother?

That's OK, that's OK, come with me—

Heyyy, Fred Shuttlesworth, goddamnit, how you been keeping?

I'm sorry we're late, I—

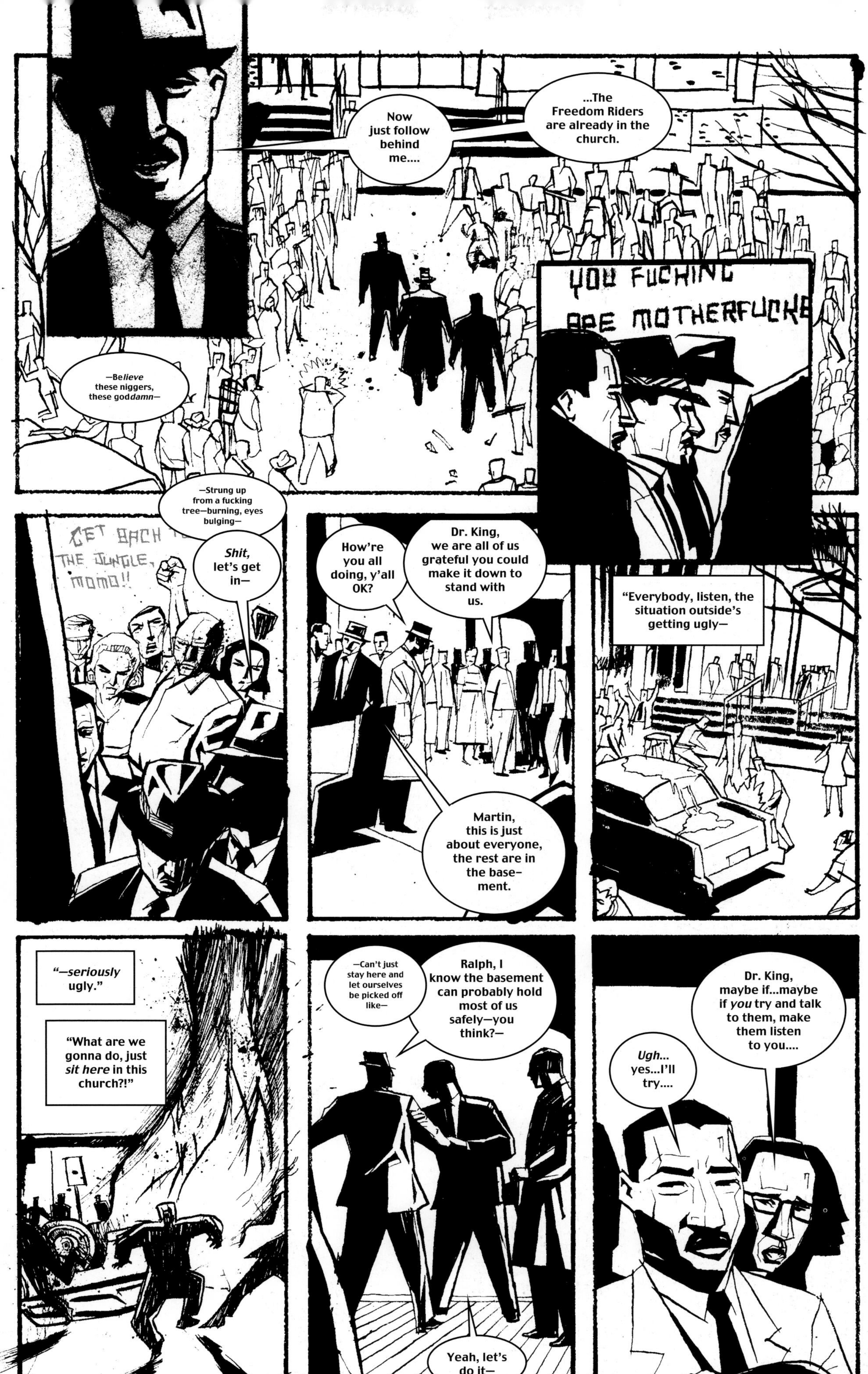
Now just follow behind me....
...The Freedom Riders are already in the church.
—Believe these niggers, these goddamn—
YOU FUCKING
ARE MOTHERFUCKE
—Strung up from a fucking tree—burning, eyes bulging—
GET BACK TO THE JUNGLE, MOMO!!
Shit, let's get in—
How're you all doing, y'all OK?
Dr. King, we are all of us grateful you could make it down to stand with us.
Martin, this is just about everyone, the rest are in the basement.
"Everybody, listen, the situation outside's getting ugly—
"—seriously ugly."
"What are we gonna do, just sit here in this church?!"
—Can't just stay here and let ourselves be picked off like—
Ralph, I know the basement can probably hold most of us safely—you think?—
Yeah, let's do it—
Dr. King, maybe if...maybe if you try and talk to them, make them listen to you....
Ugh... yes...I'll try....
WS/HCA

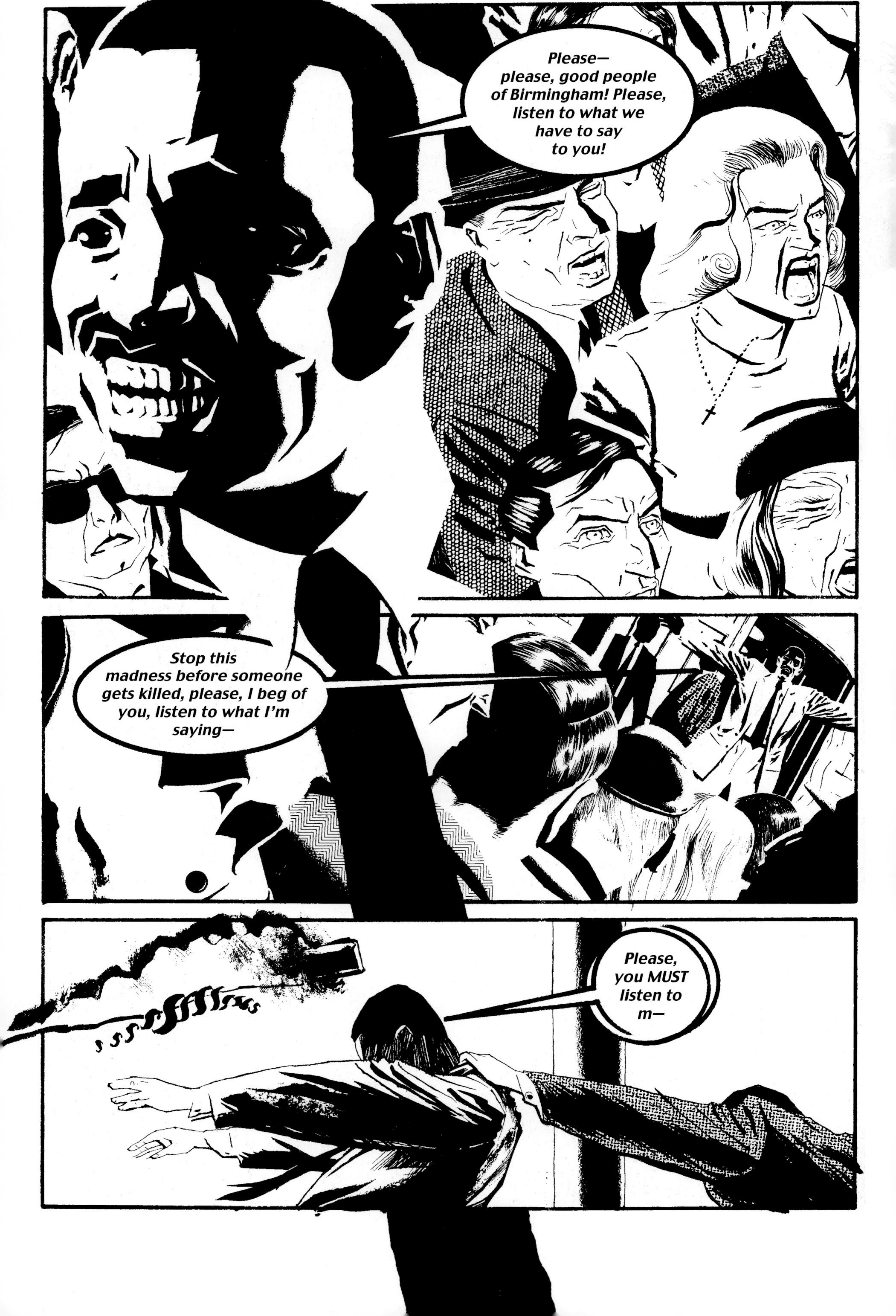
Please— please, good people of Birmingham! Please, listen to what we have to say to you!
Stop this madness before someone gets killed, please, I beg of you, listen to what I'm saying—
Please, you MUST listen to m—

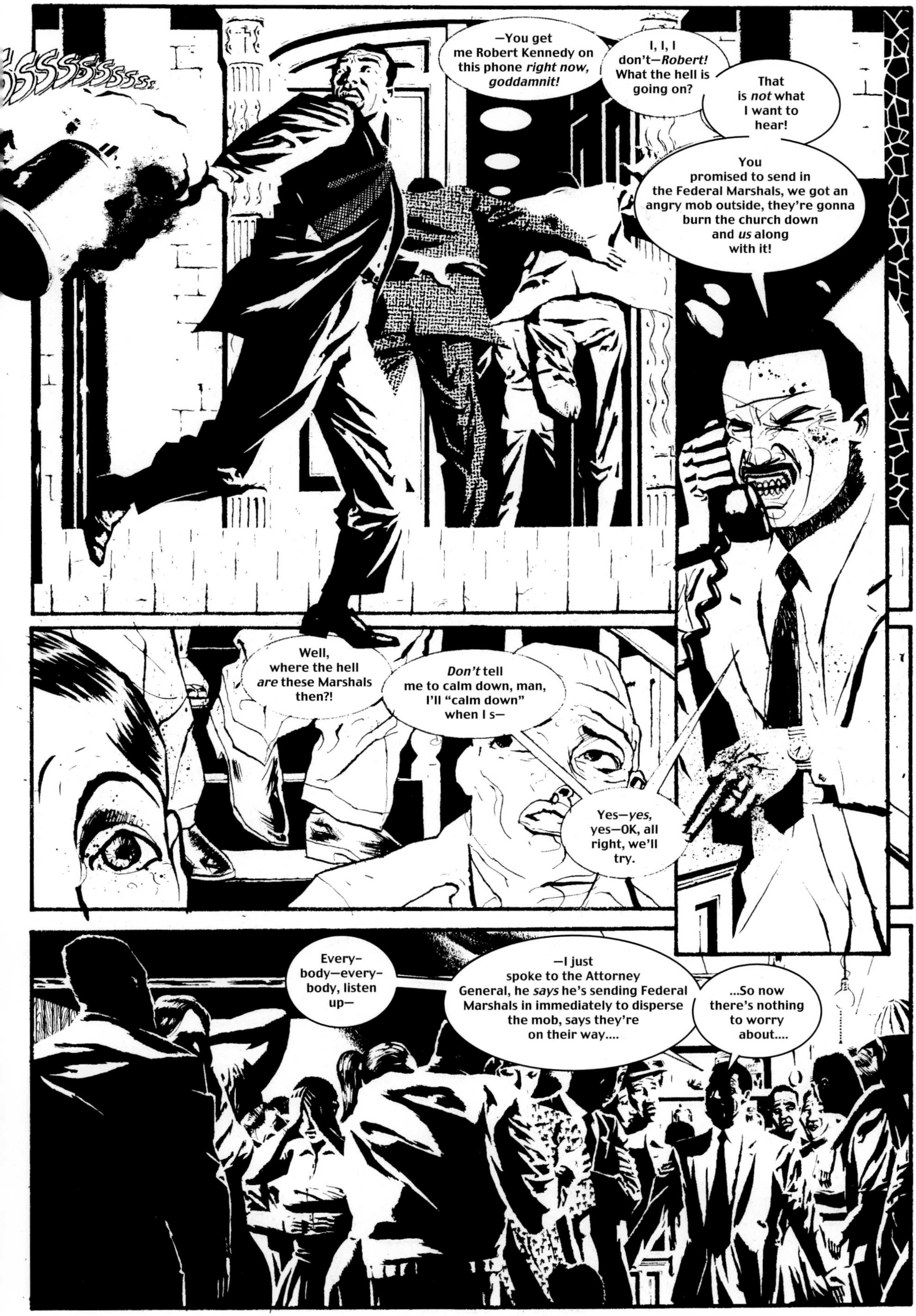
SSSSSSSSSSSS
—You get me Robert Kennedy on this phone *right now, goddamnit!*
I, I, I don't—*Robert!* What the hell is going on?
That is *not* what I want to hear!
You promised to send in the Federal Marshals, we got an angry mob outside, they're gonna burn the church down and *us* along with it!
Well, where the hell *are* these Marshals then?!
Don't tell me to calm down, man, I'll "calm down" when I s—
Yes—*yes,* yes—OK, all right, we'll try.
Every—body—every—body, listen up—
—I just spoke to the Attorney General, he *says* he's sending Federal Marshals in immediately to disperse the mob, says they're on their way....
...So now there's nothing to worry about....

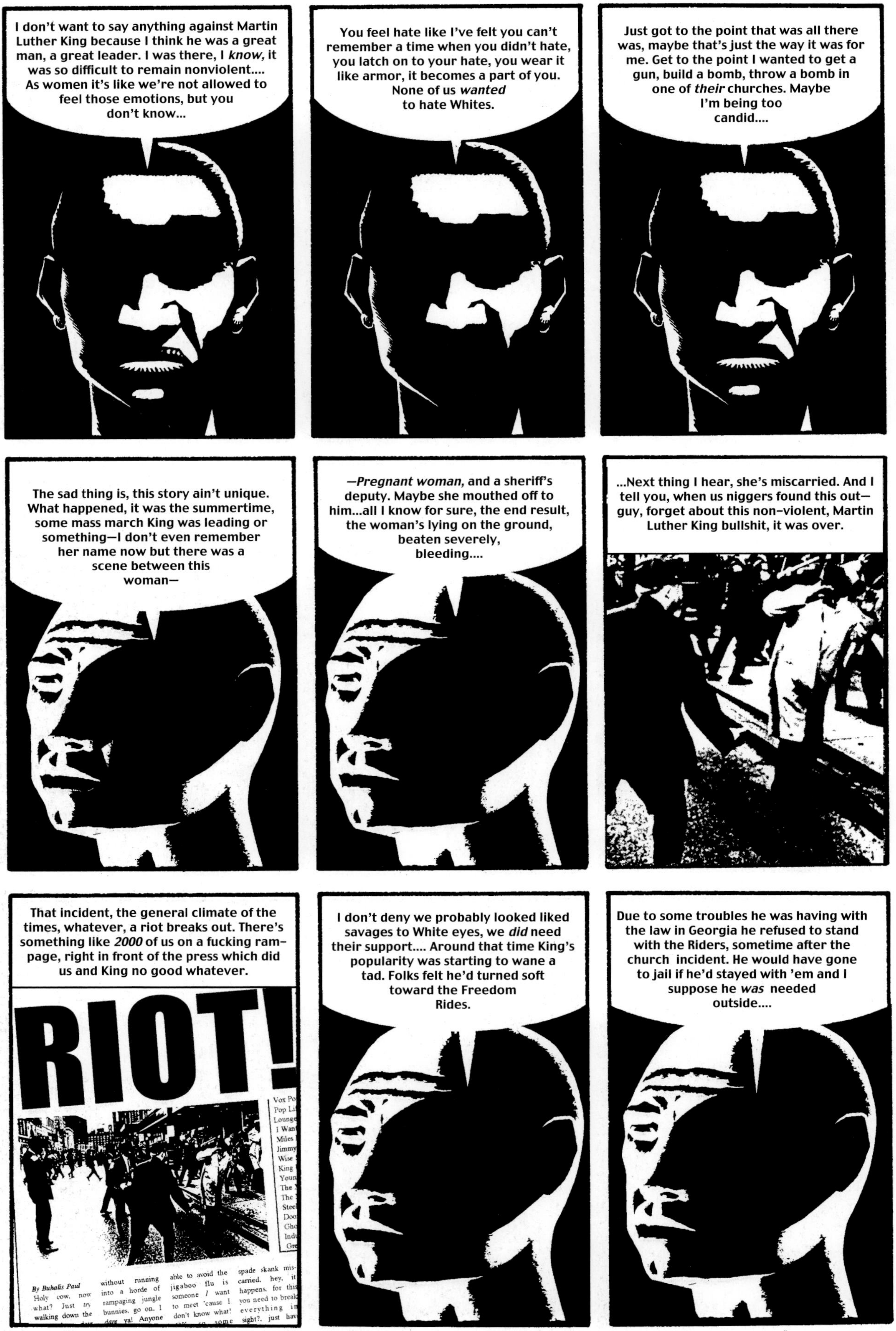
I don't want to say anything against Martin Luther King because I think he was a great man, a great leader. I was there, I *know,* it was so difficult to remain nonviolent.... As women it's like we're not allowed to feel those emotions, but you don't know...
You feel hate like I've felt you can't remember a time when you didn't hate, you latch on to your hate, you wear it like armor, it becomes a part of you. None of us *wanted* to hate Whites.
Just got to the point that was all there was, maybe that's just the way it was for me. Get to the point I wanted to get a gun, build a bomb, throw a bomb in one of *their* churches. Maybe I'm being too candid....
The sad thing is, this story ain't unique. What happened, it was the summertime, some mass march King was leading or something—I don't even remember her name now but there was a scene between this woman—
—*Pregnant woman,* and a sheriff's deputy. Maybe she mouthed off to him...all I know for sure, the end result, the woman's lying on the ground, beaten severely, bleeding....
...Next thing I hear, she's miscarried. And I tell you, when us niggers found this out—guy, forget about this non-violent, Martin Luther King bullshit, it was over.
That incident, the general climate of the times, whatever, a riot breaks out. There's something like *2000* of us on a fucking rampage, right in front of the press which did us and King no good whatever.
RIOT!
By Buhalis Paul
I don't deny we probably looked liked savages to White eyes, we *did* need their support.... Around that time King's popularity was starting to wane a tad. Folks felt he'd turned soft toward the Freedom Rides.
Due to some troubles he was having with the law in Georgia he refused to stand with the Riders, sometime after the church incident. He would have gone to jail if he'd stayed with 'em and I suppose he *was* needed outside....

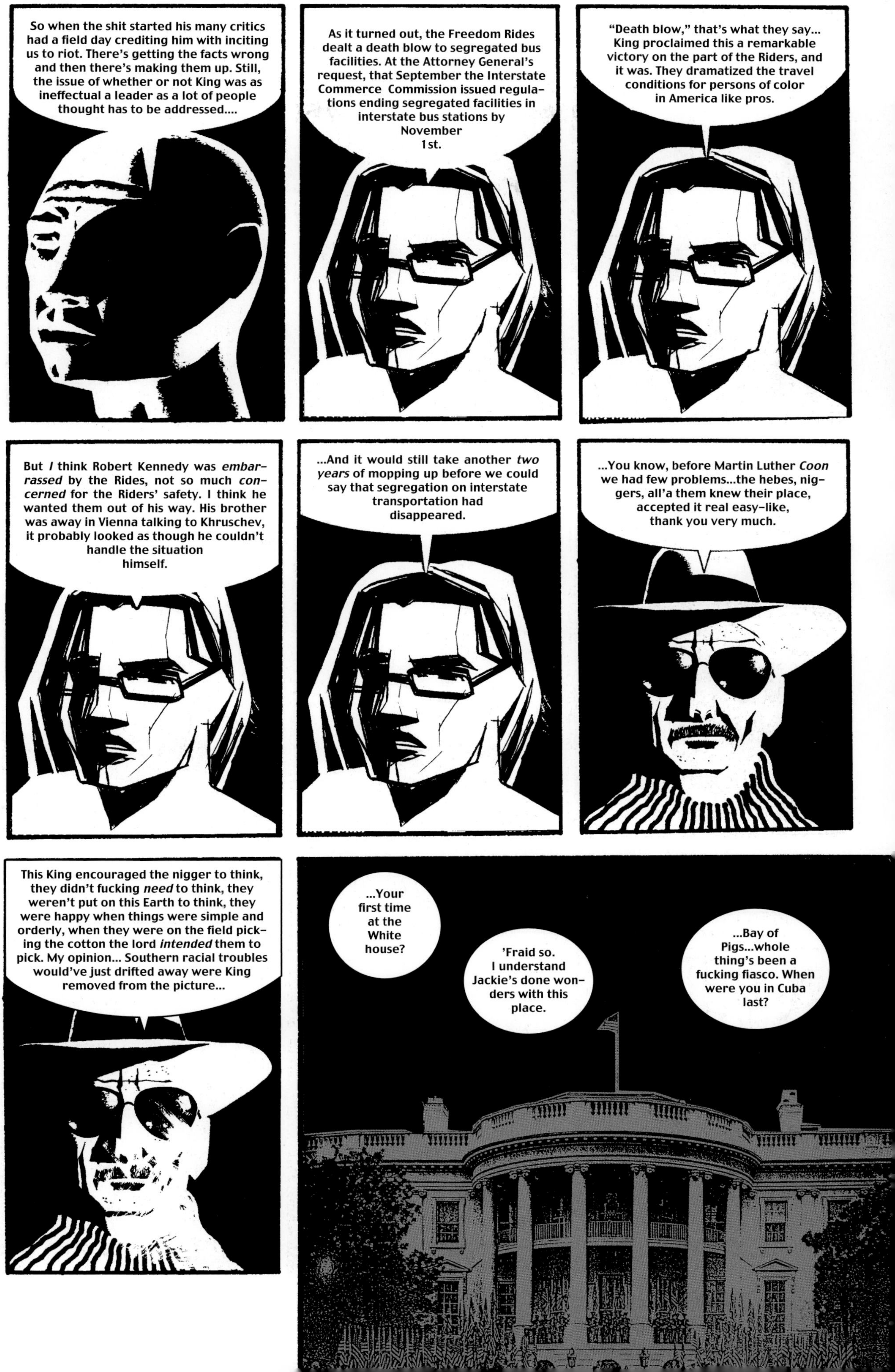
So when the shit started his many critics had a field day crediting him with inciting us to riot. There's getting the facts wrong and then there's making them up. Still, the issue of whether or not King was as ineffectual a leader as a lot of people thought has to be addressed....
As it turned out, the Freedom Rides dealt a death blow to segregated bus facilities. At the Attorney General's request, that September the Interstate Commerce Commission issued regulations ending segregated facilities in interstate bus stations by November 1st.
"Death blow," that's what they say... King proclaimed this a remarkable victory on the part of the Riders, and it was. They dramatized the travel conditions for persons of color in America like pros.
But *I* think Robert Kennedy was *embarrassed* by the Rides, not so much *concerned* for the Riders' safety. I think he wanted them out of his way. His brother was away in Vienna talking to Khruschev, it probably looked as though he couldn't handle the situation himself.
...And it would still take another *two years* of mopping up before we could say that segregation on interstate transportation had disappeared.
...You know, before Martin Luther *Coon* we had few problems...the hebes, niggers, all'a them knew their place, accepted it real easy-like, thank you very much.
This King encouraged the nigger to think, they didn't fucking *need* to think, they weren't put on this Earth to think, they were happy when things were simple and orderly, when they were on the field picking the cotton the lord *intended* them to pick. My opinion... Southern racial troubles would've just drifted away were King removed from the picture...
...Your first time at the White house?
'Fraid so. I understand Jackie's done wonders with this place.
...Bay of Pigs...whole thing's been a fucking fiasco. When were you in Cuba last?

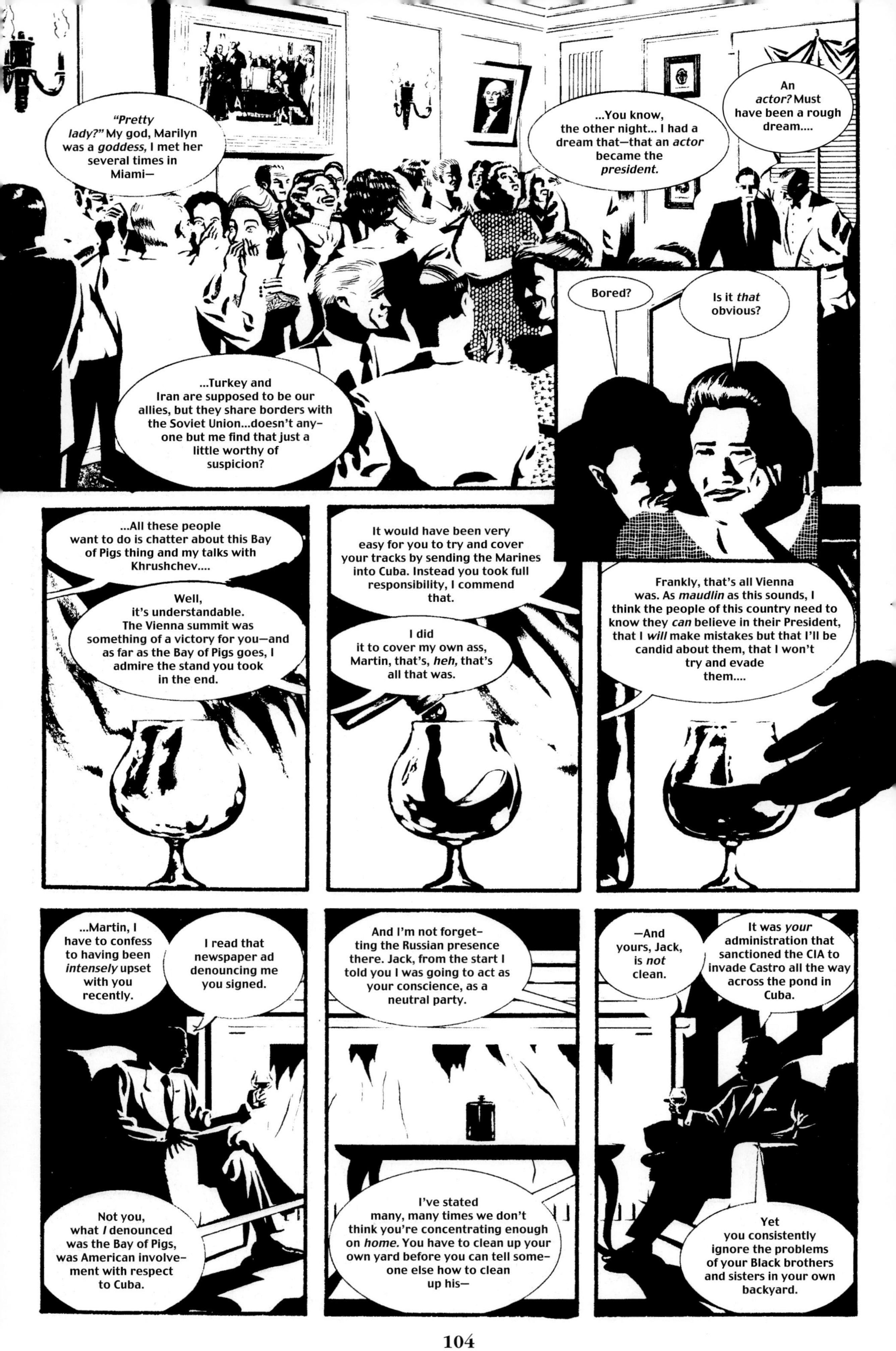
"Pretty lady?" My god, Marilyn was a goddess, I met her several times in Miami—
...You know, the other night... I had a dream that—that an actor became the president.
An actor? Must have been a rough dream....
...Turkey and Iran are supposed to be our allies, but they share borders with the Soviet Union...doesn't anyone but me find that just a little worthy of suspicion?
Bored?
Is it that obvious?
...All these people want to do is chatter about this Bay of Pigs thing and my talks with Khrushchev....
Well, it's understandable. The Vienna summit was something of a victory for you—and as far as the Bay of Pigs goes, I admire the stand you took in the end.
It would have been very easy for you to try and cover your tracks by sending the Marines into Cuba. Instead you took full responsibility, I commend that.
I did it to cover my own ass, Martin, that's, heh, that's all that was.
Frankly, that's all Vienna was. As maudlin as this sounds, I think the people of this country need to know they can believe in their President, that I will make mistakes but that I'll be candid about them, that I won't try and evade them....
...Martin, I have to confess to having been intensely upset with you recently.
I read that newspaper ad denouncing me you signed.
Not you, what I denounced was the Bay of Pigs, was American involvement with respect to Cuba.
And I'm not forgetting the Russian presence there. Jack, from the start I told you I was going to act as your conscience, as a neutral party.
I've stated many, many times we don't think you're concentrating enough on home. You have to clean up your own yard before you can tell someone else how to clean up his—
—And yours, Jack, is not clean.
It was your administration that sanctioned the CIA to invade Castro all the way across the pond in Cuba.
Yet you consistently ignore the problems of your Black brothers and sisters in your own backyard.

Y'know, you're something. You tell me you're my conscience, that you're *neutral*—yet you constantly urge me to sanction *your* agenda.... Well, what do I get from you in return?

Mr. President, this isn't just about Blacks, this concerns *everyone*—

America has only just returned from the brink of a nuclear exchange, man. *Wake up!* There very nearly was *no* backyard for me to clean up. If those *reds* hadn't backed down, by now we could've found ourselves swimming up shit's creek.

You disagree with my policies, well I just feel that the *Cold War's* a *tad* more important than your concerns.... So now we're going to ban Cuba from the OAS, so now maybe I can relax a little....

And before you start—I'm not intimating the Blacks' problems are irrelevant.... Martin... *Reverend,* what is it you would have me do?

...What would I have you do?

It's no coincidence I asked for us to come to this room.

I'm sure you know this is the room where Lincoln put forth his preliminary Emancipation Proclamation—

"—One hundred years ago. What I want, what *we* want is for *you* to promulgate a *second* Proclamation in the form of an executive order eradicating *all state segregation statutes.*"

LINCOLN SHOT!

EVER THUS TO TY- RANTS!" SHOUTS ASSA- SIN

accompanied the first lady to the Ford Theatre to see a performance of "Our Amer- ican Cousin". Witnesses to

For *you,* Mr. President, to return to this room one day and sit down at that desk and sign the order.... I wish things were different but the fact is we're all disap- pointed with your civil rights record to date.

Yes, your administration has sharply increased the number of Blacks in federal employment but it has also added Southern segregationists to the federal bench who *cheerfully* obstruct any civil rights litigation.

I *know* you know what I'm talking about. You have to accept that some of your actions have undermined the confidence negroes placed in you in 1960. This second proclamation could offset all the negati—

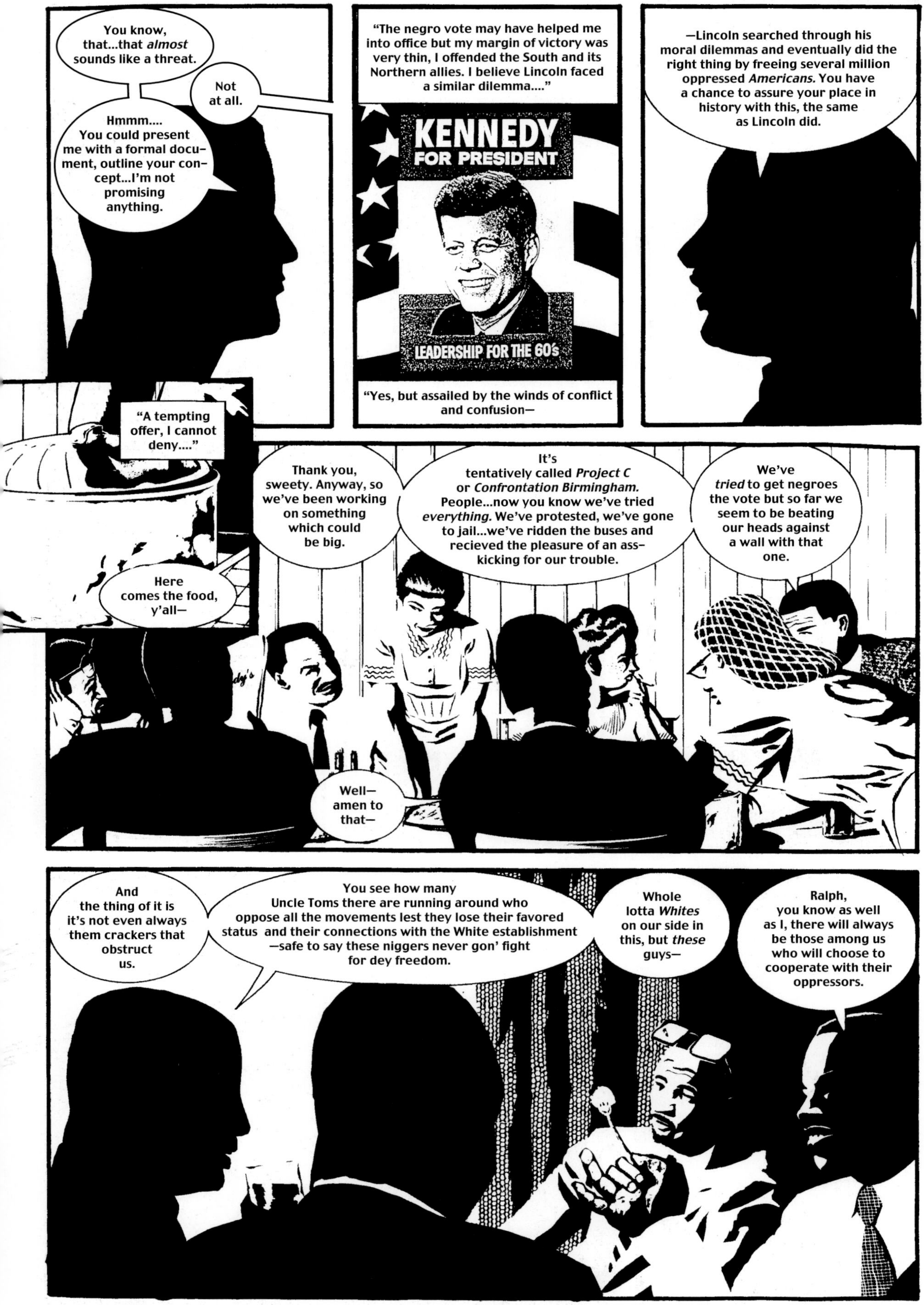
You know, that...that *almost* sounds like a threat.
Not at all.
Hmmm.... You could present me with a formal document, outline your concept...I'm not promising anything.
"The negro vote may have helped me into office but my margin of victory was very thin, I offended the South and its Northern allies. I believe Lincoln faced a similar dilemma...."
KENNEDY
FOR PRESIDENT
LEADERSHIP FOR THE 60's
"Yes, but assailed by the winds of conflict and confusion—
—Lincoln searched through his moral dilemmas and eventually did the right thing by freeing several million oppressed *Americans.* You have a chance to assure your place in history with this, the same as Lincoln did.
"A tempting offer, I cannot deny...."
Here comes the food, y'all—
Thank you, sweety. Anyway, so we've been working on something which could be big.
It's tentatively called *Project C* or *Confrontation Birmingham.* People...now you know we've tried *everything.* We've protested, we've gone to jail...we've ridden the buses and recieved the pleasure of an ass-kicking for our trouble.
We've *tried* to get negroes the vote but so far we seem to be beating our heads against a wall with that one.
Well— amen to that—
And the thing of it is it's not even always them crackers that obstruct us.
You see how many Uncle Toms there are running around who oppose all the movements lest they lose their favored status and their connections with the White establishment —safe to say these niggers never gon' fight for dey freedom.
Whole lotta *Whites* on our side in this, but *these* guys—
Ralph, you know as well as I, there will always be those among us who will choose to cooperate with their oppressors.

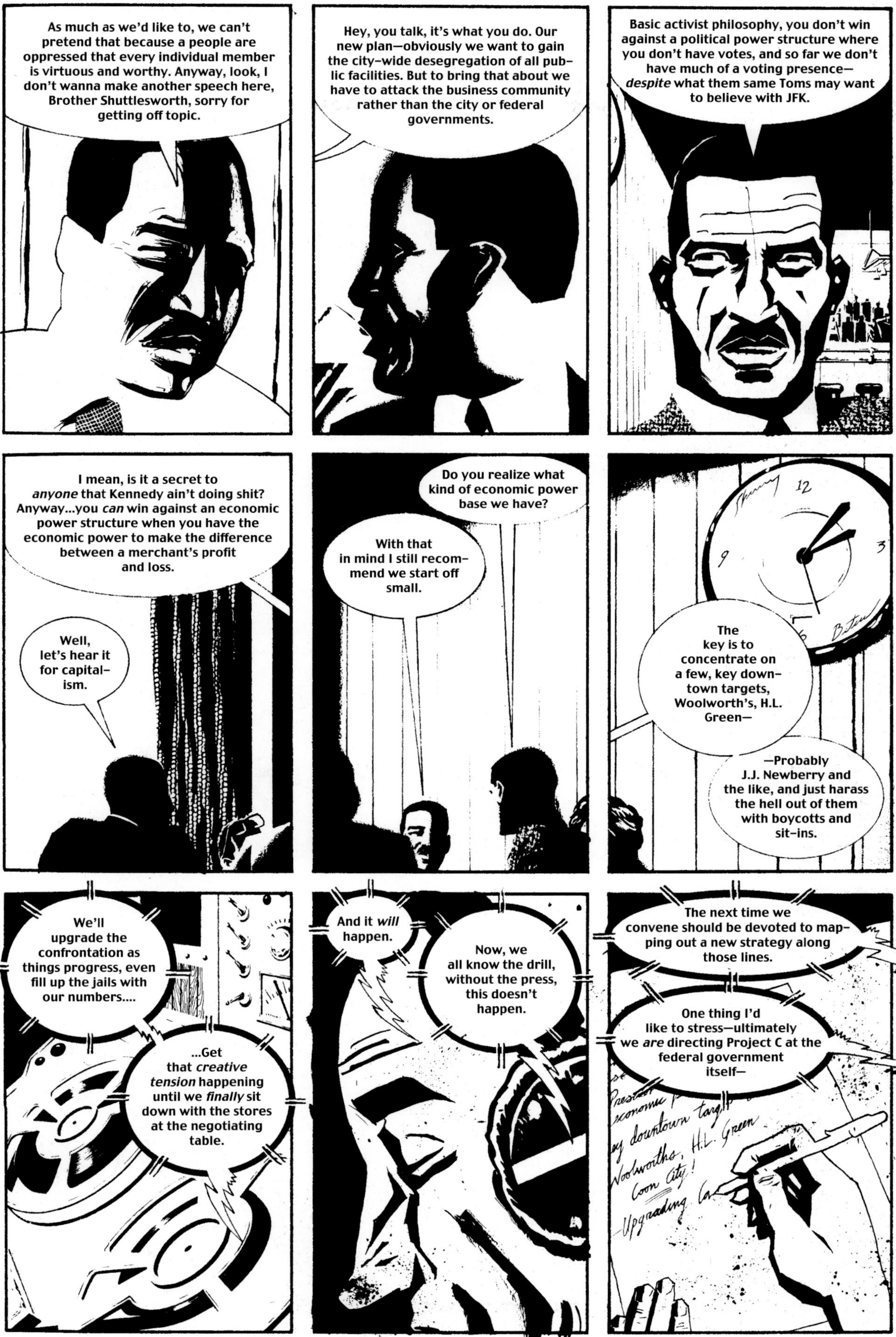

As much as we'd like to, we can't pretend that because a people are oppressed that every individual member is virtuous and worthy. Anyway, look, I don't wanna make another speech here, Brother Shuttlesworth, sorry for getting off topic.
Hey, you talk, it's what you do. Our new plan—obviously we want to gain the city-wide desegregation of all public facilities. But to bring that about we have to attack the business community rather than the city or federal governments.
Basic activist philosophy, you don't win against a political power structure where you don't have votes, and so far we don't have much of a voting presence—*despite* what them same Toms may want to believe with JFK.
I mean, is it a secret to *anyone* that Kennedy ain't doing shit? Anyway...you *can* win against an economic power structure when you have the economic power to make the difference between a merchant's profit and loss.
Well, let's hear it for capitalism.
Do you realize what kind of economic power base we have?
With that in mind I still recommend we start off small.
The key is to concentrate on a few, key downtown targets, Woolworth's, H.L. Green—
—Probably J.J. Newberry and the like, and just harass the hell out of them with boycotts and sit-ins.
We'll upgrade the confrontation as things progress, even fill up the jails with our numbers....
...Get that *creative tension* happening until we *finally* sit down with the stores at the negotiating table.
And it *will* happen.
Now, we all know the drill, without the press, this doesn't happen.
The next time we convene should be devoted to mapping out a new strategy along those lines.
One thing I'd like to stress—ultimately we *are* directing Project C at the federal government itself—
Woolworths, H.L. Green
Coon City!
Upgrading

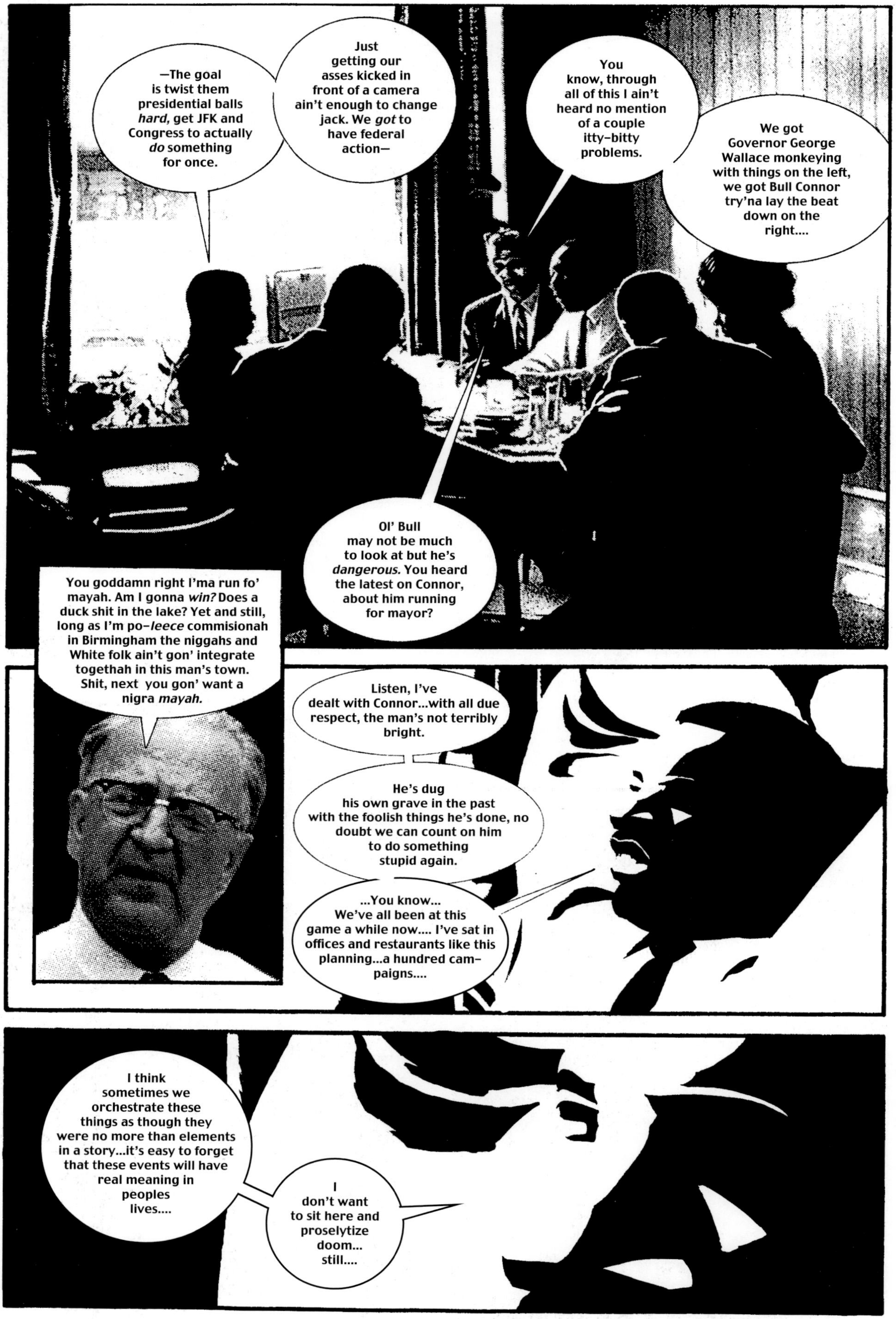
—The goal is twist them presidential balls *hard,* get JFK and Congress to actually *do* something for once.
Just getting our asses kicked in front of a camera ain't enough to change jack. We *got* to have federal action—
You know, through all of this I ain't heard no mention of a couple itty-bitty problems.
We got Governor George Wallace monkeying with things on the left, we got Bull Connor try'na lay the beat down on the right....
Ol' Bull may not be much to look at but he's *dangerous.* You heard the latest on Connor, about him running for mayor?
You goddamn right I'ma run fo' mayah. Am I gonna *win?* Does a duck shit in the lake? Yet and still, long as I'm po-*leece* commisionah in Birmingham the niggahs and White folk ain't gon' integrate togethah in this man's town. Shit, next you gon' want a nigra *mayah.*
Listen, I've dealt with Connor...with all due respect, the man's not terribly bright.
He's dug his own grave in the past with the foolish things he's done, no doubt we can count on him to do something stupid again.
...You know... We've all been at this game a while now.... I've sat in offices and restaurants like this planning...a hundred cam-paigns....
I think sometimes we orchestrate these things as though they were no more than elements in a story...it's easy to forget that these events will have real meaning in peoples lives....
I don't want to sit here and proselytize doom... still....

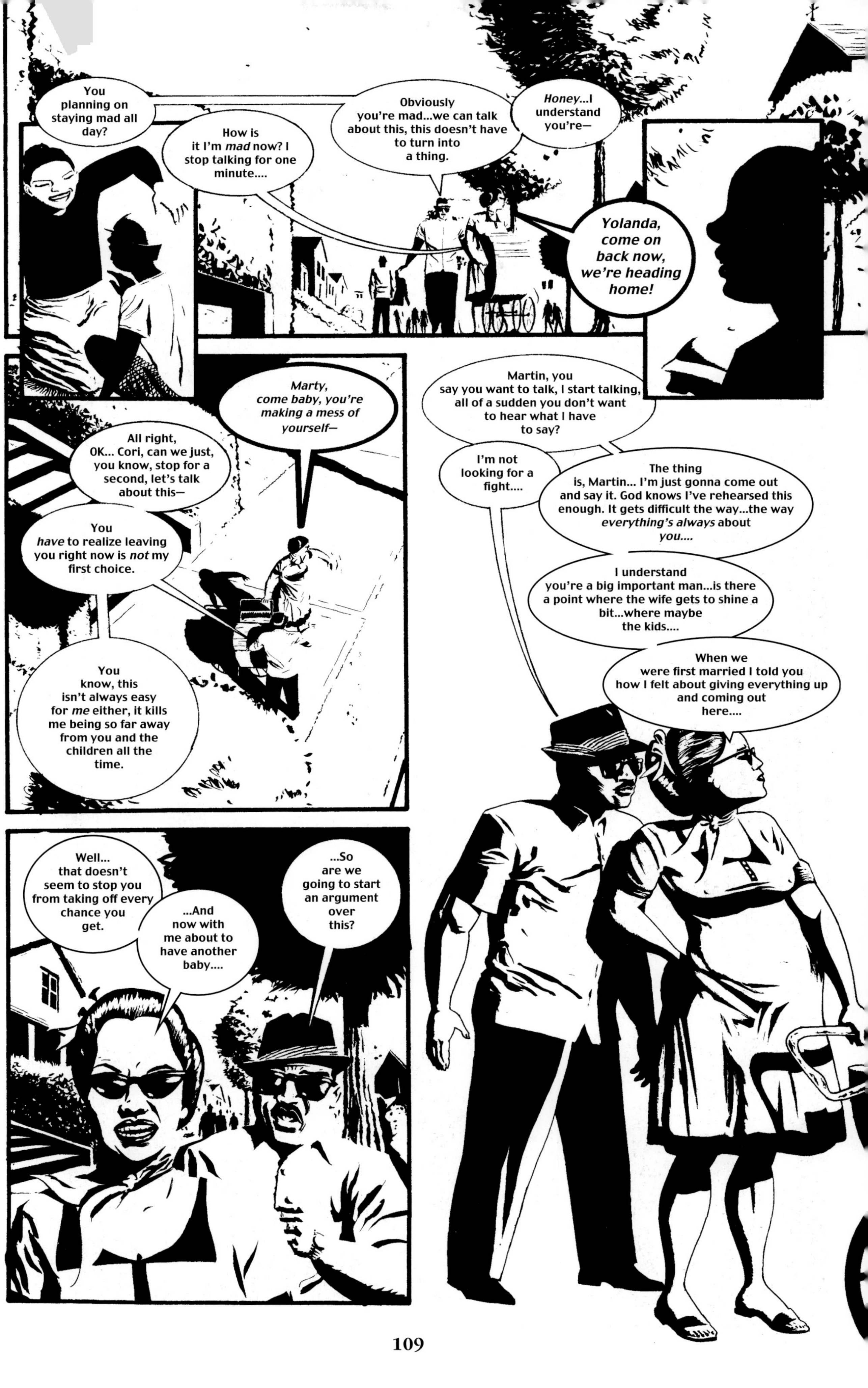
You planning on staying mad all day?
How is it I'm *mad* now? I stop talking for one minute....
Obviously you're mad...we can talk about this, this doesn't have to turn into a thing.
Honey...I understand you're—
Yolanda, come on back now, we're heading home!
Marty, come baby, you're making a mess of yourself—
All right, OK... Cori, can we just, you know, stop for a second, let's talk about this—
You *have* to realize leaving you right now is *not* my first choice.
You know, this isn't always easy for *me* either, it kills me being so far away from you and the children all the time.
Martin, you say you want to talk, I start talking, all of a sudden you don't want to hear what I have to say?
I'm not looking for a fight....
The thing is, Martin... I'm just gonna come out and say it. God knows I've rehearsed this enough. It gets difficult the way...the way *everything's always* about *you....*
I understand you're a big important man...is there a point where the wife gets to shine a bit...where maybe the kids....
When we were first married I told you how I felt about giving everything up and coming out here....
Well... that doesn't seem to stop you from taking off every chance you get.
...And now with me about to have another baby....
...So are we going to start an argument over this?

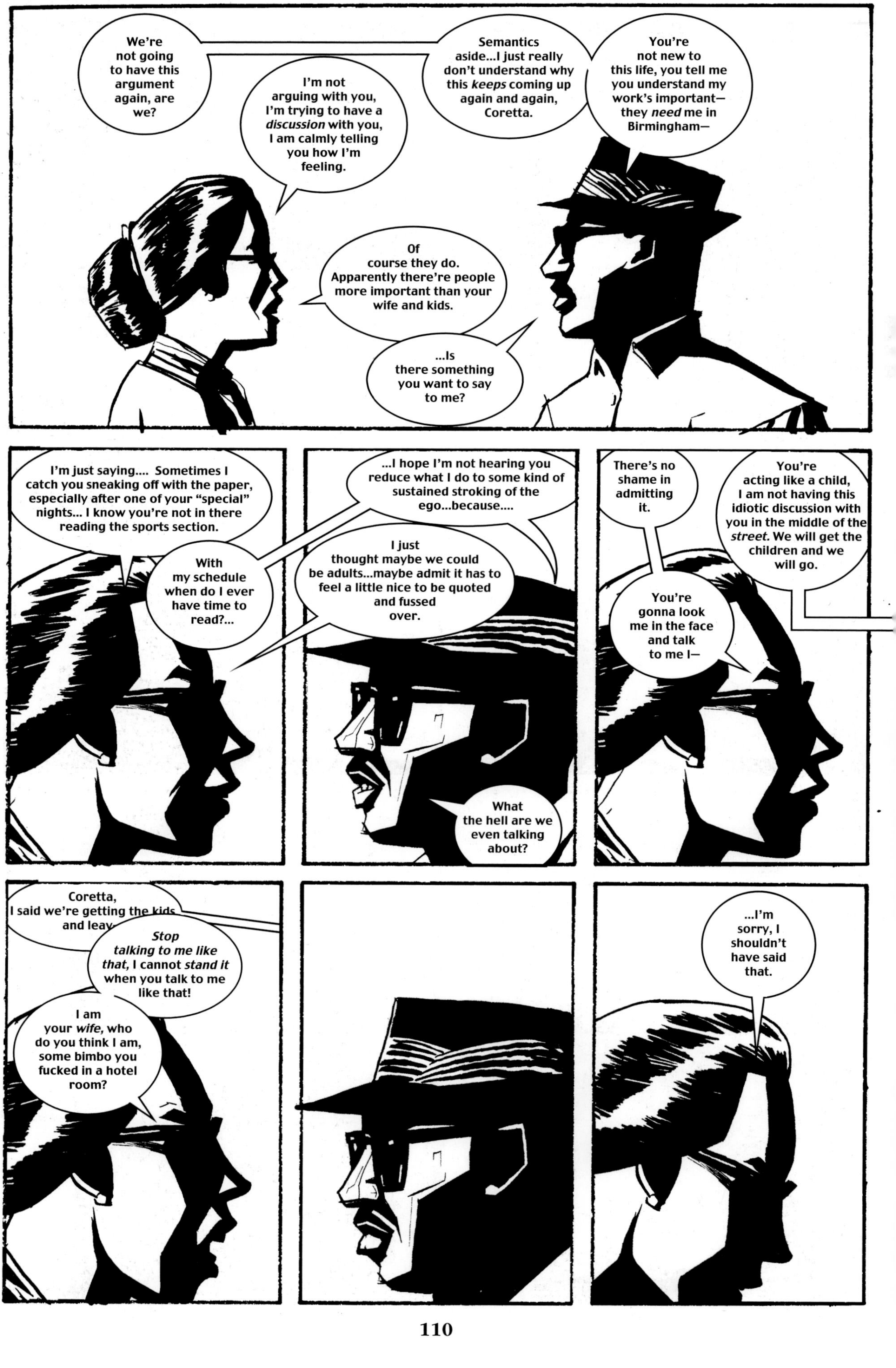
We're not going to have this argument again, are we?
I'm not arguing with you, I'm trying to have a *discussion* with you, I am calmly telling you how I'm feeling.
Semantics aside...I just really don't understand why this *keeps* coming up again and again, Coretta.
You're not new to this life, you tell me you understand my work's important— they *need* me in Birmingham—
Of course they do. Apparently there're people more important than your wife and kids.
...Is there something you want to say to me?
I'm just saying.... Sometimes I catch you sneaking off with the paper, especially after one of your "special" nights... I know you're not in there reading the sports section.
With my schedule when do I ever have time to read?...
...I hope I'm not hearing you reduce what I do to some kind of sustained stroking of the ego...because....
I just thought maybe we could be adults...maybe admit it has to feel a little nice to be quoted and fussed over.
What the hell are we even talking about?
There's no shame in admitting it.
You're acting like a child, I am not having this idiotic discussion with you in the middle of the *street*. We will get the children and we will go.
You're gonna look me in the face and talk to me I—
Coretta, I said we're getting the kids and leav—
Stop talking to me like that, I cannot *stand it* when you talk to me like that!
I am your *wife,* who do you think I am, some bimbo you fucked in a hotel room?
...I'm sorry, I shouldn't have said that.

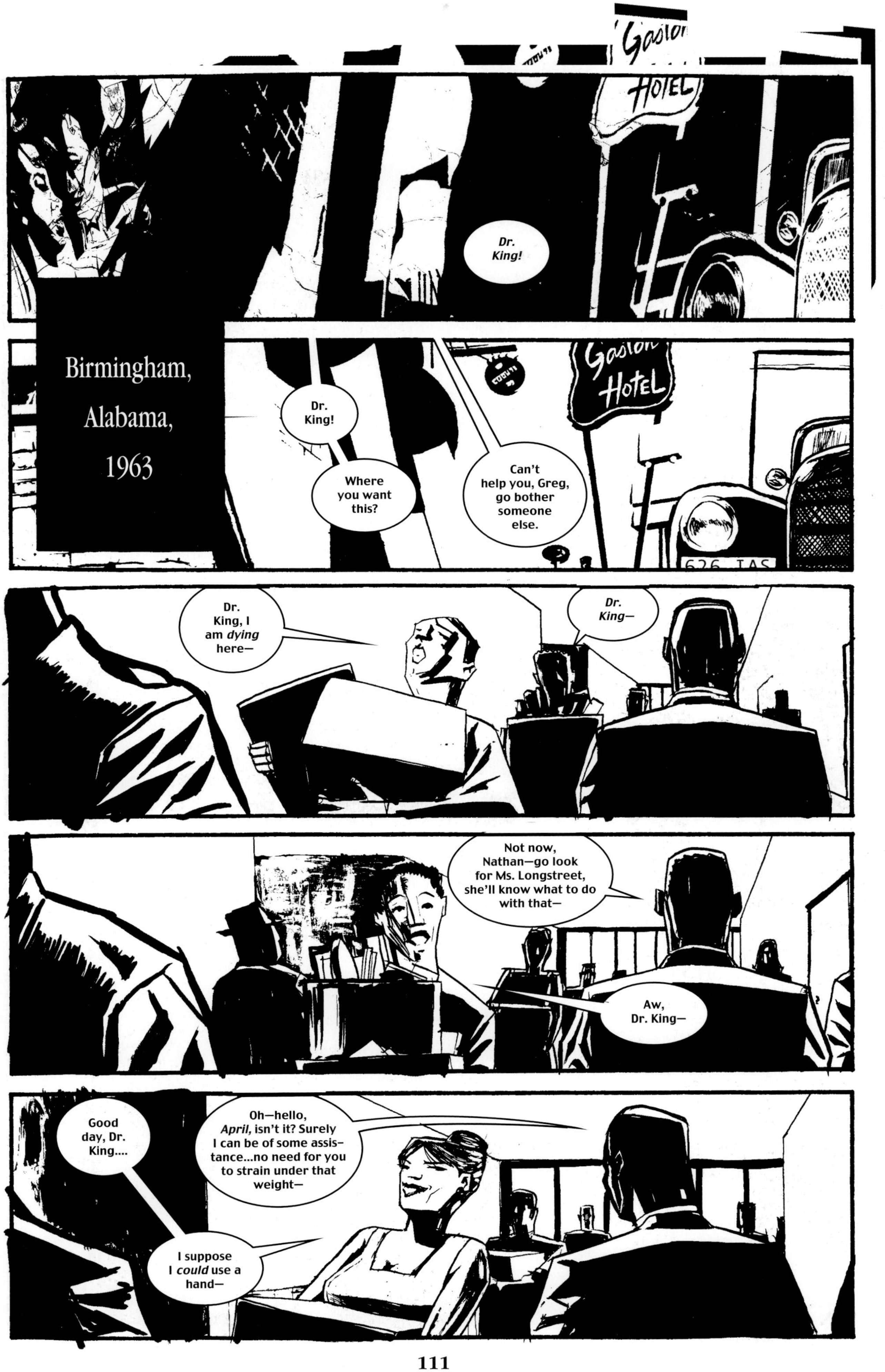
Dr. King!
Birmingham, Alabama, 1963
Dr. King!
Where you want this?
Can't help you, Greg, go bother someone else.
Gaston Hotel
Dr. King, I am *dying* here—
Dr. King—
Not now, Nathan—go look for Ms. Longstreet, she'll know what to do with that—
Aw, Dr. King—
Good day, Dr. King....
Oh—hello, *April,* isn't it? Surely I can be of some assistance...no need for you to strain under that weight—
I suppose I *could* use a hand—

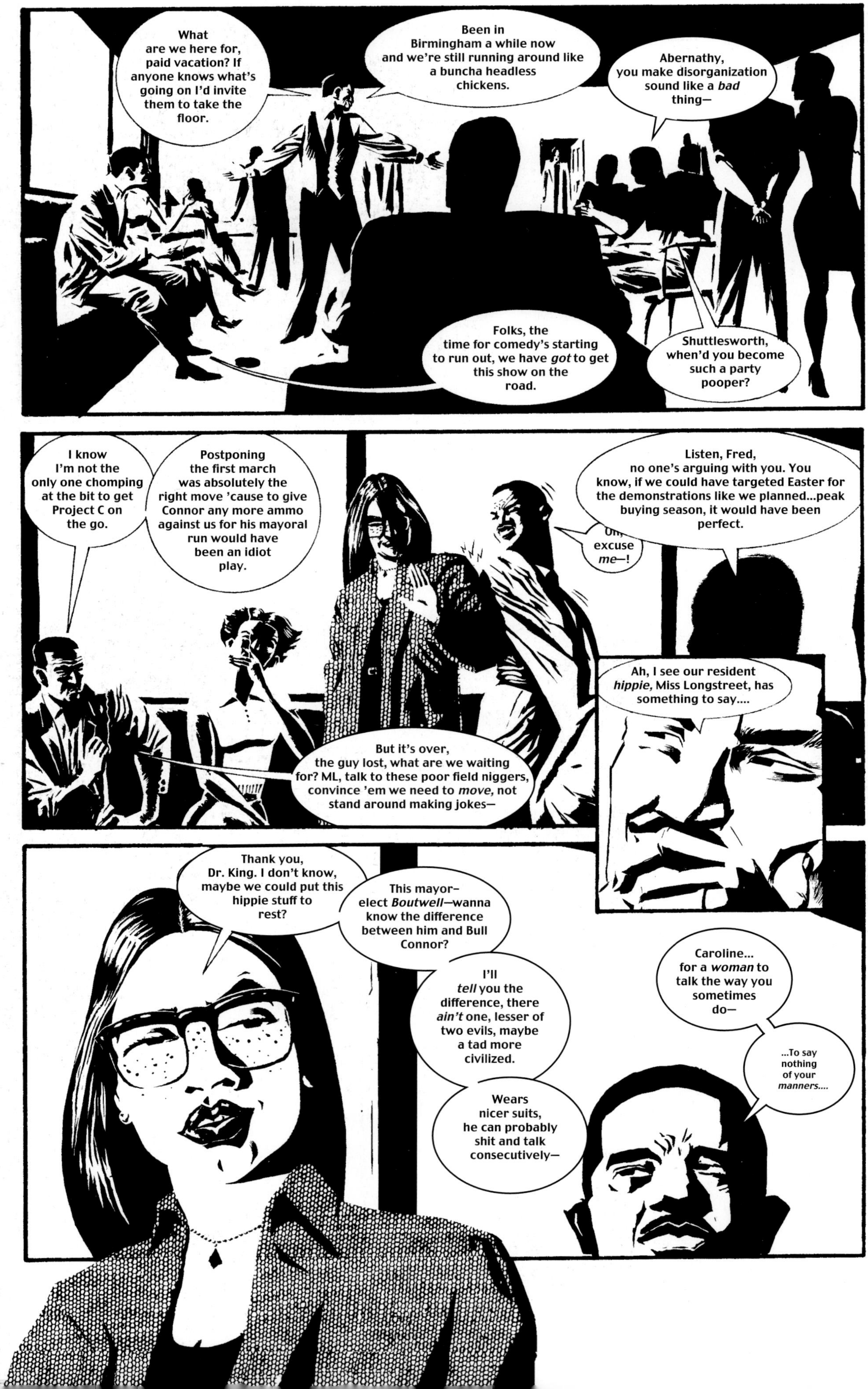
What are we here for, paid vacation? If anyone knows what's going on I'd invite them to take the floor.
Been in Birmingham a while now and we're still running around like a buncha headless chickens.
Abernathy, you make disorganization sound like a *bad* thing—
Folks, the time for comedy's starting to run out, we have *got* to get this show on the road.
Shuttlesworth, when'd you become such a party pooper?
I know I'm not the only one chomping at the bit to get Project C on the go.
Postponing the first march was absolutely the right move 'cause to give Connor any more ammo against us for his mayoral run would have been an idiot play.
Listen, Fred, no one's arguing with you. You know, if we could have targeted Easter for the demonstrations like we planned…peak buying season, it would have been perfect.
Oh, excuse *me*—!
Ah, I see our resident *hippie,* Miss Longstreet, has something to say….
But it's over, the guy lost, what are we waiting for? ML, talk to these poor field niggers, convince 'em we need to *move,* not stand around making jokes—
Thank you, Dr. King. I don't know, maybe we could put this hippie stuff to rest?
This mayor-elect *Boutwell*—wanna know the difference between him and Bull Connor?
I'll *tell* you the difference, there *ain't* one, lesser of two evils, maybe a tad more civilized.
Wears nicer suits, he can probably shit and talk consecutively—
Caroline… for a *woman* to talk the way you sometimes do—
…To say nothing of your *manners*….

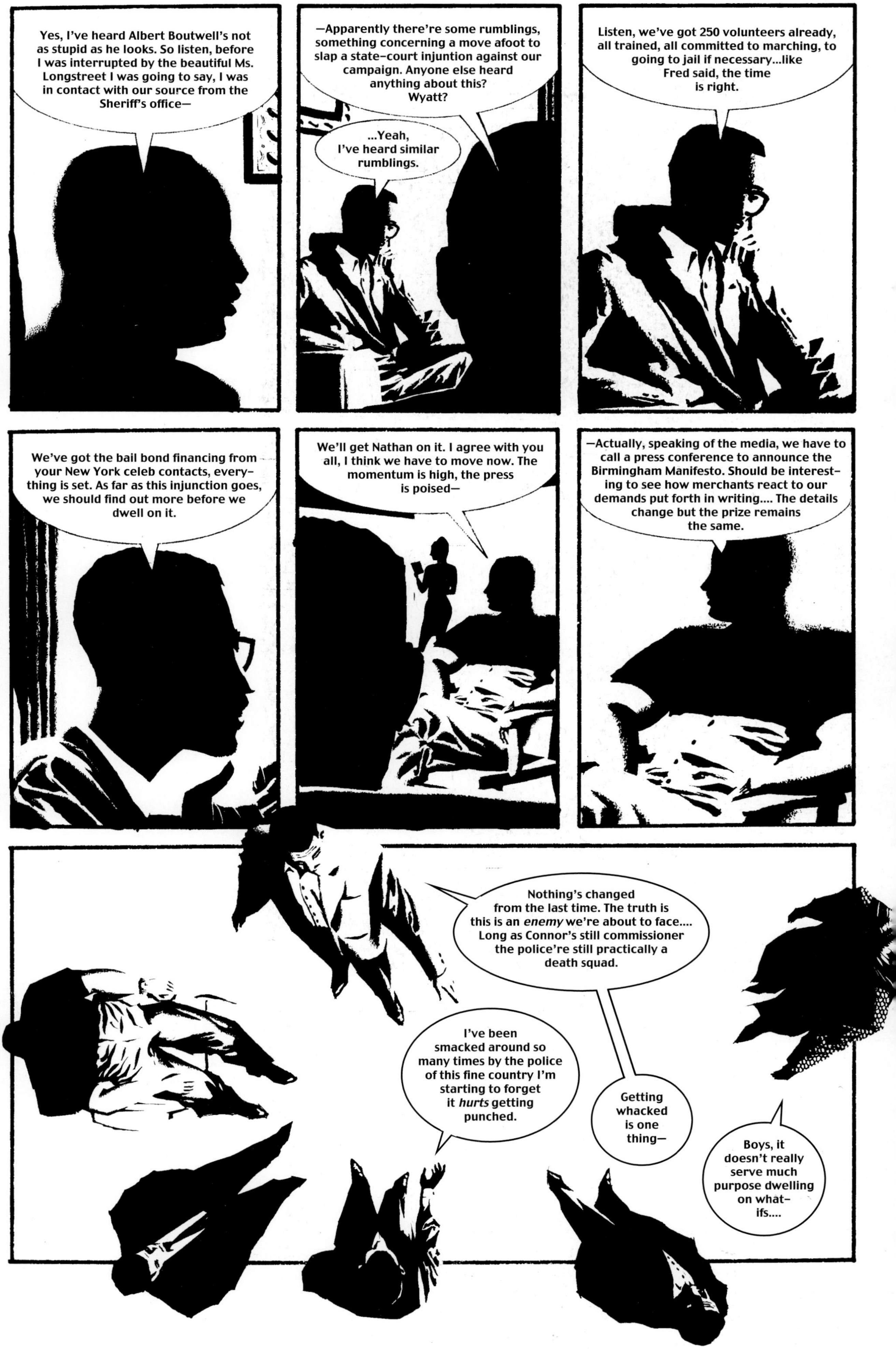
Yes, I've heard Albert Boutwell's not as stupid as he looks. So listen, before I was interrupted by the beautiful Ms. Longstreet I was going to say, I was in contact with our source from the Sheriff's office—
—Apparently there're some rumblings, something concerning a move afoot to slap a state-court injuntion against our campaign. Anyone else heard anything about this? Wyatt?
...Yeah, I've heard similar rumblings.
Listen, we've got 250 volunteers already, all trained, all committed to marching, to going to jail if necessary...like Fred said, the time is right.
We've got the bail bond financing from your New York celeb contacts, everything is set. As far as this injunction goes, we should find out more before we dwell on it.
We'll get Nathan on it. I agree with you all, I think we have to move now. The momentum is high, the press is poised—
—Actually, speaking of the media, we have to call a press conference to announce the Birmingham Manifesto. Should be interesting to see how merchants react to our demands put forth in writing.... The details change but the prize remains the same.
Nothing's changed from the last time. The truth is this is an *enemy* we're about to face.... Long as Connor's still commissioner the police're still practically a death squad.
I've been smacked around so many times by the police of this fine country I'm starting to forget it *hurts* getting punched.
Getting whacked is one thing—
Boys, it doesn't really serve much purpose dwelling on what-ifs....

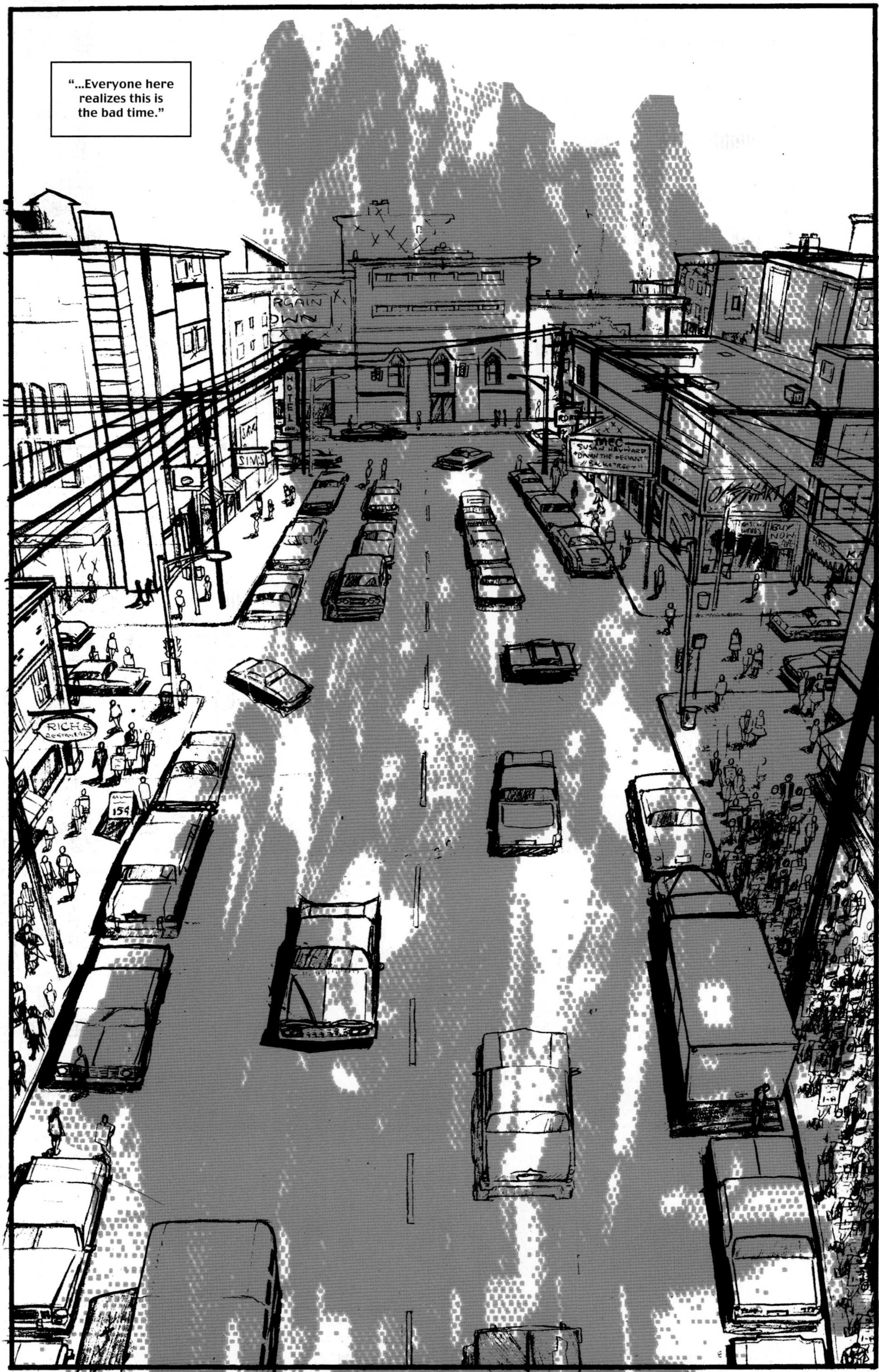
"...Everyone here realizes this is the bad time."
HOTEL
SUSAN HAYWARD
BUY NOW
RICH'S
WS/HCA

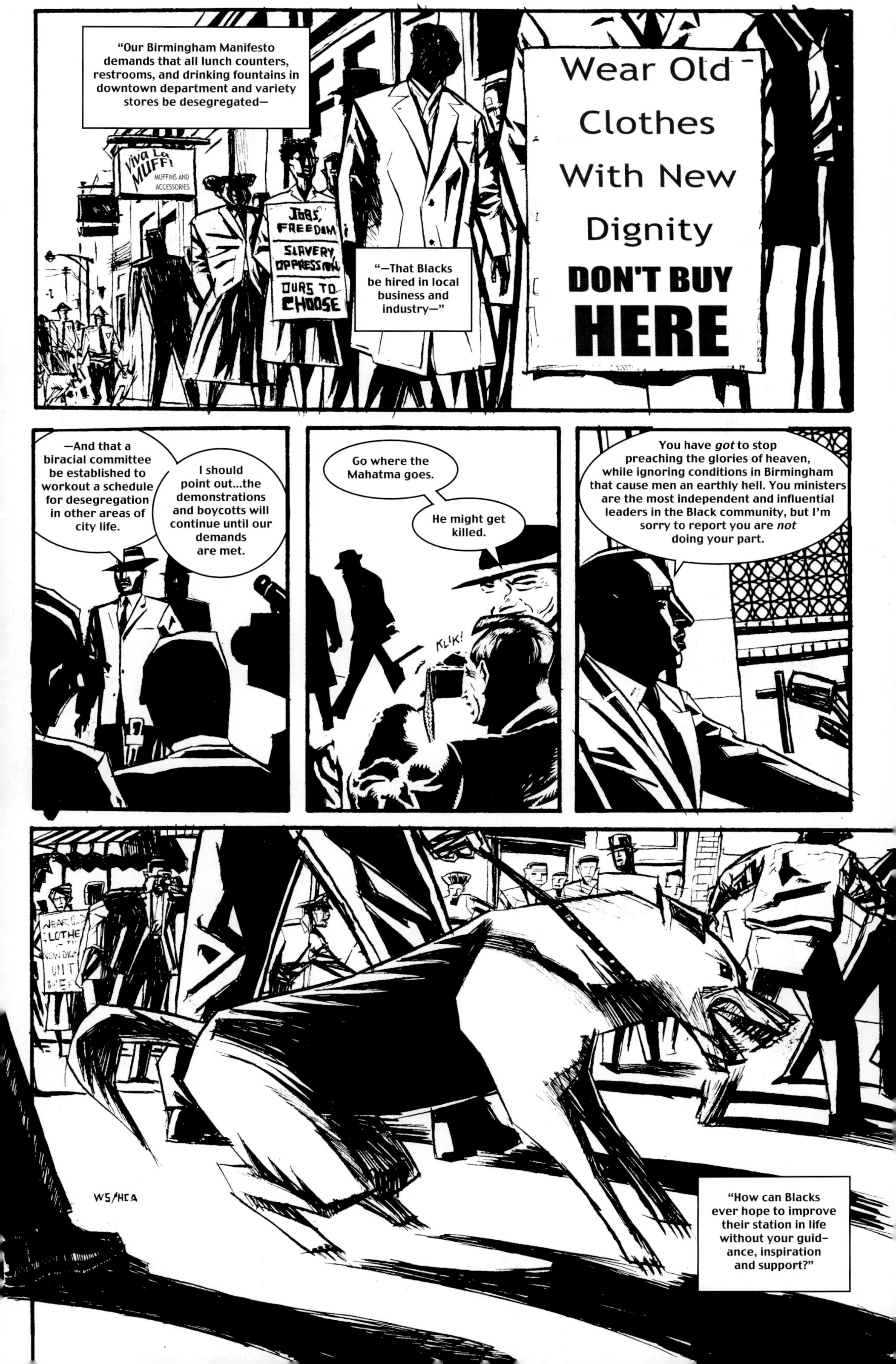

"Our Birmingham Manifesto demands that all lunch counters, restrooms, and drinking fountains in downtown department and variety stores be desegregated—
Viva La MUFF! MUFFINS AND ACCESSORIES
JOBS, FREEDOM
SLAVERY OPPRESSION
OURS TO CHOOSE
"—That Blacks be hired in local business and industry—"
Wear Old Clothes With New Dignity
DON'T BUY HERE
—And that a biracial committee be established to workout a schedule for desegregation in other areas of city life.
I should point out...the demonstrations and boycotts will continue until our demands are met.
Go where the Mahatma goes.
He might get killed.
KLIK!
You have *got* to stop preaching the glories of heaven, while ignoring conditions in Birmingham that cause men an earthly hell. You ministers are the most independent and influential leaders in the Black community, but I'm sorry to report you are *not* doing your part.
WS/HCA
"How can Blacks ever hope to improve their station in life without your guidance, inspiration and support?"

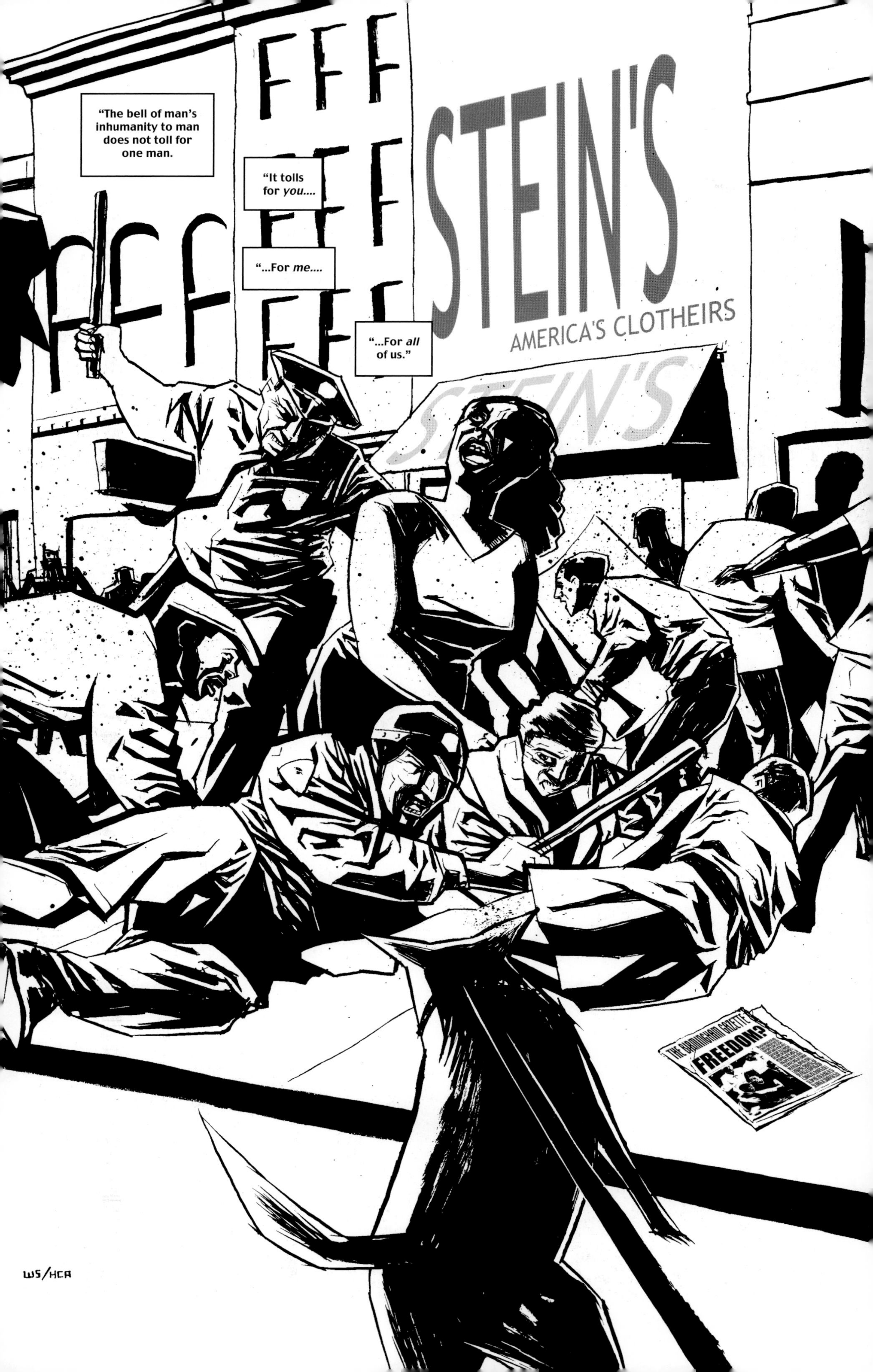

"The bell of man's inhumanity to man does not toll for one man.
"It tolls for *you*....
"...For *me*....
"...For *all* of us."
STEIN'S
AMERICA'S CLOTHEIRS
STEIN'S
THE BIRMINGHAM GAZETTE
FREEDOM?
WS/HCA

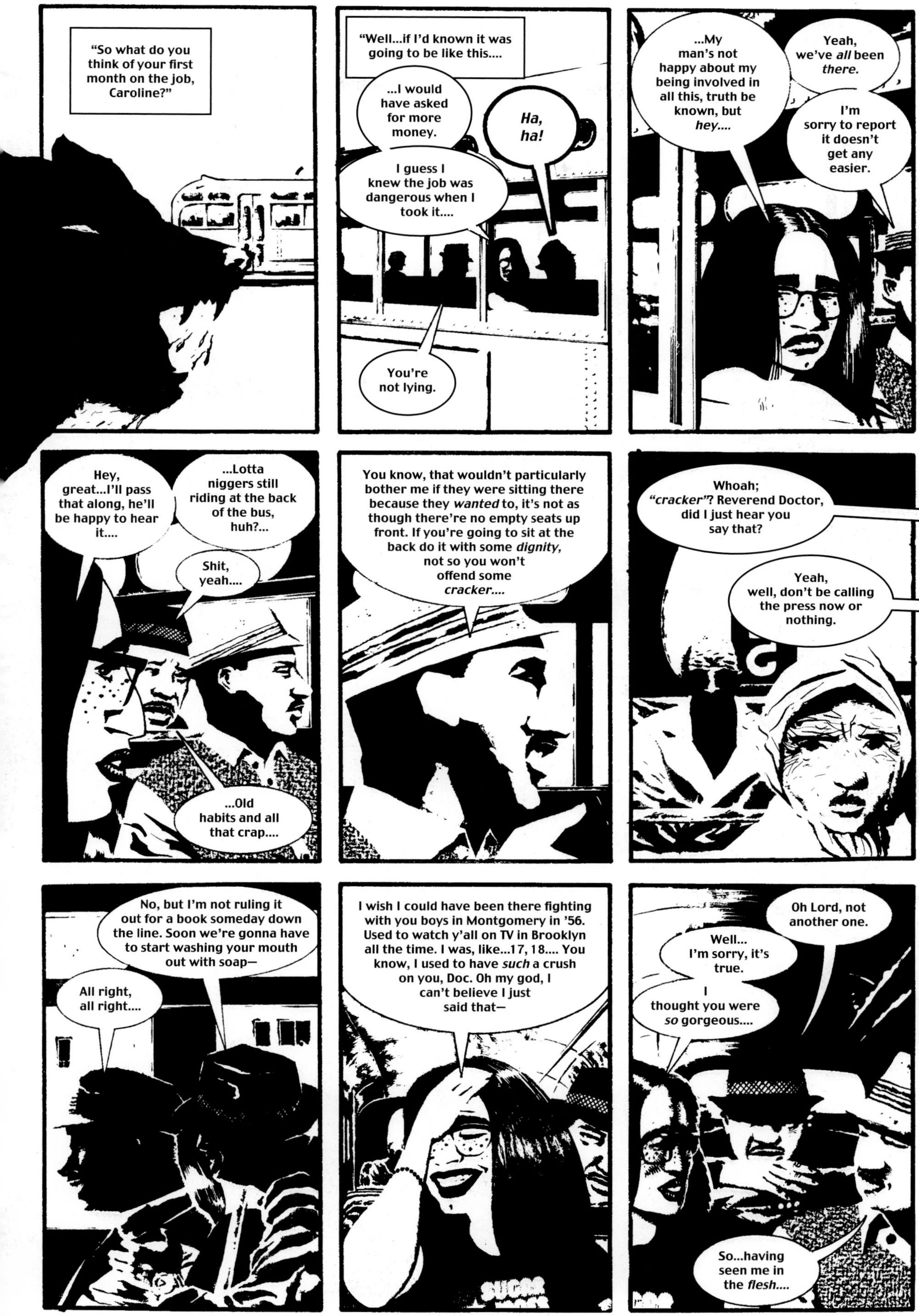
"So what do you think of your first month on the job, Caroline?"
"Well...if I'd known it was going to be like this....
...I would have asked for more money.
Ha, ha!
I guess I knew the job was dangerous when I took it....
You're not lying.
...My man's not happy about my being involved in all this, truth be known, but hey....
Yeah, we've all been there.
I'm sorry to report it doesn't get any easier.
Hey, great...I'll pass that along, he'll be happy to hear it....
...Lotta niggers still riding at the back of the bus, huh?...
Shit, yeah....
...Old habits and all that crap....
You know, that wouldn't particularly bother me if they were sitting there because they wanted to, it's not as though there're no empty seats up front. If you're going to sit at the back do it with some dignity, not so you won't offend some cracker....
Whoah; "cracker"? Reverend Doctor, did I just hear you say that?
Yeah, well, don't be calling the press now or nothing.
No, but I'm not ruling it out for a book someday down the line. Soon we're gonna have to start washing your mouth out with soap—
All right, all right....
I wish I could have been there fighting with you boys in Montgomery in '56. Used to watch y'all on TV in Brooklyn all the time. I was, like...17, 18.... You know, I used to have such a crush on you, Doc. Oh my god, I can't believe I just said that—
Oh Lord, not another one.
Well... I'm sorry, it's true.
I thought you were so gorgeous....
So...having seen me in the flesh....

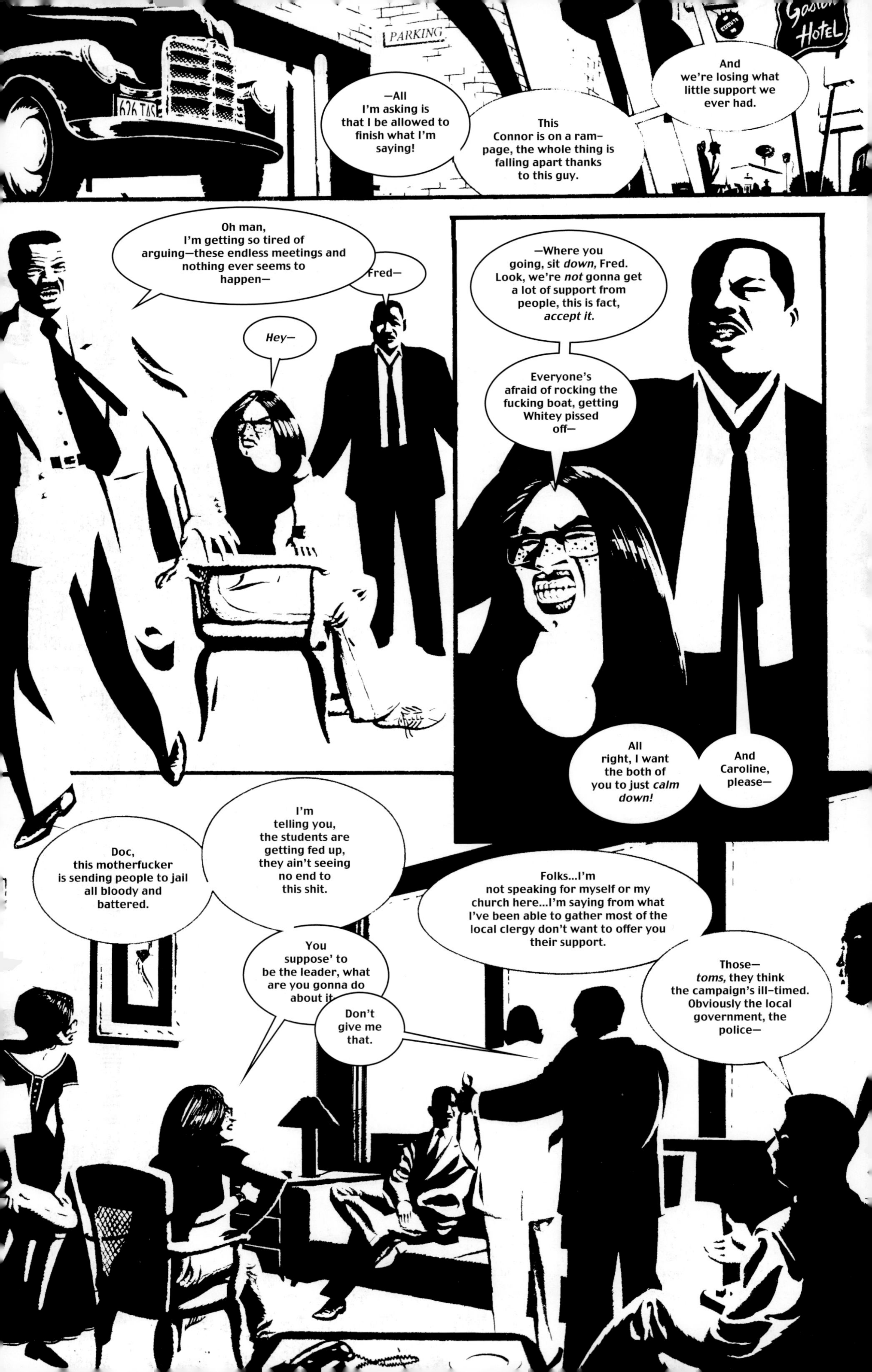
PARKING
Gaston Hotel
626 TAS
—All I'm asking is that I be allowed to finish what I'm saying!
This Connor is on a ram-page, the whole thing is falling apart thanks to this guy.
And we're losing what little support we ever had.
Oh man, I'm getting so tired of arguing—these endless meetings and nothing ever seems to happen—
Fred—
Hey—
—Where you going, sit *down,* Fred. Look, we're *not* gonna get a lot of support from people, this is fact, *accept it.*
Everyone's afraid of rocking the fucking boat, getting Whitey pissed off—
All right, I want the both of you to just *calm down!*
And Caroline, please—
Doc, this motherfucker is sending people to jail all bloody and battered.
I'm telling you, the students are getting fed up, they ain't seeing no end to this shit.
You suppose' to be the leader, what are you gonna do about it
Don't give me that.
Folks...I'm not speaking for myself or my church here...I'm saying from what I've been able to gather most of the local clergy don't want to offer you their support.
Those—*toms,* they think the campaign's ill-timed. Obviously the local government, the police—

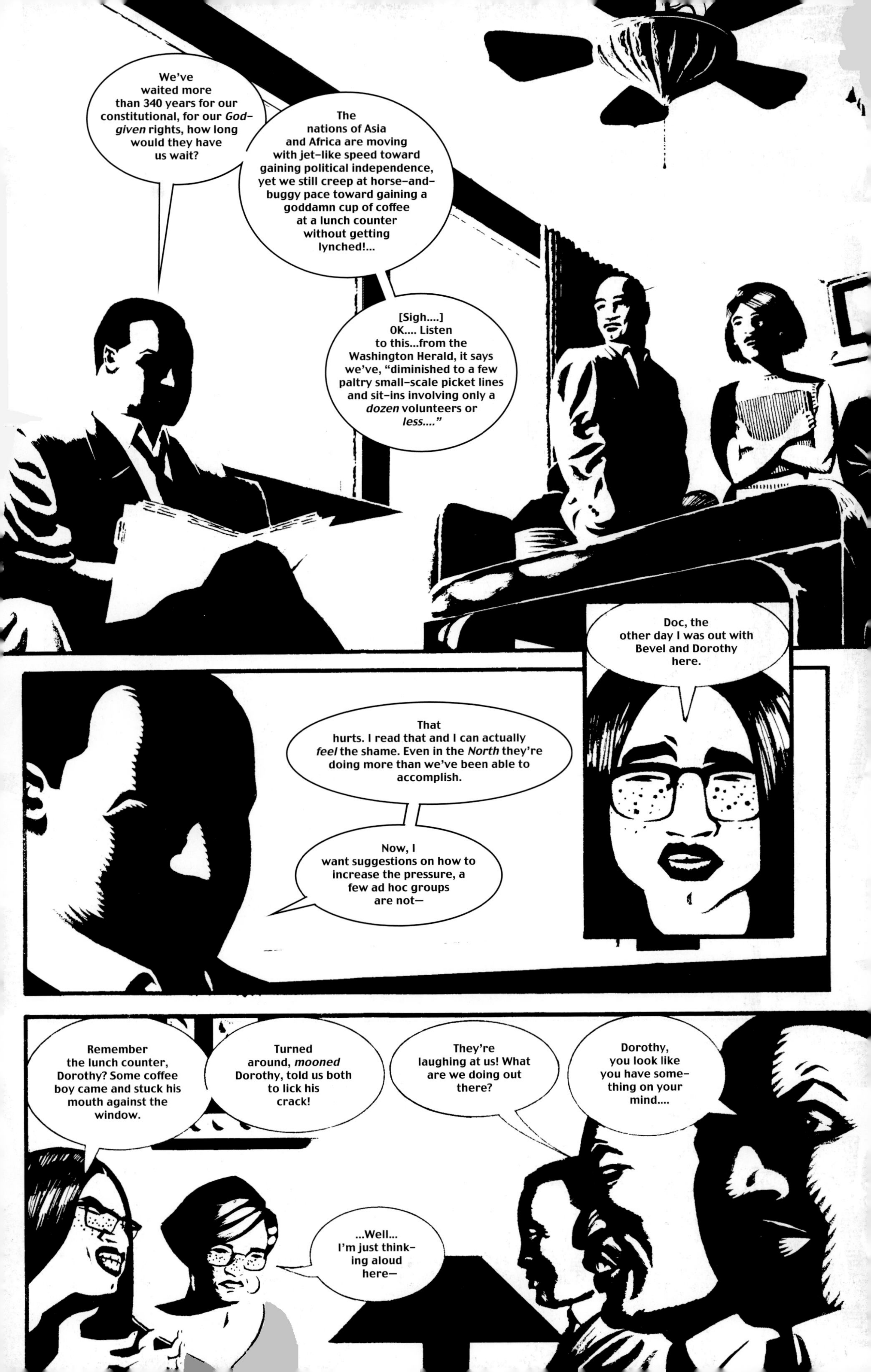
We've waited more than 340 years for our constitutional, for our *God-given* rights, how long would they have us wait?
The nations of Asia and Africa are moving with jet-like speed toward gaining political independence, yet we still creep at horse-and-buggy pace toward gaining a goddamn cup of coffee at a lunch counter without getting lynched!...
[Sigh....] OK.... Listen to this...from the Washington Herald, it says we've, "diminished to a few paltry small-scale picket lines and sit-ins involving only a *dozen* volunteers or *less....*"
That hurts. I read that and I can actually *feel* the shame. Even in the *North* they're doing more than we've been able to accomplish.
Now, I want suggestions on how to increase the pressure, a few ad hoc groups are not—
Doc, the other day I was out with Bevel and Dorothy here.
Remember the lunch counter, Dorothy? Some coffee boy came and stuck his mouth against the window.
Turned around, *mooned* Dorothy, told us both to lick his crack!
They're laughing at us! What are we doing out there?
Dorothy, you look like you have some-thing on your mind....
...Well... I'm just think-ing aloud here—

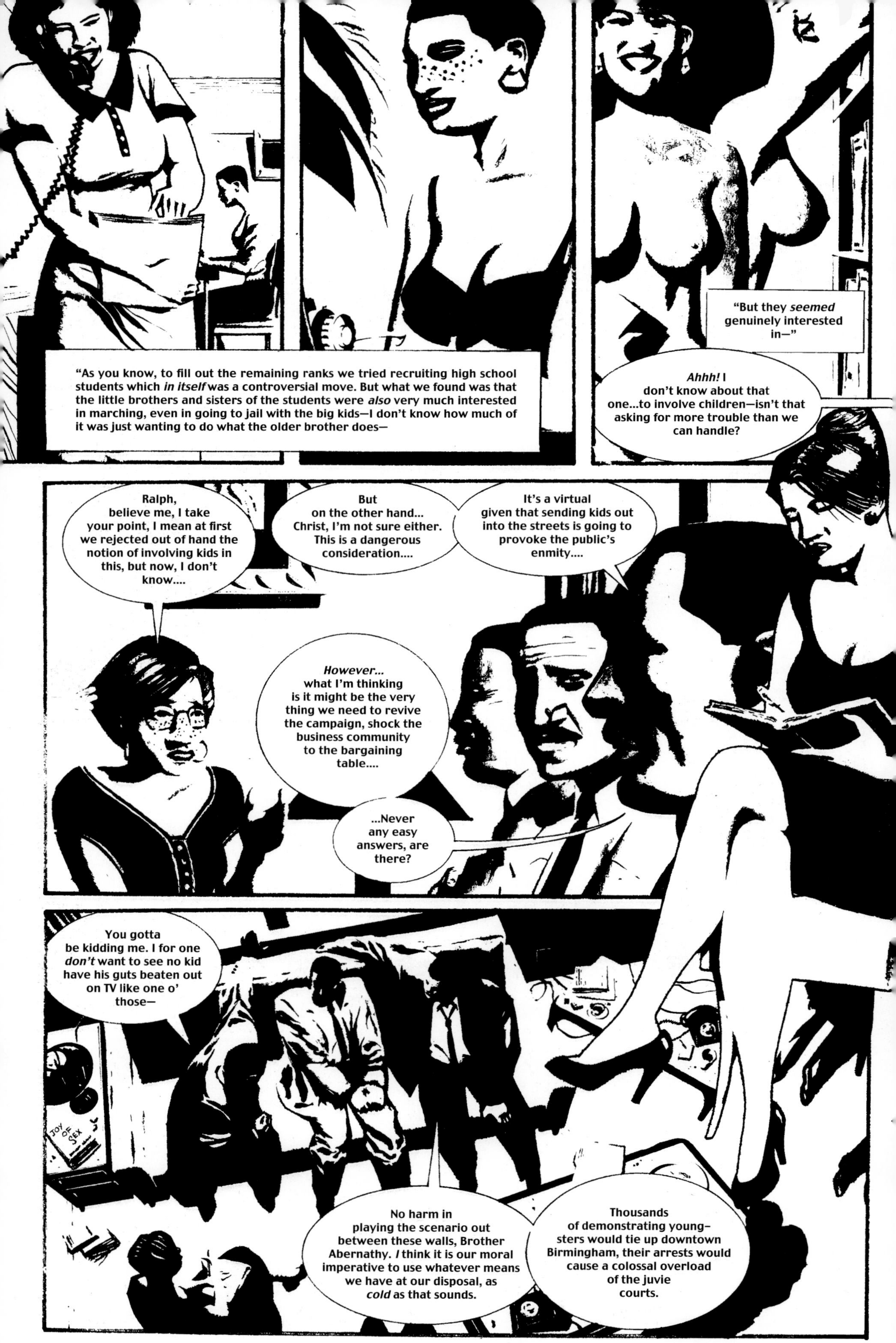
"As you know, to fill out the remaining ranks we tried recruiting high school students which *in itself* was a controversial move. But what we found was that the little brothers and sisters of the students were *also* very much interested in marching, even in going to jail with the big kids—I don't know how much of it was just wanting to do what the older brother does—
"But they *seemed* genuinely interested in—"
Ahhh! I don't know about that one...to involve children—isn't that asking for more trouble than we can handle?
Ralph, believe me, I take your point, I mean at first we rejected out of hand the notion of involving kids in this, but now, I don't know....
But on the other hand... Christ, I'm not sure either. This is a dangerous consideration....
It's a virtual given that sending kids out into the streets is going to provoke the public's enmity....
However... what I'm thinking is it might be the very thing we need to revive the campaign, shock the business community to the bargaining table....
...Never any easy answers, are there?
You gotta be kidding me. I for one *don't* want to see no kid have his guts beaten out on TV like one o' those—
JOY OF SEX
No harm in playing the scenario out between these walls, Brother Abernathy. *I* think it is our moral imperative to use whatever means we have at our disposal, as *cold* as that sounds.
Thousands of demonstrating young-sters would tie up downtown Birmingham, their arrests would cause a colossal overload of the juvie courts.

There are risks for kids in everyday life....
Hold on, what about the *injunction?* Aren't we forgetting...the thing is going into effect.
If we *march* we go to *jail.* And ML—
—If *you* go to jail then I'm sorry to say it, but the campaign's gonna head straight into the shitter. To put it bluntly.
—I've already gone on television and *proclaimed* I would march no matter what—*no matter what,* so tell me what other choice I have.
That's not true, Brother Shuttleworth. Look, if you want to give me a rundown on my options—
I back out now, I lose *all* credibility, assuming there's any *left* to lose.
Look... boys, girls, we've been working hard all day....
...Why don't we knock off for dinner, five minutes of play time....
—Will you please, *please,* keep your voice down, April, what's the matter with you? All I'm saying—

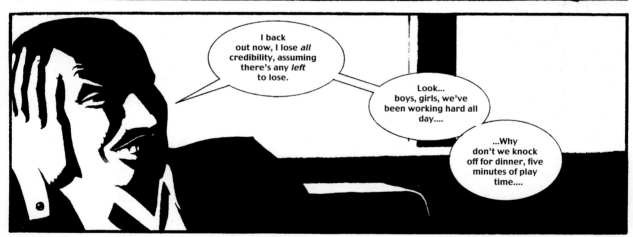

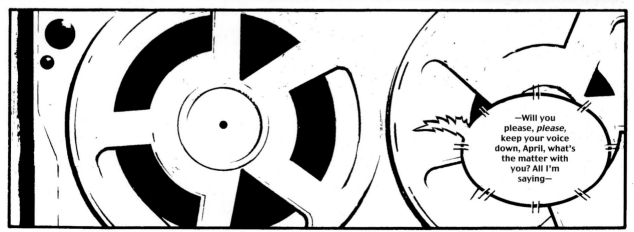

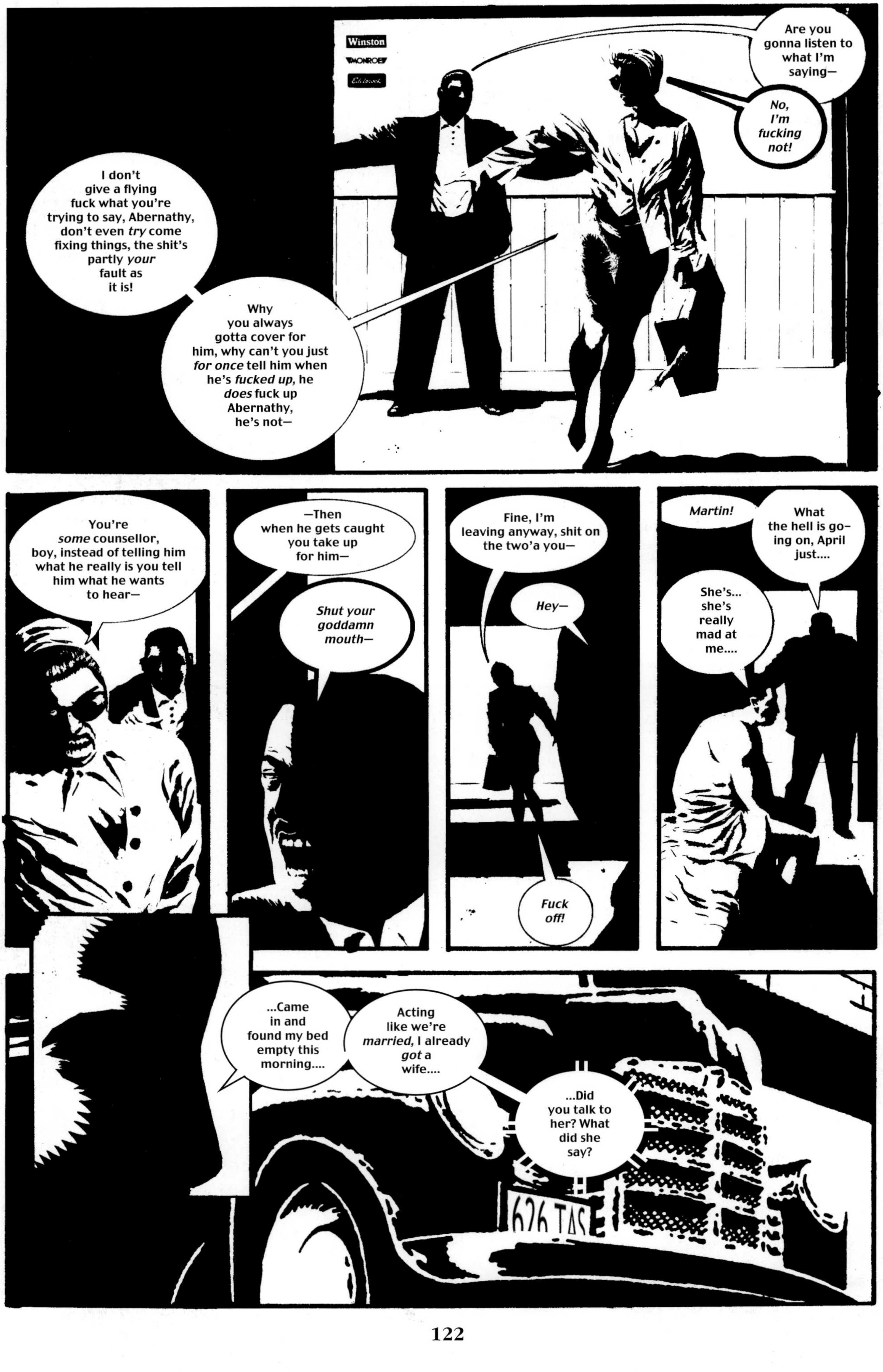
Winston
MONROE
Are you gonna listen to what I'm saying—
No, I'm fucking not!
I don't give a flying fuck what you're trying to say, Abernathy, don't even *try* come fixing things, the shit's partly *your* fault as it is!
Why you always gotta cover for him, why can't you just *for once* tell him when he's *fucked up,* he *does* fuck up Abernathy, he's not—
You're *some* counsellor, boy, instead of telling him what he really is you tell him what he wants to hear—
—Then when he gets caught you take up for him—
Shut your goddamn mouth—
Fine, I'm leaving anyway, shit on the two'a you—
Hey—
Fuck off!
Martin!
What the hell is going on, April just....
She's... she's really mad at me....
...Came in and found my bed empty this morning....
Acting like we're *married,* I already *got* a wife....
...Did you talk to her? What did she say?
626 TAS

"*Whoooff!* Boy, you *know* I let you win that one."

"[Pant....] *Heh,* yeah, I know, Brother Ralph...."

"*Heh, heh...*goddamn.... See, this party was the right idea, we need more of this kind of R&R, ML, pushing ourselves like we do, all of us, *especially* you...."

"Oh, don't start with that again, I'm not the only one working hard.

"I'm not about to start whining because I miss a few hours sleep, you said it yourself, we *all* need a rest.

"I know *you're* not getting as much sleep as you should either...."

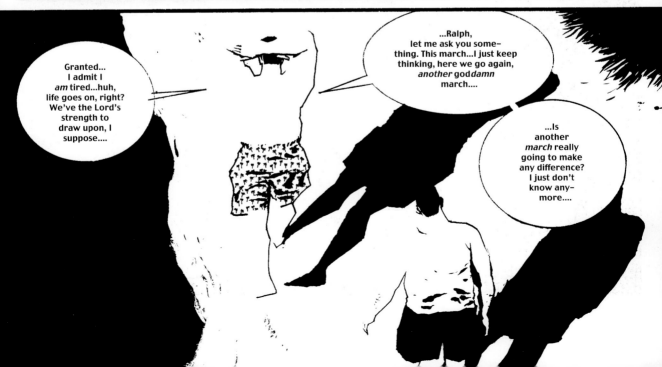

Granted... I admit I *am* tired...huh, life goes on, right? We've the Lord's strength to draw upon, I suppose....

...Ralph, let me ask you some- thing. This march...I just keep thinking, here we go again, *another* god*damn* march....

...Is another *march* really going to make any difference? I just don't know any- more....

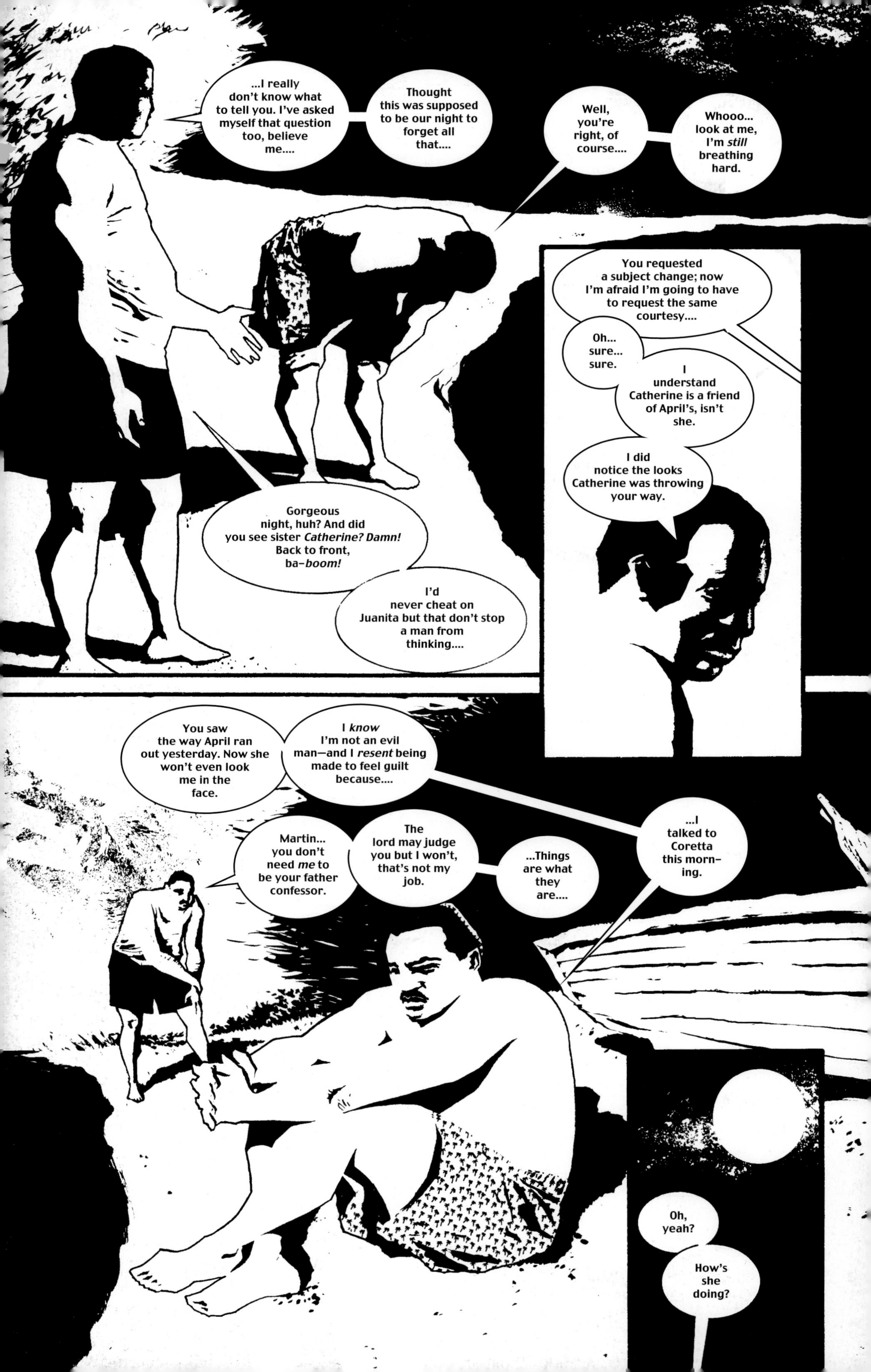
...I really don't know what to tell you. I've asked myself that question too, believe me....
Thought this was supposed to be our night to forget all that....
Well, you're right, of course....
Whooo... look at me, I'm *still* breathing hard.
Gorgeous night, huh? And did you see sister *Catherine? Damn!* Back to front, ba–*boom!*
I'd never cheat on Juanita but that don't stop a man from thinking....
You requested a subject change; now I'm afraid I'm going to have to request the same courtesy....
Oh... sure... sure.
I understand Catherine is a friend of April's, isn't she.
I did notice the looks Catherine was throwing your way.
You saw the way April ran out yesterday. Now she won't even look me in the face.
I *know* I'm not an evil man—and I *resent* being made to feel guilt because....
Martin... you don't need *me* to be your father confessor.
The lord may judge you but I won't, that's not my job.
...Things are what they are....
...I talked to Coretta this morn-ing.
Oh, yeah?
How's she doing?

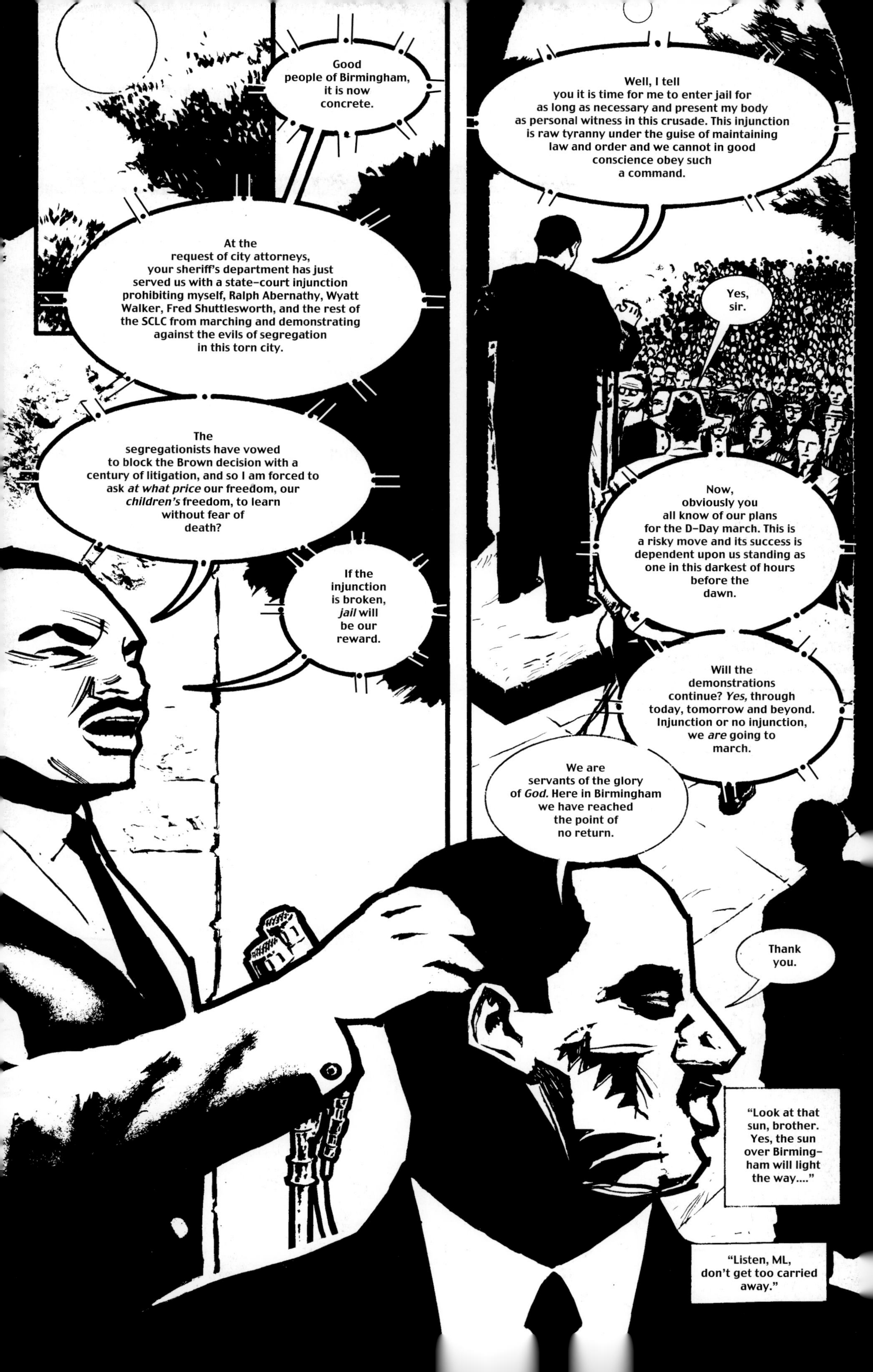
Good people of Birmingham, it is now concrete.
At the request of city attorneys, your sheriff's department has just served us with a state-court injunction prohibiting myself, Ralph Abernathy, Wyatt Walker, Fred Shuttlesworth, and the rest of the SCLC from marching and demonstrating against the evils of segregation in this torn city.
The segregationists have vowed to block the Brown decision with a century of litigation, and so I am forced to ask *at what price* our freedom, our *children's* freedom, to learn without fear of death?
If the injunction is broken, *jail* will be our reward.
Well, I tell you it is time for me to enter jail for as long as necessary and present my body as personal witness in this crusade. This injunction is raw tyranny under the guise of maintaining law and order and we cannot in good conscience obey such a command.
Yes, sir.
Now, obviously you all know of our plans for the D-Day march. This is a risky move and its success is dependent upon us standing as one in this darkest of hours before the dawn.
Will the demonstrations continue? *Yes,* through today, tomorrow and beyond. Injunction or no injunction, we *are* going to march.
We are servants of the glory of *God.* Here in Birmingham we have reached the point of no return.
Thank you.
"Look at that sun, brother. Yes, the sun over Birmingham will light the way...."
"Listen, ML, don't get too carried away."

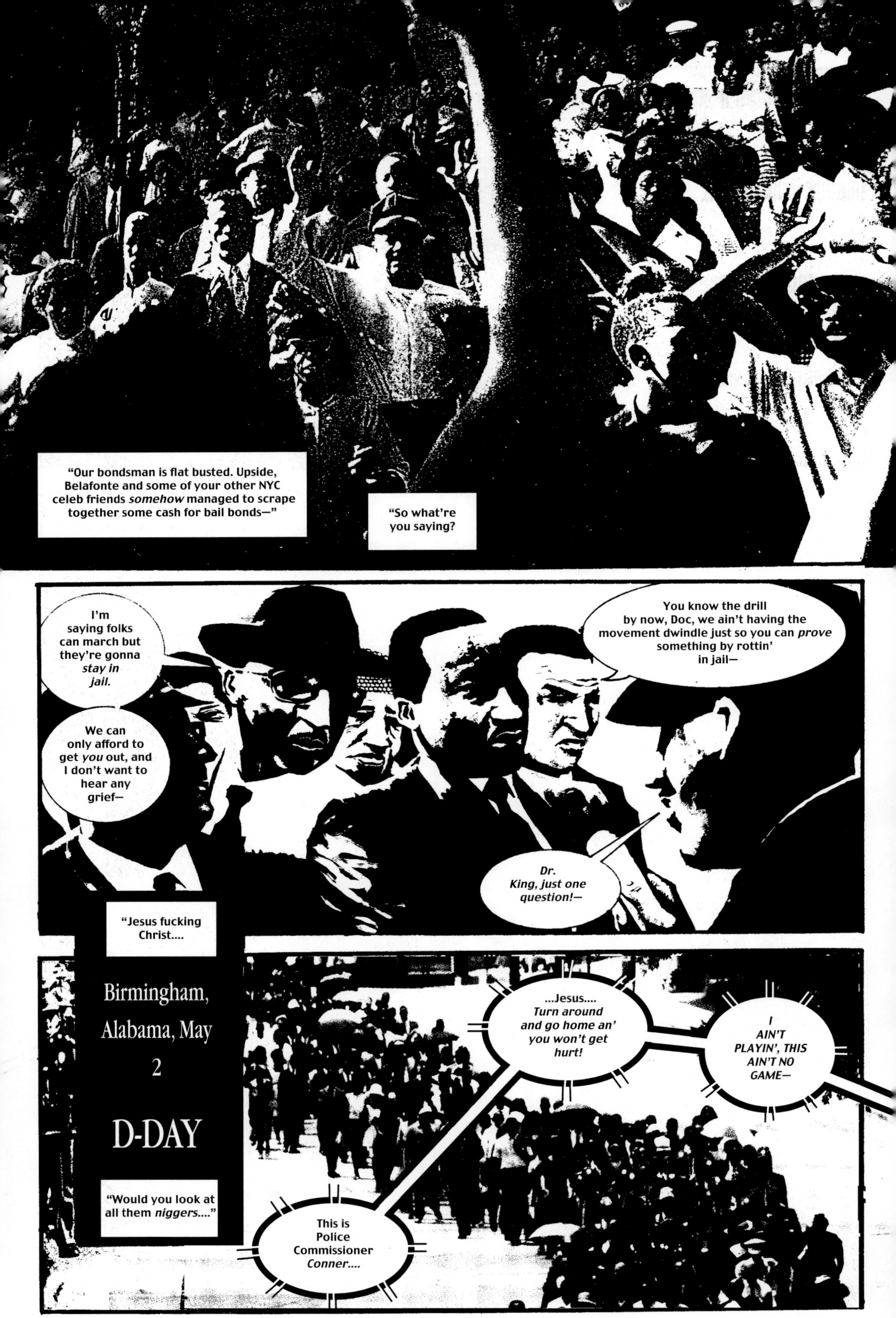
"Our bondsman is flat busted. Upside, Belafonte and some of your other NYC celeb friends *somehow* managed to scrape together some cash for bail bonds—"
"So what're you saying?
I'm saying folks can march but they're gonna *stay in jail.*
We can only afford to get *you* out, and I don't want to hear any grief—
You know the drill by now, Doc, we ain't having the movement dwindle just so you can *prove* something by rottin' in jail—
Dr. King, just one question!—
"Jesus fucking Christ....
Birmingham, Alabama, May 2
D-DAY
"Would you look at all them *niggers....*"
This is Police Commissioner *Conner....*
...Jesus.... Turn around and go home an' you won't get hurt!
I AIN'T PLAYIN', THIS AIN'T NO GAME—

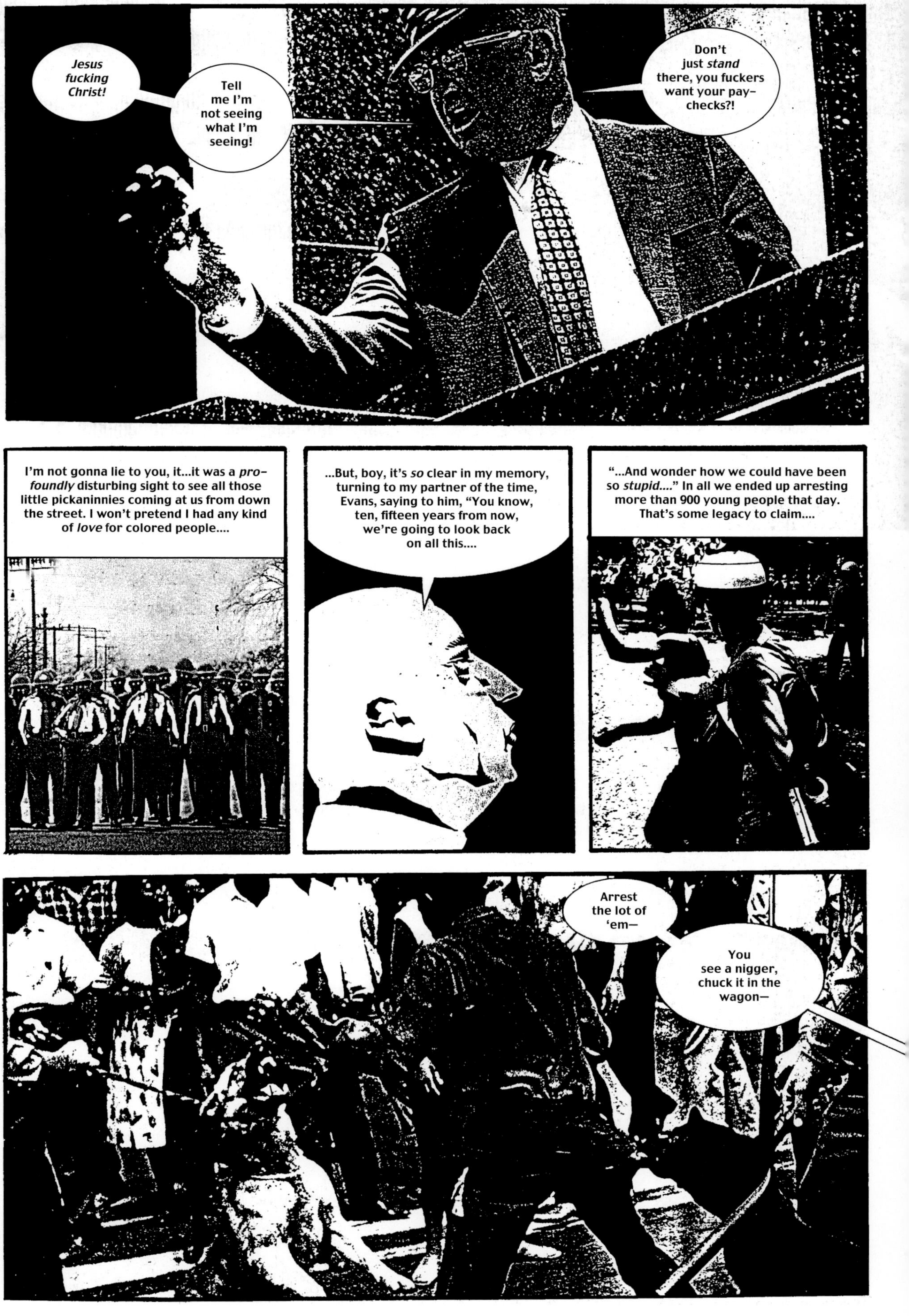
Jesus fucking Christ!
Tell me I'm not seeing what I'm seeing!
Don't just *stand* there, you fuckers want your pay-checks?!
I'm not gonna lie to you, it...it was a *pro-foundly* disturbing sight to see all those little pickaninnies coming at us from down the street. I won't pretend I had any kind of *love* for colored people....
...But, boy, it's *so* clear in my memory, turning to my partner of the time, Evans, saying to him, "You know, ten, fifteen years from now, we're going to look back on all this....
"...And wonder how we could have been so *stupid*...." In all we ended up arresting more than 900 young people that day. That's some legacy to claim....
Arrest the lot of 'em—
You see a nigger, chuck it in the wagon—

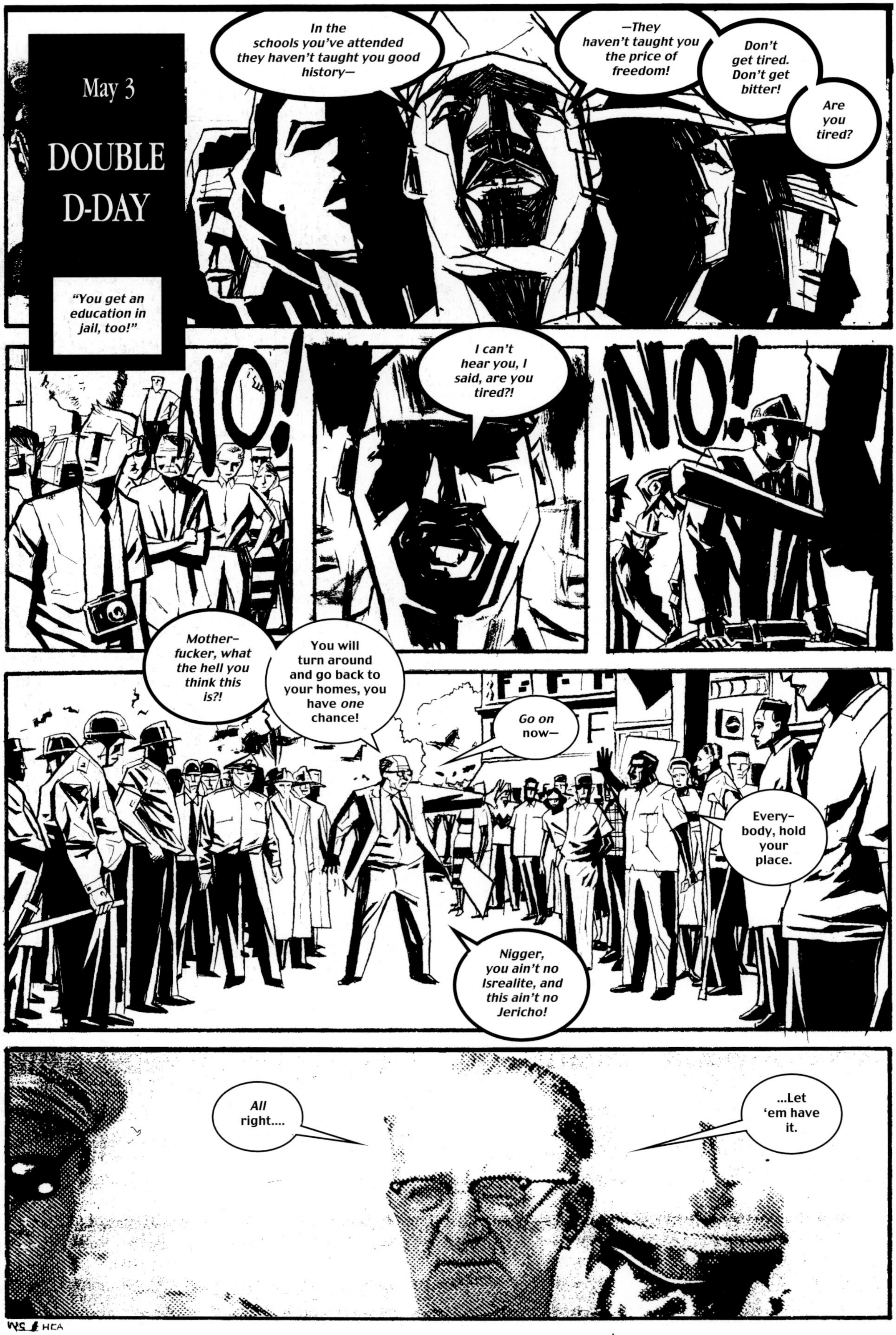
May 3
DOUBLE D-DAY
"You get an education in jail, too!"
In the schools you've attended they haven't taught you good history—
—They haven't taught you the price of freedom!
Don't get tired. Don't get bitter!
Are you tired?
NO!
I can't hear you, I said, are you tired?!
NO!
Mother-fucker, what the hell you think this is?!
You will turn around and go back to your homes, you have *one* chance!
Go on now—
Every-body, hold your place.
Nigger, you ain't no Isrealite, and this ain't no Jericho!
All right....
...Let 'em have it.

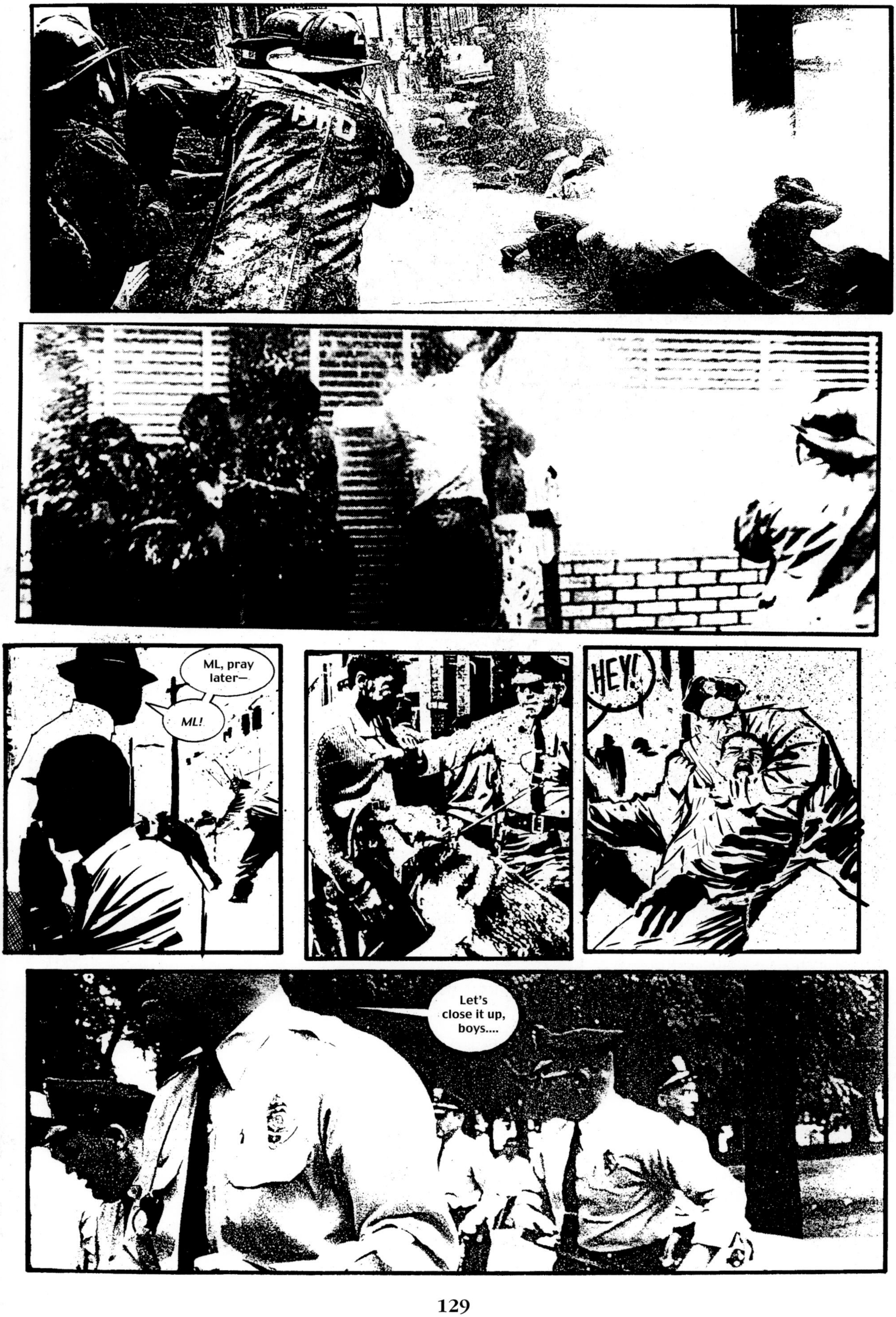
ML, pray later—
ML!
HEY!
Let's close it up, boys....

Martin King said, "Don't worry about your children in jail. The eyes of the world are on Birmingham." ...And he was right.

To see the photos of that mayhem, my kids and myself looking at them in the morning paper, and then that evening on the news... You have to wonder what it must *feel* like to be driven to that level of violence.

I never told anyone growing up I was half–negro, not even my husband, some–how I managed to pass. He's a good man, my husband...we tried to teach our kids differently, to say *colored* or *afro–American,* never that other word....

"How long we gotta put up with this *bull*shit? What, we gotta start *killing* people like Bull Connor?"

DOGS RELEASED ON INGRAM PARK PROTESTORS

By Junior Kirkpatrick

Ay yi yi, just when you think you've seen it all, straight out of left field, a boot to the head. Or in this case, a mouth on the groin—a german sheppard's mouth. Can anyone say *ouch?!* Listen, I'm no *nigger* lover but isn't this a bit much? I mean, a Negro, fine, but who's next. A dog on a Negro, I'm *talians?* Those wops got some dark skin but they're *still white.* And

"Connor, you all right, man, you doing the right thing."

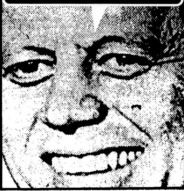

Frankly, what I saw in the papers made me sick. But unfortunately there's nothing I can legally do at this time to restrain Connor. ...In all candor, both the attorney general and myself feel the timing of this campaign

could have been handled with greater sensitivity. That said, we're not asking Dr. King or any of the other Negro leaders for patience. We can well understand why the Blacks of Birmingham have reached the limits of their patience.

THE RAMPAGE

scene ...aying dogs out of ...pitals filled ...octos ...the legs ...arts. police ...gene out the ...the ...had

who reportedly saw Connor on a Jim Bean date with an underage blonde in Vegas! Now, we're not usually ones for gossip, but c'mon, you get a story like that you tell me *you're* not gonna print it? Yeah, right. Listen, don't get all moral on me, we got reporters, we know where you live, we can find stuff out real easy–like, so keep your nose clean, nimrod.

Fellow Americans, this nation was founded on the principle that all men are created equal, that the rights of every man are diminished when the rights of one man are threatened. Every American has the right to attend any public institution, enjoy equal service in any

public facility, and register and vote without having to take to the streets or call for federal troops. We are confronted primarily with a moral issue as old as the scriptures and as dear as the American con–stitution: whether all Americans are to be afforded equal rights

and equal opportunities. We claim we're the land of the free, and we are, except for Negroes. The time has come for America to remove the blight of racial discrimination and fulfill her brilliant promise.

I shall ask Congress... to make a commitment it has not fully made in this century, to the pro-position that race has no place in American life or law.

Stay out of trouble.

Thank you, officer....

ML, my brother, you look like the scum of the Earth.

No, I mean it, you look like shit.

You *smell* great as well.

Light me one of those too. God, we both look like a couple of hobos.

And that sun, boy....

Feel the sun on your face.

Yeah, it's all right—

...The sun over Birmingham will light the way. The Lord himself will light the way....

Hey—

HONK! HONK!

How you doing, Doc?

Come to pick you up.

Baby....

To our White brothers across the South who try to keep us down, we say we will match your capacity to inflict suffering with our capacity to endure it. We will meet your physical force with soul force.

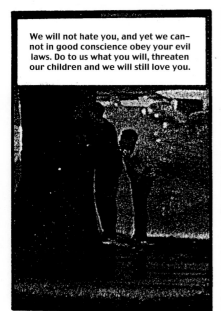

We will not hate you, and yet we can-not in good conscience obey your evil laws. Do to us what you will, threaten our children and we will still love you.

Bomb our homes and go by our churches and bomb them, and we will still love you. The victory will be *ours.* In winning this victory, we will not only win our freedom.

We will so appeal to your heart and your conscience that we will win *you* in the process. In the end the vic-tory will belong to us *all.*

I always felt that King was a god-*damn pussy.* If someone steps up to me with intent to cause bodily harm there's no way I'ma just *stand* there with my arms open, *try* 'n' explain that. Y'know, *Malcolm* once said—

May 5, it was a glorious day. By now more than 3000 of us were in jail—the demonstrations just droned on and on, we would not be discouraged. Well, this day was the largest demonstration so far, nearly 3000 strong.

We approached Connor and his wall of dogs and firemen and cops, getting to be a regular thing. Before we reached them we knelt in unison and began to pray: "We want our freedom, we've done nothing wrong, we want our freedom," the Blacks cried, you had Blacks and Whites in unison.

Well, Connor went crazy, screaming at his men to turn the dogs loose, to turn on the hoses. ...And they just *stood* there. And they let us pass, we just passed through the ranks as though.... I mean...some of the firemen were *crying.*

Can't say if it was maybe inspired by the speech Kennedy had delivered or if they were, I don't know, momentarily in touch with our plight or *what* it was. I have never seen anything like it in my life.

And I felt great for Dr. King, this was a wonderful demonstration of non-violence over violence. It was working, you could see it live in front of you.

After Birmingham a newspaper poll of Blacks indicated that 95% of us regarded King as our most successful spokesman, ahead of Thurgood Marshall, James Meredith, Roy Wilkins....

...Ahead of *Thurgood Marshall* my Black ass. King was a *tom,* intent on gaining so-called victories solely by appeasing the White man. Malcolm *also* said—

Eventually, with the aid of Assistant Attorney General for Civil Rights Burke Marshall, round-the-clock negotiations over the Birmingham Manifesto were conducted, with King and his committee—

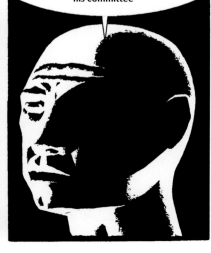

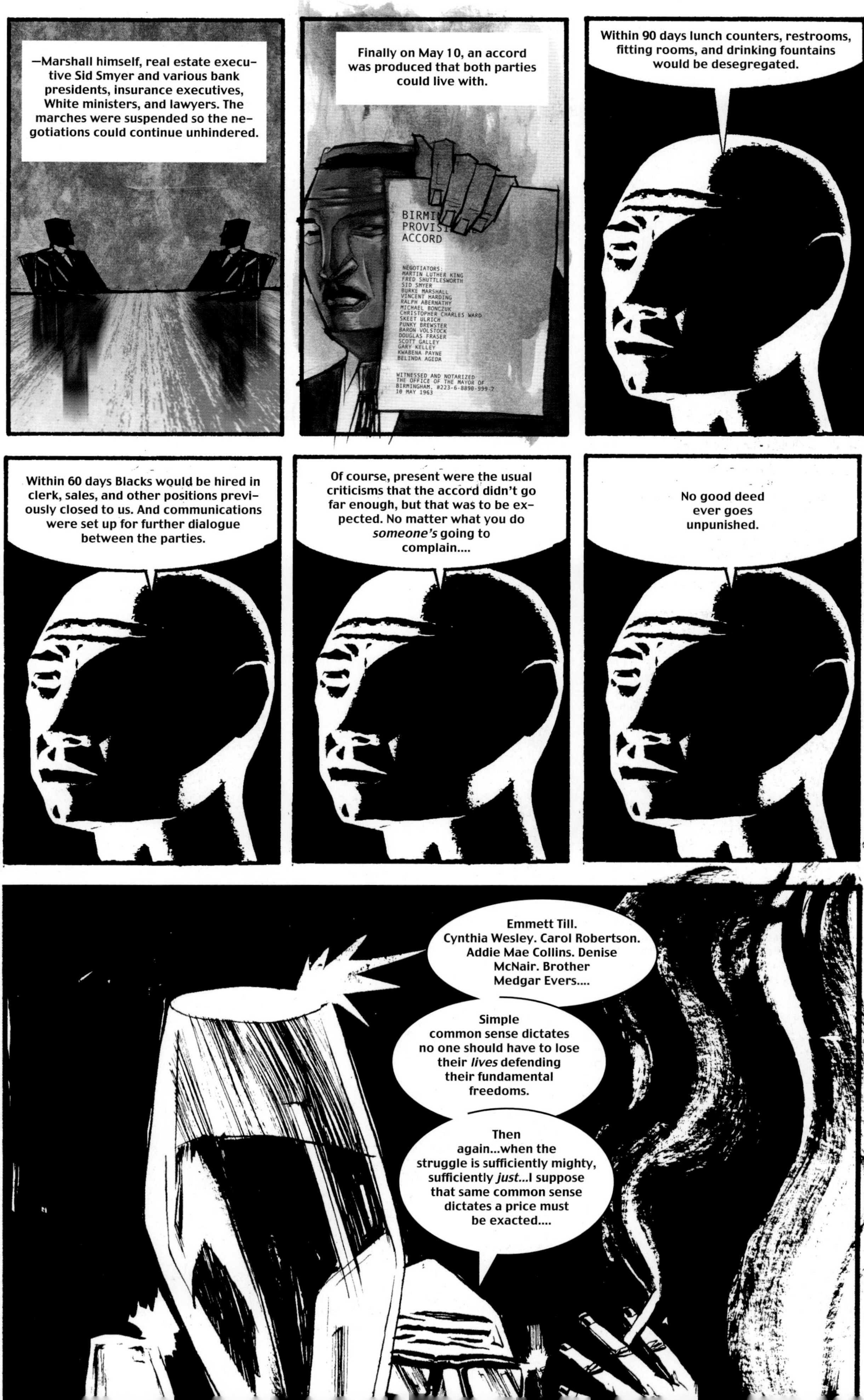
—Marshall himself, real estate executive Sid Smyer and various bank presidents, insurance executives, White ministers, and lawyers. The marches were suspended so the negotiations could continue unhindered.
Finally on May 10, an accord was produced that both parties could live with.
BIRMI
PROVISI
ACCORD
NEGOTIATORS:
MARTIN LUTHER KING
FRED SHUTTLESWORTH
SID SMYER
BURKE MARSHALL
VINCENT HARDING
RALPH ABERNATHY
MICHAEL BONCZUK
CHRISTOPHER CHARLES WARD
SKEET ULRICH
PUNKY BREWSTER
BARON VOLSTOCK
DOUGLAS FRASER
SCOTT GALLEY
GARY KELLEY
KWABENA PAYNE
BELINDA AGEDA
WITNESSED AND NOTARIZED
THE OFFICE OF THE MAYOR OF
BIRMINGHAM, #223-6-8890-999-7
10 MAY 1963
Within 90 days lunch counters, restrooms, fitting rooms, and drinking fountains would be desegregated.
Within 60 days Blacks would be hired in clerk, sales, and other positions previously closed to us. And communications were set up for further dialogue between the parties.
Of course, present were the usual criticisms that the accord didn't go far enough, but that was to be expected. No matter what you do *someone's* going to complain....
No good deed ever goes unpunished.
Emmett Till. Cynthia Wesley. Carol Robertson. Addie Mae Collins. Denise McNair. Brother Medgar Evers....
Simple common sense dictates no one should have to lose their *lives* defending their fundamental freedoms.
Then again...when the struggle is sufficiently mighty, sufficiently *just*...I suppose that same common sense dictates a price must be exacted....

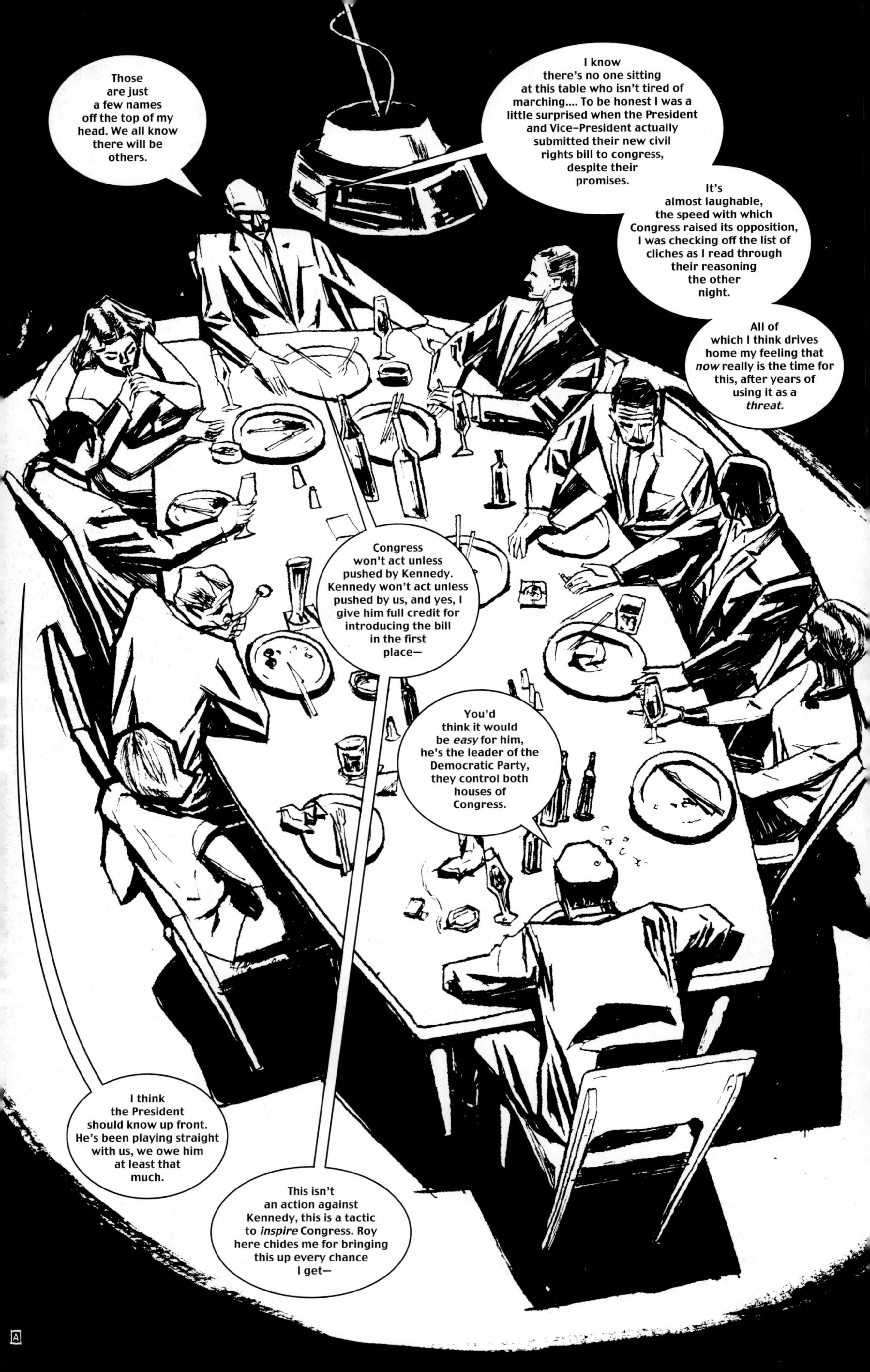
Those are just a few names off the top of my head. We all know there will be others.
I know there's no one sitting at this table who isn't tired of marching.... To be honest I was a little surprised when the President and Vice-President actually submitted their new civil rights bill to congress, despite their promises.
It's almost laughable, the speed with which Congress raised its opposition, I was checking off the list of cliches as I read through their reasoning the other night.
All of which I think drives home my feeling that *now* really is the time for this, after years of using it as a *threat.*
Congress won't act unless pushed by Kennedy. Kennedy won't act unless pushed by us, and yes, I give him full credit for introducing the bill in the first place—
You'd think it would be *easy* for him, he's the leader of the Democratic Party, they control both houses of Congress.
I think the President should know up front. He's been playing straight with us, we owe him at least that much.
This isn't an action against Kennedy, this is a tactic to *inspire* Congress. Roy here chides me for bringing this up every chance I get—

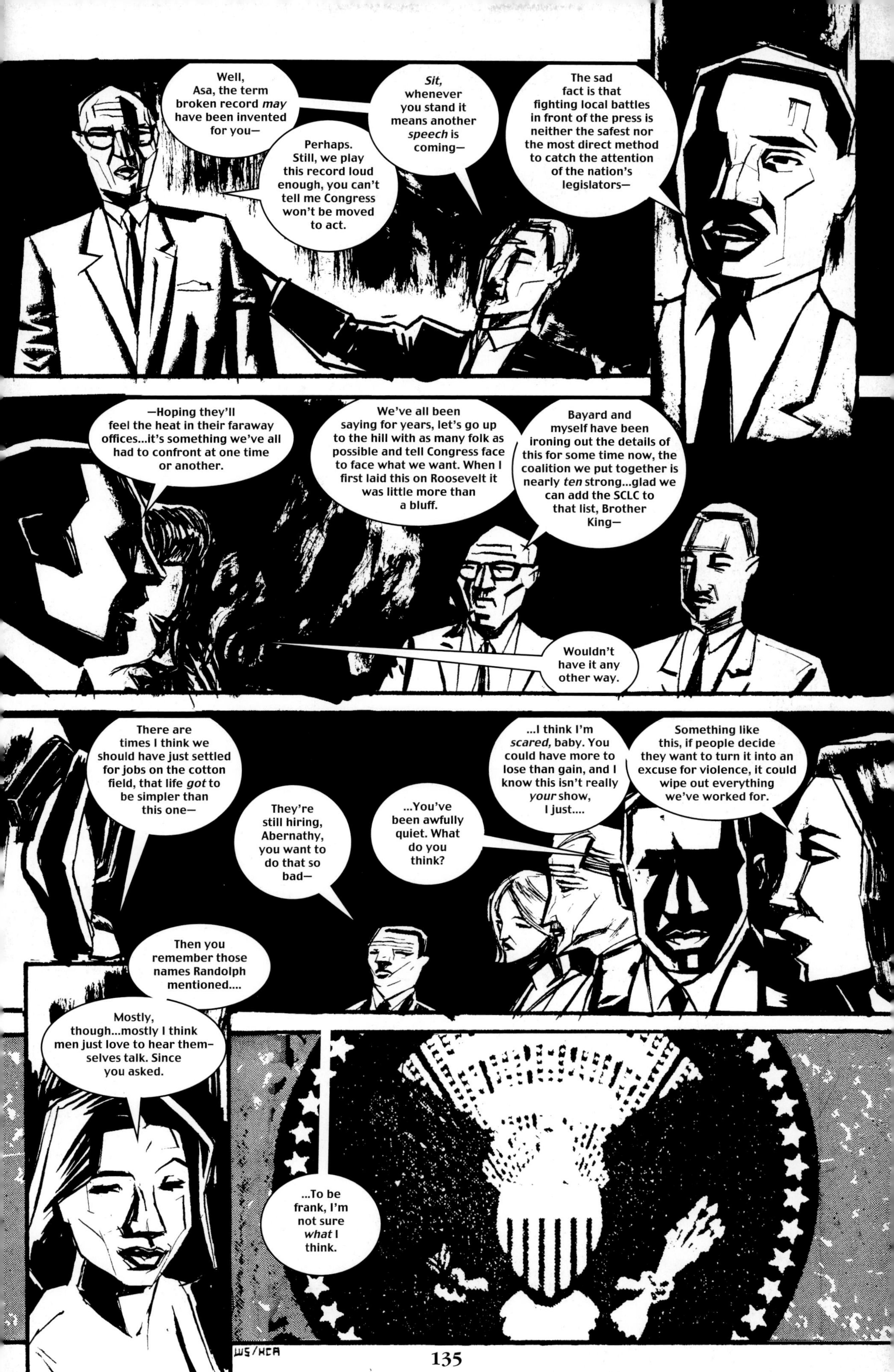
Well, Asa, the term broken record *may* have been invented for you—
Perhaps. Still, we play this record loud enough, you can't tell me Congress won't be moved to act.
Sit, whenever you stand it means another *speech* is coming—
The sad fact is that fighting local battles in front of the press is neither the safest nor the most direct method to catch the attention of the nation's legislators—
—Hoping they'll feel the heat in their faraway offices...it's something we've all had to confront at one time or another.
We've all been saying for years, let's go up to the hill with as many folk as possible and tell Congress face to face what we want. When I first laid this on Roosevelt it was little more than a bluff.
Bayard and myself have been ironing out the details of this for some time now, the coalition we put together is nearly *ten* strong...glad we can add the SCLC to that list, Brother King—
Wouldn't have it any other way.
There are times I think we should have just settled for jobs on the cotton field, that life *got* to be simpler than this one—
They're still hiring, Abernathy, you want to do that so bad—
...You've been awfully quiet. What do you think?
...I think I'm *scared,* baby. You could have more to lose than gain, and I know this isn't really *your* show, I just....
Something like this, if people decide they want to turn it into an excuse for violence, it could wipe out everything we've worked for.
Then you remember those names Randolph mentioned....
Mostly, though...mostly I think men just love to hear themselves talk. Since you asked.
...To be frank, I'm not sure *what* I think.
WS/HCA

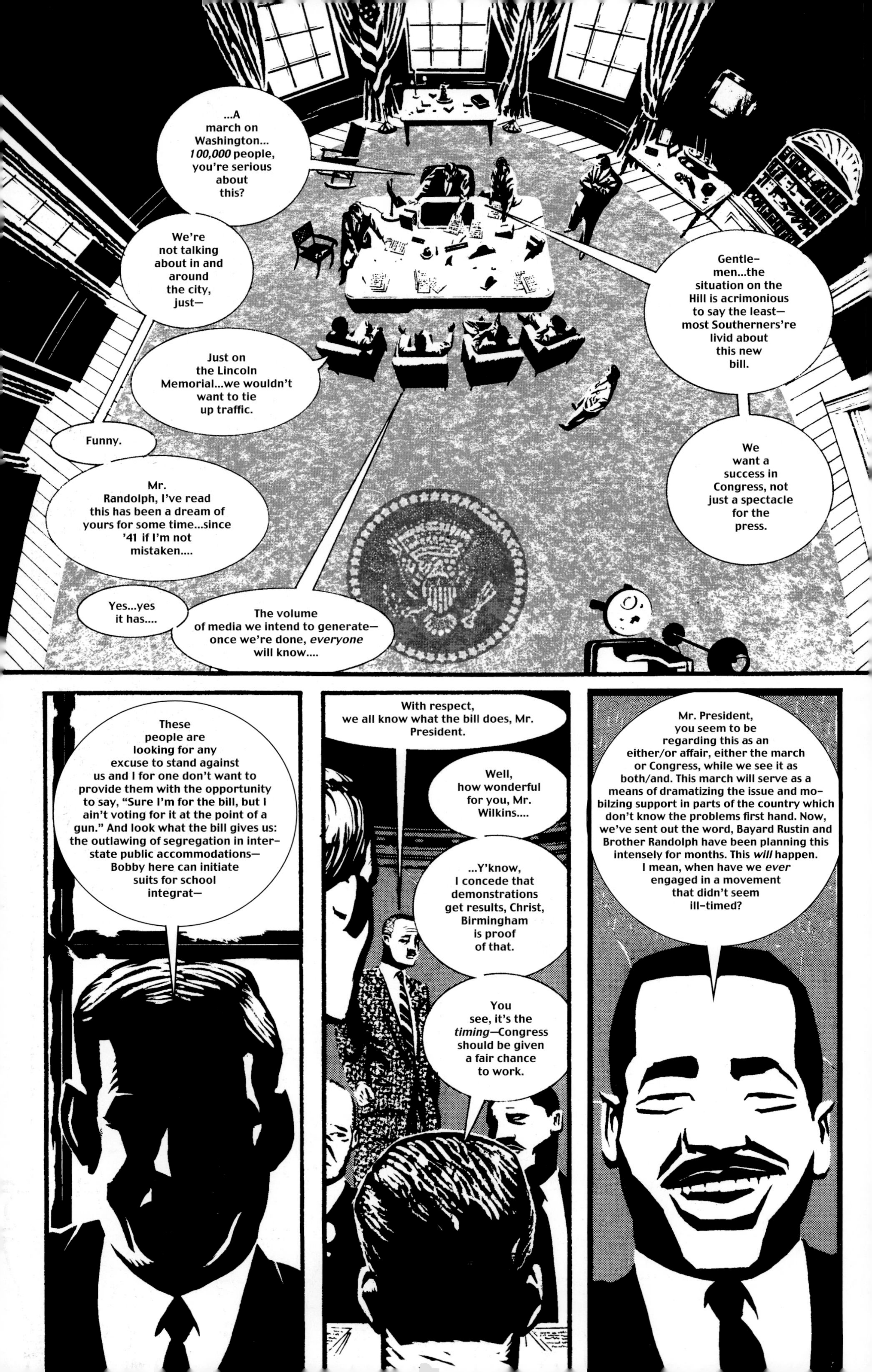
...A march on Washington... *100,000* people, you're serious about this?
We're not talking about in and around the city, just—
Just on the Lincoln Memorial...we wouldn't want to tie up traffic.
Funny.
Mr. Randolph, I've read this has been a dream of yours for some time...since '41 if I'm not mistaken....
Yes...yes it has....
The volume of media we intend to generate— once we're done, *everyone* will know....
Gentle—men...the situation on the Hill is acrimonious to say the least— most Southerners're livid about this new bill.
We want a success in Congress, not just a spectacle for the press.
These people are looking for any excuse to stand against us and I for one don't want to provide them with the opportunity to say, "Sure I'm for the bill, but I ain't voting for it at the point of a gun." And look what the bill gives us: the outlawing of segregation in interstate public accommodations— Bobby here can initiate suits for school integrat—
With respect, we all know what the bill does, Mr. President.
Well, how wonderful for you, Mr. Wilkins....
...Y'know, I concede that demonstrations get results, Christ, Birmingham is proof of that.
You see, it's the *timing*—Congress should be given a fair chance to work.
Mr. President, you seem to be regarding this as an either/or affair, either the march or Congress, while we see it as both/and. This march will serve as a means of dramatizing the issue and mobilzing support in parts of the country which don't know the problems first hand. Now, we've sent out the word, Bayard Rustin and Brother Randolph have been planning this intensely for months. This *will* happen. I mean, when have we *ever* engaged in a movement that didn't seem ill-timed?

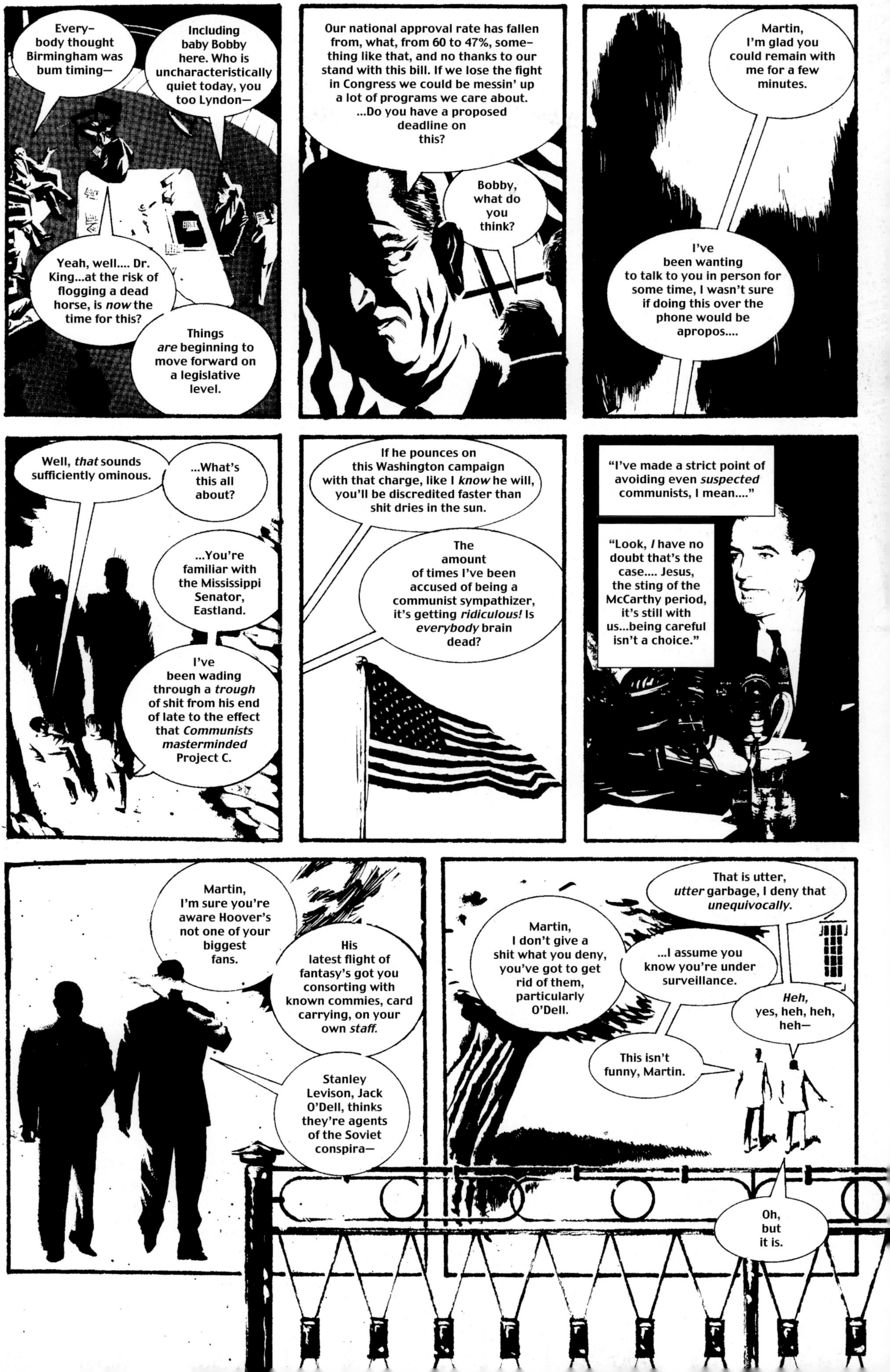

Every- body thought Birmingham was bum timing—
Including baby Bobby here. Who is uncharacteristically quiet today, you too Lyndon—
Yeah, well.... Dr. King...at the risk of flogging a dead horse, is *now* the time for this?
Things *are* beginning to move forward on a legislative level.
Our national approval rate has fallen from, what, from 60 to 47%, some- thing like that, and no thanks to our stand with this bill. If we lose the fight in Congress we could be messin' up a lot of programs we care about. ...Do you have a proposed deadline on this?
Bobby, what do you think?
Martin, I'm glad you could remain with me for a few minutes.
I've been wanting to talk to you in person for some time, I wasn't sure if doing this over the phone would be apropos....
Well, *that* sounds sufficiently ominous.
...What's this all about?
...You're familiar with the Mississippi Senator, Eastland.
I've been wading through a *trough* of shit from his end of late to the effect that *Communists masterminded* Project C.
If he pounces on this Washington campaign with that charge, like I *know* he will, you'll be discredited faster than shit dries in the sun.
The amount of times I've been accused of being a communist sympathizer, it's getting *ridiculous!* Is *everybody* brain dead?
"I've made a strict point of avoiding even *suspected* communists, I mean...."
"Look, *I* have no doubt that's the case.... Jesus, the sting of the McCarthy period, it's still with us...being careful isn't a choice."
Martin, I'm sure you're aware Hoover's not one of your biggest fans.
His latest flight of fantasy's got you consorting with known commies, card carrying, on your own *staff.*
Stanley Levison, Jack O'Dell, thinks they're agents of the Soviet conspira—
That is utter, *utter* garbage, I deny that *unequivocally.*
Martin, I don't give a shit what you deny, you've got to get rid of them, particularly O'Dell.
...I assume you know you're under surveillance.
Heh, yes, heh, heh, heh—
This isn't funny, Martin.
Oh, but it is.

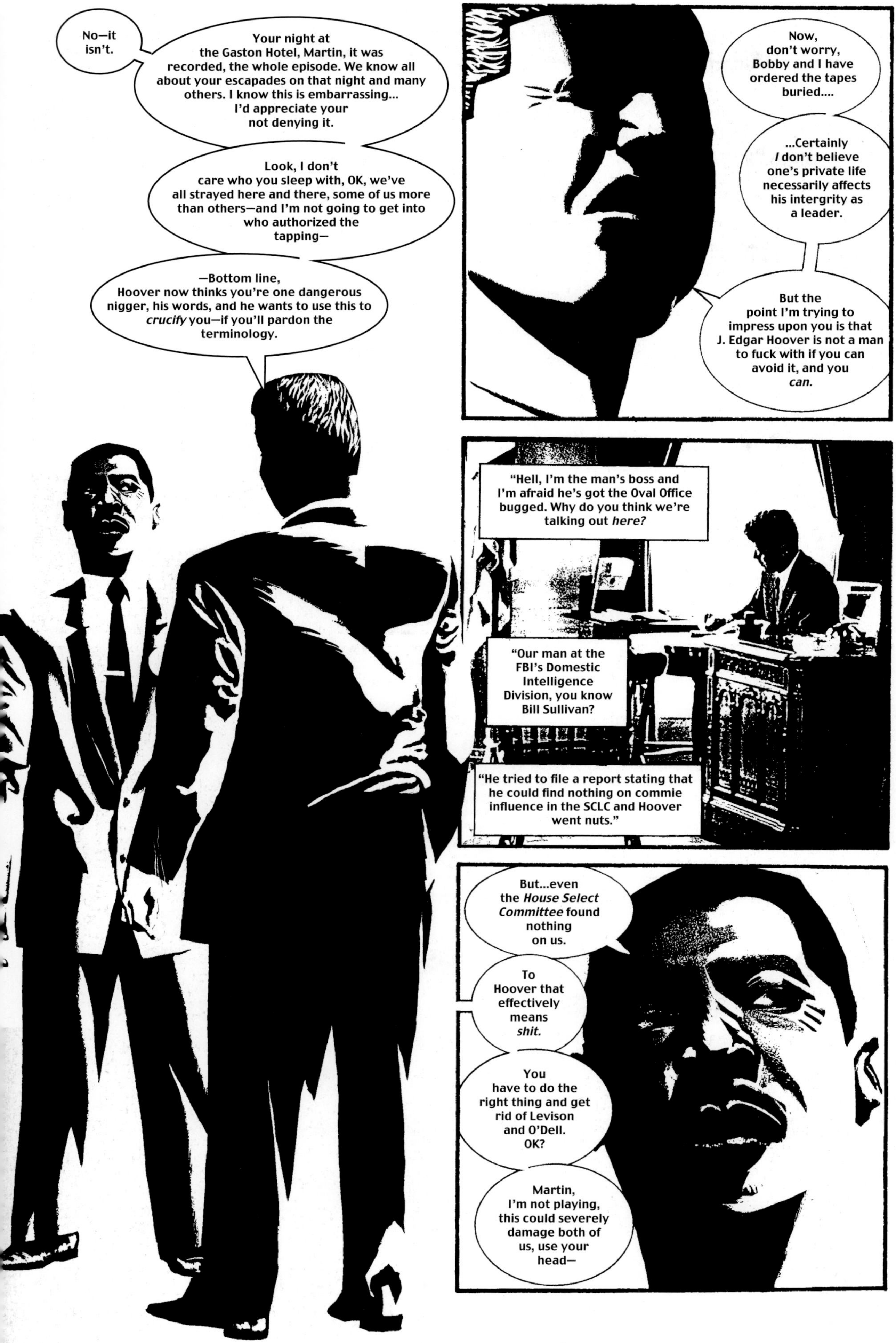
No—it isn't.
Your night at the Gaston Hotel, Martin, it was recorded, the whole episode. We know all about your escapades on that night and many others. I know this is embarrassing... I'd appreciate your not denying it.
Look, I don't care who you sleep with, OK, we've all strayed here and there, some of us more than others—and I'm not going to get into who authorized the tapping—
—Bottom line, Hoover now thinks you're one dangerous nigger, his words, and he wants to use this to *crucify* you—if you'll pardon the terminology.
Now, don't worry, Bobby and I have ordered the tapes buried....
...Certainly *I* don't believe one's private life necessarily affects his intergrity as a leader.
But the point I'm trying to impress upon you is that J. Edgar Hoover is not a man to fuck with if you can avoid it, and you *can.*
"Hell, I'm the man's boss and I'm afraid he's got the Oval Office bugged. Why do you think we're talking out *here?*
"Our man at the FBI's Domestic Intelligence Division, you know Bill Sullivan?
"He tried to file a report stating that he could find nothing on commie influence in the SCLC and Hoover went nuts."
But...even the *House Select Committee* found nothing on us.
To Hoover that effectively means *shit.*
You have to do the right thing and get rid of Levison and O'Dell. OK?
Martin, I'm not playing, this could severely damage both of us, use your head—

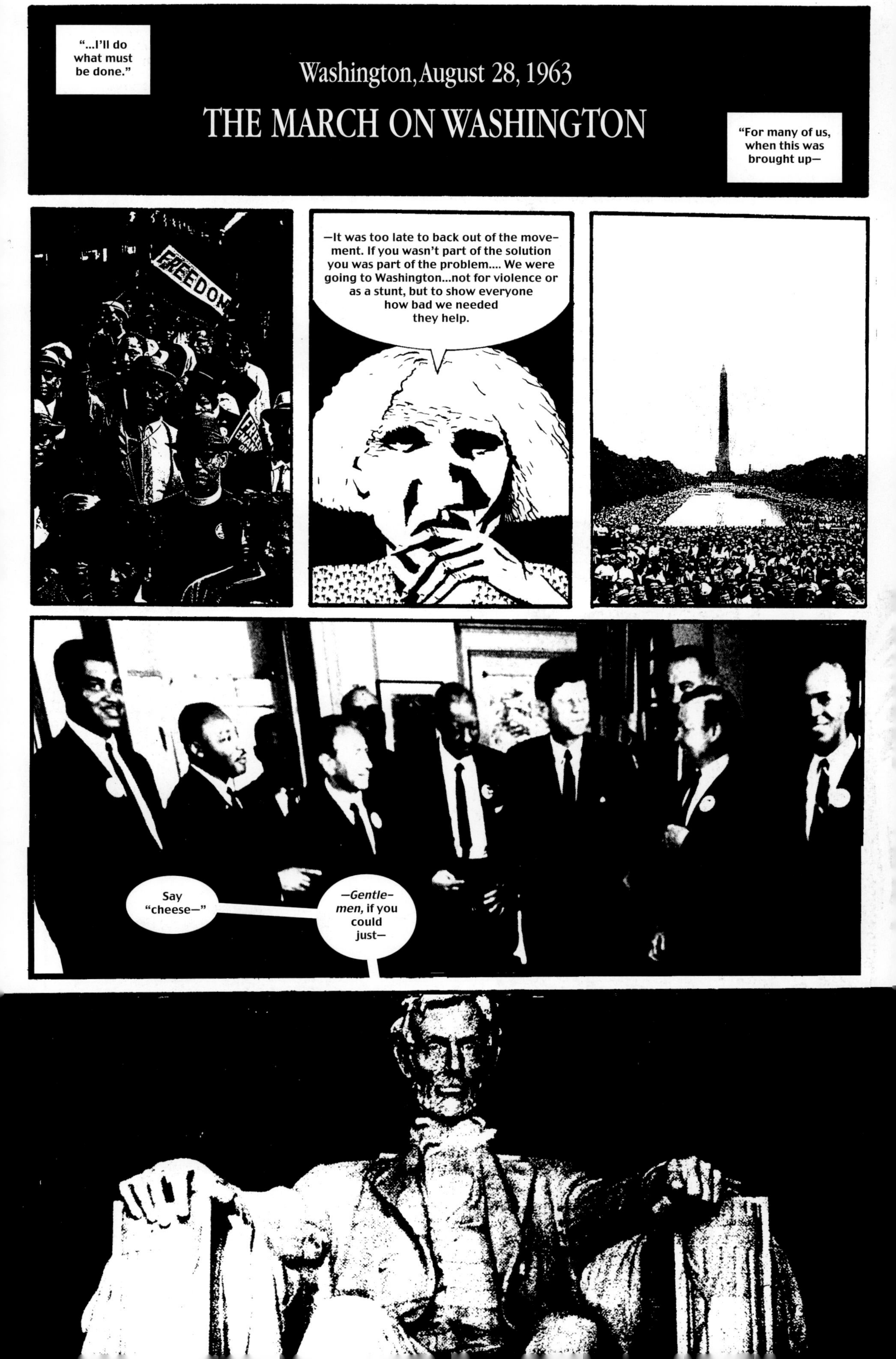
"...I'll do what must be done."
Washington, August 28, 1963
THE MARCH ON WASHINGTON
"For many of us, when this was brought up—
FREEDOM
—It was too late to back out of the movement. If you wasn't part of the solution you was part of the problem.... We were going to Washington...not for violence or as a stunt, but to show everyone how bad we needed they help.
Say "cheese—"
—*Gentlemen,* if you could just—

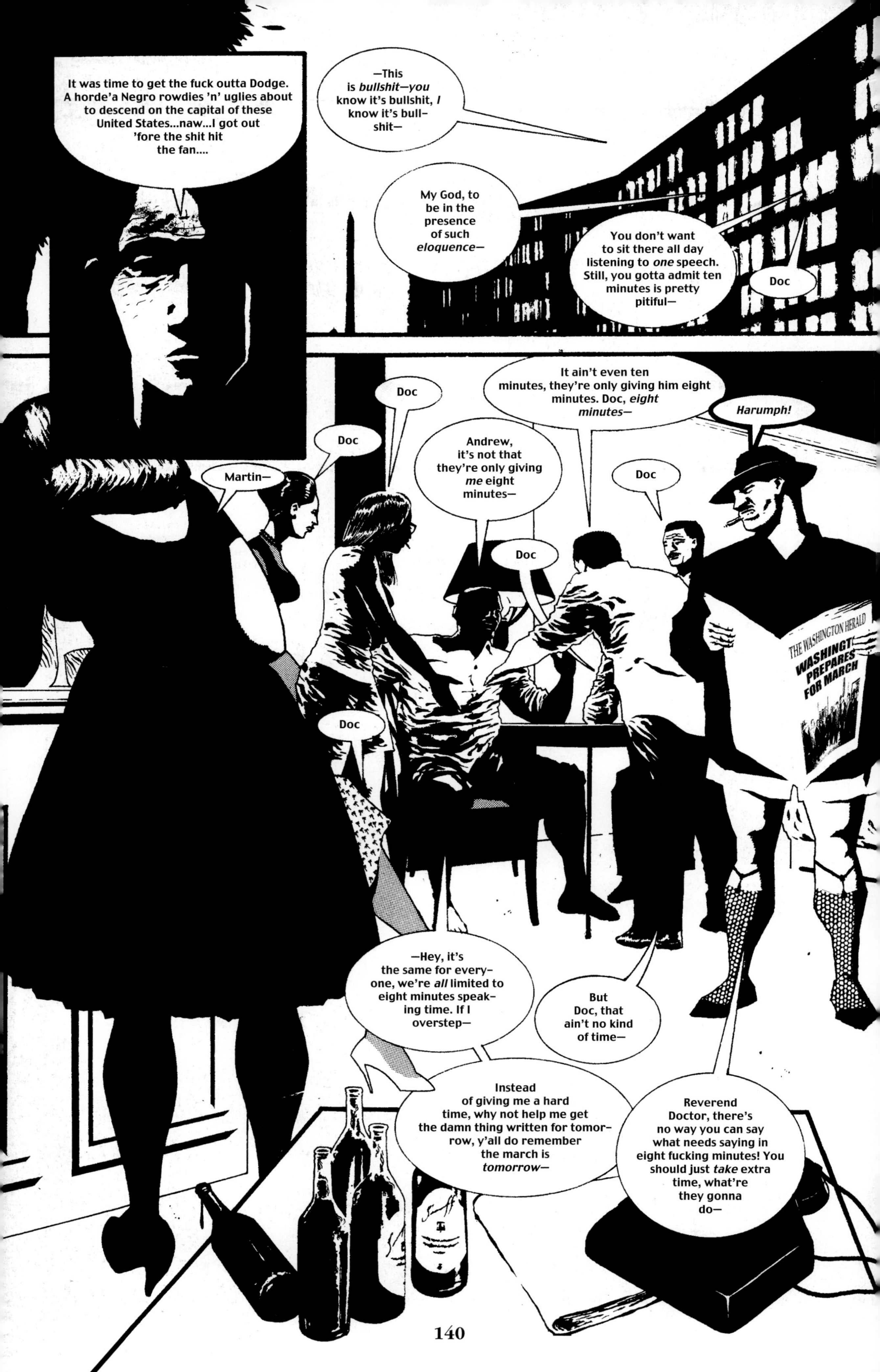

It was time to get the fuck outta Dodge. A horde'a Negro rowdies 'n' uglies about to descend on the capital of these United States...naw...I got out 'fore the shit hit the fan....
—This is *bullshit*—*you* know it's bullshit, *I* know it's bull-shit—
My God, to be in the presence of such *eloquence*—
You don't want to sit there all day listening to *one* speech. Still, you gotta admit ten minutes is pretty pitiful—
Doc
Martin—
Doc
Doc
It ain't even ten minutes, they're only giving him eight minutes. Doc, *eight minutes*—
Andrew, it's not that they're only giving *me* eight minutes—
Harumph!
Doc
Doc
THE WASHINGTON HERALD
WASHINGT PREPARES FOR MARCH
Doc
—Hey, it's the same for every-one, we're *all* limited to eight minutes speak-ing time. If I overstep—
But Doc, that ain't no kind of time—
Instead of giving me a hard time, why not help me get the damn thing written for tomor-row, y'all do remember the march is *tomorrow*—
Reverend Doctor, there's no way you can say what needs saying in eight fucking minutes! You should just *take* extra time, what're they gonna do—

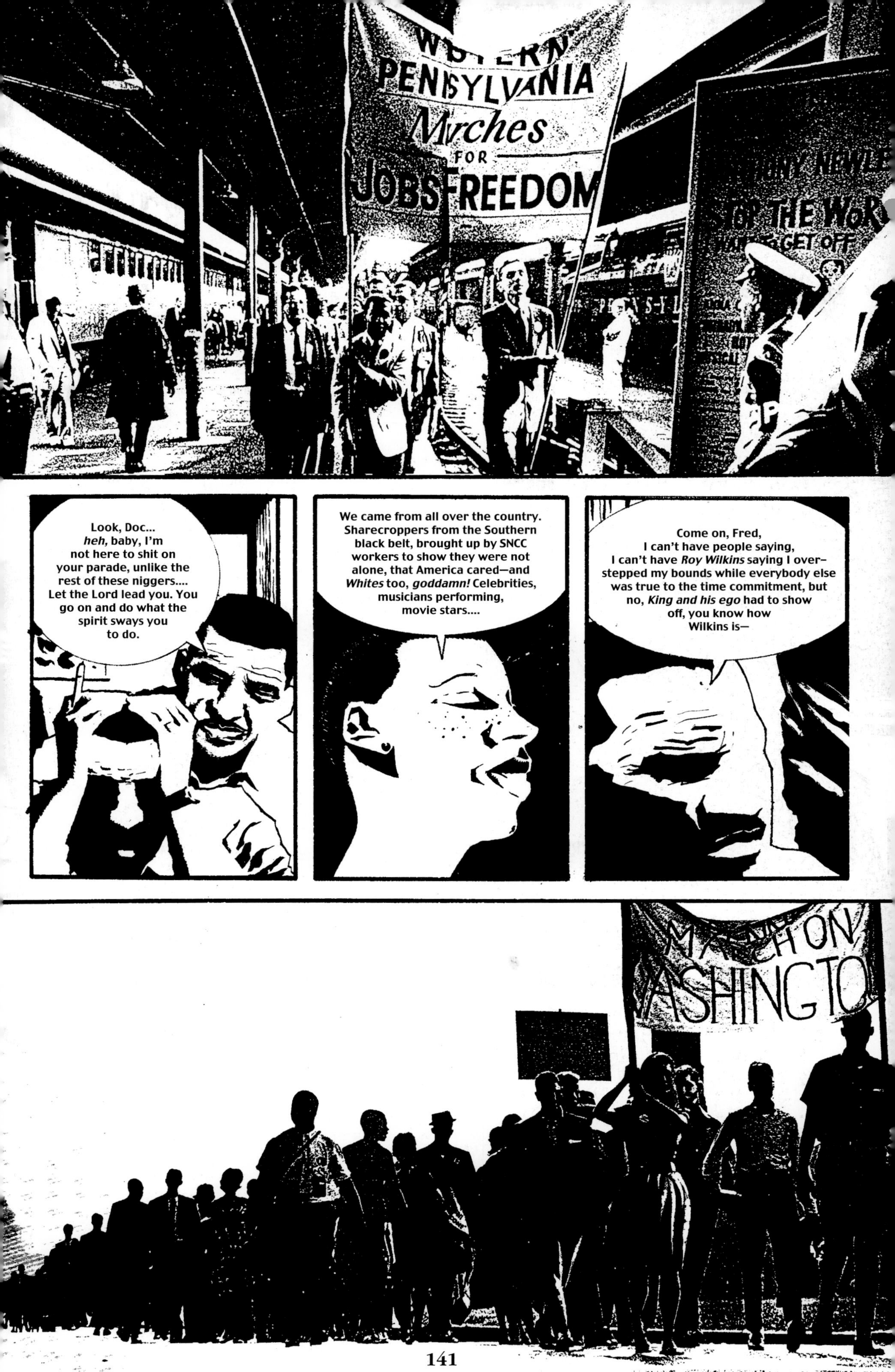
PENNSYLVANIA
FOR
JOBS FREEDOM
Look, Doc... *heh,* baby, I'm not here to shit on your parade, unlike the rest of these niggers.... Let the Lord lead you. You go on and do what the spirit sways you to do.
We came from all over the country. Sharecroppers from the Southern black belt, brought up by SNCC workers to show they were not alone, that America cared—and *Whites* too, *goddamn!* Celebrities, musicians performing, movie stars....
Come on, Fred, I can't have people saying, I can't have *Roy Wilkins* saying I over-stepped my bounds while everybody else was true to the time commitment, but no, *King and his ego* had to show off, you know how Wilkins is—

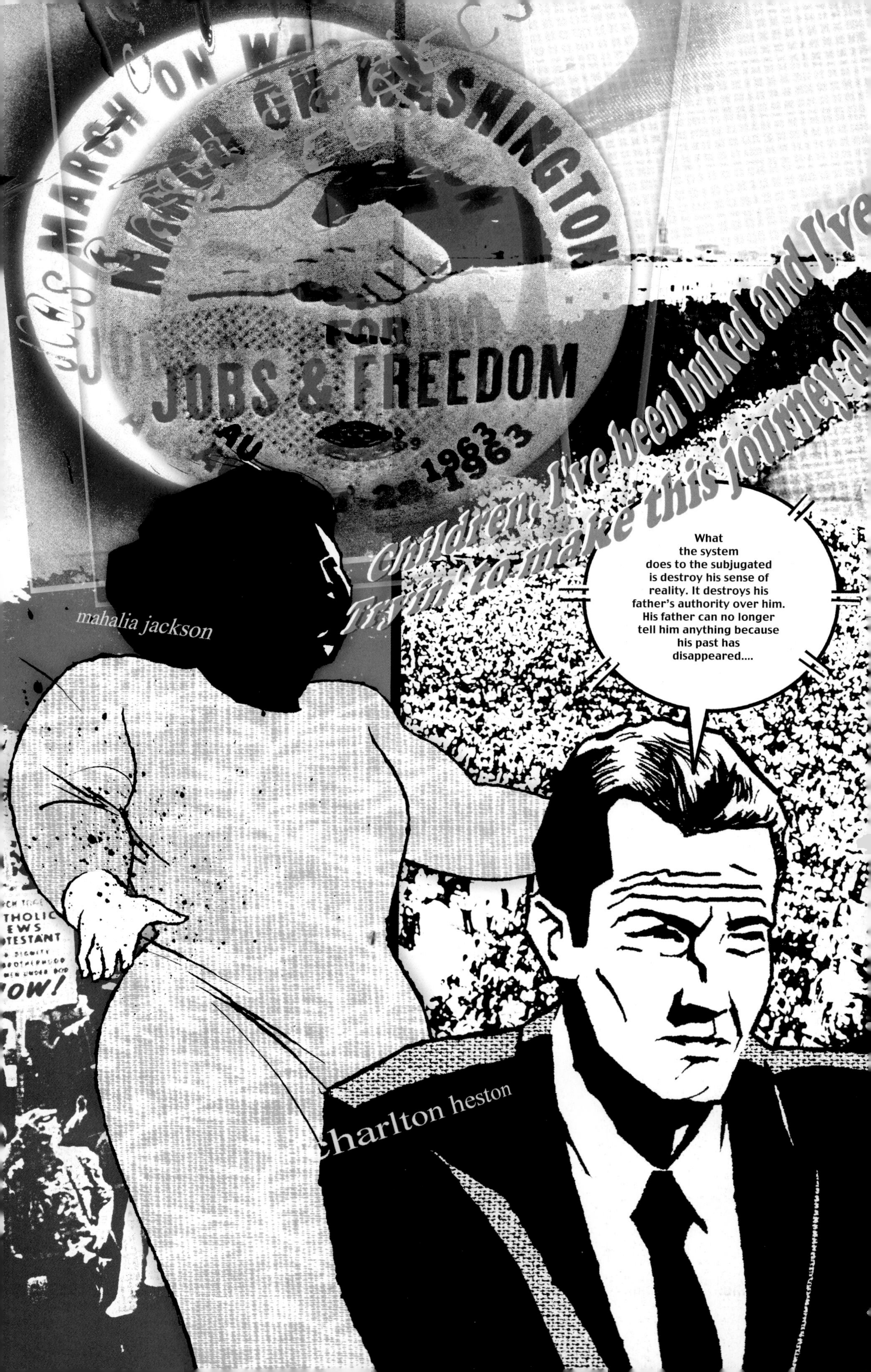

MARCH ON WASHINGTON
FOR
JOBS & FREEDOM
1963
Children, I've been buked and I've
Tryin' to make this journey al...
What the system does to the subjugated is destroy his sense of reality. It destroys his father's authority over him. His father can no longer tell him anything because his past has disappeared....
mahalia jackson
charlton heston

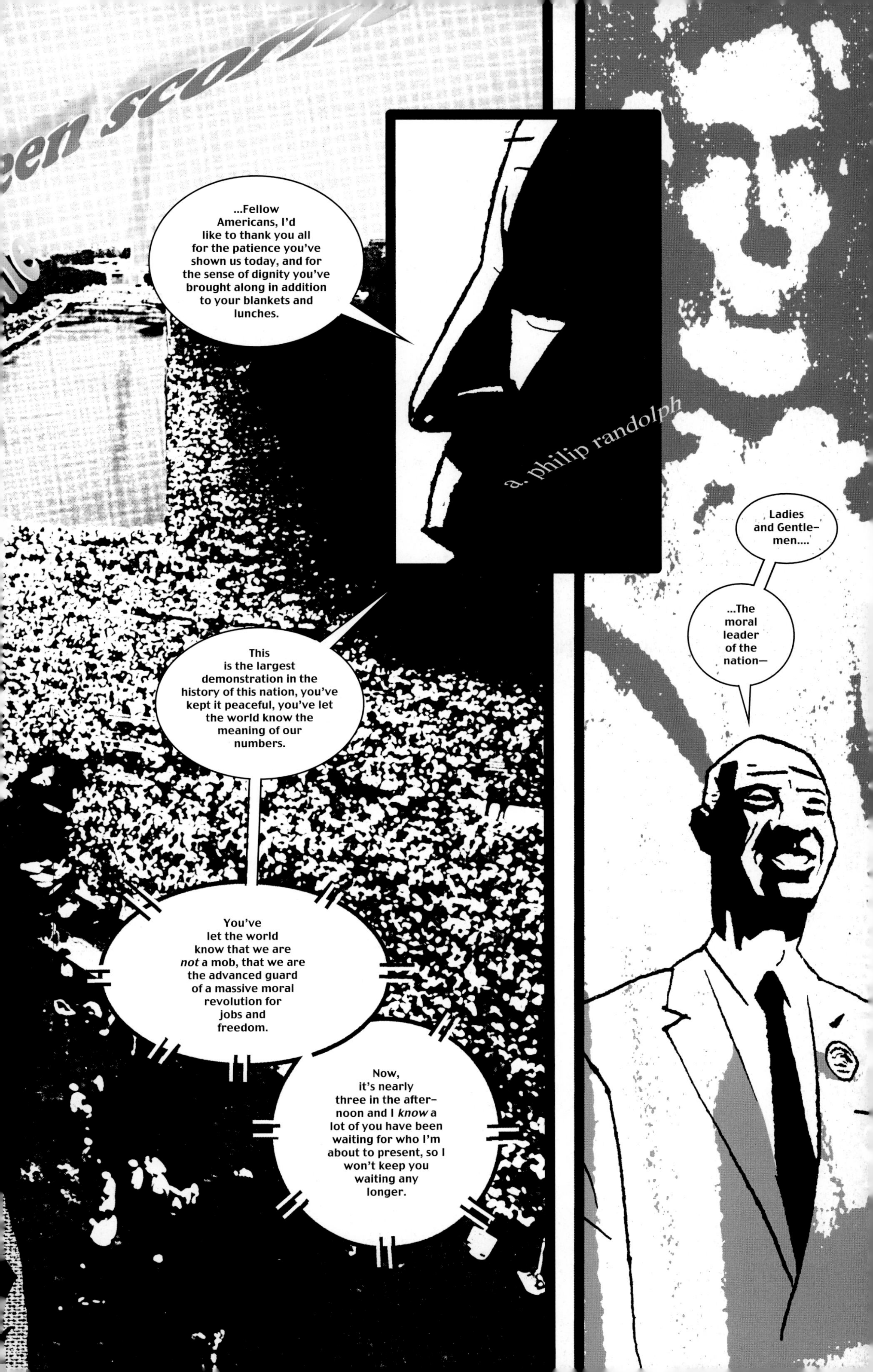

een scor
...Fellow Americans, I'd like to thank you all for the patience you've shown us today, and for the sense of dignity you've brought along in addition to your blankets and lunches.
a. philip randolph
This is the largest demonstration in the history of this nation, you've kept it peaceful, you've let the world know the meaning of our numbers.
You've let the world know that we are *not* a mob, that we are the advanced guard of a massive moral revolution for jobs and freedom.
Now, it's nearly three in the after-noon and I *know* a lot of you have been waiting for who I'm about to present, so I won't keep you waiting any longer.
Ladies and Gentle-men....
...The moral leader of the nation—

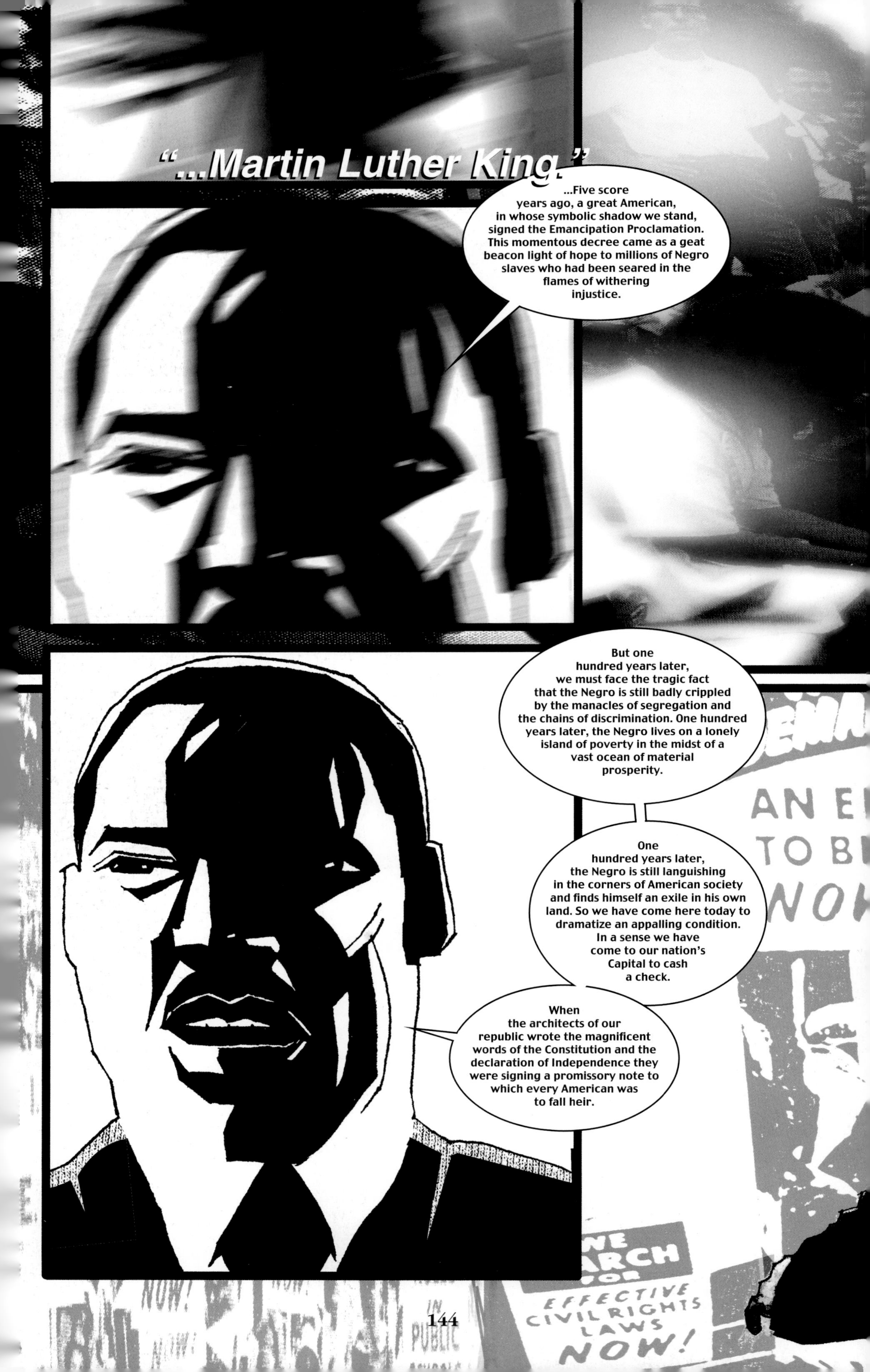
"...Martin Luther King."
...Five score years ago, a great American, in whose symbolic shadow we stand, signed the Emancipation Proclamation. This momentous decree came as a geat beacon light of hope to millions of Negro slaves who had been seared in the flames of withering injustice.
But one hundred years later, we must face the tragic fact that the Negro is still badly crippled by the manacles of segregation and the chains of discrimination. One hundred years later, the Negro lives on a lonely island of poverty in the midst of a vast ocean of material prosperity.
One hundred years later, the Negro is still languishing in the corners of American society and finds himself an exile in his own land. So we have come here today to dramatize an appalling condition. In a sense we have come to our nation's Capital to cash a check.
When the architects of our republic wrote the magnificent words of the Constitution and the declaration of Independence they were signing a promissory note to which every American was to fall heir.
AN E
TO B
NOW
WE MARCH FOR
EFFECTIVE CIVIL RIGHTS LAWS NOW!

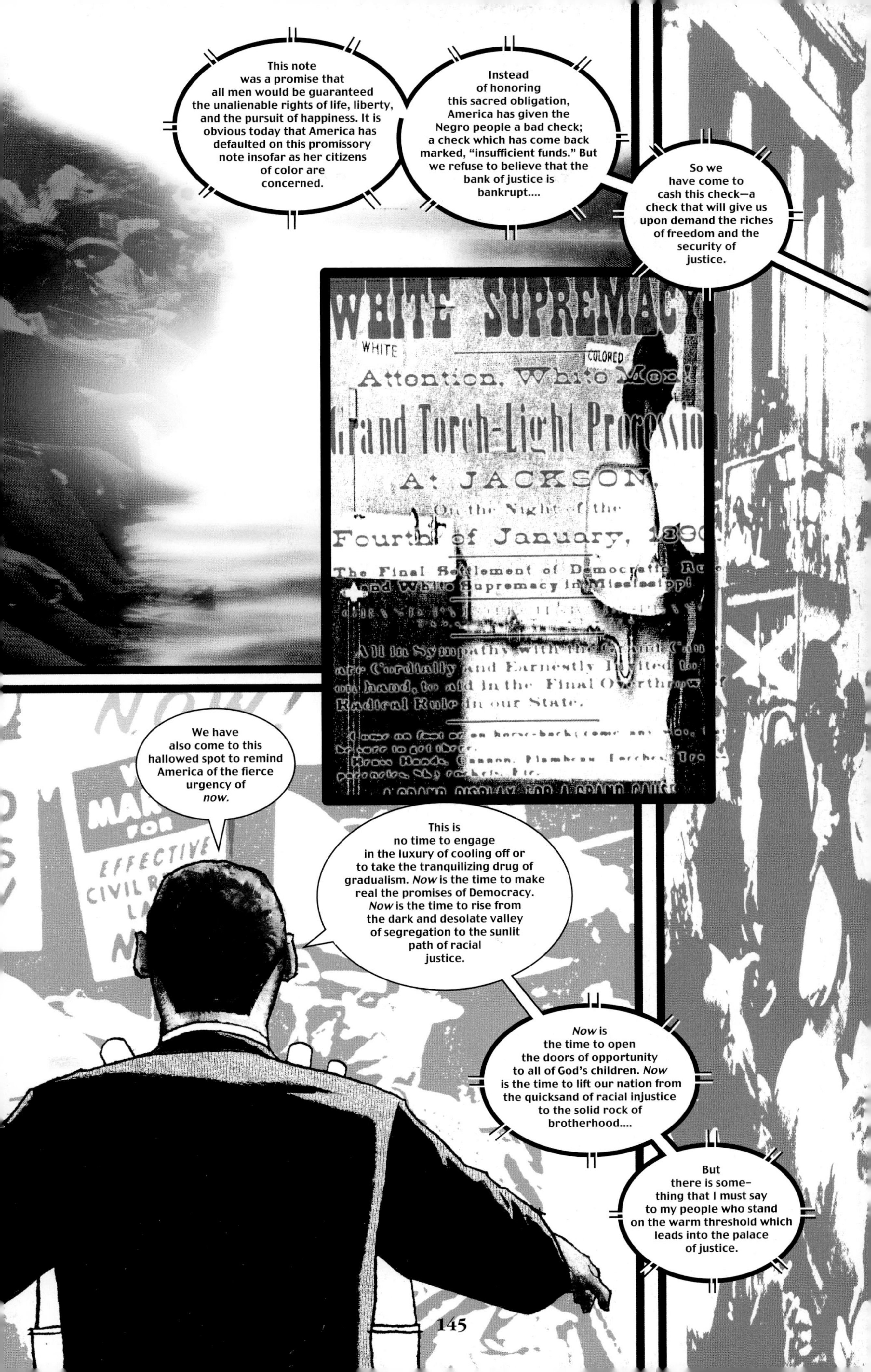
This note was a promise that all men would be guaranteed the unalienable rights of life, liberty, and the pursuit of happiness. It is obvious today that America has defaulted on this promissory note insofar as her citizens of color are concerned.
Instead of honoring this sacred obligation, America has given the Negro people a bad check; a check which has come back marked, "insufficient funds." But we refuse to believe that the bank of justice is bankrupt....
So we have come to cash this check—a check that will give us upon demand the riches of freedom and the security of justice.
WHITE SUPREMACY
WHITE
COLORED
Attention, White Men!
Grand Torch-Light Procession
At JACKSON,
Fourth of January, 189
The Final Settlement of Democratic Rule and White Supremacy in Mississippi
All in Sympathy with the Grand Cause are Cordially and Earnestly Invited to be on hand, to aid in the Final Overthrow of Radical Rule in our State.
We have also come to this hallowed spot to remind America of the fierce urgency of *now.*
EFFECTIVE
CIVIL
This is no time to engage in the luxury of cooling off or to take the tranquilizing drug of gradualism. *Now* is the time to make real the promises of Democracy. *Now* is the time to rise from the dark and desolate valley of segregation to the sunlit path of racial justice.
Now is the time to open the doors of opportunity to all of God's children. *Now* is the time to lift our nation from the quicksand of racial injustice to the solid rock of brotherhood....
But there is some-thing that I must say to my people who stand on the warm threshold which leads into the palace of justice.

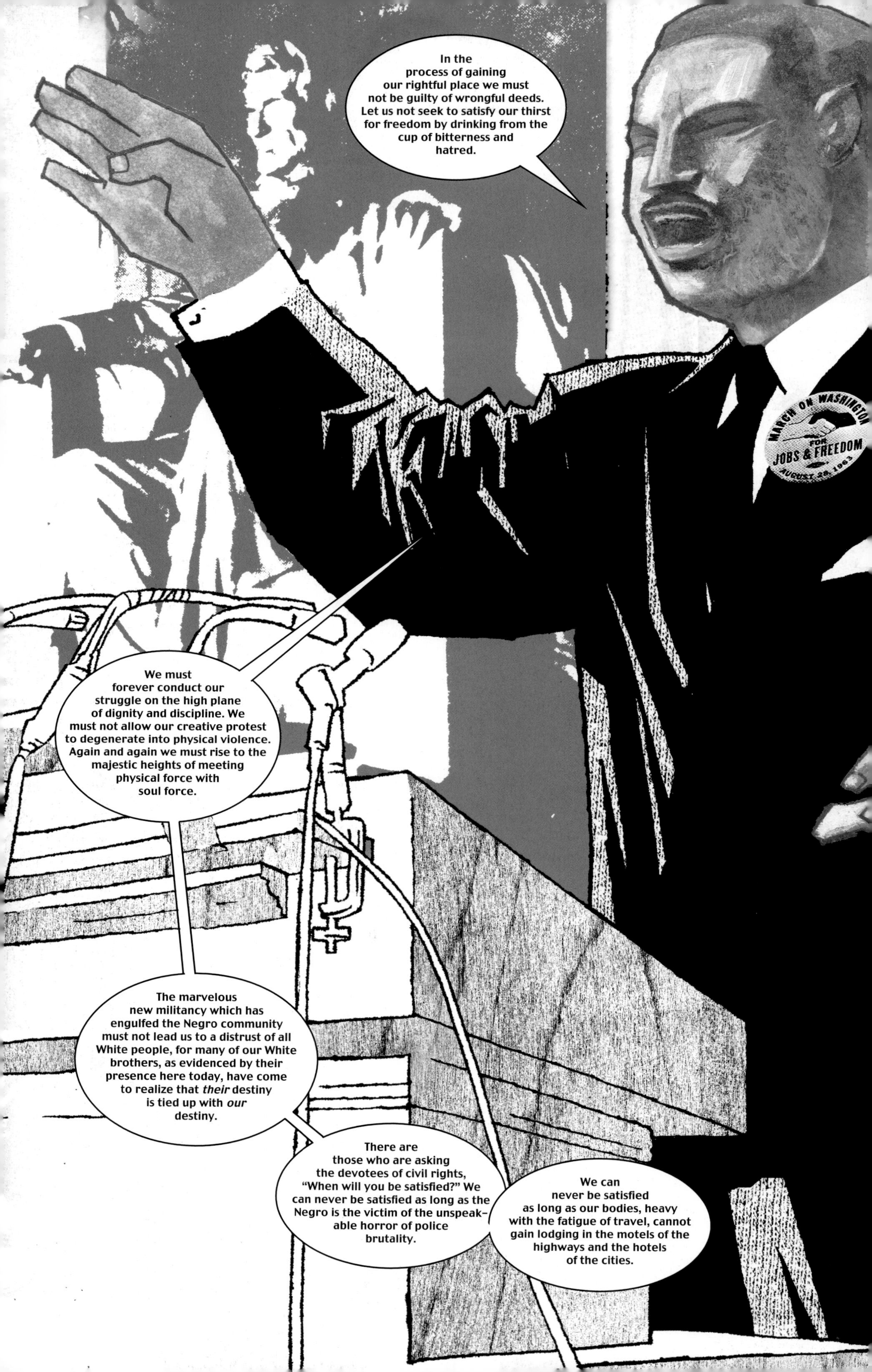
In the process of gaining our rightful place we must not be guilty of wrongful deeds. Let us not seek to satisfy our thirst for freedom by drinking from the cup of bitterness and hatred.
MARCH ON WASHINGTON FOR JOBS & FREEDOM AUGUST 28, 1963
We must forever conduct our struggle on the high plane of dignity and discipline. We must not allow our creative protest to degenerate into physical violence. Again and again we must rise to the majestic heights of meeting physical force with soul force.
The marvelous new militancy which has engulfed the Negro community must not lead us to a distrust of all White people, for many of our White brothers, as evidenced by their presence here today, have come to realize that *their* destiny is tied up with *our* destiny.
There are those who are asking the devotees of civil rights, "When will you be satisfied?" We can never be satisfied as long as the Negro is the victim of the unspeakable horror of police brutality.
We can never be satisfied as long as our bodies, heavy with the fatigue of travel, cannot gain lodging in the motels of the highways and the hotels of the cities.

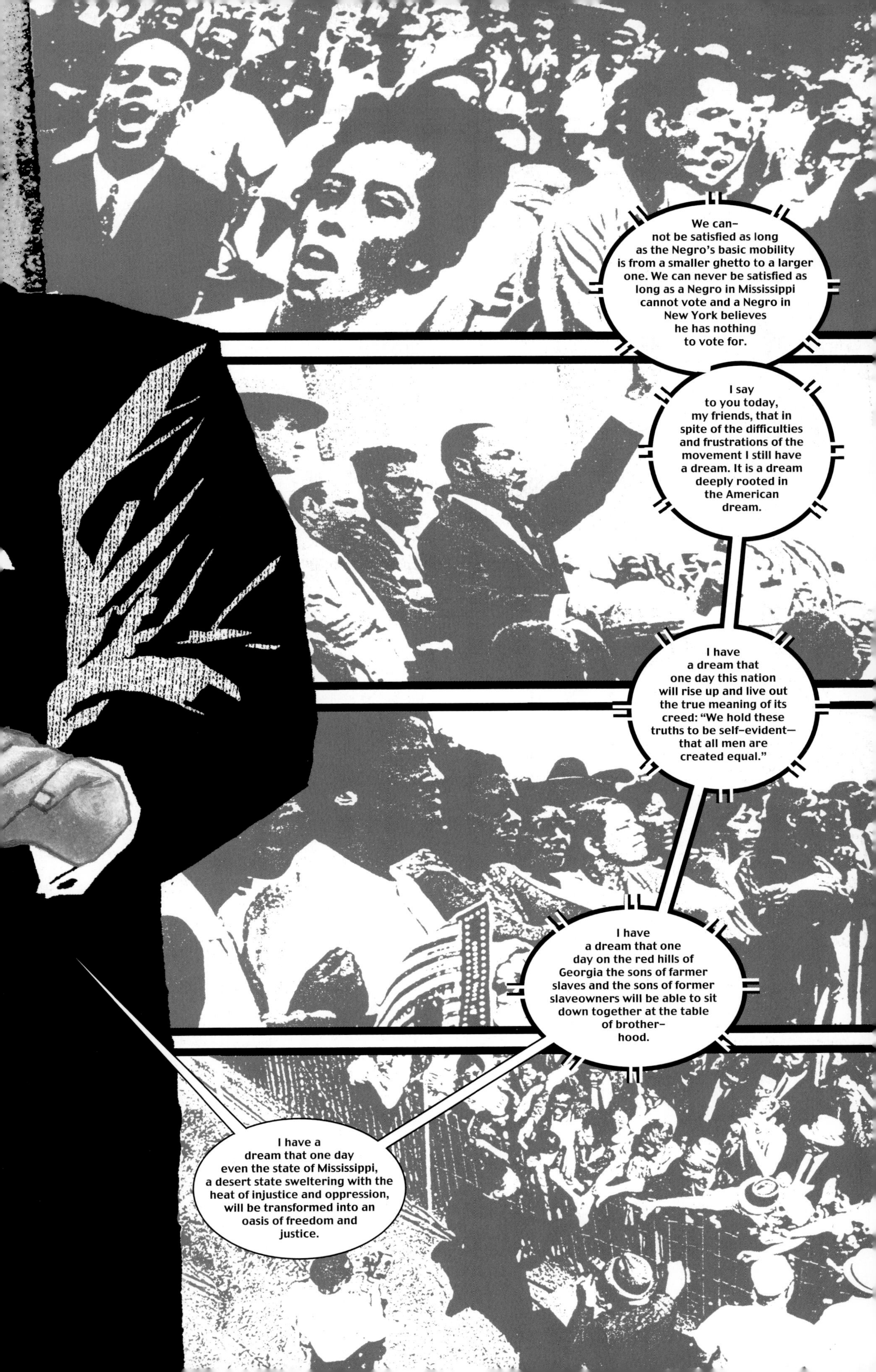
We can–not be satisfied as long as the Negro's basic mobility is from a smaller ghetto to a larger one. We can never be satisfied as long as a Negro in Mississippi cannot vote and a Negro in New York believes he has nothing to vote for.
I say to you today, my friends, that in spite of the difficulties and frustrations of the movement I still have a dream. It is a dream deeply rooted in the American dream.
I have a dream that one day this nation will rise up and live out the true meaning of its creed: "We hold these truths to be self-evident—that all men are created equal."
I have a dream that one day on the red hills of Georgia the sons of farmer slaves and the sons of former slaveowners will be able to sit down together at the table of brother–hood.
I have a dream that one day even the state of Mississippi, a desert state sweltering with the heat of injustice and oppression, will be transformed into an oasis of freedom and justice.

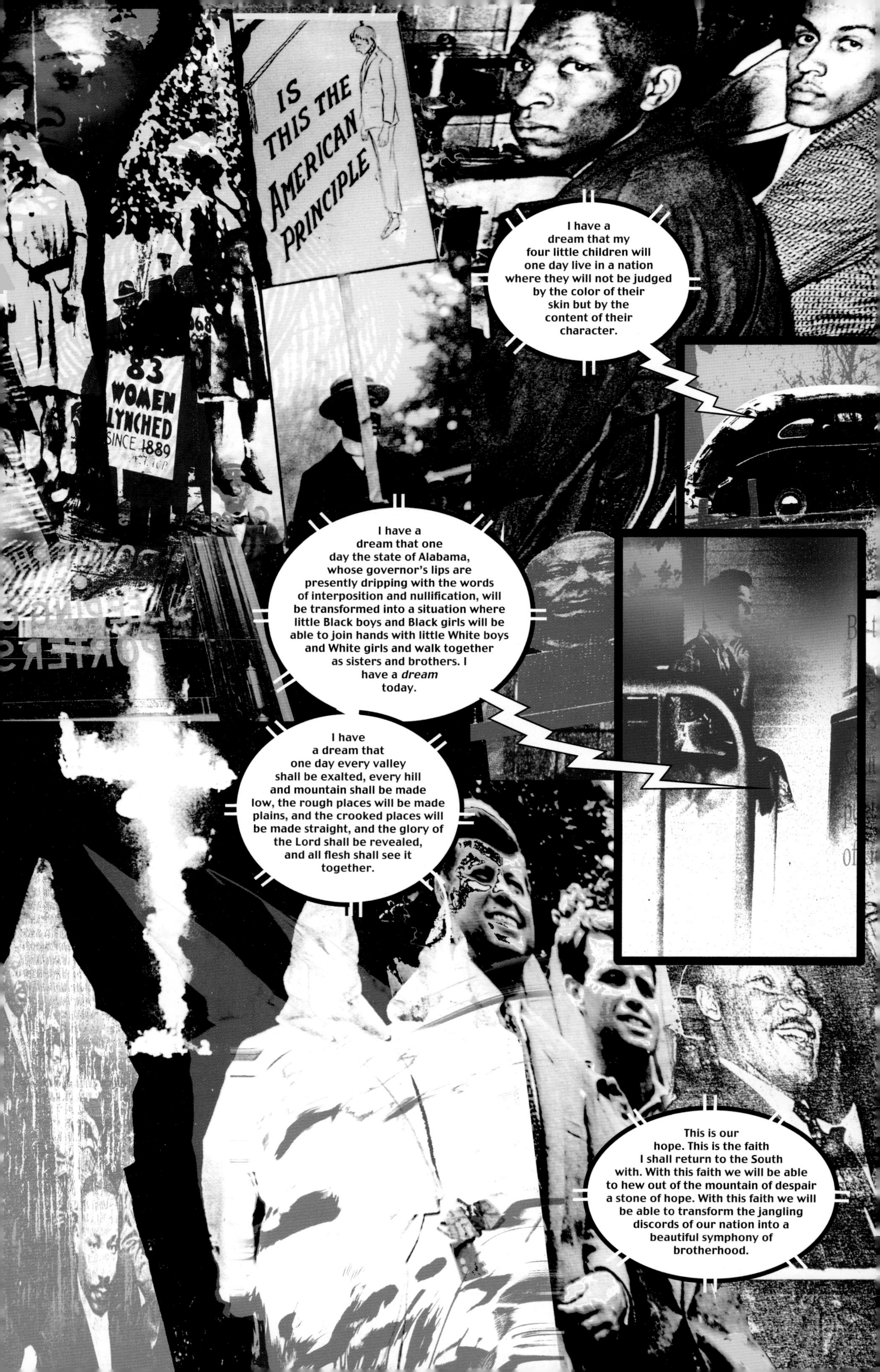

IS THIS THE AMERICAN PRINCIPLE
83 WOMEN LYNCHED SINCE 1889
I have a dream that my four little children will one day live in a nation where they will not be judged by the color of their skin but by the content of their character.
I have a dream that one day the state of Alabama, whose governor's lips are presently dripping with the words of interposition and nullification, will be transformed into a situation where little Black boys and Black girls will be able to join hands with little White boys and White girls and walk together as sisters and brothers. I have a *dream* today.
I have a dream that one day every valley shall be exalted, every hill and mountain shall be made low, the rough places will be made plains, and the crooked places will be made straight, and the glory of the Lord shall be revealed, and all flesh shall see it together.
This is our hope. This is the faith I shall return to the South with. With this faith we will be able to hew out of the mountain of despair a stone of hope. With this faith we will be able to transform the jangling discords of our nation into a beautiful symphony of brotherhood.

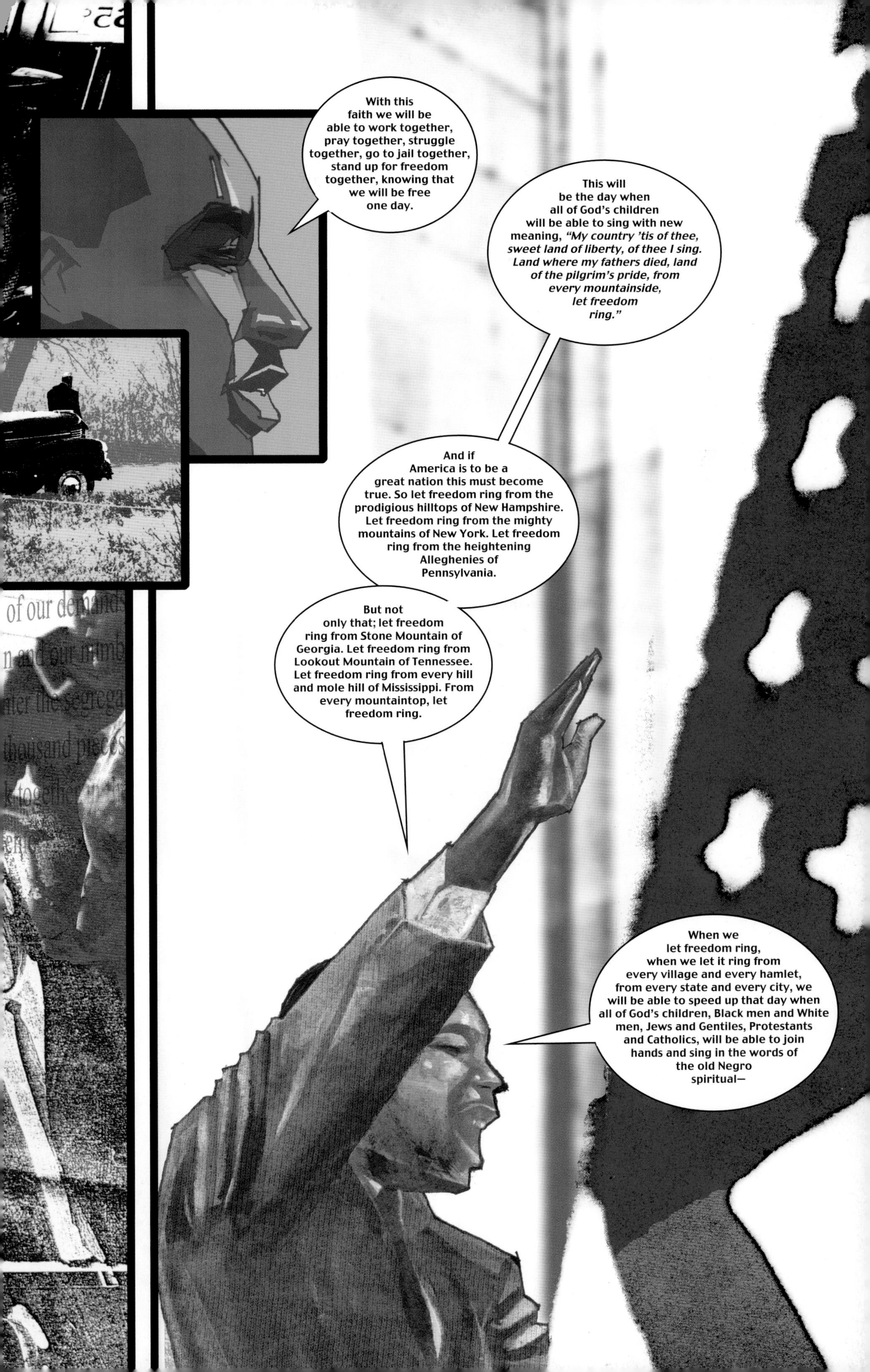
With this faith we will be able to work together, pray together, struggle together, go to jail together, stand up for freedom together, knowing that we will be free one day.
This will be the day when all of God's children will be able to sing with new meaning, *"My country 'tis of thee, sweet land of liberty, of thee I sing. Land where my fathers died, land of the pilgrim's pride, from every mountainside, let freedom ring."*
And if America is to be a great nation this must become true. So let freedom ring from the prodigious hilltops of New Hampshire. Let freedom ring from the mighty mountains of New York. Let freedom ring from the heightening Alleghenies of Pennsylvania.
But not only that; let freedom ring from Stone Mountain of Georgia. Let freedom ring from Lookout Mountain of Tennessee. Let freedom ring from every hill and mole hill of Mississippi. From every mountaintop, let freedom ring.
When we let freedom ring, when we let it ring from every village and every hamlet, from every state and every city, we will be able to speed up that day when all of God's children, Black men and White men, Jews and Gentiles, Protestants and Catholics, will be able to join hands and sing in the words of the old Negro spiritual—

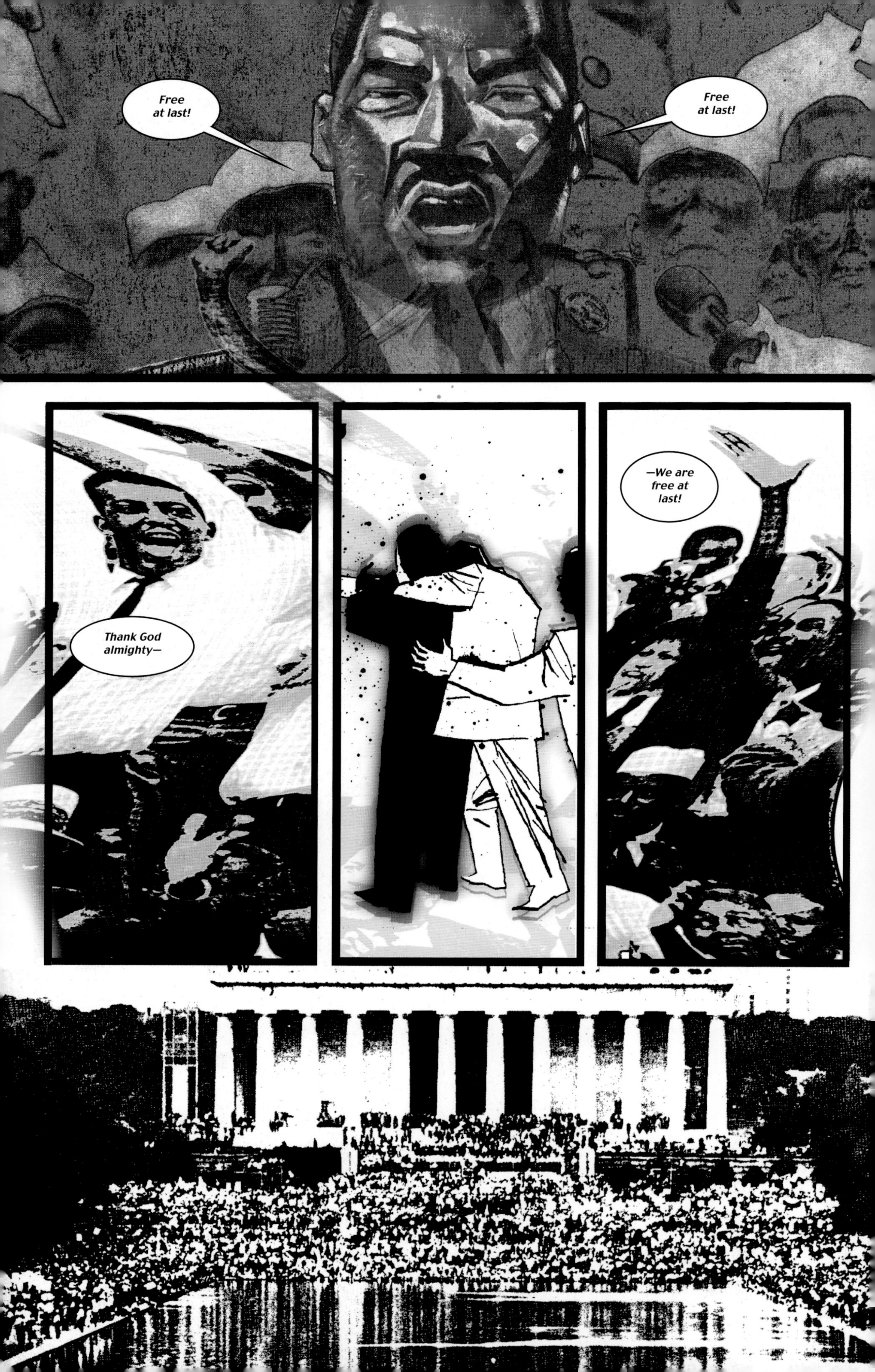
Free at last!
Free at last!
Thank God almighty—
—We are free at last!

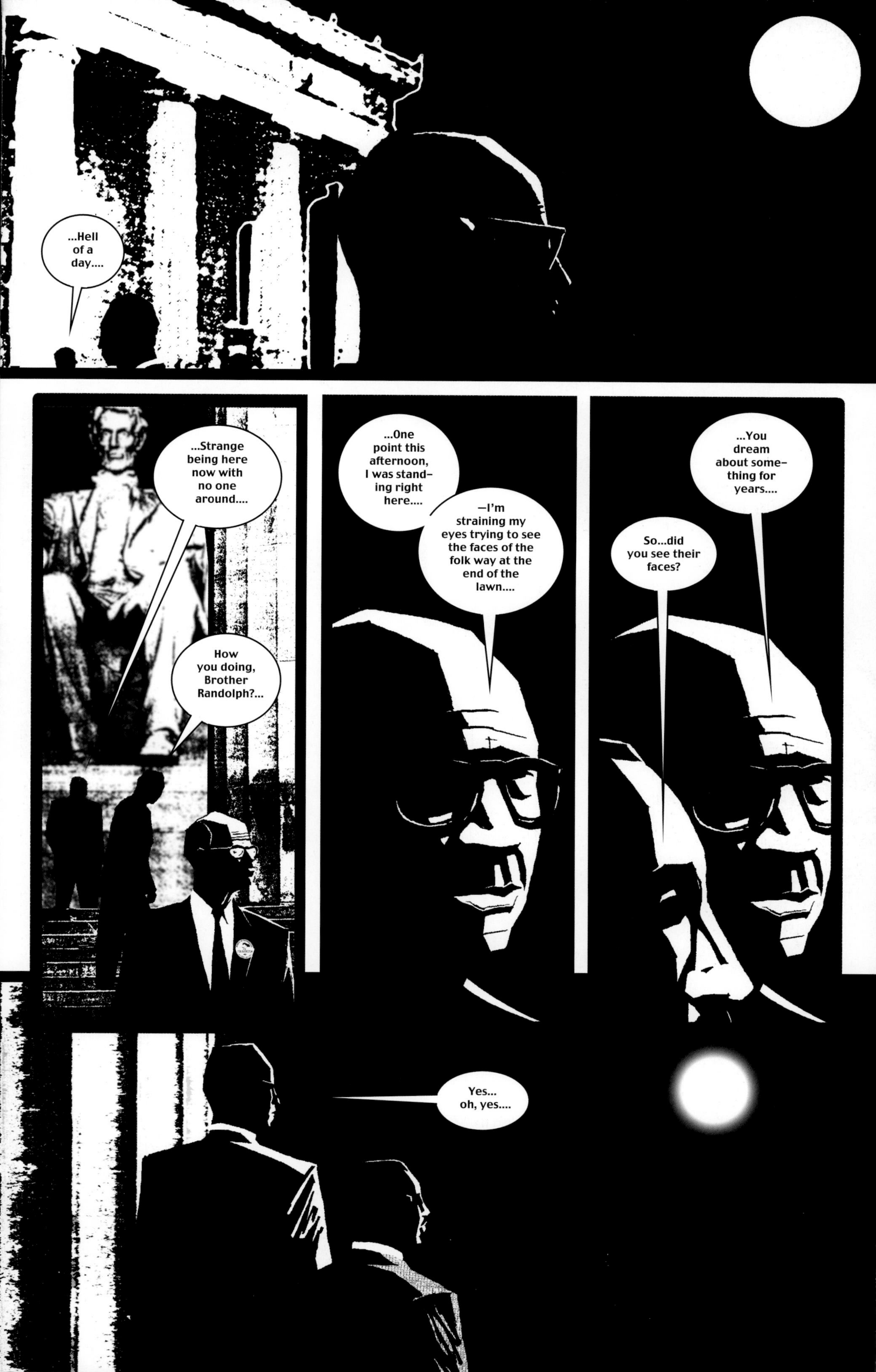
...Hell of a day....
...Strange being here now with no one around....
How you doing, Brother Randolph?...
...One point this afternoon, I was standing right here....
—I'm straining my eyes trying to see the faces of the folk way at the end of the lawn....
...You dream about something for years....
So...did you see their faces?
Yes... oh, yes....

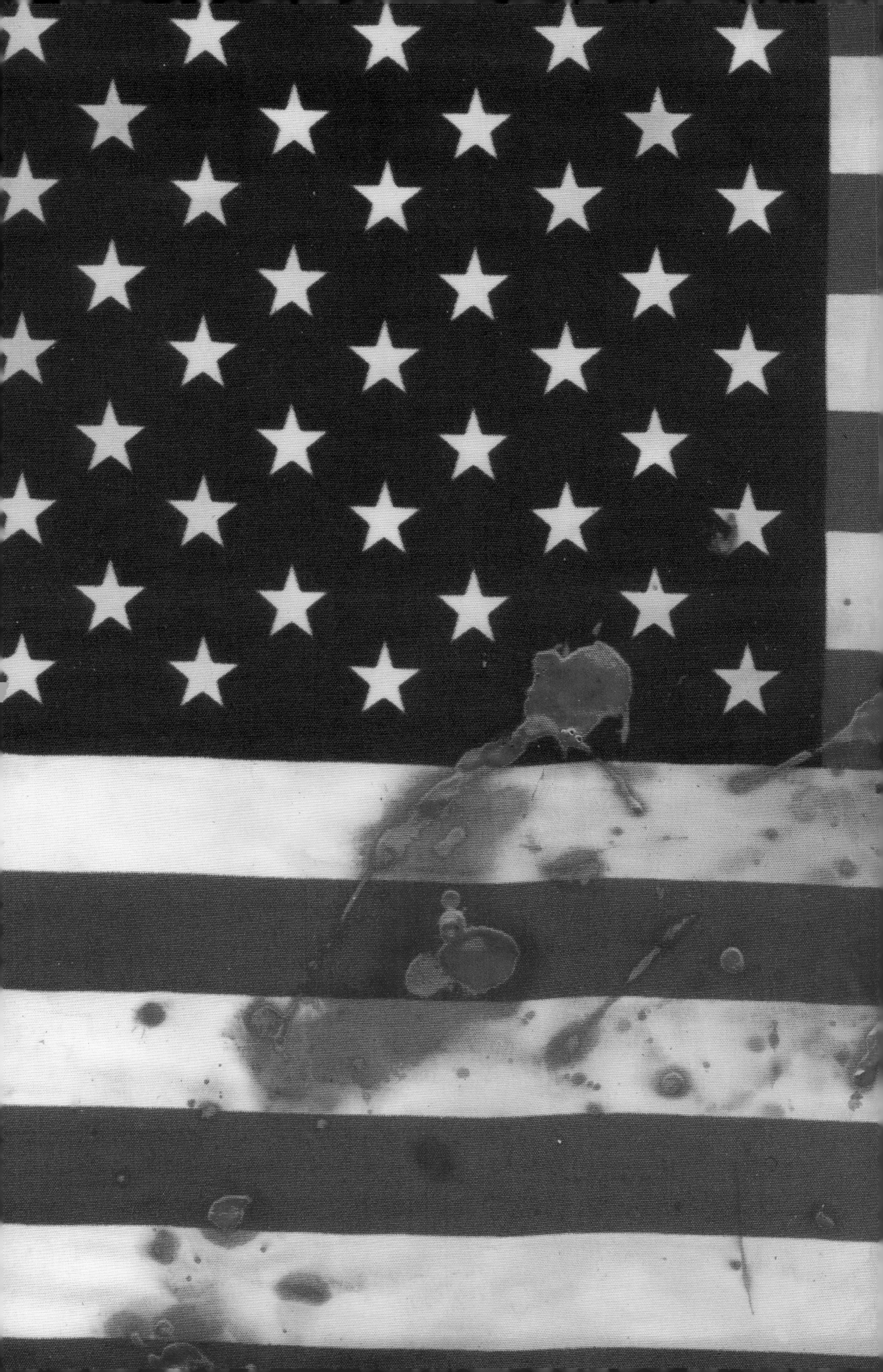

Truth or Myth—

—None of that matters.

All that matters is the legacy.

Regardless of its basis as truth or myth, Kennedy's legacy was that of a media created *Camelot*, of a man equal parts visionary, statesman and knight, passionately committed to his vision of America and its dream.

For many Americans...I daresay for all of us, Black and White, that particular dream was shattered on the 22nd of November in 1963.

I remember the entire period with profound clarity, us riveted to our television for three days and nights, watching the spectacle unfold, my sons and I. The limousine driving along the triangle at Dealey Plaza—

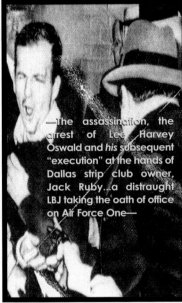

—The assassination, the arrest of Lee Harvey Oswald and *his* subsequent "execution" at the hands of Dallas strip club owner, Jack Ruby...a distraught LBJ taking the oath of office on Air Force One—

—With Jacqueline Kennedy in *shock*, still dressed in blood-stained clothes, standing beside him. And so, the former Texas senator, former Vice-President Lyndon Baines Johnson, became President by default.

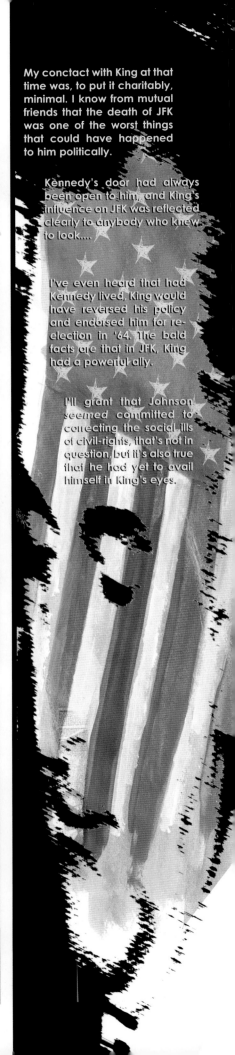

My conctact with King at that time was, to put it charitably, minimal. I know from mutual friends that the death of JFK was one of the worst things that could have happened to him politically.

Kennedy's door had always been open to him, and King's influence on JFK was reflected clearly to anybody who knew to look....

I've even heard that had Kennedy lived, King would have reversed his policy and endorsed him for re-election in '64. The bald facts are that in JFK, King had a powerful ally.

I'll grant that Johnson seemed committed to correcting the social ills of civil-rights, that's not in question, but it's also true that he had yet to avail himself in King's eyes.

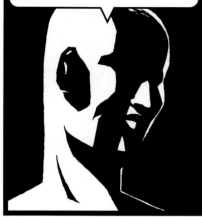

In St. Augustine, Florida, Klan activity reached an all-time high, to the point where law had effectively ceased to exist for the Blacks of that area. What you have to understand about St. Augustine was the place was probably the most permanent European community in North America.

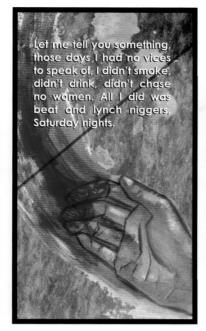

Let me tell you something, those days I had no vices to speak of, I didn't smoke, didn't drink, didn't chase no women. All I did was beat and lynch niggers, Saturday nights.

I mean, god*damn*.... Heh, I guess you never smelled a *nigger* burn.... You should though, it's an experience, 's easily one o' nature's sweetest smells, I don't mean to offend the ladies—

The SCLC set up demonstrations there in April of '64 which turned into a violent nightmare. A stalemate was eventually met between the segregationists and the demonstrators. The Johnson administration was reluctant to do anything to help at first, *refusing* to send in federal marshals to intervene—

—But eventually, partly as a tribute to the late Kennedy, partly to get the demonstrations over with, on July 2, King and other Black leaders were on hand in the east ballroom of the White House when LBJ signed into law the civil-rights bill that JFK had been trying to get off the ground.

Supposedly this was the farthest reaching civil-rights legislation since the *Reconstruction.* It *guaranteed* Blacks the right to vote and access to public accommodations—it also authorized the federal government to sue if necessary to desegregate public facilities and schools.

Afterward, Johnson reasoned the need for direct action protest was over. He actually believed that the civil-rights act eliminated the last vestiges of injustice in our *beloved* America. OK...perhaps discrimination was now *technically* illegal....

...But would the White establishment really take some *bill* seriously, as though a bill alone has any salt. To be perfectly blunt...the bill was soft, specifically on voting rights. Still, King must have realized this, he made a lot of noise trying to set up a separate voting rights bill. My boy, never enough, never satisfied....

It's no secret Martin King and J. Edgar Hoover *despised* each other. King enraged Hoover when he publicly criticized the FBI—when *Time* named King Man of the Year, Hoover's said to have responded, "They had to dig deep in the garbage for this one." This about a Nobel Laureate. It was the March on Washington that convinced Hoover the Civil Rights Movement wouldn't go away on its own, that he'd have to smash it to preserve his America.

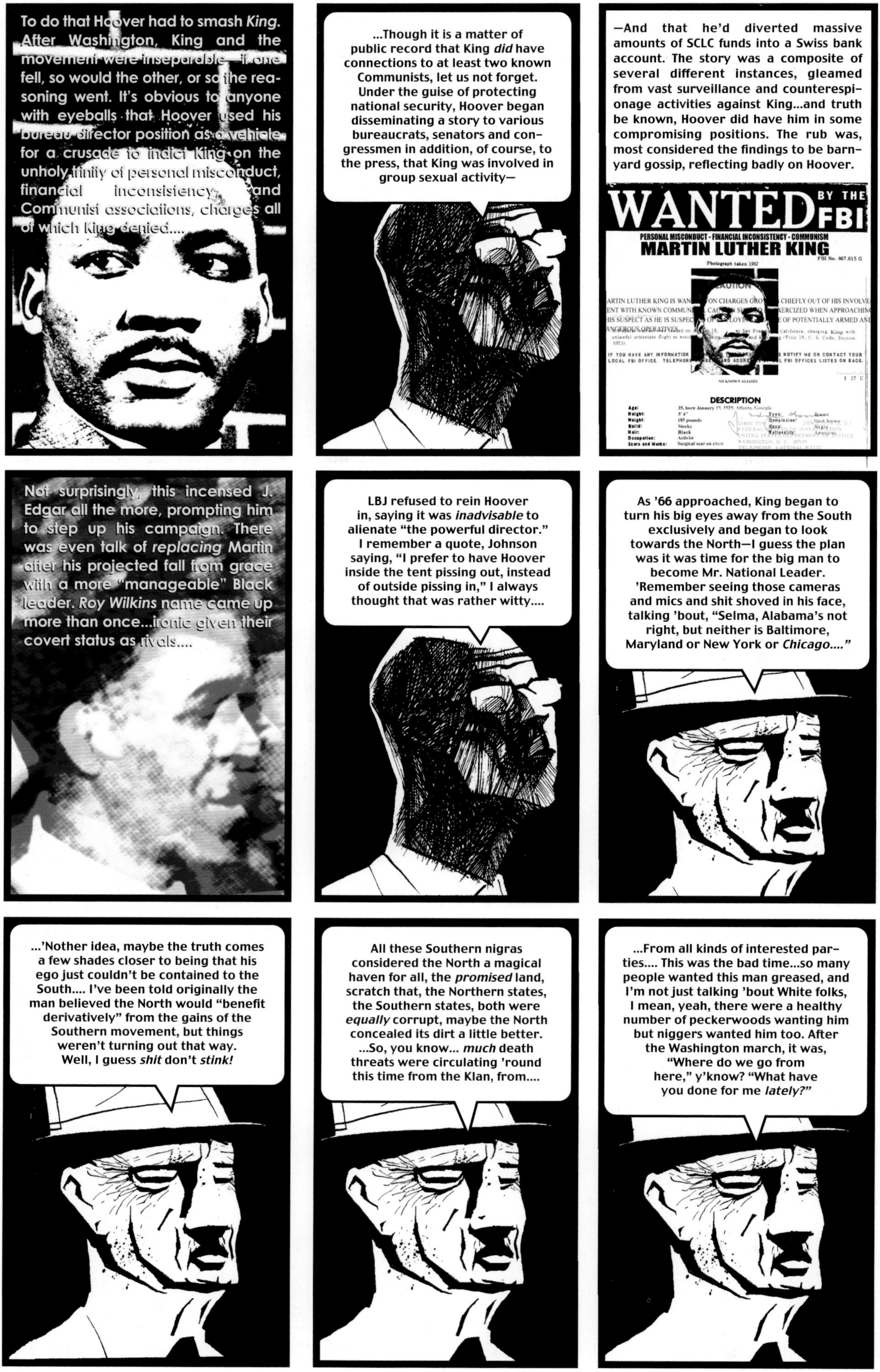

To do that Hoover had to smash *King*. After Washington, King and the movement were inseparable—if one fell, so would the other, or so the reasoning went. It's obvious to anyone with eyeballs that Hoover used his bureau director position as a vehicle for a crusade to indict King on the unholy trinity of personal misconduct, financial inconsistency, and Communist associations, charges all of which King denied....
...Though it is a matter of public record that King *did* have connections to at least two known Communists, let us not forget. Under the guise of protecting national security, Hoover began disseminating a story to various bureaucrats, senators and congressmen in addition, of course, to the press, that King was involved in group sexual activity—
—And that he'd diverted massive amounts of SCLC funds into a Swiss bank account. The story was a composite of several different instances, gleamed from vast surveillance and counterespionage activities against King...and truth be known, Hoover did have him in some compromising positions. The rub was, most considered the findings to be barnyard gossip, reflecting badly on Hoover.
WANTED BY THE FBI
PERSONAL MISCONDUCT - FINANCIAL INCONSISTENCY - COMMUNISM
MARTIN LUTHER KING
DESCRIPTION
Not surprisingly, this incensed J. Edgar all the more, prompting him to step up his campaign. There was even talk of *replacing* Martin after his projected fall from grace with a more "manageable" Black leader. *Roy Wilkins* name came up more than once...ironic given their covert status as rivals....
LBJ refused to rein Hoover in, saying it was *inadvisable* to alienate "the powerful director." I remember a quote, Johnson saying, "I prefer to have Hoover inside the tent pissing out, instead of outside pissing in," I always thought that was rather witty....
As '66 approached, King began to turn his big eyes away from the South exclusively and began to look towards the North—I guess the plan was it was time for the big man to become Mr. National Leader. 'Remember seeing those cameras and mics and shit shoved in his face, talking 'bout, "Selma, Alabama's not right, but neither is Baltimore, Maryland or New York or *Chicago....*"
...'Nother idea, maybe the truth comes a few shades closer to being that his ego just couldn't be contained to the South.... I've been told originally the man believed the North would "benefit derivatively" from the gains of the Southern movement, but things weren't turning out that way. Well, I guess *shit* don't *stink!*
All these Southern nigras considered the North a magical haven for all, the *promised* land, scratch that, the Northern states, the Southern states, both were *equally* corrupt, maybe the North concealed its dirt a little better. ...So, you know... *much* death threats were circulating 'round this time from the Klan, from....
...From all kinds of interested parties.... This was the bad time...so many people wanted this man greased, and I'm not just talking 'bout White folks, I mean, yeah, there were a healthy number of peckerwoods wanting him but niggers wanted him too. After the Washington march, it was, "Where do we go from here," y'know? "What have you done for me *lately?*"

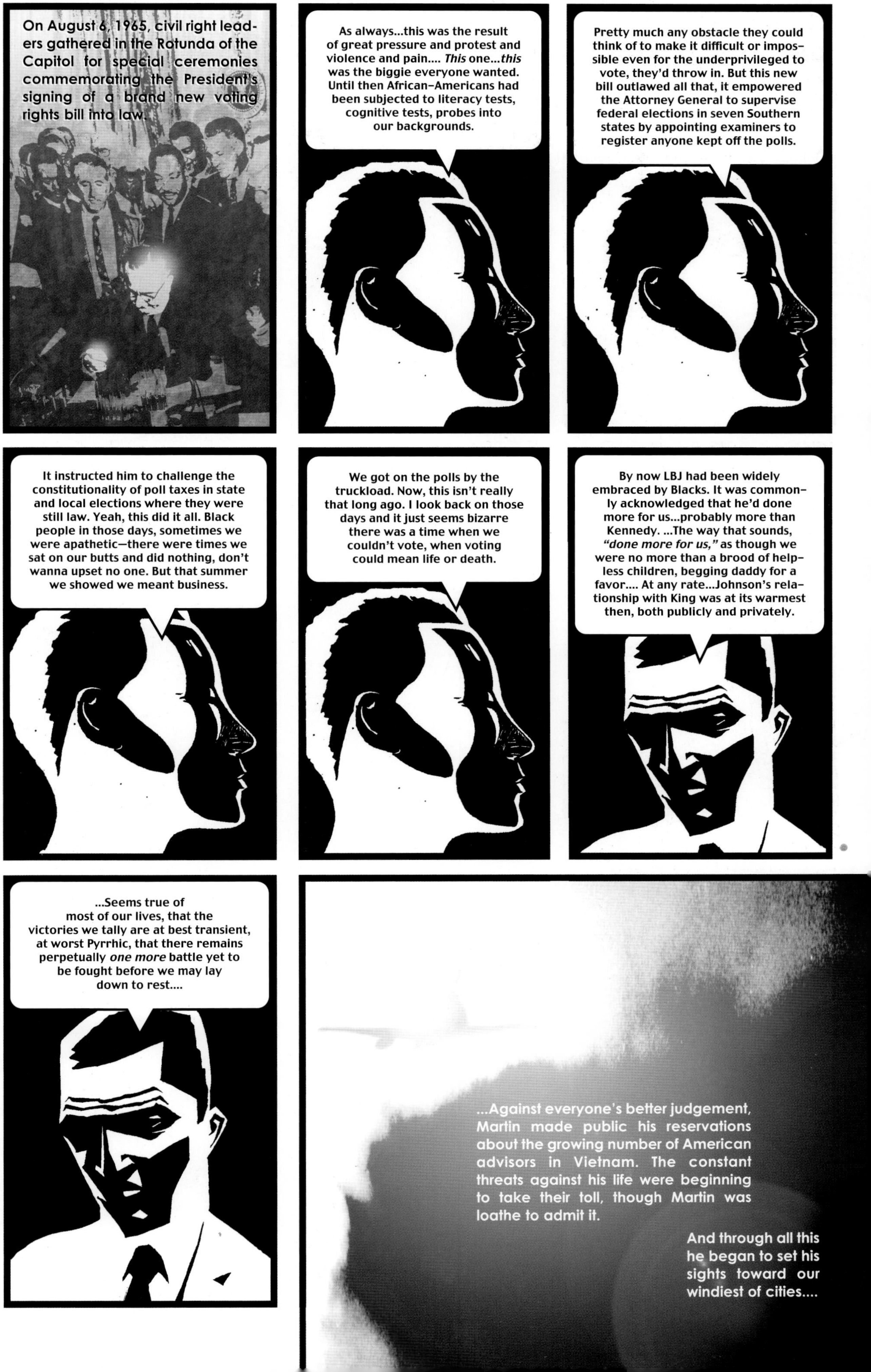
On August 6, 1965, civil right leaders gathered in the Rotunda of the Capitol for special ceremonies commemorating the President's signing of a brand new voting rights bill into law.
As always...this was the result of great pressure and protest and violence and pain.... *This* one...*this* was the biggie everyone wanted. Until then African-Americans had been subjected to literacy tests, cognitive tests, probes into our backgrounds.
Pretty much any obstacle they could think of to make it difficult or impossible even for the underprivileged to vote, they'd throw in. But this new bill outlawed all that, it empowered the Attorney General to supervise federal elections in seven Southern states by appointing examiners to register anyone kept off the polls.
It instructed him to challenge the constitutionality of poll taxes in state and local elections where they were still law. Yeah, this did it all. Black people in those days, sometimes we were apathetic—there were times we sat on our butts and did nothing, don't wanna upset no one. But that summer we showed we meant business.
We got on the polls by the truckload. Now, this isn't really that long ago. I look back on those days and it just seems bizarre there was a time when we couldn't vote, when voting could mean life or death.
By now LBJ had been widely embraced by Blacks. It was commonly acknowledged that he'd done more for us...probably more than Kennedy. ...The way that sounds, *"done more for us,"* as though we were no more than a brood of helpless children, begging daddy for a favor.... At any rate...Johnson's relationship with King was at its warmest then, both publicly and privately.
...Seems true of most of our lives, that the victories we tally are at best transient, at worst Pyrrhic, that there remains perpetually *one more* battle yet to be fought before we may lay down to rest....
...Against everyone's better judgement, Martin made public his reservations about the growing number of American advisors in Vietnam. The constant threats against his life were beginning to take their toll, though Martin was loathe to admit it.
And through all this he began to set his sights toward our windiest of cities....

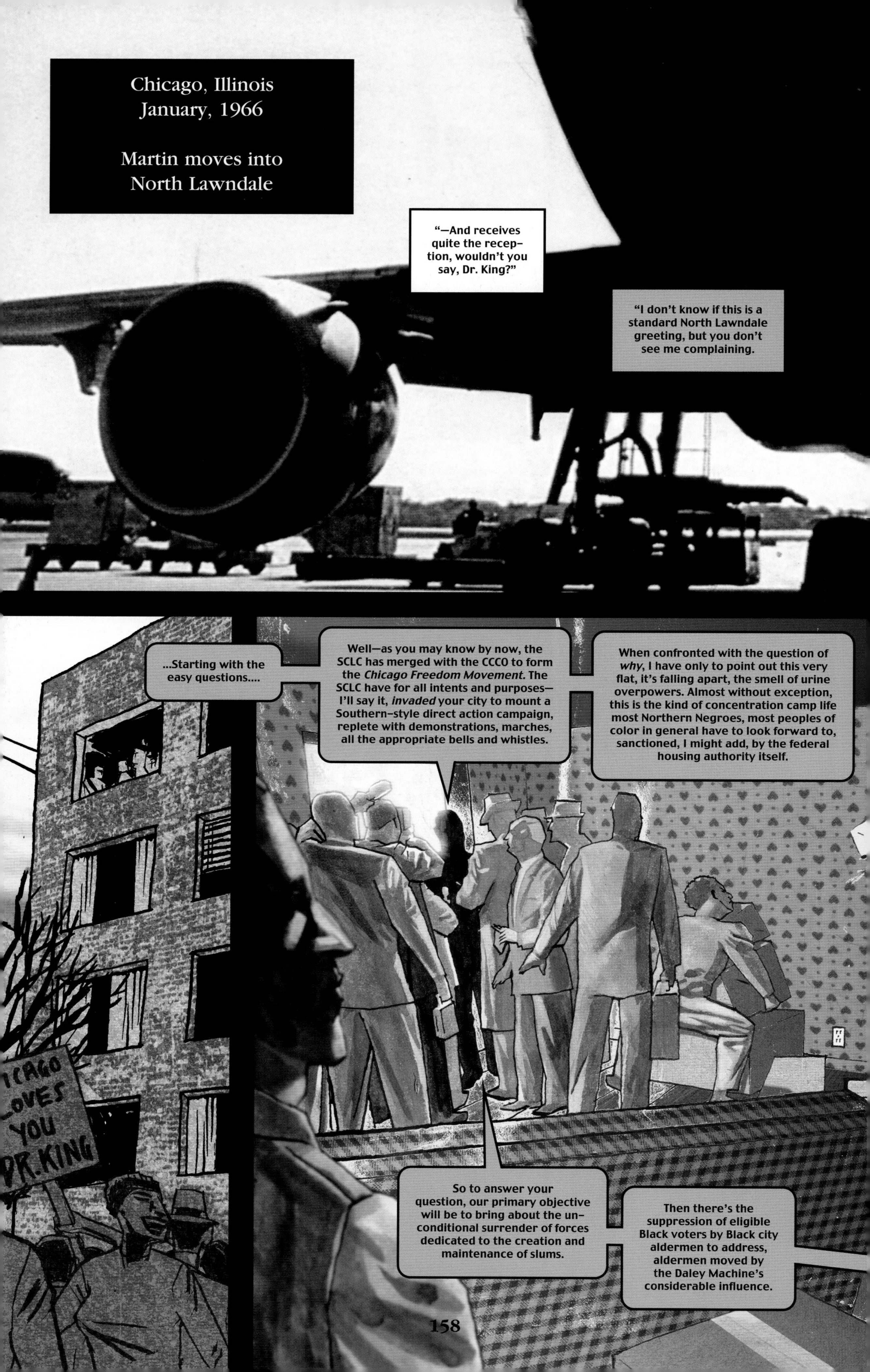

Chicago, Illinois
January, 1966
Martin moves into North Lawndale
"—And receives quite the reception, wouldn't you say, Dr. King?"
"I don't know if this is a standard North Lawndale greeting, but you don't see me complaining.
...Starting with the easy questions....
Well—as you may know by now, the SCLC has merged with the CCCO to form the *Chicago Freedom Movement.* The SCLC have for all intents and purposes—I'll say it, *invaded* your city to mount a Southern-style direct action campaign, replete with demonstrations, marches, all the appropriate bells and whistles.
When confronted with the question of *why*, I have only to point out this very flat, it's falling apart, the smell of urine overpowers. Almost without exception, this is the kind of concentration camp life most Northern Negroes, most peoples of color in general have to look forward to, sanctioned, I might add, by the federal housing authority itself.
ICAGO
OVES
YOU
DR. KING
So to answer your question, our primary objective will be to bring about the unconditional surrender of forces dedicated to the creation and maintenance of slums.
Then there's the suppression of eligible Black voters by Black city aldermen to address, aldermen moved by the Daley Machine's considerable influence.

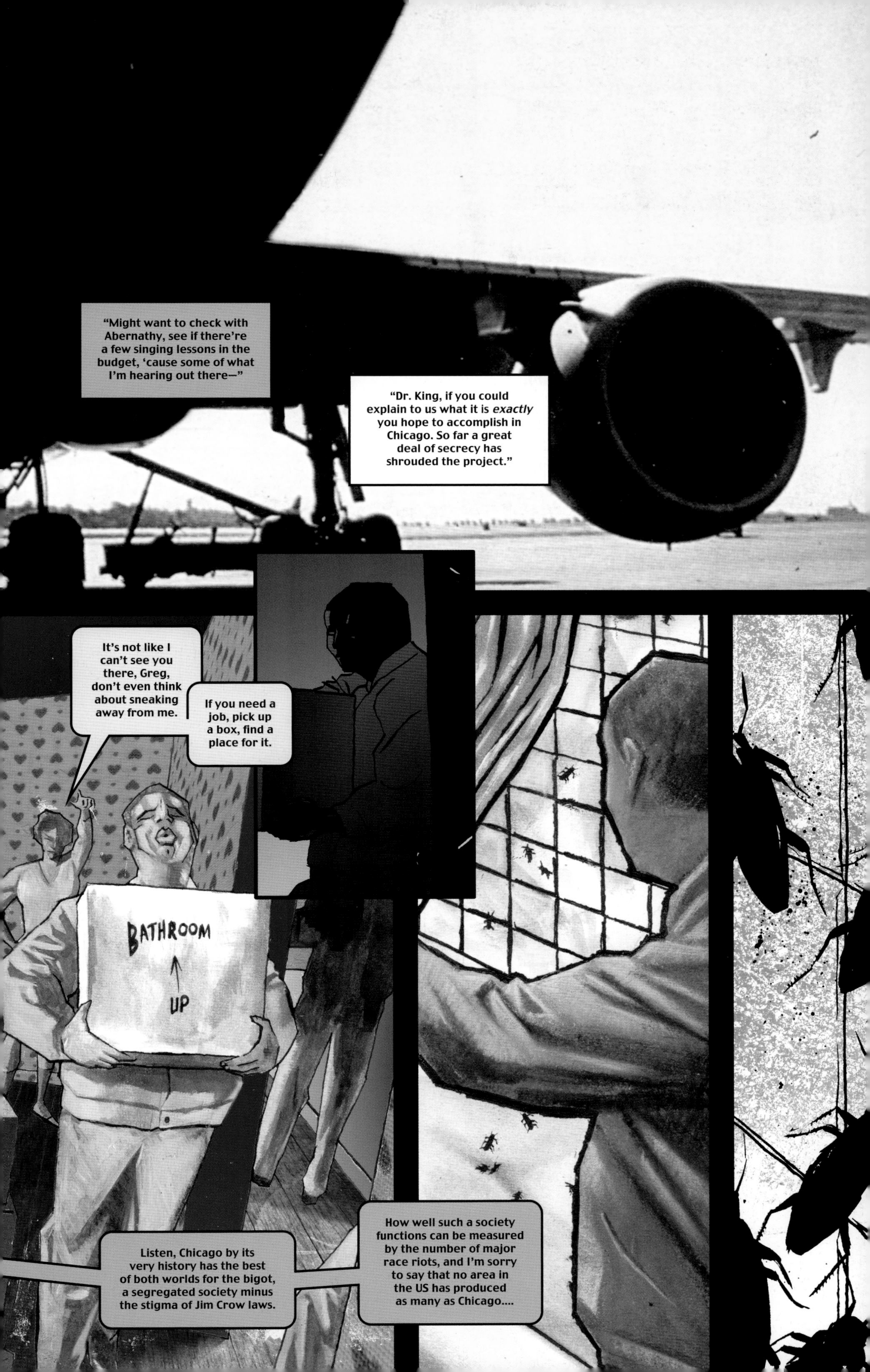
"Might want to check with Abernathy, see if there're a few singing lessons in the budget, 'cause some of what I'm hearing out there—"
"Dr. King, if you could explain to us what it is *exactly* you hope to accomplish in Chicago. So far a great deal of secrecy has shrouded the project."
It's not like I can't see you there, Greg, don't even think about sneaking away from me.
If you need a job, pick up a box, find a place for it.
BATHROOM
UP
Listen, Chicago by its very history has the best of both worlds for the bigot, a segregated society minus the stigma of Jim Crow laws.
How well such a society functions can be measured by the number of major race riots, and I'm sorry to say that no area in the US has produced as many as Chicago....

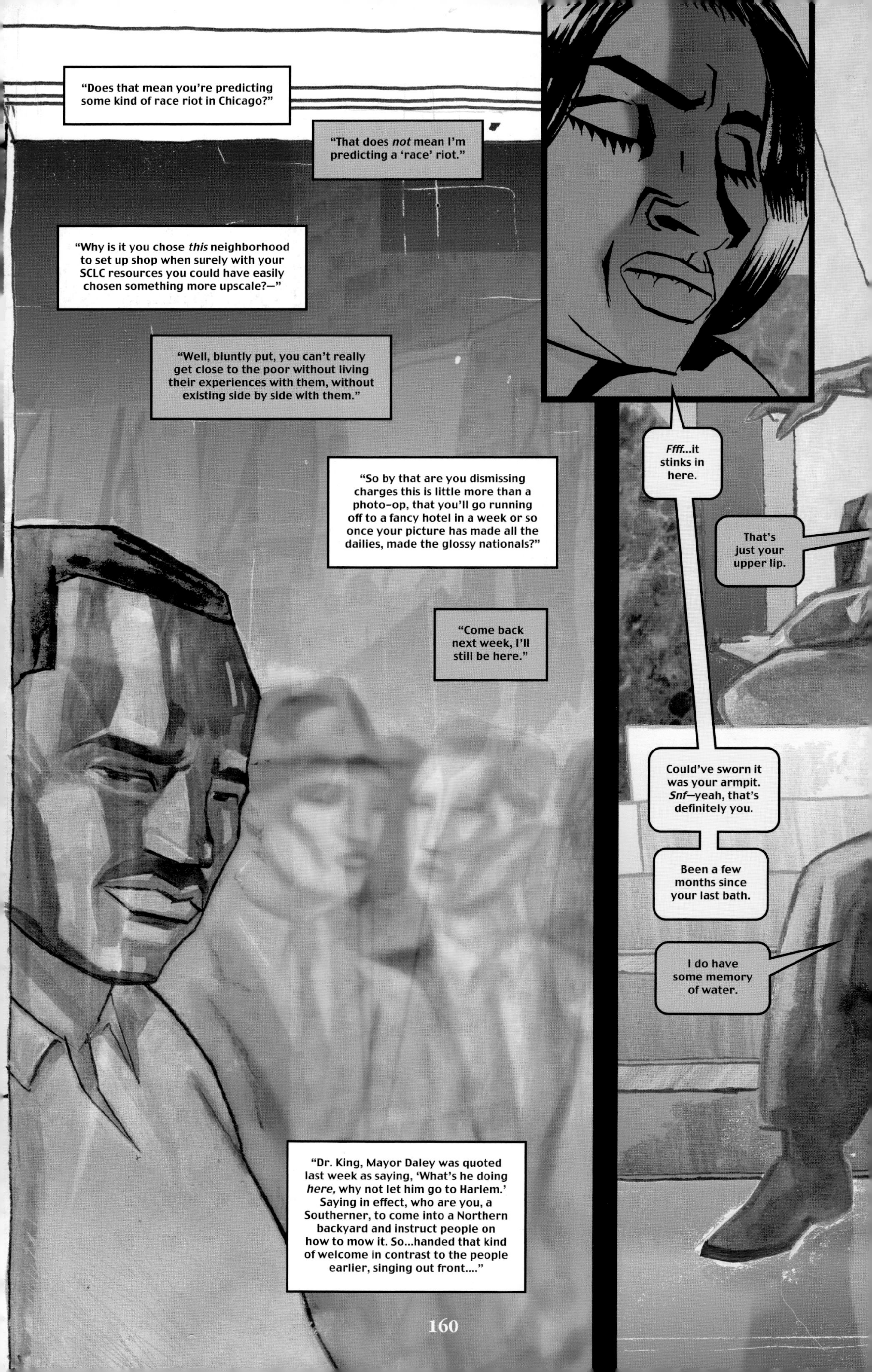

"Does that mean you're predicting some kind of race riot in Chicago?"
"That does *not* mean I'm predicting a 'race' riot."
"Why is it you chose *this* neighborhood to set up shop when surely with your SCLC resources you could have easily chosen something more upscale?—"
"Well, bluntly put, you can't really get close to the poor without living their experiences with them, without existing side by side with them."
"So by that are you dismissing charges this is little more than a photo-op, that you'll go running off to a fancy hotel in a week or so once your picture has made all the dailies, made the glossy nationals?"
"Come back next week, I'll still be here."
"Dr. King, Mayor Daley was quoted last week as saying, 'What's he doing *here,* why not let him go to Harlem.' Saying in effect, who are you, a Southerner, to come into a Northern backyard and instruct people on how to mow it. So...handed that kind of welcome in contrast to the people earlier, singing out front...."
Ffff...it stinks in here.
That's just your upper lip.
Could've sworn it was your armpit. *Snf*—yeah, that's definitely you.
Been a few months since your last bath.
I do have some memory of water.

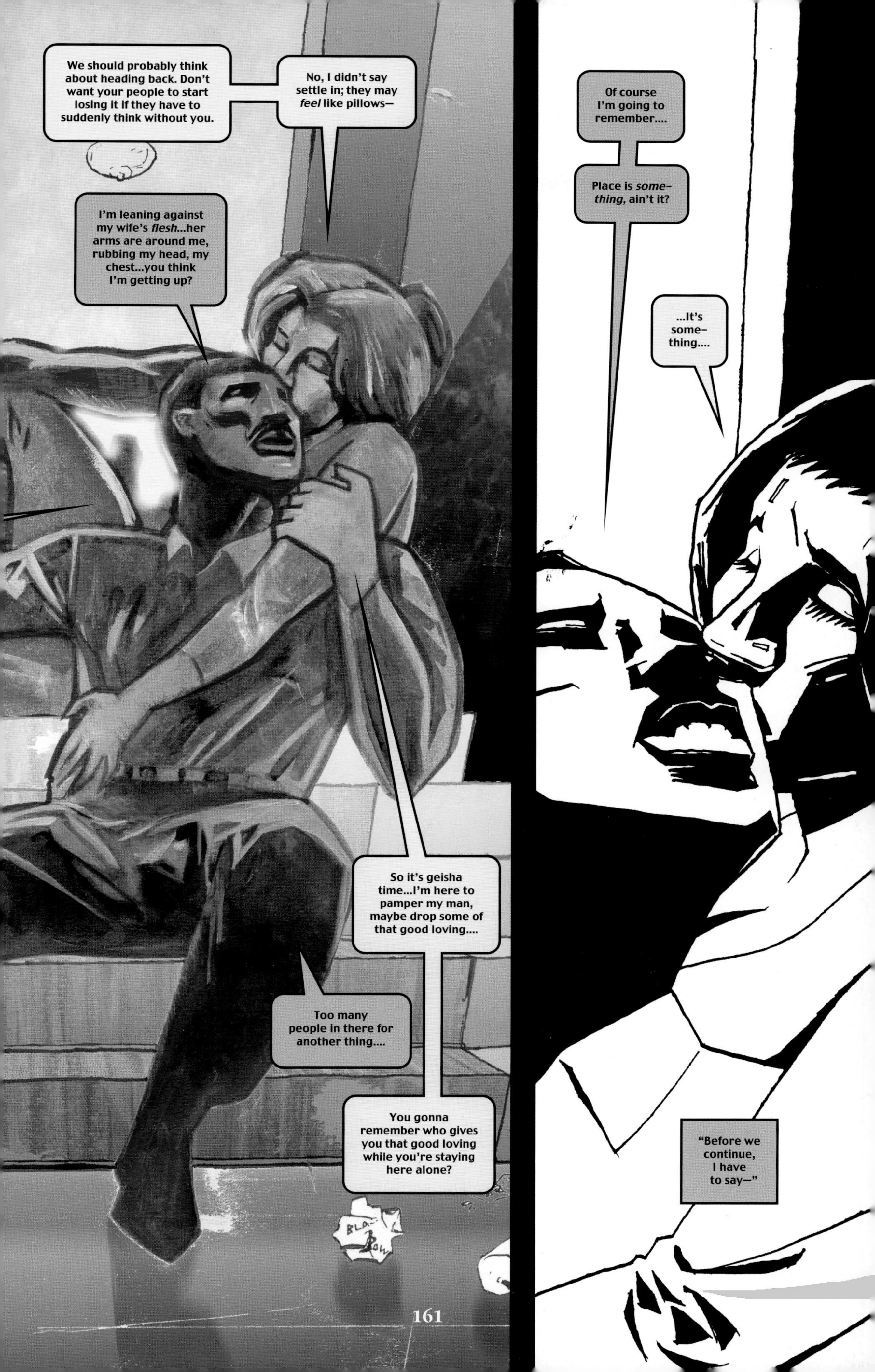
We should probably think about heading back. Don't want your people to start losing it if they have to suddenly think without you.
No, I didn't say settle in; they may *feel* like pillows—
I'm leaning against my wife's *flesh*...her arms are around me, rubbing my head, my chest...you think I'm getting up?
So it's geisha time...I'm here to pamper my man, maybe drop some of that good loving....
Too many people in there for another thing....
You gonna remember who gives you that good loving while you're staying here alone?
Of course I'm going to remember....
Place is *some-thing*, ain't it?
...It's some-thing....
"Before we continue, I have to say—"

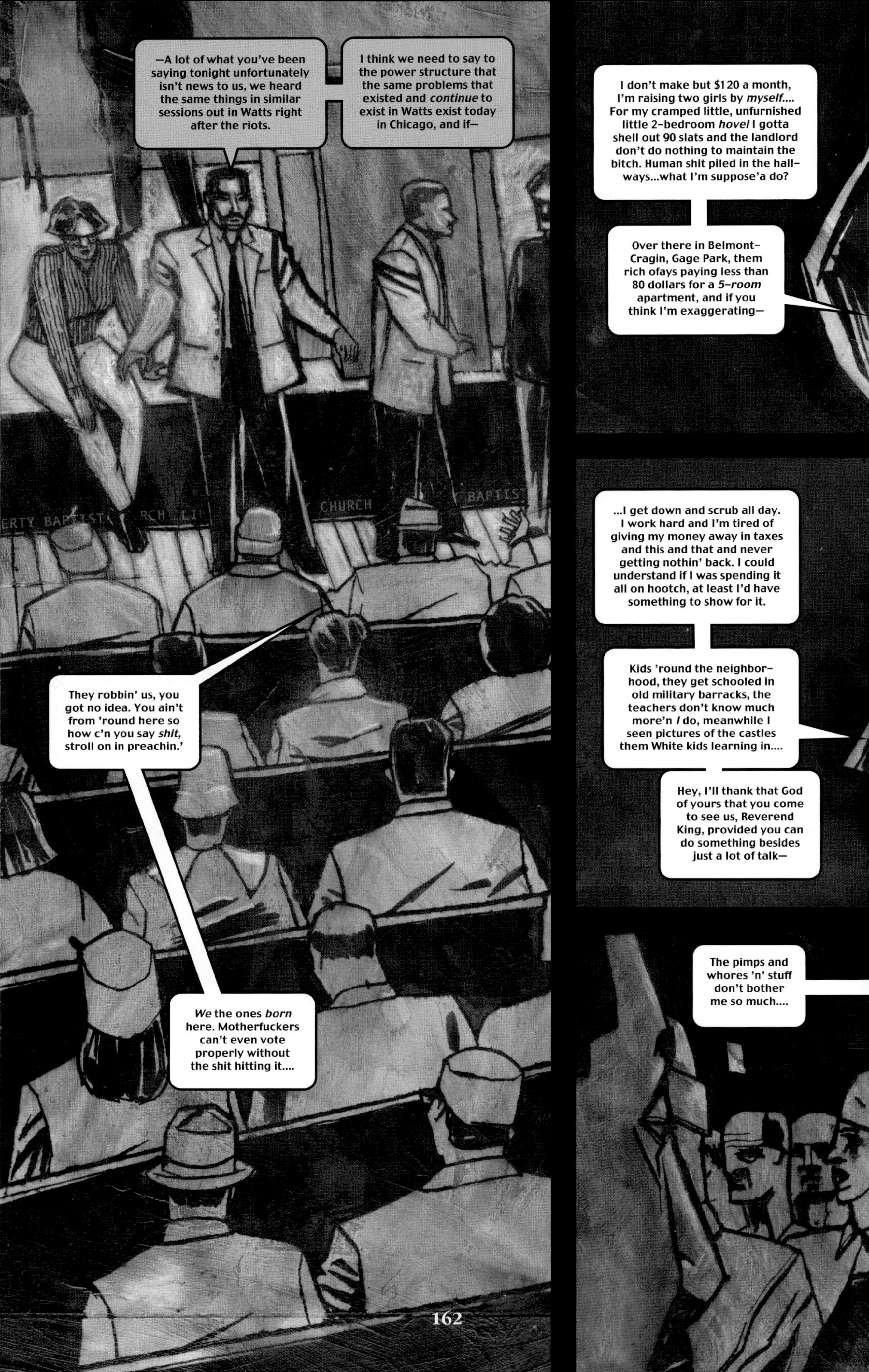
—A lot of what you've been saying tonight unfortunately isn't news to us, we heard the same things in similar sessions out in Watts right after the riots.
I think we need to say to the power structure that the same problems that existed and *continue* to exist in Watts exist today in Chicago, and if—
They robbin' us, you got no idea. You ain't from 'round here so how c'n you say *shit,* stroll on in preachin.'
We the ones *born* here. Motherfuckers can't even vote properly without the shit hitting it....
I don't make but $120 a month, I'm raising two girls by *myself....* For my cramped little, unfurnished little 2-bedroom *hovel* I gotta shell out 90 slats and the landlord don't do nothing to maintain the bitch. Human shit piled in the hall-ways...what I'm suppose'a do?
Over there in Belmont-Cragin, Gage Park, them rich ofays paying less than 80 dollars for a *5-room* apartment, and if you think I'm exaggerating—
...I get down and scrub all day. I work hard and I'm tired of giving my money away in taxes and this and that and never getting nothin' back. I could understand if I was spending it all on hootch, at least I'd have something to show for it.
Kids 'round the neighbor-hood, they get schooled in old military barracks, the teachers don't know much more'n *I* do, meanwhile I seen pictures of the castles them White kids learning in....
Hey, I'll thank that God of yours that you come to see us, Reverend King, provided you can do something besides just a lot of talk—
The pimps and whores 'n' stuff don't bother me so much....

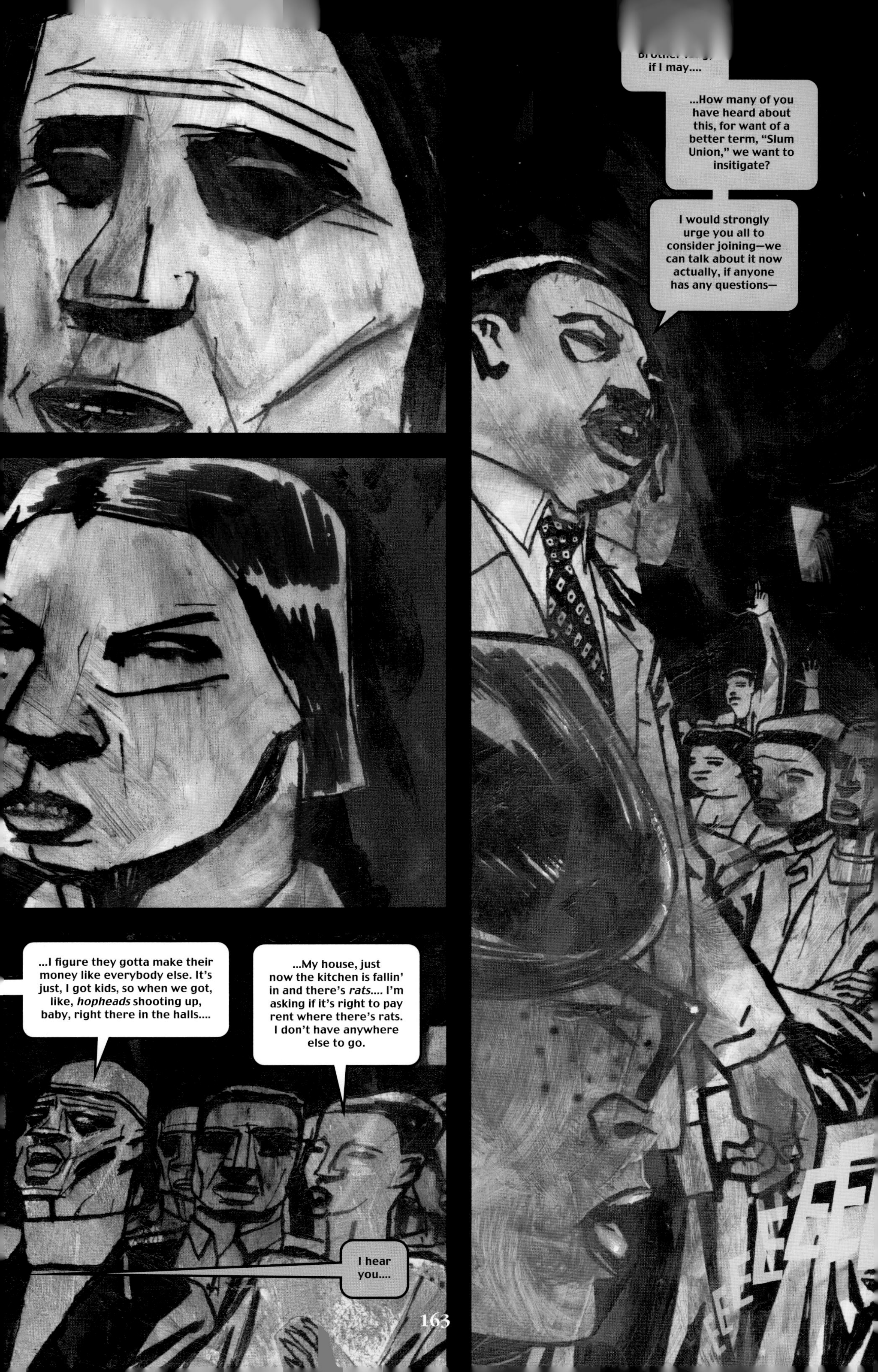
...I figure they gotta make their money like everybody else. It's just, I got kids, so when we got, like, *hopheads* shooting up, baby, right there in the halls....
...My house, just now the kitchen is fallin' in and there's *rats*.... I'm asking if it's right to pay rent where there's rats. I don't have anywhere else to go.
I hear you....
if I may....
...How many of you have heard about this, for want of a better term, "Slum Union," we want to insitigate?
I would strongly urge you all to consider joining—we can talk about it now actually, if anyone has any questions—

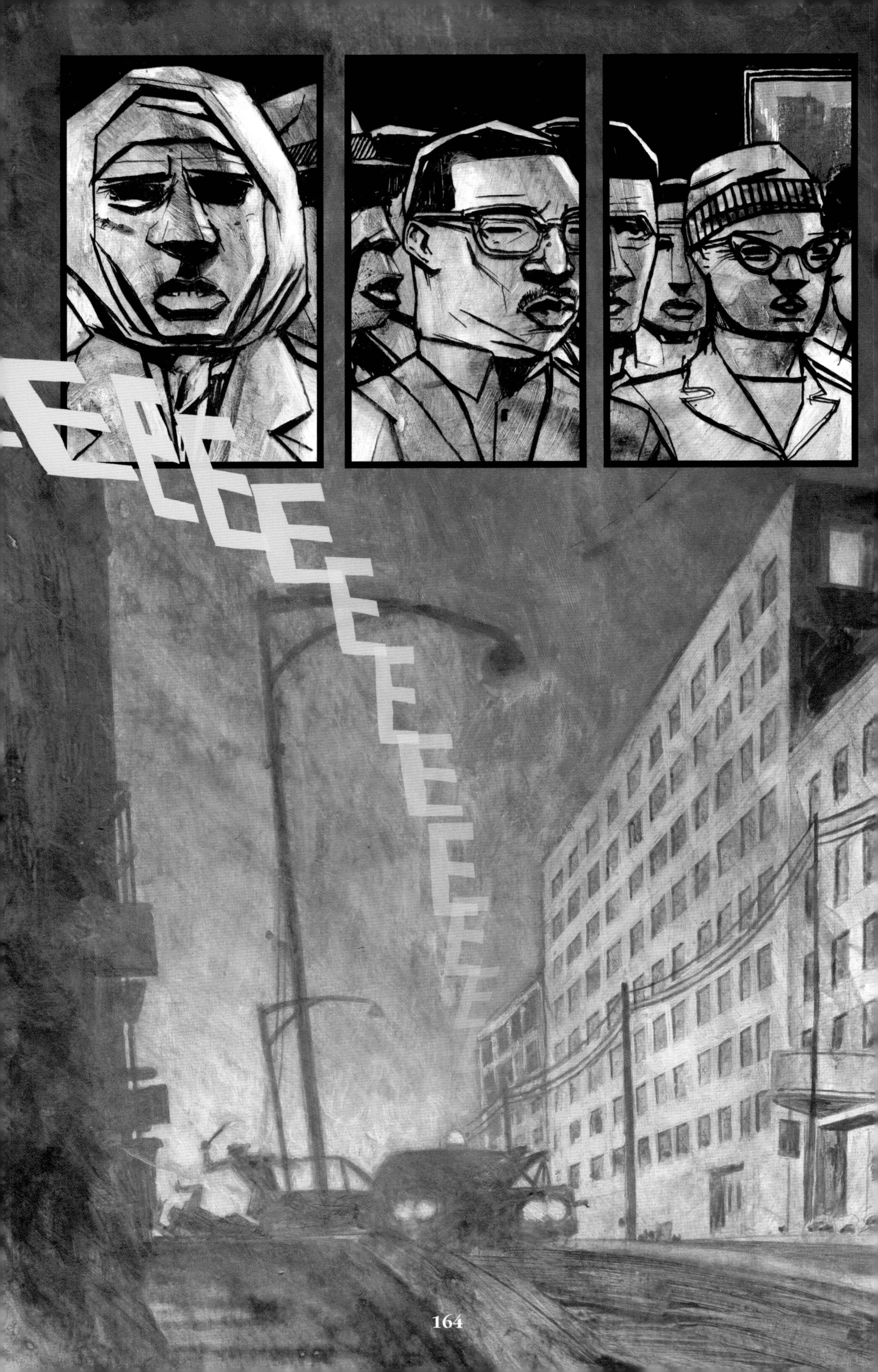
EEEEEEEEEEEEEEEEE

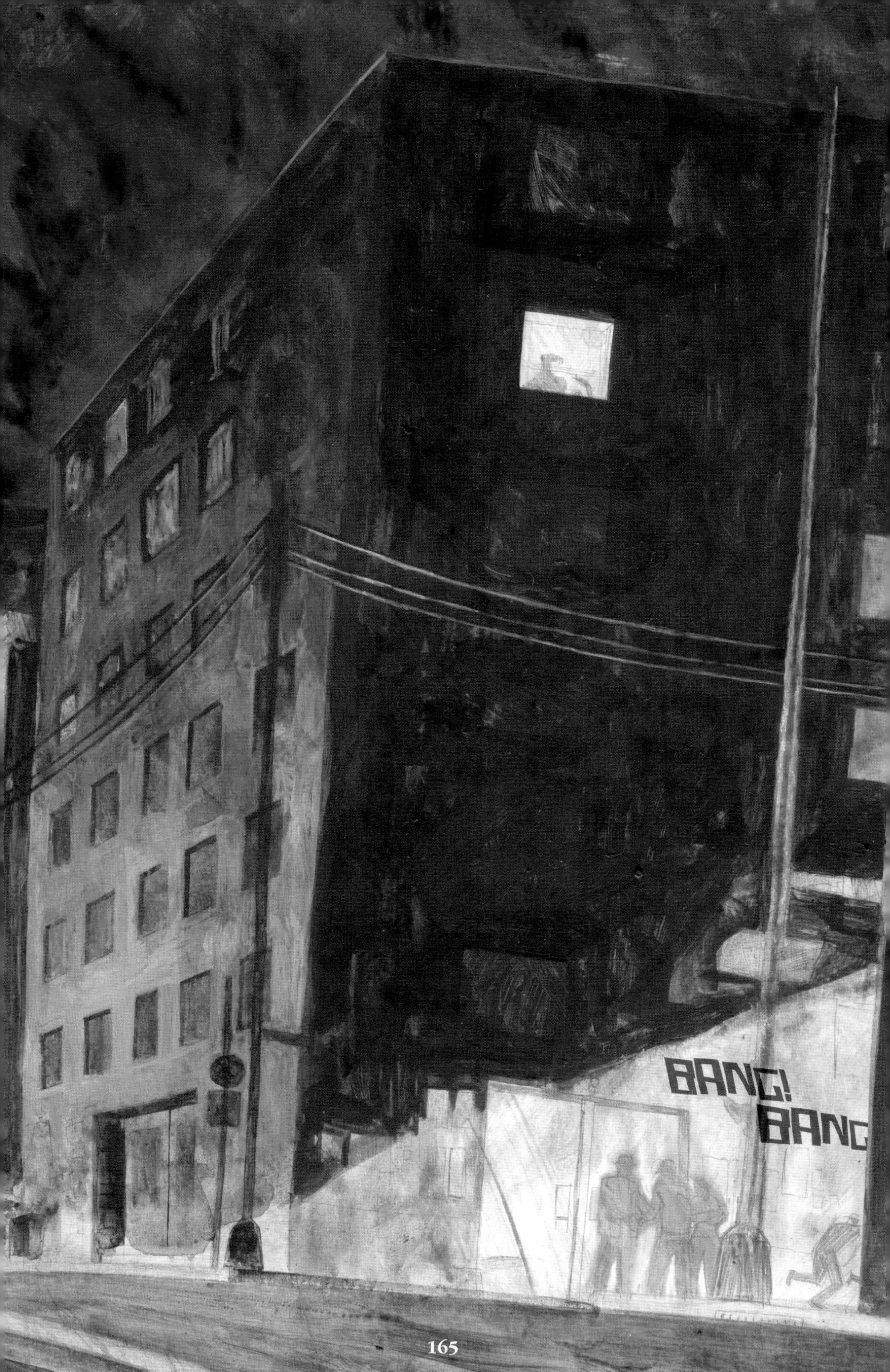
BANG!
BANG

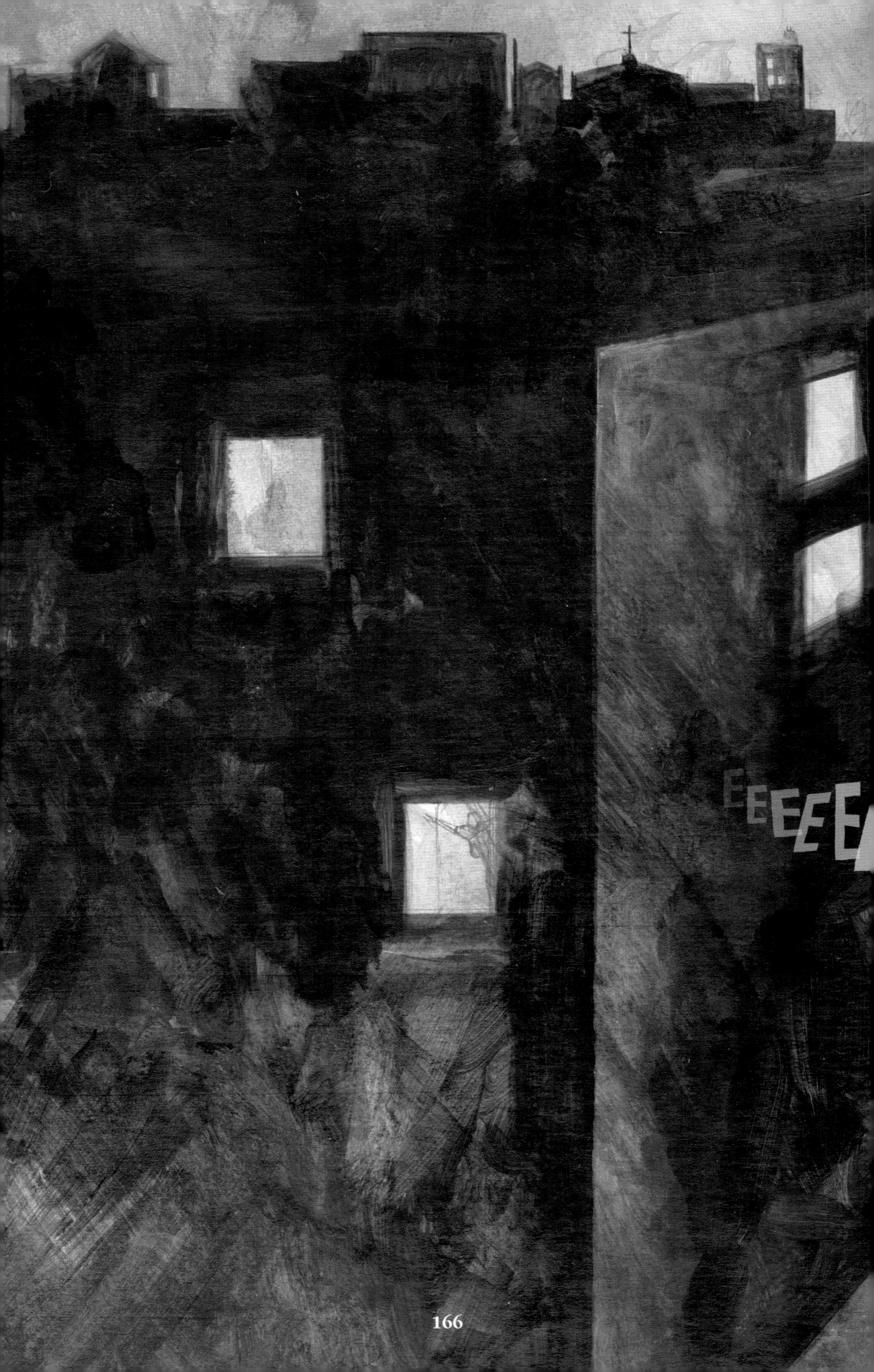
EEEEE

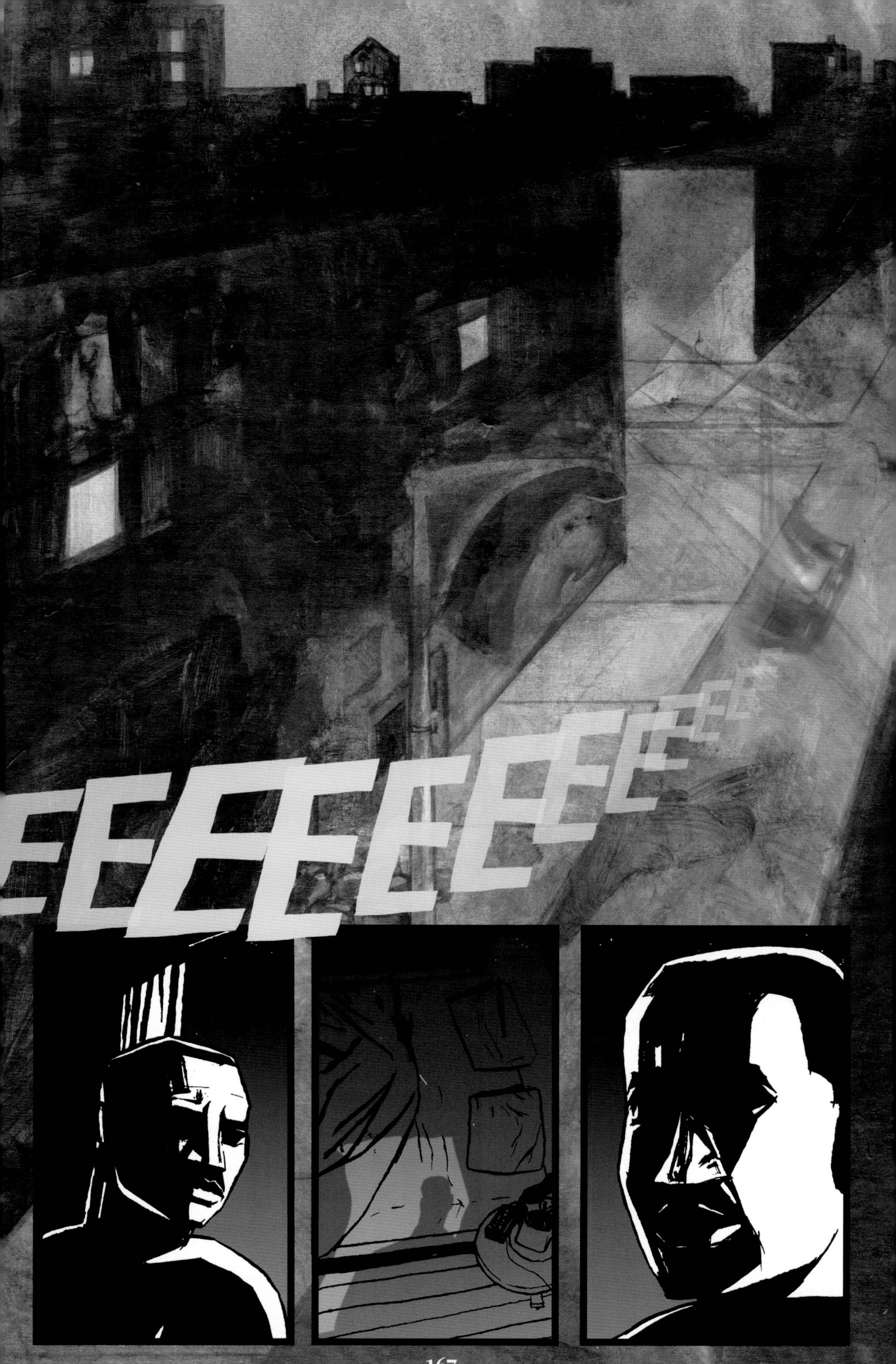
EEEEEEEEEEEEEE

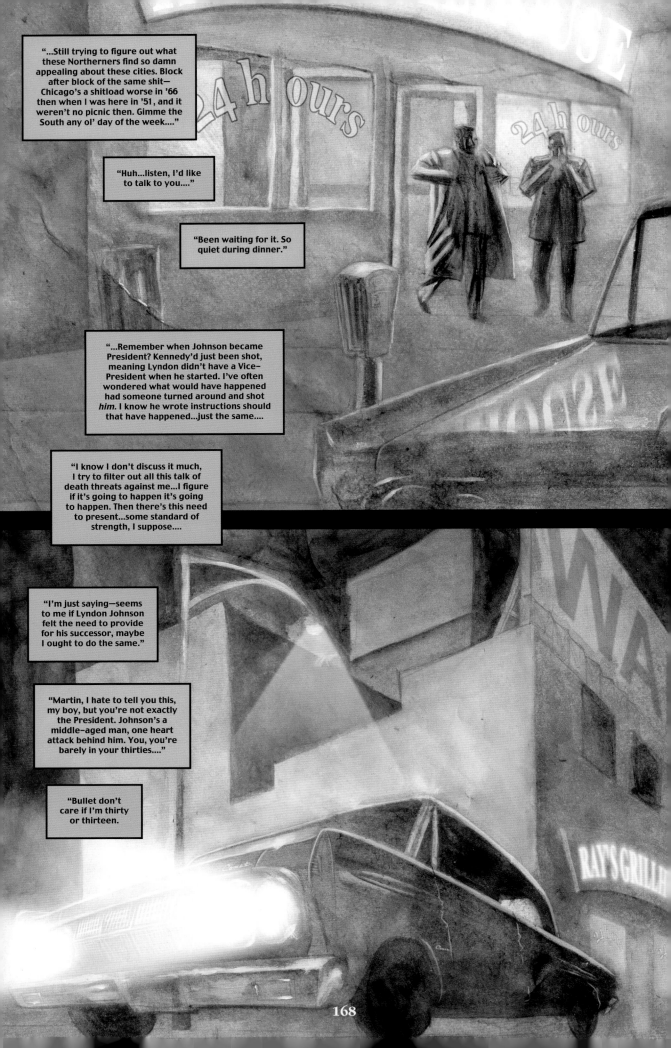

"...Still trying to figure out what these Northerners find so damn appealing about these cities. Block after block of the same shit—Chicago's a shitload worse in '66 then when I was here in '51, and it weren't no picnic then. Gimme the South any ol' day of the week...."

"Huh...listen, I'd like to talk to you...."

"Been waiting for it. So quiet during dinner."

"...Remember when Johnson became President? Kennedy'd just been shot, meaning Lyndon didn't have a Vice–President when he started. I've often wondered what would have happened had someone turned around and shot *him*. I know he wrote instructions should that have happened...just the same...."

"I know I don't discuss it much, I try to filter out all this talk of death threats against me...I figure if it's going to happen it's going to happen. Then there's this need to present...some standard of strength, I suppose...."

"I'm just saying—seems to me if Lyndon Johnson felt the need to provide for his successor, maybe I ought to do the same."

"Martin, I hate to tell you this, my boy, but you're not exactly the President. Johnson's a middle–aged man, one heart attack behind him. You, you're barely in your thirties...."

"Bullet don't care if I'm thirty or thirteen.

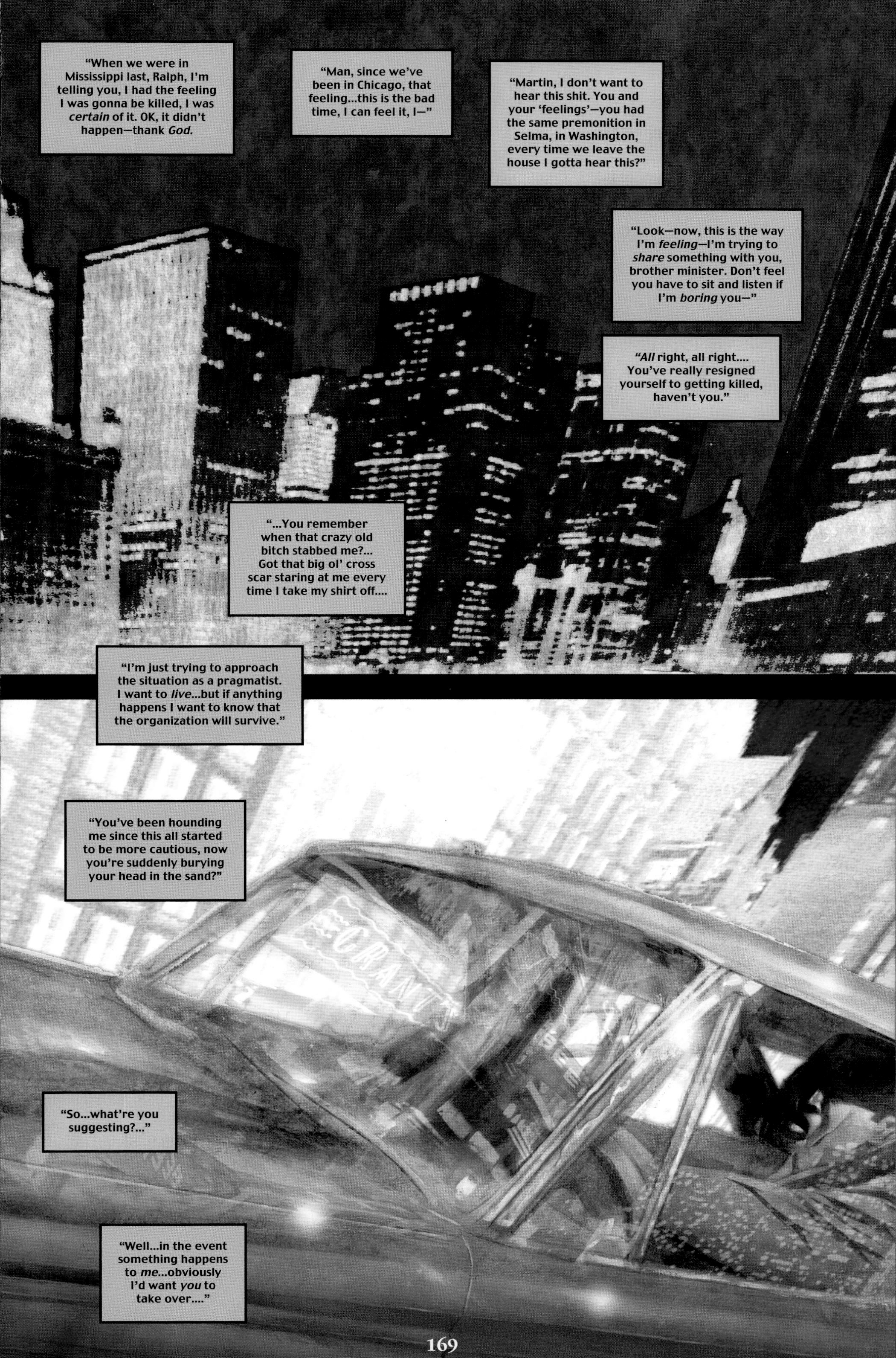
"When we were in Mississippi last, Ralph, I'm telling you, I had the feeling I was gonna be killed, I was *certain* of it. OK, it didn't happen—thank *God.*
"Man, since we've been in Chicago, that feeling...this is the bad time, I can feel it, I—"
"Martin, I don't want to hear this shit. You and your 'feelings'—you had the same premonition in Selma, in Washington, every time we leave the house I gotta hear this?"
"Look—now, this is the way I'm *feeling*—I'm trying to *share* something with you, brother minister. Don't feel you have to sit and listen if I'm *boring* you—"
"*All* right, all right.... You've really resigned yourself to getting killed, haven't you."
"...You remember when that crazy old bitch stabbed me?... Got that big ol' cross scar staring at me every time I take my shirt off....
"I'm just trying to approach the situation as a pragmatist. I want to *live*...but if anything happens I want to know that the organization will survive."
"You've been hounding me since this all started to be more cautious, now you're suddenly burying your head in the sand?"
"So...what're you suggesting?..."
"Well...in the event something happens to *me*...obviously I'd want *you* to take over...."

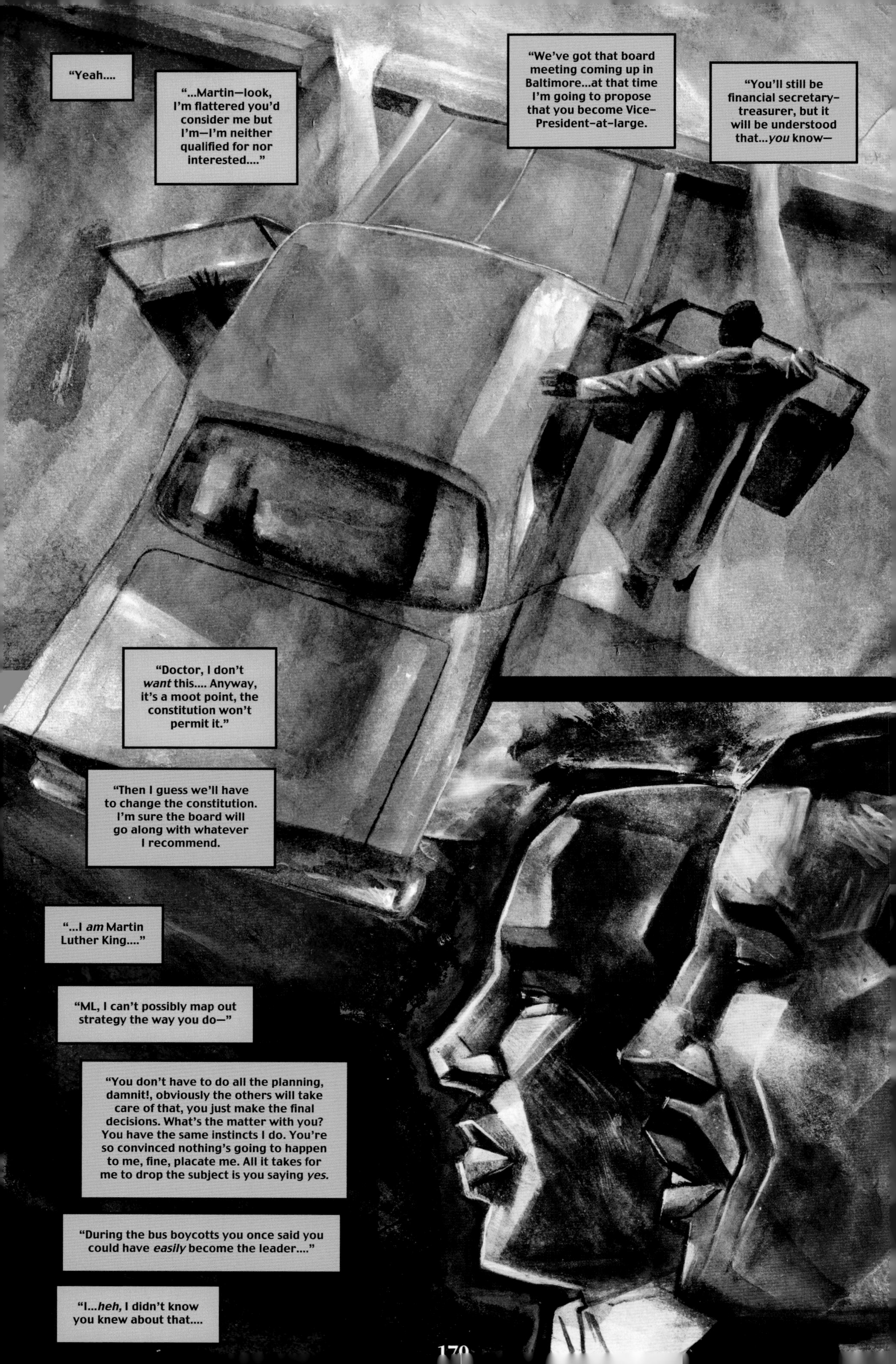
"Yeah....
"...Martin—look, I'm flattered you'd consider me but I'm—I'm neither qualified for nor interested...."
"We've got that board meeting coming up in Baltimore...at that time I'm going to propose that you become Vice-President-at-large.
"You'll still be financial secretary-treasurer, but it will be understood that...*you* know—
"Doctor, I don't *want* this.... Anyway, it's a moot point, the constitution won't permit it."
"Then I guess we'll have to change the constitution. I'm sure the board will go along with whatever I recommend.
"...I *am* Martin Luther King...."
"ML, I can't possibly map out strategy the way you do—"
"You don't have to do all the planning, damnit!, obviously the others will take care of that, you just make the final decisions. What's the matter with you? You have the same instincts I do. You're so convinced nothing's going to happen to me, fine, placate me. All it takes for me to drop the subject is you saying *yes.*
"During the bus boycotts you once said you could have *easily* become the leader...."
"I...*heh,* I didn't know you knew about that....

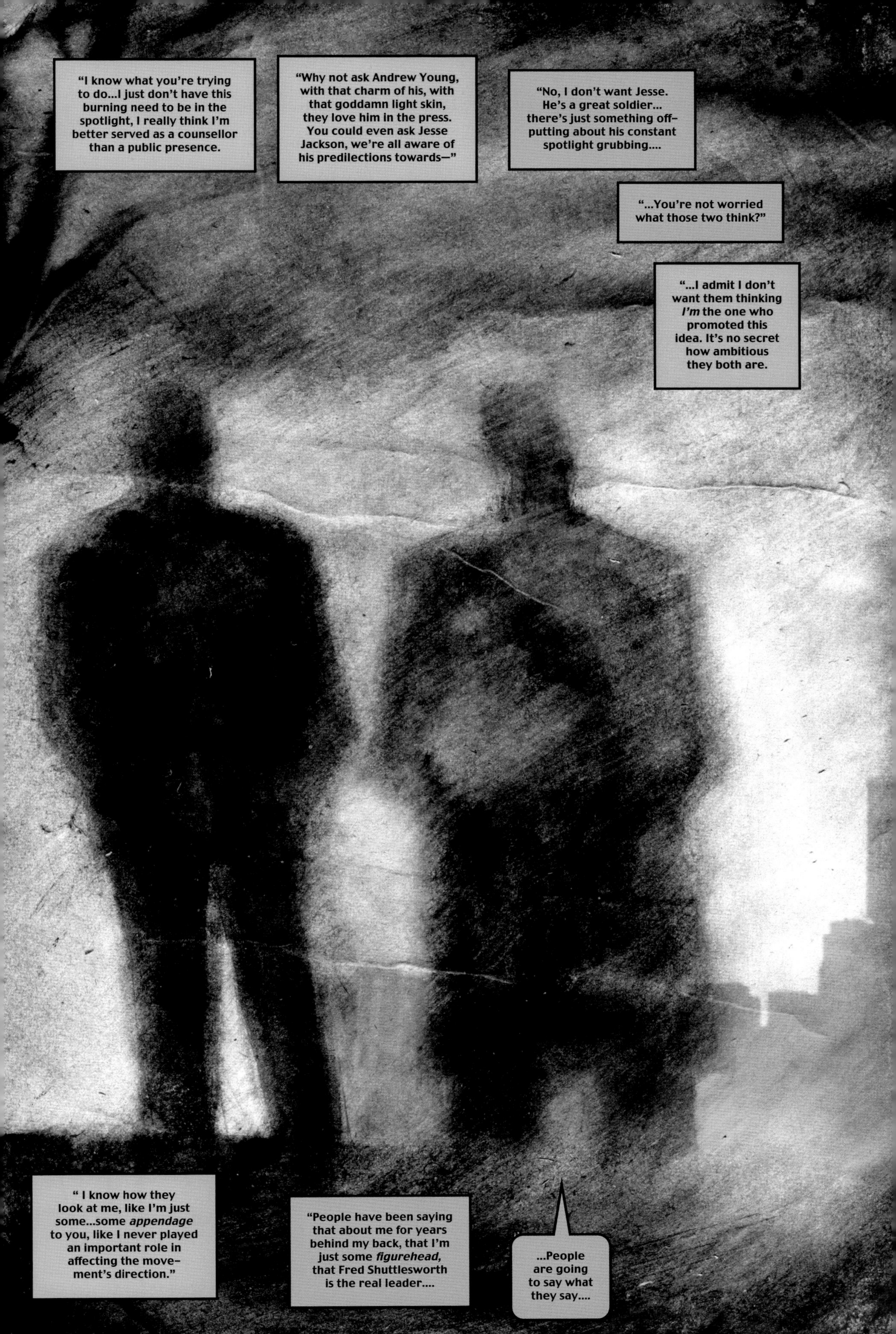
"I know what you're trying to do...I just don't have this burning need to be in the spotlight, I really think I'm better served as a counsellor than a public presence.
"Why not ask Andrew Young, with that charm of his, with that goddamn light skin, they love him in the press. You could even ask Jesse Jackson, we're all aware of his predilections towards—"
"No, I don't want Jesse. He's a great soldier... there's just something off-putting about his constant spotlight grubbing....
"...You're not worried what those two think?"
"...I admit I don't want them thinking *I'm* the one who promoted this idea. It's no secret how ambitious they both are.
" I know how they look at me, like I'm just some...some *appendage* to you, like I never played an important role in affecting the movement's direction."
"People have been saying that about me for years behind my back, that I'm just some *figurehead*, that Fred Shuttlesworth is the real leader....
...People are going to say what they say....

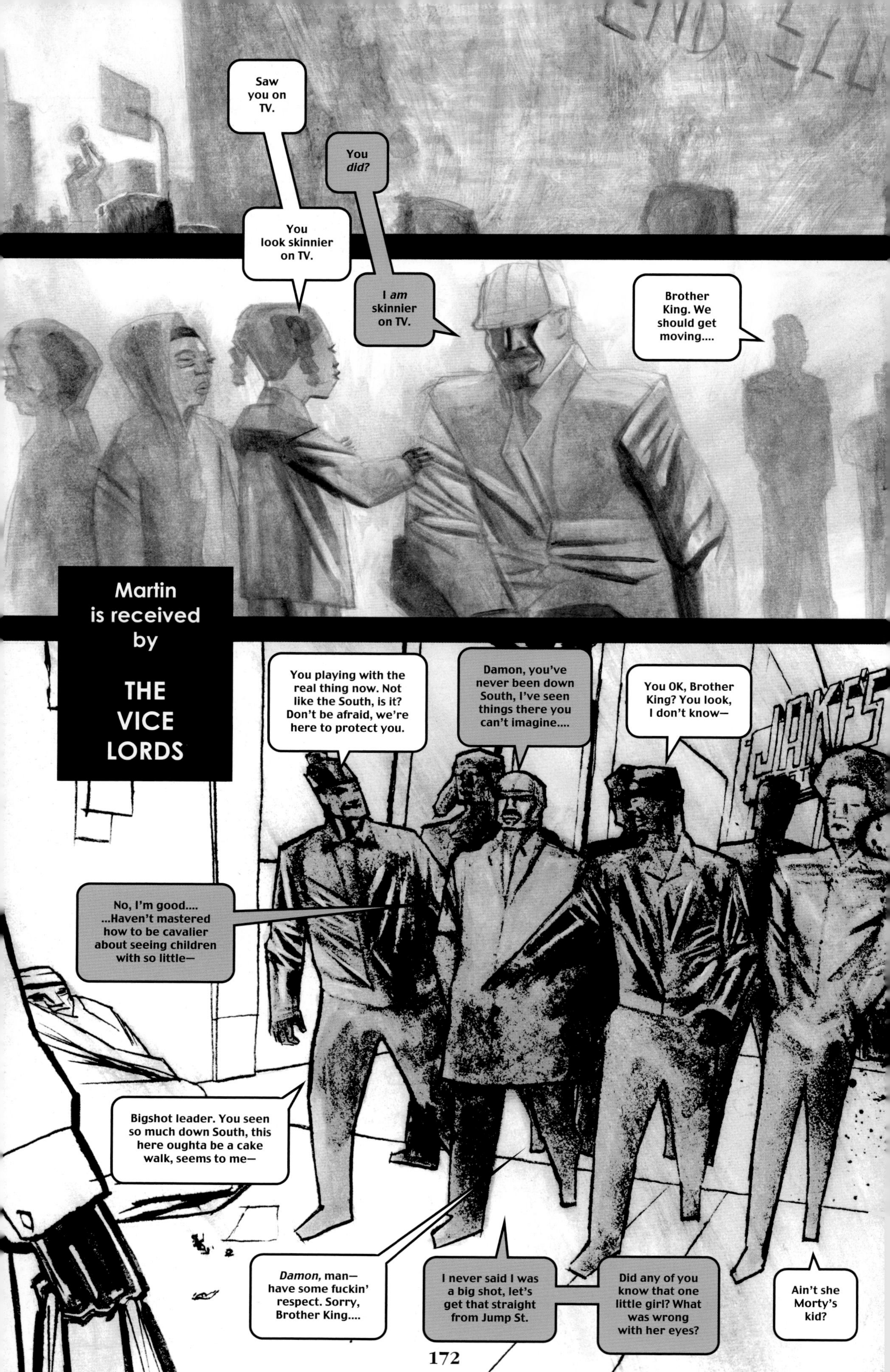

Saw you on TV.
You *did?*
You look skinnier on TV.
I *am* skinnier on TV.
Brother King. We should get moving....
Martin is received by THE VICE LORDS
You playing with the real thing now. Not like the South, is it? Don't be afraid, we're here to protect you.
Damon, you've never been down South, I've seen things there you can't imagine....
You OK, Brother King? You look, I don't know—
No, I'm good.... ...Haven't mastered how to be cavalier about seeing children with so little—
Bigshot leader. You seen so much down South, this here oughta be a cake walk, seems to me—
Damon, man—have some fuckin' respect. Sorry, Brother King....
I never said I was a big shot, let's get that straight from Jump St.
Did any of you know that one little girl? What was wrong with her eyes?
Ain't she Morty's kid?

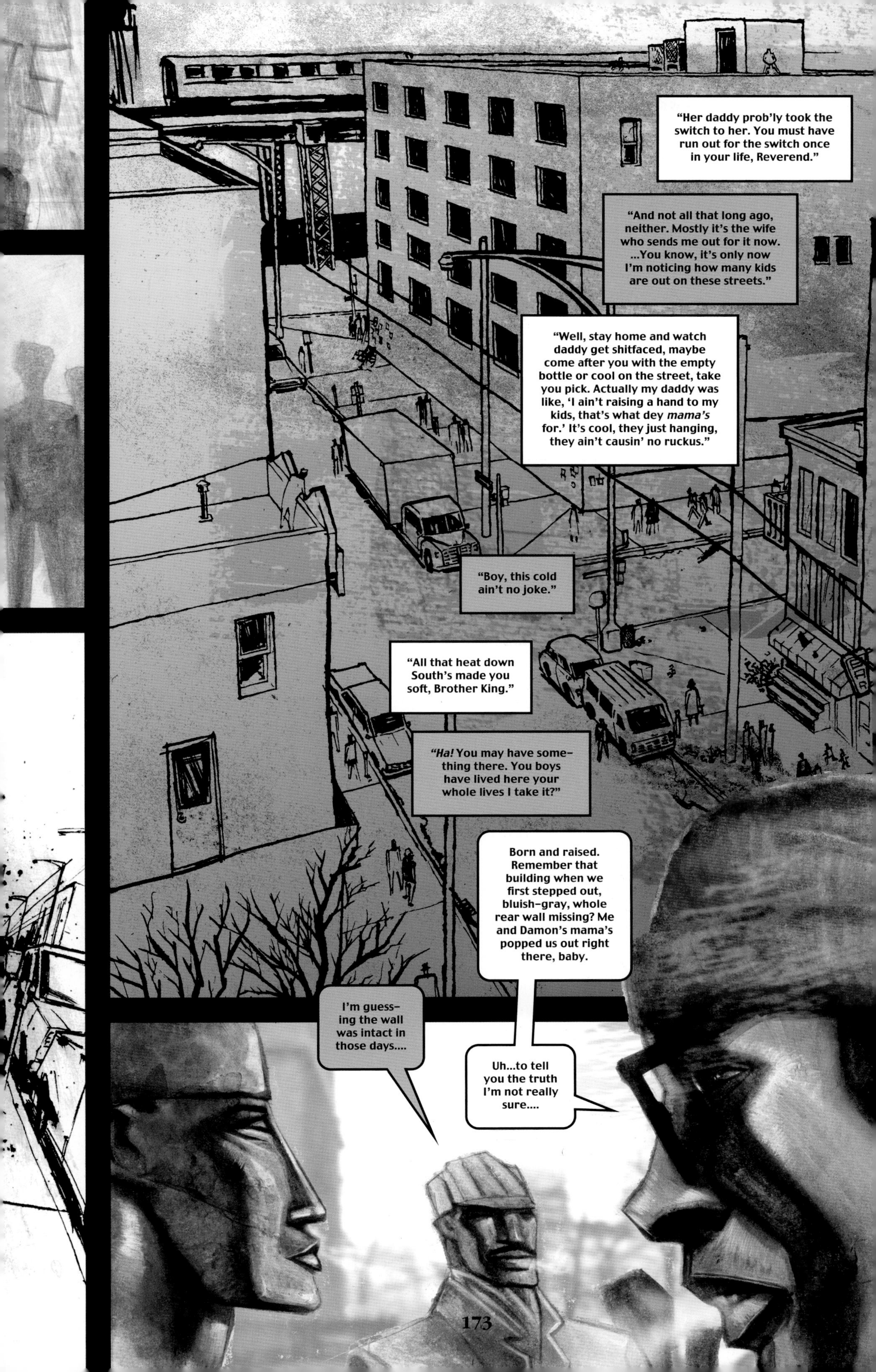
"Her daddy prob'ly took the switch to her. You must have run out for the switch once in your life, Reverend."
"And not all that long ago, neither. Mostly it's the wife who sends me out for it now. ...You know, it's only now I'm noticing how many kids are out on these streets."
"Well, stay home and watch daddy get shitfaced, maybe come after you with the empty bottle or cool on the street, take you pick. Actually my daddy was like, 'I ain't raising a hand to my kids, that's what dey *mama's* for.' It's cool, they just hanging, they ain't causin' no ruckus."
"Boy, this cold ain't no joke."
"All that heat down South's made you soft, Brother King."
"*Ha!* You may have some-thing there. You boys have lived here your whole lives I take it?"
Born and raised. Remember that building when we first stepped out, bluish-gray, whole rear wall missing? Me and Damon's mama's popped us out right there, baby.
I'm guess-ing the wall was intact in those days....
Uh...to tell you the truth I'm not really sure....

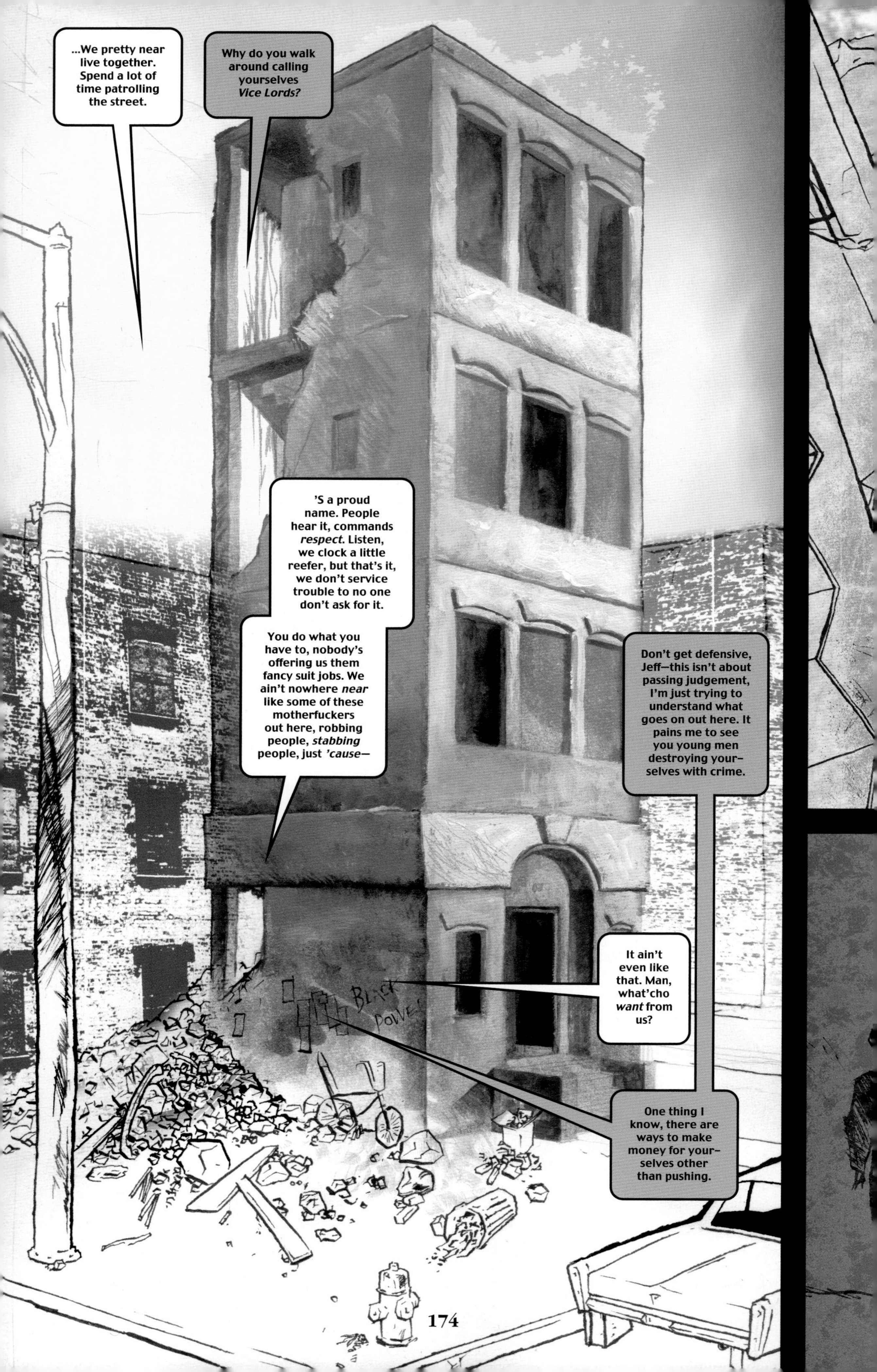
...We pretty near live together. Spend a lot of time patrolling the street.
Why do you walk around calling yourselves *Vice Lords?*
'S a proud name. People hear it, commands *respect.* Listen, we clock a little reefer, but that's it, we don't service trouble to no one don't ask for it.
You do what you have to, nobody's offering us them fancy suit jobs. We ain't nowhere *near* like some of these motherfuckers out here, robbing people, *stabbing* people, just *'cause*—
Don't get defensive, Jeff—this isn't about passing judgement, I'm just trying to understand what goes on out here. It pains me to see you young men destroying your-selves with crime.
It ain't even like that. Man, what'cho *want* from us?
One thing I know, there are ways to make money for your-selves other than pushing.

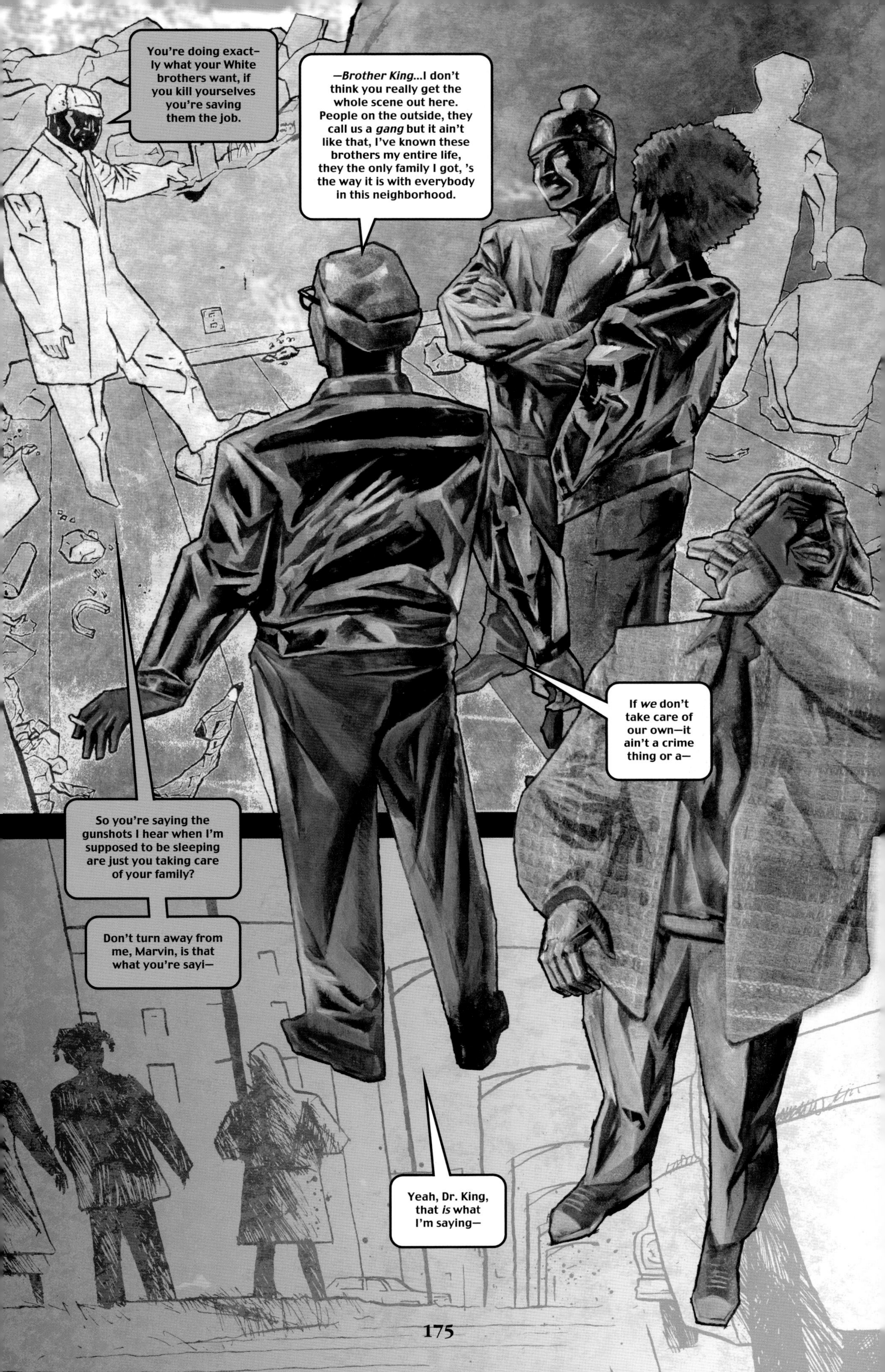
You're doing exactly what your White brothers want, if you kill yourselves you're saving them the job.
—*Brother King*...I don't think you really get the whole scene out here. People on the outside, they call us a *gang* but it ain't like that, I've known these brothers my entire life, they the only family I got, 's the way it is with everybody in this neighborhood.
If *we* don't take care of our own—it ain't a crime thing or a—
So you're saying the gunshots I hear when I'm supposed to be sleeping are just you taking care of your family?
Don't turn away from me, Marvin, is that what you're sayi—
Yeah, Dr. King, that *is* what I'm saying—

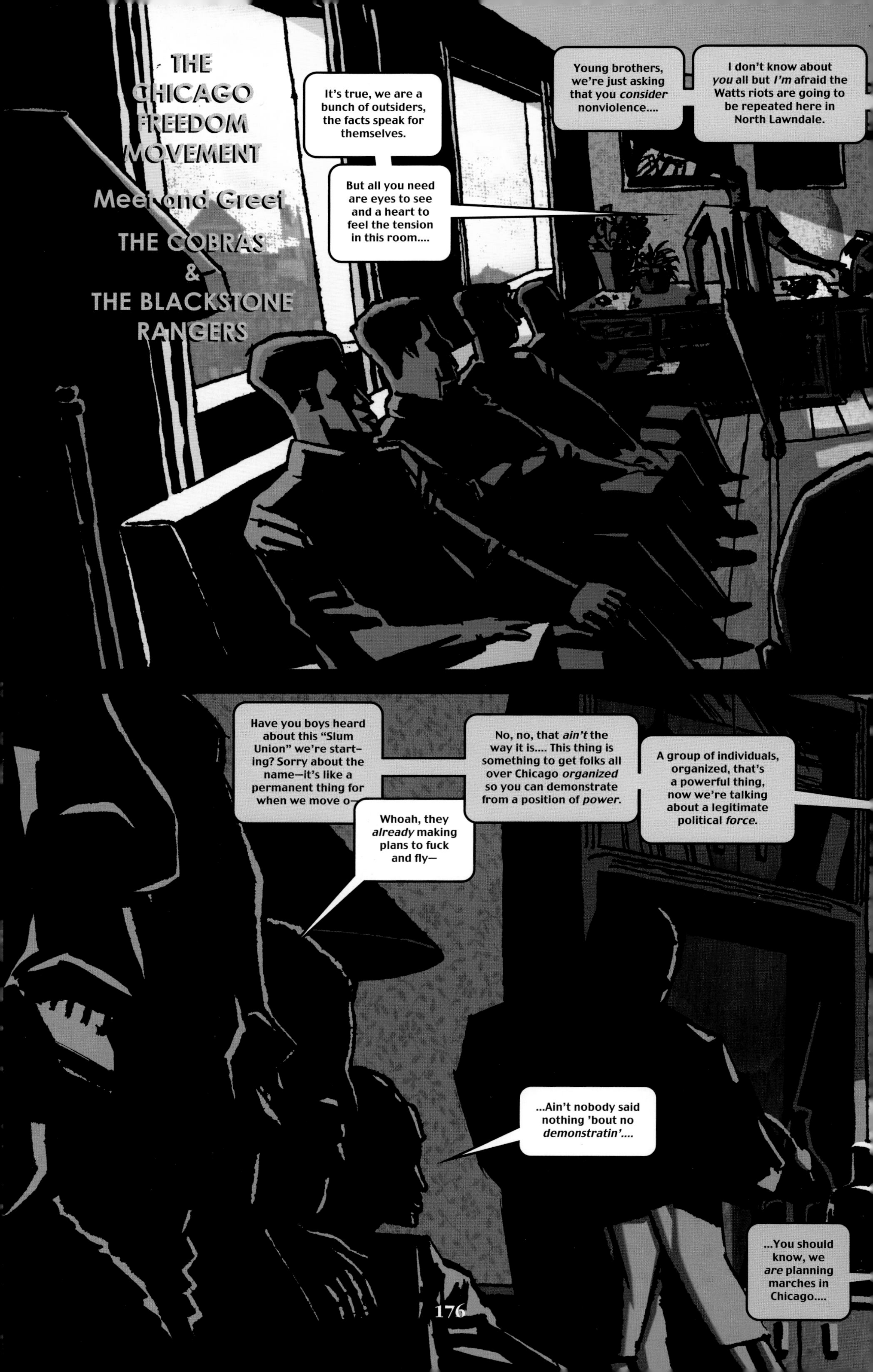
THE CHICAGO FREEDOM MOVEMENT
Meet and Greet
THE COBRAS & THE BLACKSTONE RANGERS
It's true, we are a bunch of outsiders, the facts speak for themselves.
But all you need are eyes to see and a heart to feel the tension in this room....
Young brothers, we're just asking that you *consider* nonviolence....
I don't know about *you* all but *I'm* afraid the Watts riots are going to be repeated here in North Lawndale.
Have you boys heard about this "Slum Union" we're starting? Sorry about the name—it's like a permanent thing for when we move o—
Whoah, they *already* making plans to fuck and fly—
No, no, that *ain't* the way it is.... This thing is something to get folks all over Chicago *organized* so you can demonstrate from a position of *power.*
A group of individuals, organized, that's a powerful thing, now we're talking about a legitimate political *force.*
...Ain't nobody said nothing 'bout no *demonstratin'*....
...You should know, we *are* planning marches in Chicago....

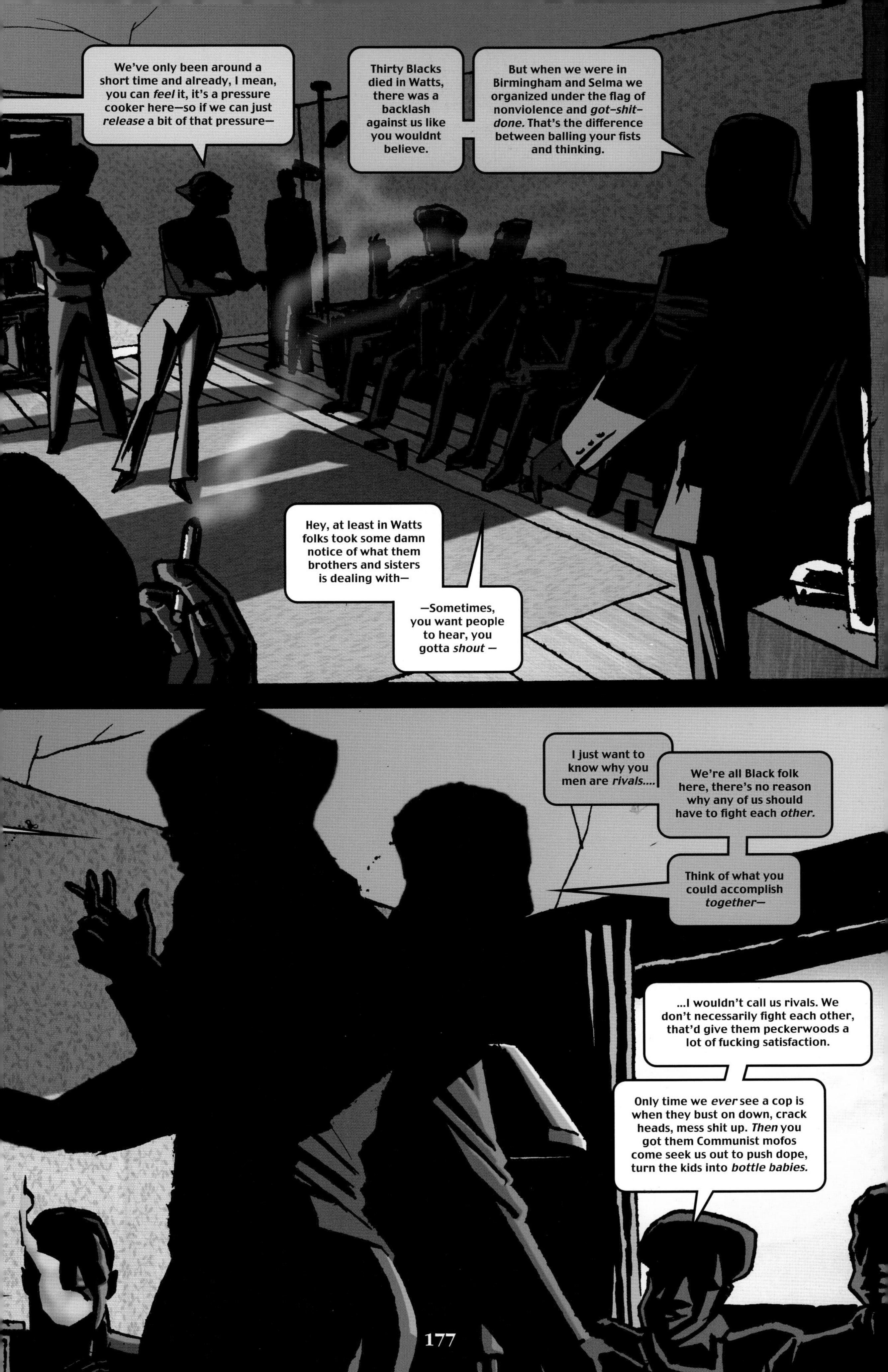
We've only been around a short time and already, I mean, you can *feel* it, it's a pressure cooker here—so if we can just *release* a bit of that pressure—
Thirty Blacks died in Watts, there was a backlash against us like you wouldnt believe.
But when we were in Birmingham and Selma we organized under the flag of nonviolence and *got-shit-done.* That's the difference between balling your fists and thinking.
Hey, at least in Watts folks took some damn notice of what them brothers and sisters is dealing with—
—Sometimes, you want people to hear, you gotta *shout* —
I just want to know why you men are *rivals....*
We're all Black folk here, there's no reason why any of us should have to fight each *other.*
Think of what you could accomplish *together—*
...I wouldn't call us rivals. We don't necessarily fight each other, that'd give them peckerwoods a lot of fucking satisfaction.
Only time we *ever* see a cop is when they bust on down, crack heads, mess shit up. *Then* you got them Communist mofos come seek us out to push dope, turn the kids into *bottle babies.*

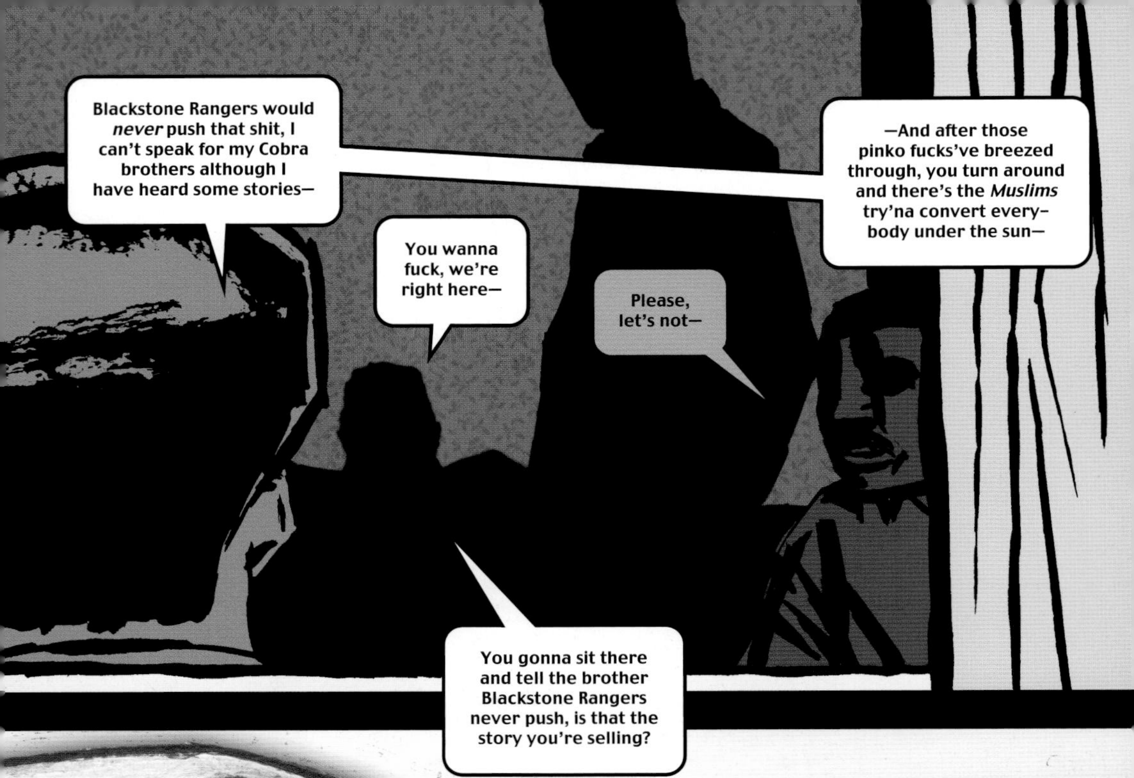
Blackstone Rangers would *never* push that shit, I can't speak for my Cobra brothers although I have heard some stories—
—And after those pinko fucks've breezed through, you turn around and there's the *Muslims* try'na convert every-body under the sun—
You wanna fuck, we're right here—
Please, let's not—
You gonna sit there and tell the brother Blackstone Rangers never push, is that the story you're selling?

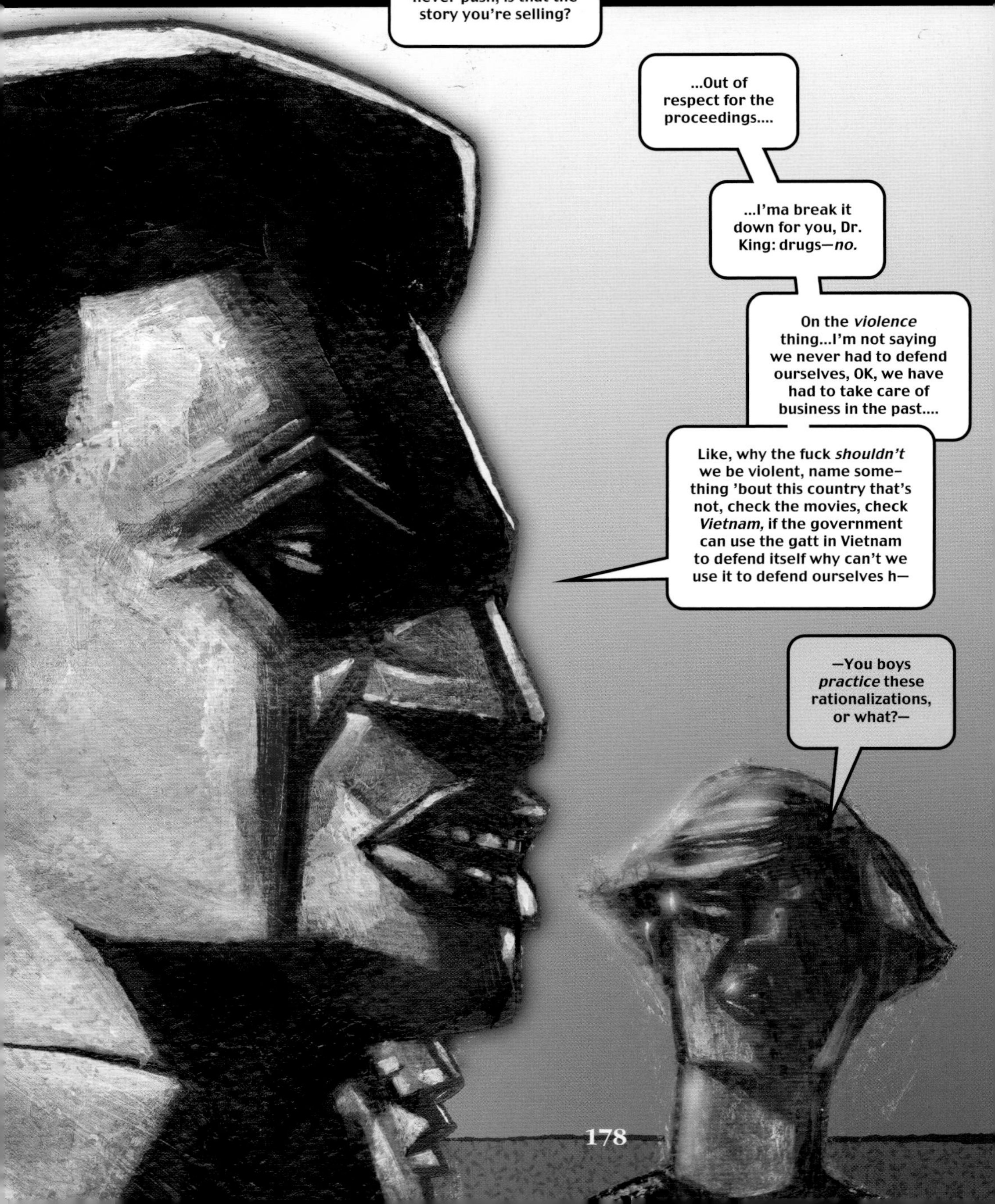
...Out of respect for the proceedings....
...I'ma break it down for you, Dr. King: drugs—*no.*
On the *violence* thing...I'm not saying we never had to defend ourselves, OK, we have had to take care of business in the past....
Like, why the fuck *shouldn't* we be violent, name some-thing 'bout this country that's not, check the movies, check *Vietnam,* if the government can use the gatt in Vietnam to defend itself why can't we use it to defend ourselves h—
—You boys *practice* these rationalizations, or what?—

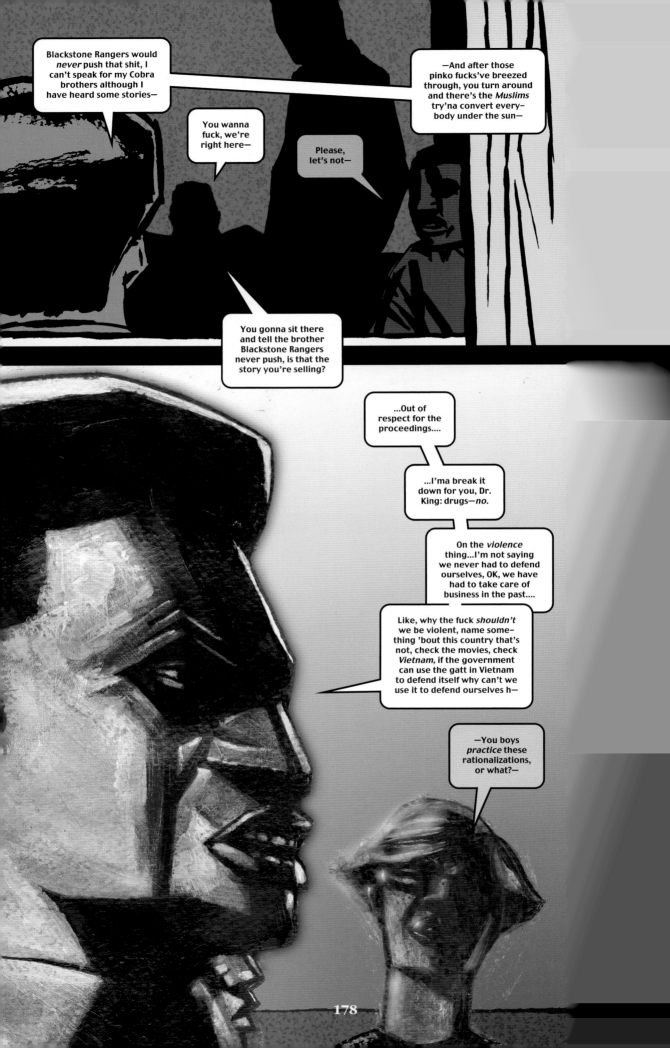

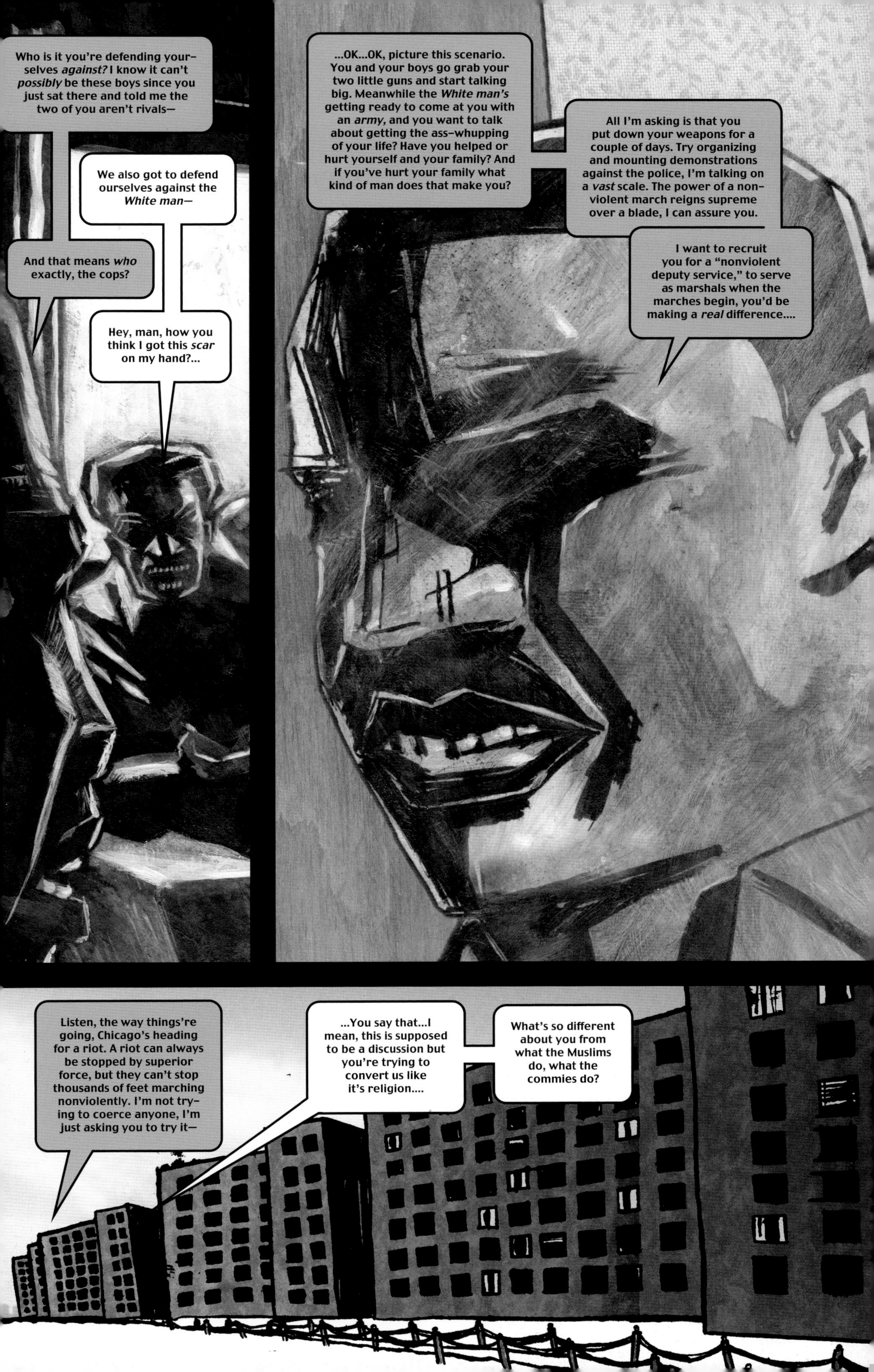
Who is it you're defending yourselves *against?* I know it can't *possibly* be these boys since you just sat there and told me the two of you aren't rivals—
We also got to defend ourselves against the *White man*—
And that means *who* exactly, the cops?
Hey, man, how you think I got this *scar* on my hand?...
...OK...OK, picture this scenario. You and your boys go grab your two little guns and start talking big. Meanwhile the *White man's* getting ready to come at you with an *army,* and you want to talk about getting the ass-whupping of your life? Have you helped or hurt yourself and your family? And if you've hurt your family what kind of man does that make you?
All I'm asking is that you put down your weapons for a couple of days. Try organizing and mounting demonstrations against the police, I'm talking on a *vast* scale. The power of a non-violent march reigns supreme over a blade, I can assure you.
I want to recruit you for a "nonviolent deputy service," to serve as marshals when the marches begin, you'd be making a *real* difference....
Listen, the way things're going, Chicago's heading for a riot. A riot can always be stopped by superior force, but they can't stop thousands of feet marching nonviolently. I'm not trying to coerce anyone, I'm just asking you to try it—
...You say that...I mean, this is supposed to be a discussion but you're trying to convert us like it's religion....
What's so different about you from what the Muslims do, what the commies do?

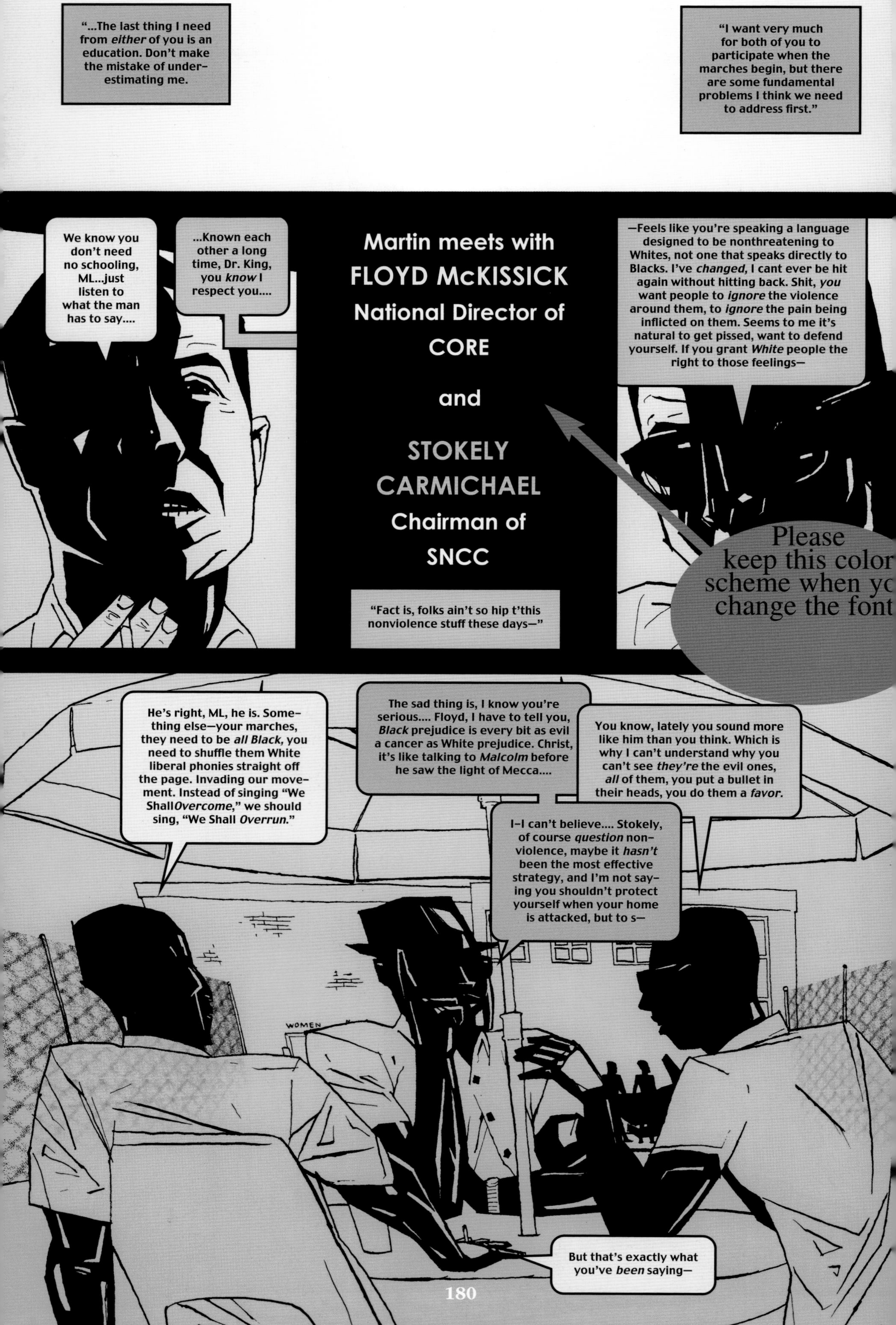
"...The last thing I need from *either* of you is an education. Don't make the mistake of under-estimating me.
"I want very much for both of you to participate when the marches begin, but there are some fundamental problems I think we need to address first."
We know you don't need no schooling, ML...just listen to what the man has to say....
...Known each other a long time, Dr. King, you *know* I respect you....
Martin meets with FLOYD McKISSICK National Director of CORE and STOKELY CARMICHAEL Chairman of SNCC
"Fact is, folks ain't so hip t'this nonviolence stuff these days—"
—Feels like you're speaking a language designed to be nonthreatening to Whites, not one that speaks directly to Blacks. I've *changed,* I cant ever be hit again without hitting back. Shit, *you* want people to *ignore* the violence around them, to *ignore* the pain being inflicted on them. Seems to me it's natural to get pissed, want to defend yourself. If you grant *White* people the right to those feelings—
Please keep this color scheme when yc change the font
He's right, ML, he is. Some-thing else—your marches, they need to be *all Black,* you need to shuffle them White liberal phonies straight off the page. Invading our move-ment. Instead of singing "We Shall *Overcome,*" we should sing, "We Shall *Overrun.*"
The sad thing is, I know you're serious.... Floyd, I have to tell you, *Black* prejudice is every bit as evil a cancer as White prejudice. Christ, it's like talking to *Malcolm* before he saw the light of Mecca....
You know, lately you sound more like him than you think. Which is why I can't understand why you can't see *they're* the evil ones, *all* of them, you put a bullet in their heads, you do them a *favor.*
I-I can't believe.... Stokely, of course *question* non-violence, maybe it *hasn't* been the most effective strategy, and I'm not say-ing you shouldn't protect yourself when your home is attacked, but to s—
WOMEN
But that's exactly what you've *been* saying—

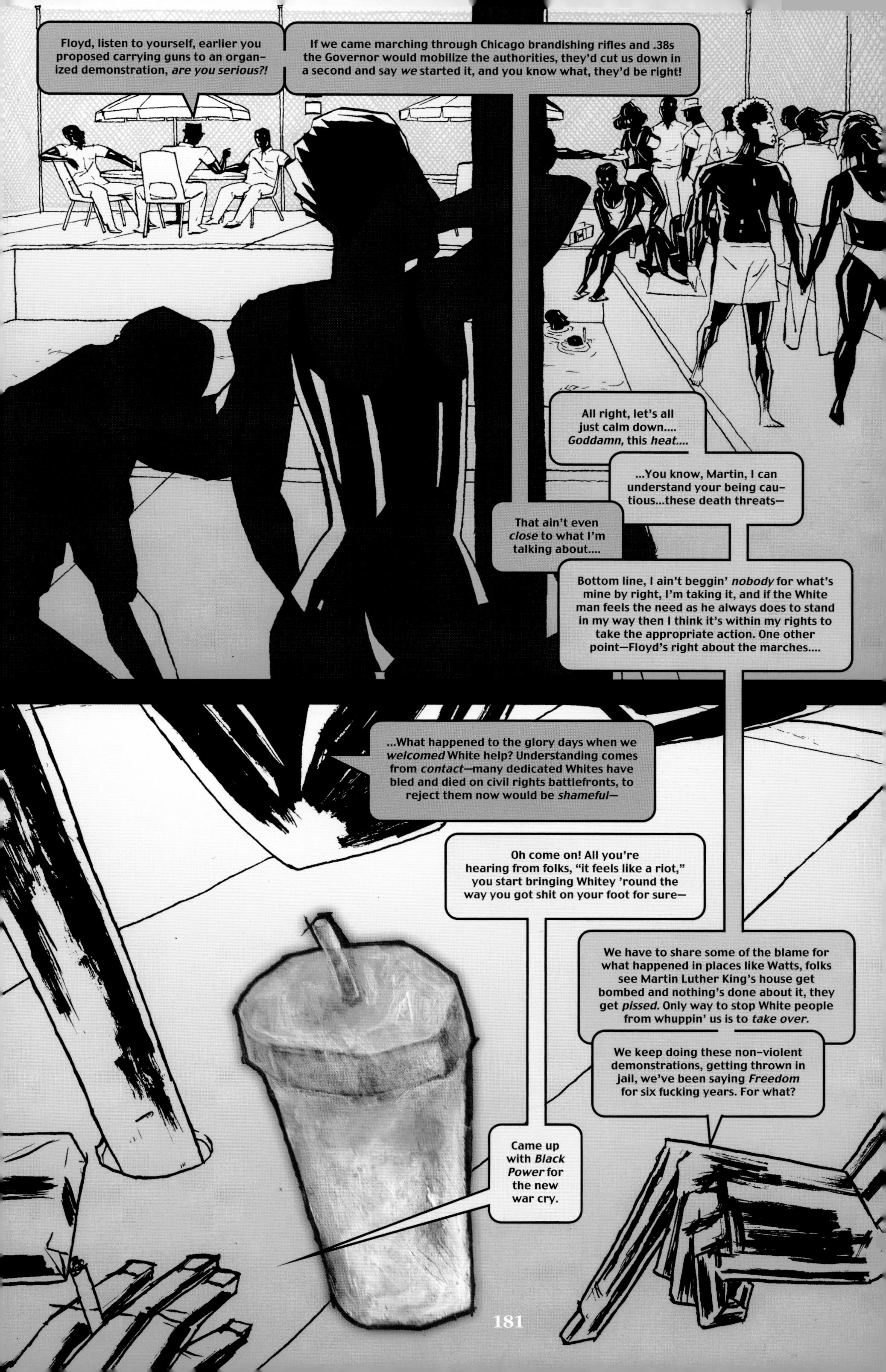
Floyd, listen to yourself, earlier you proposed carrying guns to an organized demonstration, *are you serious?!*
If we came marching through Chicago brandishing rifles and .38s the Governor would mobilize the authorities, they'd cut us down in a second and say *we* started it, and you know what, they'd be right!
All right, let's all just calm down.... *Goddamn,* this *heat....*
...You know, Martin, I can understand your being cautious...these death threats—
That ain't even *close* to what I'm talking about....
Bottom line, I ain't beggin' *nobody* for what's mine by right, I'm taking it, and if the White man feels the need as he always does to stand in my way then I think it's within my rights to take the appropriate action. One other point—Floyd's right about the marches....
...What happened to the glory days when we *welcomed* White help? Understanding comes from *contact*—many dedicated Whites have bled and died on civil rights battlefronts, to reject them now would be *shameful*—
Oh come on! All you're hearing from folks, "it feels like a riot," you start bringing Whitey 'round the way you got shit on your foot for sure—
We have to share some of the blame for what happened in places like Watts, folks see Martin Luther King's house get bombed and nothing's done about it, they get *pissed.* Only way to stop White people from whuppin' us is to *take over.*
We keep doing these non-violent demonstrations, getting thrown in jail, we've been saying *Freedom* for six fucking years. For what?
Came up with *Black Power* for the new war cry.

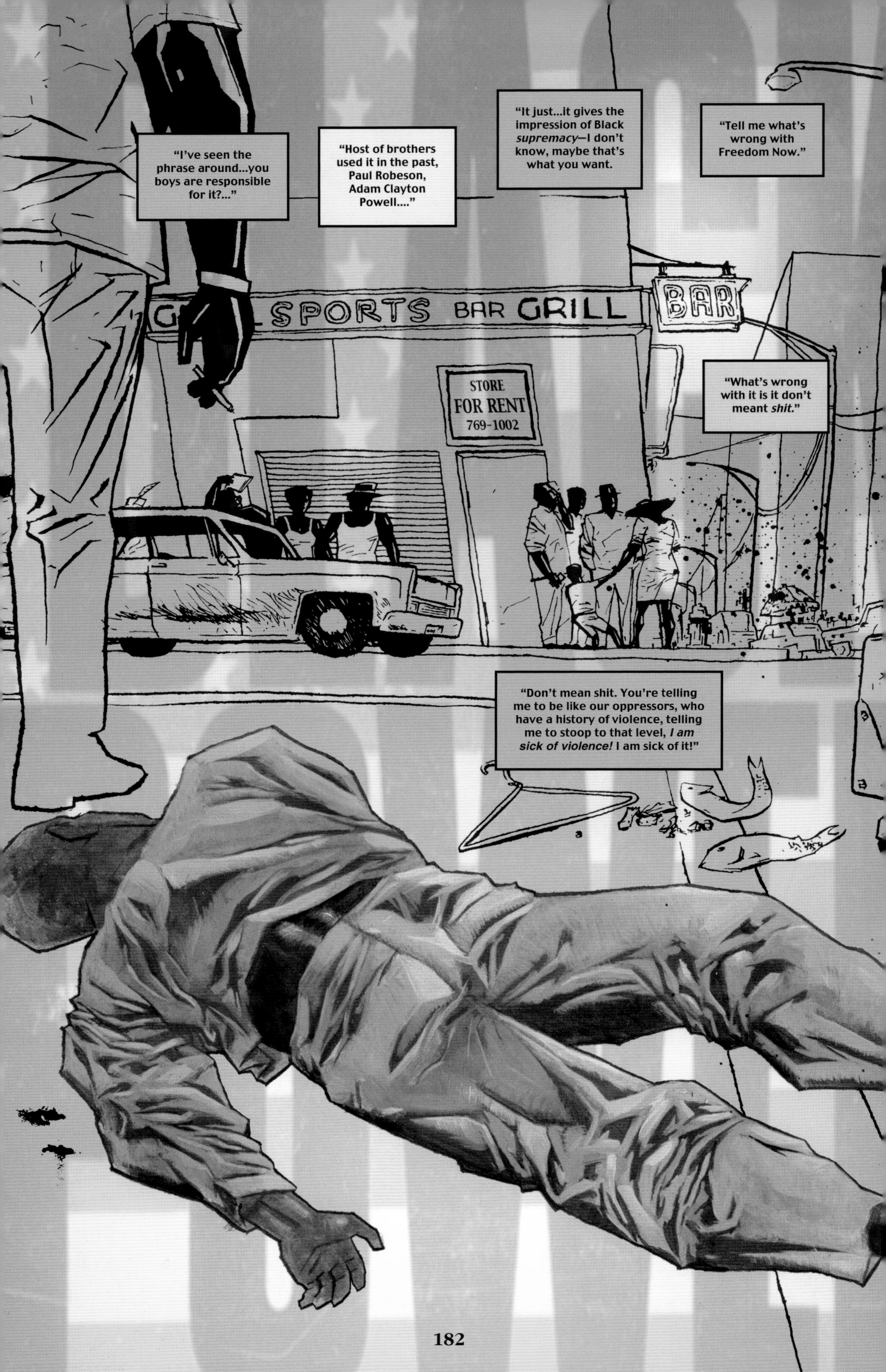

"I've seen the phrase around...you boys are responsible for it?..."
"Host of brothers used it in the past, Paul Robeson, Adam Clayton Powell...."
"It just...it gives the impression of Black *supremacy*—I don't know, maybe that's what you want.
"Tell me what's wrong with Freedom Now."
SPORTS BAR GRILL
BAR
STORE FOR RENT 769-1002
"What's wrong with it is it don't meant *shit*."
"Don't mean shit. You're telling me to be like our oppressors, who have a history of violence, telling me to stoop to that level, *I am sick of violence!* I am sick of it!"

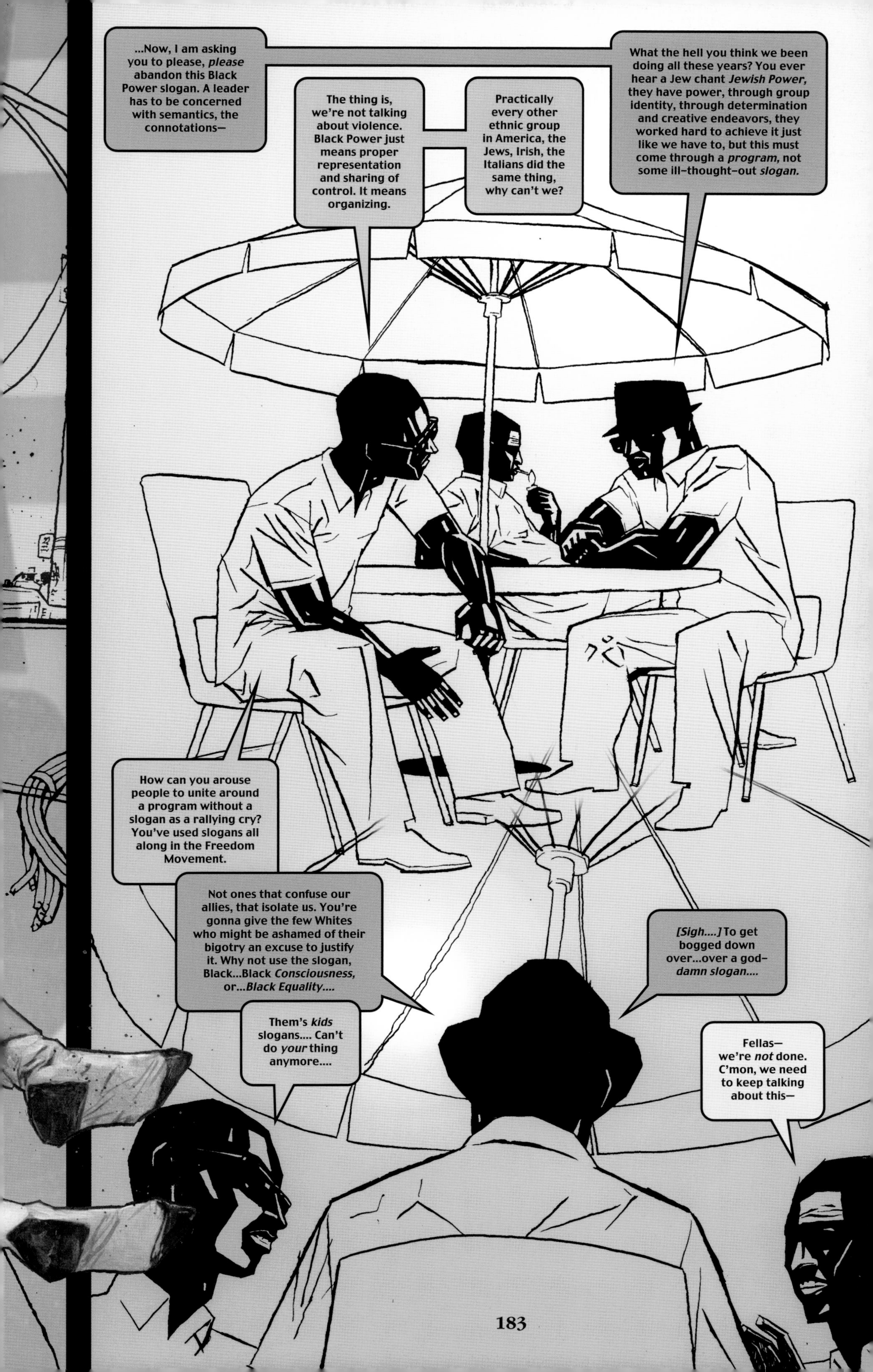
...Now, I am asking you to please, *please* abandon this Black Power slogan. A leader has to be concerned with semantics, the connotations—
The thing is, we're not talking about violence. Black Power just means proper representation and sharing of control. It means organizing.
Practically every other ethnic group in America, the Jews, Irish, the Italians did the same thing, why can't we?
What the hell you think we been doing all these years? You ever hear a Jew chant *Jewish Power,* they have power, through group identity, through determination and creative endeavors, they worked hard to achieve it just like we have to, but this must come through a *program,* not some ill-thought-out *slogan.*
How can you arouse people to unite around a program without a slogan as a rallying cry? You've used slogans all along in the Freedom Movement.
Not ones that confuse our allies, that isolate us. You're gonna give the few Whites who might be ashamed of their bigotry an excuse to justify it. Why not use the slogan, Black...Black *Consciousness,* or...*Black Equality....*
Them's *kids* slogans.... Can't do *your* thing anymore....
[Sigh....] To get bogged down over...over a god-*damn slogan....*
Fellas— we're *not* done. C'mon, we need to keep talking about this—

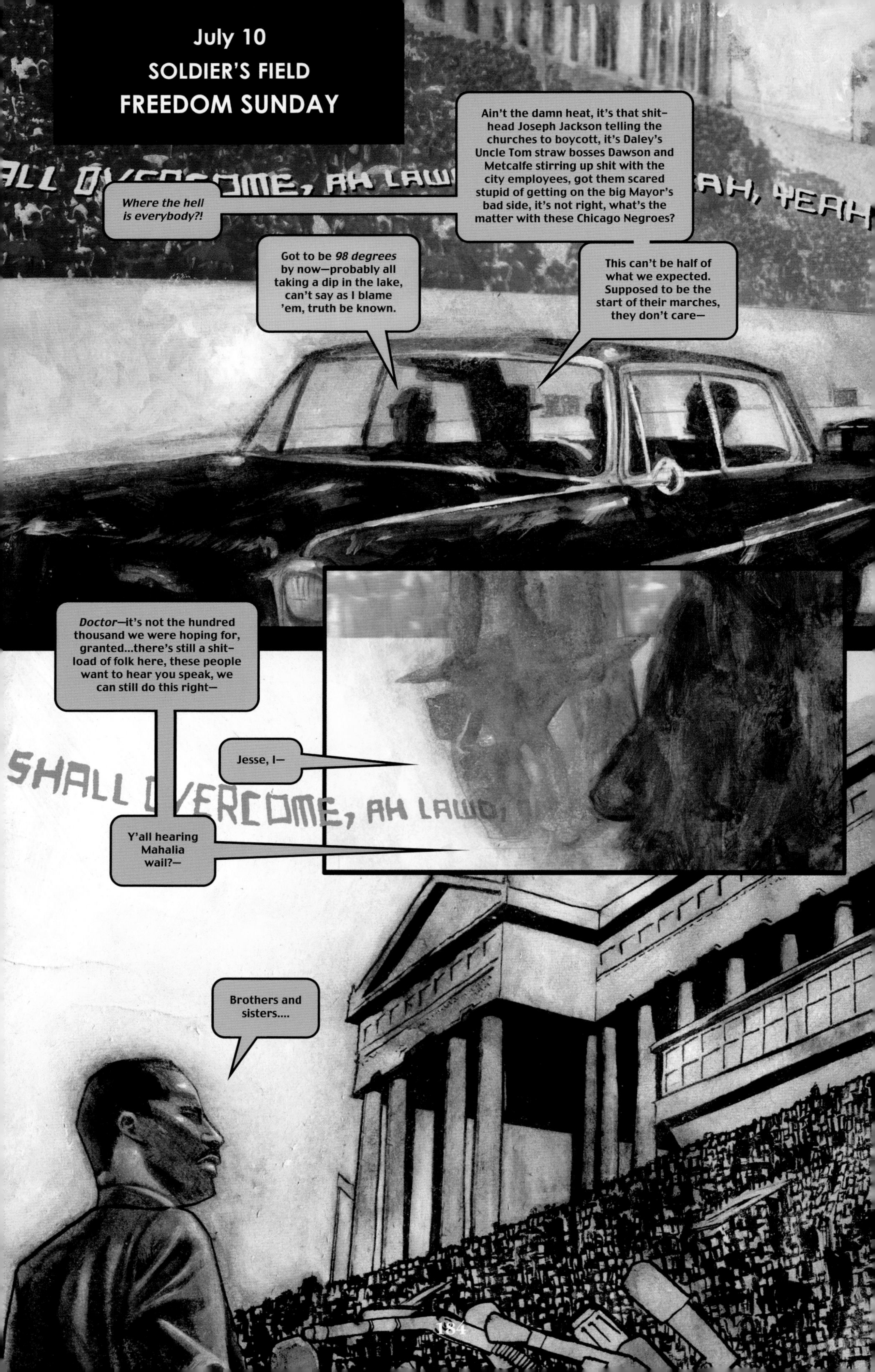
July 10
SOLDIER'S FIELD
FREEDOM SUNDAY
ALL OVERCOME, AH LAWD
AH, YEAH
Where the hell is everybody?!
Ain't the damn heat, it's that shit-head Joseph Jackson telling the churches to boycott, it's Daley's Uncle Tom straw bosses Dawson and Metcalfe stirring up shit with the city employees, got them scared stupid of getting on the big Mayor's bad side, it's not right, what's the matter with these Chicago Negroes?
Got to be 98 degrees by now—probably all taking a dip in the lake, can't say as I blame 'em, truth be known.
This can't be half of what we expected. Supposed to be the start of their marches, they don't care—
Doctor—it's not the hundred thousand we were hoping for, granted...there's still a shit-load of folk here, these people want to hear you speak, we can still do this right—
Jesse, I—
SHALL OVERCOME, AH LAWD
Y'all hearing Mahalia wail?—
Brothers and sisters....

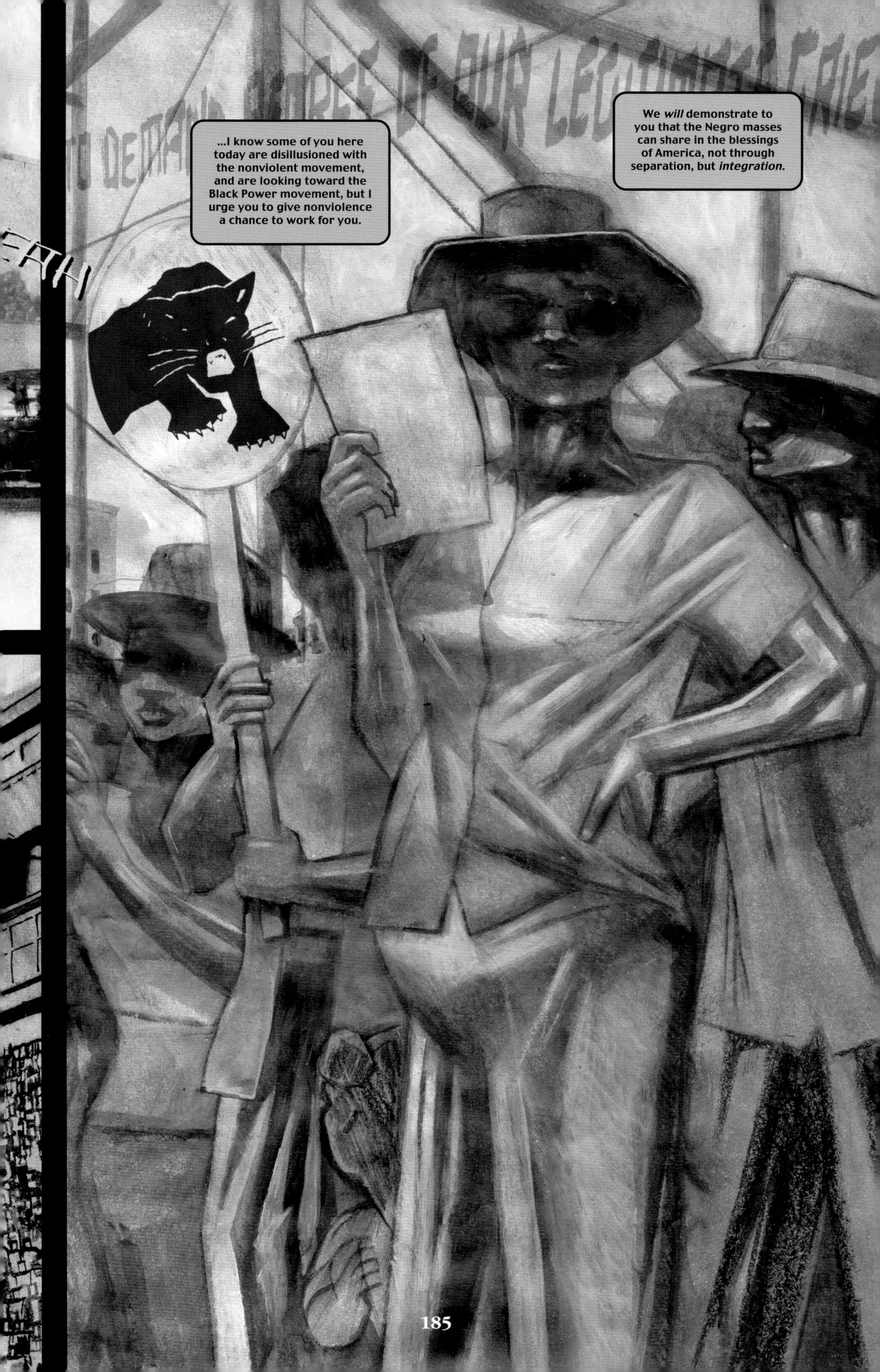
...I know some of you here today are disillusioned with the nonviolent movement, and are looking toward the Black Power movement, but I urge you to give nonviolence a chance to work for you.
We *will* demonstrate to you that the Negro masses can share in the blessings of America, not through separation, but *integration.*

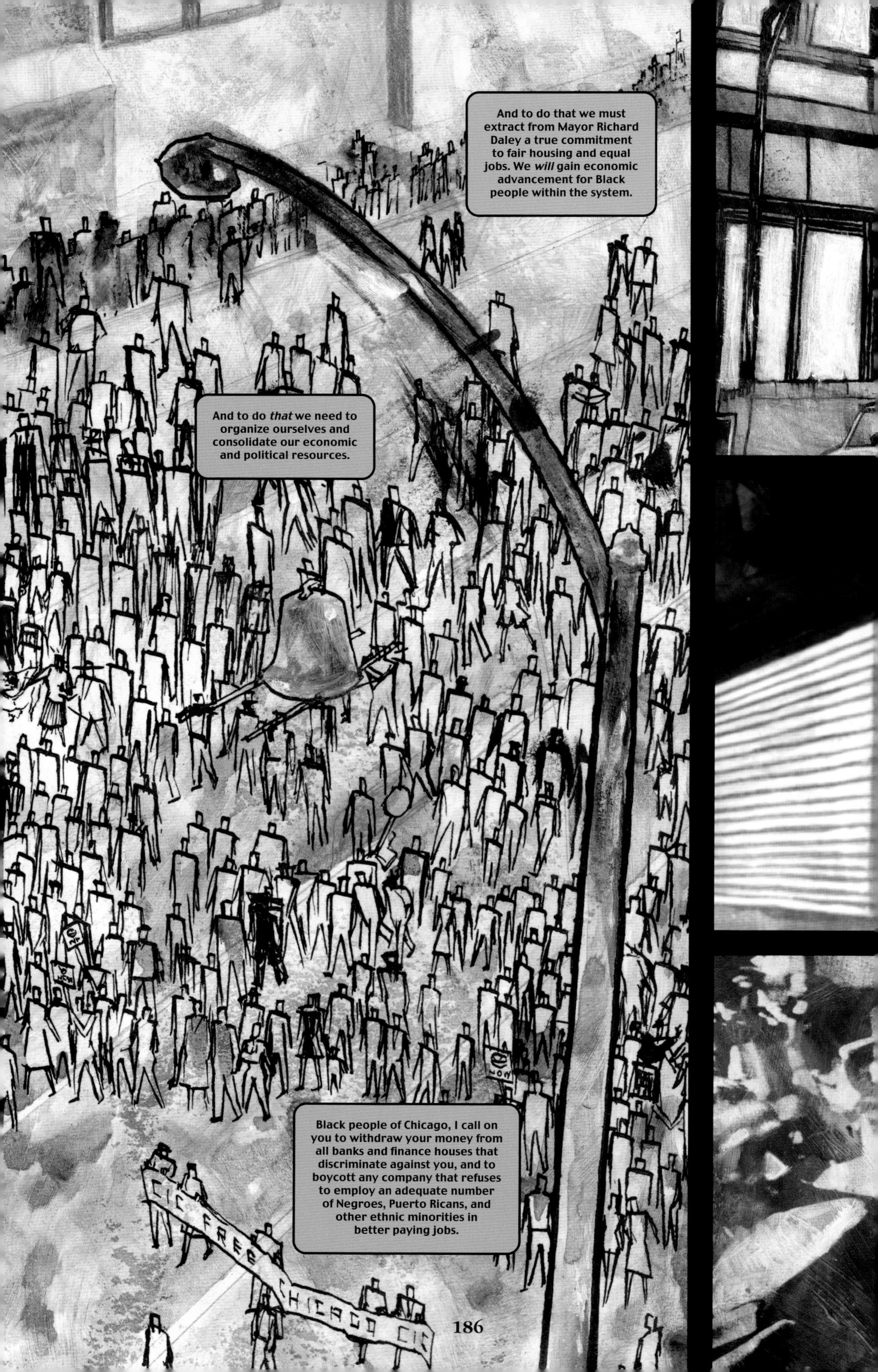
And to do that we must extract from Mayor Richard Daley a true commitment to fair housing and equal jobs. We *will* gain economic advancement for Black people within the system.
And to do *that* we need to organize ourselves and consolidate our economic and political resources.
Black people of Chicago, I call on you to withdraw your money from all banks and finance houses that discriminate against you, and to boycott any company that refuses to employ an adequate number of Negroes, Puerto Ricans, and other ethnic minorities in better paying jobs.
CIC FREE CHICAGO CIC

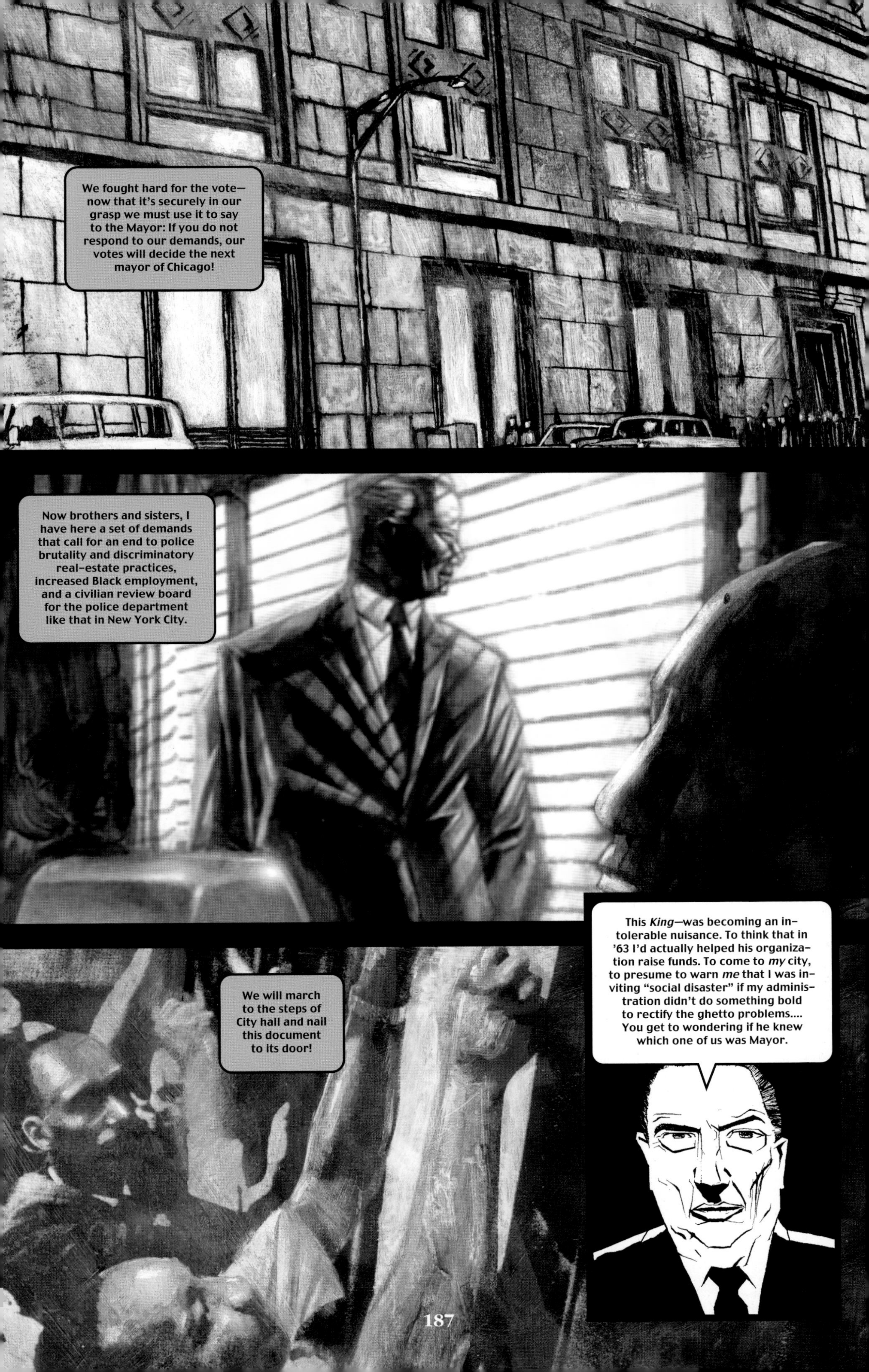

We fought hard for the vote—now that it's securely in our grasp we must use it to say to the Mayor: If you do not respond to our demands, our votes will decide the next mayor of Chicago!
Now brothers and sisters, I have here a set of demands that call for an end to police brutality and discriminatory real-estate practices, increased Black employment, and a civilian review board for the police department like that in New York City.
We will march to the steps of City hall and nail this document to its door!
This *King*—was becoming an intolerable nuisance. To think that in '63 I'd actually helped his organization raise funds. To come to *my* city, to presume to warn *me* that I was inviting "social disaster" if my administration didn't do something bold to rectify the ghetto problems.... You get to wondering if he knew which one of us was Mayor.

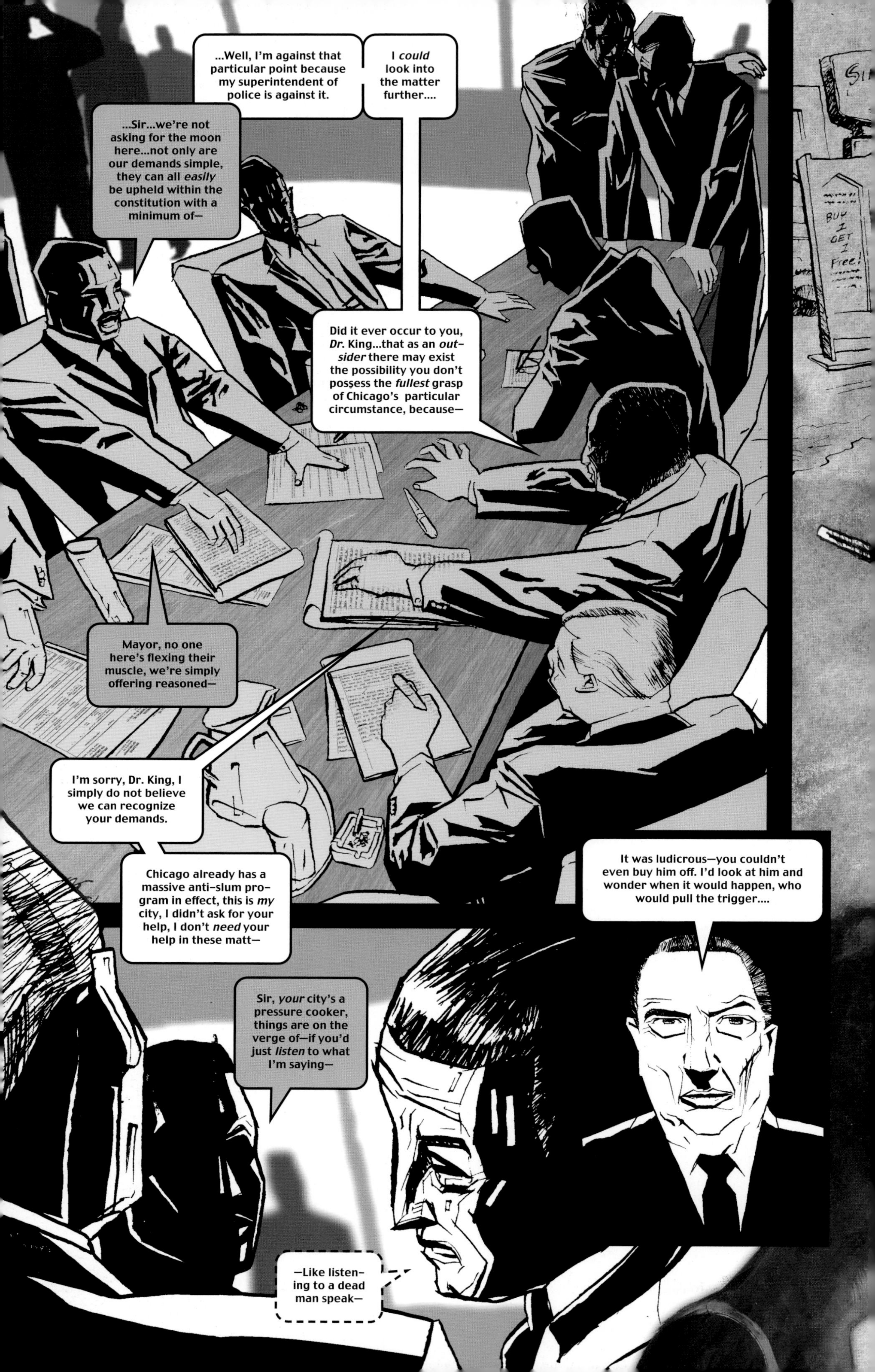
...Sir...we're not asking for the moon here...not only are our demands simple, they can all *easily* be upheld within the constitution with a minimum of—
...Well, I'm against that particular point because my superintendent of police is against it.
I *could* look into the matter further....
Did it ever occur to you, *Dr.* King...that as an *outsider* there may exist the possibility you don't possess the *fullest* grasp of Chicago's particular circumstance, because—
BUY 1 GET 1 Free!
Mayor, no one here's flexing their muscle, we're simply offering reasoned—
I'm sorry, Dr. King, I simply do not believe we can recognize your demands.
Chicago already has a massive anti-slum program in effect, this is *my* city, I didn't ask for your help, I don't *need* your help in these matt—
It was ludicrous—you couldn't even buy him off. I'd look at him and wonder when it would happen, who would pull the trigger....
Sir, *your* city's a pressure cooker, things are on the verge of—if you'd just *listen* to what I'm saying—
—Like listening to a dead man speak—

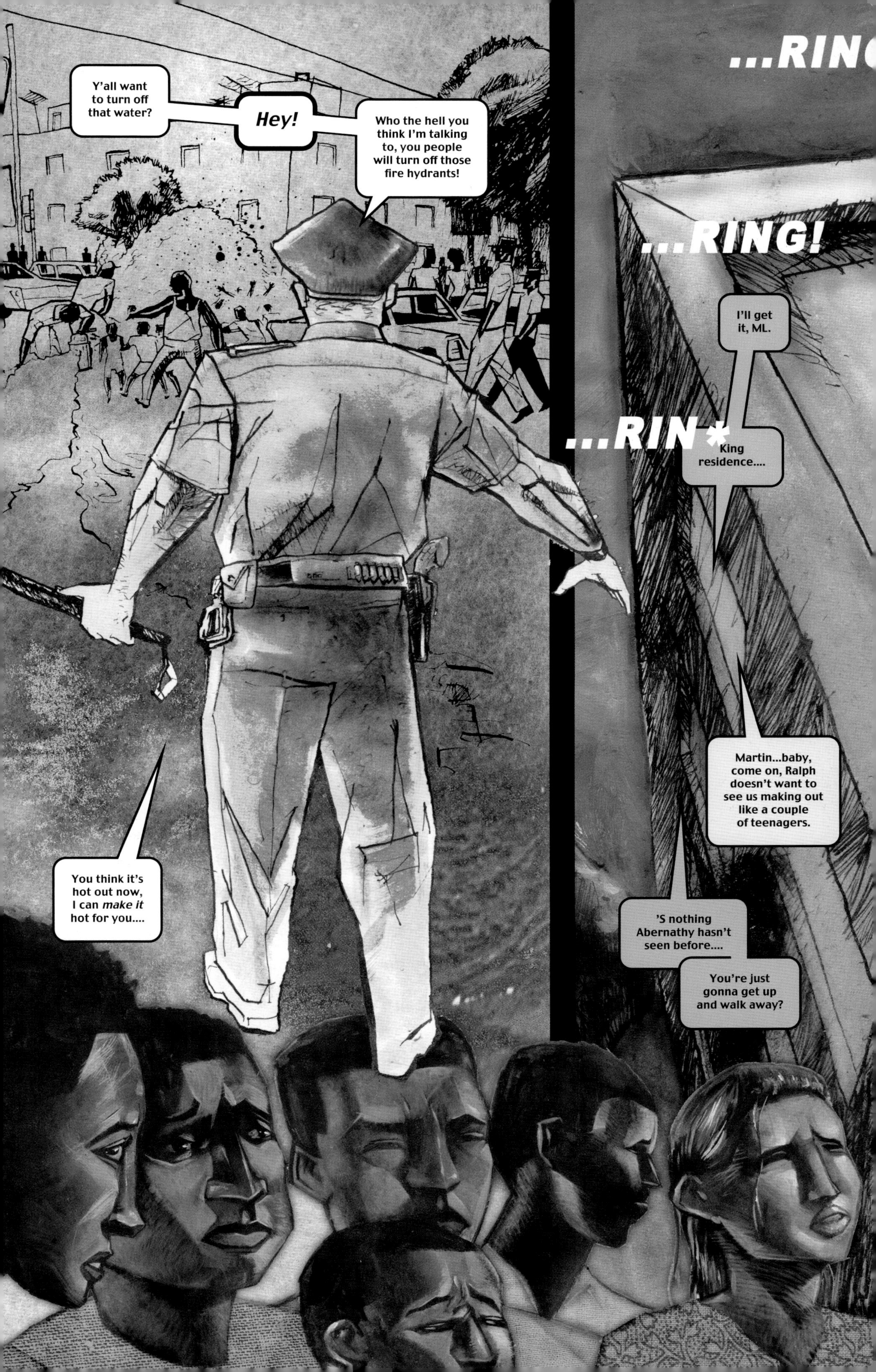
Y'all want to turn off that water?
Hey!
Who the hell you think I'm talking to, you people will turn off those fire hydrants!
You think it's hot out now, I can *make it* hot for you....
...RING
...RING!
...RIN*
I'll get it, ML.
King residence....
Martin...baby, come on, Ralph doesn't want to see us making out like a couple of teenagers.
'S nothing Abernathy hasn't seen before....
You're just gonna get up and walk away?

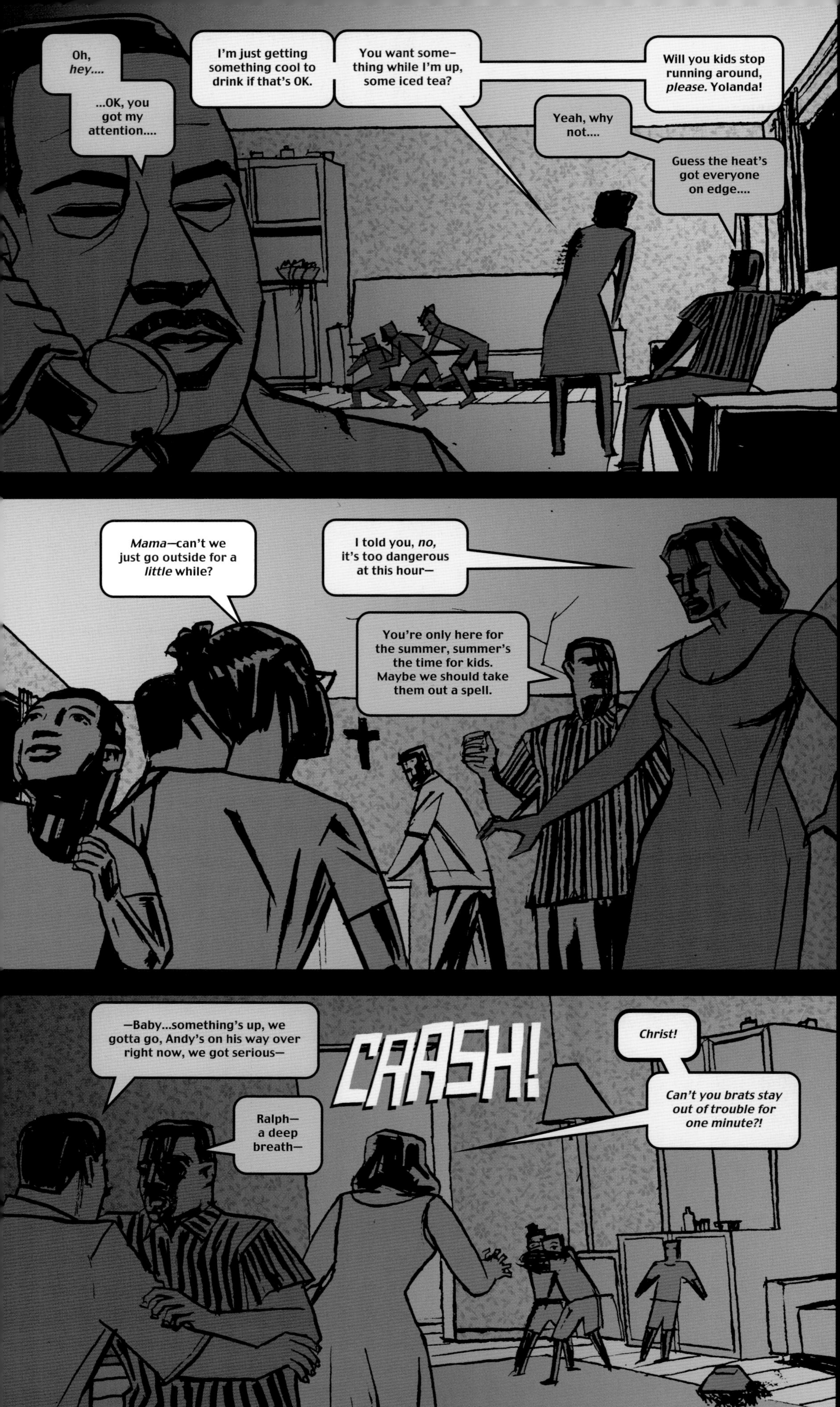
Oh, *hey....*
...OK, you got my attention....
I'm just getting something cool to drink if that's OK.
You want some-thing while I'm up, some iced tea?
Will you kids stop running around, *please.* Yolanda!
Yeah, why not....
Guess the heat's got everyone on edge....
Mama—can't we just go outside for a *little* while?
I told you, *no,* it's too dangerous at this hour—
You're only here for the summer, summer's the time for kids. Maybe we should take them out a spell.
—Baby...something's up, we gotta go, Andy's on his way over right now, we got serious—
CRASH!
Ralph—a deep breath—
Christ!
Can't you brats stay out of trouble for one minute?!

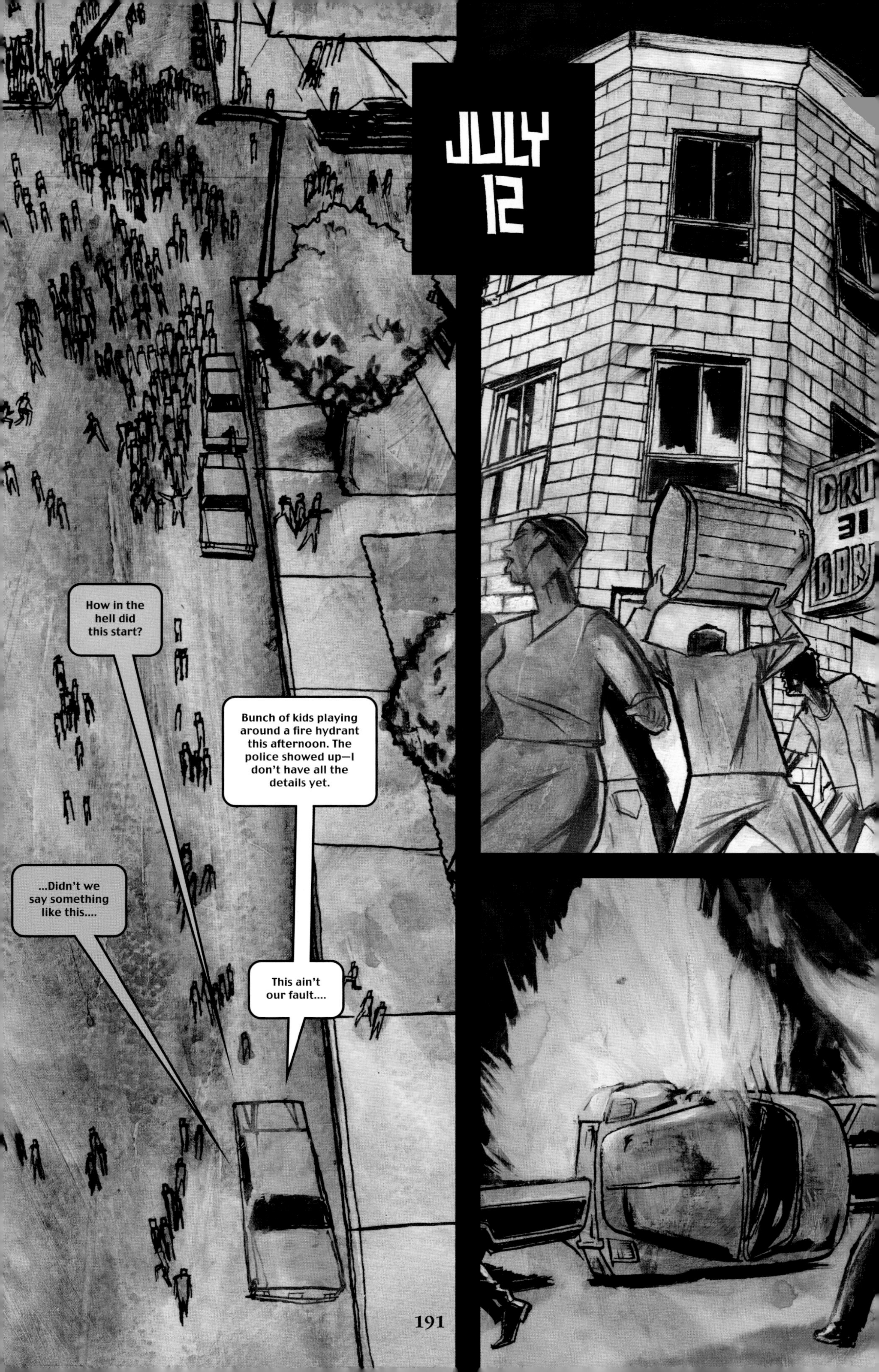
JULY 12
How in the hell did this start?
Bunch of kids playing around a fire hydrant this afternoon. The police showed up—I don't have all the details yet.
...Didn't we say something like this....
This ain't our fault....
DRU
31
BAR

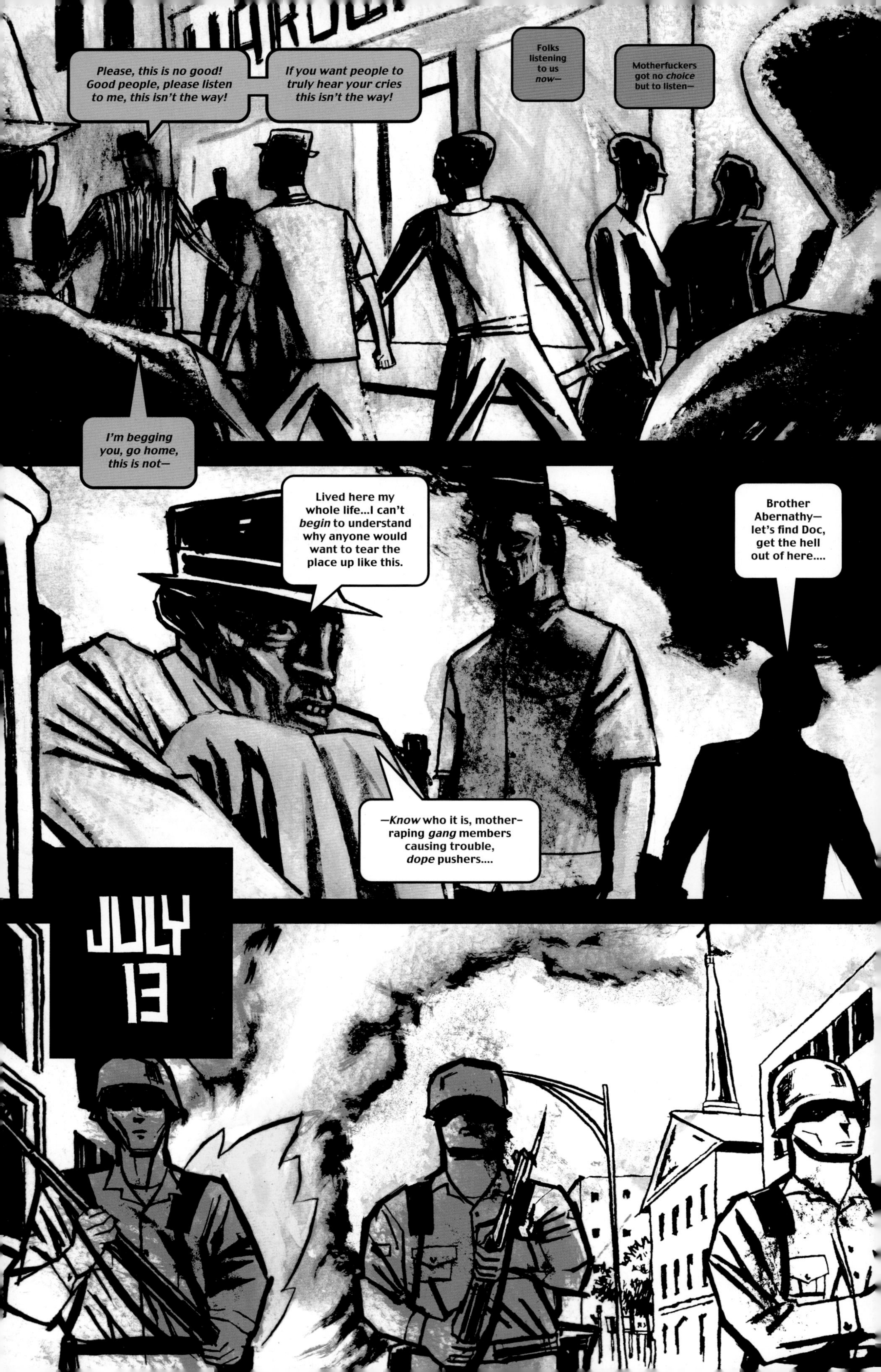
Please, this is no good! Good people, please listen to me, this isn't the way!
If you want people to truly hear your cries this isn't the way!
Folks listening to us now—
Motherfuckers got no choice but to listen—
I'm begging you, go home, this is not—
Lived here my whole life...I can't begin to understand why anyone would want to tear the place up like this.
Brother Abernathy—let's find Doc, get the hell out of here....
—Know who it is, mother-raping gang members causing trouble, dope pushers....
JULY 13

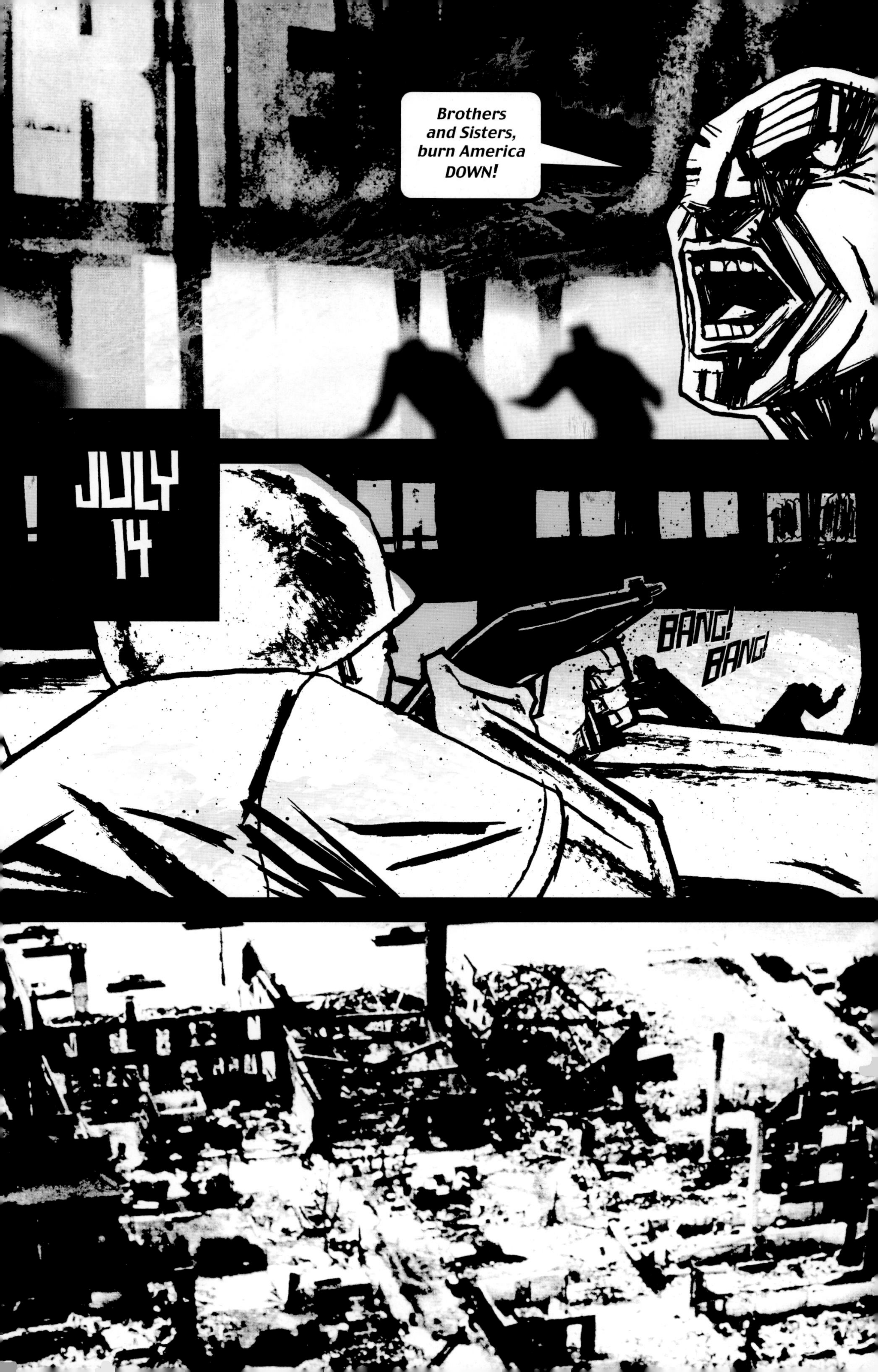
Brothers and Sisters, burn America DOWN!
JULY 14
BANG! BANG!

By and large gang members were responsible for the violence of those three nights, for actually instigating and perpetuating it, although the cops certainly provided their fair share.... I don't think it's an accident the violence followed a line to City Hall and that it was mostly White-owned stores that were bombed.

Two people were killed, I think 56 injured...272 thrown in jail, give or take.... Mayor Daley went off, he blamed the riots on anarchists, Communists, and Dr. King's own staff, something about instructing rioters on violence by showing them films on Watts.

All of a sudden Daley was eager to sit down with King and was persuaded to make *some* concessions, anything to ensure there was no more rioting. I don't remember anybody being too thrilled with what was done.

Moved in a few more swimming pools, some sprinklers on the fire hydrants, just so we could escape the heat a bit during those Chicago summers. Someone set up a citizens committee to study the police department.... But you have to ask what these so-called *concessions* really changed.... Nine months in a place, at the end you're still an outsider...I don't think the SCLC really knew what to ask for....

I believe it was probably around this time some of the youth gangs began to see that perhaps civil disobedience was slightly more effective a strategy than aimless rioting, which as a White person I couldn't agree with more, *ha, ha, ha....*

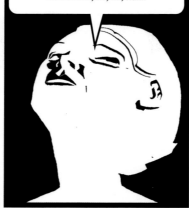

...So...some agreed to join King in the Chicago marches, that was good. ...I should point out that the initial marches proved to be among the most violent—well, certainly of anything *I've* seen, and from what I understand, certainly of *King's* career. Thousands of screaming people surrounding a couple of hundred marchers. And not just the men, you had housewives throwing rocks, you had *children....*

In retrospect I realize it was probably just plain *tough* for us Chicagoans to face up to the hate King exposed here. Newspaper editors, politicians...so many voices vilifying King, accusing *him* of creating the city's racial tensions, insisting he stop the marches. I remember thinking even at that time that his life was probably in danger.

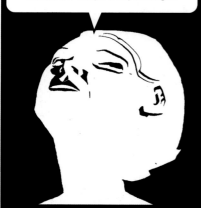

You want us to stop marching, then make justice a reality. I don't mind saying to Chicago I'm tired of marching for something that should've been mine at birth, I'm tired of living every day under the threat of death. I have no martyr complex, I want to live as long as anybody.

A new march was announced in Cicero, which is a suburb outside Cook County. Now, you have to understand about *Cicero*...if you were Black, you just didn't cross the viaduct into Cicero, driving through, you just didn't get a flat, 'cause as a nigger, they see you getting out to change your tire....

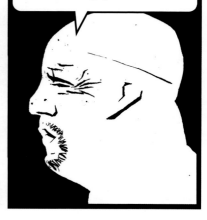

One Black kid got murdered there while looking for work. A Black family tried to move in there, had to be fifty-one, fifty-two—the shit got so bad with Whites rioting and stuff the National Guard had to be called in, serious. *One* family and this happens.

So King tells the world he's gonna march there, he's gonna show everybody how rough Chicago is and force the Mayor to fix the slums, and suddenly he's got even the Black Power guys on his side. It was something. I mean, this was a very radical fucking move. Could've embarrassed a lot of politicians.

So it comes down to a show-down between Daley and King, championship fight, going for the belt, got their poker faces on, and Daley, *pussy* that he was, backs down, hey, thank *God.* He agrees to sit down again with King which was the same as admitting there actually was something wrong with Chicago's housing policies, something he'd always denied.

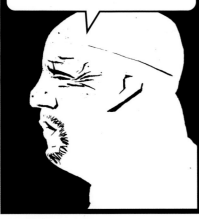

They came up with something called the *Summit Agreement.* Without getting lost in detail, this agreement was...it was *OK,* it was a good start. It helped get some families into nice homes, shit like that. But surprise, surprise, it didn't go far enough.

King had Daley on the ropes, he should've kept slugging him, not just get a few families out the ghetto, 'cause what about the rest of us left here? I mean, some of them Black Power motherfuckers even threatened to march on Cicero anyway.

Daley stood with King in front of the cameras, saying, "this is a great day for Chicago," promised to uphold his end of the agreement, turned around and did exactly jack shit. Shaking hands like they were drinking buddies or something. He was a crafty bastard, devious, an old hand at manipulating people, saying the right things to get what he wanted.

That Summit Agreement was a sell-out. Just a way for that King to bail out of Chi-town and not look like an asshole. And don't let nobody tell you it was 'cause 'a Carl Stokes' Mayoral campaign neither. You see how fast they got out of Chicago after making the agreement, tell me I'm wrong....

...If the guy had just continued to *push* Daley...but like always he backed off just when he should have fought harder. Fuck that nonviolence shit—even today, what we need to get is some of that *Black Power....*

Let's face it. Most... maybe all the people here are going to remain here until the day they meet their maker. Morally, when we *say* Freedom Now, we should *have* freedom now, we should *expect* freedom now...the fact is it doesn't all *come* now....

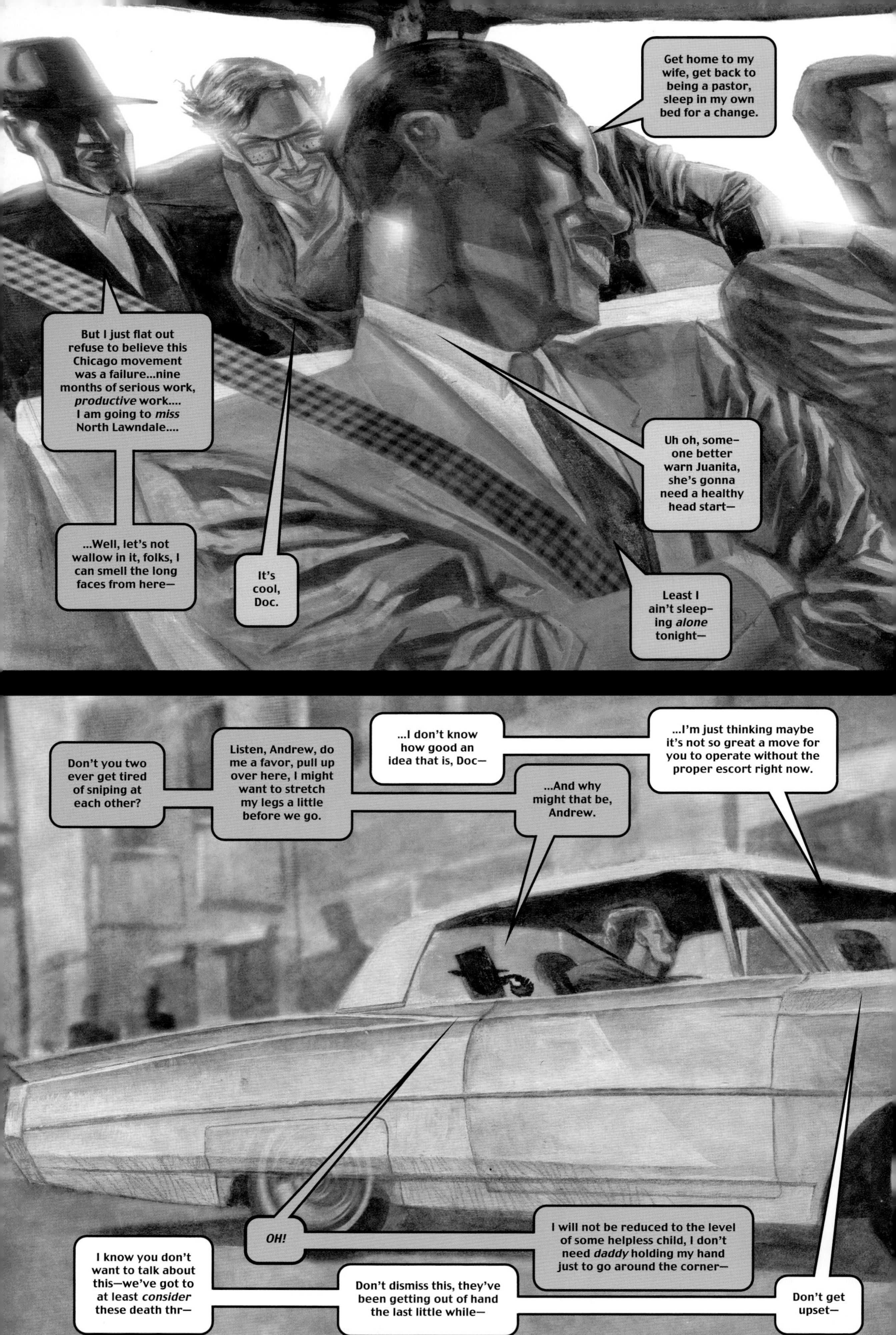
Get home to my wife, get back to being a pastor, sleep in my own bed for a change.
Uh oh, some-one better warn Juanita, she's gonna need a healthy head start—
Least I ain't sleep-ing *alone* tonight—
But I just flat out refuse to believe this Chicago movement was a failure...nine months of serious work, *productive* work.... I am going to *miss* North Lawndale....
...Well, let's not wallow in it, folks, I can smell the long faces from here—
It's cool, Doc.
Don't you two ever get tired of sniping at each other?
Listen, Andrew, do me a favor, pull up over here, I might want to stretch my legs a little before we go.
...I don't know how good an idea that is, Doc—
...And why might that be, Andrew.
...I'm just thinking maybe it's not so great a move for you to operate without the proper escort right now.
OH!
I will not be reduced to the level of some helpless child, I don't need *daddy* holding my hand just to go around the corner—
I know you don't want to talk about this—we've got to at least *consider* these death thr—
Don't dismiss this, they've been getting out of hand the last little while—
Don't get upset—

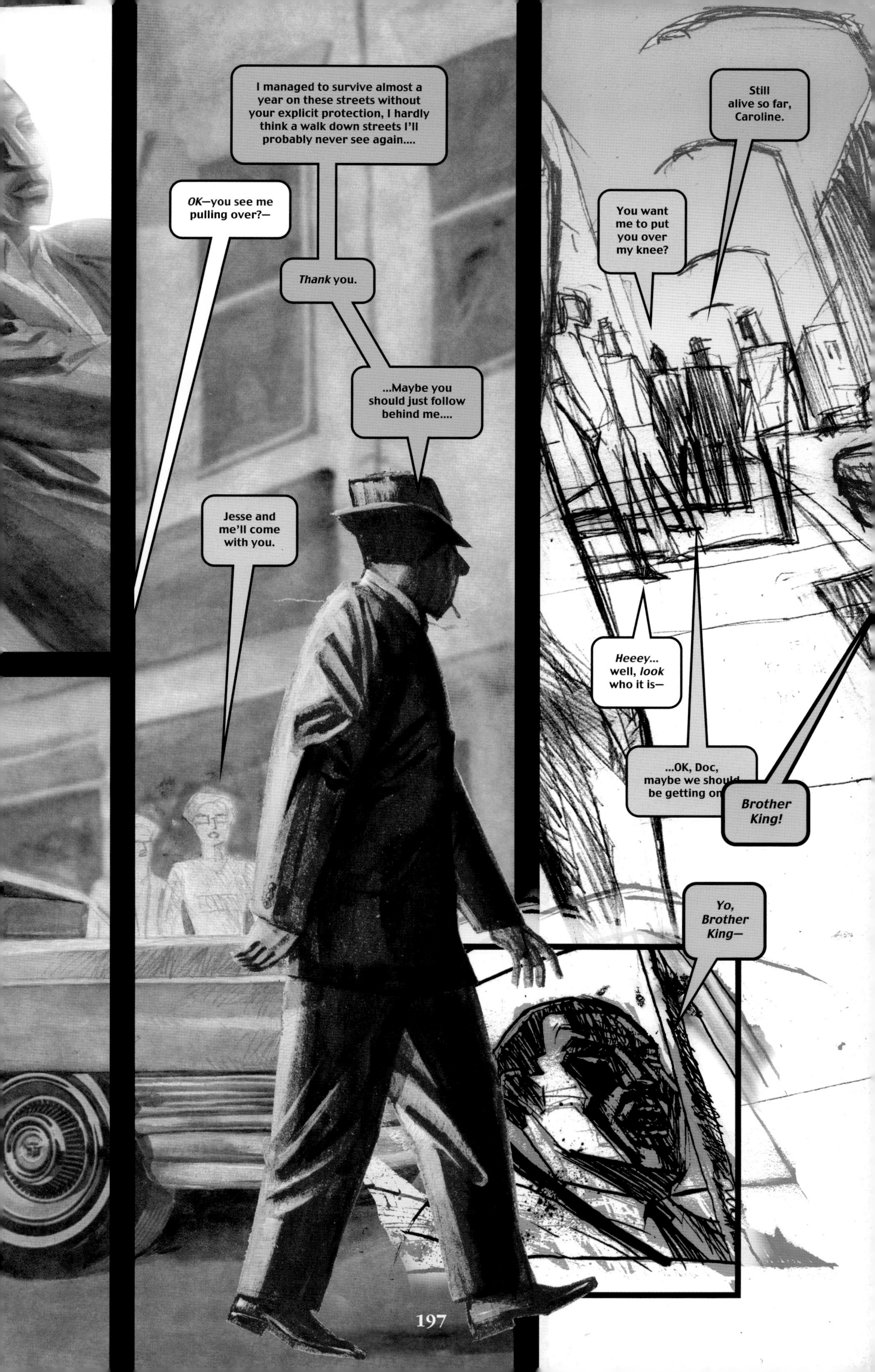
I managed to survive almost a year on these streets without your explicit protection, I hardly think a walk down streets I'll probably never see again....
OK—you see me pulling over?—
Thank you.
...Maybe you should just follow behind me....
Jesse and me'll come with you.
Still alive so far, Caroline.
You want me to put you over my knee?
Heeey... well, look who it is—
...OK, Doc, maybe we should be getting on
Brother King!
Yo, Brother King—

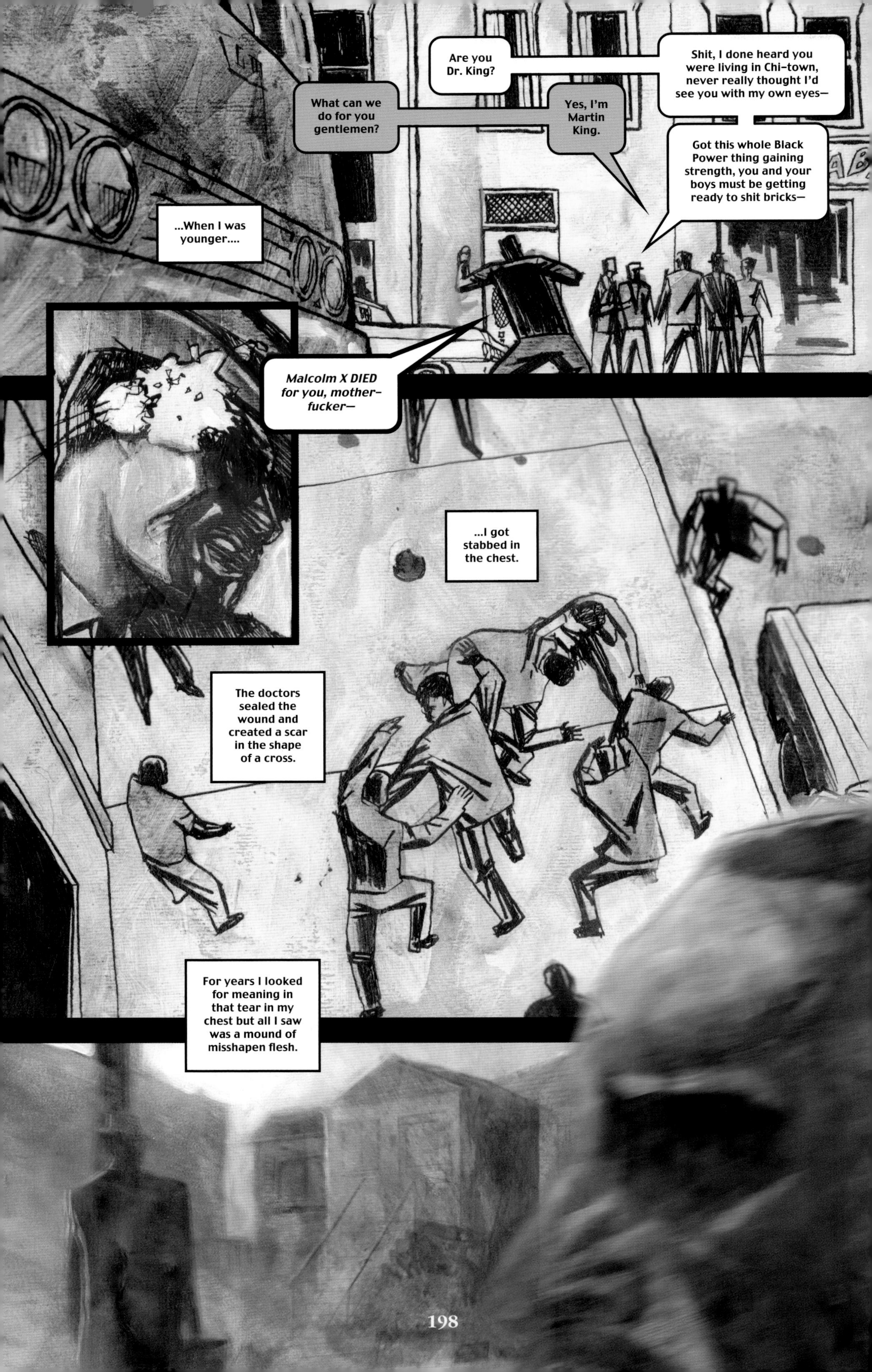

Are you Dr. King?
Shit, I done heard you were living in Chi-town, never really thought I'd see you with my own eyes—
What can we do for you gentlemen?
Yes, I'm Martin King.
Got this whole Black Power thing gaining strength, you and your boys must be getting ready to shit bricks—
...When I was younger....
Malcolm X DIED for you, mother-fucker—
...I got stabbed in the chest.
The doctors sealed the wound and created a scar in the shape of a cross.
For years I looked for meaning in that tear in my chest but all I saw was a mound of misshapen flesh.

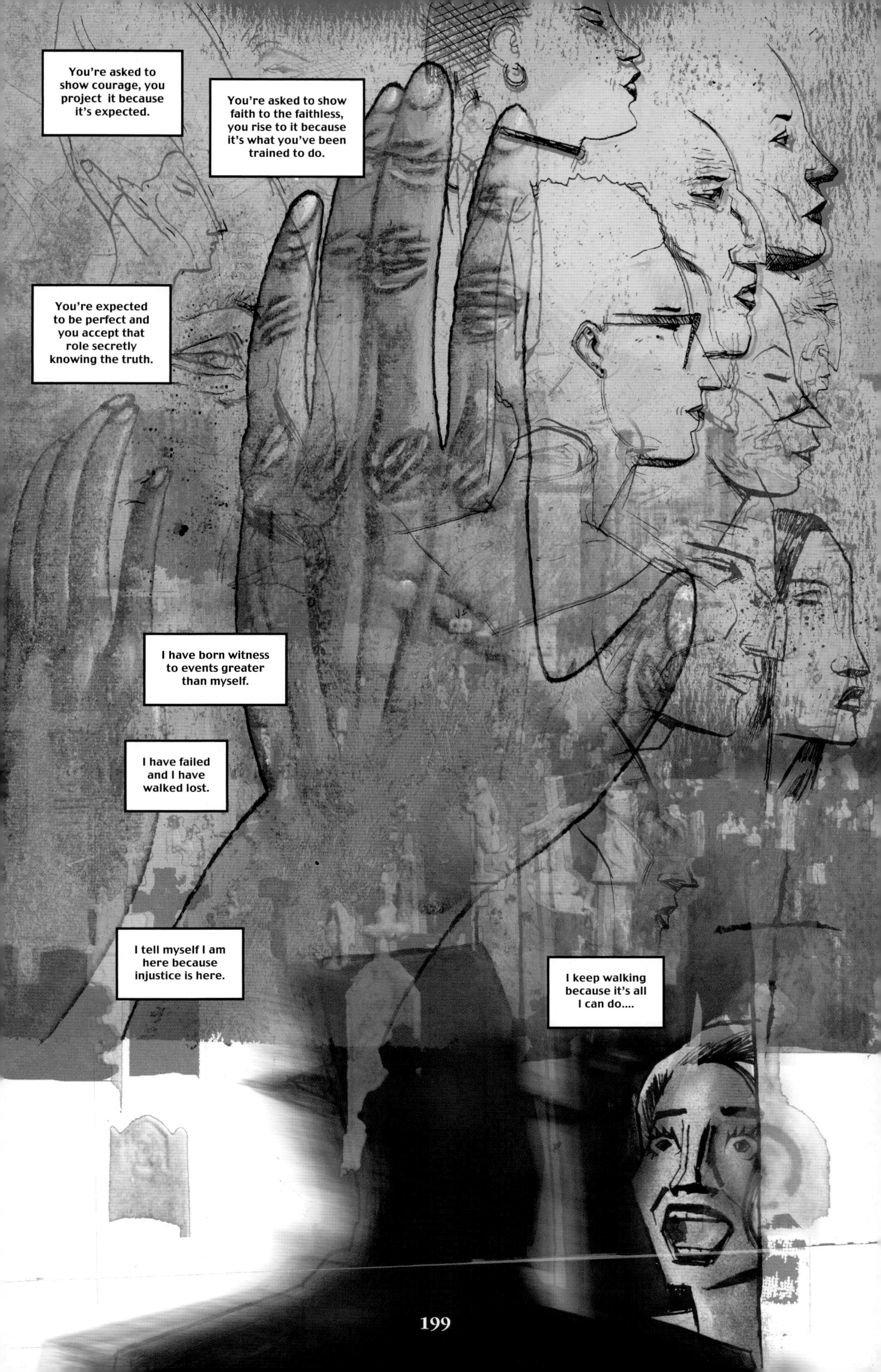
You're asked to show courage, you project it because it's expected.
You're asked to show faith to the faithless, you rise to it because it's what you've been trained to do.
You're expected to be perfect and you accept that role secretly knowing the truth.
I have born witness to events greater than myself.
I have failed and I have walked lost.
I tell myself I am here because injustice is here.
I keep walking because it's all I can do....

I have here part of the transcription of a meeting between Black Power advocates and Martin...just a suggestion of some of the feelings of the time. In the fall of sixty-six, Stokely Carmichael was crossing the country speaking out against Vietnam...

—And denouncing integration, basically championing our awakening Black masses' so-called "*revolutionary* ideology," if you will, which to my way of thinking is a catch phrase covering most of what Black Power meant.

The sentiment was that violence was psychologically healthy and tactically sound, that only violence could bring about Black liberation. The feeling was that nonviolence, that "progress" belonged to *middle-class* Blacks and Whites. So, reading Martin's reply, it says here,

The courageous efforts of our own insurrectionist brothers, such as Denmark Vesey and Nat Turner should be eloquent reminders that violent rebellion is doomed from the start. Negroes in this country are outnumbered ten to one,

so what are the chances and potential casualties of a minority rebellion against a rich and heavily armed majority with a fanatical right wing that would delight in exterminating thousands of Black people? Violence only multiplies hate, intensifying the brutality

"—of the oppressor and the bitterness of the oppressed. Only *love* can drive out *hate*." Had to be rough. After the failure of the Chicago movement...and I see no need to be charitable, let's confront the issue head on, it *was* a failure—Martin's credibility was sorely challenged.

The torch seemed to be passing to a new generation of leaders. More and more people were extolling the virtues of violence, "by any means necessary." Martin was accused of being out of step with the time, an anachronism of sorts.

In those appalling popularity polls his esteem was being challenged, even among prominent leaders; Adam Clayton Powell comes to mind, he publically derided him, called him Martin Loser King. Very depressing, *galling* time for him....

On April 4 of 1967, King delivered an address at my church, *Riverside* Church in New York, that put down *hard* America's growing involvement in Vietnam, 'cause by now there were 350,000 troops overseas. He said that America was spending too much time, money—

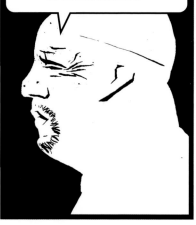

—And *attention* on an unjust war while ignoring problems at home that also demanded attention. He said the war was killing our young men, that Black men and White men fought and died together but couldn't walk down the street together at home.

He said that we went to Vietnam to liberate it and instead we were destroying it, how we were converting a civil war over national unification into an American war over Communism. He likened Americans in Vietnam to nazis in concentration camps.

The minute he spoke in support of letting Ho Chi Minh unify his own country it started up once again in earnest, that old talk about pinko influence in the King camp. Listen, there was a *serious* stink over this speech—

—So-and-so saying the guy didn't know what he was talking about, just stick to what you get and leave the rest to the experts, this kind of thing. I'm reading the papers and now it's obvious that the cozy relationship Doc Martin had with the President is over 'cause he's mad at King's stand on Vietnam.

Also...I think that LBJ felt that after all he'd done for him, King was being ungrateful. How this powerful man's words must have shaken the corridors of power... that people might actually be moved to think their *own* thoughts...to challenge the sanctioned doctrine of the nation's elite....

A few days after River-side the President received an expanded edition of the FBI's report on King and allowed Hoover to circulate it in and out of Washington. Stories about King conspiring with Elijah Muhammed and the Muslims, all this shit about sexual escapades and violence—

—And Communism and embezzle-ment were circulated to the entire intelligence community, the Secretary of State, the Joint Chiefs of Staff, army and naval commanders. Hoover up to his ways. It's all garbage, smear tactics, King never cheated on his wife, he certainly never embezzled money.

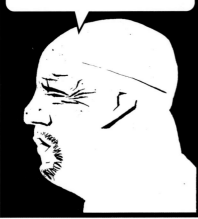

I think also a lot of LBJ's problem with King was that even though the war was largely supported, just the same, there he was slow-ly losing credibility, partly *because* of King. Bobby Kennedy said, "Can America survive another five years of this crazy fool?"

Then, at the end of 1967 the SCLC announced plans for a dramatic new campaign.

Beginning in early April of 1968, SCLC will undertake a strong, dramatic, and attention-getting campaign of mass civil disobedience in Washington, D.C., to force the federal gov-ernment to guarantee jobs or incomes for all Americans, and to start tearing down the slums once and for all. SCLC is planning to recruit three thousand slum dwellers, in effect a "poor peoples" army, from five rural areas and ten major cities, to be named later.

We'll train them for three months in the techniques of non-violence, and then bring them to Washington to disrupt transportation and government operations until America responds to the needs of her poor.

This announcement resulted in the usual criticisms: it was ill–timing, potential provocation of riots, blah, blah, blah. Some even felt this was a move towards Black Power on King's part. This had to be Martin's *lowest* ebb professionally.

Everybody was attacking him! Young Black militants for his stubborn adherence to nonviolence, moderate and conservative Blacks for going too far, the FBI for Vietnam and whatever else they could cobble together. I imagine he must have been desperate for a victory that would silence his critics and save his crumbling movement.

After all, it had been a couple of years since his last concrete victory. By sixty-eight the FBI had logged *fifty* assassination threats against him, and the Klan and other hate groups had him targeted for violence.

I felt that this "poor peoples" campaign would hurt Capitalism. Frankly, it reeked of a kind of *Communist* social order, I mean, if you listened closely you could actually *hear* the death knell of free enterprise.... Sure there was money on King's head, but it was *business,* not some...some *personal* vendetta....

I'm not afraid to admit I might have supported his being eliminated, I may have been present during certain discussions.... I'm not here to name names...one gentleman, someone high up in the Secretary General's office, something about a standing offer of $20,000 for King's assassination.

Another gentleman claimed he had $30,000 to spread around. Another offered *$50,000!,* this was one *serious* nigger to command sums of that caliber.... I guess it's fair to say I wouldn't be surprised to discover there were still others willing to go further.

When you want a man dead....

"...Martin we go back...you don't have to hold nothing back with *me,* I know we've both witnessed more comforting times....

"The glory days, huh?"

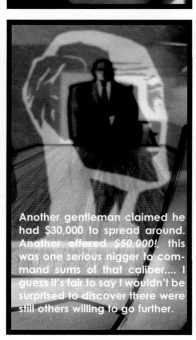

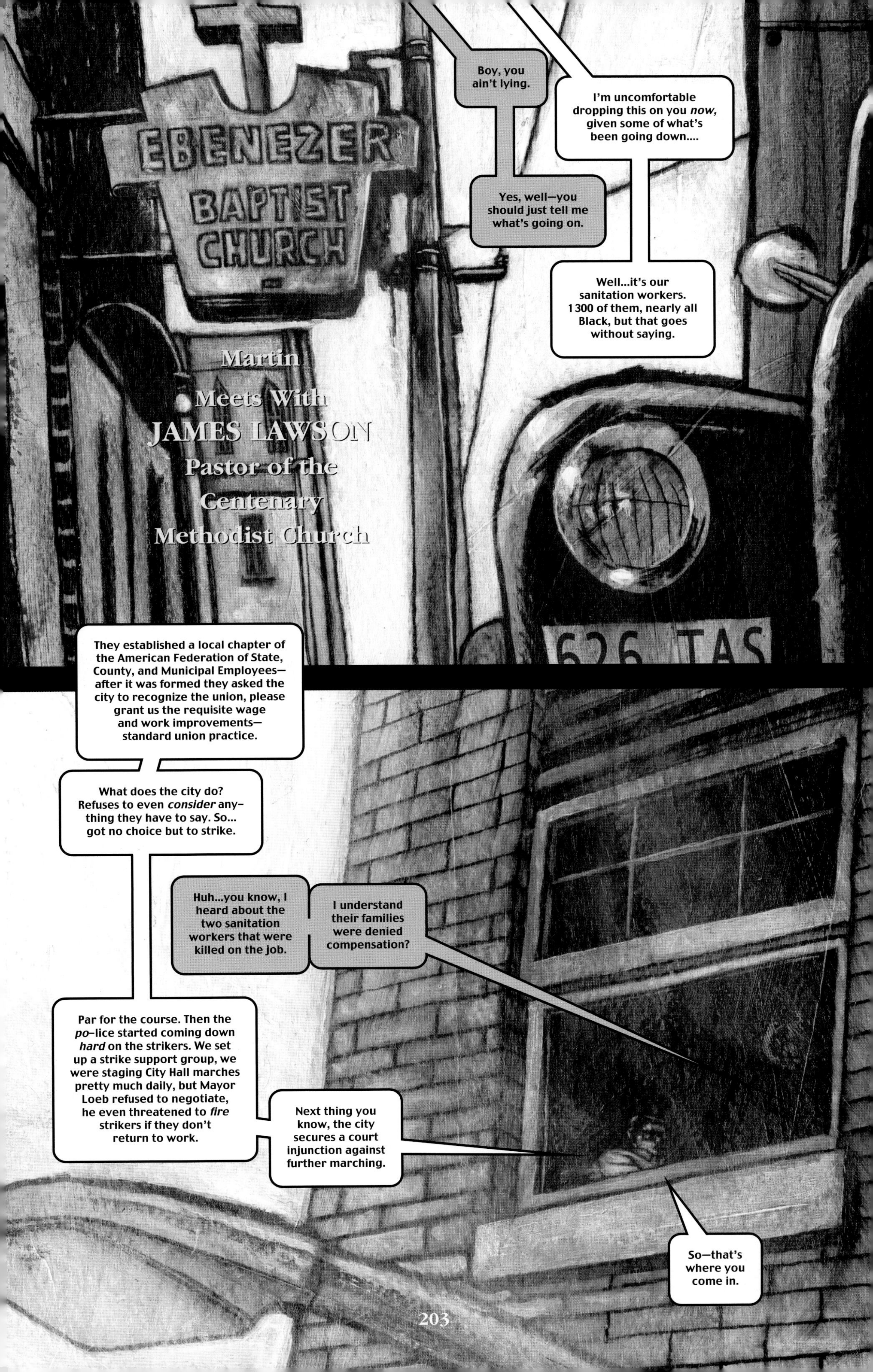
EBENEZER BAPTIST CHURCH
Boy, you ain't lying.
I'm uncomfortable dropping this on you *now,* given some of what's been going down....
Yes, well—you should just tell me what's going on.
Well...it's our sanitation workers. 1300 of them, nearly all Black, but that goes without saying.
Martin Meets With JAMES LAWSON Pastor of the Centenary Methodist Church
626 TAS
They established a local chapter of the American Federation of State, County, and Municipal Employees—after it was formed they asked the city to recognize the union, please grant us the requisite wage and work improvements—standard union practice.
What does the city do? Refuses to even *consider* any-thing they have to say. So... got no choice but to strike.
Huh...you know, I heard about the two sanitation workers that were killed on the job.
I understand their families were denied compensation?
Par for the course. Then the *po*–lice started coming down *hard* on the strikers. We set up a strike support group, we were staging City Hall marches pretty much daily, but Mayor Loeb refused to negotiate, he even threatened to *fire* strikers if they don't return to work.
Next thing you know, the city secures a court injunction against further marching.
So—that's where you come in.

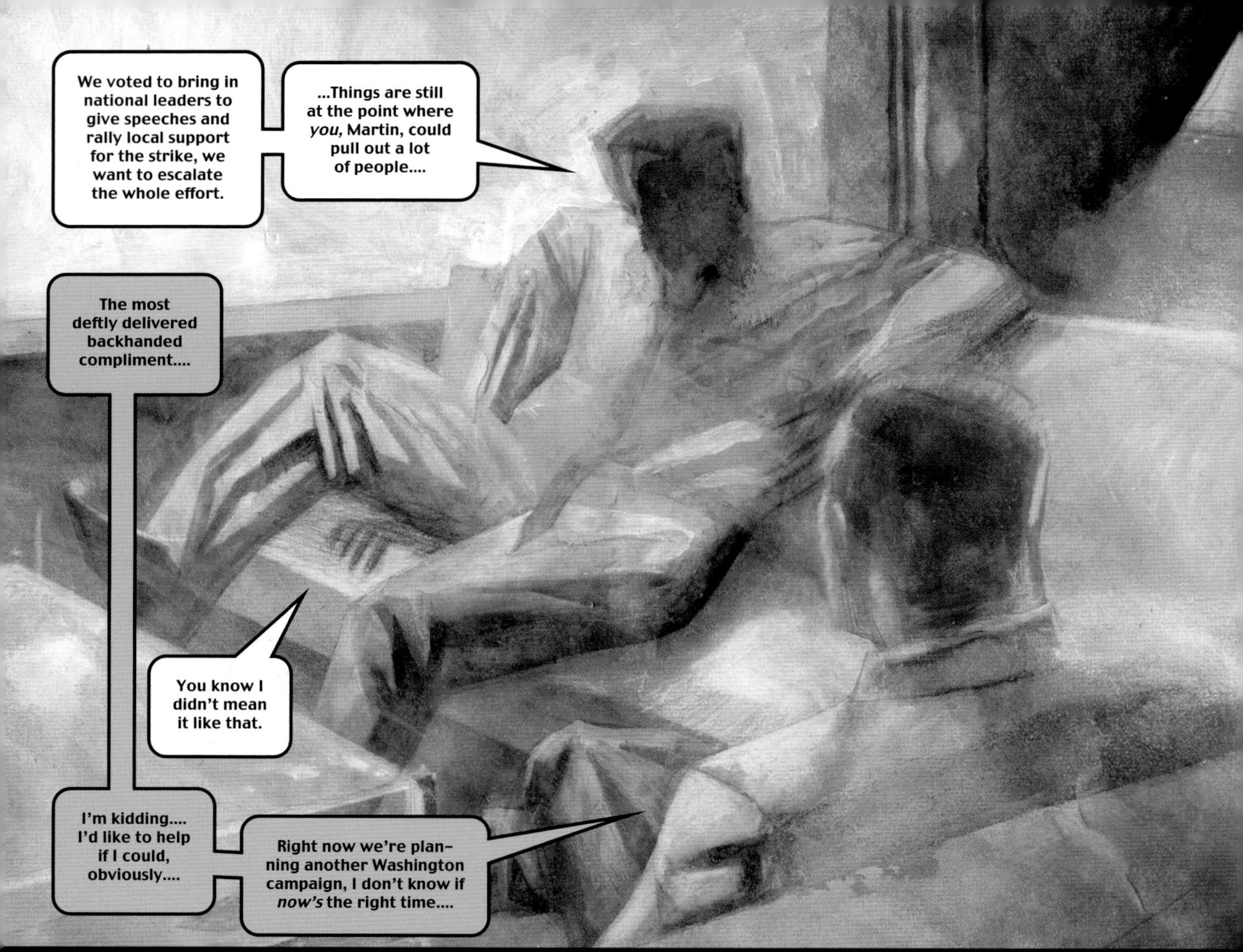
We voted to bring in national leaders to give speeches and rally local support for the strike, we want to escalate the whole effort.
...Things are still at the point where *you,* Martin, could pull out a lot of people....
The most deftly delivered backhanded compliment....
You know I didn't mean it like that.
I'm kidding.... I'd like to help if I could, obviously....
Right now we're planning another Washington campaign, I don't know if *now's* the right time....

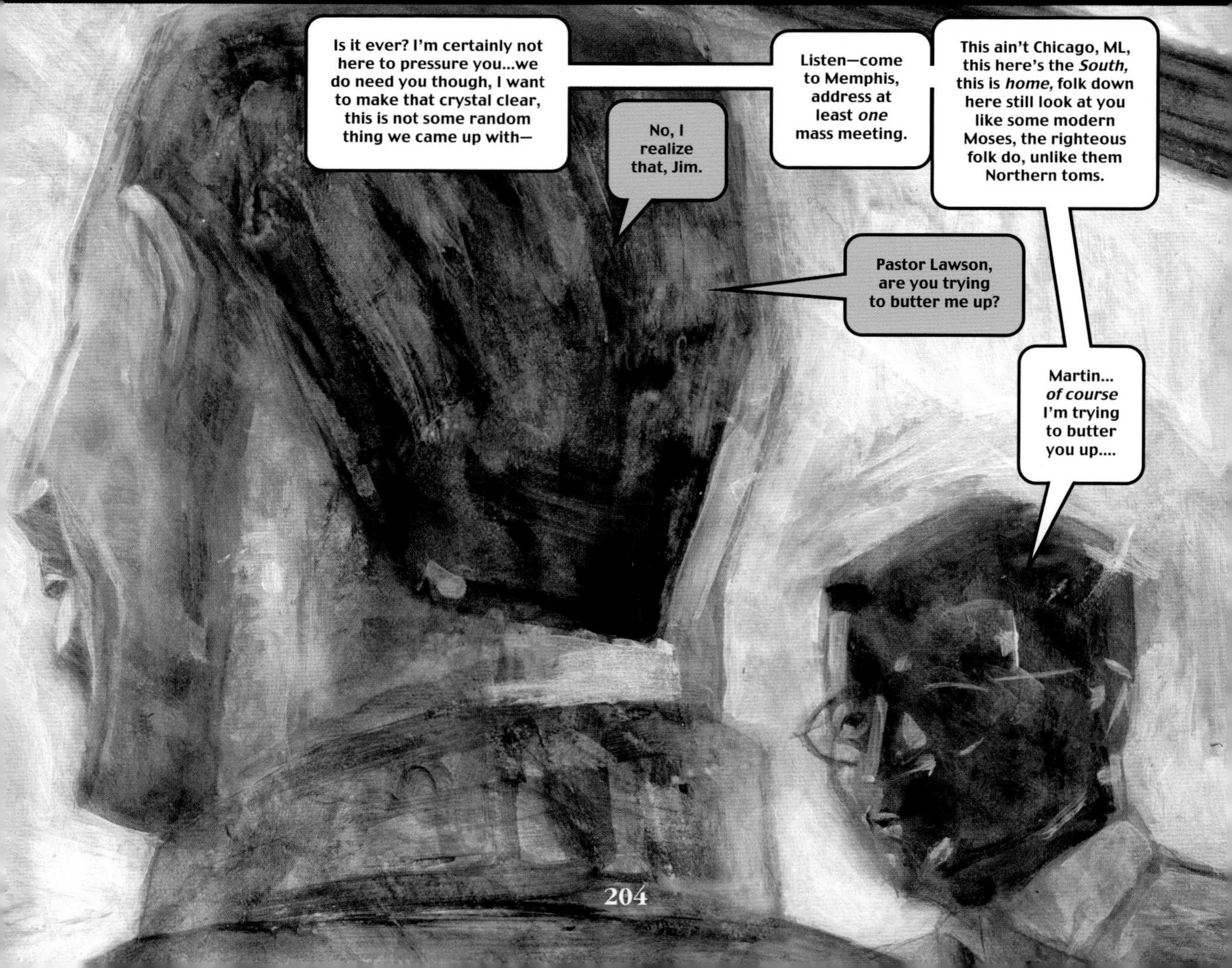
Is it ever? I'm certainly not here to pressure you...we do need you though, I want to make that crystal clear, this is not some random thing we came up with—
No, I realize that, Jim.
Listen—come to Memphis, address at least *one* mass meeting.
This ain't Chicago, ML, this here's the *South,* this is *home,* folk down here still look at you like some modern Moses, the righteous folk do, unlike them Northern toms.
Pastor Lawson, are you trying to butter me up?
Martin... *of course* I'm trying to butter you up....

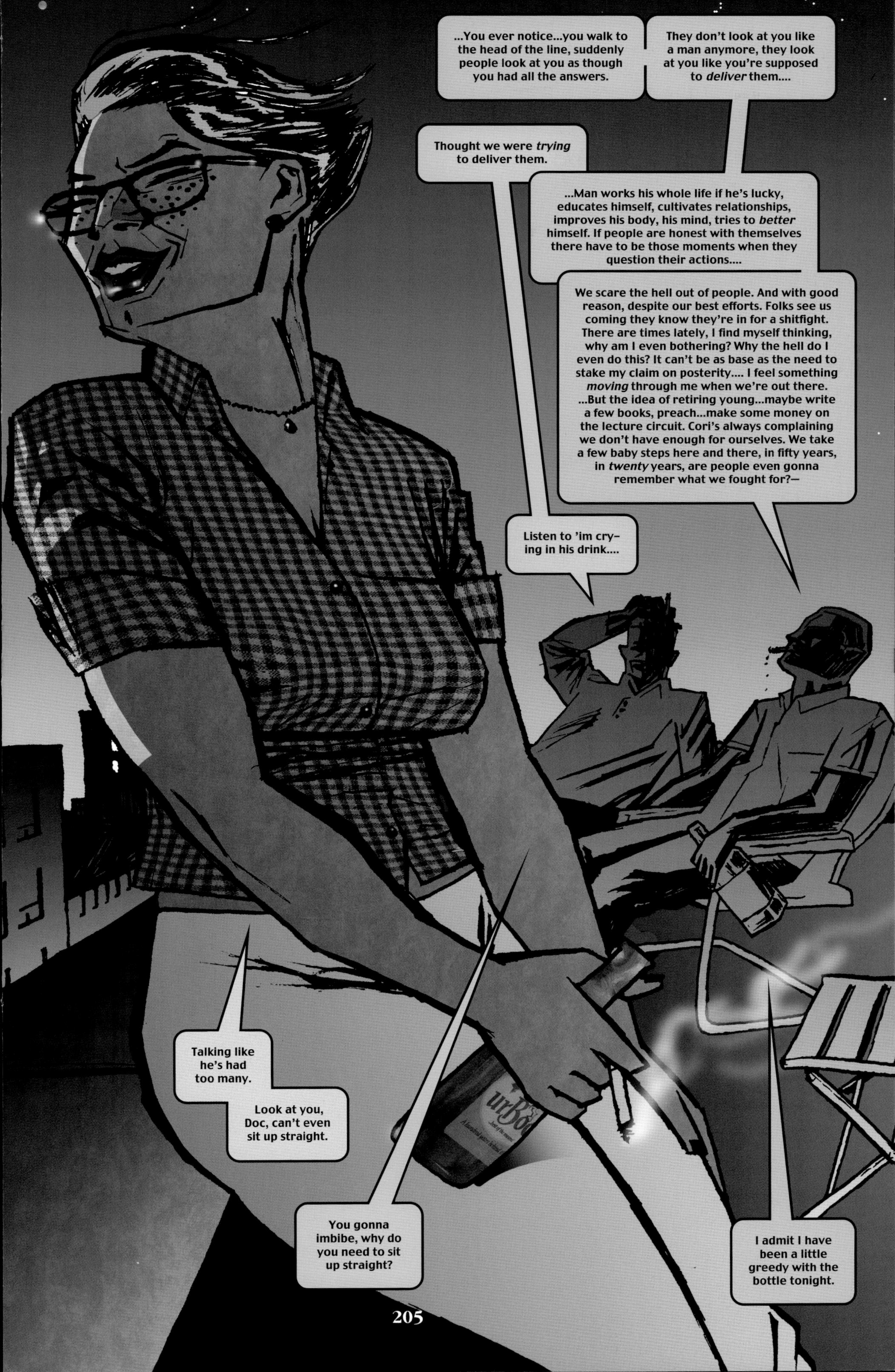
...You ever notice...you walk to the head of the line, suddenly people look at you as though you had all the answers.
They don't look at you like a man anymore, they look at you like you're supposed to *deliver* them....
Thought we were *trying* to deliver them.
...Man works his whole life if he's lucky, educates himself, cultivates relationships, improves his body, his mind, tries to *better* himself. If people are honest with themselves there have to be those moments when they question their actions....
We scare the hell out of people. And with good reason, despite our best efforts. Folks see us coming they know they're in for a shitfight. There are times lately, I find myself thinking, why am I even bothering? Why the hell do I even do this? It can't be as base as the need to stake my claim on posterity.... I feel something *moving* through me when we're out there. ...But the idea of retiring young...maybe write a few books, preach...make some money on the lecture circuit. Cori's always complaining we don't have enough for ourselves. We take a few baby steps here and there, in fifty years, in *twenty* years, are people even gonna remember what we fought for?—
Listen to 'im crying in his drink....
Talking like he's had too many.
Look at you, Doc, can't even sit up straight.
You gonna imbibe, why do you need to sit up straight?
I admit I have been a little greedy with the bottle tonight.

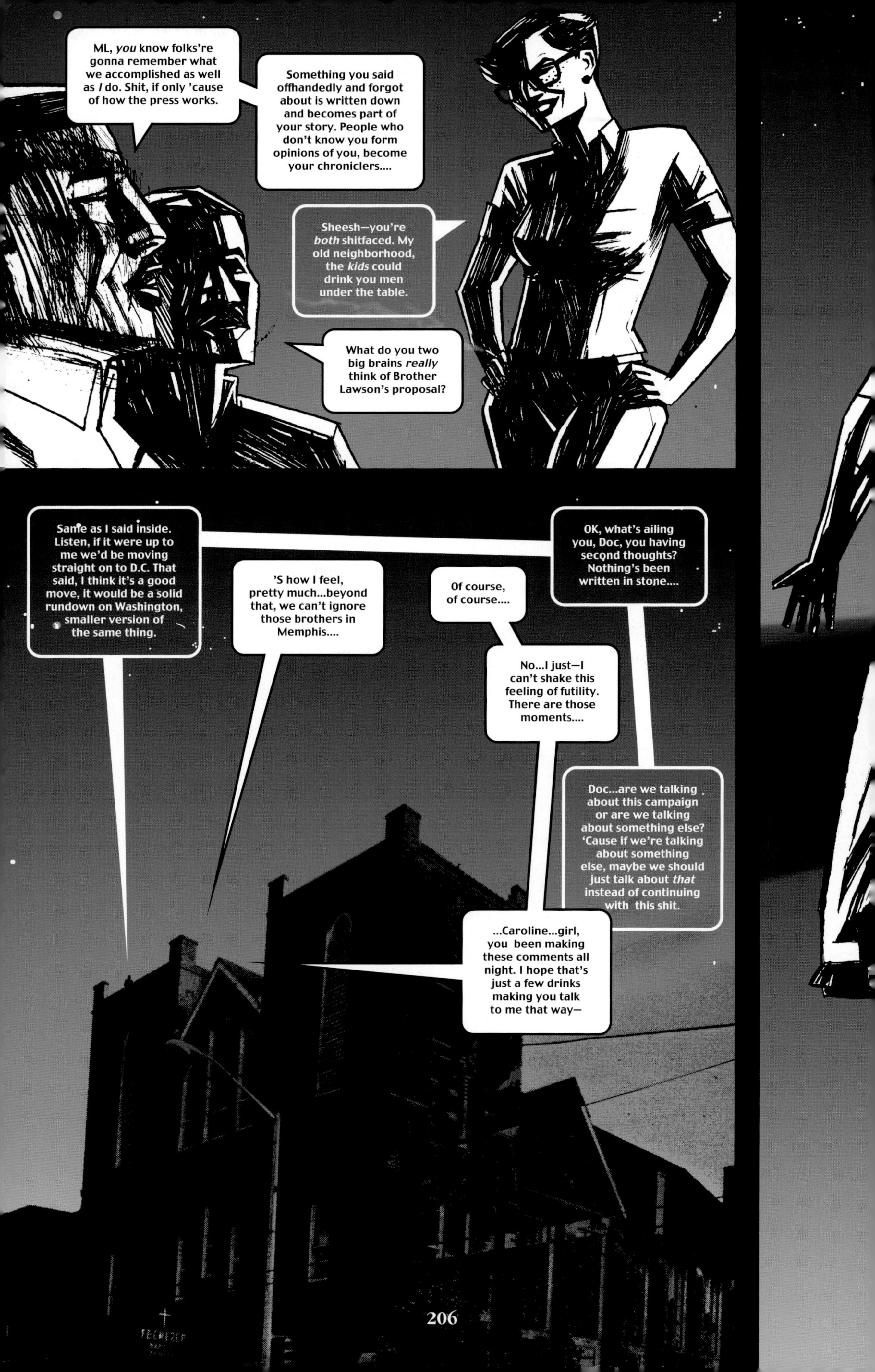
ML, *you* know folks're gonna remember what we accomplished as well as *I* do. Shit, if only 'cause of how the press works.
Something you said offhandedly and forgot about is written down and becomes part of your story. People who don't know you form opinions of you, become your chroniclers....
Sheesh—you're *both* shitfaced. My old neighborhood, the *kids* could drink you men under the table.
What do you two big brains *really* think of Brother Lawson's proposal?
Same as I said inside. Listen, if it were up to me we'd be moving straight on to D.C. That said, I think it's a good move, it would be a solid rundown on Washington, smaller version of the same thing.
'S how I feel, pretty much...beyond that, we can't ignore those brothers in Memphis....
Of course, of course....
OK, what's ailing you, Doc, you having second thoughts? Nothing's been written in stone....
No...I just—I can't shake this feeling of futility. There are those moments....
Doc...are we talking about this campaign or are we talking about something else? 'Cause if we're talking about something else, maybe we should just talk about *that* instead of continuing with this shit.
...Caroline...girl, you been making these comments all night. I hope that's just a few drinks making you talk to me that way—

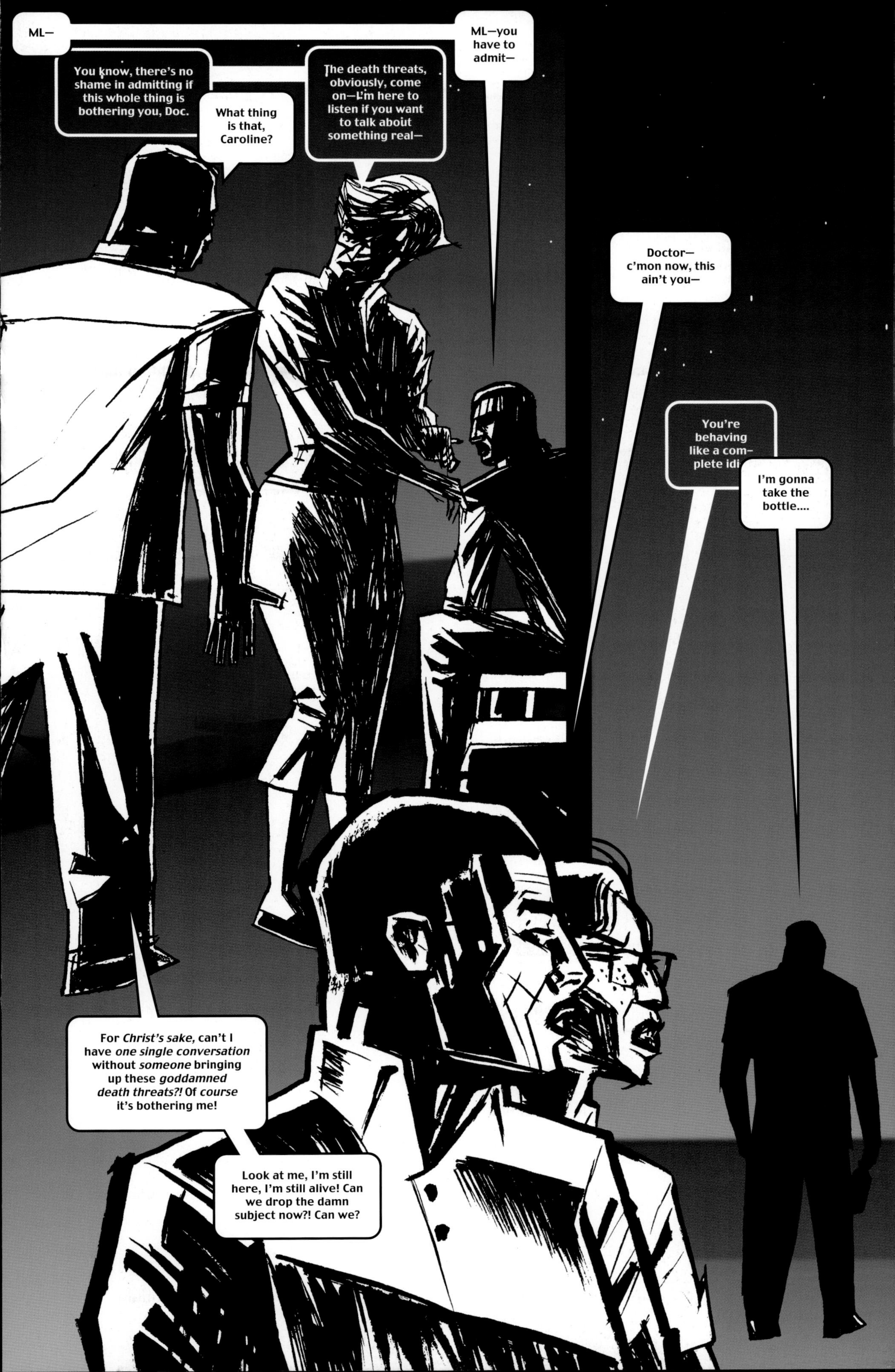
ML—
ML—you have to admit—
You know, there's no shame in admitting if this whole thing is bothering you, Doc.
The death threats, obviously, come on—I'm here to listen if you want to talk about something real—
What thing is that, Caroline?
Doctor— c'mon now, this ain't you—
You're behaving like a complete idi—
I'm gonna take the bottle....
For *Christ's sake,* can't I have *one single conversation* without *someone* bringing up these *goddamned death threats?!* Of *course* it's bothering me!
Look at me, I'm still here, I'm still alive! Can we drop the damn subject now?! Can we?

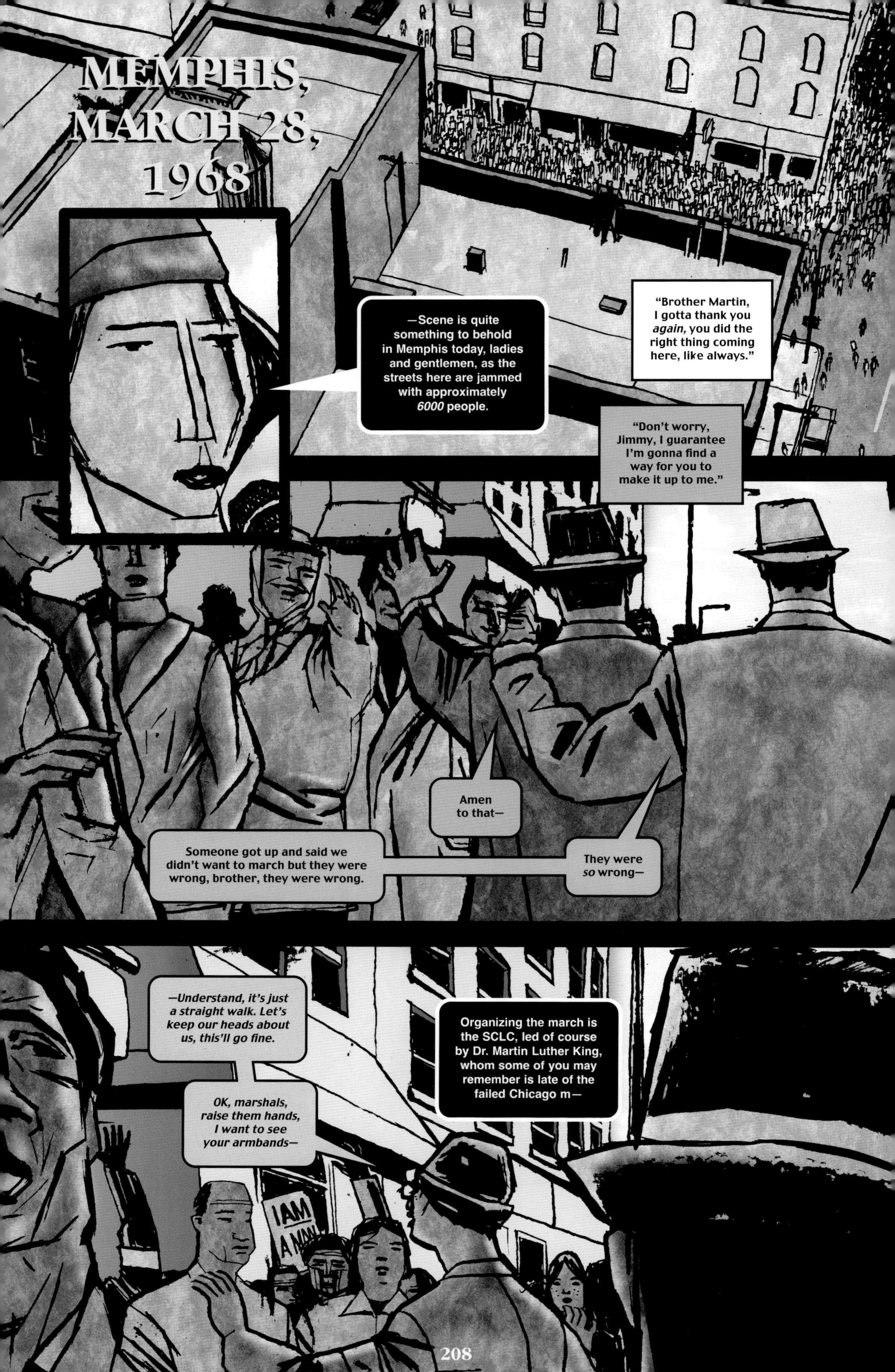
MEMPHIS, MARCH 28, 1968
—Scene is quite something to behold in Memphis today, ladies and gentlemen, as the streets here are jammed with approximately 6000 people.
"Brother Martin, I gotta thank you again, you did the right thing coming here, like always."
"Don't worry, Jimmy, I guarantee I'm gonna find a way for you to make it up to me."
Amen to that—
Someone got up and said we didn't want to march but they were wrong, brother, they were wrong.
They were so wrong—
—Understand, it's just a straight walk. Let's keep our heads about us, this'll go fine.
OK, marshals, raise them hands, I want to see your armbands—
Organizing the march is the SCLC, led of course by Dr. Martin Luther King, whom some of you may remember is late of the failed Chicago m—
I AM A MAN

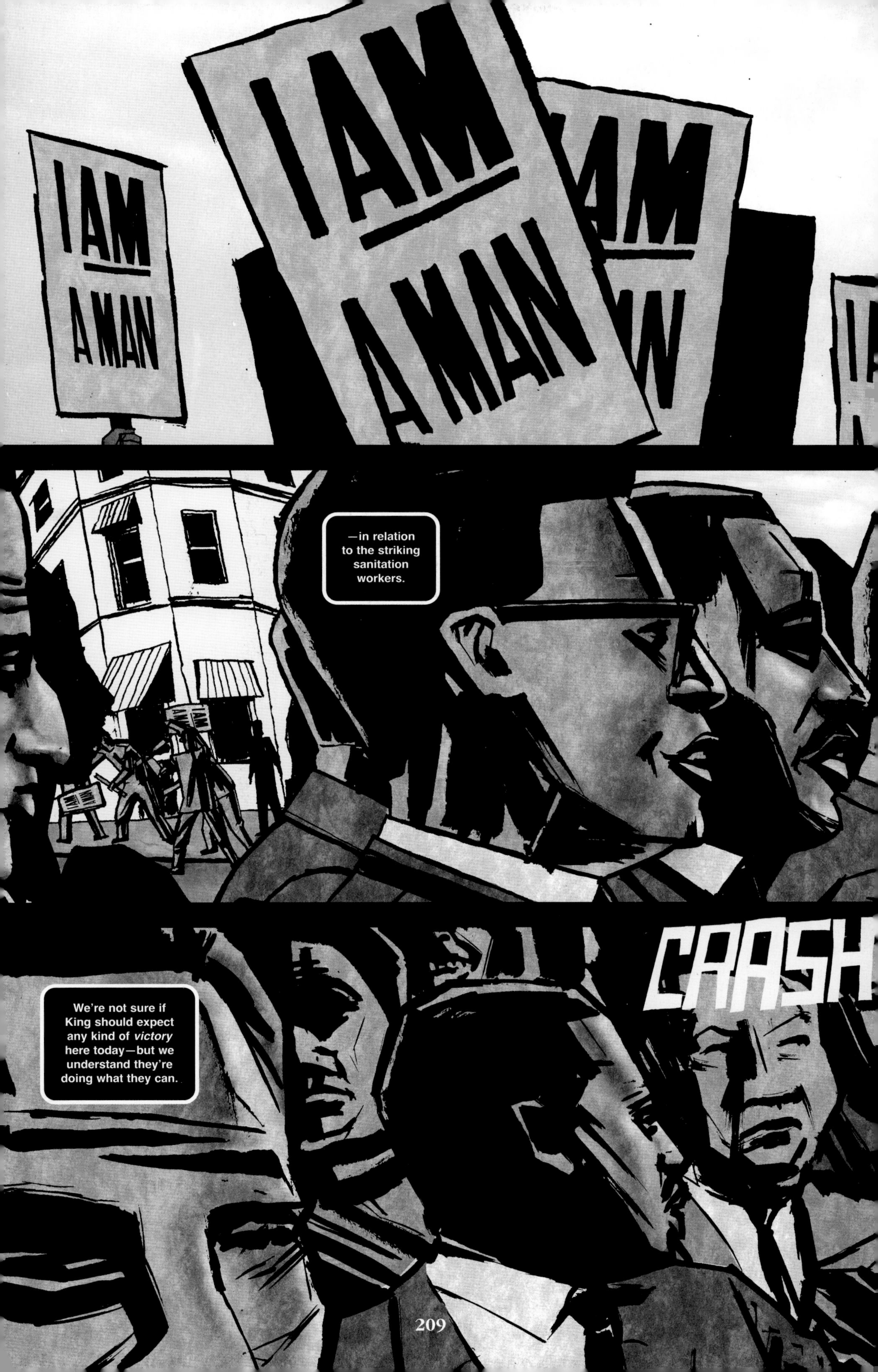
I AM A MAN
I AM A MAN
—in relation to the striking sanitation workers.
CRASH
We're not sure if King should expect any kind of *victory* here today—but we understand they're doing what they can.

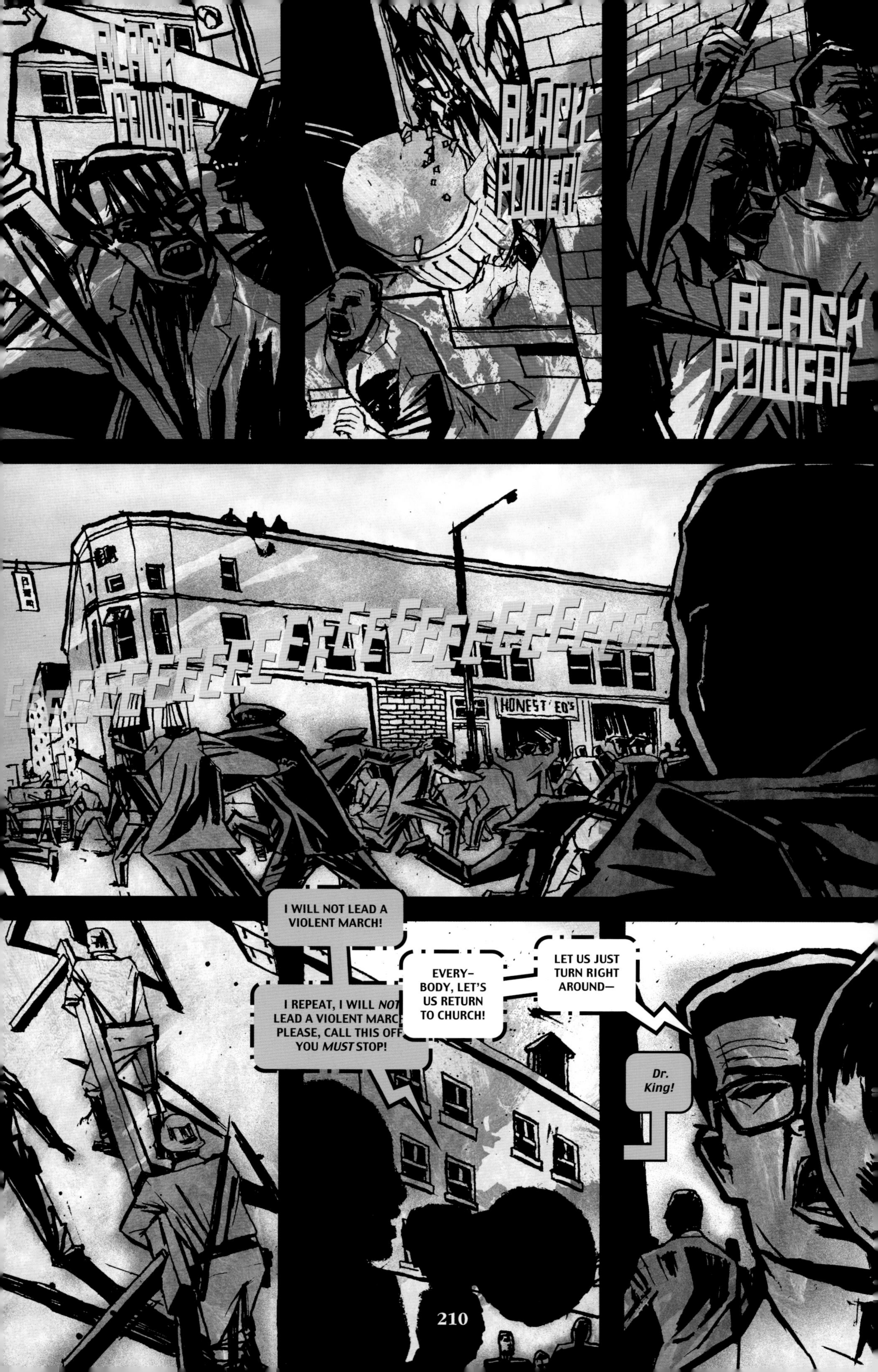
BLACK POWER!
BLACK POWER!
BLACK POWER!
EEEEEEEEEEEEEEEEEEEEEEE
HONEST ED'S
I WILL NOT LEAD A VIOLENT MARCH!
I REPEAT, I WILL *NOT* LEAD A VIOLENT MARCH! PLEASE, CALL THIS OFF! YOU *MUST* STOP!
EVERY-BODY, LET'S US RETURN TO CHURCH!
LET US JUST TURN RIGHT AROUND—
Dr. King!

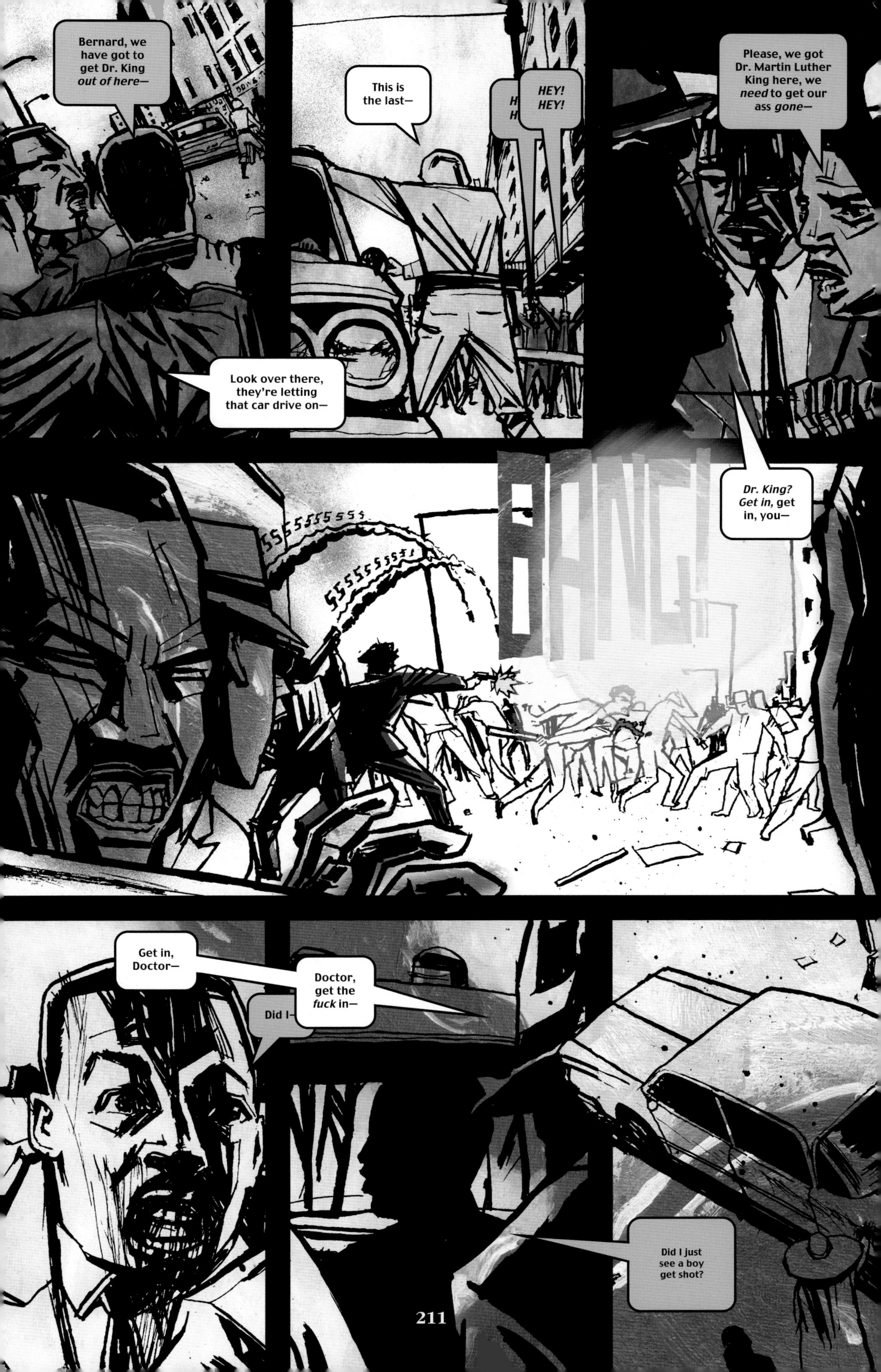

Bernard, we have got to get Dr. King *out of here—*
Look over there, they're letting that car drive on—
This is the last—
HEY! HEY!
Please, we got Dr. Martin Luther King here, we *need* to get our ass *gone—*
Dr. King? *Get in,* get in, you—
BANG!
SSSSSSSSS
SSSSSSSSS
Get in, Doctor—
Did I—
Doctor, get the *fuck* in—
Did I just see a boy get shot?

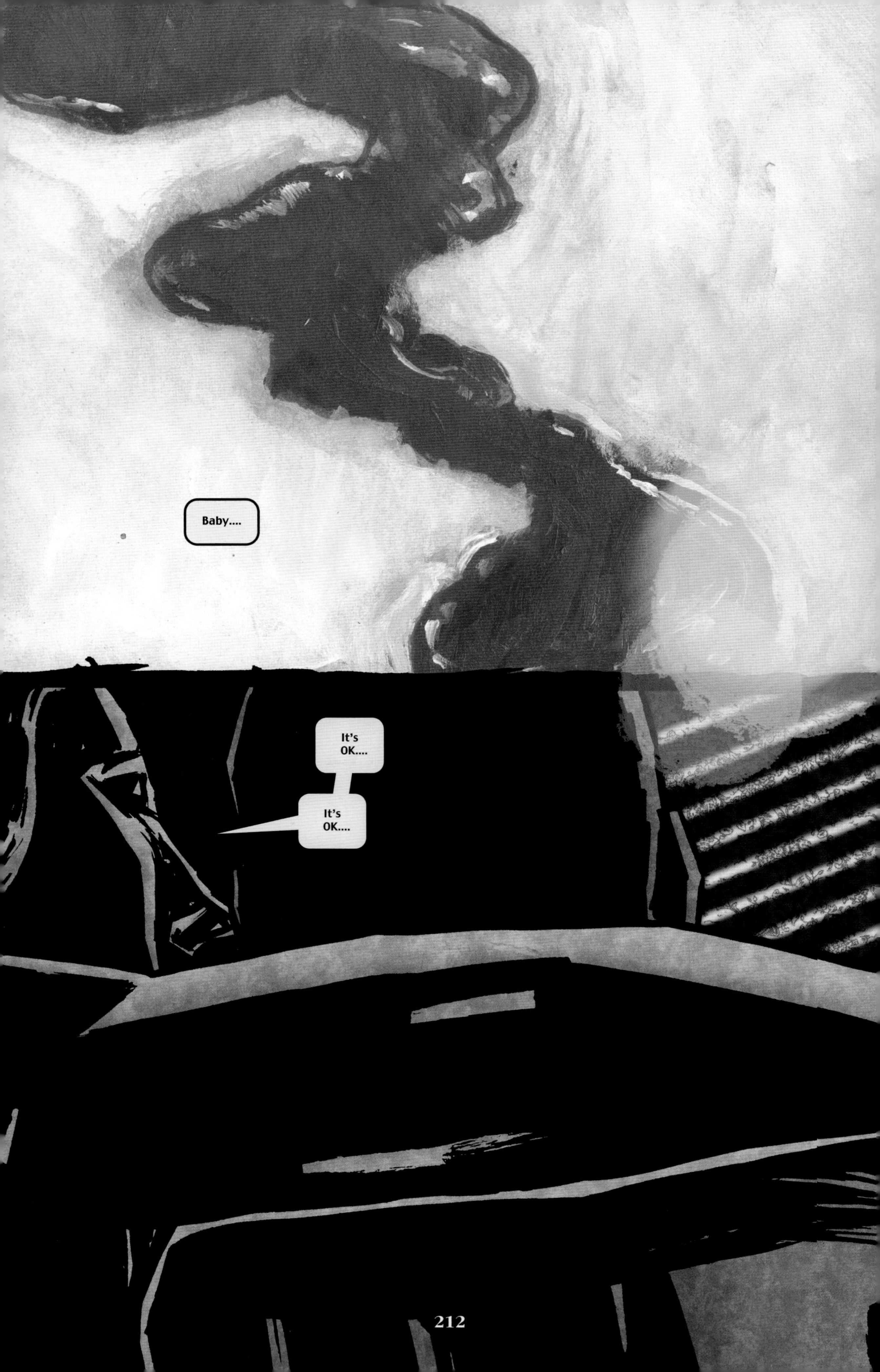
Baby....
It's OK....
It's OK....

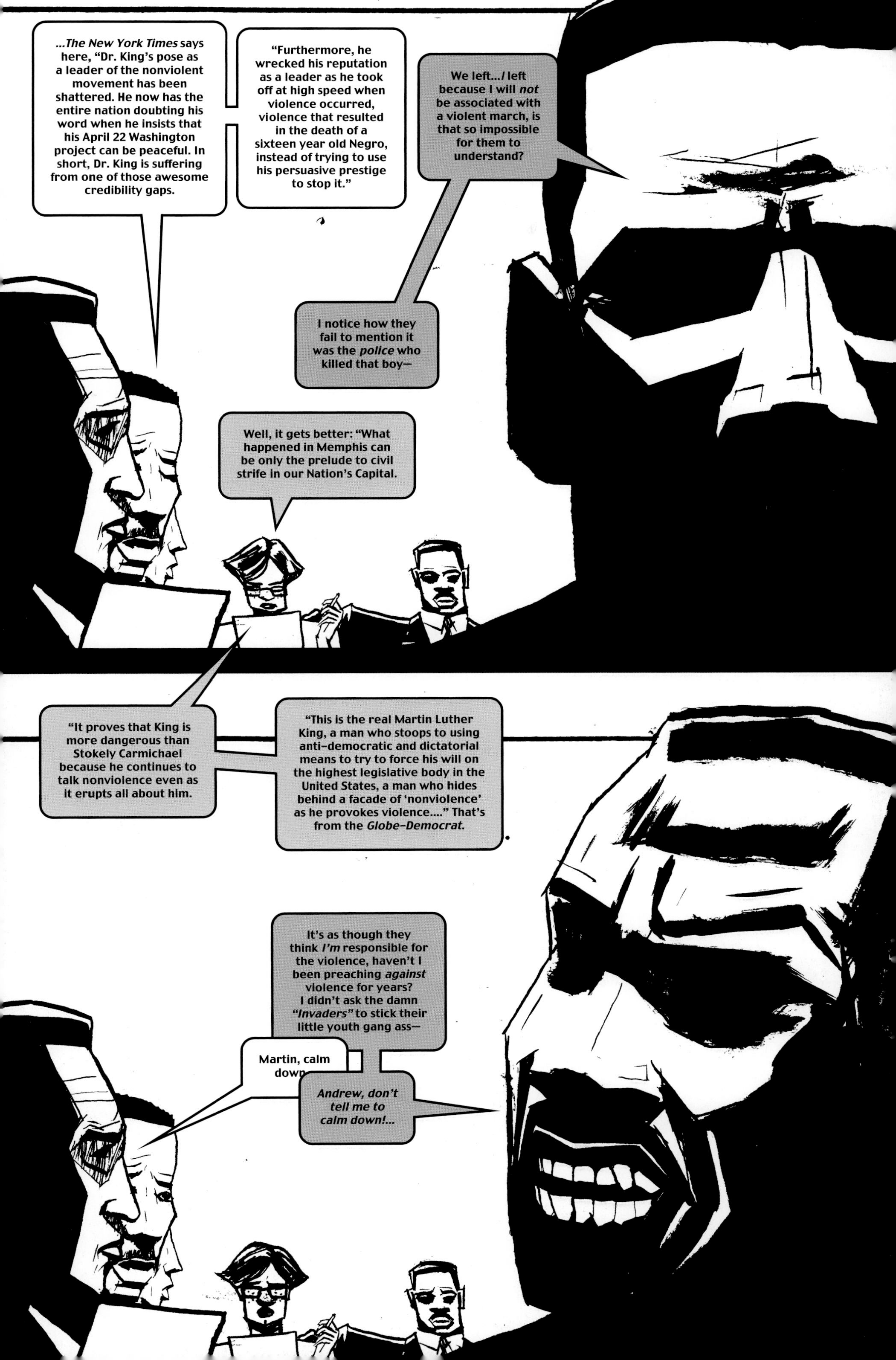
...The New York Times says here, "Dr. King's pose as a leader of the nonviolent movement has been shattered. He now has the entire nation doubting his word when he insists that his April 22 Washington project can be peaceful. In short, Dr. King is suffering from one of those awesome credibility gaps.
"Furthermore, he wrecked his reputation as a leader as he took off at high speed when violence occurred, violence that resulted in the death of a sixteen year old Negro, instead of trying to use his persuasive prestige to stop it."
We left... I left because I will not be associated with a violent march, is that so impossible for them to understand?
I notice how they fail to mention it was the police who killed that boy—
Well, it gets better: "What happened in Memphis can be only the prelude to civil strife in our Nation's Capital.
"It proves that King is more dangerous than Stokely Carmichael because he continues to talk nonviolence even as it erupts all about him.
"This is the real Martin Luther King, a man who stoops to using anti-democratic and dictatorial means to try to force his will on the highest legislative body in the United States, a man who hides behind a facade of 'nonviolence' as he provokes violence...." That's from the Globe-Democrat.
It's as though they think I'm responsible for the violence, haven't I been preaching against violence for years? I didn't ask the damn "Invaders" to stick their little youth gang ass—
Martin, calm down
Andrew, don't tell me to calm down!...

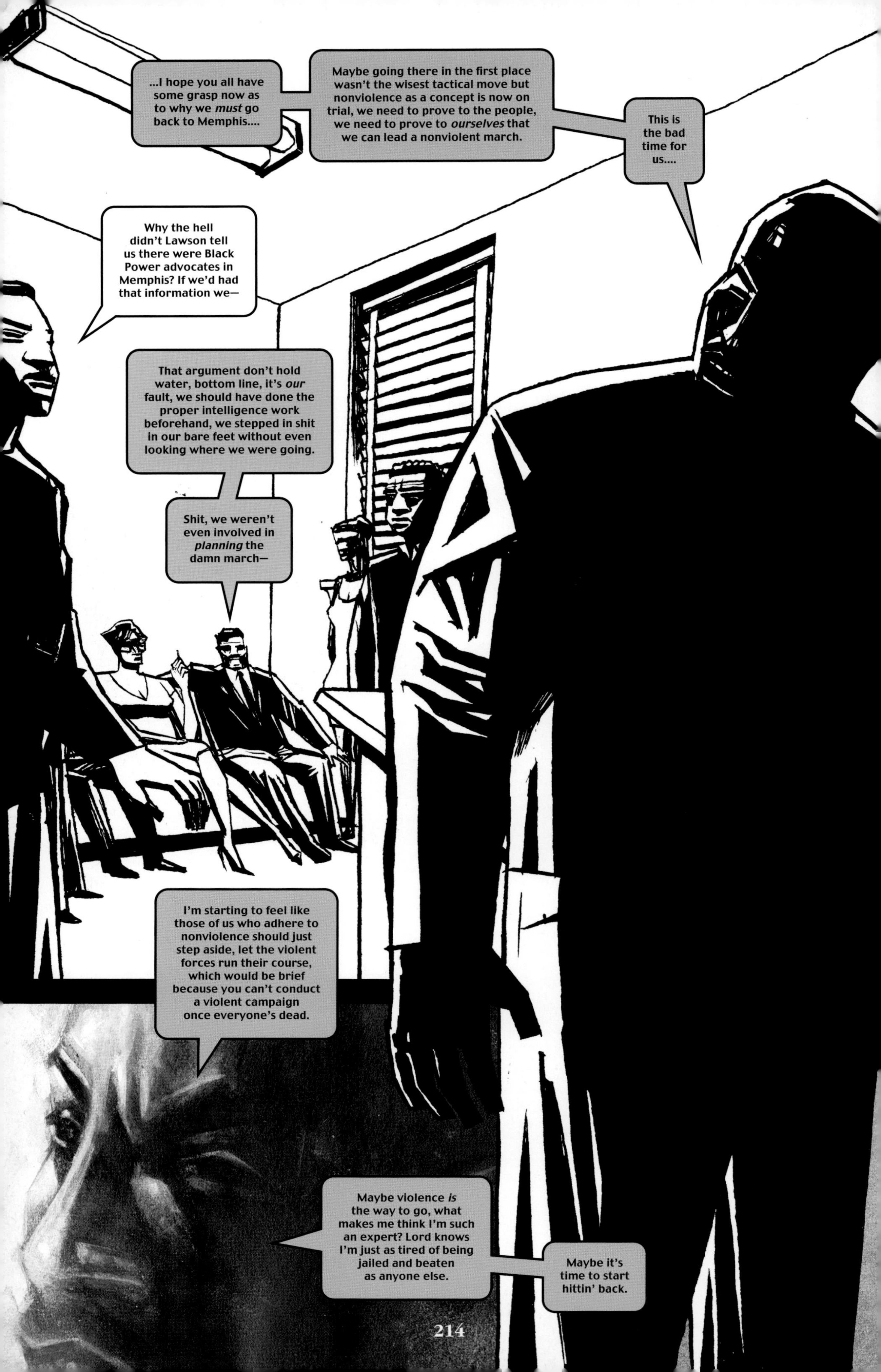

...I hope you all have some grasp now as to why we *must* go back to Memphis....
Maybe going there in the first place wasn't the wisest tactical move but nonviolence as a concept is now on trial, we need to prove to the people, we need to prove to *ourselves* that we can lead a nonviolent march.
This is the bad time for us....
Why the hell didn't Lawson tell us there were Black Power advocates in Memphis? If we'd had that information we—
That argument don't hold water, bottom line, it's *our* fault, we should have done the proper intelligence work beforehand, we stepped in shit in our bare feet without even looking where we were going.
Shit, we weren't even involved in *planning* the damn march—
I'm starting to feel like those of us who adhere to nonviolence should just step aside, let the violent forces run their course, which would be brief because you can't conduct a violent campaign once everyone's dead.
Maybe violence *is* the way to go, what makes me think I'm such an expert? Lord knows I'm just as tired of being jailed and beaten as anyone else.
Maybe it's time to start hittin' back.

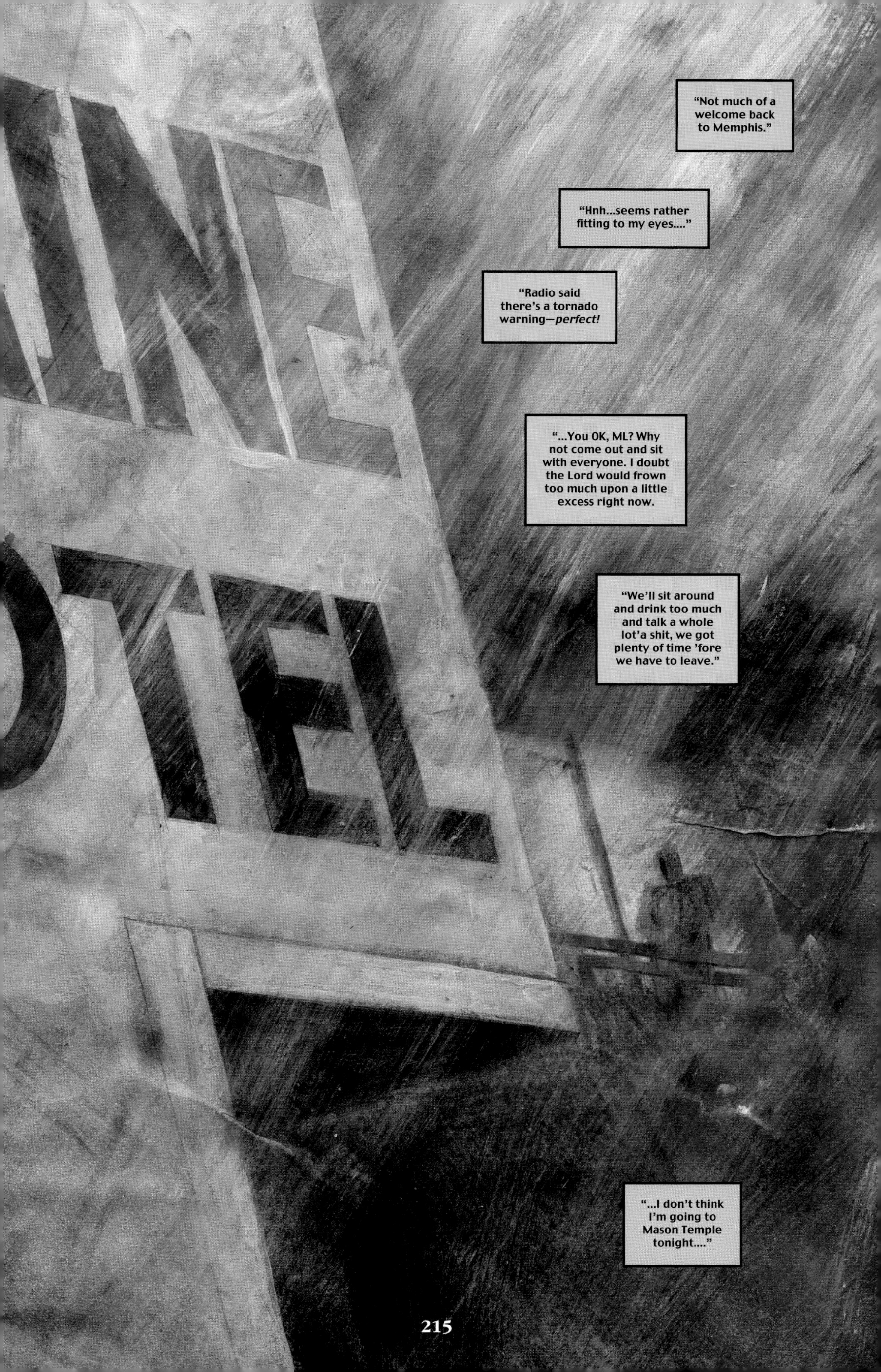
"Not much of a welcome back to Memphis."
"Hnh...seems rather fitting to my eyes...."
"Radio said there's a tornado warning—*perfect!*
"...You OK, ML? Why not come out and sit with everyone. I doubt the Lord would frown too much upon a little excess right now.
"We'll sit around and drink too much and talk a whole lot'a shit, we got plenty of time 'fore we have to leave."
"...I don't think I'm going to Mason Temple tonight...."

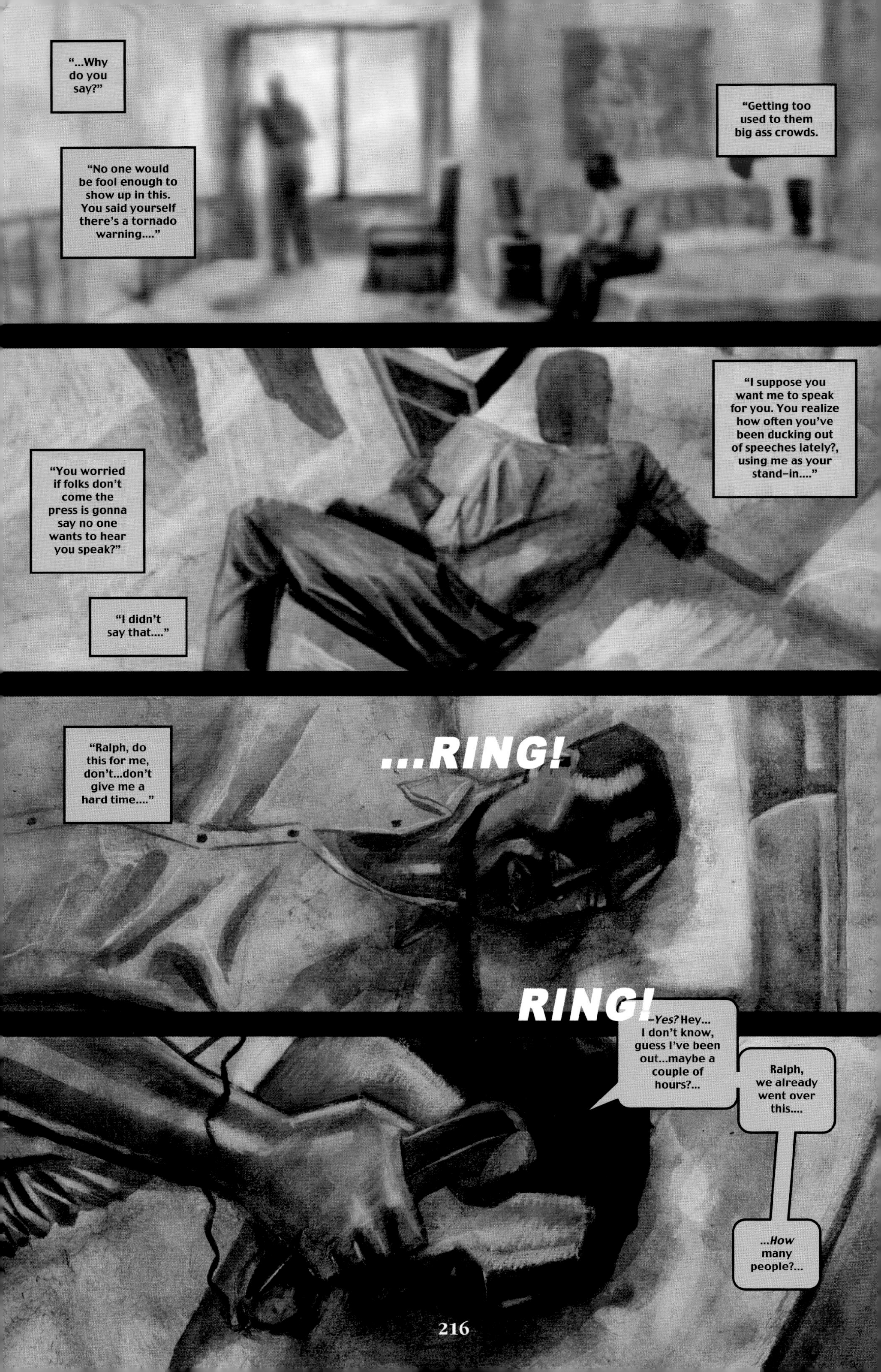
"...Why do you say?"
"Getting too used to them big ass crowds.
"No one would be fool enough to show up in this. You said yourself there's a tornado warning...."
"I suppose you want me to speak for you. You realize how often you've been ducking out of speeches lately?, using me as your stand-in...."
"You worried if folks don't come the press is gonna say no one wants to hear you speak?"
"I didn't say that...."
"Ralph, do this for me, don't...don't give me a hard time...."
...RING!
RING!
–*Yes?* Hey... I don't know, guess I've been out...maybe a couple of hours?...
Ralph, we already went over this....
...*How* many people?...

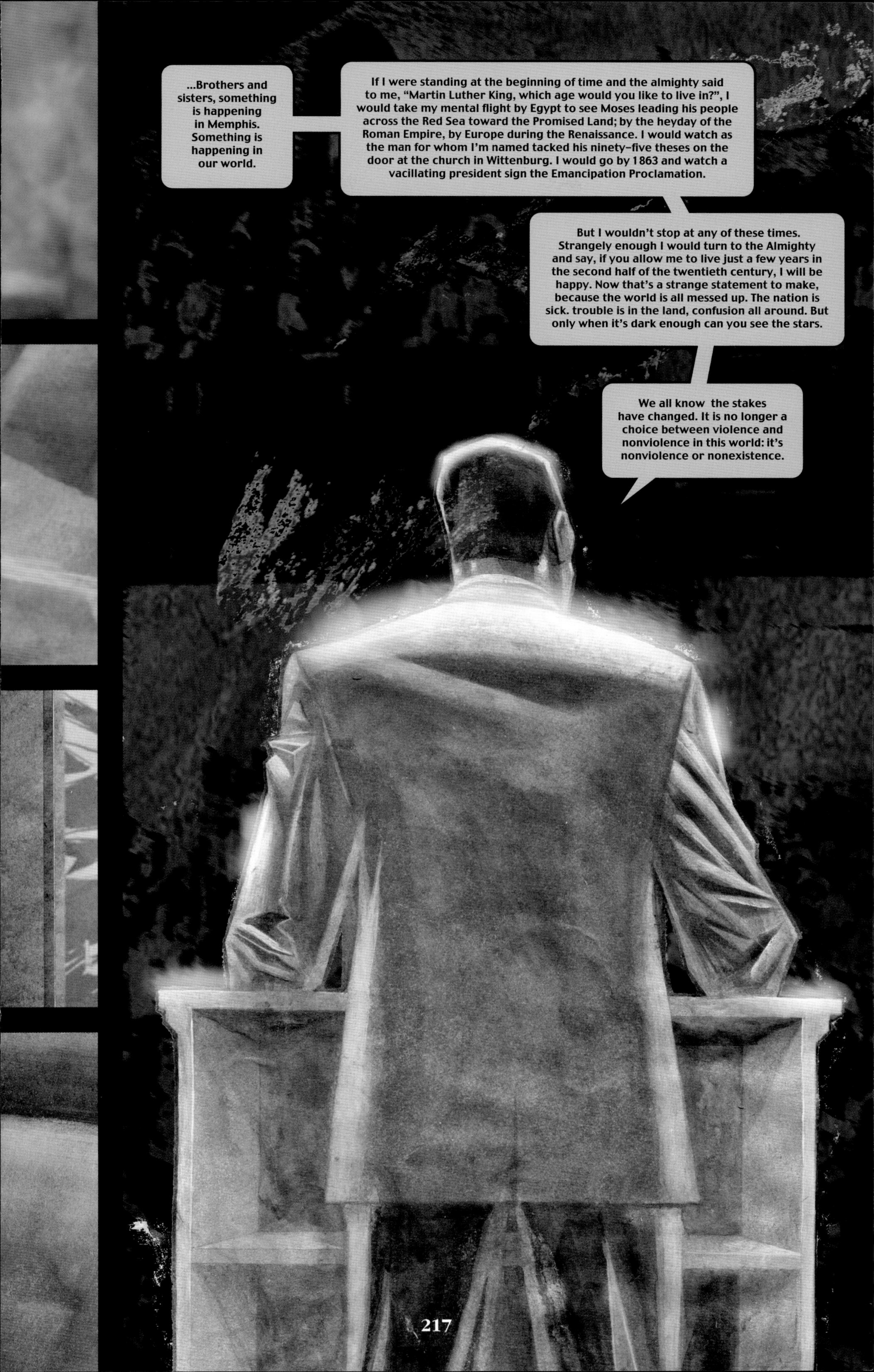
...Brothers and sisters, something is happening in Memphis. Something is happening in our world.
If I were standing at the beginning of time and the almighty said to me, "Martin Luther King, which age would you like to live in?", I would take my mental flight by Egypt to see Moses leading his people across the Red Sea toward the Promised Land; by the heyday of the Roman Empire, by Europe during the Renaissance. I would watch as the man for whom I'm named tacked his ninety-five theses on the door at the church in Wittenburg. I would go by 1863 and watch a vacillating president sign the Emancipation Proclamation.
But I wouldn't stop at any of these times. Strangely enough I would turn to the Almighty and say, if you allow me to live just a few years in the second half of the twentieth century, I will be happy. Now that's a strange statement to make, because the world is all messed up. The nation is sick. trouble is in the land, confusion all around. But only when it's dark enough can you see the stars.
We all know the stakes have changed. It is no longer a choice between violence and nonviolence in this world: it's nonviolence or nonexistence.

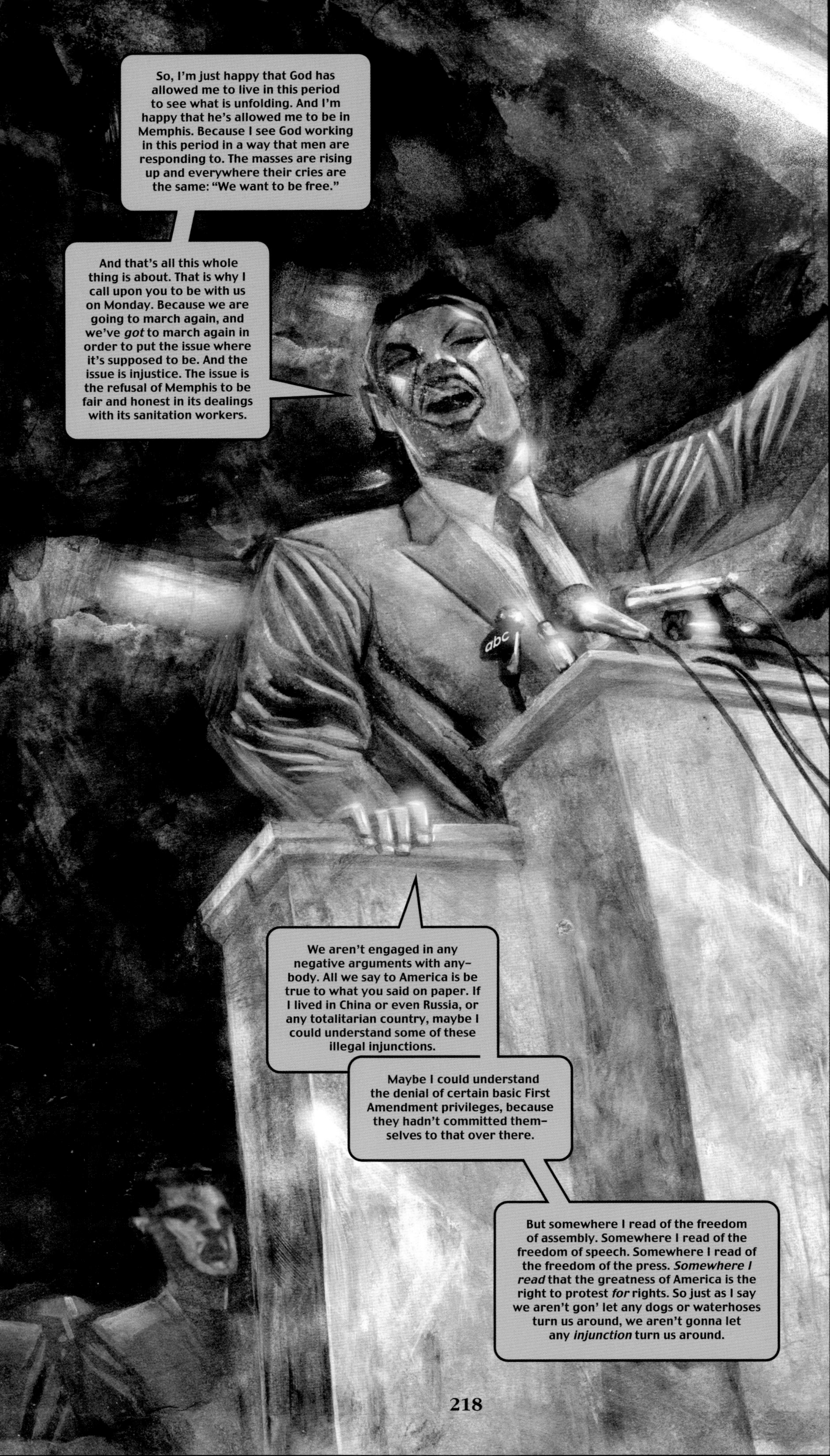
So, I'm just happy that God has allowed me to live in this period to see what is unfolding. And I'm happy that he's allowed me to be in Memphis. Because I see God working in this period in a way that men are responding to. The masses are rising up and everywhere their cries are the same: "We want to be free."
And that's all this whole thing is about. That is why I call upon you to be with us on Monday. Because we are going to march again, and we've *got* to march again in order to put the issue where it's supposed to be. And the issue is injustice. The issue is the refusal of Memphis to be fair and honest in its dealings with its sanitation workers.
abc
We aren't engaged in any negative arguments with any-body. All we say to America is be true to what you said on paper. If I lived in China or even Russia, or any totalitarian country, maybe I could understand some of these illegal injunctions.
Maybe I could understand the denial of certain basic First Amendment privileges, because they hadn't committed them-selves to that over there.
But somewhere I read of the freedom of assembly. Somewhere I read of the freedom of speech. Somewhere I read of the freedom of the press. *Somewhere I read* that the greatness of America is the right to protest *for* rights. So just as I say we aren't gon' let any dogs or waterhoses turn us around, we aren't gonna let any *injunction* turn us around.

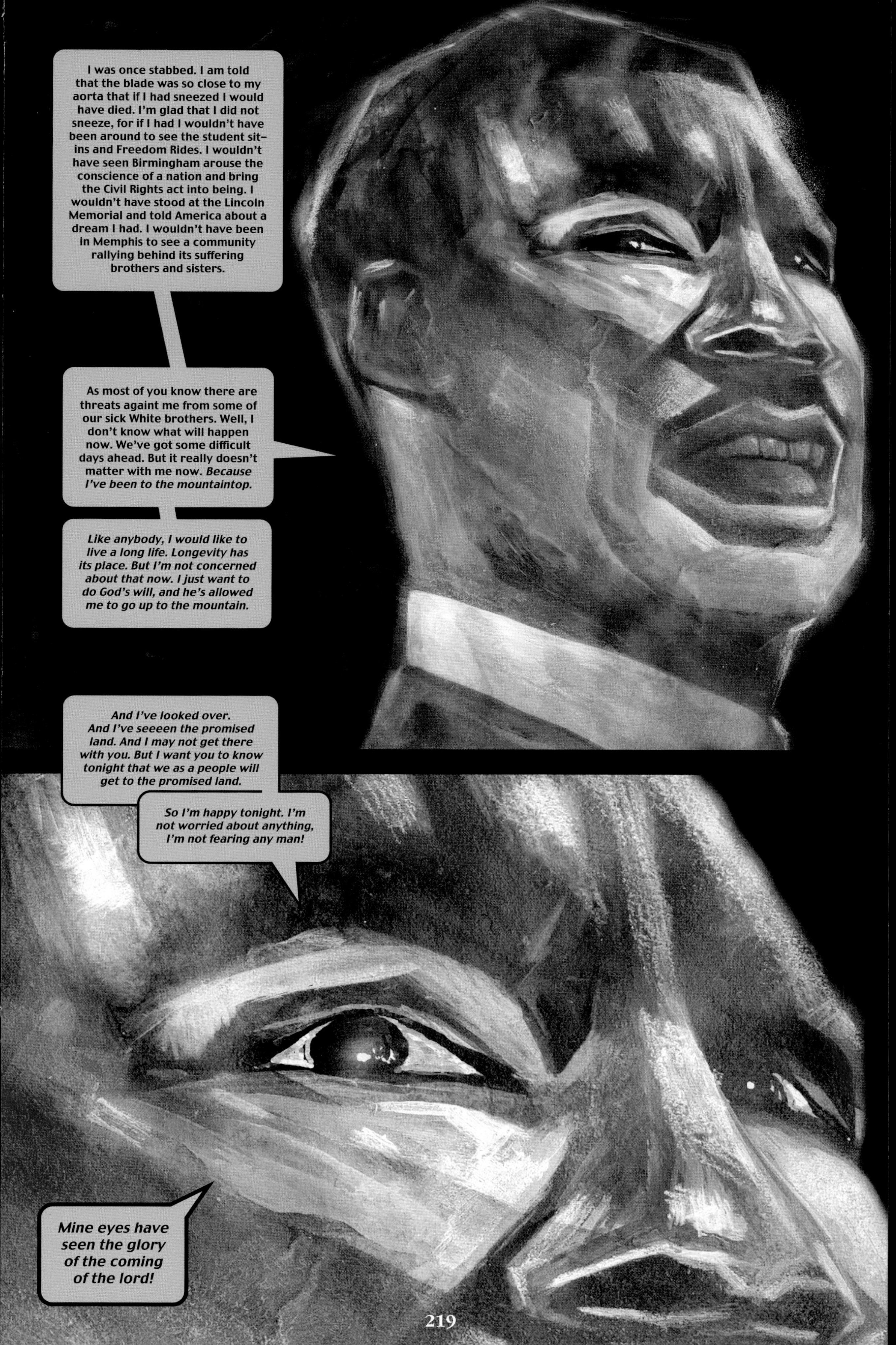
I was once stabbed. I am told that the blade was so close to my aorta that if I had sneezed I would have died. I'm glad that I did not sneeze, for if I had I wouldn't have been around to see the student sit-ins and Freedom Rides. I wouldn't have seen Birmingham arouse the conscience of a nation and bring the Civil Rights act into being. I wouldn't have stood at the Lincoln Memorial and told America about a dream I had. I wouldn't have been in Memphis to see a community rallying behind its suffering brothers and sisters.
As most of you know there are threats againt me from some of our sick White brothers. Well, I don't know what will happen now. We've got some difficult days ahead. But it really doesn't matter with me now. Because I've been to the mountaintop.
Like anybody, I would like to live a long life. Longevity has its place. But I'm not concerned about that now. I just want to do God's will, and he's allowed me to go up to the mountain.
And I've looked over. And I've seeeen the promised land. And I may not get there with you. But I want you to know tonight that we as a people will get to the promised land.
So I'm happy tonight. I'm not worried about anything, I'm not fearing any man!
Mine eyes have seen the glory of the coming of the lord!

Memphis, April 4, 1968

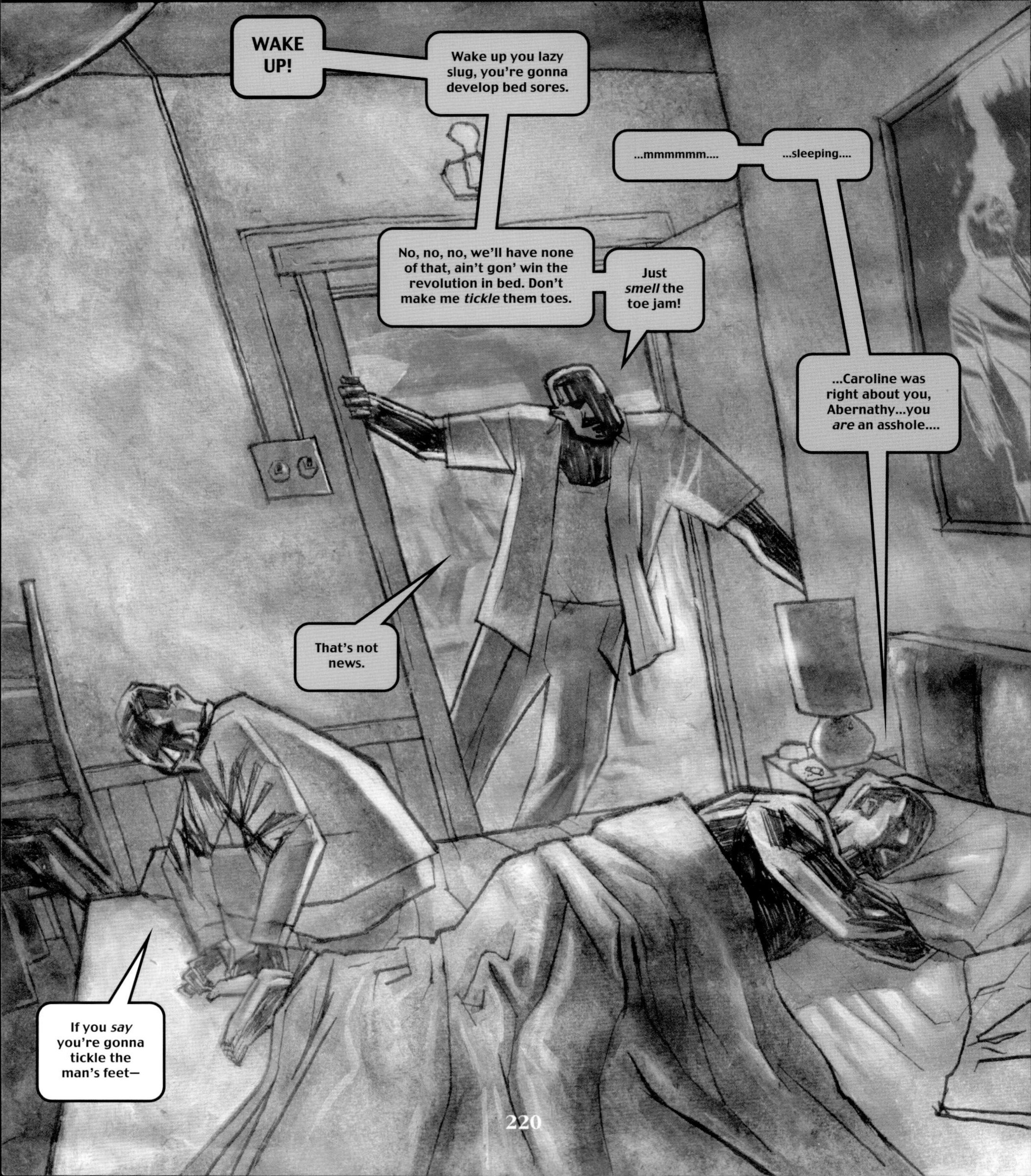

WAKE UP!
Wake up you lazy slug, you're gonna develop bed sores.
...mmmmmm....
...sleeping....
No, no, no, we'll have none of that, ain't gon' win the revolution in bed. Don't make me *tickle* them toes.
Just *smell* the toe jam!
...Caroline was right about you, Abernathy...you *are* an asshole....
That's not news.
If you *say* you're gonna tickle the man's feet—

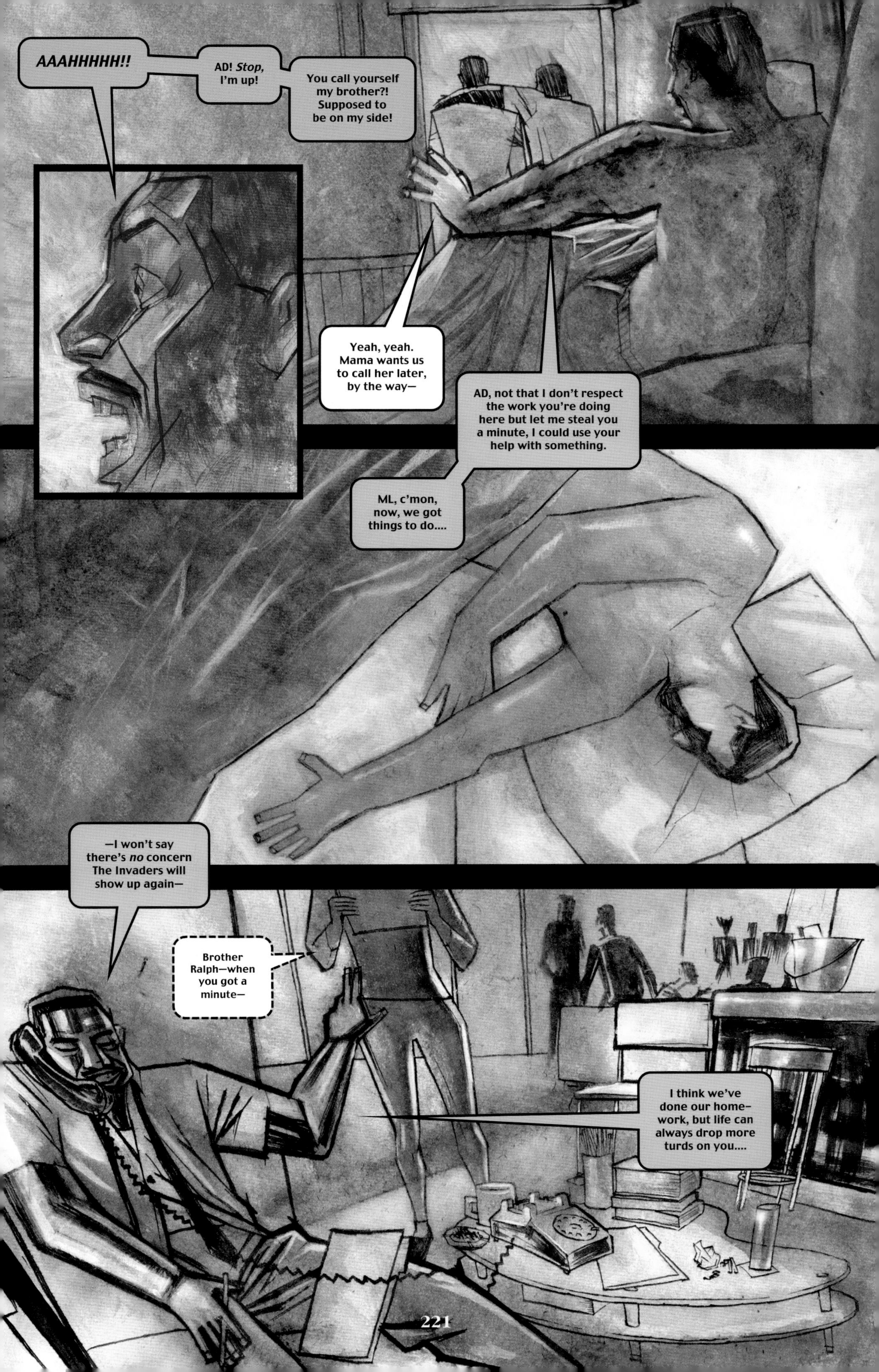
AAAHHHHH!!
AD! *Stop,* I'm up!
You call yourself my brother?! Supposed to be on my side!
Yeah, yeah. Mama wants us to call her later, by the way—
AD, not that I don't respect the work you're doing here but let me steal you a minute, I could use your help with something.
ML, c'mon, now, we got things to do....
—I won't say there's *no* concern The Invaders will show up again—
Brother Ralph—when you got a minute—
I think we've done our home-work, but life can always drop more turds on you....

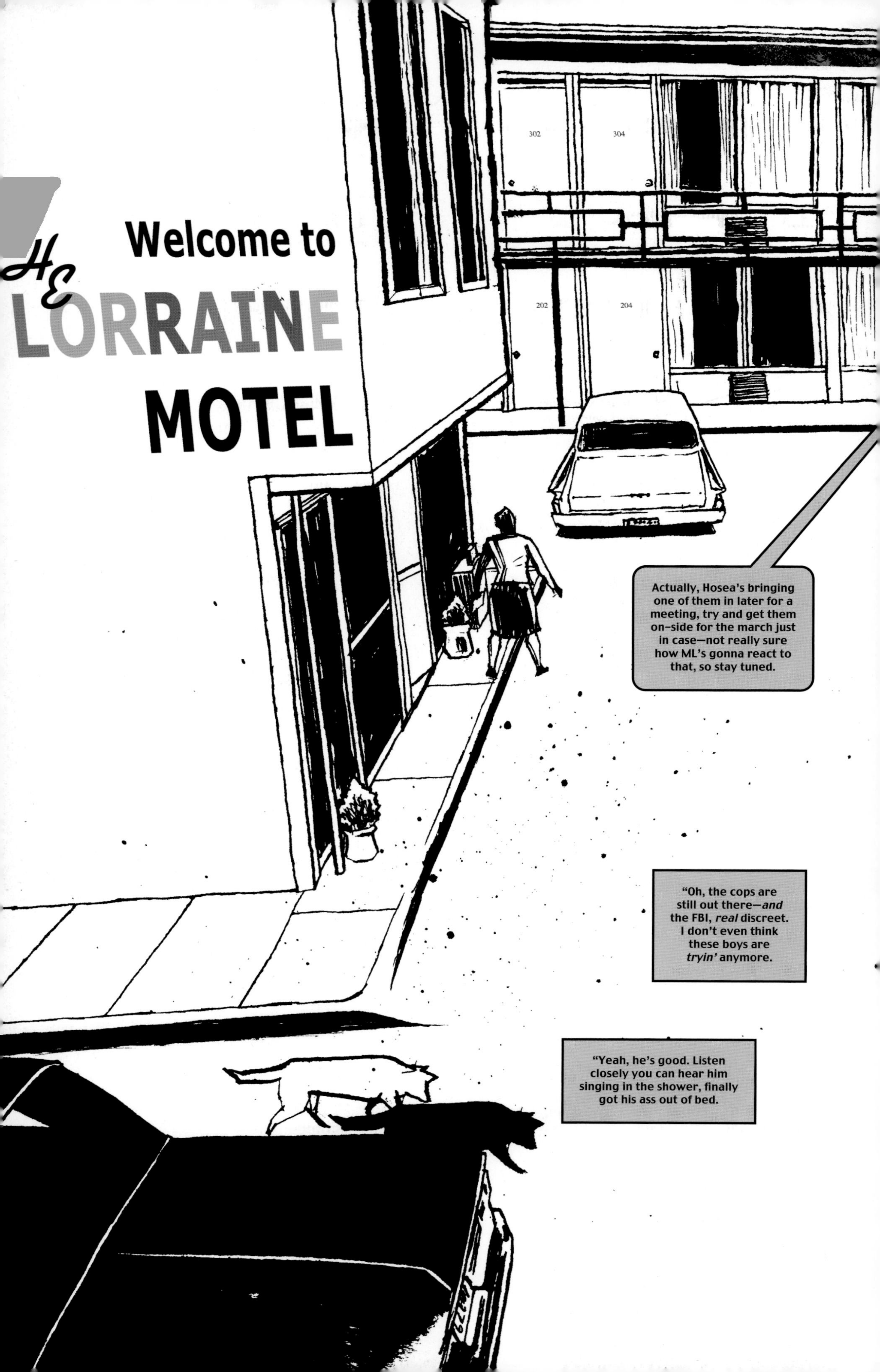
Welcome to
THE
LORRAINE
MOTEL
302
304
202
204
Actually, Hosea's bringing one of them in later for a meeting, try and get them on-side for the march just in case—not really sure how ML's gonna react to that, so stay tuned.
"Oh, the cops are still out there—*and* the FBI, *real* discreet. I don't even think these boys are *tryin'* anymore.
"Yeah, he's good. Listen closely you can hear him singing in the shower, finally got his ass out of bed.

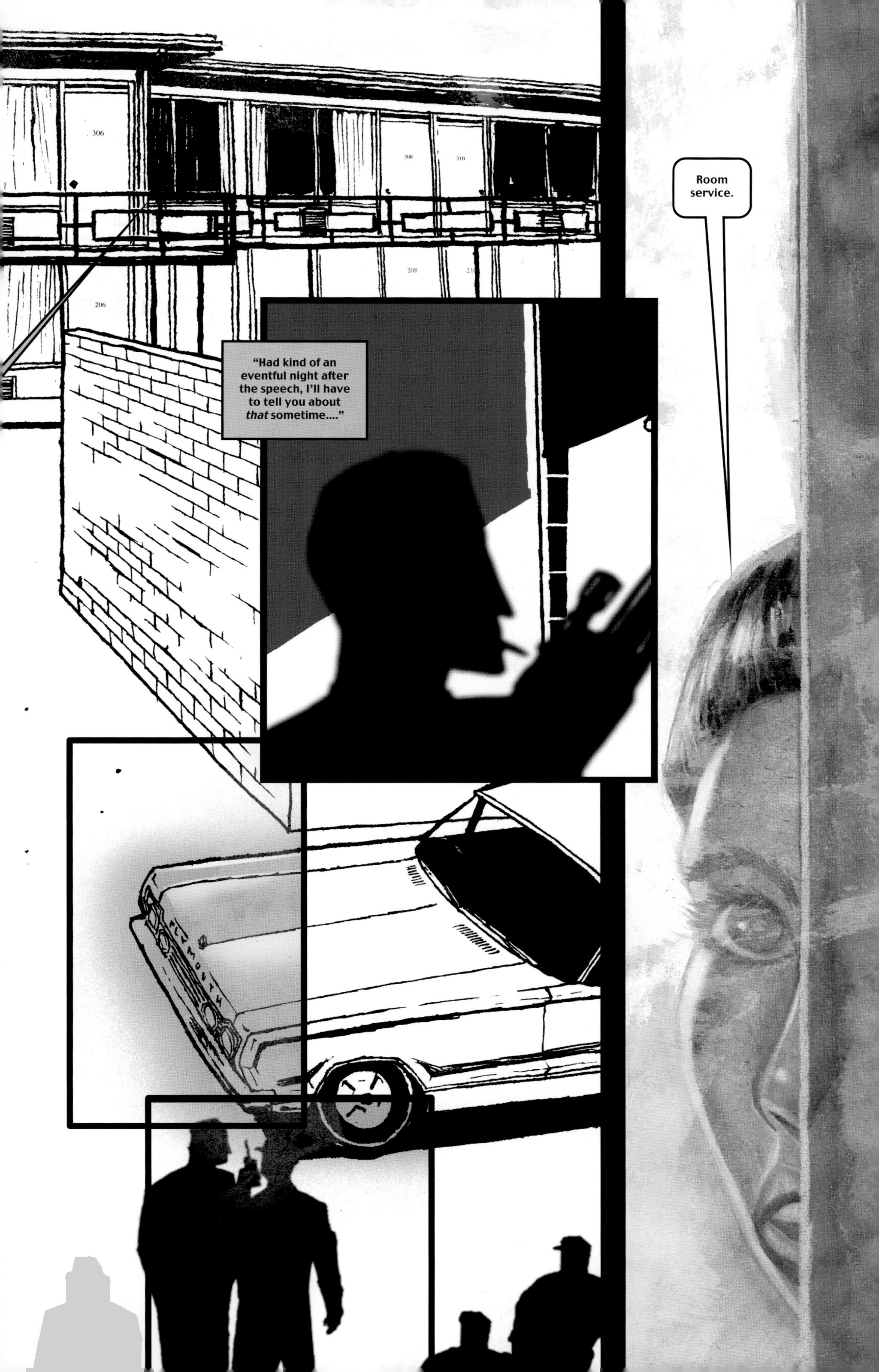
306
308
310
208
206
"Had kind of an eventful night after the speech, I'll have to tell you about *that* sometime...."
PLYMOUTH
Room service.

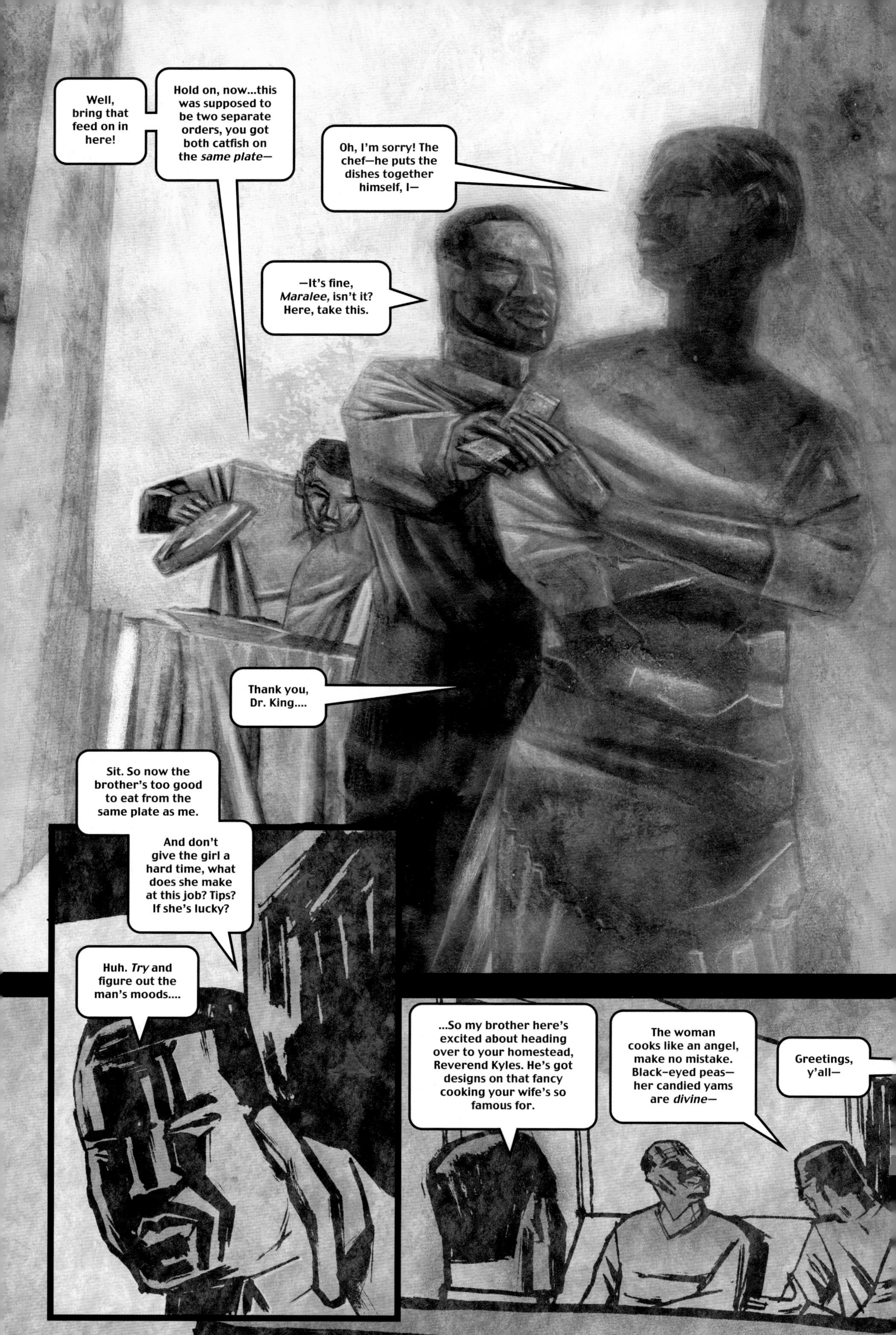
Well, bring that feed on in here!
Hold on, now...this was supposed to be two separate orders, you got both catfish on the *same plate*—
Oh, I'm sorry! The chef—he puts the dishes together himself, I—
—It's fine, *Maralee,* isn't it? Here, take this.
Thank you, Dr. King....
Sit. So now the brother's too good to eat from the same plate as me.
And don't give the girl a hard time, what does she make at this job? Tips? If she's lucky?
Huh. *Try* and figure out the man's moods....
...So my brother here's excited about heading over to your homestead, Reverend Kyles. He's got designs on that fancy cooking your wife's so famous for.
The woman cooks like an angel, make no mistake. Black-eyed peas—her candied yams are *divine*—
Greetings, y'all—

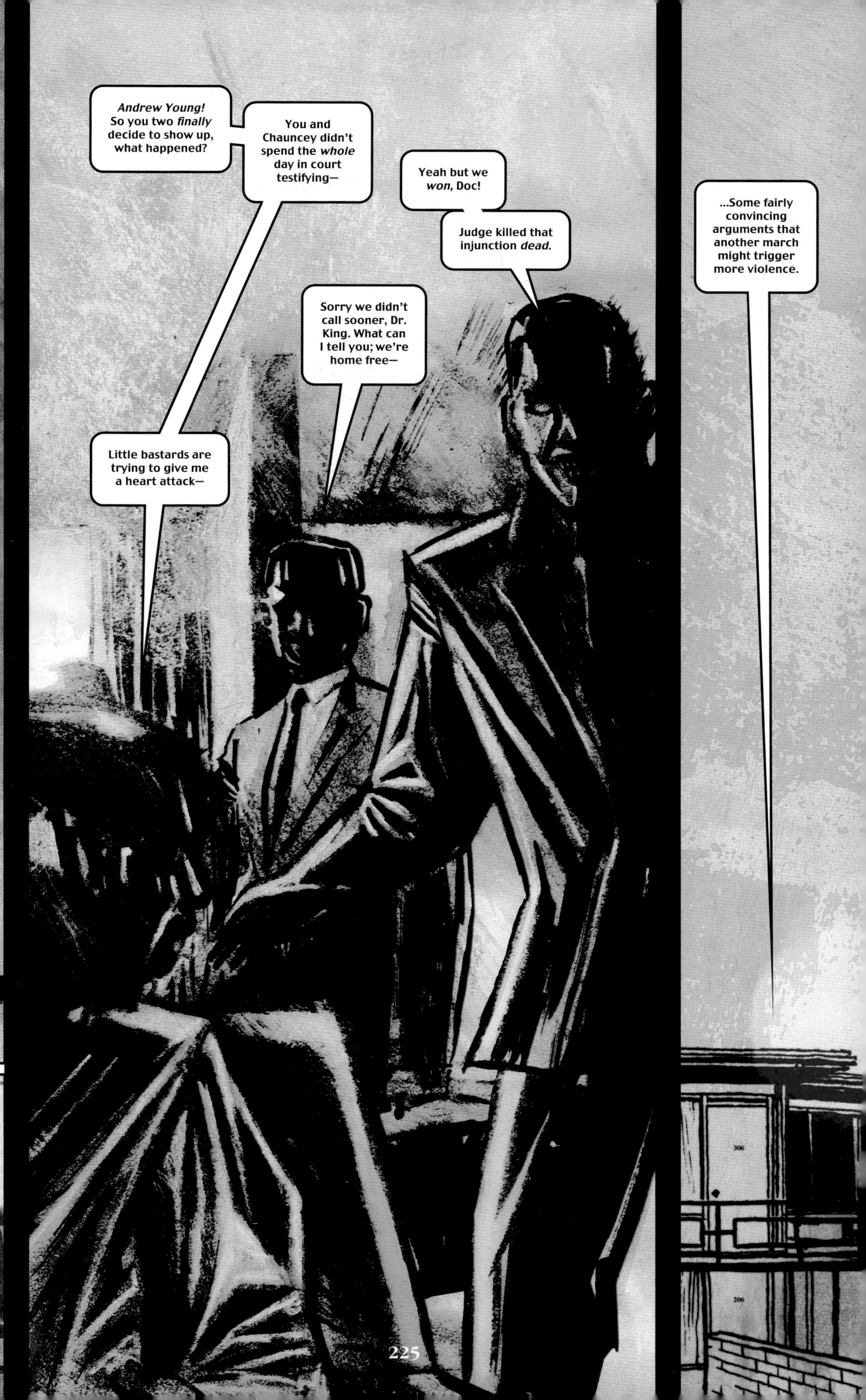
Andrew Young! So you two *finally* decide to show up, what happened?
You and Chauncey didn't spend the *whole* day in court testifying—
Little bastards are trying to give me a heart attack—
Sorry we didn't call sooner, Dr. King. What can I tell you; we're home free—
Yeah but we *won,* Doc!
Judge killed that injunction *dead.*
...Some fairly convincing arguments that another march might trigger more violence.
306
206

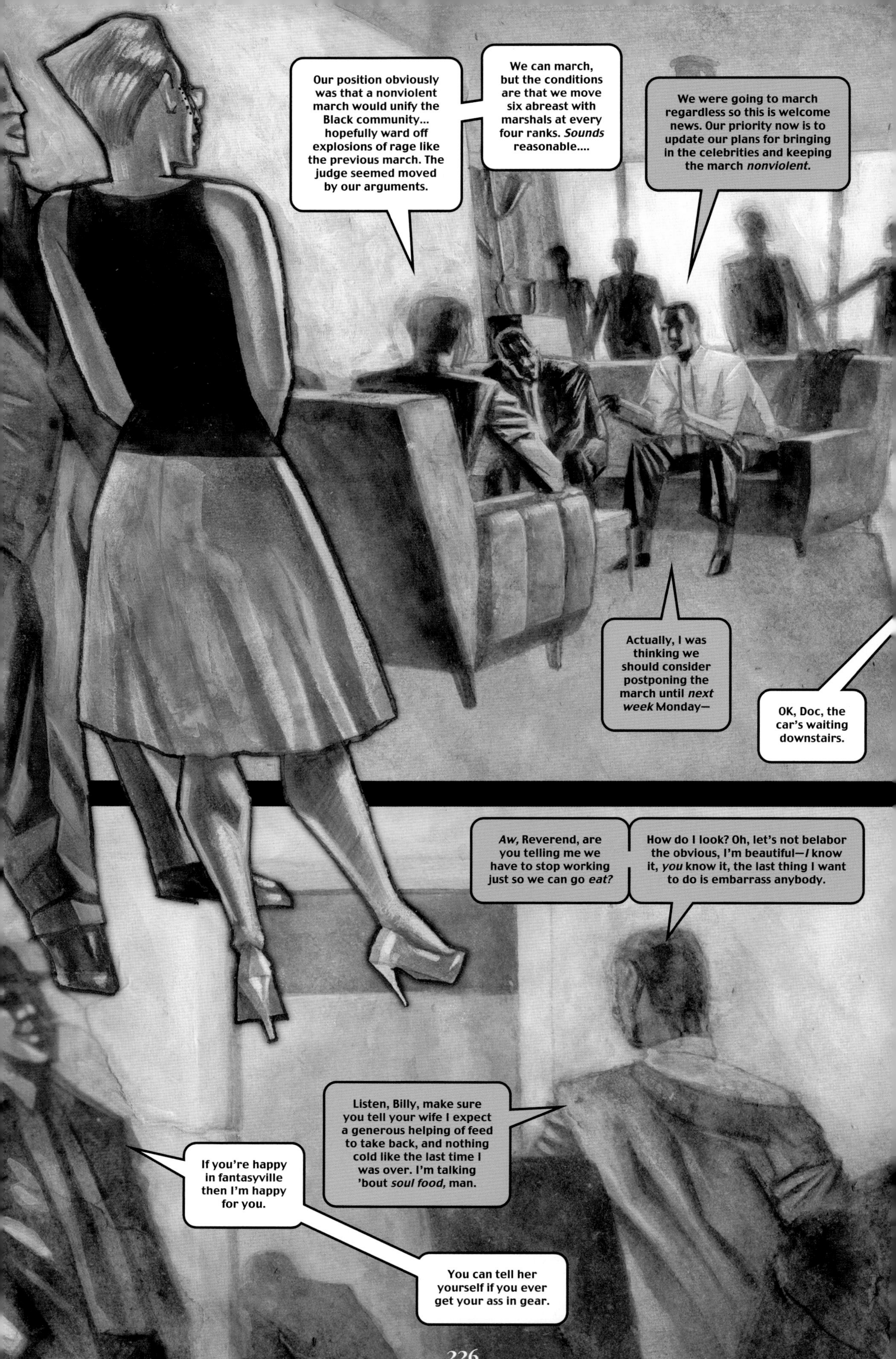
Our position obviously was that a nonviolent march would unify the Black community... hopefully ward off explosions of rage like the previous march. The judge seemed moved by our arguments.
We can march, but the conditions are that we move six abreast with marshals at every four ranks. *Sounds* reasonable....
We were going to march regardless so this is welcome news. Our priority now is to update our plans for bringing in the celebrities and keeping the march *nonviolent.*
Actually, I was thinking we should consider postponing the march until *next week* Monday—
OK, Doc, the car's waiting downstairs.
Aw, Reverend, are you telling me we have to stop working just so we can go *eat?*
How do I look? Oh, let's not belabor the obvious, I'm beautiful—*I* know it, *you* know it, the last thing I want to do is embarrass anybody.
Listen, Billy, make sure you tell your wife I expect a generous helping of feed to take back, and nothing cold like the last time I was over. I'm talking 'bout *soul food,* man.
If you're happy in fantasyville then I'm happy for you.
You can tell her yourself if you ever get your ass in gear.

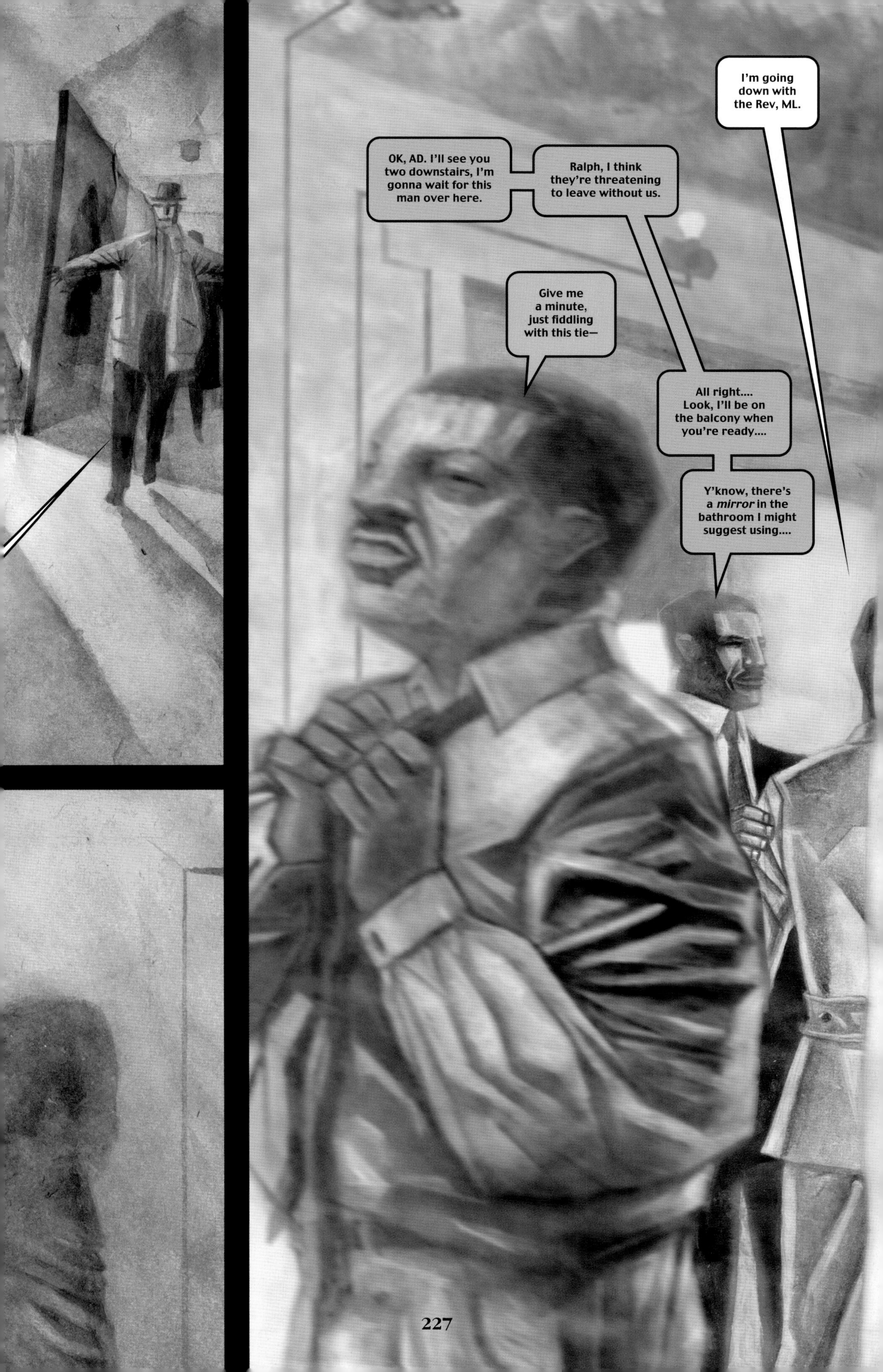
I'm going down with the Rev, ML.
OK, AD. I'll see you two downstairs, I'm gonna wait for this man over here.
Ralph, I think they're threatening to leave without us.
Give me a minute, just fiddling with this tie—
All right.... Look, I'll be on the balcony when you're ready....
Y'know, there's a *mirror* in the bathroom I might suggest using....

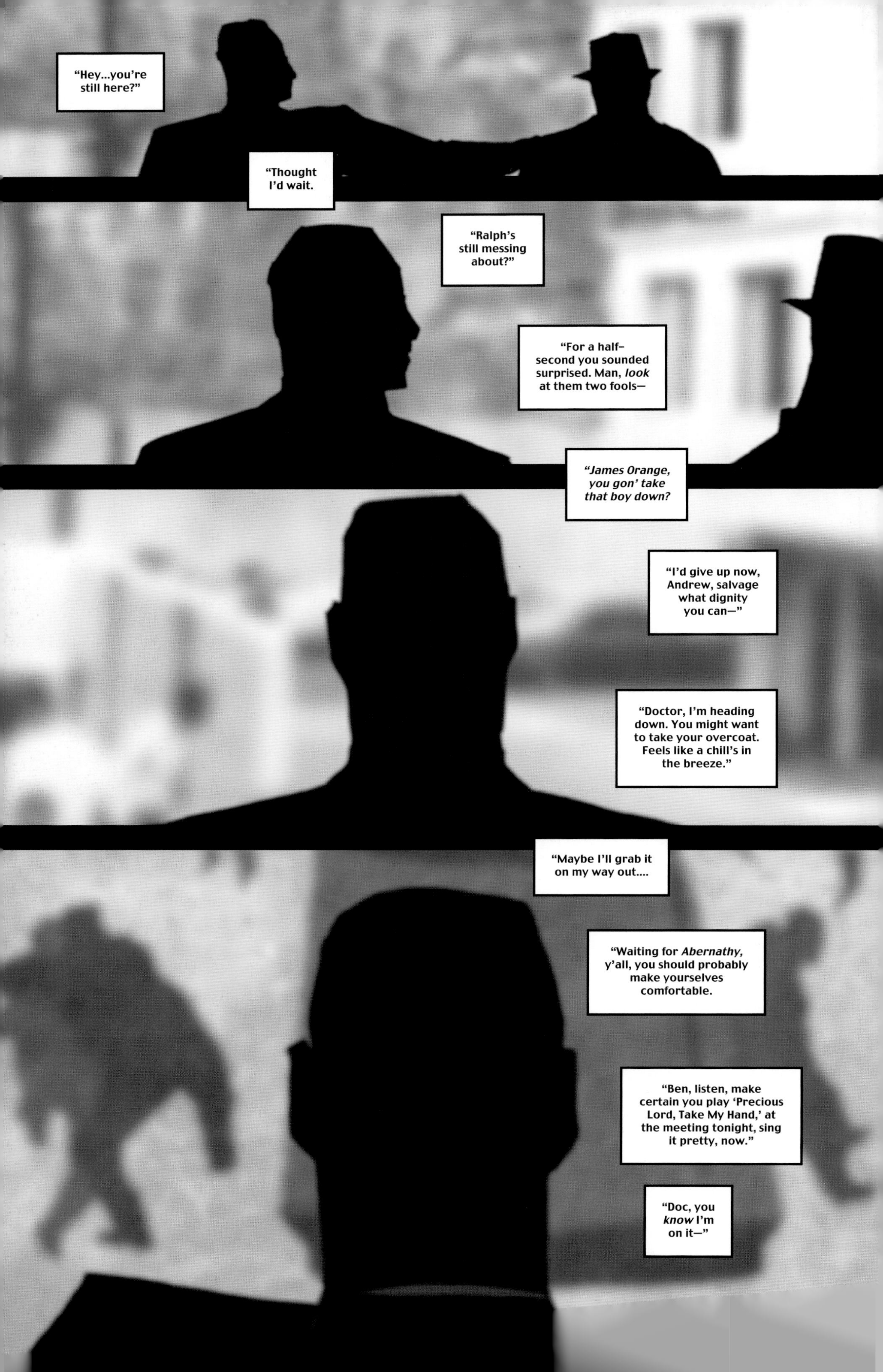
"Hey...you're still here?"
"Thought I'd wait.
"Ralph's still messing about?"
"For a half-second you sounded surprised. Man, *look* at them two fools—
"James Orange, you gon' take that boy down?
"I'd give up now, Andrew, salvage what dignity you can—"
"Doctor, I'm heading down. You might want to take your overcoat. Feels like a chill's in the breeze."
"Maybe I'll grab it on my way out....
"Waiting for *Abernathy,* y'all, you should probably make yourselves comfortable.
"Ben, listen, make certain you play 'Precious Lord, Take My Hand,' at the meeting tonight, sing it pretty, now."
"Doc, you *know* I'm on it—"

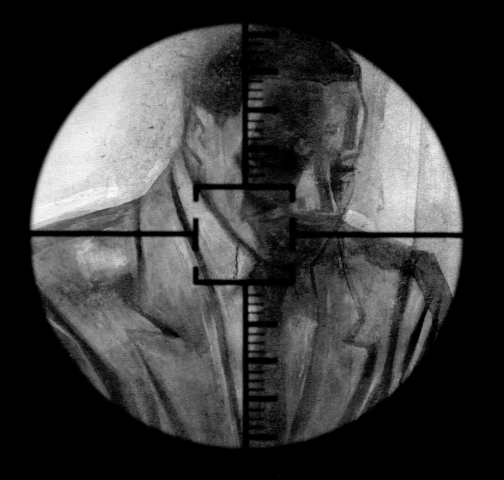

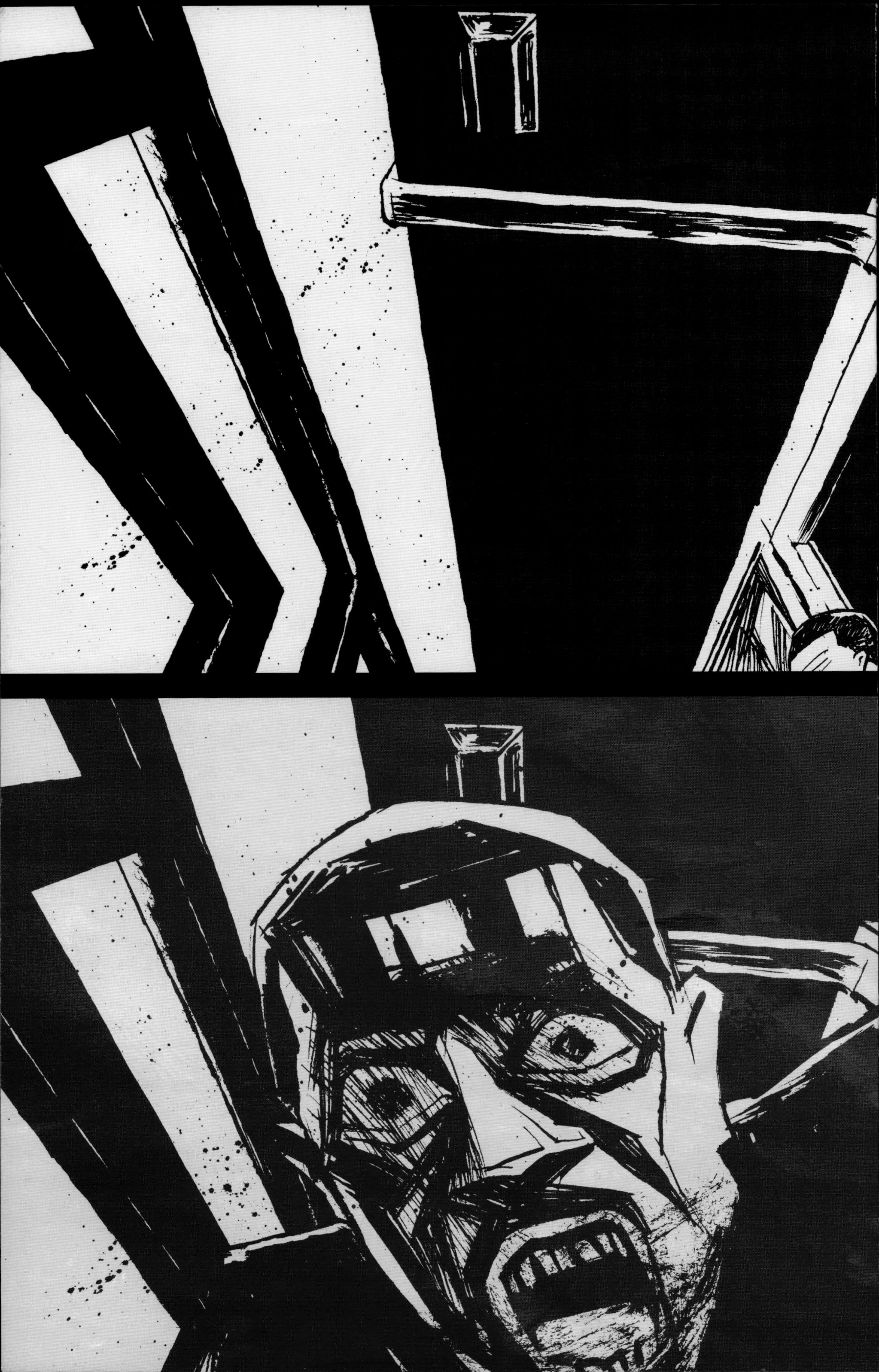

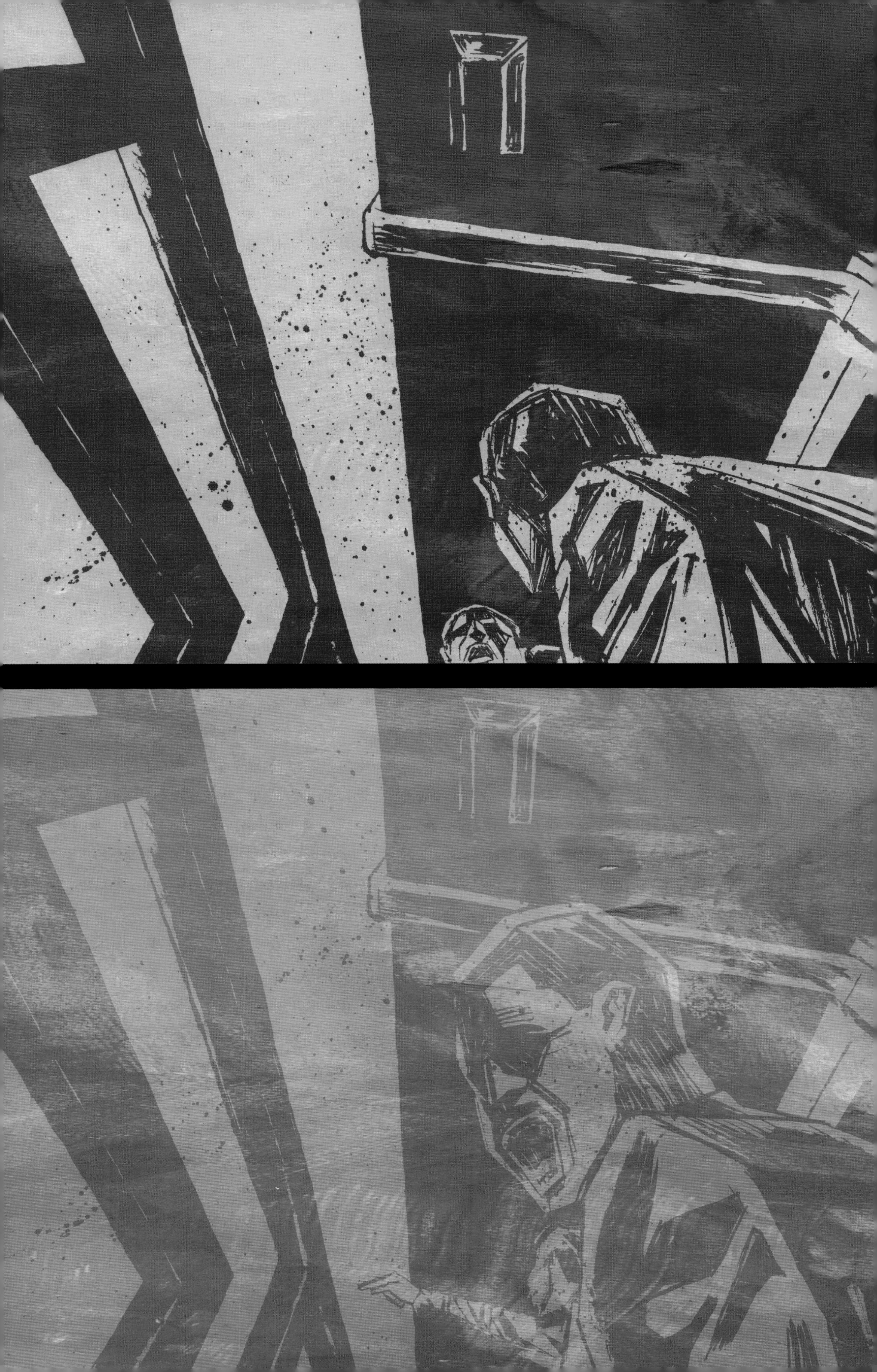

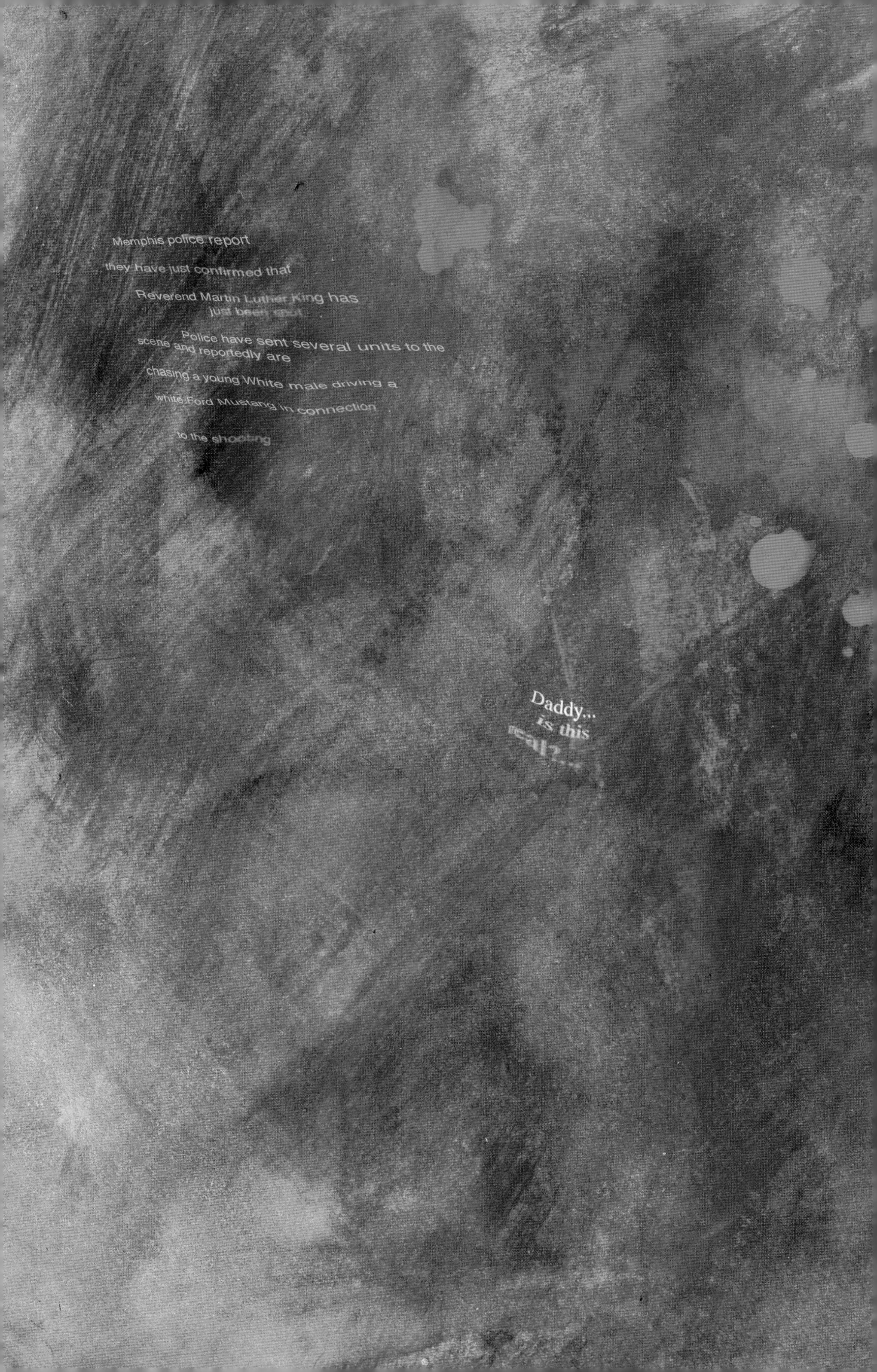
Memphis police report
they have just confirmed that
Reverend Martin Luther King has
just been shot
Police have sent several units to the
scene and reportedly are
chasing a young White male driving a
white Ford Mustang in connection
to the shooting
Daddy...
is this
real?...

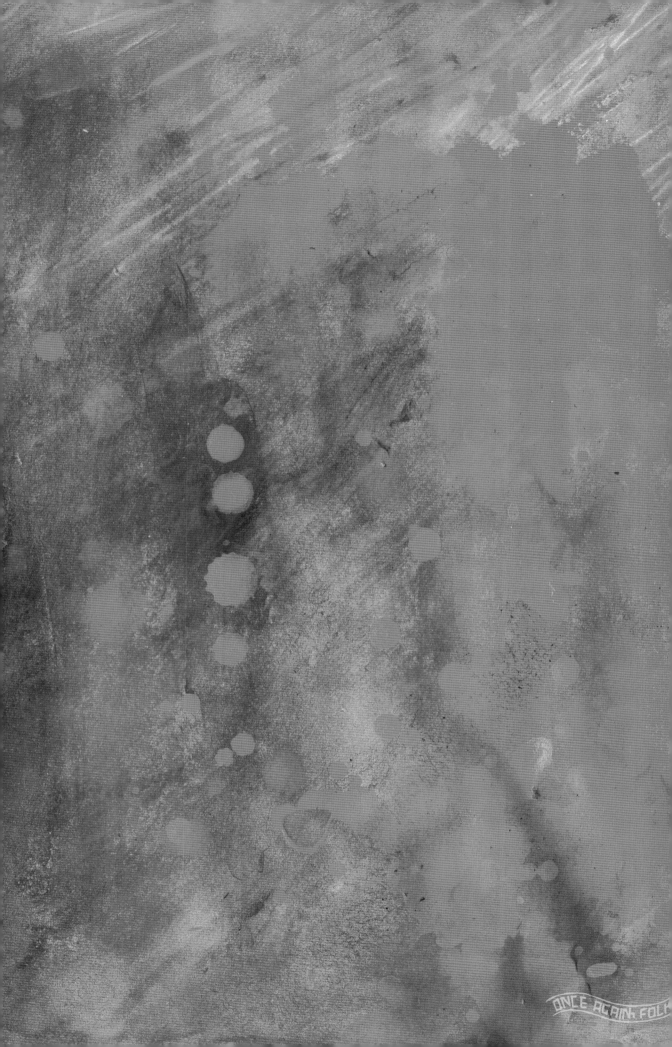

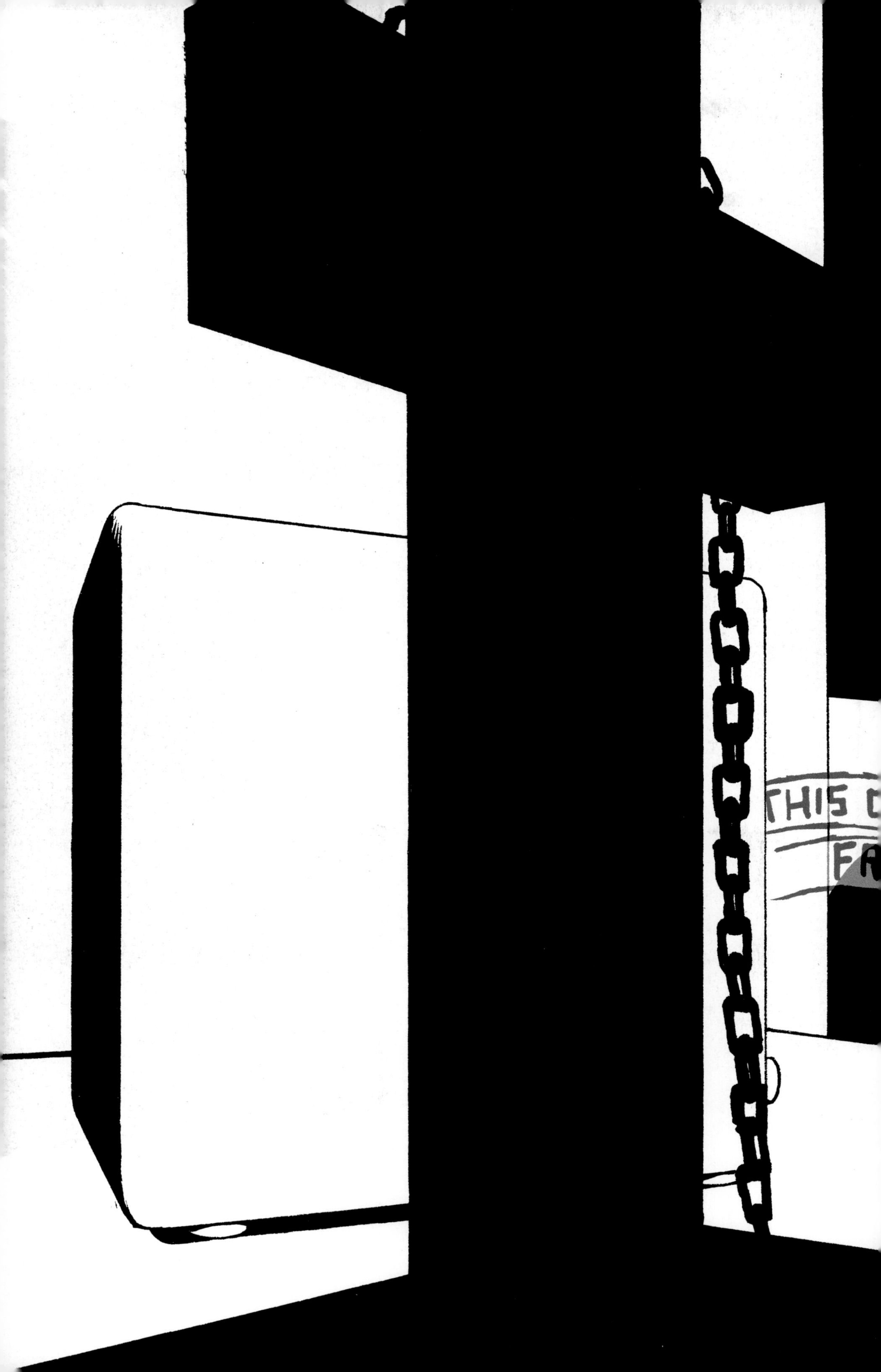
THIS

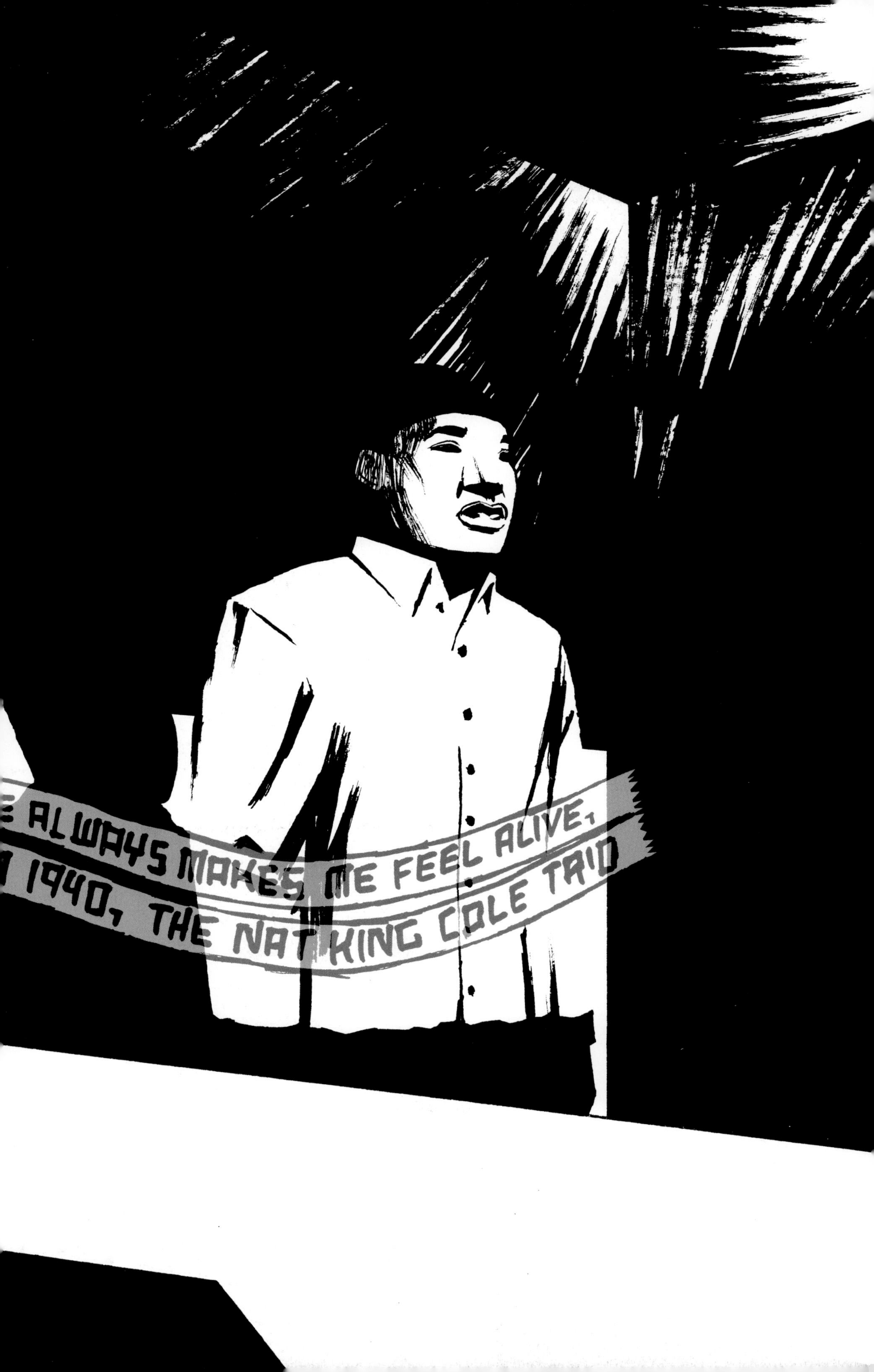
E ALWAYS MAKES ME FEEL ALIVE,
1940, THE NAT KING COLE TRIO

T FOUND JOY, I'M
PPY AS A BABY B
TH A BRAND N
OO-CHOO TOY, WH
MET MY SWEET LO
LORRAINE, LORRAINE

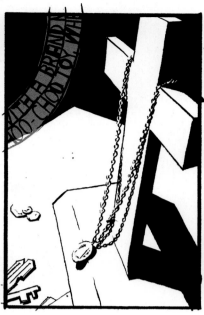

STEPHEN B. OATES   RALPH DAVID ABERNATHY   JUAN WILLIAMS   ALEX HALEY
MARK LANE   DICK GREGORY   STOKELY CARMICHAEL   MARTIN LUTHER KING

BY THE SAME PERPETRATOR

I WANT TO BE YOUR DOG	WISE SON	POP LIFE (WITH WILFRED SANTIAGO)
THE MUSE	YOUNG HOODS IN LOVE	
ZANANA X	TEMPLE DUNCAN	STEEL DRUMS & ICE SKATES (WITH DIRK MCLEAN)
BLACK DOGS	THE NO-BOYS CLUB	SCREAM QUEEN

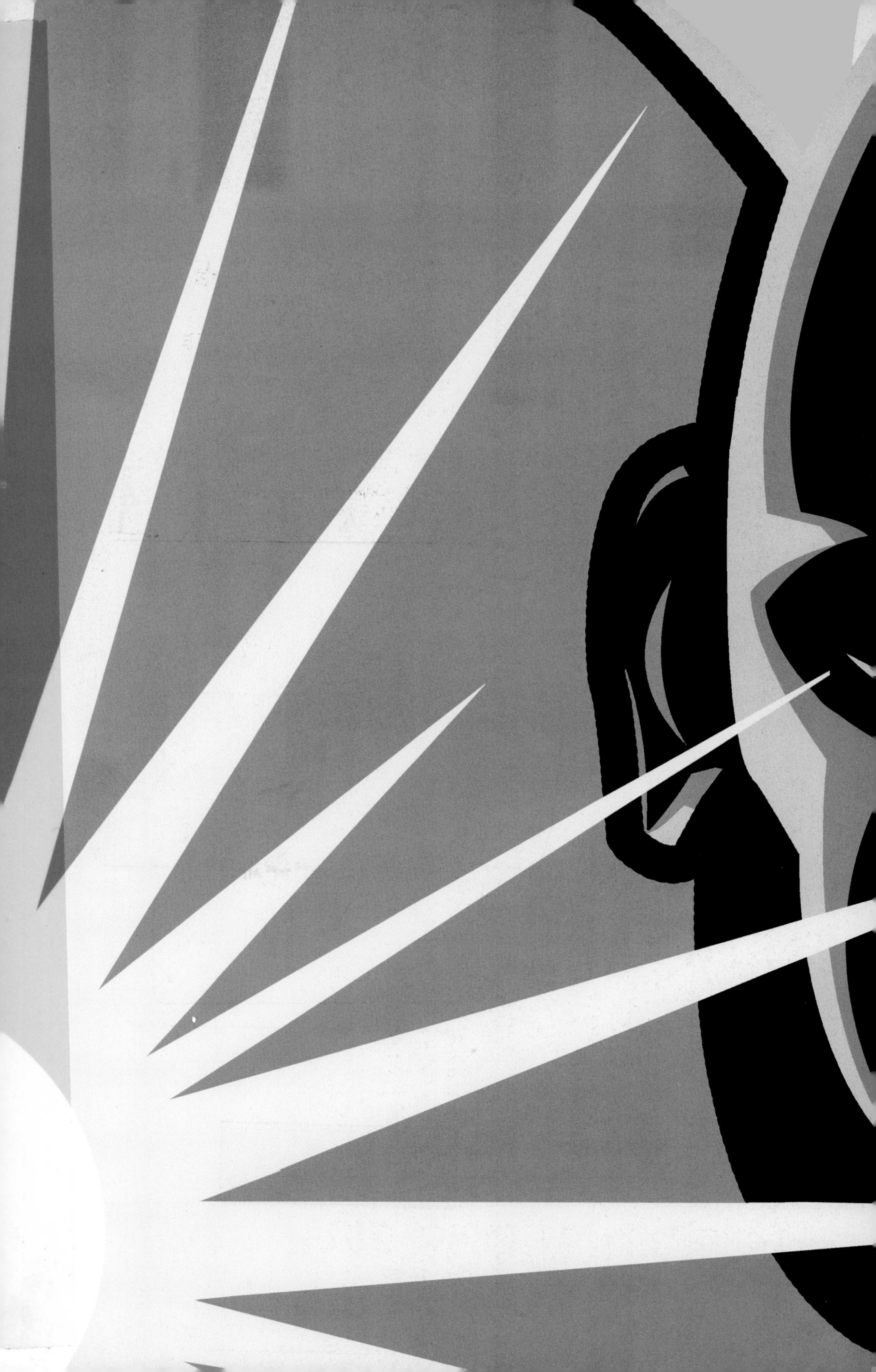

THE VOLUME COVERS FOR KING 1-3

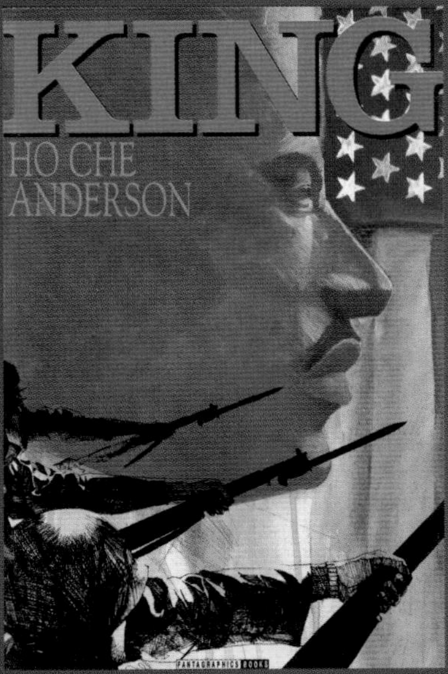
KING
HO CHE
ANDERSON
FANTAGRAPHICS BOOKS

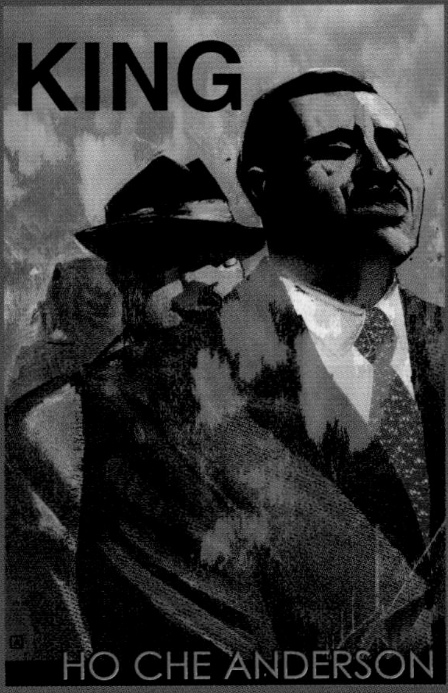
KING
HO CHE ANDERSON

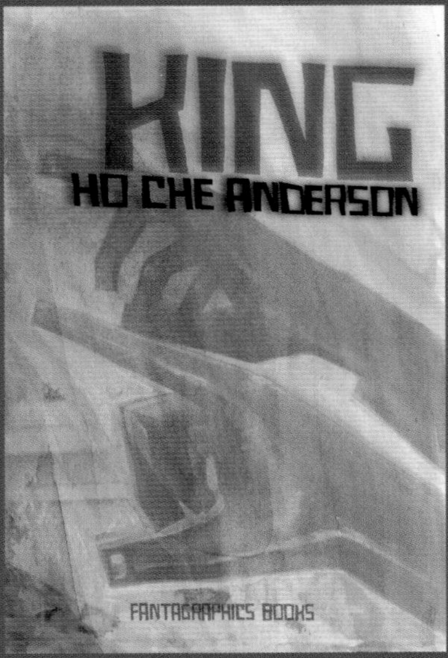
KING
HO CHE ANDERSON
FANTAGRAPHICS BOOKS

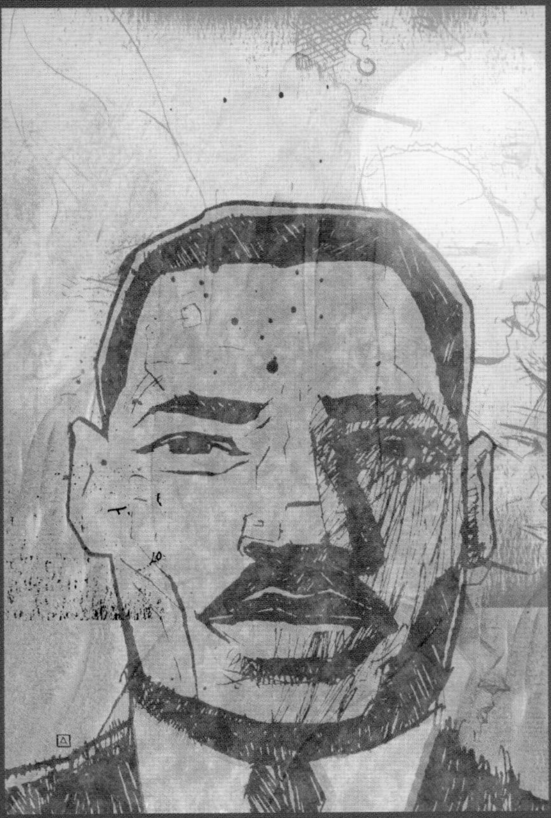

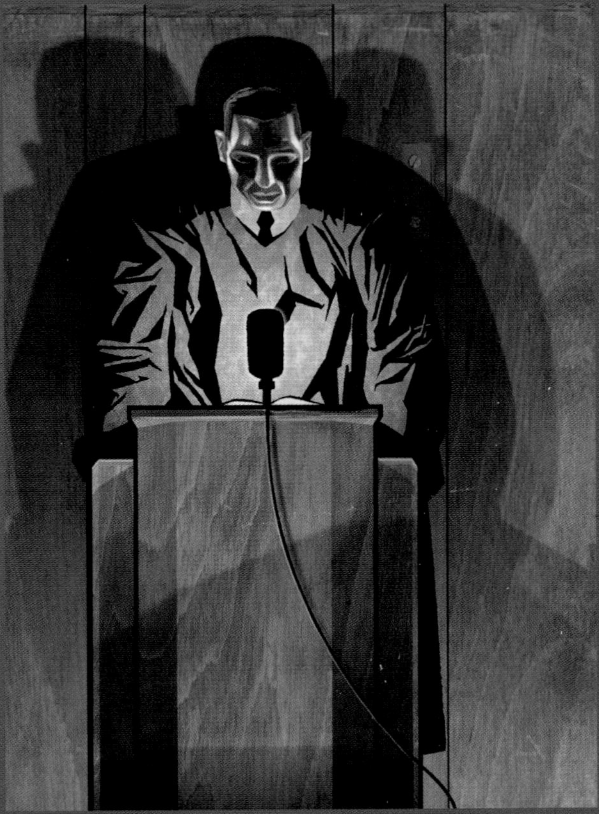